Negroes and the New Southern Politics

# Negroes
# and the
# New Southern Politics

## Donald R. Matthews
## James W. Prothro
UNIVERSITY OF NORTH CAROLINA

HARCOURT, BRACE & WORLD, INC.
NEW YORK / CHICAGO / BURLINGAME

© 1966 by Harcourt, Brace & World, Inc.

Library of Congress Catalog Card Number: 66–28289

PRINTED IN THE UNITED STATES OF AMERICA

*For two pioneers in the study*
*of southern politics—*

*G. Alexander Heard* AND *V. O. Key, Jr.*

# Preface

This book is about a revolution in process—the growing participation of southern Negroes in the politics of the 1960's.

For generations after Reconstruction, the eleven states of the former Confederacy excluded Negroes from active citizenship. But in recent years United States Supreme Court decisions and federal legislation—to say nothing of pressures from southern Negroes themselves—have broken the barriers to political participation by Negroes in the South. Southern Negroes are beginning to vote in impressive numbers. Front-page news stories announce the election of a Negro county sheriff in Alabama and of Negro state legislators in Georgia. Boycotts, sit-ins, demonstrations, and mass marches have become almost routine occurrences. Obviously, southern politics is rapidly changing in fundamental ways.

The classic works on the Negro—Gunnar Myrdal's *An American Dilemma* (1944)—and on southern politics—V. O. Key, Jr.'s *Southern Politics* (1949) —describe a "Negro problem" and a South that bear little resemblance to present realities. The new southern politics has yet to be described and analyzed. Although writing about a revolution in process is almost as uncomfortable and risky as living through one, the job badly needs to be done. With this book we have tried to make a start.

Our focus is on Negro political participation and its consequences. How much do southern Negroes participate in the politics of the 1960's? In what ways? Why do some Negroes participate while others do not? What are likely to be the consequences of Negro political activity for southern politics and race relations?

Our effort to answer these questions is based on perhaps the largest collection of systematic data on Negro political behavior ever compiled. About two thousand southerners, from Texas to Virginia to Florida, were interviewed.

Detailed social, economic, and political data were collected on more than a thousand counties. Four widely differing local communities were studied in detail. More than a hundred persons—interviewers, coders, data processors, and the like—were directly involved in collecting and processing this material at one time or another over the last six years. Even this large staff would not have been able to cope with this quantity of facts without the help of high-speed computers.

Political science has changed almost as much as the South since Professor Key wrote *Southern Politics*; the fruits of modern political research are not easily presented to a general audience. Nonetheless, we are convinced that our subject is the most crucial domestic problem facing the United States, so we have tried to deal with it in terms that are comprehensible to the general reader. The more technical underpinnings of the research have been relegated to appendixes, but the general reader may wish to skip Chapters Two and Eleven, which are unavoidably technical.

Our largest and most tangible debt is to the Rockefeller Foundation, which made this study possible through two grants to the Institute for Research in Social Science of the University of North Carolina at Chapel Hill. The Foundation's confidence in our ability to conduct a study of this magnitude will always be a source of personal satisfaction to us. The Social Science Research Council and the Center for Advanced Study in the Behavioral Sciences, by supporting leaves of absence for both of us, greatly speeded the lengthy process of analysis and writing.

The dedication of this volume suggests something of our indebtedness to the late Professor V. O. Key, Jr., of Harvard University and to Chancellor G. Alexander Heard of Vanderbilt University. Professor Key was the premier teacher of an entire generation of political scientists, including many, such as ourselves, who never set foot in his classroom. Chancellor Heard was a colleague in the Department of Political Science and Dean of the Graduate School at the University of North Carolina when we launched this inquiry. During the critical early months of this work, both men gave us more time than they should have and more wisdom than we had the wit to absorb.

This study could not have been conceived or completed without the help and encouragement of Frederic N. Cleaveland of the University of North Carolina. As an extraordinarily creative departmental chairman he provided us with plentiful resources and an ideal work environment. As an old friend and close professional colleague he gave us sound advice on virtually every major problem we encountered. Professor Warren E. Miller of the Survey Research Center of the University of Michigan also served as a close adviser during the entire study. While he and his collaborators at the Survey Research Center—Angus Campbell, Philip Converse, and Donald Stokes—have been most helpful throughout our work, we particularly wish to acknowledge Professor Miller's contribution to the overall research design. Daniel O. Price, Director of the Institute for Research in Social Science during the period of this study, far exceeded the bounds of his official responsibilities to advise us on particularly knotty problems of statistical analysis. Charles E. Bowerman of the Department of Sociology at North Carolina and John Gilbert of the Center for Advanced Study in the Behavioral Sciences also helped greatly with statistical problems.

Our two principal assistants were R. Lewis Bowman, Staff and Field Director of our study, who carried much of the administrative burden during the interviewing and coding stages and played a major role in preparing the four community studies, and Barbara Bright, Office Manager and Research Analyst, whose duties have been so numerous and varied that no title adequately describes them. Next to the authors, this capable pair devoted more time, energy, and emotion to this study than anyone else.

Twiley W. Barker, Jr., John R. Larkins, Charles U. Smith, and the late I. Gregory Newton served as consultants to the study and prepared valuable memoranda on the Negro political community in the four counties we studied intensively.

The following graduate assistants carried out interviewing, editing, and coding chores at various times in the course of the study: Lawton E. Bennett, G. Robert Boynton, Charles Cnudde, William J. Crotty, Jr., Jack D. Fleer, Donald M. Freeman, David M. Kovenock, Ann Lulka Lewis, Charles J. Parrish, Ronald C. Semone, Richard L. Sutton, and Jon Van Til. Our principal data processors were Richard Ames, Ted Cooper, Toni Koh, and Karen Lawrence.

For aid in typing various versions of the manuscript we are indebted to Ann Lester, Rita Snyder, and Hildegarde Teilheit.

Most of the interviewing for this study was conducted under the supervision of Morris Axelrod, then Assistant Head of the Field Section, Survey Research Center, University of Michigan. Mrs. Goldina Powell and Mrs. Mary Pass of SRC served as field supervisors and took part in the final pretesting and training of Negro interviewers. The forty-five professional interviewers they directed were, for all practical purposes, our eyes and ears.

J. David Barber, Arnold Rose, Allan Sindler, and several other colleagues mentioned above read portions of the manuscript and gave us the benefit of their comments and criticisms. Fred I. Greenstein read the manuscript from beginning to end with his usual attention to detail and sensitivity to the larger theoretical problems.

To all these people, we extend our warm thanks. We could not have asked for more, or better, advice and assistance. The defects of this work are obviously ours alone.

Finally, our thanks go to Maggie, Molly, and Jonathan Matthews and Mary, Pamela, Barbara, and Susan Prothro for putting up with "the project" for so long. Until the next study begins, they will have to put up with us.

D R M
J W P

*Chapel Hill, N. C.*
*June 1966*

# Contents

PART TWO

## Influences on Negro Political Participation 61

## 4. Who Are the Participants? 65

## 5. The Community Setting: Social and Economic Aspects 101

## 6. The Community Setting: Political Aspects 137

## 7. Negro Leaders   175

## 8. Negro Political Organizations   203

## 9. Mass Communications and Negro Political Participation   237

Negroes and the New Southern Politics

Part One

# Introduction

On August 18, 1961, John W. Jones, a 21-year-old Negro from Nashville, Tennessee, opened a voter registration school for Negroes at the Mount Zion Baptist Church in rural Crayfish County, Mississippi. Mr. Jones, a student at Tennessee Agricultural and Industrial University and an active member of the Student Non-violent Coordinating Committee, spent several weeks training a dozen or so Negroes in Mississippi's literacy test and other registration requirements. Up to that time these requirements (and their administration) had proved so intricate that not one of the 2,500 Negroes of voting age in Crayfish County had been able to satisfy them. After about two weeks of instruction, four Negro graduates of the training school—one a college student and another a former school teacher—presented themselves to the registrar of voters, Circuit Court Clerk Jim Rock, in the county courthouse in Breedville. The next day Mr. Rock announced that all four Negroes had failed to meet the legal qualifications for registration.

A week later two more graduates of the school, this time accompanied by Mr. Jones, tried to register. Mr. Rock declined to administer the test because he did not want to affect the outcome of a Justice Department suit just filed against him for discriminatory treatment of potential Negro voters. Rock and Jones fell into an argument. Finally, the registrar reached into his desk, pulled out a gun, and ordered the three Negroes to leave. After they had turned toward the door, Rock struck Jones on the head with his pistol. As the youth staggered from the office assisted by his companions, County Sheriff Ted White arrived on the scene, arrested him for disturbing the peace, and threatened to "beat him within an inch of his life."

•　　•　　•

Political interest among Negroes in Farmington, a small city in rural Bright

3

Leaf County, was unusually intense as the municipal election of 1960 approached. A young Negro lawyer, Howard Alden, was running for a seat on the city council and victory seemed within his reach. He was not the first Negro to run for public office in Farmington in modern times. But before 1960 the few Negro candidacies had been token affairs, for only about 250 Negro voters were registered in the city. The situation was changed by pressure from the federal government, a bitter campaign for county sheriff in 1956 during which one of the white candidates systematically sought to get his Negro supporters on the voting lists, and by the excitement and organizational activity engendered by Alden's campaign. By 1960 the number of registered Negro voters in Farmington had swelled to 2,500, most of them concentrated in the ward in which Alden was running. Alden was playing the game to win. And if he could attract to the polls a large majority of the registered Negroes in his ward, he was virtually certain of victory.

Alden's fellow Negroes let him down. Until only a few months before, the political leadership of Farmington's Negro community had been monopolized by the Civic Association, a self-perpetuating group of Negro ministers and businessmen with access to the leaders of the white community. Early in 1960 eight leaders of the Association, without consulting the others, selected their president as the informal "Negro nominee" for the city council race. This proved to be an unpopular decision, and another Negro group—a fraternal organization called the Benevolent Brothers—named Alden as the candidate of the Negro community. To support his candidacy, they formed a new and more aggressive political organization, the Progressive Voters League. The older leaders of the Civic Association eventually gave in, but the struggle left lasting scars. The "Negro bloc vote"—about which Alden's white opponent complained so bitterly—was not so "solid" as it seemed.

A few days before the election, a white supporter of Alden's opponent made substantial cash contributions to two churches in Alden's ward. The ministers of these churches were leaders of the discredited Civic Association. They were assured that if Alden's opponent were elected, he would use his influence to see that a pending urban renewal project would not break up their congregations or force them to move their churches and cemeteries.

The two ministers lost all interest in the electoral fray. The Sunday before election day their sermons dealt with the delights of another world, not with the grubby business of electing a Negro to the city council the following Tuesday. They made no effort to encourage voter turnout from their large and strategically located parishes.

On election day Howard Alden polled 1,500 votes—about 200 fewer, it turned out, than he needed to win. A few weeks later the newly elected, all-white city council ruled that henceforth all candidates for the city council would have to run from the city at large. No Negro candidate, the councilmen assured themselves, would soon again come that close to the portals of power.

•   •   •

On May 27, 1956, two coeds from Peripheral State A. and M. College, an all-Negro institution located in Capital City (population, 35,000)—the county seat of Camellia County and the state capital—boarded a bus, paid their ten-cent fares, and sat down in the only two empty seats, which happened to be in the front of the bus on a three-passenger bench occupied by a white woman. The bus driver asked them to move to the rear, where there was standing room only. The Negro girls refused but offered to leave the bus if the driver would refund their fares. The driver said no. The girls sat tight. The driver then drove to a nearby filling station and called the police, who proceeded to arrest the girls on charges of violating a local ordinance that required segregated seating in public transportation. That night a cross was burned in front of the dormitory where the two students—released on bond—were living.

The next day at noon the students of Peripheral State A. and M. held a mass meeting. After listening to several speeches they voted unanimously "to refrain from riding city busses" for the rest of the school term. That afternoon crowds of students stopped the busses running through the campus and "asked" the Negro passengers to disembark. The dean and the president of the College soon put a stop to this practice, but the Negro community got the message. By midafternoon, almost no Negroes—students or adults—were riding the city busses.

On May 29 a citywide mass meeting called by the Negro Ministerial Association was held at the Baptist Church. The overflow crowd of Negro adults voted unanimously to boycott the city busses, formed a new organization called the Inter-Civic Council, and elected the young and militant Reverend K. C. Stone as its president. The ICC immediately pledged itself to the nonviolent pursuit of three objectives: the seating of all bus passengers on a "first come, first served" basis, the hiring of Negroes as bus drivers, and more courteous treatment of Negro passengers.

During the next few days an elaborate car pool was set up to get Negroes to their jobs. The managers of the local bus company, whose busses on most routes were now almost empty, claimed that their hands were tied so long as the segregation ordinance remained in effect.

After several tense weeks the city commissioners took action. They got in touch with the long-established (Negro) Civic League, which historically had taken a very "accommodating" position on racial problems, and suggested a compromise. They proposed that only the first three seats on each bus be kept segregated and promised that in the future bus drivers would be hired on the basis of job qualifications alone. Most of the Civic League officers were officials and employees at the state-supported Negro college and were fearful that the boycott would lead to budget cuts and political reprisals. So they recommended that the compromise be accepted and that the boycott be terminated at once.

The leaders of the ICC promptly denounced the Civic League as "traitors" and implored the Negro rank and file to carry on their fight for equal treatment on the city's busses. The next day the busses were as empty as before. Two weeks later, the boycott still in effect, the bus company suspended service throughout the city.

Capital City was not to have desegregated bus service for years—and then thanks to a federal court order. But the city had an entirely new group of leaders, young, articulate, demanding, militant, uncompromising, and black. And Capital City had entered a new era of racial crisis marked by shootings, cross-burnings, mass arrests, legal harassment of car-pool drivers, near riots, and festering ill will from which it has not yet, a decade later, emerged.

• • •

Tom Scott left the office of one of Urbania's largest and most prosperous law firms, in which he was a junior partner, and walked several blocks to the Workingman's Bank on Church Street. Exchanging greetings with the tellers as he strode across the marble floor of the bank, he headed toward the mahogany-paneled room in which the board of directors usually met. The others were already there, seated in leather-upholstered chairs around the large conference table—the president of the Workingman's Bank, a city councilman, several lawyers, a labor union official, a college professor, and several others. Every one of them was a Negro. And the Workingman's Bank, so similar in appearance to most other banks in medium-sized cities, was owned and operated entirely by Negroes.

Tom Scott was a white man. He was also a candidate for the Democratic nomination for state representative from Piedmont County, in which Urbania is located. The nomination was tantamount to election, and the competition for it in 1964 was vigorous. Scott believed that he had little chance of winning without the endorsement of the Urbania League for Negro Affairs. He had, therefore, requested this opportunity to meet with the Political Committee of ULNA to ask for its support in the upcoming campaign. That was why they all were there.

The distinguished-looking chairman introduced Scott to the few members of the Committee whom he had not met before. Scott shook hands all around and then took a seat near the head of the conference table. He had done his homework. For about 15 minutes he presented his case without interruption. Then the questioning began—polite, but probing. After a while the questions ceased, Scott was shown to the door, and he went back to his office.

Then the waiting began. Evidently, ULNA was giving serious consideration to other candidates as well. Several weeks later a member of the Political Committee came to Scott's office and advised him that ULNA had decided to endorse him for the office. Scott's elation was not diminished by the detailed financial discussion that followed. ULNA does not sell its endorsements, but it does expect the candidates whom it endorses to contribute to its campaign work. A ward and block organization of the size and complexity of ULNA's is an expensive piece of human machinery.

ULNA's endorsement of Scott remained secret until election day. If word had leaked out, the white segregationists of Piedmont County would have had a chance to organize a massive vote against Scott.

The night before the election, a slate of ULNA-endorsed candidates was printed in a Negro-owned and Negro-operated print shop and distributed to the organization's workers. The next day these workers, armed with the printed slate and experienced in election-day campaigning, sprang into action. In the Negro sections of the city the voter turnout was higher than in the predominantly white wards—and 90 per cent of the Negro votes were cast for Tom Scott. Without the support of the Negroes he would have gone back to writing wills, searching titles, and preparing briefs. With their support he had become Piedmont County's representative in the state legislature.

· · ·

Although the names of people and places have been changed, all four of these stories are true.[1] No one of them alone is "typical" of the South today, but taken together they indicate the extraordinarily wide range of Negro political participation in the region.[2] At one end of the continuum (represented by Crayfish County) no Negroes have yet voted, politics is the white man's preserve, and the whites are willing to resort to violence and intimidation to keep out interlopers. At the other end (represented by Piedmont County) Negroes have achieved near parity at the ballot box, a few Negroes

[1] These case studies are based partly on the public record but primarily on our own observations and interviews with the participants and local observers. The interviews were conducted with the understanding that neither our informants nor their communities would be identified; hence we use pseudonyms for the communities and their inhabitants throughout the book. With one exception, we also use fictitious names for the states in which the four community studies were conducted. Since Mississippi is unique, we must identify it as the state in which Crayfish County is located in order to explain the politics of that community.

[2] The South has been defined, for purposes of this study, as the former Confederate states: Alabama, Arkansas, Florida, Georgia, Louisiana, Mississippi, North Carolina, South Carolina, Tennessee, Texas, and Virginia. The boundaries of "the South" have been variously defined, but this definition is the standard one for purposes of political analysis. See V. O. Key, Jr., *Southern Politics in State and Nation* (New York: Alfred A. Knopf, 1949). H. Douglas Price presents an interesting scale of "Southernness" in *The Negro and Southern Politics: A Chapter of Florida History* (New York: New York University Press, 1957), pp. 8–9.

have been elected to public office, and the Negro community plays an active and powerful role in the process of self-government. Not just the relationships between black and white are at issue. As the brief accounts of Bright Leaf and Camellia counties suggest, southern Negro communities are also in the midst of internal political upheavals.

# Chapter One

# Negroes in Southern Politics

If the incidents described in the Introduction are not necessarily "typical" of the South, what is? How much do Negroes participate in southern politics? In what ways? How common are situations like those in Crayfish, Bright Leaf, Camellia, and Piedmont counties? And why are the political status and power of the Negro so different in each of these communities?

Although the differences are large, all four communities have one important characteristic in common: Negroes consistently vote in smaller proportions and less often than do whites. Why? If all southern communities were like Crayfish County, the answer would be distressingly obvious. But in Bright Leaf County, for example, voters are registered with no noticeable racial bias—at least in the city of Farmington. Yet only 27 per cent of the Negro adults in the county have ever voted, compared to 82 per cent of the whites. In the two urban counties of Camellia and Piedmont, voter registration is clearly conducted without regard to race; in Piedmont County most of the electoral officials in Negro residential areas are themselves Negro. But in Camellia County only 61 per cent of the adult Negroes have voted, compared to 91 per cent of the voting-age whites. The comparable figures for Piedmont County are 75 per cent for Negroes and 82 per cent for whites.

What explains these differences in rates of political activity between the races? And what would southern politics be like if this racial gap were eliminated, if the Negroes' political power became roughly proportional to their numbers? Are whites' fears of Negro voting power in places like Crayfish County justified? And how much impact would increases in Negro political activity and power have on the region's historic patterns of social and economic segregation? These are the questions we shall try to answer in this book.

9

## The significance of the problem

These questions should be of considerable interest to students of political science, because their significance extends beyond Negro political behavior alone. If we are to answer them, we must use techniques and examine propositions that help us understand the political behavior of any group. Most studies of political behavior have focused on groups that have little in common with the American Negro, and they have been conducted in social and economic contexts that differ sharply from the American South. We can learn a great deal about political life *in general* from studying the exceptions to the well-established general rule—from examining the atypical situation.[1] At the most obvious level, we can determine whether some of the accepted generalizations about political behavior are truly general. To test such generalizations in the South is almost as demanding (if not nearly so exotic) as to test them in India or Thailand.

The South and the Negro are the great "deviant cases" in American life. The American political system has demonstrated, over its relatively short history, an extraordinary ability to absorb new groups and new peoples. One minority group after another—Irish, German, Italian, Polish—have become full and effective members of the political cast. No group has experienced such difficulty in achieving "first-class citizenship" as the most "American" of all these newcomers, the Negro. No group, save the Puerto Ricans, has undergone the painful process of political assimilation at a time when social scientists were so well equipped to study the operation in depth and with precision.

Finally, political scientists are rightly preoccupied with problems of change and "modernization" in a world that is in desperate need of both. But why study these phenomena in other cultures and ignore the revolutionary changes that are occurring in America's own "underdeveloped area"? For some reason most political scientists seem willing to leave the description and analysis of the South's political revolutions to today's journalists and tomorrow's historians.[2]

[1] On the utility of "deviant" case analysis, see P. F. Lazarsfeld and M. Rosenberg (eds.), *The Language of Social Research: A Reader in Methodology of Social Research* (Glencoe, Ill.: The Free Press, 1955), pp. 167–74.
[2] Among the exceptions, the most important are V. O. Key, Jr., *Southern Politics in State and Nation* (New York: Alfred A. Knopf, 1949); Alexander Heard, *A Two-Party South?* (Chapel Hill, N.C.: University of North Carolina Press, 1952); H. D. Price, *The Negro and Southern Politics: A Chapter of Florida History* (New York: New York University Press, 1957); James Q. Wilson, *Negro Politics* (Glencoe, Ill.: The Free Press, 1960); Bradbury Seasholes, "Negro Political Participation in Two North Carolina Cities" (Ph.D. dissertation, University of North Carolina, 1962); A. Sindler (ed.), *Change in the Contemporary South* (Durham, N.C.: Duke University Press, 1963); A. Leiserson (ed.), *The American South in the 1960's* (New York: Praeger, 1964). Several dissertations at the University of North Carolina based on our data have been helpful: L. Bennett, "The Political Competence of Southern Negroes";

The questions we shall try to answer in this book are not merely of academic significance. They address the central issues of domestic politics in mid-century America: the demands of Negroes for full participation in American life and the responses of the political system to those demands. Answers to these questions will affect not only those who support or oppose civil rights reform but also every participant in the political process.

Journalists, civil rights leaders, and politicians regard the vote as the southern Negro's strongest and most accessible weapon in his struggle for full citizenship and social and economic equality. They argue that "political rights pave the way for all others."[3] Once Negroes in the South vote in substantial numbers, politicians, be they white or black, will respond to the desires of the Negro community. Also, the white South—and southerners in Congress—will oppose federal action on voting less vigorously than they will oppose action on schools, jobs, or housing.

Such, at least, seems to have been the reasoning behind the four civil rights acts passed since 1957. All have dealt primarily with the right to vote. Presidents Eisenhower, Kennedy, and Johnson and every attorney general since Herbert Brownell have said that the vote provides the southern Negro with his most effective means of advancing toward equality.[4] Most Negro leaders share this belief in the overriding importance of the vote. Hundreds of registration drives have been held in southern cities and counties since 1957.[5] Martin Luther King, usually regarded as an advocate of direct protest, recently remarked that the biggest step Negroes can take is in the "direction of the voting booths."[6] The National Association for the Advancement of Colored People, historically identified with courtroom attacks on segregation, is now enthusiastically committed to a "battle of the ballots."[7] The Congress of Racial Equality, the National Urban League, and the Student Non-violent Co-

---

R. L. Bowman, "Negro Politics in Four Southern Counties"; G. R. Boynton, "Southern Republican Voting in the 1960 Election"; E. Dreyer, "A Study of the Patterns of Political Communication in the South"; D. M. Freeman, "Religion and Southern Politics: The Political Behavior of Southern White Protestants"; J. M. Orbell, "Social Protest and Social Structure: Southern Negro College Student Participation in the Protest Movement." Members of other social-science disciplines have devoted a good deal of attention to the problems of the Negro in the South.

[3] *New York Times*, January 7, 1962. On March 17, 1965, the *Times* concluded an editorial on the incidents in Selma, Alabama, by referring to the vote as ". . . the most powerful of democracy's weapons."

[4] *New York Times*, January 7, 1962; Louis E. Lomax, "The Kennedys Move in on Dixie," *Harper's*, May 1962, pp. 27–33; James Reston, "A Just and Compassionate Society," *New York Times*, March 17, 1965.

[5] For general survey articles on these registration drives, see *Wall Street Journal*, November 6, 1961, and *New York Times*, July 10, 1961.

[6] "Civil Right No. 1—The Right to Vote," *New York Times Magazine*, March 14, 1965, pp. 26ff.

[7] The 1962 NAACP National Convention had "Battle of the Ballots" as its theme. *Raleigh News and Observer* (N.C.), June 24, 1962.

ordinating Committee have also been fighting for the right of southern Negroes to vote.

The focus on the vote for Negroes in the South is understandable. Yet some thoughtful observers are skeptical about how much registration drives and federal legislation can add to the number of Negroes who are already voting. Most southern Negroes have low social status, relatively small incomes, and limited education received in inferior schools. These attributes are associated with low voter turnout among all populations.[8] The low voting rates of Negroes in the South are, to perhaps a large extent, a result of these factors rather than of *direct* political discrimination by the white community. Moreover, the low status, income, and education of the southern whites themselves foster racial prejudice.[9] Thus poverty and ignorance may have a double-barreled effect on Negro political participation: they may decrease the Negroes' desire and ability to participate effectively while increasing white resistance to Negro participation. Negro voting in the South is not, according to this reasoning, easily increased by political or legal means. The rise of a large, active, and effective Negro electorate in the South may have to await substantial social and economic change.

Northern and western Negroes have been voting in substantial numbers for generations, but they have yet to vote themselves social or economic equality. Nonsouthern Negroes are certainly better off than their counterparts below the Mason-Dixon Line. But most still live in ghettos, most hold low-paying jobs that no one else wants, most receive inferior educations in segregated schools, and so on and on.[10] If the vote has not solved the Negroes' problems in the North, why should we expect it to in the South?[11]

The future role of the Negro in southern politics hinges on questions that political scientists ought to be able to answer. Can registration drives, legal pressure on voter registrars or their actual displacement by federal officials, the abolition of the poll tax, the revision or suspension of literacy tests, and similar political and legal reforms really change Negro political activity enough

[8] For some useful summaries of the literature, see S. M. Lipset *et al.*, "The Psychology of Voting," in G. Lindzey (ed.), *Handbook of Social Psychology* (Cambridge, Mass.: Addison-Wesley Publishing Co., 1954), Vol. 2, pp. 1126–34; and Robert E. Lane, *Political Life* (Glencoe, Ill.: The Free Press, 1959), ch. 16.

[9] B. Bettelheim and M. Janowitz, *The Dynamics of Prejudice* (New York: Harper & Brothers, 1950); Herbert H. Hyman and Paul B. Sheatsley, "Attitudes Toward Desegregation," *Scientific American*, Vol. 195 (1956), pp. 35–39; Melvin M. Tumin, *Desegregation: Resistance and Readiness* (Princeton, N.J.: Princeton University Press, 1958). For somewhat contrary findings, see James W. Vander Zanden, "Voting on Segregationist Referenda," *Public Opinion Quarterly*, Vol. 25 (1961), pp. 92–105.

[10] The classic study of the Negro's position in American life is Gunnar Myrdal, *An American Dilemma* (New York: Harper & Brothers, 1944), 2 vols. A shorter, more popular, and more up-to-date treatment of the Negro problem (mostly in the North) today is Charles E. Silberman, *Crisis in Black and White* (New York: Random House, 1964).

[11] For a thoughtful analysis, see William R. Keech, "The Negro Vote as a Political Resource" (Ph.D. dissertation, University of Wisconsin, 1966).

to reshape southern politics? Or do the social and economic realities of the region make the goal of Negro parity at the ballot box impossible to achieve for generations and, once won, of little value?

To date, political scientists have not come up with firm answers to these questions. History does provide some clues, but they are confusing, ambiguous, and seemingly contradictory.

## Some contradictory lessons of history

Shortly after the end of the Civil War, southern Negroes were enfranchised by the Reconstruction Act of 1867. Then the Fourteenth and Fifteenth Amendments to the Constitution (ratified in 1868 and 1870) forbade the states to discriminate "on account of race, color, or previous condition of servitude" in setting suffrage requirements.[12] For a time, the southern electorate was predominantly black; the South was ruled by a coalition of former slaves and their northern sympathizers. Even friendly observers agreed that the government of the region was extravagant, corrupt, and incompetent.[13]

Although these charges are undoubtedly accurate, they may exaggerate the contribution of the new Negro voters to the South's postwar difficulties. How would a region disrupted militarily, politically, economically, and socially have fared under any rulers? "In fact," an eminent Negro scholar has observed, "if the situation in the South is compared with revolutionary situations in other parts of the world, the Negroes exhibited considerable restraint and intelligence during the transition to their new status."[14] Given the abruptness of the change, and the fact that the Negroes were almost totally uneducated, impoverished, and lacking in governmental experience, perhaps what should surprise us is that the reconstructed state governments functioned as well as they did.

### THE DISFRANCHISEMENT OF SOUTHERN NEGROES

These regimes soon fell. United by fear of Negro domination and hatred of a seemingly vengeful North, the southern whites struck back any way they could. As they regained their political rights, the number and proportion of white voters swelled. The whites controlled the region's economy and its

12 Northern Negroes were thereby enfranchised, too. Prior to the Civil War, Negroes were disfranchised by the constitutions of all states save Maine, Massachusetts, New Hampshire, Rhode Island, and Vermont. In practice, "the free exercise of the suffrage by the Negroes was said to be restricted to Maine." V. O. Key, Jr., *Politics, Parties, and Pressure Groups,* 4th ed. (New York: Thomas Y. Crowell Co., 1962), p. 604.

13 See, for example, Paul Levinson, *Race, Class, and Party* (New York: Oxford University Press, 1932), ch. 2. We have relied heavily on this volume in preparing this section.

14 E. Franklin Frazier, *The Negro in the United States* (New York: Macmillan, 1957), p. 136.

social institutions, and they used their power ruthlessly to discourage Negro participation. The Ku Klux Klan and other terrorist organizations sprang up to intimidate real or imagined Negro agitators and activists. Finally, when President Hayes withdrew federal troops from the South in 1877, he knocked the last prop from under the Negro-carpetbagger regimes, and the whites quickly recovered their control of the region's government.[15] Thus "... within 10 to 15 years after 1867 the premature enfranchisement of the Negro was largely undone, and undone by a veritable revolution."[16]

Now the southern whites began to experiment with ways to disfranchise Negroes permanently. The effort called for solidarity and legal ingenuity. When bitter controversy broke out between white factions, the temptation to seek Negro support at the polls was overwhelming. This is exactly what happened during the Populist rebellion of the 1890's.

> The Farmers Alliance and the Populist party generated a dispute among whites whose outcome was of such deep concern that both factions breached the consensus to keep the blacks from the polls. Both Democrats and Populists were willing to bid for Negro support. According to southern tradition Negroes were in a position to hold the balance of power between white factions. The degree to which Negroes actually voted *en bloc* and participated in the elections of the agrarian uprising has never been adequately investigated. . . . Nevertheless, the Populists, either alone or in combination with Republicans, threatened Democratic supremacy, and a situation emerged in which the plea for white supremacy could be made effectively.[17]

Led by Mississippi in 1890, most of the southern states changed their constitutions so as to disfranchise Negroes without apparent conflict with the Fifteenth Amendment. Without even mentioning Negroes, many states lengthened their residential requirements for voting—on the assumption that Negroes were more mobile than whites—and made the payment of cumulative poll taxes a precondition for voting. A variety of elaborate literacy tests were written into the state constitutions. In most cases these required that fledgling voters to be able to read a section of the state constitution aloud and/or to demonstrate that they understood its provisions.[18] The southern lawmakers could, of course, rely on local registrars to see that no Negroes met these requirements but that most whites did. Partly as a result of these new require-

---

15 On the politics of this period, see C. Vann Woodward, *Reunion and Reaction* (Garden City, N.Y.: Doubleday, Anchor, 1956).

16 Key, *Southern Politics,* p. 536.

17 V. O. Key, Jr., *Southern Politics* (New York: copyright © 1949 by Alfred A. Knopf), p. 541, reprinted by permission of the publisher.

18 A chronological listing and description of these constitutional changes may be found in U.S. Commission on Civil Rights, *1959 Report* (Washington, D.C.: U.S. Government Printing Office, 1959), pp. 31–32. Disfranchisement was but one part of a larger movement to require racial segregation by law. See C. Vann Woodward, *The Strange Career of Jim Crow* (New York: Oxford University Press, 1955),

ments, the number of Negro voters in the region dwindled to insignificance.[19]

Negro litigants urged the United States Supreme Court to look behind the legal verbiage of these state constitutional provisions and decide whether or not they violated the Fifteenth Amendment. The Supreme Court refused to respond.[20] In *Williams* v. *Mississippi*, for example, the Court held that Mississippi's suffrage requirements did "not on their face discriminate between the races" and that it had "not been shown that their actual administration was evil, only that evil was possible under them." Southern generals may have lost the battles but southern politicians had won "The War."

What lesson can we learn from this brief historical sketch? "The right to vote" is not the same thing as the effective exercise of that right. To give the franchise to an uneducated and impoverished minority in the face of vehement opposition from a united majority that controls the economic and social life of a region is likely to be fruitless—unless the minority is supported by force of arms from "outside." The vote alone—*without* other sources of power, *without* education or wealth or status, and *without* armed support—is not a sufficient resource for effective citizenship. Without other resources, southern Negroes in the 1890's were not able to protect their vote, let alone use it to advance themselves.[21]

This chapter of southern history is sobering indeed to those who place infinite faith in the efficacy of legal reforms and Negro ballots as "solutions" to the racial problems of the South today. The legal right to vote appears to be an insufficient condition for effective citizenship. But the history of Negro voting in the South since the turn of the century suggests a contrary conclusion.

## THE DEATH OF THE WHITE PRIMARY

As the spokesmen for "white supremacy," the southern Democrats had virtually liquidated their Populist and Republican opposition by the time the

[19] How influential the constitutional changes actually were in producing the result is still in dispute. Key, in *Southern Politics*, pp. 533ff., argues, on the basis of Texas election data, that the constitutional changes merely "legitimized" Negro disfranchisement which had already been brought about through violence and the collapse of Populism after 1896. Levinson, *op. cit.*, p. 81, using Louisiana voter registration figures, concludes that the new constitutions were primarily responsible for the precipitous decline in Negro voting.

[20] *Williams* v. *Mississippi*, 170 U.S. 213 (1898); *Giles* v. *Harris*, 189 U.S. 475 (1903). In *Guinn* v. *United States*, 238 U.S. 347 (1915), the Supreme Court did declare Oklahoma's "grandfather clause" unconstitutional, but this clause was merely a way of exempting whites from the difficult tests placed between Negroes and the ballot box. Before any of these decisions, the Court had narrowed the impact of the Fourteenth Amendment in the *Civil Rights Cases*, 109 U.S. 3 (1883), and it had ruled that the Amendment permitted racial segregation on a "separate but equal" basis in *Plessy* v. *Ferguson*, 163 U.S. 537 (1896).

[21] See Key, *Politics, Parties, and Pressure Groups*, pp. 628–29.

disfranchising constitutions were adopted. The Republicans were identified with military defeat and Negro domination during Reconstruction. The Populists had demonstrated that any real party competition would lead to Negro voting. As a result, the whites were now almost all Democrats. The Democratic primary elections had become the "real" elections in which the effective choices between competing candidates and policies were made. The postwar amendments to the Constitution prohibited *states* from denying the vote on the basis of color, but the Democratic party, as a "private" association, could discriminate against Negroes if it so desired. By the prohibition of Negroes from taking part in any Democratic primary, Negroes could be denied a voice in the government of the region even if they somehow managed to register as voters.[22]

At first the "white primary," as this racially exclusive nominating device came to be called, was merely a continuation of local practice and custom— southern Negroes were all Republicans anyway. But over the years the notion that only whites could participate in Democratic party affairs was written into state party rules in most southern states (in Florida, North Carolina, and Tennessee county option prevailed). Despite a few local exceptions in three states, and occasionally lax enforcement elsewhere, the white primary quickly became the most common—and seemingly the most invulnerable—means of disfranchising Negroes in the South.

The Texas legislature of 1923, however, unwittingly made the white primaries vulnerable to attack as unconstitutional by requiring them *by statute.* Court cases were immediately brought by Texas Negroes who had been denied access to the primary.[23] The Texas Negroes argued that the Texas Democratic party was, in fact as well as in law, an agent of the state and hence was bound by the federal prohibition against racial discrimination in setting voting requirements. Each time a Negro plaintiff won a case of this sort, southern legislatures changed the legal and party rules to bring the white primary into technical compliance with the decision, thus requiring still another return to the courtroom. Finally, in 1944, the Supreme Court handed down a decision (in *Smith* v. *Allwright*[24]) that seemed to make the white primary unconstitutional under almost any conceivable condition.

> The Court reasoned that the primary in Texas was an integral part of the machinery of choosing officials. Although the Democratic state convention had acted on its own authority and not as an agent of the state in excluding Negroes

[22] On the origins and characteristics of the "white primary," see Key, *Southern Politics,* ch. 29 and *passim;* and Levinson, *op. cit.,* ch. 3.

[23] *Nixon* v. *Herndon,* 273 U.S. 536 (1927); *Nixon* v. *Condon,* 286 U.S. 73 (1932); *Grovey* v. *Townsend,* 295 U.S. 45 (1935).

[24] 321 U.S. 649 (1944). This decision was anticipated by *United States* v. *Classic,* 313 U.S. 299 (1941), in which the Supreme Court held that a primary in a one-party state (Louisiana) was bound by the United States Constitution. This decision, however, did not concern racial exclusion from the primary.

from the primary, in other respects the primary was regulated by state law and the state provided procedure by which the party certified its nominees for inclusion on the general election ballot. By such action the state itself endorsed and enforced the party's discrimination against Negroes. Under these circumstances, discrimination by the party had to be treated as discrimination by the state.[25]

More legal maneuvering followed. Various states probed for loopholes in the decision and sought to salvage some measure of racial exclusion from the wreckage. But by now the Court had substantially expanded its concept of "state action" and had shown that it was willing to look at the political facts behind the legal technicalities. One after another of these ignoble experiments fell before court attack. Thus, after more than twenty years of litigation, the 1944 decision had signaled the death of the white primary. Subsequent decisions buried it.

### THE RISE IN NEGRO VOTING SINCE 1944

Once the white primary had been killed, the number and proportion of Negroes registered to vote in the southern states increased with startling speed (see Table 1–1). According to the best estimates available—they are often only informed guesses—about 250,000 Negroes (5 per cent of the adult nonwhite population) were registered voters before the historic decision of 1944. Most of them were allowed to vote only in meaningless general elections and usually unimportant nonpartisan contests and referenda. Three years after *Smith* v. *Allwright*, both the number and the proportion of registered Negro voters had doubled. By 1952 about 20 per cent of the Negro adults, compared to over 60 or 70 per cent of voting-age whites, were registered voters. At that time, however, the growth of Negro voter registration began to slow down. By 1956, the authoritative Southern Regional Council estimated that about 25 per cent of the Negro adults in the region were registered; four years later the estimate was only 28 per cent.

One major reason for this slowdown was the racial crisis precipitated by the Supreme Court's *Brown* v. *Board of Education*[26] decision of 1954, which outlawed racial segregation in the public schools. At first the white South seemed stunned by the decision and the magnitude of change it demanded; when the reaction came, it was vehement. Racial tensions grew alarmingly, and white resistance to Negro advancement stiffened in every realm, including the political. Several states adopted new and more demanding voter requirements, and others applied old requirements more strictly.

But some gave other reasons for the declining rate of growth in Negro voter registration. By the early 1950's the "natural" voters among southern

---

[25] V. O. Key, Jr., *Southern Politics* (New York: copyright © 1949 by Alfred A. Knopf), p. 624, reprinted by permission of the publisher. For legal developments following *Smith* v. *Allwright*, see *ibid.*, pp. 625–43.

[26] 347 U.S. 483 (1954).

TABLE 1-1.   *Estimated number and percentages
of voting-age Negroes registered to vote
in eleven southern states, 1940–1966*

| Year | Estimated number | Percentage |
|------|-----------------|------------|
| 1940 | 250,000 | 5% |
| 1947 | 595,000 | 12 |
| 1952 | 1,008,614 | 20 |
| 1956 | 1,238,038 | 25 |
| 1958 | 1,266,488 | 25 |
| 1960 | 1,414,052 | 28 |
| 1964 | 1,907,279 | 38 |
| 1966 | 2,306,434 | 46 |

SOURCES: U.S. census data on nonwhite population and Negro registration estimates in G. Myrdal, *An American Dilemma* (New York: Harper & Brothers, 1944), p. 488; M. Price, *The Negro Voter in the South* (Atlanta: Southern Regional Council, 1957), p. 5; "The Negro Voter in the South—1958," *Special Report* (Atlanta: Southern Regional Council, 1958), p. 3; U.S. Commission on Civil Rights, *1959 Report* (Washington, D.C.: U.S. Government Printing Office, 1959), and *Voting* (Washington, D.C.: U.S. Government Printing Office, 1961); *New York Times*, August 8, 1965 (official U.S. Civil Rights Commission estimates for 1964); Southern Regional Council, *New South*, Vol. 21 (Winter 1966), p. 88.

Negroes—the well-educated, politically involved middle class—seemed to have gotten their names on the voters' lists throughout most of the region. The non-registered Negroes were relatively apathetic. According to this view, the slow-down was the result of social, economic, and psychological factors rather than of "legal" and administrative barriers. Although this was a plausible interpretation, its validity was soon in serious doubt.

Between 1960 and 1964 the number of registered Negroes in the South increased by about 500,000—the most startling increase during any four-year period since the death of the white primary. If all the "natural" Negro voters were on the books in 1960, something had caused an incredible number of "unnatural" voters to register. In the Johnson-Goldwater election of 1964, almost two million southern Negroes—about 38 per cent of all those of voting age—were registered to vote. By early 1966 the number had climbed to 2,306,434, or 46 per cent of all voting-age Negroes.

The causes of this sharp increase are difficult to untangle. The Negro Protest Movement, which began in earnest in 1960, stimulated unprecedented political interest among Negroes during these years. A massive Voter Education Project, conducted under the auspices of the Southern Regional Council, helped to increase greatly the organizational activity and effectiveness of Negro communities in the region. Gradual social and economic change, especially after the start of the Second World War, undoubtedly had a delayed effect on Negro political activity. And, beginning in 1957 with the passage of the first civil rights act since Reconstruction, the federal government again drastically altered the legal setting in which Negroes were seeking effective suffrage in the South.

The major goal of the civil rights acts of the late 1950's and the 1960's was to eliminate racial discrimination in voter registration in the southern states. The 1957 act had empowered the Attorney General of the United States to seek court injunctions when an individual was deprived, or was about to be deprived, of his right to vote. The 1960 civil rights act went one step further, by providing for the appointment of federal voter "referees" to register potential voters when the courts determined that there was a "pattern or practice" of depriving Negroes of their vote in a specified area. In 1962 Congress proposed a constitutional amendment outlawing the poll tax in federal elections (but *not* in state or local contests); this proposal became the Twenty-fourth Amendment to the United States Constitution early in 1964.

Later that same year Congress passed a third civil rights act. This law dwarfed the earlier ones in scope and importance, but its primary aim was still to ensure Negroes easy and equal access to the ballot. Among other things, it made the unequal administration of voting requirements a federal crime, prohibited the denial of the right to vote on the basis of minor errors or omissions in the process of applying to vote, required that all literacy tests be given in writing and that applicants be able to examine these tests after taking them, and stated that a sixth-grade education must be considered proof of literacy.

To political leaders outside the South, these efforts to eliminate the alleged abuses of southern electoral administration appeared inadequate. Consequently the House of Representatives on August 3, 1965, and the Senate on August 4 overwhelmingly passed the administration-backed voting rights bill. The act:

1. Suspended literacy tests and similar devices in all states or counties in which less than 50 per cent of the voting-age residents were registered to vote on November 1, 1964. This clause initially affected 26 counties in North Carolina and the entire states of Alabama, Georgia, Louisiana, Mississippi, South Carolina, and Virginia.
2. Provided for the appointment of federal examiners to register persons in these areas to vote.
3. Directed the Attorney General "forthwith" to institute court action against the enforcement of poll taxes as a prerequisite to voting in state and local elections.[27] (In 1966 the federal courts upheld these efforts, thereby outlawing the poll tax in all elections.)

[27] Brief, nontechnical summaries of the legislative history and contents of the civil rights acts of 1957, 1960, and 1964 and the Voting Rights Act of 1965 may be found in Congressional Quarterly Service, *Congress and the Nation, 1945–1964* (Washington, D.C.: U.S. Government Printing Office, 1965), pp. 1615–41, and *Congressional Quarterly Weekly Report*, August 6, 1965, pp. 1539–40.

On August 6, 1965, President Johnson signed the bill into law in the ornate President's Room of the Capitol Building. In the same room, 104 years ago to the day, President Lincoln had signed a bill freeing slaves who had been forced into Confederate Army service. President Johnson commemorated the occasion by calling the act "one of the most monumental laws in the entire history of American freedom."[28]

But is it? How much difference will it really make? In the 13 southern counties to which federal examiners were immediately sent to register new Negro voters, 19,178 Negroes were registered to vote in the first ten days. About a month later, federal officials had registered 41,500 Negroes in 14 counties. By mid-March, 1966, the best estimates were that over 100,000 Negroes had been registered by the "feds" and over 200,000 by regular local registrars since passage of the 1965 act.[29] This was a large increase, but many observers were disappointed that it was not larger. Many had hoped for a million or more new voters in the first few months under the new act.

How much of the remaining gap in political participation between white and black in the South is actually the result of discriminatory voter registration? Our glance at the four southern communities of Piedmont, Camellia, Bright Leaf, and Crayfish counties suggests that other inhibitions are involved. Only in Crayfish County is the system of voter registration clearly aimed at keeping Negro voters off the books. But in all four counties Negroes participate in politics less than do the local whites.

Federal legislation and court decisions since 1944 have substantially increased Negro voter registration in the South. But how much more can the size of the Negro vote in the South be increased without *first* revolutionizing the social and economic structure of the region, without *first* altering the pattern of subordination within which southern Negroes live? And, even if the Negro vote does continue to increase rapidly and substantially, will Negroes be able to vote themselves equality in other realms of life? Despite drastic changes since the Reconstruction era, the basic question remains unanswered: Is the vote the golden key that will unlock the door to full citizenship and to social and economic equality for southern Negroes?

Only an entirely new examination of Negro political participation in the South—one that employs systematic empirical data—can throw much light on these perplexing questions. They pose the most urgent domestic problem the United States faces today.

[28] *New York Times,* August 8, 1965.
[29] See *New York Times,* August 22, 1965; September 12, 1965; and March 13, 1966.

# Chapter Two

# The Approach and the Data

We shall try to do four things in this book. First, we shall *describe* the political activities of the ten million adult Negroes in the South as fully and as accurately as we can. Second, we shall *explain* why some Negroes do, while many do not, participate in the political life of the region. Third, we shall try to *predict* the future of Negro political participation in the South. Finally, we shall explore the probable *consequences* of these current and future activities for the South and its racial problems.

## Describing Negro political participation

Before we can begin to talk about Negro political participation in the South, we must specify what we include in the concept of political participation. With the idea of political participation clearly fixed, we can find out what it is like for southern Negroes—that is, we can describe the political actions of all adult[1] Negroes living in the 11 states of the former Confederacy. Ideally, of course, this description would require observing and talking with every one of them—such a vast enterprise that only the federal government has the resources to carry it out, and then, only once every decade.

Fortunately, however, one can estimate—within small and known limits of accuracy—the characteristics of large groups of people by studying a relatively small sample of them. The theory of sampling is so esoteric, and sampling practices so complex, that we have relegated a full description of our sample to Appendix A. Perhaps here we need only say that the 618 voting-age Negroes interviewed for this study form a representative cross sec-

[1] The minimum voting age is 18 in Georgia; in the other states it is the usual 21.

tion of Negro southerners that can safely be considered to "stand for" all Negro adults living in private households in the region.[2]

When we try to describe such phenomena as political attitudes and behavior, we have to get along without absolute criteria for evaluation. There are simply none available. If we find, for example, that about 30 per cent of southern Negroes have a great deal of interest in politics (as we shall),[3] we can express the finding in quantitative terms, but the finding by itself is hard to evaluate. Is this level of interest unusually high, about average, or unusually low? Only if we have some bench mark for comparison can we interpret the finding. We can compare some of our findings with those from national studies conducted by others, but many of the attitudes with which we are concerned have not been investigated in other studies.

Moreover, the regional peculiarities of the South might account for any differences that were found in the attitudes of southern Negroes and other Americans. The political interest of Negroes in the South might appear high (or low) in comparison with that of the national population but quite normal in comparison with that of southern whites. To meet the need for a bench mark uncontaminated by "nonsouthern" influences, we undertook a parallel survey of southern voting-age whites. From the 694 respondents in that sample we discovered that about 30 per cent of the white adults in the South express a great deal of interest in politics. When we juxtapose this finding to that for Negroes, interpretation of both becomes possible.

Both samples of southerners were interviewed during the late winter and early spring of 1961 by professional interviewers of their own race and region.[4] The schedule of questions used by the interviewers, which the authors had "pretested" twice, appears in Appendix B.

Analyzing such a large body of data takes time—over four years in this case. Meanwhile, of course, the phenomena under study are changing. This is a significant limitation of survey research and, perhaps, is particularly serious when a rapidly changing subject is under examination. In order to compensate for this limitation, we have supplemented our 1961 data whenever possible with information collected by the Survey Research Center of the University of Michigan in their presidential election study of 1964. The directors of that study were kind enough to use in identical form a number of the questions developed for the present analysis. Thanks to their data, we are able to extend our analysis where necessary to include 1964 opinions.

[2] Most national samples contain from 1,500 to 2,500 respondents, of which about 200 to 250 are Negroes. Our sample of southern Negroes, therefore, is three times as large as that ordinarily employed for nationwide studies. In the usual national sample survey, the component of southern Negroes is so small that little analysis of them is possible.
[3] See Table 10–1.
[4] The field phase of this study is described in Morris Axelrod, Donald R. Matthews, and James W. Prothro, "Recruitment for Survey Research on Race Problems in the South," Public Opinion Quarterly, Vol. 26 (1962), pp. 254–62.

# Answering the "why?" questions: The analysis scheme

Once we have described the subject of study, we come to the more difficult problem of analysis. Why are some southern Negroes active in politics while others fail to participate?

Most attempts to explain political behavior have employed only one type of explanatory factor or, in the language of social science, one class of "independent variables." Thus political participation is often explained entirely in terms of individual motivations and attitudes, or entirely on the basis of individual social and economic characteristics, or entirely on the basis of community characteristics. This kind of approach can sometimes explain a great deal. But no such simple explanatory scheme is adequate to deal with Negro political participation in the South.

Individuals with strong political motivations, for example, normally are active and involved citizens. But one cannot make this assumption for southern Negroes: strong political motivations do not necessarily lead to voting if the individual happens to be a Negro living in Crayfish County, Mississippi. On the other hand, in Piedmont County, where white-imposed restraints on Negro political participation are slight, some Negroes are thoroughgoing political activists while others are as politically inert as any Negro in Crayfish County. Obviously *both* individual *and* community characteristics affect Negro political activity in the South. To rely exclusively on one class of variables is to run the risk of being spectacularly wrong in explaining Negro participation in southern politics.

On both the community and the individual level, some factors are more immediately and directly related to Negro political activity, or the lack of it, than others. Some factors have as immediate and direct an effect on Negro participation as the crack on the head Jim Rock gave John Jones in Crayfish County, or as the presence of a Negro candidate on the ballot in Farmington, the largest city in Bright Leaf County. In such cases, the time lag between "cause" and "effect" or between "stimulus" and "response" is neglible; the link between the two is direct rather than circuitous.

But not all the variables that presumably affect Negro participation are so immediate or direct in their impact. Other scholars have demonstrated, for example, that the level of Negro voter registration in southern counties *today* is related to the extent of cotton production in those counties many years ago,[5] or to the relative size of Negro and white populations *in 1900*.[6] We

[5] U.S. Commission on Civil Rights, *1961 Report* (Washington, D.C.: U.S. Government Printing Office, 1961), Vol. I, Part 3.
[6] H. Douglas Price, *The Negro and Southern Politics: A Chapter of Florida History* (New York: New York University Press, 1957), pp. 41ff.

cannot fully understand the political role of the southern Negro today without some comprehension of the particularly vicious form slavery took in the United States,[7] and of the varying impact of the Civil War and Reconstruction on different parts of the South. "The War" and Reconstruction converted Urbania in Piedmont County, for example, from a sleepy crossroads village into a thriving tobacco-processing center. In Camellia County, however, white memories are dominated by southern heroism in nearby battles and the alleged horrors of a black-controlled state government in Capital City. The political consequences of these different historical backgrounds are still evident in the two communities.

Perhaps Figure 2–1 will help the reader visualize the complex system of variables that we believe affect Negro political activity in the South. At the extreme right (G) is our "dependent variable," Negro political participation. All the other boxes in the diagram represent different types of independent variables; the solid lines represent flows of influence or "causation." Note that the different classes of variables are arranged along the two dimensions discussed above: individual Negro attributes appear at the top of the diagram, and community characteristics at the bottom. The variables toward the right have a more immediate and direct impact on Negro activity than those toward the left.

We view the determinants of political activity (in the present case, of southern Negroes, but in principle of anyone anywhere) as falling into four major classifications. The importance of each of these sets of variables for political participation has been demonstrated in other studies, although this may be the first effort to examine all of them in a single study.

First, the individual's social and economic attributes (B)—age, sex, education, occupation, and the like—are strongly associated with the level of his political participation. So we shall turn first to how these individual characteristics are related to the political activity of southern Negroes.

Second, the structure of the community (C) in which an individual Negro lives has an effect on whether or not he engages actively in its political life. Here we are concerned with such matters as the proportion of Negroes in the local population, whether the Negro lives in an urban or rural area, and the occupation and education of his neighbors, white and black. We hypothesize that these community characteristics have an effect on the individual's political participation, regardless of his own personal attributes: that a college-educated Negro, for example, will participate less if he lives in a rural, black-belt community than if he lives in a city; that he will participate less if he lives in a community with a low general level of education than

[7] Stanley M. Elkins, *Slavery: A Problem in American Institutional and Intellectual Life* (Chicago: University of Chicago, 1959).

FIGURE 2–1. *Classes of variables affecting Negro political participation*

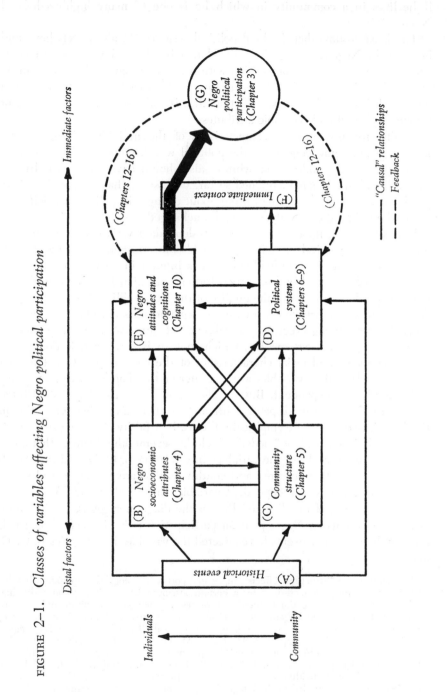

Individuals ⟷ Community

Distal factors ⟶ Immediate factors

(A) Historical events

(B) Negro socioeconomic attributes (Chapter 4)

(C) Community structure (Chapter 5)

(D) Political system (Chapters 6–9)

(E) Negro attitudes and cognitions (Chapter 10)

(F) Immediate context

(G) Negro political participation (Chapter 3)

(Chapters 12–16)

(Chapters 12–16)

——— "Causal" relationships
– – – Feedback

if he lives in a community in which he is one of many highly educated Negroes.[8]

Third, we assume that the local political system (D) also affects how, and how much, Negroes engage in political activity. Formal voter requirements and their administration, competition within and between parties, the quantity and quality of Negro political organization and leadership, and so on, should have an impact on Negro participation that is independent of individual or community social and economic attributes.

Finally, the psychological characteristics of the individual Negro (E)— interest in and knowledge about the political world, sense of political competence and efficacy, and fear of whites—also should have an impact. In this case, as in all the others mentioned so far, we assume that changes in Negro psychological characteristics will bring about changes in political participation even when the other variables remain unchanged.

We assume that these four classes of independent variables are related not only to Negro political participation but also to one another. Thus, for example, the extent of an individual Negro's interest in an election campaign (E) is probably shaped by how much formal education he has received (B), which is partly a function of the quality of the local public school system (C). An election contest between two white segregationists is not likely to stimulate much interest among Negroes: this absence of any real choice is a product of the local political system (D), which in turn is partly a reflection of the social, economic, and racial characteristics of the community (C). The four classes of independent variables at the center of the diagram, then, are likely to be highly interdependent. But we also assume that they are *not* so interdependent that we can dispense with any of them altogether. Our aim in this book is to demonstrate empirically the truth or falsity of these assumptions.

Our analysis scheme—or "model"—includes several other features that a full explanation requires. First, the variables in categories B, C, D, and E were all shaped by events that occurred and conditions that arose many decades ago. Thus a fifth category of independent variables, historical events (A), appears at the extreme left of the diagram. But, as the diagram suggests, the influence of historical events on Negro political participation today is never *direct*; it is felt only because those events have affected the variables in categories B, C, D, and E.

[8] The literature on "structural effects" in contemporary sociology demonstrates that belonging to a group characterized by a certain attribute has an impact on individual behavior over and above the influence of possessing that same attribute oneself. See Peter M. Blau, "Formal Organizations: Dimensions of Analysis," *American Journal of Sociology*, Vol. 63 (1957), pp. 58–69, and "Structural Effects," *American Sociological Review*, Vol. 25 (1960), pp. 178–93. James M. Davis, Joe L. Spaeth, and Carolyn Huson, "Analyzing Effects of Group Composition," *American Sociological Review*, Vol. 26 (1961), pp. 215–25, and Arnold S. Tannenbaum and Jerald G. Bachman, "Structural Versus Individual Effects," *American Journal of Sociology*, Vol. 69 (1964), pp. 585–95, suggest useful methodological improvements on Blau's seminal work.

Second, the variables in A, B, C, and D all must be filtered through individual Negro minds (E) before they can affect Negro participation. Our model therefore includes no direct causal links between political participation (G) and any of the other classes of independent variables (A, B, C, D).

Finally, a sixth box, labeled "immediate context" (F), intervenes between the psychological attributes of Negroes and political action. Most of these factors are random and idiosyncratic—rain on election day, for example. Those immediate-context variables that can be analyzed by social scientists are mostly offshoots of the political system (D)—the nature of the candidates and the attitudes of the local registrar of voters, for example, might be part of the immediate context of the act of voting. The immediate context, however, is less likely to produce action than it is to stop or reshape action; hence it is represented in the diagram as a screen that reduces or redirects the action flowing from E to G, rather than as one of the multiple "causes" of Negro participation.

## Answering the "why?" questions: The data

To devise a logical scheme of analysis like the one shown in Figure 2–1 is much easier than to apply it to reality. One reason is that no single research technique is equally well suited to studying *all* the types of variables that we believe affect Negro participation. The sample survey, for example, is an ideal way to collect information on present-day individual attributes, attitudes, and behavior. It is far less powerful as a tool for analyzing the effects of historical events or community characteristics. But the research techniques usually employed in historical or community studies lack the descriptive and analytic power that the sample survey has in the study of individuals. Thus to rely on a single research technique is dangerous: it may bias our analysis in the direction of those factors that the technique most easily accommodates.

The best way to find out about the political life of Negroes in the South is to ask them about it. But this is not enough. We are convinced that community characteristics have an impact on individual behavior that is not revealed simply by analyzing individual responses to questions. To some extent we can relate the characteristics of different communities to individual behavior by taking the average response of all interviewees in a community as a general characteristic of the entire community.[9] But the respondents in the usual sample survey are so widely scattered throughout the area being studied that too few interviews are taken in any single community to be of much use. Our interviews with southern Negroes were taken in 24 counties in

[9] See the literature cited in footnote 8. A. Campbell *et al.*, *The American Voter* (New York: John Wiley & Sons, 1960), have pioneered in the use of survey research techniques in analyzing community-based political variables.

all 11 states. From time to time we shall look at the characteristics of these counties—using either nonsurvey data about the community collected by the survey interviewing staff[10] or the average of responses obtained from all the individuals interviewed in the community. But if these were all the data on community and political structure at our command, we could say very little about communities as such, and we would have to restrict our analysis of why Negroes do and do not participate in southern politics almost entirely to individuals. So we looked beyond our survey data for additional information on community characteristics and how they are related to Negro political participation.

For the first of these supplementary sources of information we conducted detailed community studies in the counties of Crayfish, Camellia, Bright Leaf, and Piedmont.

Two considerations led us to choose these four counties out of the 1,136 counties in the South. First, we wanted the communities to be widely separated and very different in their social and political characteristics. Crayfish and Camellia counties are in the Deep South,[11] while Bright Leaf and Piedmont are in the Peripheral South; Crayfish and Bright Leaf are predominantly rural, while Camellia and Piedmont are each dominated by a medium-sized city.

At the time our research began, the Civil Rights Commission estimated that the following percentages of voting-age Negroes were registered to vote in each county: Crayfish, 0 per cent; Bright Leaf, 13 per cent; Camellia, 36 per cent; Piedmont, 61 per cent. Thus these four communities differ from one another in a number of attributes relevant to politics, namely:

| SUBREGION | NATURE OF COUNTY | |
|---|---|---|
| | Urban | Rural |
| Peripheral South | Piedmont (61% of Negroes registered) | Bright Leaf (13% of Negroes registered) |
| Deep South | Camellia (36% of Negroes registered) | Crayfish (0% of Negroes registered) |

Any number of other counties would have fitted this scheme equally well. Thus our second criterion of selection was one of convenience: we tried to pick the four counties for detailed study from among those represented in

10 Interviewers are seldom used to collect nonsurvey community data. We instructed our interviewers to fill out a brief questionnaire on the political system and social practices of each county in which they conducted interviews. They collected this information by visiting the county courthouse and local library and by interviewing, informally, public officials and such local leaders as the president of the local League of Women Voters and the minister of the largest Negro church.

11 Camellia County is in a state that we would classify as Peripheral South, but it is in a tier of counties that can definitely be classified as Deep South.

our southwide sample survey.[12] The reason for restricting our choice in this way was largely economic. We knew that we would be conducting a good many interviews with local residents in these communities as part of our southwide survey. By conducting a few more interviews in each, we saw that we could get representative samples of Negroes and whites *for each county* at bargain-basement prices, because we would be counting most of the interviews in *both* the southwide *and* the county samples. These small county samples,[13] then, permit us to make generalizations about the attitudes and behavior of voting-age residents of these four counties as well as of the South as a whole.

We did not confine our study of Crayfish, Camellia, Bright Leaf, and Piedmont counties to these systematic opinion surveys. We visited each county during 1961 and 1962 to observe them at first hand and personally to conduct semifocused interviews with local leaders and politically prominent persons.[14] We read the local newspapers carefully before and after our field trips. To ensure that we obtained roughly equal access to the leaders of both races, and to check against possible bias, we enlisted the help of four trained, experienced Negro social scientists. Each conducted a separate inquiry into the Negro community in one of the counties, following general instructions and using a common outline prepared for their use. We have drawn freely on their reports in our own interpretation of these four communities.

The four community studies gave us a good "feel" for the wide variety of political and racial situations that exist in the South today. They tended to correct the inherent qualitative limitations of our southwide sample survey, and they served as a constant reminder that generalizations about the South as a whole inevitably blur local differences. On the other hand, the community studies suffer from a major weakness that the regional sample survey does not have. Crayfish, Camellia, Bright Leaf, and Piedmont counties were arbitrarily selected for four case studies. We cannot generalize from them to all southern communities; they are illustrative, not representative.

To correct for this inherent limitation of case studies, we also collected aggre-

[12] A good example of a Peripheral South urban area with a high rate of Negro voter registration that was, in addition, convenient for detailed study did not appear in the southwide sample. So we selected Piedmont County for study, even though it was not one of the sampling points in the southwide survey.

[13] The sizes of these county samples are:

| County | Negro respondents | White respondents |
|---|---|---|
| Piedmont | 100 | 96 |
| Camellia | 77 | 68 |
| Bright Leaf | 75 | 82 |
| Crayfish | 48 | 56 |

The remarkably homogenous nature of the respondents in Crayfish County enabled us to rely on a smaller sample.

[14] Incumbents of certain social and political positions—mayor, police chief, county sheriff, chairman of the Democratic party, and so forth—were invariably interviewed. The interviewers in our sample surveys asked respondents to nominate "leaders"; the authors interviewed those most frequently mentioned in each county.

gate information on *all* biracial southern counties. Obviously, we could not make sample surveys in each county; nor could we personally conduct community studies. The United States Commission on Civil Rights, however, shortly after it was created by the Civil Rights Act of 1957, collected and published voter registration figures, by race, for every county in the South.[15] Although these data are approximate at best, and although voter registration is not the only form of political activity in which we are interested, they do furnish information on all the 997 counties in the region whose population contains more than 1 per cent Negroes. We also correlated the social, economic, and political characteristics of these counties as reported by the United States Census and other reference sources[16] with the rate of Negro voter registration for the entire region.

In addition to community studies and a massive analysis of aggregate data on all counties, we supplemented our survey of Negro political participation with an equally extensive survey of whites. We said earlier that the white survey was necessary for adequate description of Negro participation. It was also necessary for adequate explanation. The so-called Negro problem has long been recognized as at least equally a white problem. We could not hope to gain an understanding of Negro political participation in the South without also examining the context of white hopes, fears, prejudices, and expectations within which Negro political activity takes place.

Thus we were able to obtain all the data that our model of the processes determining Negro political participation required. This is probably the largest body of systematic political data on the American Negro ever collected.

Each of these different research techniques and bodies of data has strengths and limitations. The southwide aggregrate data permit conclusions of maximum generality. But they do not get at individual attitudes (except through perilous inference), and they include only limited information on the political characteristics of communities. Although the community studies lack generality, they furnish information on such community characteristics as historical background and qualities of local leadership. The southwide survey permits only limited analysis of community factors, but it gives us individual reports of attitudes and behavior, which are our ultimate concern. We hope that the weaknesses of each body of data are compensated for by the strengths of others. If so, we should be able to make the first reasonably complete explanation of Negro political participation in the South.

[15] U.S. Commission on Civil Rights, *1959 Report* and *1961 Report,* Vol. 1, "Voting" (Washington, D.C.: United States Government Printing Office, 1959 and 1961 respectively). The 1958 registration data, contained in the earlier report, are more complete and were used for all states except Tennessee. The 1960 figures, printed in the *1961 Report,* are the only ones available for Tennessee. For comments on the accuracy of these data, see our "Social and Economic Factors and Negro Voter Registration in the South," *American Political Science Review,* Vol. 57 (1963), pp. 25–26.
[16] A mimeographed list of these sources will be supplied on request.

# Predicting the future of Negro political participation

If accurate prediction is the hallmark of science, then political science has a long way to go before it deserves to be called a science. Given the present state of the discipline, prediction is a hazardous undertaking which the prudent practitioner avoids when he can. But southern politics and race relations are so difficult to accept as they exist that most students of the South eventually become preoccupied with the region's future. We are no exception.

Perhaps the best way to go about predicting Negro political participation in the South would be to conduct several studies like this one over a period of years. Then, with a "panel study" design,[17] we could measure rates of change precisely and discover the variables that are most closely associated with change. But a panel study was not feasible in this case: the subject we were studying required such a complex research design that the costs of such a study would have been prohibitive. We are forced, therefore, to try to make predictions about the future primarily on the basis of a single study conducted at one point in time.

The data collected during the 1964 presidential election permit some analysis of changes since 1961. But the Goldwater-Johnson contest was an aberrant affair. So the 1961 data appear—especially because they were collected in a noncampaign period—to constitute a better bench mark for projections into the future.

Our analysis of the factors that determine current rates of Negro political participation provides one useful, if by no means infallible, clue to the future. If the variables we find to be positively related to Negro political participation are increasing in number and value, while those we find to be negatively related are on the decline, then we can reasonably expect Negro participation to increase in the future. This expectation is based on the sometimes unrealistic assumption that relationships between independent and dependent variables will remain the same over time, despite changes in their value. Obviously, this reasoning pushes the problem of prediction back from the dependent to the independent variables. And the future values of the independent variables in this study can often be predicted with greater accuracy and certainty than can the future of Negro political participation outright.

A second clue to the future lies in the attitudes and behavior of today's young people: they will soon be the region's adult population. People change as they grow older, and today's young Negroes cannot be expected to carry all their present attitudes and beliefs with them unchanged into adult life.

[17] In a panel study the same respondents are interviewed several times at regular intervals. It is a particularly useful technique for analyzing short-run changes in attitudes or behavior. See P. F. Lazarsfeld and M. Rosenberg (eds.), *The Language of Social Research: A Reader in Methodology of Social Research* (Glencoe, Ill.: The Free Press, 1955), pp. 231–60.

Even so, we know a good bit about the political effects of maturation and aging. By taking into account the probable changes resulting from aging, we can roughly estimate what today's young people will be like in ten or twenty years.

Other factors underscore the need to include the region's youth in our study. Ever since early 1960, students in the predominantly Negro colleges in the South have been at the forefront of the civil rights struggle. They are likely to provide a disproportionate share of the future Negro leadership in the region. Because most of these students are not of voting age, they are not represented in our southwide sample of Negro adults.

But we wanted to learn something about the future Negro leaders of the region and about today's active militants. So we asked our Negro field staff to interview a representative sample of 264 Negro students attending accredited, predominantly Negro institutions of higher learning in the South during the early months of 1962. The staff used a modified version of our adult questionnaire. The technical features of the sample are described in Appendix A; the schedule of questions appears in Appendix B.

## The future consequences of Negro political participation

We are interested not merely in predicting the future of Negro political participation in the South. We are also interested in the *effects* of anticipated changes in Negro activity and power. To study such effects, we must reorient our thinking: now Negro political participation becomes an independent variable—a "causal" factor. We must try to find out how changes in Negro participation "feed back" to change the factors and conditions that determined it in the first place. We must now read Figure 2–1 from right to left, because the flow of influence in the system of variables has been reversed.

We cannot, of course, consider *all* the possible consequences of future changes in the level of Negro political activity in the South. We shall therefore concentrate on the possible consequences in only two realms of southern life—politics, and patterns of social and economic segregation.

Our conclusions on these matters are the most speculative and debatable in the book. They are, after all, predictions based on predictions, and thus doubly suspect. Nonetheless, they are more solidly based on factual analysis than previous thinking about these matters has been. And the compelling necessity to understand and anticipate the future problems of the South exceeds the possible embarrassment of being proved wrong by subsequent events. Contemporary political science is caught between the desire to be rigorous and the desire to be relevant. We have tried to be both. But we have been prepared in this study to sacrifice a good deal of rigor in order to achieve relevance.

Chapter Three

# Levels of Participation

Political participation is many things. Old men talking politics in the shade of a crossroads store, housewives discussing the local schools over a cup of coffee, a farm family attending a campaign barbecue, a Negro student joining the "sit-in" at a drugstore lunch counter, a union member contributing his dollar to a labor political committee—all are taking part in the daily round of democratic government. Elections are the most dramatic and visible political events, and voting may well be the most obvious form of political action. But voting is not the only kind of mass political participation, and it is best understood within the context of these other, more continuous ways of influencing public policy.

Very little attention has been paid to the civic participation of southern Negroes in this broad sense. The Negroes' struggle for a meaningful suffrage has been so prolonged, and their *de facto* disfranchisement has been so at odds with American ideals, that both scholarly and popular attention has focused on Negro efforts to qualify for and utilize the ballot. How much—or how little—southern Negroes participate in ways other than voting has been ignored.

Just what, then, do we want to cover in a study of "political participation"? Or, in the language of social science, precisely what is the *dependent variable* that this book promises to describe and explain? We could answer, "Just the act of voting," and let it go at that. But we would be excluding much of the behavior that makes up the political life of Americans.[1]

We define political participation as *all behavior through which people directly express their political opinions*. This definition is broad enough to cover all expressions of political opinion, from merely talking about politics

[1] For an overall picture of the extent of political participation by all American adults, see J. L. Woodward and E. Roper, "Political Activity of American Citizens," *American Political Science Review,* Vol. 44 (1950), pp. 872–85.

to seeking political office. But it is narrow enough to exclude purely private behavior. Thus, if a citizen gets a headache from watching a political speech on television, his trip to the medicine cabinet for an aspirin is *not* political action. But if he complains to his wife, "That man gives me a headache," he *is* participating in the political process to a minimal degree. Only when a person acts on his views—at least verbally—does he become a part of the political process.

In this chapter we shall describe the different ways in which southern Negroes participate in politics, and how much they participate. We shall compare these findings with those for southern whites and—whenever possible—for northern Negroes and whites as well. In later chapters we shall try to explain the differences between Negro and white rates of political participation. But description must precede explanation.

## Talking politics

The most ubiquitous form of participation in the governmental process is "talking politics." Everyday political discussions, gossip, and arguments between ordinary citizens are not just meaningless chatter. Rather, this political talk—even of the most superficial and ill-informed sort—helps form the climate of opinion in which politicians make decisions. Hence it is part of the process of self-government.[2]

One might reasonably expect southern Negroes not to be active participants in the political conversation of the region. Politics has been "the white man's business" in most of the South for well over half a century. Why should a man who has never voted bother to discuss public problems he can do so little about? Studies of the general public tell us that political participation of all sorts increases with improvement in education, occupation, and social status: the more educated and the more highly placed a person is in the social structure, the more likely he is to take an active part in the political process. But southern Negroes tend to receive relatively little education, in inferior schools, and they tend to be lumped in an undifferentiated mass at the bottom of the social scale. A Negro maid in Camellia County fits these expectations:

> I don't have time for talk. I have to work so hard I don't even see them [friends] 'til I git a chance to go to church. Then we don't be talking 'bout things like that. Ain't you talking 'bout things like the wars and prices and stuff? Well, I ain't got no money and talking won't git me none. I ain't got no son to go to the army, so I don't worry none 'bout the war taking 'em; and if we was to ever have a war and they shoot one of them bombs I hear people talking 'bout, we gonna all be

[2] An early recognition of the influence of informal conversation on political attitudes is P. F. Lazarsfeld, B. Berelson, and H. Gaudet, *The People's Choice* (New York: Columbia University Press, 1948). The first edition of this book appeared in 1944.

dead and gone anyhow, so why talk 'bout 'em and worry 'bout 'em 'fore they git here? I just cross my bridges as I come to 'em.

To have so little leisure that one does not have time to talk with friends precludes every form of political activity.[3] And low levels of education—the maid quoted above has had four years of formal schooling—produce a feeling of inability to cope with "wars and prices and stuff."

But we could argue just the opposite: if people are denied the ballot, we might expect them to express their political opinions in other ways. Because the whole structure of segregation was imposed by force of government, government should have extraordinary salience for Negroes. We know that ethnic groups in other countries have thrown themselves into politics once they became the targets of punitive government action.[4] Denied the ballot because of their skin color but still exposed to the American ideal of citizen participation, southern Negroes might seek other outlets for political self-expression. "We talk about the affairs of wages, and socialism, and what's going to become of us," said a Mississippi farm Negro who has never voted. "We [in this county] don't have no jobs much and what jobs we do have the whites have them. We stand around and look at them work." In contrast to the Florida maid, this Mississippian is free to spend all his time on politics—he has nothing else to do.

To what extent, then, does the extraordinary relevance of politics for Negroes overcome their low levels of income, status, and education to produce political discussion?

On the whole, southern whites talk about public problems more often than Negroes do (see Figure 3–1). In the less public settings for such discussions, however, the difference between the two races is small. Eighty-four per cent of the whites say they talk politics with friends, as compared to 76 per cent of the Negroes; 76 per cent of the whites and 64 per cent of the Negroes report talking about these matters with members of their families. The disparity between white and Negro rates of political discussion is larger in the work situation: three whites report talking about public problems with their co-workers for every two Negroes who do. Of course, Negroes probably have fewer opportunities to talk about *any* subject on the job—more of them are unemployed or work at such jobs as farming, where conversation is difficult or discouraged. But the frequency of political conversation declines more rapidly for Negroes than for whites as the forum of discussion shifts to other more public settings as well.

[3] This might be viewed as an extreme lack of the "role dispensability" usually necessary to engage in extensive political activity. See Max Weber, "Politics as a Vocation," in H. Gerth and C. W. Mills (eds.), *From Max Weber: Essays in Sociology* (New York: Oxford University Press, 1946), pp. 77–128.

[4] S. M. Lipset *et al.*, "The Psychology of Voting," in G. Lindzey (ed.), *Handbook of Social Psychology* (Cambridge, Mass.: Addison-Wesley Publishing Co., 1954), Vol. 2, pp. 1126ff.

The greatest disparity between the races in talking about politics and public problems is in talking with government officials and politicians. The Negroes' need for government action is often great, but the rewards for approaching men of power—who are almost always white—are typically small. An elderly Negro farmer in Crayfish County illustrated both points when he said:

> We talk about the roads that lead to our house—you can't even get in. When I was sick a car couldn't even get here. That's the main problem I talk about. I've talked to the road superintendent about five or six times. I even asked some of his friends, and the superintendent said he doesn't give a damn about a nigger road.

There are two exceptions to the tendency of southern whites to talk politics more than southern Negroes. First, Negroes report talking about public problems with Negro community leaders much more frequently than whites talk with their leaders. This deviation from the normal pattern reflects the subordinate social and political position of the Negro in the South. The southern Negro, typically suffering from severe and cumulative deprivations, often does not feel that he can take his problems directly to the white men who hold the

FIGURE 3–1.  *Percentages of Negro and white southerners who ever talk about public problems*

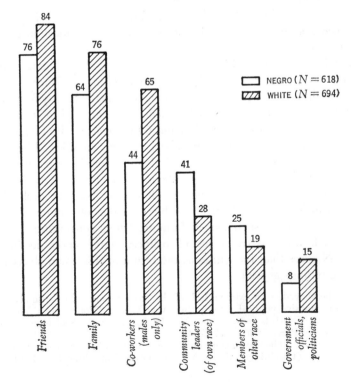

power in the community. Instead, he often works through intermediaries, the leaders of the Negro community. These leaders may be of much higher status than the average Negro; yet they cannot isolate themselves physically from the black ghetto, nor can they join the white leaders in their flight to the suburbs.[5] No matter how successful, wealthy, or esteemed a Negro leader may be, he is a Negro first. Leaders are therefore more necessary and more accessible in the Negro community than in the white.

Second, about a quarter of the voting-age Negroes in the South say they have talked directly with whites about public issues and problems, while only 19 per cent of the whites say they have had such discussions with Negroes. Negroes are perhaps more likely than are whites to remember or even to exaggerate the extent of political communication across race lines.[6] More significant than these small differences is the substantial agreement between Negroes and whites that almost all political talk takes place *within* racial groups and very little *between* them.

A young Negro maid in Florida made the point neatly when she was asked if she discussed public affairs with the people she works for: "I don't talk to them because they are Crackers!" A 28-year-old white laborer in North Carolina, when asked if he ever talked about public problems with "any colored people," said: "I've always called them *niggers* and I'll keep on calling them that. I call them that to their faces. Might get knocked down one day for doing it, but that won't stop me. I just ain't got no use for them." These are not ideal attitudinal conditions for the democratic dialogue.

Figure 3–2 shows the kinds of public problems that southerners discuss. Negroes discuss racial problems more than any other issue. Race ranks either first or second among the public problems Negroes discuss with everyone—friends, family, co-workers, community leaders, white people, government officials, and politicians. Economic problems (jobs, unemployment, the cost of living, taxes, and the like) and community problems (schools, housing, and so forth) rank next. Because these "economic" and "community" problems have heavy racial overtones, the southern Negroes' concern about race appears to be all-pervasive. Other public affairs—"politics" narrowly defined; international politics; such "style" issues (those related to *how* government is carried on) as corruption, efficiency, communism, and individual freedom—make up less than one third of the public problems southern Negroes talk about.

Southern whites are somewhat less preoccupied with race and its conse-

[5] James Q. Wilson stressed this point in *Negro Politics: The Search for Leadership* (Glencoe, Ill.: The Free Press, 1960), pp. 101–10.

[6] Robert E. Lane, *Political Life* (Glencoe, Ill.: The Free Press, 1959), p. 89, says "the lower-status person is more likely to remember and value the conversation than the upper-status person." See also B. Berelson, P. F. Lazarsfeld, and W. N. McPhee, *Voting* (Chicago: University of Chicago Press, 1954), pp. 101–17. Among other things, Berelson and his collaborators found that married women remember political discussions within the family more often then do married men.

quences. The public problems they most frequently discuss are local community problems (especially public schools), economic problems, and "politics" and government. However, a full 15 per cent of the problems they mention are clearly racial ones—as large a proportion of all issues as international affairs. And because southern community, economic, and political problems are so heavily influenced by racial concerns, race is a major topic of discussion among southern whites, too. Yet the political interests of southern whites—at least as reflected by their reports of what they talk about—are broader, more cosmopolitan, and less bound by the immediate and personal problems of existence in a segregated society than is true for southern Negroes.

Considerable variety from one community to another is concealed beneath this southwide pattern of political communication. In both Crayfish and Piedmont counties, for example, whites are as likely as Negroes to have discussed public affairs with such community leaders as club or church leaders, but the rates for both races in Crayfish are about twice as high as in Piedmont. In the rural environment of Crayfish, white community leaders have the same physical and social proximity to their followers that characterizes their Negro counterparts. In the urban environment of Piedmont, on the other hand, whites talk with community leaders at about the same rate as southerners in general. Piedmont also differs from Crayfish in the fact that its Negroes' rate of contact with leaders is lower than for southern Negroes in general; the rate is about the same as for whites. The more highly differentiated Negro com-

FIGURE 3–2. *Types of public problems talked about by Negro and white southerners, as percentage of all problems discussed*

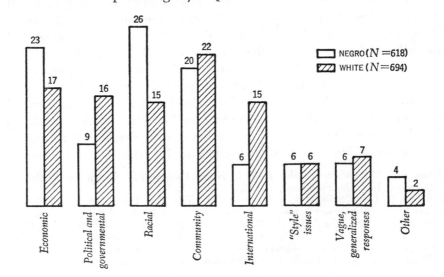

munity in Urbania, the central city of Piedmont County, apparently leads to a pattern of leader-follower communication similar to that of southern whites. Community variations, then, do not negate the southwide generalization that Negro leaders are more accessible than white leaders. Rather, they support the generalization by suggesting the conditions under which it holds.

As in the South as a whole, very few Negroes in our four communities ever talk about public affairs with government officials or politicians. In Piedmont County 8 per cent, exactly the same as in the South as a whole, report such conversations. Because Negroes hold public office in Urbania and are active and articulate in local politics, one might expect even more Negroes there than in the South in general to talk with public officials. But the unusual permissiveness of the environment may be balanced by the greater size of the population. With about the same number of officials as a small town, a relatively large city offers less mathematical chance for any one member of its population to have talked with an official.

The proportion of Negroes ever having talked with an official drops to 4 per cent in Camellia County, to 3 per cent in Bright Leaf, and to 2 per cent in Crayfish. The elderly Negro farmer who lamented the road superintendent's lack of interest in a "nigger road" suggests why. In none of the other three counties is there a single Negro who holds a government or party office. To talk with an official, then, is to talk with a white person who is likely to be unsympathetic and perhaps insulting as well. This lack of contact with public officials clearly does not stem from a lack of problems. In all three of these counties the rate of discussion with Negro community leaders is higher than it is in Piedmont, and in Crayfish it is the highest of all.

What kinds of public affairs do Negroes talk about in different communities? In Piedmont County, even more than in the South as a whole, racial problems dominate the discussions in which Negroes take part. These problems make up 46 per cent of all the topics mentioned by Piedmont Negroes. This concentration on race almost doubles that for the entire South, and it is much higher than in the counties of Camellia (32 per cent), Bright Leaf (19 per cent), and Crayfish (16 per cent). In Piedmont, the least repressive county, Negroes talk much more about race problems than they do in more repressive areas—not because they have more race problems, but because they have some chance to alleviate the ones they do have. An elderly unemployed doorman in Urbania, asked what he talked about with his friends, said: "Well, just first one thing and another. Mostly about the picketing of Piedmont Theater. They shot me out of a job. [Who is that?] The young folk what picket the theater. I had worked there 16 years and they closed the colored balcony. Course it's all right, though."

Camellia, Bright Leaf, and Crayfish offer sharp contrasts to Piedmont. Race is the most common public problem discussed by Negroes in Camellia, where vigorous but largely unsuccessful efforts have been made to end public segregation. In Bright Leaf and Crayfish counties, however, economic problems emerge as the number-one topic of discussion among Negroes. In these primarily rural counties, the basic problems of food and clothing are so pressing for Negroes, and the attainment of status needs so unlikely, that discussion focuses primarily on such things as jobs and pay. In talking with white people, Negroes in these counties are much less likely than in Piedmont to bring up racial problems. The frequency with which Negroes mention race as the topic of conversation with whites drops from 61 per cent in Piedmont to 36 per cent in Camellia, and on down to 24 per cent in Crayfish and 21 per cent in Bright Leaf.

A retired farmer in Crayfish, explaining why he had never known a white person well enough to talk to him as a friend, suggests the extreme difference between his environment and that of the doorman in Urbania: "I am scared of them [laugh]. They'll get you and try to make you talk and go tell their friends you're one of them 'niggers' that's got big ideas. Then they'd want to run you out of town or beat you up and will even kill you!" For the millions of people who have never visited Crayfish, this may sound like an old man's hyperbole; for the few people who have visited the place, however, it sounds entirely reasonable.

We do not have the data we would need to make a precise comparison between the amount and the content of political talk in the North and the South. However, 33 per cent of the northern Negroes reported talking to someone during the 1960 presidential election in an effort to influence his vote. Thirty-four per cent of the northern whites said that they engaged in this form of political talk.[7] In this respect, at least, Negroes in the North participate about as much as do whites. In the South, the gap between whites and Negroes is considerably larger, but it is also far smaller than we might assume from differences in white and Negro rates of registration and voting.

## Voting

The difference in political participation by southern whites and Negroes becomes much more extreme when participation is defined as voting rather than as talking about politics. *Eighty-six per cent of the voting-age whites in the South have voted in at least one election; only 41 per cent of the adult Negroes have ever voted.* This two-to-one ratio holds for registration as well: 66 per cent of the voting-age whites but only 33 per cent of the voting-age Negroes were registered to vote at the time of our survey.[8] In the nonsouthern

[7] This and all subsequent references to the 1960 presidential election are based on data collected by the University of Michigan's Survey Research Center.

[8] Before the poll tax was declared unconstitutional (in elections for national office by the Twenty-fourth Amendment in 1964, and in elections for state and local office by

FIGURE 3-3.  *Frequency of voting in presidential elections,*
*by region and race*

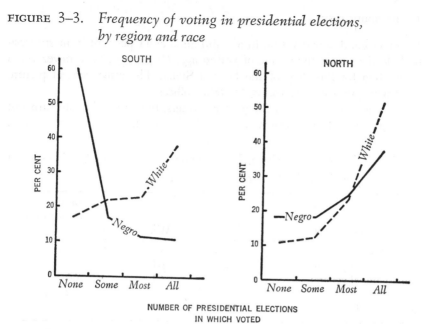

NUMBER OF PRESIDENTIAL ELECTIONS
IN WHICH VOTED

states almost no difference exists in the rates at which Negroes and whites register to vote—80 per cent of the voting-age whites and 78 per cent of the voting-age Negroes were registered to vote in 1960.

When we plot the frequency of voting in presidential elections by Negroes and whites for both the North and the South (Figure 3-3), the southern Negroes stand out in stark contrast to the three other groups. The frequency of generally approved behavior tends, when presented graphically, to take the shape of a J; this is the shape of the curves representing turnout in presidential elections for northern Negroes and for both southern and northern whites. Most people act in the approved way—in this case, they vote regularly. So the highest point is to the right of the graph. But the frequency of Negro voting in the South completely reverses the pattern. Judging from these findings alone, we would conclude that the institutionally approved behavior for southern Negroes is abstention from voting, and that the least-approved behavior is regular voting.

Northern whites are the most regular voters in presidential elections; 52 per cent report having voted in all presidential elections since they were old enough to vote, and only 11 per cent report having voted in none. Northern Negroes and southern whites have almost identical records: 38 per cent of both groups say they have voted in all presidential elections, and 17 or 18 per cent say they have voted in none. Only 11 per cent of southern Negroes,

court decisions in 1966), formal voter registration did not exist in the poll-tax states. A "registered voter" in these states is, for our purposes, one who *believes* he has met all the legal qualifications for voting and could vote in the next election if he chose to. As was indicated in Chapter One, Negro registration has increased (18 percentage points) since 1961, but the Negro-white disparity has not been greatly reduced.

on the other hand, report voting in all, and another 11 per cent in most, presidential elections since they came of voting age; 60 per cent have never voted in an election for President of the United States. The same general picture emerges when we examine voting for other offices.

Not only are most southern Negroes nonvoters; those who do vote turn out less regularly than do southern whites (see Table 3–1). The less elevated and

TABLE 3–1.   *Percentages of southern voters participating in all or most elections, by type of election and race*

| TYPE OF ELECTION | Negro | White | NEGRO RATE AS PERCENTAGE OF WHITE RATE |
|---|---|---|---|
| Presidential | 55% | 71% | 78% |
| Gubernatorial primary[a] | 42 | 61 | 69 |
| Gubernatorial general | 40 | 61 | 66 |
| Local | 39 | 66 | 59 |
| School board | 28 | 48 | 58 |

[a] Registered Democrats only.

visible the office, the more intermittent becomes the voting of southern Negroes. Thus 55 per cent of the Negro voters have voted in all or most presidential elections, yet only 28 per cent have voted in all or most elections for school board. The regularity of white turnout decreases too as the importance of the elections diminishes. But the decline is far less severe. In presidential elections Negro voters participate with about three quarters of the regularity of white voters, but in local and school board elections their regularity of voting is only about half that of their white neighbors.

So far as voting is concerned, then, the participation of southern Negroes is a great deal less than that of whites in the South or North and of Negroes living outside the former Confederate states. This disparity shows itself in all four of the communities we studied in detail, but it almost disappears in Piedmont County and it reaches its most exaggerated form in Crayfish County. In Piedmont, three fourths of the Negroes have voted at one time or another, and 69 per cent are currently registered; compared with the whites in Piedmont, Negro voting is at 91 per cent and current registration is at 95 per cent of the white rates. In Crayfish, on the other hand, only 6 per cent of the Negroes have ever voted, and that was while they lived somewhere else! Not a single Negro is registered in the county; indeed, the white residents boast that no Negro has ever voted in Crayfish.[9] Negroes in Camellia County par-

[9] Crayfish County was not established until 1914, but the claim is extended back through Reconstruction for the territory of the county.

ticipate much more and in Bright Leaf County somewhat less than in the South as a whole.[10]

The gap between Negro and white participation thus varies greatly in the four counties. The variation is clearly revealed by current Negro registration as a percentage of white registration: Piedmont, 95 per cent; Camellia, 89 per cent; Bright Leaf, 32 per cent; Crayfish, 0 per cent. Although Camellia Negroes have not achieved the extremely high levels of voting achieved by the Negroes in Piedmont County, they are closer to Piedmont than to the South in general. A 55-year-old lumber grader, a man with a third-grade education who has never voted, suggests why Camellia County has approached the Piedmont model:

> Well, I hadn't given much thought [to voting] 'til here lately. You know, you can live in a place where everything is at a standstill, nobody doing nothing, and you will be in the rut with them. But there ain't nothing that's keeping us from it, so the next time they be voting, I'll be there, too. I been thinking 'bout it seriously here of late. This is all our problem, and if some is going to jail, the least I could do is vote.

Negro voting rates differ so markedly from one community to another that we clearly must take community factors into account when we try to explain rates of Negro political participation in later chapters. Piedmont and Camellia suggest that white pressure against Negro voting (something "keeping us from it") and Negro organization and activity ("nobody doing nothing" versus "some . . . going to jail") are among the factors that we must examine.

When we confine our attention to those who have ever voted, we discover additional community differences. Whereas Piedmont County has far more Negroes registered to vote than do the other counties, Camellia County has the largest proportion of regular voters among those Negroes who are registered. If we define a regular voter as one who has voted in all or most elections since reaching voting age, we find that Camellia has more regular Negro voters for every type of contest—presidential elections, gubernatorial primaries and general elections, local elections, and school board elections. The number of regular white voters in the two counties is about the same, but roughly 10 per cent more of the Negro voters in Camellia vote regularly. The difference is smallest for presidential elections (47 per cent regular Negro voters in Piedmont to 53 per cent in Camellia) and greatest for local elections (28 per cent to 45 per cent). The registration of Negroes in Piedmont is unusually high, and apparently more voters with low motivation are registered there than are registered in Camellia. In other words, the smaller proportion of Negroes registered in Camellia may represent a more highly motivated group.

[10] The proportions ever voting and currently registered in Camellia are 61 and 55 per cent; in Bright Leaf, 27 and 23 per cent.

But Bright Leaf County suggests that the explanation is more complex: although only 23 per cent of its Negroes are registered, this small group includes few regular voters (30 per cent for presidential elections, 5 per cent for local elections).

The white voters in these counties, as in the South as a whole, tend to vote more regularly than do the Negroes. Only in Camellia does the regularity of turnout of Negro voters approach that of whites. The racial difference is greatest, of course, in Crayfish, where no Negroes vote; but it is also extreme in Bright Leaf. Crayfish also has a very high frequency of voting in local elections—86 per cent of its white electorate vote in all or most local or county elections, and 77 per cent in school board elections. White voters in the other three counties turn out much less regularly for local elections, although they equal or surpass Crayfish in their regularity of voting in presidential elections. The peculiarity of Crayfish is that its voters participate more regularly in local than in presidential elections. This extreme provincialism is not simply a product of rurality. Bright Leaf County is also predominantly rural, but for local elections it has the smallest proportion of regular voters, both white and Negro, to be found in our four counties.

## Participating in political campaigns

Americans probably spend more time, lung power, and money on campaigning than do any other democratic people.[11] The vast size of the American electorate, the large number of elective offices, the system of holding elections at fixed intervals without regard to crises or issues, the nomination of candidates through primary elections—all help explain why. Presidential campaigns and general elections for state office are waged less vigorously in the South, for the South is predominantly a one-party region. But the flamboyant, no-holds-barred battles in the Democratic primaries may make up for that lack. Indeed, some people maintain that the South is peculiarly politicized, that southerners take to politics as enthusiastically as they do to hominy grits and black-eyed peas.

Despite the elaborate nature of American campaigns, most of the activity is created by a small proportion of the citizenry. In the heat of the 1960 Kennedy-Nixon battle, for example, only 12 per cent of the adult citizens in the United States engaged in one of the most common forms of campaign participation—attending campaign meetings or rallies. Most Americans are sufficiently aware of politics to mention it occasionally in casual conversation,

[11] At least in absolute terms. The per-capita expenditure of time, effort, and money may well be higher in several other countries. On financial expenditures, see Alexander Heard, *The Costs of Democracy* (Chapel Hill, N.C.: University of North Carolina Press, 1960), ch. 14.

and most of these go to the trouble of voting on election day; but participating in a campaign is a more demanding activity. Only a minority of Americans take any part in a campaign, even when participation is very broadly defined.

Only a minority of southern Negroes (41 per cent) said they had ever voted, and even fewer (33 per cent) said they were currently registered. So we would expect to find that only an infinitesimal number had ever participated in campaigns. Our findings on southern whites reinforce this expectation: although 86 per cent have voted and 66 per cent are currently registered, only 45 per cent have *ever* taken any part in a political campaign. When we remember, however, that the low voting rates of southern Negroes may stem from a repressive environment rather than simply from lack of interest, and that campaign participation does not require the formal approval of a local official, a different expectation becomes plausible.

The data support the latter expectation: 35 per cent of southern Negroes report that they have engaged in some kind of campaign participation. *The number of adult Negroes in the region who took part in campaigns was as great as the number who were registered voters at the time of our interviews.* Whereas Negroes vote at only 48 per cent of the rate of whites, their campaign participation is 78 per cent as high as that of whites. Instead of widening, the gap between Negro and white participation thus decreases startlingly when we shift from voting to campaign activity as the measure of participation.

As Figure 3–4 indicates, the greatest difference between southern whites and Negroes in campaign participation is found in the most visible form of activity (attending meetings and rallies), and the smallest difference is found in the least visible form (giving money and buying tickets). Thirty-four per

FIGURE 3–4.    *Participation in political campaigns, by region and race*

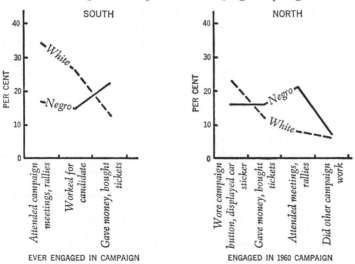

cent of the whites but only 17 per cent of the Negroes have attended campaign meetings, rallies, barbecues, fish fries, and the like. In volunteer work for a candidate or party, white participation drops more sharply than does Negro participation, reducing the difference to 11 percentage points. In giving money or buying tickets to help a candidate, white participation drops still more sharply while Negro participation increases to the point where *Negroes participate more than do whites.* Giving money is ordinarily a high-income activity, and southern Negroes are one of the lowest-income groups in the country. When we add this consideration to the fact that southern Negroes vote at only half the rate of whites, the rate at which they give money becomes all the more impressive. As we have suggested, however, monetary contributions are a relatively anonymous form of participation that is possible for a subordinate minority that cannot participate more openly.[12] People who think that they need government action to improve their lot will normally participate more actively than those who depend less directly on government. Anonymous donations represent the only form of active participation that is possible for many southern Negroes.

We find support for this interpretation in our nonsouthern data and in the community studies. During the 1960 presidential election, nonsouthern Negroes participated more than did whites in almost every aspect of the campaign—more gave money, attended meetings or rallies, engaged in direct campaign work, and reported contact with a party worker.[13] Only in wearing campaign buttons or displaying car stickers did white participation exceed that of Negroes in the North—and fewer Negroes have automobiles.

The contrasts between urban Piedmont and Camellia counties on the one hand, and rural Bright Leaf and Crayfish on the other, also support the interpretation. In the two rural counties, campaign rallies are generally for "whites only"; in the two urban counties, Negroes are not excluded from rallies. Indeed, any candidate for office in Urbania must actively seek Negro support; somewhat more covertly, candidates in Capital City also try to win a Negro following, and the entire slate of candidates appears at special Negro rallies. Accordingly, a fourth to a fifth of the Negroes in Piedmont and Camellia have attended political meetings, compared with less than 10 per cent in Bright Leaf and Crayfish. But *the highest proportion of campaign contributors (29 per cent) is found in Crayfish, where no Negro is allowed to vote!*

In view of the inhibitions Negroes in Crayfish feel about voting—such as the fear of getting slugged with a pistol—and the uniformly anti-Negro position of local candidates, the meaning of this finding is not immediately clear.

[12] See Heard, *op. cit.,* pp. 154–68, for a discussion of underworld participation in American politics through campaign contributions.
[13] R. A. Dahl, *Who Governs?* (New Haven, Conn.: Yale University Press, 1961), pp. 293ff., suggests some of the reasons for the high participation of northern Negroes despite relatively low socioeconomic levels, especially in areas of "machine-style" local politics.

An alternative to the interpretation of campaign contributions as a substitute for more open participation seems plausible. Crayfish Negroes are subjected to extreme subordination, and it may be that the local whites force those who are more vulnerable to contribute to political campaigns. In that event we would have to interpret campaign contributions as a form of "Uncle Tom-ism" rather than as a sign of independent political action. But such is not the case. The Negro campaign contributors in Crayfish have talked politics with whites less frequently than have the noncontributors, and they have talked politics with other Negroes more frequently. On the whole, they seem less sympathetic to or dependent on white people than do the noncontributors. Uncle Toms apparently have other, less expensive ways of ingratiating themselves with their white superiors than giving money.

Our first interpretation—that anonymous and covert forms of political participation by southern Negroes, such as giving money, are encouraged by the repression of Negro voting—is thus given additional weight by the bizarre popularity of political money-giving by the impoverished Crayfish Negroes.

These findings indicate pretty clearly that the low *voting* rate of southern Negroes is not an adequate index of their overall political participation. So far, we have found that the gap between white and Negro political activity in the region is relatively small *except when it comes to voting*. If the low rate of Negro voting were merely a matter of personal choice—of apathy and ignorance, of not being "ready" for the responsibilities of full citizenship— we would not have found this pattern. Rather, Negro participation rates would have lagged about the same amount behind white rates for *all* forms of political activity; or, even more likely, the gap between white and Negro participation rates would have widened as the forms of political action grew more and more demanding.

# Belonging to political associations
# or holding party or public office

Southerners have regular opportunities to vote or to participate actively in political campaigns. These opportunities occur only at intervals, however, depending on the electoral calendar of their state. Talking politics is a more continuous process, although it too tends to reach a peak during the election season. But talking demands a very slight investment of political interest and involvement. The forms of political participation to which we now turn our attention are both more taxing and more continuous than any we have considered so far. They are, therefore, the least common ways in which both whites and Negroes take part in the political processes of the South.

Southerners may be "different," but they are as often joiners as are other

Americans. All but 9 per cent of the Negroes and 15 per cent of the whites belong to some kind of association, club, or formal group. Most of these groups are not overtly political. Churches, fraternities, lodges, and PTA's are the most popular groups among both races. Although these nonpolitical groups sometimes get into politics,[14] their political activity is so infrequent and so peripheral to their main purpose that belonging to them cannot reasonably be counted as a form of political action. Membership in groups like the Young Democrats or the Young Republicans, the League of Women Voters, the NAACP, white citizens councils, and various civic leagues, on the other hand, represents a clear-cut and conscious involvement in the world of politics.

About 10.5 per cent of the voting-age Negroes in the South belong to political organizations and associations—most commonly the NAACP. Only 2.5 per cent of the whites are similarly involved. *Thus we find that, at this extremely demanding level, Negroes in the South participate more than do southern whites.* Moreover, this finding holds up in a wide variety of southern locales. In Piedmont County, for example, 18 per cent of the Negroes but only about 4 per cent of the whites belong to the wide range of political organizations existing there. In Camellia County, 6.5 per cent of the Negroes and 1.5 per cent of the whites report membership in political associations. For once, the picture is the same in Bright Leaf and Crayfish counties—5 and 9 per cent of the Negroes are members of political groups, while not one white respondent in either county reported such membership. The rich and active associational life of American Negroes has often been noted. Less widely recognized is that their group activity carries over into the political arena, despite their low rate of voting.

Officeholding in political parties and government is quite another matter. Since the end of Reconstruction holding party and public office has been almost entirely a white prerogative. This situation is gradually changing, but Negro officeholding is still so rare that not one Negro in our sample had ever held a public office of any kind; 2 per cent of the whites had been federal, state, or local officials at some point in their lives. Officeholding in political parties is almost as one-sided. One Negro respondent was a precinct committeeman; six white respondents had held office in the Democratic or Republican party. On this level, southern politics is still a white man's game.

## The Political Participation Scale

So far in this chapter we have discussed the different ways in which southern whites and Negroes participate in the political process. In this concluding

---

[14] See especially S. M. Lipset, M. Trow, and J. Coleman, *Union Democracy* (Glencoe, Ill.: The Free Press, 1965), sect. 2, and David B. Truman, *The Governmental Process* (New York: Alfred A. Knopf, 1951), parts 1 and 4.

section we shall suggest that talking politics, voting, taking part in campaigns, belonging to political organizations, and holding party or public office are not only related to one another but are, in fact, different forms of the same phenomenon.

If all these activities are different kinds of political participation, then knowing about a person's participation in one activity should enable us to predict whether he will participate in another activity. Those who engage in the most "difficult" form of participation should also participate in the less demanding ways, just as a strong man who raises a 300-pound weight above his head should be able to raise a 150-pound weight as well. The heaviest weight the strong man lifts tells us—assuming he does not exhaust himself in the process—that he can lift everything that weighs less.[15] And when he fails to lift the next weight, we know he cannot lift any that are still heavier.

The most infrequent and therefore the "hardest" form of activity we have examined is holding party or public office; the next most uncommon form is belonging to political groups. These are followed by taking part in electoral campaigns, voting, and talking politics (the most ubiquitous form of all). An ideal "cumulative pattern" of these behaviors—with officeholding and membership in political groups lumped together, because so few southerners do either—would be as follows:

| Talks? | Votes? | Participates in campaigns? | Holds office or belongs to political group? |
|--------|--------|----------------------------|---------------------------------------------|
| Yes | Yes | Yes | Yes |
| Yes | Yes | Yes | No |
| Yes | Yes | No | No |
| Yes | No | No | No |
| No | No | No | No |

In this ideal cumulative scale, knowing the "highest" form of participation an individual engages in always tells us the *entire* pattern of his behavior. Thus, if Mr. A holds a public office or belongs to a political organization, he *also* participates in political campaigns *and* votes *and* talks politics. If Mr. B does not hold an office or belong to a political group but does participate actively in campaigns, he also votes and talks politics. (All those who vote also talk about political events and problems.) If, on the other hand, Mr. C does not even talk about politics—the "easiest" and most common form of participation —he does not participate in any other way. If the facts conform to this logical scheme or model, then we have reason to believe that all these actions probably are different forms of the same thing—political participation. If the facts con-

[15] This approach was initially devised by L. Guttman in the field of attitude measurement. See S. A. Stouffer *et al., Measurement and Prediction* (Princeton, N.J.: Princeton University Press, 1950), chs. 3–9.

flict with this model, we can be certain that no single concept such as "political participation" underlies all the behavior we have described so far.

When asked about the kinds of political activities they had engaged in, 95 per cent of the Negro responses and 98 per cent of the white responses fell into one of the five "pure" scale types listed above. A batting average over 90 per cent is usually considered an adequate demonstration of the existence of a scale. That is, such a high rate of conformity to the expected pattern of behavior suggests that the different tests are probably measuring the same thing and that they differ only in being harder or easier to pass. So we can safely say that people who vote but do not take part in campaigns *will* also talk politics but *will not* hold office or belong to a political organization. At least we can "safely" say this in the sense that we will be correct for over 90 per cent of the responses. Such a scale is extremely useful, because it permits us to talk about political participation as a general phenomenon rather than forcing us to discuss each discrete political act in unique terms.[16]

The relatively few "errors"—or behavioral patterns that deviate from the ideal scale—are often the result of interviewer mistakes or quixotic interpretations of questions by some respondents. A respondent, for example, who says that he is the mayor of his home town but has never talked about public problems or campaigned is either a congenital liar or has misunderstood the questions. Thus the 2 per cent of the white and 5 per cent of the Negro answers that do not conform to one of the five ideal patterns were assigned to the "pure" pattern they most closely approximated. (This is a standard procedure in scaling analysis.) As we shall see, some of the scale "errors" are large enough and regular enough to suggest that something more than clerical or perceptual mistakes were involved. Actually, these deviations from a "pure" scale pattern are of great help in understanding differences between Negro and white political participation in the South.

A comparison of the overall rates of political participation of Negro and white southerners is presented in Figure 3–5, which is based on the Political Participation Scale (PPS) we just described. We have arranged the different scale types along the bottom of the graph, starting with those who engaged in none of the political actions making up the scale (Type I) and ending with those who engaged in all (Type V). The vertical axis represents the percentage of the Negro and white adult populations found in each participation type.

The most obvious fact about the political participation of Negroes and whites is also the most far-reaching: the overall pattern of political participation is very different for the two races. Very few whites are completely

---

[16] The construction of a single scale to describe the behaviors of two populations as different as southern Negroes and southern whites requires the sacrifice of some technical refinements in the interests of comparability. See Appendix C for a technical discussion of the Political Participation Scale.

FIGURE 3–5.   *Political participation scale types, by race*

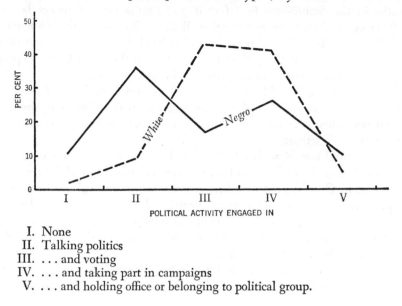

I. None
II. Talking politics
III. . . . and voting
IV. . . . and taking part in campaigns
V. . . . and holding office or belonging to political group.

inactive (2 per cent) or content merely to talk about politics and public problems (9 per cent). An equally small number of whites are extreme political activists (5 per cent). Thus about 84 per cent of the whites either talk politics and vote (43 per cent) or talk politics, vote, and occasionally take part in political campaigns (41 per cent). The line representing white participation approximates the contours of a bell-shaped, normal-distribution curve—the same sort of curve we would get if we plotted the physical heights of southerners. Most people would be clustered near the average height, and very few would turn out to be potential basketball stars or circus midgets.

The curve for Negroes is startlingly different. It has two peaks separated by a deep valley at the voting stage. Political participation rates are far less uniform among southern Negroes than among southern whites. A large number of Negroes are politically inert or nearly so—11 per cent never have talked about politics or public affairs, and 36 per cent have talked about these things but have never voted. On the other hand, twice as many Negroes as whites, proportionately, are thoroughly political activists (Type V). And 26 per cent of the Negroes report taking part in some way in political campaigns. Most Negroes who become registered voters do not restrict themselves to voting alone; they *also* become active in political campaigns and organizations, at least occasionally. The most common degree of white participation, on the other hand, is to vote but to go no further.

Now let us shift our attention from the South as a whole to the four counties we studied in detail (see Figure 3–6). In Piedmont County—no racial utopia by anyone's standards, and yet one of the more racially enlightened counties in the South—we find few if any significant differences between the two races in patterns of participation. Both the Negro and the white curves are bell-shaped. The sharp dip at the voting level and the bifurcation of the Negro population are entirely absent. Apparently in Piedmont County "people are people" when it comes to participating in government.

The picture is slightly different in Camellia County. Both racial curves are more or less bell-shaped, but the Negro population contains many more inactive persons than does the white and about the same proportion of campaign participants and activists.

The two rural counties—Bright Leaf and Crayfish—show the same sharp division between the inactive and active Negro that we found for the South as a whole. In Crayfish, the void between the Negroes who have never voted (62 per cent) and those who have campaigned (23 per cent) or have belonged to political groups (4 per cent) is almost incredible. Underscoring these wild differences in patterns of Negro participation is the similarity of the white patterns in the four counties.

The PPS scores for the South as a whole and for our four counties indicate, without any further analysis, that southern political systems facilitate white

FIGURE 3–6. *Political participation scale frequencies,*
*by county and race*

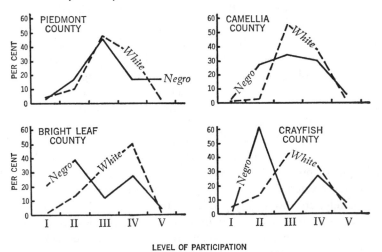

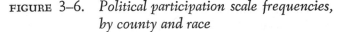

I. None
II. Talking politics
III. . . . and voting
IV. . . . and taking part in campaigns
V. . . . and holding office or belonging to political group.

participation and throw up major barriers to Negro participation. This is hardly news! But our analysis further demonstrates that these barriers are more effective in impeding voting—especially in counties like Bright Leaf and Crayfish—than they are in blocking other kinds of political activity. The minority of Negroes who do become voters must be unusually dedicated and determined citizens—a greater proportion of them than of white voters go on to more demanding forms of participation. And most of the non-voting Negroes demonstrate at least enough political interest to talk about public affairs.

Additional support for this interpretation of the data is given by an examination of "scale errors." As we explained above, a scale is based on the assumption that the highest and most demanding form of political participation a person engages in perfectly predicts his other forms of participation. Thus someone who takes part in campaigns also votes and also talks about politics. Although we found this true for a vast majority of southerners, we did find a few anomalies or "errors." Most of these scale errors for Negroes came from responses to the question about voting. Specifically, the largest single cause of scaling error was Negroes who had never voted but who had taken part in campaigns, or had belonged to political groups, or had held party or public office.

TABLE 3–2.   *Percentages of respondents who have held public office, belonged to a political group, or participated in an election campaign but who have never voted, by county and race*

| County | Negro | White |
|---|---|---|
| Piedmont | 5% | 3 % |
| Camellia | 9 | 1.5 |
| Bright Leaf | 15 | 4 |
| Crayfish | 31 | 3.5 |
| The South as a whole | 12 | 2 |

Table 3–2 shows the proportion of all Negroes and whites with this apparently anomalous pattern of behavior in our four counties and in the South as a whole. In Piedmont County only 5 per cent of the Negroes have engaged in the more demanding forms of political action without voting—only 2 percentage points more than was true for the whites. In Camellia and Bright Leaf counties, on the other hand, nonvoting activists comprised 9 and 15 per cent of the Negro populations while only a small handful of whites reported such extraordinary behavior. Finally, in rural Deep South Crayfish County, almost a third of the Negroes participated in campaigns (largely through

anonymous gifts of money) or belonged to political organizations (usually the NAACP) even though they were nonvoters.

If the South as a whole displayed as much "error" as does Crayfish County, we could not combine other political activities with voting in a single measure of political participation. In Crayfish, we cannot assume that Negroes who engage in the most demanding form of political activity (membership in a political organization) have also been active as voters. Thus the scale requirement of predictability from more to less demanding forms of participation is not met.

Because all these forms of participation are closely related for whites and for Negroes in the South as a whole, however, we conclude that the failure of politically active Negroes in Crayfish to vote is indeed a manifestation of error rather than of a defective scale. These people in scale types IV and V *ought* to be voters. If they lived in Piedmont County—or in some other less repressive environment—most of them would be voters. The defect or "error" is in the Crayfish political system, not in the answers of its Negro citizens. "Artificial" barriers to normal participation by Negroes thus seem to account for most of the seeming errors in our scale. As these barriers are removed, southern Negroes should begin to show a more normal pattern of participation, one that includes a great deal more voting than has characterized the political behavior of southern Negroes in the past.

We have gone into the technicalities of scales and scale errors only because they furnish clues for understanding political behavior. The points on our scale represent the behavior of millions of southerners, white and Negro. What are the people at each point like? What puts them there? The following chapters are addressed to these questions.

Part Two

Part Two

# Influences on Negro Political Participation

Now that we have described the modes and rates of Negro political participation in the South, we turn to the difficult task of explaining them. *Why* are southern Negroes, in most but not all respects, less politically active than are southern whites? *Why* do some Negroes participate in politics while others do not?

Our description in Chapter Three of the patterns of Negro political participation, and our comparison of those patterns with the patterns for southern whites and northern whites and Negroes, indicate that political activity—particularly voting—has a special meaning for southern Negroes. But the description and comparison do not tell us a great deal more than that. In order to answer the "why?" questions, we must establish *empirically* the relationships between Negro political activity and the factors that produce or inhibit it.

We shall begin, in Chapter Four, by examining the personal characteristics of southern Negroes and how those characteristics are related to their participation in politics. For Americans in general, political involvement and activity are known to vary with age, sex, education, occupation, and income. These demographic characteristics can safely be assumed to have political consequences —although not necessarily the same ones—for southern Negroes, too. Our southwide sample survey provides rich data for such an analysis.

But this is merely a beginning: southern Negroes live in a wide

61

variety of communities whose nature undoubtedly shapes Negro political participation. The next five chapters will be devoted to an examination of how community structure affects Negro participation in political life. In Chapters Five and Six we shall analyze the effects of the social and economic structure and of the political system on Negro rates of participation; our analysis will be based primarily on aggregate data from all biracial counties in the South. In Chapters Seven and Eight, with our focus narrowed to the four counties we have studied personally and in detail, we shall examine the impact of local leadership and political organization on Negro civic participation. The mass media of communications—newspapers, magazines, television, and radio— are generally thought to have a great impact on men's minds and behavior. In Chapter Nine, using both community study materials and southwide sample data, we shall look at the impact of mass communications on southern Negroes, particularly on their political activity or lack of it. Then, in Chapter Ten, we shall try to probe the "Negro mind," using our interviews with the southwide sample to see how Negro attitudes and cognitions affect political behavior.

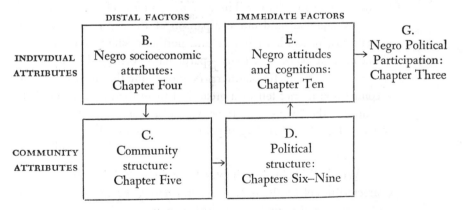

This order of topics matches the map of variables affecting Negro political participation given in Chapter Two:[1]

[1] Sharp-eyed readers will note that we have omitted two types of influence—(A) historical events and (F) the immediate context—from this abbreviated version of Figure 2–1. The omission is intentional. We believe that both have effects on Negro participation (G) only through their impact on the variables in B, C, D, and E, and this makes them very difficult to discuss separately. Discussions of the impact of historical events and the immediate context will be found, where appropriate, in chapters on the other independent variables.

We might have adopted almost any other order of presentation, because these classes of variables are linked together in a rather tightly knit "system." The order adopted here has one merit: it begins with those variables thought to be most remotely and indirectly related to Negro political activity and works toward those thought to be most closely linked to it. Our search for explanation begins and ends at the individual level of analysis. That is entirely appropriate, for individual behavior is what we seek to explain.

In the chapters that follow, we shall discover dozens of factors belonging to all four classes of independent variables which are related either positively or negatively to Negro political activity. Most of these factors are also related to one another, and this makes the drawing of causal inferences exceedingly difficult. So many factors prove to be related to Negro participation that we cannot, in the statistical approximation of a controlled experiment, hold all but one independent variable constant in order to probe its singular effect on Negro activity. In Chapters Four through Ten, we shall attempt to control for as many of these "third" variables as possible, drawing them primarily from others of the same class. This procedure ensures that we do not unnecessarily proliferate independent variables within each class, but it tells us little about the relationships *among* the four classes of independent variables and how, all together, they produce the present degree of Negro political participation in the South. This problem will be dealt with separately in Chapter Eleven, which provides an overview of the entire analysis up to that point and an estimation of the relative contribution of each *class* of variable to understanding and predicting Negro participation. The general reader should be forewarned that this chapter is unavoidably technical. It may be skimmed or skipped by those whose interest in this book is exclusively substantive.

Given the fact that we must try to predict the future on the basis of a study conducted at one point in time, the isolation of variables most strongly associated with Negro participation, or the lack of it, provides all the "hard" evidence we have about the future of Negro political activity in the South. We shall, therefore, point out the probable implications of our findings for the future as we go along. By the time the reader has finished Part Two, the likely direction and rate of change in Negro political activity in the future South should be quite clear. Then, in Part Three, we shall be in a position to look at the consequences of these anticipated changes for southern politics and race relations.

# Chapter Four

# Who Are the Participants?

Most Americans feel that the South is somehow "different" without knowing precisely how or in what ways it is different. Professional students of political behavior are not much better off. V. O. Key and his students have made brilliant studies of southern politics on the elite level, but our knowledge about the political behavior of rank-and-file southerners is scant. This is particularly true for Negro southerners. Most of the "well-established" generalizations about political participation, for example, are based on local northern samples or on nationwide samples in which the southern component is too small to permit detailed analysis. Yet these generalizations are applied to all Americans, regardless of race or region. Most of the best research on mass political behavior is thus highly vulnerable to the charge, "But *not* among Negroes in the South." To date, no one has known whether this charge is justified or whether it is merely "one-upmanship."

So we must begin our inquiry into the influences on Negro political activity in the South at a quite elementary level. In the present chapter we shall talk about the simplest and most "obvious" characteristics of southern Negroes—their sex, age, education, occupations, and income—and how these are related to their civic activity.

## Sex and political participation

Women all over the world are less active in politics than men. In some countries they are not allowed to vote, but even where they have access to the ballot they use it less than men do.[1] In the United States, although the gap appears to be decreasing, the voting rate of women is typically about

[1] Robert E. Lane, *Political Life* (Glencoe, Ill.: The Free Press, 1959), pp. 209–16.

65

10 per cent below that of men.[2] Most of this difference comes from lack of participation by lower-status women. At the highest status levels, among those with a college education, for example, women participate about as much as men do; at lower status levels fewer men and women take part in politics, but the decrease is much sharper for women than for men. Political sex roles seem to be so defined that women need feel no shame in saying, "I don't know a thing about politics—I leave that to my husband." This view of politics as peculiarly masculine has largely disappeared among higher-status groups, but it lingers on in varying degrees throughout American society. We have never known an interviewer to quote a husband, at any status level, as saying, "I can't answer questions about politics—I leave those to my wife."[3]

We might expect sex differences in political participation among southern Negroes to be even greater than among Americans in general. Negroes tend to be disproportionately clustered at the lowest status levels, where the general deficit in female participation is greatest. Moreover, if we assume that the southern-Negro subculture shares the general belief that women should be protected from unpleasantness, we might expect Negro women to be less likely than men to risk challenging white restraints on political activity.

But we might, with equal logic, expect just the opposite. Much has been said about the peculiarly matriarchal character of the Negro family in the South.[4] If the mother is an unusually dominant figure in the Negro family, one might infer that women represent family aspirations more accurately than men do in relation to the outside world, including the world of politics. There is support for this line of reasoning: a larger proportion of Negro women (39 per cent) than of white women (28 per cent) report that they are the heads of their households. A majority of Negro women (68 per cent) report some occupation other than housewife, whereas only 45 per cent of the white women have ever had any occupation outside the home.

Without concerning ourselves with the experiences and attitudes that produce contrasting political sex roles, we can lay to rest any belief that the usual American differences are reversed among southern Negroes. More Negro men than women take part in southern politics, and the gap is far greater than it is for southern whites. For the moment, let us regard as politically active all people who have voted, or who have taken some part in a campaign, or who hold political office or membership in a political group. Within this definition, 63 per cent of the Negro males and 47 per cent of the Negro females are active in the politics of the South. The contrast between

[2] A. Campbell et al., The American Voter (New York: John Wiley & Sons, 1960), p. 484.

[3] This is not simply a matter of generalized masculine dominance: in other roles, such as the selection of art objects or nonpatio culinary skills, the American husband gladly defers to his wife.

[4] See, for example, E. Franklin Frazier, The Negro Family in the United States (Chicago: University of Chicago Press, 1939).

male and female rates of participation among Negroes (see Figure 4-1) is almost as stark as the contrast between races that we discovered in Chapter Three. This contrast becomes even more impressive when we realize how little difference there is between male and female participation among whites: 90 per cent of the white males and 87 per cent of the white females qualify as politically active under our definition.

Were we to rely simply on voting as a measure of political participation, the difference in political sex roles for Negroes would not appear nearly so great as it actually is. In terms of voting alone, 47 per cent of the Negro males and 38 per cent of the Negro females would qualify as participants. The extreme disparity comes mostly, then, from the failure of Negro women to engage in higher forms of participation. In Figure 4-1, notice that the Negro males are the only group with a distribution that radically differs from a "normal," bell-shaped curve. The curve for the Negro women has a single peak at Political Participation Scale (PPS) Type II, those who talk about public affairs but have never taken a more active part in politics. The peak for white women is one scale type higher, those who talk about politics and vote but do not go beyond voting in their political activity. The peak for white men is still another scale type higher, those who talk politics, vote, and take part in campaigns but do not hold an office or belong to a political group.

Aside from the fantastically low rate of Negro female participation, what is impressive about these distributions is the peculiar bimodal curve for Negro

FIGURE 4–1. *Political participation scale types, by sex and race*

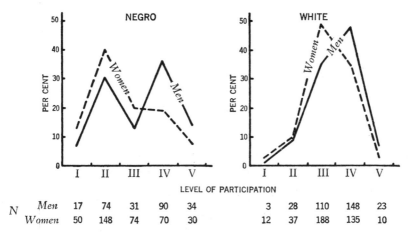

| N | | I | II | III | IV | V | | I | II | III | IV | V |
|---|------|----|-----|----|----|----|---|---|----|-----|-----|----|
| | *Men* | 17 | 74 | 31 | 90 | 34 | | 3 | 28 | 110 | 148 | 23 |
| | *Women* | 50 | 148 | 74 | 70 | 30 | | 12 | 37 | 188 | 135 | 10 |

I. None
II. Talking politics
III. . . . and voting
IV. . . . and taking part in campaigns
V. . . . and holding office or belonging to political group.

men—with one peak or concentration at PPS Type II and another at PPS Type IV. Negro women tend to be frozen out of southern politics; Negro men tend either to be frozen out or, if they overcome the inhibitions of the system, to participate beyond merely voting.

For Americans in general, the old notion of politics as a man's business is retained only among those in lower status levels. Women of higher status are about as active in politics as men—except when it comes to holding public office. But the old sex differences still show up among southern Negroes at all status levels. If we take education as an index of social status and compare the political participation of those with the same amount of schooling (see Table 4–1), the male-female differences among Negroes are reduced but not

TABLE 4–1.   *Percentages of southern whites and Negroes participating in politics at different levels, by sex and education*

| EDUCATION AND SEX | PARTICIPATION BEYOND TALKING POLITICS[a] | | PARTICIPATION BEYOND TALKING AND VOTING[a] | | N | |
|---|---|---|---|---|---|---|
| | Negro | White | Negro | White | Negro | White |
| *Grade school* | | | | | | |
| Male | 56% | 87% | 46% | 47% | 159 | 102 |
| Female | 37 | 83 | 19 | 22 | 202 | 103 |
| *High school* | | | | | | |
| Male | 73 | 90 | 56 | 60 | 71 | 125 |
| Female | 56 | 87 | 34 | 40 | 131 | 179 |
| *College* | | | | | | |
| Male | 88 | 94 | 69 | 58 | 16 | 83 |
| Female | 73 | 95 | 52 | 54 | 33 | 93 |

[a] Each percentage entry in this table represents the percentage of people in the group who take part in politics at the indicated level. The first figure in the first column, for example, means that 56 per cent of the Negro males with grade-school education not only talk politics but also vote, take part in campaigns, or hold political group membership, and that 44 per cent fall below this level of participation. The two righthand columns give the bases on which the percentages were computed.

eliminated. *At every level of education*, and *for all forms of political participation*, more Negro men than women are active. The greater increase in participation by Negro women than men as education increases results simply from the fact that women have such extremely low rates of participation at the low education levels.

For southern whites, the relationship between sex and political activity conforms to the national pattern. At the highest educational level, about as many white women as white men are active in politics, whether we focus on more or less demanding forms of participation. But at lower educational levels, our conclusion about sex differences depends on the way we view participation. In terms no more demanding than having once voted, about as many white women as white men take part. Voting thus appears to be a "cheaper" activity for whites than for Negroes, a nearly uniform attribute of adulthood that varies little with sex or education. Going beyond voting, however, is still much more likely for white men than for white women at the grade-school or high-school level.

Both the sex and the race differences in participation are greatest at the lowest educational level. We would expect traditional patterns to change more slowly among those with least education. With the tradition of politics as the white people's business added to the broader tradition of politics as the man's domain, Negro women have a double barrier to overcome. And the racial barrier is not merely an internalized restraint; in places like Crayfish County it carries a very genuine threat of bodily harm. Hence Negro women at lower educational levels are much less likely than Negro men or white women to take part in politics; most of them "stay in their place," which is definitely not the polling booth. A great impetus is needed to overcome these barriers. But once Negro women break through them to participate as voters, a large proportion go on to participate still more actively— enough to make the total proportion of Negro women active *beyond voting* almost the same as the proportion of white women, particularly at the higher educational levels.

The idea that responsibility for acting as head of the household might carry over into political activity receives uneven support. Negro women who are heads of their households exceed Negro housewives in political activity by only a very small margin. (Their average scores on the 5-point PPS are 2.8 and 2.7, respectively.) The very lowest rate of participation (2.1) is that of women who are head of their household but have no other employment. These people are "out of it" politically as well as economically. But women who are somewhat more successful as heads of households—those who have jobs—have a higher participation rate (3.1) than do housewives, both those with no other occupation (2.5) and those who are employed (2.8).[5] Being head of the house does not necessarily increase the probability that Negro women will become politically active, but the combination of such responsibility with outside employment does seem to lead to a modest increase in political participation.

[5] Controlling for level of employment does not reduce this difference: the mean PPS score for female heads with unskilled jobs is 3; for nonheads with unskilled jobs, 2.7; for heads with white-collar or skilled jobs, 4.4; for nonheads with white-collar or skilled jobs, 3.4. So few Negro women are employed in white-collar or skilled jobs that the last two figures should be taken as merely suggestive—they include only 6 per cent of all Negro women ($N = 24$).

Women outnumber men throughout the United States, but the disparity is even greater among Negroes in the South. Whereas women accounted for 52 per cent of the national (and of the southern white) adult population in the 1960 census, they accounted for 54 per cent of the adult Negro population of the South.[6] The voting-age population of Negroes in the South thus differs from the general American electorate in two respects: sex differences in participation are greater, and women make up a larger proportion of the total. Both these facts depress the overall rate of Negro political activity.

## Age and political participation

National studies have found that as people grow older, they vote more often; the frequency reaches a peak around the age of 60 and gradually decreases with old age. But the decrease normally is not sharp enough to return the elderly to the very low turnout rates of youth; even the elderly vote more often than those who have just reached adulthood.[7]

Why should older people be more regular in their voting than young people? Lane, in his careful survey of the literature, suggests a number of possible reasons:

> In maturity certain things occur in the normal lifetime which tend to increase motivation and the pressure to take part in the political life of the community. A person acquires property, hence one of the most important forces politicizing the local citizen comes to bear upon him—the question of the assessment and tax on his house. Then, too, the family includes children who need playgrounds and schools and therefore the mother finds new stakes in politics. Because of the children . . . the parents become conscious of themselves as civic models. . . . They are geographically less mobile. Dreams of solving status and income problems through rapid personal mobility may suffer erosion, and a more solid alignment with class and ethnic groups emerges. Vocational interests become more salient. The increased economic security associated with middle age provides freedom of attention and psychic energy for political matters often not available at an earlier stage in life.[8]

Political activity is habit-forming—older people have had more opportunities to acquire the habit.

[6] Within our sample the proportion of women is still higher—60 per cent. Although this difference appears to be large, it is about what would be expected. Our samples are not of the total population of adults in the South but of the populations of adult Negroes and whites living in private households. More Negro males than females (and than white males) tend to be excluded, because—as residents of military posts, logging and mining camps, penal institutions, and so forth—they are not a part of the private-household population. Females make up 55 per cent of our white sample, which is the same proportion they have consistently represented in the national surveys of the University of Michigan's Survey Research Center.

[7] See, for example, Campbell *et al.*, *op. cit.*, pp. 493ff., and Lane, *op. cit.*, pp. 209ff.

[8] Robert E. Lane, *Political Life* (Glencoe, Ill.: copyright © 1959 by The Free Press), p. 218, reprinted by permission of the publisher.

FIGURE 4–2.   *Age and political participation in the South, by race*

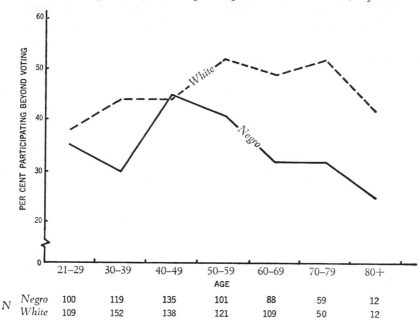

|   | | 21–29 | 30–39 | 40–49 | 50–59 | 60–69 | 70–79 | 80+ |
|---|---|---|---|---|---|---|---|---|
| N | Negro | 100 | 119 | 135 | 101 | 88 | 59 | 12 |
|   | White | 109 | 152 | 138 | 121 | 109 | 50 | 12 |

Figure 4–2, which shows the proportion of Negro and white political activists in the South at different age levels, gives the expected pattern for whites.[9] Marred only by one dip, the curve rises until it reaches the seventies and then gently drops. The smallest proportion of white activists is found among those in their twenties. The Negro curve, however, is markedly different. The highest proportion of Negro activists is found at a much earlier age than for southern whites or for Americans in general. Many more Negroes in their forties take an active part in politics than at any other age. Beyond the forties, the curve drops sharply. Unlike the whites, Negroes are more likely to be activists in their twenties than they are from sixty on.

Here we seem to have a "generational effect"—a result produced not by aging as such but by the experiences peculiar to a given age level. Before *Smith* v. *Allwright* (1944), Negroes were routinely denied the right to vote in most of the South. A southern Negro who is in his sixties today probably had no chance to vote until he was in his forties. Elderly Negroes have lived almost all their lives in a condition of open and often official repression. It is not surprising that some are Uncle Toms, some apathetic, and some too ill informed to participate. The age group with the highest proportion of

[9] We focus here on those who participate beyond voting, but the form of the white and Negro distributions would be the same if we were considering participation merely as voting. The gap between the proportions of white and Negro participants, however, would be much greater.

activists at the time of our survey were in their twenties or early thirties when the Supreme Court ruled the "white primary" unconstitutional. Since they were at the age when they were most likely to be affected by the promise of the decision, they may constitute a special generation of Negro activists. They are the only age group that includes a larger proportion of activists than is found among whites of the same age. And the other group of Negroes closest to whites in its proportion of activists is made up of those in their twenties. Whereas gaining legal access to the ballot marked the generation of Negroes now in their middle age, school desegregation and other promises of full citizenship rights may mark the newest generation of Negro adults. If we assume the "normality" of an increase in participation with age, we can attribute deviations of southern Negroes from the normal pattern to peculiar generational experiences. This interpretation implies that Negro rates will take on the normal pattern once the present generation of older Negroes passes from the scene.

But we must not leap to conclusions. The notion of "generational effects" merely explains the deviation of the Negro pattern from the normal one in a way that is consistent with the hypothesis that aging leads to heightened political participation. We have yet to demonstrate that this is, in fact, the case for Negroes in the South. The Negro curve in Figure 4–2 certainly seems to suggest the contrary.

The normal statistical association of advancing years and high political activity might be explained in several ways. It may be the result of cumulative political experience—the longer a person is actively involved in politics, the more interested and active he becomes. But age and length of political experience are not the same thing; people can and do become politically active at different stages in life. Those who become active in politics for the first time during or after middle age might be so numerous and so highly active that they increase the average participation rates of the older group. Years of political experience need have no effect at all; the "late bloomers" merely have to be more active than those who become involved in politics early in their adult lives. This explanation, though logically possible, does not seem psychologically convincing. But we must remember that political participation by southern Negroes may have much less to do with individual motivations than is usually the case. Let us not, therefore, reject this possibility out of hand.

Very few southern whites are "late bloomers." Of those southern whites who have ever voted, about half (49 per cent) first registered to vote during the first year they became eligible;[10] 82 per cent were registered before they were 30 years of age. Late-starting whites accordingly do not appear numerous enough to account for the steady growth in white participation rates up to the age of 70 plotted in Figure 4–2.

[10] At age 18 in Georgia; at 21 in the other southern states.

As might be expected, however, the Negro pattern is different. Only 5 per cent of those southern Negroes who have ever voted registered during the first year they were eligible; only 48 per cent registered while they were still in their twenties. This delay in registering was not, of course, necessarily a voluntary act. Indeed, 8 per cent of the Negroes who tried to register were unsuccessful. Regardless of causes, however, late-starting Negro voters *are* numerous enough profoundly to affect the average participation rates of the older Negro age groups.

Moreover, voter registration seems to be a far more purposive and less routine act for Negroes than for whites. The two races give quite different reasons for trying to register (see Table 4–2). Most whites seem to have

TABLE 4–2. *Reasons given for registering for the first time*

| REASONS | Negroes who tried to register but failed | Registered Negroes | Registered whites |
|---|---|---|---|
| Came of age, first chance | 5% | 5% | 34% |
| Interest in contest or issues that year | 15 | 20 | 12 |
| Urged by candidate, organization, or leader | 25 | 7 | 1 |
| Urged by spouse, friend, or relatives | 15 | 5 | 7 |
| Other—"to be a citizen," "to be a man," etc. | 25 | 32 | 13 |
| No special reason, don't know | 15 | 31 | 33 |
| TOTAL | 100% | 100% | 100% |
| N | 20 | 244 | 602 |

registered because it was expected of them when they became adults—34 per cent said they registered because they had come of age, and 33 per cent ventured no particular reason at all. For Negroes, on the other hand, registering seems to have been a much more meaningful act that required either strong personal motivation or direct external stimulus. Some 20 per cent of the Negro registrants cited interest in a particular election, and 25 per cent mentioned things like "to be a man"; Negroes who tried unsuccessfully to register most often mention the promptings of some organization or a friend or relative as the reason for making the attempt when they did.

This pattern of findings is consistent with the notion that the massive introduction of highly motivated, late-starting Negro voters into the southern electorate causes Negro participation to increase among older age groups, *even in the absence of any effects from cumulative political experience.* The embarrassing thing about this interpretation, however, is that Negro participation does *not* increase among Negro age groups the way it *does* increase

TABLE 4–3.  *Percentages of political activists[a] among southern Negro voters, by proportion of adult life and number of years as a registered voter*

| NUMBER OF YEARS AS REGISTERED VOTER[b] | PROPORTION OF ADULTHOOD AS REGISTERED VOTER[c] | | | | ALL VOTERS |
|---|---|---|---|---|---|
| | Small | Medium small | Medium large | Large | |
| Low | 40% (20) | 33% (9) | 50% (8) | 67% (9) | 46% (46) |
| Medium low | 57% (7) | 68% (25) | 45% (11) | 57% (7) | 60% (50) |
| Medium high | 67% (6) | 60% (10) | 52% (23) | 82% (11) | 62% (50) |
| High | — (0) | 60% (10) | 80% (15) | 73% (22) | 72% (47) |
| ALL VOTERS | 48% (33) | 59% (54) | 58% (57) | 71% (49) | |
| N | 33 | 54 | 57 | 49 | |

[a] Political activists are those who take part in politics beyond the act of voting, at least to the point of participating in some way in campaigns.
[b] In determining the low to high categories we divided Negro voters into four roughly equal groups by number of years registered: "low" means 1 to 7 years as a registered voter; "medium low," 8 to 12; "medium high," 13 to 16; "high," 17 and over.
[c] In determining the small to large categories, we divided Negro voters into four roughly equal groups by proportion of adulthood as a registered voter: "small" means 1 to 29 per cent of adulthood as a registered voter; "medium small," 30 to 49 per cent; "medium large," 50 to 79 per cent; "large," 80 per cent or more.

for whites—very few of whom become politically active for the first time after 30!

Table 4–3 clarifies this situation considerably and demonstrates beyond reasonable doubt that cumulative experience is the primary reason for the tendency of political participation to increase with age. This table compares the rates of participation beyond voting of Negroes, both by the number of years and by the proportion of their adult lives they have been registered voters. Reading across the "all voters" row near the bottom of the table, we see that the percentage of activists increases markedly as the proportion of adult life as a registered voter goes up. Only 48 per cent of the Negro voters who have been registered for a small part of their adult lives (the "late bloomers") are active beyond voting, whereas 71 per cent of those registered a large part of their adult lives (the "early starters") are activists.

Reading down the "all voters" column at the right reveals an equally impressive increase in the percentage of activists with an increase in the absolute number of years as a voter, from 46 to 72 per cent. And, regardless of the proportion of their adulthood spent as voters, the proportion of southern Negroes active beyond voting goes up as the actual number of years as a voter goes up. These increases are substantial (27 to 30 percentage points) *within* each proportion-of-adult-life category except the very highest. The few young

Negroes who register almost immediately upon coming of age, then, appear almost as active as the oldsters who registered early.

Reading across the table, with number of years as a voter held constant, we see that the proportion of adult life as a voter makes less difference than does cumulative experience. Only for those who have been voters for a relatively few years does proportion of adulthood as a voter make a substantial difference. Older Negroes who registered only recently appear to be less active than young Negroes whose equally few years in politics represent most of their adulthood. But this does not blur the basic finding: the southern Negro becomes more politically active the longer his experience at participation, regardless of the age at which he first officially enters the political world.[11]

Political activity thus does seem to have a cumulative effect. When the present generation of Negro voters in their middle and early years gain more experience, the overall gap between white and Negro activity can be expected to narrow.

## Education and political participation

As in the nation as a whole, people in the South participate more in politics as they get more education. The proportion of both white and Negro participants increases with almost every increase in education, even when it is divided into very small categories of school years completed (see Figure 4–3). The extraordinary gap between white and Negro participation *at every level of education* is, of course, the gross point made by the figure. The gap is greater at lower educational levels; but, even among those with college educations, the proportion of participants is far greater among whites than among Negroes. We think of education as the great leveler of group distinctions, and yet *a greater proportion of semiliterate whites (with four to six years of schooling) than of college-trained Negroes participate in southern politics at the level of voting or above.* The only white educational group with a lower participation rate than Negro college graduates is made up of those with less than four years of schooling.

We cannot appreciate the monumental effects of these disparities without an awareness of the tremendous difference in educational level between the southern Negro and white populations. The percentages of each sample at different educational levels are given in the following table.

11 Because 49 per cent of the white voters in the South have been registered for 100 per cent of their adult lives, and 63 per cent for over 90 per cent of their adult lives, a directly comparable analysis of white participation by proportion of adult life and number of years as a voter is not possible. Even so, if white voters are divided into two groups by proportion of adult life as a registered voter (100 per cent, less than 100 per cent) and into four groups by actual number of years registered, the nature of the findings is the same: absolute years in politics is more strongly related to political participation than is proportion of adult life in politics.

|  | Negro | White |
|---|---|---|
| 0–3 grades | 21% | 2% |
| 4–6 grades | 21 | 11 |
| 7–8 grades | 17 | 16 |
| Some high school | 13 | 14 |
| High-school graduate | 20 | 31 |
| Some college | 4 | 16 |
| College graduate | 4 | 10 |
|  | 100% | 100% |

Even if as large a proportion of Negroes as of whites with the same education participated in politics, the overall proportion of white participants would still be much greater, because Negroes rank so much lower in education. In fact, only 4 per cent of the Negroes are in the one educational category—college graduates—that includes a proportion of participants approaching the magnitude found among *all* white educational groups.

Education is widely recognized as a powerful influence on political behavior,

FIGURE 4–3. *Education and political participation in the South, by race*

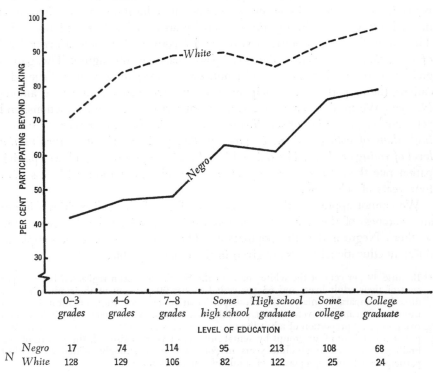

|  |  | 0–3 grades | 4–6 grades | 7–8 grades | Some high school | High school graduate | Some college | College graduate |
|---|---|---|---|---|---|---|---|---|
| N | Negro | 17 | 74 | 114 | 95 | 213 | 108 | 68 |
|  | White | 128 | 129 | 106 | 82 | 122 | 25 | 24 |

but the actual meaning of the concept "education" is vague. It is easier for the researcher simply to note that political participation goes up as education goes up than it is to look behind the number of years in school in an effort to identify what it is about educational experience that stimulates political participation. The usual presumption is that schooling imparts knowledge and intellectual skills that broaden a student's horizon and strengthen his ability to cope with abstract problems. In addition to its cognitive content, schooling has a motivational content; it imparts general feelings of patriotism and a specific interest in public affairs.

Are the vast differences in Negro and white participation at each level of schooling a result of noneducational factors? To some extent they must be, since even the best-informed and most highly motivated citizens are excluded from politics in some parts of the South if they happen to be Negroes. But perhaps some of the racial contrast in participation results from the fact that the same number of years in different schools may not result in an equal amount of education. Almost all Negro voters in the South grew up under a segregated educational system in which "separate" by no means meant "equal." The disparity in the quality of Negro and white schools in the South requires that we push beneath the usual concern with mere number of years in school to examine the motivational and informational consequences of schooling.

A convenient way of examining the motivational effects of education is in terms of interest in politics. Education normally develops political interest, and political interest normally leads to political participation. But civics-book preachments about the duty of citizens to participate must have a hollow ring for many Negro youngsters. In an area where uncounted elections have been won by the candidate who is most convincingly anti-Negro, members of the race have little incentive to develop an interest in politics. "Heads I win, tails you lose." And while it may be a civic duty for whites to vote, it is sometimes a personal danger for Negroes to do so. Withdrawal from an unrewarding or threatening realm of activity is, after all, a common psychological phenomenon.

The actual distribution of Negro interest runs completely counter to these speculations (see Figure 4–4). When the proportions of whites and Negroes expressing a "great deal" of interest in politics are compared, with education held constant, *Negro interest exceeds that of whites at every level of education except one.* The excess of Negro over white expressions of great interest in politics is not large, but even an equal degree of interest would have been impressive. Education thus seems to perform its usual motivational function for southern Negroes despite their lower levels of participation. The very forces militating against participation by Negroes may enhance their interest by making government highly relevant to the Negro citizen. Classroom exposure to national ideals of citizenship may furnish a standard against which to judge the southern scene and thereby kindle Negro interest in politics.

FIGURE 4–4. *Percentages of southern whites and Negroes with a "great deal" of interest in politics, by education*

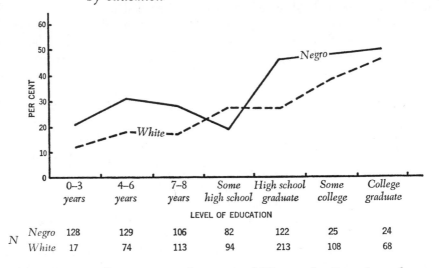

| | Negro | 128 | 129 | 106 | 82 | 122 | 25 | 24 |
| N | White | 17 | 74 | 113 | 94 | 213 | 108 | 68 |

Peculiarities in the motivational content of Negro schooling, then, do not account for the failure of Negro participation to approach that of whites with equal schooling. Perhaps differences in informational content will. To avoid exclusive reliance on formal schooling as a measure of education, we asked respondents seven factual questions about government; these questions were designed to be simple enough to ensure a substantial number of correct responses.[12] If we regard six or seven correct answers as a high score on political information, three to five as medium, and zero to two as low, the rankings are:

| | Negro | White |
|---|---|---|
| High | 8% | 23% |
| Medium | 53 | 69 |
| Low | 39 | 8 |
| | 100% | 100% |

Southern Negroes clearly command fewer political facts than southern whites. This is partly a result of lower levels of schooling, but it also reflects lower levels of informational content with a given amount of formal schooling (see Figure 4–5). At every level of schooling except the very highest, Negroes have less political information than whites.

Thus the cognitive rather than the motivational content of Negro education

[12] See Chapter Ten for these questions and for the proportions of Negroes and whites answering each correctly.

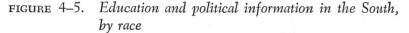

FIGURE 4–5. *Education and political information in the South, by race*

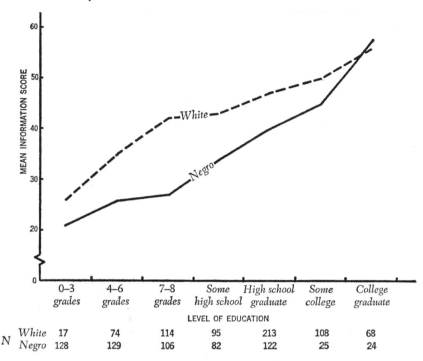

| N | | 0–3 grades | 4–6 grades | 7–8 grades | Some high school | High school graduate | Some college | College graduate |
|---|---|---|---|---|---|---|---|---|
| | White | 17 | 74 | 114 | 95 | 213 | 108 | 68 |
| | Negro | 128 | 129 | 106 | 82 | 122 | 25 | 24 |

in the South may account for the failure of schooling to level out racial differences in political participation. Although Negro schooling instills as much political interest as does white schooling, it results in less political information, even of a fairly simple kind.[13] When we compare political participation by Negroes and whites with equal *schooling*, then, we are not comparing groups with equal *education*, in the informational sense. Table 4–4 compares white and Negro participation at equal levels of political information rather than at equal numbers of school years. With political information held constant, the percentage of Negroes is still much smaller than the percentage of whites participating beyond merely talking about politics, except at the high level of information. Among those deemed highly informed by our simple test, 90 per cent of the Negroes and 97 per cent of the whites go beyond talking in their political participation, at least to the point of voting. This 7-percentage-point difference is much smaller than the 18-percentage-

[13] Negro children in the ninth grade might score as high on our information test as would white ninth-graders. Remember that we queried adults and tested not what they learned a number of years ago but what they recall today. Information is less likely to be remembered if it is not employed in daily life, and Negroes in the South have less opportunity than do whites to put political information to use.

TABLE 4–4. *Political participation of southern Negroes and whites, by level of political information*

| POLITICAL INFORMATION | PERCENTAGE PARTICIPATING BEYOND TALKING | | PERCENTAGE PARTICIPATING BEYOND VOTING | | N | |
|---|---|---|---|---|---|---|
| | Negro | White | Negro | White | Negro | White |
| High | 90% | 97% | 62% | 57% | 52 | 159 |
| Medium | 61 | 87 | 41 | 44 | 325 | 470 |
| Low | 35 | 78 | 24 | 29 | 237 | 58 |

point spread between Negro and white college graduates (see Figure 4–3). At the medium and low levels of information the excess of white over Negro participation is as great as we found for medium and low levels of formal schooling.

Even when informational content is substituted for formal schooling, then, the proportion of Negroes who reach the voting stage of participation approaches that of whites only for those who are most highly informed. Table 4–4 includes an additional measure of participation (columns 3 and 4), the proportion of the two races who reach the point of taking some part in campaigns. This shift to a more demanding measure of participation greatly changes the findings. Smaller numbers of Negroes reach the voting stage of political activity but, of those who do, a much larger proportion go on to more active involvement. With political information controlled, more Negro than white activists are found at the high level of information and almost as many at the medium and low levels. Once again we find that the southern political setting seems either to exclude Negroes or—especially if they are politically knowledgeable—to stimulate them to high levels of political activity.

When our measures of education are considered separately, political information appears to be more predictive of political activity than is formal schooling. But the only way we can be certain is to examine participation with both formal schooling and political information controlled or held constant. Table 4–5 presents the percentages of southern whites and Negroes who take part in politics for different levels of both education and information.[14] Reading down the columns provides a picture of the influence of formal schooling with political information held constant. The third column, for example,

---

[14] Interracial comparison is not the primary point here, for we already know that more whites than Negroes reach this stage of political activity under controls for either formal education or political information. Hence it is no surprise to discover that the percentage of Negro participants exceeds the percentage of white participants in only one of our eight education-information categories. If we had presented the relationships in terms of a higher level of participation, however, the interracial comparison would look quite different. The percentage of political activists (participants beyond the stage of voting) would be greater for whites than for Negroes in only three of the eight education-information categories.

TABLE 4–5.    *Percentages of southern whites and Negroes participating in politics beyond talking, by formal schooling and political information*

|  | INFORMATION[a] | | | | | |
|  | NEGRO | | | WHITE | | |
| FORMAL SCHOOLING | Low | Medium | High | Low | Medium | High |
| Grade school | 31% (184) | 58% (166) | 91% (11) | 75% (40) | 85% (137) | 100% (26) |
| High school | 48% (82) | 60% (126) | 96% (25) | 92% (13) | 86% (236) | 93% (57) |
| College | — (0) | 76% (33) | 81% (16) | — (4) | 93% (95) | 99% (76) |

a Each entry represents the percentage of people in the group who take part in politics at least at the stage of voting—for example, the first figure in the first column means that 31 per cent of the Negroes with no more than grade-school education and a low score on the political-information test not only talk politics but also vote or take a more active part in politics. The numbers in parentheses are the bases on which the percentages were computed. "Low," "medium," and "high" indicate levels of political information.

includes only Negroes with high scores on political information; 91 per cent of the highly informed Negroes who have no more than grade-school education are political participants, compared with 96 per cent who have high-school training and 81 per cent who have college training. For those with high information, then, the amount of schooling makes little difference for political participation. Reading across the rows, we see the effect of different levels of political information on people with the same amount of formal schooling. Everyone in the first row, for example, has only grade-school education; the percentage of Negroes who participate increases from 31 per cent to 91 per cent as their level of political information rises.

Our illustrative readings of the findings have dealt with extreme cases that suggest—to the point of exaggeration—that information is far more important than formal schooling. In terms of average difference, greater information brings a mean increase in participation by Negroes, at all levels of schooling, of 38 percentage points. Greater education, on the other hand, brings a mean increase in participation by Negroes, at all levels of information, of only 8 percentage points. The differences are smallest for those in the highest information and education categories: if a southern Negro has college training, he will participate almost as much if he has only a moderate amount of political information as he would if he had a large quantity of such information; and if he has a large store of political information, he will participate regardless of his amount of formal schooling. Even at the highest levels, information appears somewhat more important than schooling; for the vast majority of Negroes, information far outweighs schooling as a factor predictive of political activity.

The schooling-information relationship is quite different for southern whites:

participation at the level of voting is much more nearly uniform for them. The average increase in participants found along each dimension, when the other is held constant, is identical—8 percentage points. Just as the examination of age and political activity suggested that political participation is a more purposive act for Negroes, here the stronger relationhip between participation and information for Negroes than for whites points in the same direction. Even if our measure of participation were in terms of activity beyond voting, the conclusion would have been similar: information is again more important than schooling.

Education in the sense of actual command of political information thus makes much less difference for whites than for Negroes. Southern whites engage in the least demanding forms of participation as a matter of course, almost regardless of information or schooling. And they engage in more demanding forms of participation somewhat more in response to status (formal schooling) than to information. More Negroes are found in all forms of participation, on the other hand, if they have more information, regardless of their formal schooling.

## Occupation and political participation

Most southern Negroes get the kinds of jobs nobody else wants. As Table 4–6 indicates, 34 per cent of the adult whites in the South are engaged in professional or white-collar occupations, which include jobs ranging from accountants to veterinarians, from buyers for stores to self-employed proprietors, from attendants in libraries to typists, from advertising agents to salesmen. Only 8 per cent of the Negro adults in the South have similar jobs, and two fifths of these are schoolteachers or administrators whom the whites

TABLE 4–6.  *Occupations of southern adults,*
*Negro and white*

| OCCUPATION | Negro | White |
|---|---|---|
| Professional and white-collar workers | 8% | 34% |
| Skilled and semiskilled workers | 27 | 25 |
| Unskilled nonfarm workers | 28 | 2 |
| Farm owners and managers | 5 | 5 |
| Farm tenants, sharecroppers, laborers | 12 | 3 |
| Housewives | 19 | 30 |
| Refusal, don't know, not ascertained | 1 | 1 |
| TOTAL | 100% | 100% |
| N | 618 | 694 |

need to maintain segregated public schools. Some of the rural southern counties, such as Crayfish, contain not a single Negro professional worker outside the school system, and the claim of schoolteachers to professional qualifications is weak—the retired superintendent of Negro schools in Crayfish, for example, is only semiliterate. At the other extreme, 40 per cent of the adult Negroes are employed in unskilled labor, either on farms or in menial nonfarm tasks. If we exclude housewives and consider only adults in the labor force, we find that unskilled laborers constitute almost half the Negro labor force, whereas professional and white-collar workers make up almost half the white labor force.

Even if Negroes were as active in politics as are whites with the same occupations, great disparities in overall rates of participation would remain. In fact, as Figure 4-6 reveals, a greater percentage of whites than of Negroes are participants in every occupational category. On quick inspection, racial differences in participation seem much more erratic with controls for occupation than they did with controls for education. But with education we were dealing with a continuous variable, however imperfect the measure in terms of school years, whereas our occupational categories are broad groupings of a noncontinuous sort. We could say that college graduates had definitely been

FIGURE 4-6.   *Occupation and political participation*
*by southern whites and Negroes*

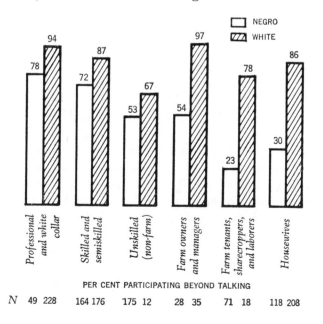

exposed to "more education" than had high-school graduates, but it would be senseless to say that professional and white-collar workers have "more occupation" than do farm owners and managers. We can sensibly say that professional and white-collar workers have more occupational *status* and *more politically relevant job activities* than unskilled laborers, but we can hardly make even this rough ranking in comparing farm and nonfarm occupations. Even when we translate occupation into a status ranking, then, we have two separate rankings—one for farm and another for nonfarm occupations—as well as the residual unranked category of housewives. Recognizing that occupational classes cannot be ordered like educational classes, and that rough rankings must be in terms of two separate sets of occupations, we must compare the percentages of Negro and white participants in each set of occupations rather than simply compare the curves as a whole.

Such a detailed examination of Figure 4–6 produces a different sort of conclusion. For the three nonfarm occupational categories, the gap between white and Negro participants is slightly smaller than we found at the very highest levels of education (see Figure 4–3). Among college graduates, the white-Negro difference in percentage of participants beyond the level of talking was 18 percentage points. This is greater than the racial difference for those in professional and white-collar employment (16 points), skilled and semiskilled work (15 points), and even unskilled nonfarm labor (14 points). The extreme racial differences in proportion of participants are in the other three occupational categories: farm owners and managers (43 percentage points); farm tenants, sharecroppers, and laborers (55 points); and housewives (50 points). The low participation of Negro women has already been accounted for. Both the other categories include rural farm people, among whom the high participation of whites and the minimal participation of Negroes may well reflect nonoccupational factors.

Except for housewives and for the purely rural occupations, then, occupation appears to be a more significant force than education in explaining racial differences in participation. We have not said that Negroes in these nonfarm occupations are as likely as Negro college graduates to participate in politics. They are not. We have said that the *racial difference* in proportion of participants is slightly less within these occupational groups than within the highest educational groups. The low rates of participation by Negroes can thus be attributed to their poor occupations no less than to their educational handicaps. It is difficult to say which is more influential, partly because education and occupation are so closely linked, and partly because farm and nonfarm occupations cannot realistically be combined in a single status ranking.

Table 4–7 therefore reports participation by education separately for each

TABLE 4–7.   *Percentages of southern Negroes participating in politics beyond talking, by education and occupation*

| | NONFARM OCCUPATIONS | | | FARM OCCUPATIONS | |
| EDUCATION | Unskilled labor | Skilled and semiskilled labor | Professional and white-collar workers | Tenants, laborers, and sharecroppers | Owners and managers |
|---|---|---|---|---|---|
| Grade school | 46% (109)ᵃ | 70% (83) | —   (6) | 27% (64) | 58% (26) |
| High school | 62%   (60) | 70% (69) | 76% (17) | —   (7) | —   (2) |
| College | —   (6) | 100% (12) | 73% (26) | —   (0) | —   (0) |

ᵃ The numbers in parentheses are the bases on which the percentages were computed.

of five occupational categories.[15] This division of the sample into 15 combinations of education and occupation gives us some highly unlikely combinations. No Negro in the sample, for example, was both a college graduate and a farmer, and only six respondents with no more than grade-school education had secured white-collar or professional employment. Nevertheless, a close reading of the table indicates that both education and occupation are independently related to participation, with the occupation relationship somewhat the stronger. A sizable majority of southern Negroes are concentrated in the four cells of the table that include those with grade-school or high-school education who are laborers in nonfarm occupations. Focusing on this fourfold grouping, we find a considerably larger percentage of participants among semiskilled and skilled laborers than among unskilled laborers, regardless of education. Holding occupation constant and reading down the first two columns, we find the pattern less regular: an increase from grade-school to high-school education brings an increase in proportion of participants among unskilled laborers but not among the skilled and semiskilled.

This limited analysis points to occupation as slightly more influential than education for Negro political participation, but for the most part the two vary together. The relatively few Negroes in the highest levels of occupation and education present a picture that is clear in its central point but fuzzy around the edges. The central point is simply that southern Negroes who acquire *either* a college education *or* employment in professional or white-collar jobs are much more likely than other Negroes to have taken some part in politics. Among those with college training, the percentage of participants is high regardless of occupation. And the same is true for people with professional or white-collar employment: whether they have college or only high-school education, they tend to participate.

[15] The residual "housewife" category is dropped here because it cannot be fitted into either the farm or the nonfarm ranking.

The puzzling part is, however, that such variation as exists within these high overall rates of participation is in a direction opposite to that expected. Among professional and white-collar Negroes, those with only high-school training include a slightly greater proportion of participants than those with college training. This difference is hardly large enough to be of concern. But look at those with college training: Why should so many more participants be found among those with skilled or semiskilled jobs than among those in professional or white-collar positions? The fact that the same anomaly is not found among whites suggests something peculiar to the Negro occupational structure.

Negroes have been largely excluded from the more desirable forms of employment in the South, but a thin stratum of Negro professionals and white-collar workers is essential to the maintenance of a segregated society. In Crayfish County, for example, no white undertaker would be expected to prepare a Negro corpse for burial in the segregated Negro cemetery—if segregation is a satisfactory way of life, it is also a satisfactory way of death. Hence a Negro undertaker maintains one of the few Negro business establishments in the county. We have already noted that 40 per cent of all southern Negroes in professional and white-collar employment are schoolteachers or administrators, the largest and most essential professional group for the perpetuation of segregation. These professionals have college training, but they depend on the white community for their positions. When they were interviewed individually, only 65 per cent reported that they had ever gone beyond talk in their political activity. This is a high percentage for Negroes in general, but it is far below that of college-trained Negroes in skilled or semiskilled occupations.

These vagaries should not be taken as discounting the significance of personal characteristics like education and occupation for political behavior. But they can be taken as underscoring the need for going beyond individual attributes to examine the social, economic, and political structures of different communities, for these community characteristics limit the meaning of individual characteristics for political behavior.

## Income and political participation

Inevitably, the low education and poor occupations of southern Negroes produce extremely low incomes. Indeed, the southern Negro's financial status is even worse than his educational and occupational status. The southern system may grudgingly permit—or even require—a small minority of Negroes to attain college training and professional positions, but it is much less inclined to accord them high incomes. Eight per cent of the Negro adults of the South have had college training, and 8 per cent are in professional or white-collar employment. These figures are pitiably small, but the income figures are even smaller: only 2 per cent of the Negro families in the South have incomes over $7,500 a year, and 34 per cent have incomes under $1,000 a year.[16] By way of contrast, 24 per cent of the southern white families have annual incomes over $7,500, and only 9 per cent have incomes under $1,000.

If we lay these disparities aside, as we have in Figure 4–7, to compare the political participation of Negroes and whites with the same income, a new pattern emerges. The lower graph, in which participation is defined as activity beyond talking, shows the now familiar gap between proportions of whites and Negroes participating at the lower levels of income. As with education and occupation, the gap is reduced as higher levels of income are reached. But with income the reduction is much more acute: *the white-Negro differ-ence virtually disappears at the $4,000 income level and reaches a point of greater Negro than white participation at the highest income level. More Negroes than whites with incomes over $7,500 a year take part in politics.* To be sure, this is "more" out of 2 per cent of the Negroes and 24 per cent of the whites, but income still emerges as the most effective leveler of racial differ-ences in participation examined so far.

As we discovered in Chapter Three, voting is a harder step for Negroes than for whites; but of those who vote, a larger percentage of Negroes than of whites go on to other activities. Whatever the social characteristic we con-trolled, then, we would find a smaller gap between white and Negro partici-pation in terms of activity beyond voting. The upper graph in Figure 4–7 defines participation in these terms and holds income constant. In this graph the racial differences are particularly striking, because of the consistent *excess of Negro over white participation* at the $4,000 income level and beyond. At the lower income levels, a smaller proportion of Negroes than of whites are political activists; but the reversal at the higher income levels brings an even greater excess of Negro over white activists.

Another way of describing these findings is to say that, although income

[16] In the interest of consistency, and because all relationships between income and indi-vidual political behavior must be based on the survey data, we are relying on our survey rather than on the census in discussing income distribution. In any case, the survey and the census findings are very similar.

| Income | Negro sample | Nonwhite census | White sample | White census |
|---|---|---|---|---|
| Under $1,000 | 33.8% | 32.5% | 9.0% | 14.0% |
| $1,000–$1,999 | 24.2 | 23.0 | 8.7 | 11.8 |
| $2,000–$2,999 | 13.7 | 17.2 | 10.9 | 10.8 |
| $3,000–$3,999 | 12.4 | 11.2 | 11.2 | 11.1 |
| $4,000–$4,999 | 5.1 | 6.8 | 12.8 | 10.7 |
| $5,000–$5,999 | 6.4 | 3.8 | 12.2 | 10.2 |
| $6,000–$7,499 | 2.6 | 2.7 | 11.6 | 11.2 |
| $7,500 + | 1.8 | 2.8 | 23.6 | 20.2 |
| | 100% | 100% | 100% | 100% |

is more strongly related than other social characteristics to political participation by southern Negroes, it makes little difference for white participation. The difference between the highest and lowest income levels in percent-

FIGURE 4–7.   *Income and political participation in the South, by race*

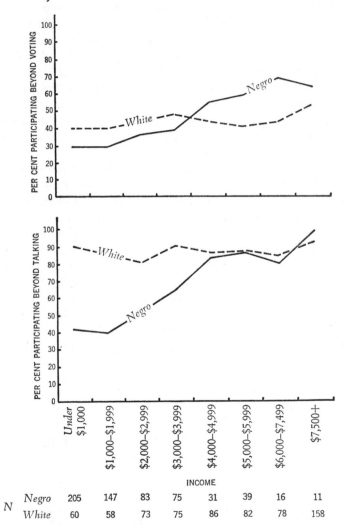

| N | | Under $1,000 | $1,000–$1,999 | $2,000–$2,999 | $3,000–$3,999 | $4,000–$4,999 | $5,000–$5,999 | $6,000–$7,499 | $7,500+ |
|---|---|---|---|---|---|---|---|---|---|
| | Negro | 205 | 147 | 83 | 75 | 31 | 39 | 16 | 11 |
| | White | 60 | 58 | 73 | 75 | 86 | 82 | 78 | 158 |

age of participants who go beyond talking is 4 percentage points for whites and 58 for Negroes. Of course, such an overwhelming majority of southern whites at all income levels have voted at least once that little increase is possible.

When we consider only political activists—people who go beyond talking and voting in political participation—we are dealing with activities pursued by a minority of whites as well as Negroes. Here, too, we find greater variation with changes in income among Negroes, not only because of smaller proportions of activists at the lower income levels but because of greater proportions at the upper income levels. The range in proportion of Negro activists from lowest to highest income levels is 35 percentage points, compared with a range of 14 percentage points for whites. In this case, however, the larger percentage of Negro activists at the "highest" income level stems partly from the fact that the highest income level for southern Negroes is only a moderately high level for southern whites. Family incomes of $10,000 and above are not included in Figure 4–7, because they are attained by too few Negroes. But 13 per cent of southern whites report incomes above $10,000; if they were separately reported rather than included in the category "$7,500 and above," we would find that 60 per cent of them are political activists, virtually as large a proportion as found for Negroes at the $7,500 level.

Income thus has a peculiarly strong impact on political participation by southern Negroes. A vast majority of Negroes at the lowest income levels appear to be frozen completely out of southern political life. But those with reasonably decent family incomes—$4,000 or above—get into southern politics as voters in proportions as great as do whites, and as political activists in greater proportions than do the whites.

"Money talks." But does it speak for itself or for something else? Students of political behavior generally think of income simply as a measure of something else—they think of it as speaking for (or representing) some other, more "basic," variable such as occupation or education. The link between these basic variables and political participation is easy to see. Certain occupations require more political skill and entail greater contact with and dependence on government than others, and education increases political information and interest. But, at least above the subsistence level, income tends to be thought of as an indicator of social status (including education and occupation) rather than as an independent influence on political participation. Accordingly, our discovery of strong relationships between income and political participation by southern Negroes might be expected to disappear when we control for occupation and education.

Southern Negroes engaged in farm occupations are so heavily concentrated in the lower income levels that we can control only for nonfarm occupational status in comparing the relation of occupation and income to political participation. As Table 4–8 indicates, the increase in the percentage of Negroes who take part in politics beyond talking is both greater and more regular along the income dimension than along the occupation dimension. With occupation

TABLE 4–8.   *Percentages of southern Negroes participating in politics beyond talking, by occupation and income*

| ANNUAL HOUSEHOLD INCOME | NONFARM OCCUPATIONS | | |
|---|---|---|---|
| | *Unskilled labor* | *Skilled and semiskilled labor* | *Professional and white-collar workers* |
| Less than $1,000 | 42%  (57)ᵃ | 69%  (40) | —    (6) |
| $1,000–$2,999 | 51%  (72) | 57%  (75) | 46%  (13) |
| $3,000–$4,999 | 73%  (20) | 82%  (54) | 86%  (15) |
| $5,000 + | 77%   (9) | 89%  (40) | 94%  (13) |

ᵃ The numbers in parentheses are the bases on which the percentages were computed.

held constant, the average increase in percentage of participants from low to high levels of income is 34 percentage points. With income held constant, the average increase in percentage of participants from unskilled labor to professional and white-collar workers is 13 percentage points. Although participation is independently related to both occupation and income when the other is taken into account, the participation-income relationship is much stronger.

Education is no more successful than occupation in accounting for the increase in Negro political participation with increases in income (see Table 4–9). Regardless of their level of education, the higher the income of southern Negroes, the more likely they are to take part in politics. The differences are particularly great among Negroes with grade-school and high-school education, but even among those with college training we find a considerably larger percentage of participants in the high than in the low income levels. The deviant cases also attest to the greater effects of income: southern Negroes who combine low education with high income participate more than those who combine high education with low income.

Must we conclude that money *in and of itself* leads to greater political

TABLE 4–9.   *Percentages of southern Negroes participating in politics beyond talking, by income and education*

| ANNUAL HOUSEHOLD INCOME | EDUCATION | | |
|---|---|---|---|
| | *Grade school* | *High school* | *College* |
| Under $1,000 | 41%  (161) | 45%  (40) | —    (4) |
| $1,000–$2,999 | 40%  (141) | 49%  (72) | 69%  (16) |
| $3,000–$4,999 | 66%   (29) | 73%  (62) | 73%  (15) |
| $5,000 + | 79%   (24) | 93%  (28) | 93%  (14) |

participation by southern Negroes? An affirmative answer somehow runs against the American grain. Despite our great emphasis on materialism, Americans have argued since the days of the Puritan oligarchs that financial gain should be interpreted primarily as evidence of something else. That "something else" may be God's favor (as in early New England), natural selection as one of the fit (as in Social Darwinism), service to one's fellow man (as in laissez-faire economics and the Gospel of Wealth), or simply social status (as in most contemporary behavioral research). In view of these precedents, we must make some effort to explain away our finding.

One possible explanation is technical in nature. As southern Negroes have long observed, money is the one commodity that has never been segregated in the South. It moves freely across race lines. Although most of the money flows into white hands, a thousand dollars of "Negro income" means about the same as a thousand dollars of "white income."[17] But ten years of Negro schooling does not have the same meaning as ten years of white schooling; nor do Negro and white claims to a law practice or a business proprietorship usually carry the same meaning. Thus dollars may come closer than any other unit of measure to having identical value across racial lines in the South.

If this line of reasoning is correct, and it certainly seems plausible, then we are saying that income is not *truly* an independent factor but that, for southern Negroes, it more accurately measures the "something else" that is normally represented by other status attributes. This would be a convincing explanation if income were more powerful than other variables only in interracial comparisons. But it is also more powerful than education or occupation in explaining differences among Negroes themselves. *Interracial* differences in the meaning of occupational status and education cannot account for their lesser explanatory power for differences *within* the Negro population.

We cannot, then, explain away the relationship of income to Negro political participation in purely technical terms. So let us try an explanation that is partly substantive and partly technical. In and of itself, what does income represent? The power to buy things. One of the things that money can buy is a ticket for a fund-raising event to help a candidate in an election campaign. Or it can be used for a direct campaign contribution. Such a use of money is a form of political participation that is included in our Political Participation Scale: one way of qualifying as a participant in election campaigns (PPS Type IV) is by giving an affirmative answer to the question, "Have you ever given any money or bought tickets or anything to help someone who was trying to win an election?" People with high income can spend money more easily than can their poorer friends. Monetary contributions are clearly a form

---

[17] Not, however, completely identical: among other exceptions, $5 of Negro income may not, like $5 of white income, be exchanged for a dinner in many restaurants of the South, and $50,000 of Negro income may not suffice to buy a house that could be purchased with $30,000 of white income.

of political participation. But the inclusion in the PPS of an item dependent on income could have a self-fulfilling quality: higher-income people will be found to include more participants if participation is defined so as to require higher income.

The proportions of southern Negroes at each income level who report having "given money or bought tickets" in a campaign are: low, 17; medium low, 10; medium high, 13; high, 27. The increase in percentage of contributors with increases in income is by no means regular, although those in the highest income category are more likely to contribute than are others. But so are they more likely to participate in other ways. High-income Negroes did not simply "buy" their positive scores on the campaign-participation item of the Political Participation Scale: most (83 per cent) of the high-income Negroes who reported participation in the form of giving money have also taken some other part in campaigns, either by attending political meetings or by working for a candidate. In the other income groups, the proportions who have given money and have also taken some other part in campaigns are: low, 63; medium low, 61; medium high, 54. In fact, then, more of the high-income Negroes than of those in other income groups would have qualified as campaign participants if we had not counted monetary outlay as a form of participation.

The impact of income on Negro political participation apparently cannot be explained away. Can it be explained? Can we specify characteristics of income that have direct consequences for political participation by southern Negroes? We think we can, in terms of several links between income and participation.

Money can buy a number of things that are conducive to political participation but that are unavailable to many southern Negroes. The minority who receive adequate incomes can join other middle-class Americans in subscribing to newspapers and buying magazines, television sets, and radios. A few can also afford to speculate about whether to vacation in Bermuda, New York City, or Los Angeles, and where (outside the South) they should send their children to college. All these fruits of high income have some kind of direct or indirect educational effect. Southern Negroes tend to be intellectually, socially, and physically isolated, but those with incomes above the subsistence level can afford to buy their way—at least vicariously—into the main stream of American life. Exposure to national media of communication may bring more of Matt Dillon than of Huntley and Brinkley, but even popular entertainment programs carry some incidental information as well as insight into the white man's daydreams.

The seven-item test of political information reveals that political knowledge does increase with income. Southern Negroes at the low income level achieved an average score of 2.3 correct answers; those at the medium low level, 3.1; and those at the medium high and high levels, 4. Information is primarily a product of formal schooling, but the informal education that occurs in daily life is richer for those with high incomes than for those with low incomes. Remembering how truly low are the family incomes in our "low" and "medium low" categories—under $1,000 and $1,000 to $2,999 a year—and that 72 per cent of all southern Negroes fall into these categories, we can understand that many southern Negroes are totally impoverished, culturally no less than financially. If we examine mean political-information scores with controls for both education and income, as in Table 4–10, we see that formal schooling

TABLE 4–10.   *Mean political-information scores of southern Negroes, by income and education*

| ANNUAL HOUSEHOLD INCOME | EDUCATION | | |
|---|---|---|---|
| | *Grade school* | *High school* | *College* |
| Under $1,000 | 2.1 (161)[a] | 2.9 (40) | — (4) |
| $1,000–$2,999 | 2.6 (141) | 3.7 (72) | 4.9 (16) |
| $3,000–$4,999 | 3.3  (29) | 4.1 (62) | 5.0 (15) |
| $5,000 + | 3.1  (24) | 3.8 (29) | 5.8 (14) |

[a] The numbers in parentheses are the bases on which the means were computed.

produces higher scores with income held constant than does income when education is held constant. Nevertheless, political information does go up in every education category as income increases. Both formal schooling and reasonably high incomes appear to be necessary to gain a command of even the most elemental facts of political life.

Income thus leads to political participation among southern Negroes by permitting them to buy access to minimum political information. But this is not the only way in which income increases political participation. In Table 4–11 we see that information is powerfully related to participation—so much so that the percentage of political participants increases markedly as information goes up, even when income is held constant. Neither formal education nor occupation holds up equally well as a facilitator of participation with similar controls for income; so information is a primary independent variable in relation to Negro political activity. But the income-information nexus does not account for the whole income-participation relationship. Reading down the columns of Table 4–11, we see that the proportions of Negro participants increase with information held constant and income varying. These increases are as great as those for information. *Regardless of their amount of political information, more Negroes at high than at low income levels engage in political activity.*

What, in addition to better informal education, can income buy that leads southern Negroes into political participation? First, it can pay a poll tax. It can also pay for a baby sitter and for transportation to political meetings or to

TABLE 4–11. *Percentages of southern Negroes participating in politics beyond talking, by income and political information*

| ANNUAL HOUSEHOLD INCOME | INFORMATION | | |
|---|---|---|---|
| | Low (0–2) | Medium (3–5) | High (6–7) |
| Under $1,000 | 29% (115) | 58% (84) | — (5) |
| $1,000–$2,999 | 31% (85) | 49% (132) | 85% (13) |
| $3,000–$4,999 | 42% (19) | 73% (67) | 89% (19) |
| $5,000 + | 87% (16) | 86% (35) | 93% (15) |

the polling station, and it can pay for membership fees and appropriate attire to wear to meetings of organizations like the NAACP. Moreover, spare time is needed to participate, and Negroes with better incomes are more likely to enjoy some leisure, or at least greater flexibility in their work schedules, than are those at the subsistence level.[18]

At a less tangible level, higher income undoubtedly leads to greater self-confidence in coping with one's environment. And, in view of the peculiar impediments to active participation by Negroes in the politics of the South, southern Negroes need more self-confidence than do Americans in general if they are to become politically active. The Negro with greater financial status also has more daily experience in making decisions. Those who exist at the subsistence level may have little opportunity to make choices even about what they will do without, because they must settle for absolute necessities. Although economic choices are made on different grounds from political choices, at least the higher-income Negroes are not confronted with a novel situation when an election gives them a chance to weigh alternatives.

In addition to the effect on the Negro himself, higher income has an effect on the way he is viewed by others. In buying the trappings and the experiences of the "American way of life," income may buy at least a modicum of respect from the whites. Income produces more visible badges of status than either education or occupation. It is more difficult for a voter registrar summarily to dismiss a well-dressed Negro than one clad in tattered overalls.[19]

[18] Some of these points are suggested in Bradbury Seasholes, "Negro Political Participation in Two North Carolina Cities" (Ph.D. dissertation, University of North Carolina, 1963), pp. 68–69.

[19] To be sure, white reactions are quite complex. Dean R. B. Brazeal, of Morehouse College, reports that Negroes cannot wear neckties on weekdays in some areas of the South without endangering themselves. M. Price, *The Negro and the Ballot in the South* (Atlanta: Southern Regional Council, 1959), pp. 58–59. The "pistol-whipping" of the Student Non-violent Coordinating Committee representative by the voter registrar of Crayfish County received added justification in the minds of some of the whites when they learned that the Negro youth was wearing Bermuda shorts. The lesson appears to be that Negroes may dress well but that, at least in rural areas, their attire should not deviate from the prescriptions of local custom.

Negroes who win the appurtenances of middle-class American life are regarded as "different," as somehow less Negro than their poverty-stricken fellows; "un-Negro" activities such as political involvement evidently are somehow less inappropriate for Negroes who look, act, and spend money like most whites rather than like most Negroes.

Income thus buys many things, including political information, leisure, self-confidence, experience in making choices, and recognition by whites. Through these and similar mechanisms, it buys a place in the political life of the South.

## Negro political participation as it might be

The main drift of this chapter is plain: the social and economic attributes of individual Negroes are strongly related to the extent of their participation in the civic life of the South. Indeed, the apparent influence of these factors is much greater among southern Negroes than among southern whites, who tend—especially when compared with their Negro neighbors—to take some part in political life regardless of their sex, age, education, occupation, or income.

Our measures of status—education, occupation, and income—are particularly demanding for southern Negroes. As between a Negro laborer and a white laborer of equal competence, the Negro is less likely than the white to be promoted to a higher position. Almost anyone who has been in the South has witnessed a slovenly, incompetent white man "bossing" Negroes who appeared superior to him on any objective basis. Similarly, Negroes of low education or income are more likely than whites to be in the lower position for reasons unrelated to their basic ability. Accordingly, we might have expected smaller differences than we found in participation by Negroes and whites at low status levels. Whatever their native abilities, most Negroes who are deprived of status are also deprived of active citizenship. But the few Negroes who gain high status—especially as measured by income—must have unusual talent. Their higher levels of participation may thus be explained by their ability no less than by other marks of accomplishment.

Given their individual social and economic attributes, the "normal" condition for most southern Negroes is political inactivity. In the southern political environment, the factors that depress political activity among other populations depress Negro activity even more. But the very few Negroes in the South with status attributes roughly comparable to those of most whites approach white rates of participation in talking politics, voting, and taking part in political campaigns. They consistently *exceed* whites at the highest levels of participation—primarily through membership in the NAACP. Moreover, Negro political participation appears more purposive than that of whites.

To what extent do the individual demographic attributes we have examined in this chapter explain the low rates of political participation by southern Negroes? Or the participation gap between whites and Negroes? A final answer to the first question will have to await Chapter Eleven, where we are able to examine the impact of different types of variables on Negro participation, controlling for the effects of all the others. In the meantime, we can give a preliminary answer to the second question—how much of the participation gap between southern Negroes and whites results from their different personal characteristics?

The most direct way to approach this problem is to "reconstruct" the Negro population arithmetically so that it has the same sex, age, education, occupation, and income distributions as the white population, and then to see what pattern of civic participation the Negroes would have. For example, 34 per cent of the Negroes have family incomes of less than $1,000 per year, and the participation of this group is understandably very low. Only 9 per cent of the southern whites are equally poverty-stricken. What would happen to the overall pattern of Negro political participation if only 9 rather than 34 per cent of them "enjoyed" an income of less than $1,000? We cannot say for sure, because such a startling change in Negro income might well change the relationship of income to political participation. But we can say what would happen if the income distribution of the two races were in all other respects identical and if the relationship between income and Negro civic participation remained the same. With a little tedious but simple arithmetic we have created a hypothetical world in which the income gap between southern Negroes and whites has been erased.[20] With a few more calculations we have matched the Negro and white voting-age populations as to their sex and age distributions and their educational and occupational attainments as well.

As we have already seen, income makes the most difference (see Table 4–12). If Negroes had the same incomes as whites—and if Negro participation continued to vary with income as it now does—then 73 per cent of southern Negroes would be voters or more active political participants. This is considerably more than the actual proportion of Negro participants (53

[20] This is accomplished by ascertaining the proportion of Negroes at each level of participation within each category of these demographic variables, multiplying this proportion by the percentage of whites in the demographic category, and summing the products. This procedure gives the percentage of Negroes that could be expected at each level of participation if the distribution of the variable were the same for Negroes as whites and *if the relation of this variable to Negro participation were unchanged by the change in its distribution.* This last assumption is, no doubt, unrealistic to some unknown degree. If the *relationship* between income, for example, and political participation became the same for Negroes as for whites—and if the income *distribution* of the two races were identical—then the two races would participate to exactly the same degree. The hypothetical reconstruction reported in the text varies only one of the two factors—frequency, but not relationship to PPS—which result in differences between the two races.

TABLE 4–12.　*Predicted political participation of southern Negroes,
assuming the same distribution of attributes among
Negroes as among whites*

| DEMOGRAPHIC ATTRIBUTE | PPS TYPE: HIGHEST LEVEL OF ACTIVITY | | | | | TOTAL (N = 618) |
| | I Nothing | II Talk | III Vote | IV Campaign | V Office holder or group member | |
| --- | --- | --- | --- | --- | --- | --- |
| Sex | 10% | 35 | 17 | 27 | 11 | 100% |
| Age | 11% | 36 | 17 | 26 | 10 | 100% |
| Education | 7% | 32 | 19 | 26 | 16 | 100% |
| Occupation of respondent | 7% | 33 | 19 | 25 | 16 | 100% |
| Occupation of head of household | 7% | 27 | 22 | 28 | 16 | 100% |
| Income | 5% | 22 | 22 | 32 | 19 | 100% |

per cent) but still less than the white proportion (89 per cent). The findings
demonstrate that no real difference in Negro participation rates would be
achieved if the Negro population were somehow reshuffled to have the same
sex ratio and the same age pattern as whites. Although the *relationships* between age and sex and participation are different for the two races, age and

FIGURE 4–8.　*Political participation scale scores of southern
whites and Negroes, actual and predicted
if Negroes had the same educational, income, and
occupational distributions as whites*

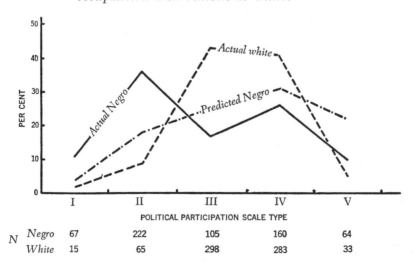

sex *distributions* of the two races are too similar for such a reconstruction to have much effect. Comparable education and occupation structures would produce more Negro participants but not to the extent that a redistribution of income would.

So far we have reconstructed the Negro population one feature at a time. A more realistic procedure is to consider the combined effect of these variables. Figure 4–8 shows the percentage of Negroes who could be expected to participate in each form of political activity if southern Negroes had the same income, occupational, and educational characteristics as southern whites. (Sex and age are dropped, because adjustments to produce corresponding sex ratios and age distributions had no effect on the percentage of Negro participants.) Such a redistribution of these variables, taken together, would greatly increase Negro participation—with 78 per cent rather than 53 per cent qualifying as participants at the voting level or above. Moreover, such a reconstruction eliminates the peculiar bimodal shape of the Negro distribution; Negro political participants would be normally distributed if they had incomes, occupations, and educations comparable to those of whites.

Despite the great effect of financial, occupational, and educational deprivations on Negro participation, we can sweep these deprivations away (mathematically, at least) *without producing Negro political activity comparable to that of whites.* An analysis of the individual attributes of southern Negroes *alone* is not enough to explain their political behavior.

# Chapter Five

# The Community Setting: Social and Economic Aspects

Willy Clayton has all the individual attributes usually found among active participants in politics. He is a 36-year-old male with three and a half years of college training. A high-school social-studies teacher, he and his school-teacher wife earn an annual income of between $5,000 and $6,000. Mr. Clayton has traveled in England, France, and Germany—thanks to the U.S. Army. And he reads, more or less regularly, two daily newspapers, a Negro weekly, *Jet, Ebony,* and *Reader's Digest.* He listens to the radio and watches TV fairly regularly.

Yet he never discusses public problems with his family, the people with whom he works, or any white people; he has *never* voted or even tried to register; he has *never* gone to a political meeting, talked to people to try to influence their vote, bought tickets or given money to help a candidate, or done any other work in a campaign. He *has* talked about public problems with his friends and with Negro community leaders; so he qualifies as a political participant at the lowest level (Type II).

What manner of social-studies teacher is this? The answer is simple: he is a social-studies teacher who lives and works in Crayfish County, Mississippi. This one fact tells more about his political participation than any of his personal characteristics except the color of his skin, which is very dark. Although 33 per cent of the Negroes in the South as a whole were registered as voters in 1961, and almost 50 per cent in 1966, no Negro has yet voted in Crayfish County.

Obviously, Negro political participation is not simply a product of personal attributes like sex, age, education, occupation, and income. It is also a product of the kind of community in which Negroes live.

What kind of county is Crayfish? The rural part of Crayfish, where Mr. Clayton lives, is attractive country; most of it is gently rolling pasture land, with patches of row crops. Crayfish is a black-belt county, with Negroes making up 45 per cent of its population. Although the proportion of Negroes in most southern counties is declining, Crayfish has a slightly larger proportion of Negroes now than it had in 1900—not from any influx of Negroes, but from the more rapid emigration of whites. The county population as a whole declined by 11 per cent from 1940 to 1950, and by 13 per cent from 1950 to 1960.

Mr. Clayton is one of the few Negroes in Crayfish who have ever been to college—the median school years completed by adult Negroes is 5.3 compared to 10.1 years for the average white adult. Thus almost half of the Negro population is functionally illiterate. A man who reads magazines like *Jet*, *Ebony*, and *Reader's Digest* and who subscribes to more than one newspaper enjoys a distinct intellectual advantage. Clayton was the only Negro respondent in Crayfish to answer all seven of the information test questions correctly. His advantage in terms of income is also great: the median annual family income for Negroes is $468, about as much as the Claytons earn in one month. For that matter, the Claytons' income is about five times as large as the median for white families. Most Crayfish Negroes are engaged in menial labor, and only 3 per cent have white-collar jobs of any kind. Clayton's status as a professional man thus puts him in a rare category for local Negroes. Nevertheless—or, perhaps, therefore—our interviewer reported that Willy Clayton "seemed to be very evasive on certain questions, for he felt, seemingly, that a direct and frank opinion might jeopardize his position as a teacher."

Crayfish is farm country with 68 per cent of its total labor force engaged in agriculture. The tenancy rate remains high—29 per cent of the farms are operated by tenants. Breedville, the county seat and the only town in Crayfish, has only 1,200 residents. It strikes the outsider as a small-town slum. The business district is slovenly, with stores badly in need of paint and streets badly in need of sweeping. The white middle-class residential areas look like those in many other small towns—except, perhaps, for the frequent presence of Negro "yard men" conspicuously, if reluctantly, working outside many of the less pretentious homes.

Breedville's city fathers have set aside some land which they optimistically call an industrial park, and they have managed to attract a clothing plant by furnishing a tax-free building to a national concern. The clothing plant and Crayfish's only other "industry," a pickle-processing plant, employ about 10 per cent of Crayfish workers. But the only Negro to win such "manufacturing" employment is a female washroom attendant. And she knows not to seek membership in the company-dominated union, because her predecessor was discharged for that act of effrontery.

Like most Negroes and whites of Crayfish, Willy Clayton is a Baptist, and he attends church regularly. But the church does not fill the political void in his life. He says that problems of race relations and election campaigns are never discussed at church, and he does not know whether his minister believes that Christianity and the Bible favor segregation or integration. Clayton himself is in favor of integration, but he judges that "less than half" of the other Negroes in Crayfish favor integration and that "all" whites favor "strict segregation." Despite his schooling, his travel, and his teaching experience, the most perfect kind of race relations he can imagine is one "where there is equal protection under the law. . . . I believe that would cover it." Rating his community in terms of this ideal, he places it near the very worst imaginable.

Clayton misjudges his fellow Negroes: rather than a majority favoring segregation, 92 per cent actually favor integration. But he is right about the whites: 98 per cent favor strict segregation, 2 per cent "something in between," and none favors integration. Whatever the views of the majority of Crayfish Negroes, they count for little in local politics. Most informed leaders feel that the county's white schools should be consolidated, but this reform is blocked by sentimental and economic attachments to scattered village schools. The Negro schools, however, were quickly consolidated. As a white leader laughingly explained, "We didn't have to ask the niggers; we just did it."

Despite the relatively high educational level of Crayfish whites, the social and economic characteristics of the county apparently are not conducive to Negro political activity. The large percentage of Negroes; their lack of educational, occupational, and financial resources; the rural way of life; the lack of religious heterogeneity—these factors seem to add up to an environment in which Negroes are kept in "their place." It is not a community in which a Negro, even a social-studies teacher, should take part in politics unless he has ambitions to martyrdom.

·   ·   ·

Joe Barton of Bright Leaf County would appear to be a less likely prospect for political participation than Willy Clayton. A 47-year-old sharecropper, he manages with his wife and seven children to earn an income between $4,000 and $5,000 a year from his 60 acres of corn, cotton, peanuts, tobacco, sweet potatoes, and cucumbers. While this places him in a relatively high income category among local Negroes, he has had only seven years of schooling. Not having been in the army, Mr. Barton has never been abroad; the farthest he has ever been away from "home"—geographically and culturally—was while on a trip to Washington, D.C. He reads a daily paper and two farm journals, and he watches TV fairly regularly—news programs in particular.

Although Barton lacks a good many of Clayton's advantages, he leads a more active community life. Whereas Clayton claimed to be only "somewhat" interested in politics, Barton says he has "a great deal" of interest and that he has talked to people to try to get them to vote for or against specific candidates.

As a young man he registered to vote while living in the county next to Bright Leaf, because "the [white] man I farmed with told me I ought to." Despite this prompting, he thought it an important step in his life, and he has voted in several presidential elections.

Barton is not currently registered in Bright Leaf, "because the place I went to to register was the wrong place and I never did find the right place." He was able to answer only four of our seven political-information items, which suggests that he might have difficulty coping with the intricacies of his state's registration scheme. Although he is not registered now, Barton's past record of voting and his discussion of politics qualify him for the middle level of participation (Type III).

Unlike Clayton, Barton lives in a place where Negro voting is common— 23 per cent of the voting-age Negroes were registered in 1961. Bright Leaf County, which lies in the flat plain of the Atlantic coast, has small but relatively prosperous farms—largely in tobacco. Negroes constitute 44 per cent of the population, almost exactly the same as in Crayfish. But in Bright Leaf the proportion of Negroes has declined slightly since 1900, when it was just over 50 per cent. And the total Bright Leaf population is slowly increasing— 4 per cent from 1940 to 1950 and 10 per cent from 1950 to 1960. Mr. Barton's seven years of schooling put him ahead of most Bright Leaf Negroes: the median schooling of Negroes is 4.9 years; of whites, 9.2 years. While both whites and Negroes in Bright Leaf fall below those in Crayfish in education, their incomes are considerably higher: the median family income of Negroes is $861; of whites, $1,754. Thus Barton is relatively well-to-do: his hopes of building a home of his own are not just dreams. Almost 9 per cent of Bright Leaf Negroes enjoy white-collar employment, however, so that Barton does not enjoy a position of distinction comparable to Clayton's.

Bright Leaf is less dominated by agriculture than is Crayfish—not quite half the labor force (49 per cent) is employed in agriculture. Moreover, many more of its farms are absentee-owned, with almost three fourths being operated by tenants. Almost a third of Bright Leaf's population is urban, and Farmington, the county seat, would look like a metropolis to most Crayfish residents. Farmington's population of 23,000 is increased during the school year by some 10,000 students at the bustling state teachers college, and it boasts such advantages as fairly decent restaurants, motels, and a daily newspaper.

Joe Barton seems to feel that he has access at least to the commercial advantages of the nearby city. If he were not "treated right at some white store," he says, "I'd do something about it. I'd go to the authorities and talk to them. That's why colored folk are treated the way they are today, because they don't say nothing when they ain't treated right." This is in marked contrast to Willy Clayton's more grammatical and more circumspect comment: "I would contact the manager of the store and talk to him—that is, if I were mistreated by one of the employees; otherwise, I would do nothing."

Like most Negroes in Bright Leaf, Joe Barton is a Baptist. Among the whites, too, the Baptists make up the largest denomination, but Bright Leaf has enough religious heterogeneity for the Baptists to constitute a plurality rather than a majority of the whites. Mr. Barton does not attend church regularly, but he goes often enough to report that race relations and election campaigns are discussed at church and that his minister believes that religion and the Bible favor integration. Mr. Barton himself favors "something in between" strict segregation and integration, but his comment— "down here that's about all you can be for"—suggests that he is manfully adjusting his preferences to harsh realities. In marked contrast to Crayfish Negroes, 45 per cent of those in Bright Leaf say they favor "strict segregation"; 87 per cent of the whites (as compared with 98 per cent in Crayfish) agree with them.

The environments in which Willy Clayton and Joe Barton live are very similar in racial composition, but they are different in a number of other respects. Bright Leaf's residents have slightly lower average educational levels, but more Negroes there have white-collar jobs, both whites and Negroes have higher incomes, not quite half the labor force is in agriculture, almost a third of the population is urban, and there is less religious homogeneity. Somehow, in this environment, personal attributes seem to have greater relevance to political behavior. It is hard to imagine that Willy Clayton would be a nonvoter if he lived in a more progressive community than Crayfish. But if Joe Barton lived in a more permissive environment, his participation would probably still be sporadic and limited.

• • •

Tom Johnson, of Capital City in Camellia County, is another southern Negro who is fairly well off financially. Fifty years old, he owns a shoe repair shop that—supplemented by his wife's income as a schoolteacher—brings his family an annual income of $7,500 to $9,000. Mr. Johnson, a college graduate, is an extremely talkative and well-informed businessman. He has traveled widely in the United States and demonstrates the transferable confidence of the skilled craftsman in discussing public affairs of all kinds. He reads the Capital City daily newspaper and—"to find [out] the truth about Negroes"—the *Pittsburgh Courier*, the Baltimore *Afro-American*, and the *Chicago Defender*. Two magazines he reads more or less regularly are *Jet* and a professional journal for shoemakers. He listens to the radio and watches TV, paying special attention to news and to the commentary on the "Today Show."

Fairly bristling with ideas and advice, Johnson has engaged in all forms of political activity except actually holding office. He discusses public problems at length with his family, friends, customers, and Negro community leaders. As for white people, he reports that "once in a while you find a broad-minded white man" with whom you can talk. But he adds, "You have to let him have the lead or you'll be labeled Communist. I can't *really* talk because they don't want to treat the Negro the way they should."

Johnson registered to vote shortly after the Supreme Court declared the "white primary" unconstitutional, or, as he put it, "when they stopped threatening to beat colored people for registering." Since then he has voted in all elections for local, state, and national office. He contributes money to candidates, puts campaign cards in his customers' packages, talks to people to try to influence their vote, and attends political meetings. He does not approve of political barbecues, however, because "they serve moonshine under the table." Mr. and Mrs. Johnson are both members of the NAACP, but in talking about it he urged, "Please be careful because of the witch-hunt here." All these forms of activity qualify Mr. Johnson as a political participant at the highest level (Type V).

Despite being the site of the state capital, Camellia County was almost entirely farm land in 1900, with 80 per cent of its population Negro. In recent decades its population has increased at a breathtaking pace—63 per cent from 1940 to 1950, and 44 per cent from 1950 to 1960. Capital City itself has grown from a village to a city of 50,000. Since most of the new people were whites moving into the county, Negroes constituted only a third of the population by 1960. About two thirds of Camellia's population are now urban, and only 8 per cent of the labor force works in agriculture. The efforts of the Chamber of Commerce to attract light industry have not been conspicuously successful: only 7 per cent of the labor force is employed in manufacturing. The principal employers are the state government and the two state universities, one of which is Negro, and one primarily white but with token integration. The county also serves as a wholesale and trading center for surrounding rural counties and as regional headquarters for a number of businesses.

Capital City is thus primarily a white-collar town full of professors, lawyers, bureaucrats, and clerks; even among Negroes, 17 per cent are in white-collar employment. It is also a weird mixture of old South and non-South. Natives of Capital City like Mr. Johnson grew up in a typically Deep South environment, but the influx of government, university, and business employees mixes the local southern accent with homogenized American and a variety of other accents. White educational levels are unusually high in Camellia: the median number of school years its residents have completed is 12.6, which means that over half the whites have had some college training. The median schooling of Negroes is more typical—5.4 years—but the presence of the Negro college makes the range considerably greater than in most southern counties. Camellia residents are not much better off financially, however, than the people of Bright Leaf. The median family income of whites is $1,803; of Negroes, $879. The Johnsons fare handsomely by local standards.

Most of the Negroes in Capital City are Baptists, as elsewhere in the South; the Johnsons are Methodists, but Mr. Johnson seldom accompanies his wife to church. He does attend CORE-sponsored mass meetings at the church. Through such meetings, his minister has played a prominent role in organizing a bus boycott and sit-in demonstrations. Not surprisingly, the minister has clearly indicated that "segregation is morally and spiritually wrong." He also discusses election campaigns—among them his own recent unsuccessful bid for a seat on the city commission.

The heterogeneity of Capital City is underscored by the variety of religious preferences among whites. Baptists make up the largest denomination, but all major religions are represented in the city. Moreover, 10 per cent of the whites say they have no religious preference at all, an admission that very few whites in the other communities were willing to make.

Johnson is only one among many Negro political participants in Camellia, where a majority (55 per cent) of the adult Negroes are currently registered to vote. As such, he would not hesitate to approach elective officials if he had a problem they could help with—"they are in by popular vote, so they will help." Although he knows that his minister and other Negro leaders have received threatening telephone calls and have been subjected to such acts of vandalism as broken windows, he feels that "bread-and-butter" needs can be met. He explains, for example, how Camellia Negroes finally got a public swimming pool. "We got one after the Korean War on the basis of an agreement with Reverend Sampson [the minister of the largest Baptist church for whites]. He asked the Negroes to vote the county dry. We voted the county dry—we got the swimming pool (and awful moonshine)."

The Negro community in Capital City is complex and differentiated. Mr. Johnson is thus able to think of different strata of Negroes in a fashion that would hardly occur to Mr. Clayton in Crayfish. Johnson reported, for example, that he did not think of himself as being in the middle class or the working class, although we shall see below that he does think of himself as being in the "better class." Asked which he would call himself if he had to make a choice, he selected working class, on the grounds that "professional people are in the middle class—I'm a workingman." Earlier, in naming Negro community leaders, he had said, "I'm not talking about the people at the college; they have a cushion seat." As professional people, college professors occupy a higher status, but Mr. Johnson clearly does not lump working businessmen like himself with the mass of Negroes. The most perfect race relations he could imagine, for example, call for selective and gradual integration:

> Forgetting the social end, when it comes to living, the better class [of whites] should take into consideration that the average Negro hasn't lived like them. Integrate the better classes first, then the masses will come in time. [Cites Jackie Robinson as an example.] The trash are getting together on their level now— you know that—just like in slavery times. Give qualified Negroes chances at jobs and houses and land.

Camellia County not only permits Negro political participation but, granted a good education and varied interests like Tom Johnson's, the local environment positively encourages a high level of political participation.

•   •   •

George Hopkins, a 28-year-old insurance agent, lives in the suburban fringe of a city where Negroes have made even more social and economic progress—Urbania, a city of 75,000 that dominates Piedmont County. A young married man without children, Mr. Hopkins has lived in Urbania all his life, has completed three years of training at the local Negro college, and receives a salary between $5,000 and $6,000 a year. Hopkins is one of a number of Negroes employed by the Urbania Insurance Company to maximize sales to Negroes and to demonstrate the liberalism of company management. He has visited such American cities as New York but, a nonveteran, he has never been abroad. Hopkins is both less talkative and less well informed than Johnson; he answered six of the seven political-information questions correctly (almost equaling the perfect scores of Clayton and Johnson). He reads Urbania's daily morning newspaper and its Negro weekly, as well as *Life, Sports Illustrated,* and *Ebony,* and he listens to the radio and watches TV.

With his wife and friends and with his white co-workers at the insurance company, Hopkins talks about "current events and international affairs, such as the Cuban and Berlin crises," and about "segregation against Negroes." He has also discussed politics with Negro officeholders and party leaders in Urbania. This simple feat is impossible in the other three counties, because they had no Negro officeholders. Unlike Clayton, Barton, and Johnson, George Hopkins registered to vote as soon as he was of age. Unlike them, he could take the franchise for granted as a right that comes with adulthood. Asked if there was any special reason why he registered at that time, he could reply—without Barton's reference to the advice of a white plantation owner or Johnson's reference to threats of beatings—"Only that I was of age, and registration was required before one could vote." Nevertheless, he felt that registration was "most important" to him. Hopkins has not contributed money, gone to political meetings, worked for a candidate in a campaign, or held public or party office, but he is a member of the NAACP. He thus qualifies as a high-level participant (PPS Type V), although his lack of campaign activity represents an "error" in the scale.

Unlike Camellia County, Piedmont has no history of old-South plantation days when Negroes greatly outnumbered whites. In 1900, Negroes made up only 37 per cent of the Piedmont population, a smaller proportion than in Crayfish and Bright Leaf today. By 1960 that proportion had decreased to 32 per cent Negro, almost identical to the proportion in Camellia. The overall population of Piedmont increased 27 per cent from 1940 to 1950, and 10 per cent from 1950 to 1960. About three fourths of the county's population are urban, with only 5 per cent of the labor force employed in agriculture. Large tobacco and textile companies in Urbania dominate the county's economy, and 30 per cent of the labor force is employed in manufacturing.

Before the Civil War, Piedmont County was an area of poor, small farms. Late in the nineteenth century it turned to industry. So it has neither a need nor a basis for exaggerated memories of a patrician past. Urbania is an ugly, smelly city, but its ugliness and its smell are products of money-making. Piedmont seems less concerned with or hampered by its past than any of the other three counties. Already enjoying the blessings and hardships of industry, it has a nearby research center that has actually attracted a few of the national concerns for which business leaders in the other counties yearn.

Alone among the four communities we studied, Urbania has large-scale Negro business establishments. The top officers of the Negro insurance company and bank in Urbania have national stature—as is indicated by their appointment to national committees and commissions by several presidents of the United States. These people are invited to dinner at the White House, and the local paper prints their pictures as they fly off to winter vacations in the Caribbean. (Only recently, however, have these same Negro leaders gained entry into the local chamber of commerce!) The major Negro businesses in Urbania produce not only a thin stratum of truly wealthy Negroes but also an unusually large proportion (18 per cent) of Negroes in white-collar jobs. The result is a large, well-educated, economically independent group of Negroes with leadership skills and proclivities. White leaders cannot afford to ignore them in politics or in business. Competition from the Negro insurance company helps, for example, to account for the eagerness of Urbania's "white" insurance company to add Negroes like George Hopkins to its staff.

White educational levels are not so high in Piedmont (9.9 median school years) as in Camellia (12.6) or even in Crayfish (10.1), but Negroes have more schooling in Piedmont (6.5 median school years) than in the other three communities. Hopkins, like many local Negroes, attended a state Negro college in Urbania. The income of both whites and Negroes in Piedmont is much higher than in the other areas; the median family income for whites is $2,599 a year—for Negroes, $1,584. The average Negro family in Piedmont thus receives a higher income than the average white family in Crayfish! The religious composition of Piedmont is similar to that of Camellia. George Hopkins and his wife both belong to the Baptist Church, and he claims to attend services often. Like Johnson, he reports that race relations and election campaigns are discussed at church and that his minister believes in integration.

A large majority (69 per cent) of the adult Negroes in Piedmont are registered to vote; a young businessman like Hopkins would be quite out of step if he were totally uninvolved in politics. Unlike the three other Negro citizens we have described, Hopkins recalls that his father also voted; he would be violating family no less than community tradition if he abstained. Hopkins is politically active because it is expected of him, and he shares the view that it should be expected. If he was concerned about a traffic safety problem, he states, "I'd contact my city councilman and see what could be done." In his case, *my* city councilman refers not only to someone for whom he has voted (which Johnson could say as well) but also to a fellow Negro (which Johnson could not say). Perhaps this is why Hopkins does not feel impelled to add comments about whether or not politicians respond to voters; he can more nearly take the working of the democratic process for granted.

## Community characteristics and political participation: Problems of analysis

This glimpse into the way of life of four men suggests that local community characteristics influence Negro political participation in the South. The community makes itself felt in several ways. First, *the nature of the community in which Negroes live affects their personal characteristics, and—*as we saw in Chapter Four and shall see again in Chapter Ten*—these in turn affect political participation.* George Hopkins, for example, could not be an insurance salesman and live in Crayfish County: the only white-collar occupations open to Negroes in this county are schoolteacher or proprietor of a small retail and service establishment with exclusively Negro clientele. Given the size and poverty of the Negro market in Crayfish, a shoe repairman like Tom Johnson could not earn $7,500 a year there; he does in Capital City. In some southern communities, then, Negroes have a reasonable chance to achieve the occupational, educational, and income levels that facilitate civic activity; in other communities they have virtually no chance at all. The same is true of individual psychological attributes: the motivational and cognitive preconditions for active citizenship are much more likely to be achieved in some community settings than in others.

If this were the only way in which community structure affected Negro political participation, we would hardly need to consider *both* individual *and* community variables in our research. The analysis of one set of variables would tell us all we needed to know about Negro political behavior without looking at the other set. But local community structure does not completely determine the personal characteristics of every local Negro, and the characteristics of communities are more than the sum (or average) of the personal characteristics of the people who live in them. The average Negro in Crayfish County, for example, is a semiliterate, poverty-ridden farmer: these personal attributes are scarcely conducive to active citizenship anywhere. But Willy Clayton is a moderately well-paid, politically knowledgeable schoolteacher who happens to live in Crayfish too. We cannot explain his lack of political activity on the basis of personal characteristics. If Clayton taught school in Piedmont or Camellia counties, chances are he would lead a quite active political life. Or if Tom Johnson or Joe Barton moved to Crayfish County, Mississippi, their present levels of political activity would probably (and prudently) be reduced. Thus, at least in such extreme situations, *the characteristics of the communities in which Negroes live affect their political participation regardless of the personal characteristics of individual Negroes.*[1]

If this is true, then why have community characteristics been so largely ignored in studies of political participation? One reason is that students of politics tend, like others, to be influenced by the technology of their trade. The opinion survey is the most efficient current tool for the collection of data on political behavior. Accordingly, the variables that are most easily measured in surveys—social status and party identification, for example—have been analyzed with rich rewards. But variables that do not lend themselves to survey research design, such as community characteristics, tend to be neglected. A sample of a population of *citizens* includes too few *communities* for the researcher to make any extensive analysis of aggregate community characteristics. But even the limited analysis that is possible is rarely undertaken.[2]

Another common research technique is the intensive community study, which often includes an opinion survey. This approach permits detailed analysis of community characteristics. But, because the researcher usually lacks comparative data on other communities, he cannot handle the community as the analytical unit.

Our data on four communities suggest some of the difficulties. Although the data are highly useful—indeed, indispensable—for examining such factors as leadership styles, the number of communities studied is too small for us to generalize safely. No Negroes vote in Crayfish County, for example, and the county has a high proportion of Negroes in its population. Does this mean that, when the number of local Negroes rises to a certain proportion of the total population, Negroes are excluded from southern politics? The current registration of 23 per cent of the Negroes in Bright Leaf, which has the same

---

[1] We shall not attempt to distinguish between these two types of effect in this chapter. The independent effects of community factors will be isolated and measured in Chapter Eleven.

[2] The neglect of community factors does not stem simply from the nature of the research instrument; it also stems from the particular research design and the substantive interests of those who pioneered in the use of the instrument. In the case of survey research on voting behavior, the pioneering study was carried out in a single county by researchers with little interest or sophistication in politics *per se*. See P. F. Lazarsfeld *et al.*, *The People's Choice* (New York: Duell, Sloan & Pearce, 1944). Subsequent research using national samples and showing a greater concern for political variables demonstrates that the analysis of community characteristics can enrich survey findings. See A. Campbell *et al.*, *The American Voter* (New York: John Wiley & Sons, 1960), especially chs. 11, 14, 15, and 16.

racial composition as Crayfish, suggests not. Which is the deviant county? What is the relevance of other variables? Even as many as four community studies do not permit an answer.

A more promising approach is to consider all counties within the total area of study. This is what we propose to do for those county characteristics on which data are available for all counties in the South. In shifting from survey data on individuals to aggregate data on all counties, we must, of course, also shift to a measure of Negro political participation that is available for all counties. The percentage of Negro adults registered to vote appears to be the best such measure. When the item is of the sort (such as the nature of registration procedures) not reported in census-type sources, we shall supplement this collection of aggregate county data with additional information on the 25 counties we used as sampling points for the southwide survey.

Although, so far as we know, no comprehensive effort has been made to explain community variations in Negro voter registration in the South, earlier studies of southern politics suggest a number of partial explanations. Drawing on these studies and on hypotheses derived from our four community studies, we collected data on 21 social and economic characteristics of southern counties (counting Virginia's independent cities as counties). We took some of these characteristics, such as percentage of population Negro and percentage of population urban, directly from the United States census. Others, such as percentage of nonwhite labor force in white-collar occupations, and white and nonwhite median incomes, we derived from census figures that required calculations of varying degrees of complexity for each county. Still other items, such as percentage of the white population belonging to a church, and the number of Negro colleges in each county, came from noncensus sources.[3]

Because our focus is on Negroes, we excluded from our analysis 108 counties with populations containing less than 1 per cent Negroes. All other counties for which 1958 registration data were available by race we included.[4] This selection procedure gave us a total of 997 counties for the analysis of Negro registration and 822 for the analysis of white registration.[5]

Studying almost a thousand counties seems obviously preferable to studying only four, but the data on such a large number of counties cannot be as good. To begin with, the measure of political participation in terms of percentage of registered voters in each county is cruder and less reliable than the

---

[3] A complete list of sources used to obtain county frequencies for the independent variables used in this analysis would be too lengthy to reproduce here. A mimeographed list will be supplied upon request.

[4] Voter registration rates, by race, are presented in U.S. Commission on Civil Rights, *1959 Report* (Washington, D.C.: U.S. Government Printing Office, 1959) and "Voting," *1961 Report*, Vol. 1. The 1958 registration data, contained in the *1959 Report*, are more complete and were used for all states except Tennessee. The 1960 figures, printed in the *1961 Report*, are the only ones available for Tennessee.

[5] The 11 southern states contain 1,136 counties, 1,028 of which have populations containing at least 1 per cent Negroes.

Political Participation Scale derived from interviews. Virtually all Negroes who are registered to vote in the South have voted at least once.[6] So to use voter registration rates is roughly equivalent to dividing all Negroes into two groups, with the division between Type II and Type III on the Political Participation Scale. This means that we cannot distinguish between non-voters who discuss politics (Type II) and those who do not even do that (Type I). Nor can we differentiate between those who merely talk and vote (Type III) and those who engage in politics even more actively (Types IV and V).

The reported percentage of Negroes registered to vote is not highly reliable. In some cases, the figures obviously exaggerate the extent of Negro voter registration: when we compare them with census data on total nonwhite population, we find that in a number of southern counties over 100 per cent of the adult Negroes are said to be registered! Apparently some local officials decided they would "look good" in the eyes of the U.S. Civil Rights Commission if they inflated the number of Negro voters. In other counties, especially in rural areas, voting lists may simply be out of date, carrying the names of many bona fide residents of New York, Detroit, and Los Angeles, not to speak of local graveyards.

In some states, the payment of a poll tax (since outlawed) was the nearest equivalent of voter registration, but exemptions from the tax were so numerous that the number of poll-tax payers was much smaller than the number of voters. Moreover, statewide statistics on voter registration (or poll-tax payment) by race are collected only in Arkansas, Florida, Georgia, Louisiana, South Carolina, and Virginia. In the remaining states, the number of registered Negro voters must be obtained from estimates made by county registrars, newsmen, politicians, and the like.

Nevertheless, when we correct for obvious error and reduce reported figures so that no county is recorded as having over 100 per cent of its Negroes registered, we find that the proportions of voting-age Negroes reported by these sources as registered in 1958 (28 per cent) and by our 1961 survey (33 per cent) are quite close.

The use of these county data poses conceptual as well as measurement difficulties. Ultimately, we are interested in determining the impact of *community* factors on *individual* behavior. But our county data do not permit us to do this directly, because our measure of political participation is an aggregate figure—the percentage of all voting-age Negroes in the county registered to vote. This gives us a single measure of Negro political participation for thousands of people in an entire county. Similarly, the community characteristics we examined as possible influences on political participation—median income, for example—are merely aggregate figures. A relationship between

[6] Among Negroes who have *ever* registered, 96 per cent have also voted. The 4 per cent who have never voted were not asked if they were currently registered.

two such "averages" can obscure a wealth of variation among individuals.

To go from county averages to individual behavior is not quite like trying to divide apples into oranges; in the first case we are dealing with different levels of measurement of the same phenomenon, not—as in apples-oranges arithmetic—with different phenomena. Nevertheless, we must be extremely cautious in drawing inferences about individual behavior from information about such large aggregates of people as the populations of counties.

A final limitation lies in the statistical approach we employed here, which is that of correlation and regression analysis. The coefficient of correlation ($r$) is a measure of the association between variables when each variable is expressed as a series of observations of a quantitative characteristic. The value of $r$ varies from 0 (no association between independent and dependent variables) to 1.0 (one variable perfectly predicts the other).[7] A positive correlation indicates that as one variable increases the other also increases; a negative correlation indicates an inverse relationship—as one variable increases, the other decreases.

We shall first consider simple correlations, describing the association between percentage of Negroes registered and each of the social and economic characteristics of southern counties. In order to make a better estimate of the independence of these relationships, we shall also present partial correlations, which measure the association between two variables that remains after we have taken into account the contribution of a third variable.

Although these measures do enable us to determine the strength and direction of association between variables, a warning is in order: correlations do not reflect the *absolute level* of the variables. Thus, a given amount and regularity of change in Negro registration will produce the same correlation whether the actual level of Negro registration is high or low. Only for the more powerful variables shall we look beneath the correlations to examine the *level* of Negro registration.

Despite these problems and limitations, the sometimes crude and refractory county data on Negro voter registration still reveal much about Negro political participation in the South today.

---

[7] Correlations between aggregate measures tend to be artificially inflated by the elimination of individual variations around the group norm. Thus, for example, the relationship between median income and registration rates *of a group* is likely to appear larger than the relationship between individual income and individual participation, because much random or idiosyncratic variation is eliminated by the group measures.

For a technical discussion of the limitations of correlation analysis using aggregate data, see W. S. Robinson, "Ecological Correlations and the Behavior of Individuals," *American Sociological Review*, Vol. 15 (1950), pp. 351–57; L. A. Goodman, "Ecological Regression and the Behavior of Individuals," *ibid.*, Vol. 18 (1953), pp. 663–64; O. D. Duncan and B. Davis, "An Alternative to Ecological Correlation," *ibid.*, Vol. 18 (1953), pp. 665–66; L. A. Goodman, "Some Alternatives to Ecological Correlation," *American Journal of Sociology*, Vol. 64 (1959), pp. 610–25.

# Negro concentration

The concentration of an ethnic or an occupational group in a geographical area tends to increase communication among the group's members, to nurture feelings of "belonging," and to provide social reinforcement for the political expression of common interests. Consequently, the geographical concentration of a group usually results in more political participation by its members than would be the case if they were widely dispersed.[8]

Just the opposite seems true for southern Negroes: *the larger the proportion of Negroes in a southern community, the smaller the proportion who are politically active.* The coefficient of correlation between the percentage of Negroes in the 1950 population of southern counties and the percentage of their voting-age Negroes registered to vote is —.46. This correlation is larger than that between any other county characteristic (of those we have been able to measure) and Negro voter registration.[9] This does not mean, however, that the decline in Negro registration associated with increasing Negro concentration occurs at a constant rate. If we examine the relationship between these two variables over the entire range of southern counties, we see that increases in the proportion Negro up to about 30 per cent are *not* accompanied by substantial declines in Negro registration (see Figure 5–1). As the proportion Negro increases beyond 30 per cent, however, Negro registration rates begin to decline very sharply until they approach 0 at about 60 per cent Negro and above.

Correlations tell us that two factors vary together; they do not tell us which is "cause" and which is "effect" or why the two variables are associated. What do these statistics mean?

First of all, Negro concentration clearly appears to be the independent variable ("cause") and Negro voter registration the dependent variable ("effect"). It boggles the imagination to think that Negroes might move into a county because it is an area where Negroes do not, or cannot, vote. But *how* does the presence of a high proportion of Negroes in a county reduce the likelihood that they will register to vote? We can hardly infer that Negroes are discouraged from voting because they have lots of Negro neighbors, or that they crowd one another out of registration queues!

[8] S. M. Lipset *et al.*, "The Psychology of Voting," ch. 30 in G. Lindzey (ed.), *Handbook of Social Psychology* (Cambridge, Mass.: Addison-Wesley Publishing Co., 1954), Vol. 2, pp. 1126–34.

[9] For a more complete and technical discussion of the analysis undergirding this chapter, see D. R. Matthews and J. W. Prothro, "Social and Economic Factors and Negro Voter Registration in the South," *American Political Science Review*, Vol. 57 (1963), pp. 24–44. The correlations of 20 independent variables and Negro registration rates are there presented in Table II, p. 29.

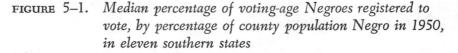

FIGURE 5–1.  *Median percentage of voting-age Negroes registered to vote, by percentage of county population Negro in 1950, in eleven southern states*

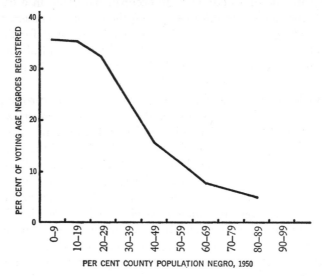

One reason Negro concentration is such a powerful explanatory factor in analyzing southern politics may be that it is related to so many other social and economic characteristics of the region's counties. Percentage Negro in 1950 is strongly related, for example, to the percentage of farms operated by tenants (+.49), nonwhite median income (—.40), nonwhite school years completed (—.47), percentage of the labor force in agriculture (+.30), and percentage of the white population belonging to a church (+.38). Such characteristics as these are in turn related to variation in rates of Negro voter registration.[10] These related factors, rather than Negro concentration, might account for the —.46 correlation between percentage Negro and percentage registered to vote. One might say, for example, that low levels of Negro education actually account for low levels of registration, and that Negro education is particularly low in the most heavily Negro counties.

When we control separately for the contribution of all other county characteristics, the partial correlation between Negro registration and Negro concentration reveals that this is not the case: Negro registration in southern counties goes down as the proportion of Negroes goes up regardless of the other characteristics of the counties. The correlation is reduced only to —.41, for example, when we take variations in Negro education into account. Only one county characteristic is so closely related to both Negro registration in 1958 and Negro concentration in 1950 that the strength of their association

[10] The respective correlations are —.32, +.19, +.22, —.20, and —.17.

drops when we take its contribution into account—and this characteristic is an earlier measurement of the same independent variable. Controlling for percentage of Negroes in the population in 1900 reduces the correlation between 1950 Negro concentration and registration to —.21. Even with this control, the independent tendency of Negro registration to decrease in counties currently containing more Negroes is not eliminated, although it is reduced substantially.

*Thus southern counties containing a large proportion of Negroes tend to be rural, tenant-farming, tradition-bound communities in which local Negroes are poorly educated and have very low incomes. But these other community characteristics do not always accompany high Negro concentration, and, where they do not, Negro voter registration is still responsive to the proportion of Negroes in the population.*

We must therefore look beyond these associated community characteristics for an explanation of why Negro concentration depresses Negro political activity.

The usual explanation of this relationship is that as the proportion of Negroes in southern communities increases, so do the racial anxieties and fears of southern whites. These white attitudes engender race relations and political practices that inhibit Negro political activity regardless of Negro desires.[11] By shifting our attention from all southern counties to the 25 survey counties on which we have attitudinal data, we can test these heretofore unverified inferences.

The American political system places a high value on the right of every citizen to vote, and an overwhelming majority of Americans endorse this principle in the abstract, even those who deny its specific application.[12] In the South as a whole, for example, 87 per cent of the adult whites agree that "colored people ought to be allowed to vote" (73 per cent agree "quite a bit," 14 per cent agree "a little," 4 per cent disagree "a little," and 7 per cent disagree "quite a bit").[13] The percentage of whites in each county who agree

[11] V. O. Key, Jr., *Southern Politics* (New York: Alfred A. Knopf, 1949), gives little attention to Negro voting, because it was of little importance at the time he wrote (see, however, his p. 518). His stress on the overriding importance of Negro concentration for all aspects of southern politics makes his study highly relevant, nonetheless. Other works specifically on Negro voting that stress the importance of Negro concentration include: James F. Barnes, "Negro Voting in Mississippi" (M.A. thesis, University of Mississippi, 1955); H. D. Price, *The Negro and Southern Politics, A Chapter of Florida History* (New York: New York University Press, 1957); Margaret Price, *The Negro and the Ballot in the South* (Atlanta: Southern Regional Council, 1959); U.S. Commission on Civil Rights, "Voting," *1961 Report* (Washington, D.C.: U.S. Government Printing Office, 1961); Donald Strong, "The Future of the Negro Voter in the South," *Journal of Negro Education,* Vol. 26 (1957), pp. 400–07.

[12] James W. Prothro and Charles M. Grigg, "Fundamental Principles of Democracy: Bases of Agreement and Disagreement," *Journal of Politics,* Vol. 22 (1960), pp. 276–94.

[13] Two per cent said they "don't know" or gave no answer.

"quite a bit" that Negroes should be allowed to vote may be taken as a rough index of a permissive local attitude toward Negro registration. Relating this aggregate figure for each county to the percentage of Negroes in its population, we find a strong negative correlation (—.51) for the 25 counties in the survey. The more Negroes in the population of a county, the fewer the whites who give even abstract endorsement to the right of Negroes to vote.

Moreover, when we examine in detail the relationship between Negro concentration and white attitudes toward Negro voting, we find much the same pattern as that presented in Figure 5–1 for the relationship between Negro concentration and Negro registration rates. The whites in counties with less than 30 per cent Negroes in their populations overwhelmingly favor Negro suffrage—at least in the abstract. But as the proportion of Negroes climbs beyond 40 per cent toward an absolute majority, the proportion of whites favoring the abstract notion of Negro voting drops very rapidly.

Piedmont and Camellia counties, for example, both have Negro populations of about 35 per cent; in both counties an overwhelming majority of whites still accept the idea of Negro voting without qualification. Bright Leaf and Crayfish counties have only about 10 percentage points more Negroes than Piedmont and Camellia, but only half the whites in Bright Leaf and less than 10 per cent in Crayfish approve of Negro voting without qualification. In the range between 30 and 60 per cent Negro, then, small increases in the proportion Negro have large effects on white attitudes. In the counties at the two extremes—with less than 30 or more than 60 per cent Negroes—further differences in racial proportions have little effect: the whites are overwhelmingly in favor of Negro voting in the former case and overwhelmingly opposed in the latter.

Do these changes in white attitudes affect merely the rate of participation by local Negroes, or do they affect Negro attitudes toward participation as well? Although only 41 per cent of the adult Negroes in the South have ever voted, a vast majority (73 per cent) say that they have either voted or wanted to vote. Thus their low level of participation appears to result more from external restrictions than from lack of concern. But when we look at these responses on a county basis, we find that Negro commitment to voting declines as white disapproval of Negro voting increases. Not only are fewer Negroes registered where white attitudes are less permissive, but fewer Negroes express a desire to vote. The correlation between Negro commitment to voting and white attitudes toward Negro voting is +.57. Some of the inhibitions to Negro voting thus take the form of internalized restraints.

The lack of desire to vote where white attitudes are most repressive no doubt represents in part a realistic adjustment to the environment and in part the psychological mechanism of rationalization. Some Negroes will realistically calculate that they do not want to vote if the costs in terms of possible social, economic, or physical reprisals are too great. Others will rationalize by deciding that they would not want to vote even if they could—the familiar "sour grapes" reaction. Still others may simply have no desire to vote because of lack of interest or information. Regardless of the psychological mechanisms involved, the proportion of Negroes in southern counties has a slightly larger impact on Negro attitudes toward voting than it does on white attitudes toward Negro voting.

The proportion of the southern population which is Negro has been steadily declining since before the turn of the century. This great emigration will undoubtedly continue, although perhaps at a less rapid rate in the years ahead. As the proportion of Negroes in the black-belt counties decreases, can we expect a less repressive environment to emerge? The great impact of Negro concentration on rates of Negro voter registration and on corresponding white and Negro attitudes would suggest that we could. But attitudes and behavior patterns can persist for generations after their initial cause disappears. Perhaps white racial attitudes will not change quickly as the proportion of Negroes declines. Let us examine these alternative possibilities as best we can.

When we correlate the percentage of Negroes in southern counties in 1900 with the percentage of voting-age Negroes registered to vote in 1958, we find a correlation of —.41. Negro population concentration around the turn of the century—when southern political practice crystallized into its strongly anti-Negro pattern—seems to be almost as good a predictor of contemporary Negro political participation as is current Negro concentration! The sharp decrease in correlation between 1950 Negro concentration and registration when we control for 1900 concentration (from —.46 to —.21) is also impressive evidence of the stability of southern racial practices.[14]

It would be a mistake, however, to conclude either that 1900 Negro concentration is as successful as 1950 Negro concentration in predicting contemporary Negro registration, or that decreases in Negro concentration are not associated with increasing Negro voter registration. When we reverse the partialing process and control for Negro concentration in 1950, the correlation between current Negro registration and 1900 Negro concentration disappears (it becomes —.01). The 1900 simple correlation accordingly seems to come from stable racial practices that in turn reflect a large measure of stability in Negro concentration and related county characteristics. In itself, the proportion of Negroes in southern counties in 1900 has no autonomous relationship to present rates of Negro registration.

The effects of decreases in Negro concentration since 1900 on Negro political activity today are a little more difficult to describe and understand, because they are quite different in different situations. Briefly, such decreases

[14] A point to keep in mind in connection with such partial correlations is that controlling for a third variable also has the effect of controlling for all the other variables related to it. Thus the difference in the magnitude of a simple correlation and a partial correlation cannot be attributed exclusively to the influence of the third variable.

make no apparent difference where the Negro portion of the population was so large in 1900 that it remains large today; they make a slight difference where Negroes were a small part of the population in 1900; and they make a great deal of difference in those counties where Negroes made up between 40 and 70 per cent of the population in 1900.[15] If history is a trustworthy guide—and it by no means always is—future decreases in Negro concentration should result in further increases in Negro political activity, especially in counties in the critical medium range of Negro-white population ratios.

Although the —.46 correlation between Negro concentration and voter registration is large, it still leaves unexplained a great deal of the county-by-county variation in Negro voter registration. Piedmont and Camellia counties, for example, have nearly identical proportions of Negroes within their respective boundaries—69 per cent of them are registered to vote in the first county and only 55 per cent in the other. Bright Leaf and Crayfish counties have nearly identical ratios between whites and Negroes, too. Twenty-three per cent of the voting-age Negroes in Bright Leaf and none in Crayfish are eligible to vote. Obviously, we must look to other factors to explain these differences in Negro political activity in counties with nearly identical concentrations of Negro citizens.

## The Negro middle class

Southern Negroes, like Americans in general, are more likely to participate in politics if they enjoy higher levels of education, occupation, and income. In aggregate terms, these three factors are probably the best indexes of the size of a county's Negro middle class. Many students of Negro politics believe that the low rate of voter registration by southern Negroes results in part from lack of leadership.[16] Only when there is a pool of educated and skillful leaders whose means of livelihood is not controlled by whites can sufficient leadership and political organization develop to ensure a relatively high rate of Negro registration in the South.

Our data support this line of argument. The three largest positive correlations with Negro voter registration we obtained in this analysis are with percentage of the nonwhite labor force in white-collar occupations (+.23), the median number of school years completed by nonwhites (+.22), and the median income of nonwhites (+.19). These are simple correlations, however, and small ones at that. They may be largely, if not entirely, the result of

15 For full details, see Matthews and Prothro, op. cit., pp. 24–44; see particularly pp. 30–32.
16 For an extreme statement of this position, see E. Franklin Frazier, Black Bourgeoisie: The Rise of a New Middle Class in the United States (Glencoe, Ill.: The Free Press, 1957). Less exaggerated statements to the same effect may be found in the literature cited in footnote 11.

some third factor associated both with Negro registration rates and with Negro education, occupation, and income. The large negative correlation of Negro concentration with Negro registration suggests that the percentage of the population Negro in 1950 is the most likely prospect as a key third variable. This expectation is heightened by the fact that Negro concentration is also substantially correlated with Negro school years completed (—.47), income (—.40), and white-collar workers (—.23). When we introduce controls for percentage of Negroes in the population, the positive association of Negro registration with both income and education almost disappears. Thus county averages of Negro income and education are intervening community variables. They help explain why more Negroes are registered in counties with fewer Negroes in their population, but in themselves they have no independent association with county differences in Negro registration. In the few counties with large Negro concentrations but high Negro income and education, no more Negroes are registered than in similar counties with lower Negro income and education.

The explanatory power of our county occupational measure—the percentage of nonwhite labor force in white-collar occupations—also diminishes when we take percentage of Negroes into account, but much less. It becomes +.15. Although this a small partial correlation, it is one of the higher partials we obtained in this study while controlling for Negro concentration. The proportion of employed Negroes in white-collar jobs does, therefore, have a small but discernible independent association with Negro voter registration.

Moreover, small increases in the proportion of Negro white-collar workers are associated with large increases in Negro voter registration (Figure 5–2), and we cannot attribute these higher rates simply to the registration of the white-collar workers themselves. A very small increase in the size of the Negro middle class seems to produce a substantial increase in the pool of qualified potential leaders. Middle-class Negroes not only tend to register, but they also seem to stimulate working-class Negroes to follow their example.

In the average southern county with 1 per cent of its nonwhite labor force in white-collar jobs, only 4 per cent of its voting-age Negroes are registered to vote; at 5 per cent white-collar, 15 per cent of the Negroes are registered; and so on. Each percentage-point increase in white-collar occupation is associated with an increase of 3 to 4 percentage points in voter registration. This trend continues until 12 per cent of the nonwhites are in white-collar jobs and 42 per cent of the potential Negro electorate is registered. After this point, additional increases in the proportion of Negroes in white-collar jobs are no longer associated with increases in voter registration; indeed, voter registration actually declines as percentage white-collar increases.

Perhaps when the Negro middle class becomes fairly large, it tends to become more isolated from other Negroes, more preoccupied with the middle-

FIGURE 5-2.   *Median percentage of voting-age Negroes registered to vote, by percentage of nonwhite labor force in white-collar occupations*

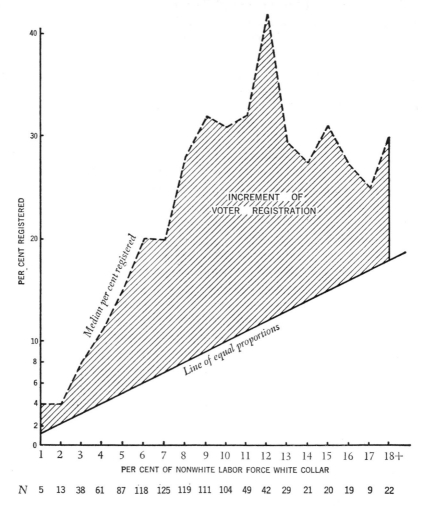

class round of life, less identified with the black masses.[17] A sharpening of class cleavages within the Negro community may lead to some loss of political effectiveness. Even so, this decline in effectiveness is not enough to wipe out the added increment from jobs to registered votes; it merely declines (as the

[17] This is the basic argument of Frazier, *op. cit.* A more mundane explanation would be called for if counties from particular states were clustered at particular points on the curve in Figure 5-2, but examination of the same relationships for each state reveals no such state-by-state clustering.

size of the middle class increases beyond 12 per cent) from three or four votes for every white-collar job to about two.

Despite the independent association of Negro white-collar employment with voter registration, the correlations between county variations in Negro registration and Negro education, income, and occupation are far smaller than many of the correlations between Negro registration and the characteristics of the white-dominated community. The level of Negro voter registration in southern counties has far less to do with the characteristics of the Negro sub-community than it does with the characteristics of the white population and of the total community.

## Agrarianism, urbanization, and industrialization

Many observers believe that the relatively poor agricultural economy of the South depresses the level of Negro political participation.[18] People living in poverty are unlikely candidates for active citizenship anywhere. The Negroes' economic dependence on local whites in the rural South serves as a potent inhibition to those few who are not otherwise discouraged from voting. Rural whites who oppose Negro voting are in a better position to do something about it than are their urban kin.

Our correlations tend to support this line of reasoning. Two measures included in the analysis were the percentage of labor force in agricultural employment and the percentage of farms operated by tenants.[19] The negative relationship of both these attributes to Negro voter registration (—.20 and —.32, respectively) indicates that Negro registration is lower in the old-style agrarian counties. But the region's Negro population is still primarily rural: the simple correlation between percentage in agriculture and percentage Negro is +.30; that between farm tenancy and Negro concentration is +.49.

Are these two county characteristics still associated with low Negro voter registration when Negro concentration is controlled? The partial correlation between farm tenancy and Negro registration is —.13 when Negro concentration is controlled; between percentage in agriculture and registration it is reduced even further, to —.07. The tendency for Negro voter registration to decline as agricultural employment and farm tenancy increase does not disappear even when we take into account differences in Negro concentration from one county to the next. Nonetheless, agrarianism is a far less powerful factor than Negro concentration, and it is no more important a factor than

[18] See especially U.S. Commission on Civil Rights, "Voting," *1961 Report* (Washington, D.C.: U.S. Government Printing Office, 1961), Vol 1, pp. 143–99.
[19] This and other measures of countywide characteristics might better be considered separately for Negroes and whites, but they are not separately reported in the census.

the size of the Negro middle class in explaining Negro participation and nonparticipation.

If the South's agrarian economy tends to discourage Negro registration and voting, then industrialization and urbanization should facilitate them. The urban-industrial life is more rational, impersonal, and less tradition-bound; both Negroes and whites enjoy more wealth and education; the Negroes benefit from a concentration of potential leaders and politically relevant organizations in the cities; the urban ghetto may provide social reinforcement to individual motivations for political action. Many other equally plausible reasons might be suggested for the belief that urbanization and industrialization should foster Negro registration.[20] Our southwide correlations, however, cast serious doubt on this entire line of reasoning.

The simple correlation between the percentage of the county population living in urban areas and Negro registration is a mere +.07; between percentage of the labor force in manufacturing and Negro registration the correlation is +.08. When we calculate partial correlations, controlling for Negro concentration, the association between urbanization and Negro registration completely disappears, a fact which suggests that the initial +.07 simple correlation results from the low proportion of the urban population which is Negro, and from other associated factors. The partial correlation between percentage in manufacturing and Negro registration goes up slightly to +.09 when we add controls for Negro concentration. Partial correlations figured after controlling for many other social and economic variables do not significantly increase either correlation.

What accounts for these surprising findings? One possible explanation is the imperfections of the statistical measures we used. The census definition of "urban," for example, includes all places of 2,500 plus the densely settled fringe around cities of 50,000 or more. Many "urban" places in the South are therefore exceedingly small. From the potential Negro voter's point of view, it may make little difference whether he lives in a town of 5,000 or in the open country. And yet one place is classified as "urban" and the other as "rural." Moreover, a county with a relatively small population concentrated in two or three small towns may possess a higher "urban" percentage than a very large county with a medium-sized city in it. A more meaningful

[20] On Negro voting in urban settings, see Harry J. Walker, "Changes in Race Accommodation in a Southern Community" (Ph.D. dissertation, University of Chicago, 1945); George A. Hillery, "The Presence of Community Among Urban Negroes: A Case Study of a Selected Area in New Orleans" (M.A. thesis, Louisiana State University, 1951); Charles D. Farris, "Effects of Negro Voting Upon the Politics of a Southern City: An Intensive Study, 1946–1948" (Ph.D. dissertation, University of Chicago, 1953); Cleo Roberts, "Some Correlates of Registration and Voting Among Negroes in the 1953 Municipal Election of Atlanta" (M.A. thesis, Atlanta University, 1954); Leonard Reissman et al., "The New Orleans Voter: A Handbook of Political Description," *Tulane Studies in Political Science*, Vol. 2 (New Orleans: Tulane University Press, 1955).

classification of counties along an urban-rural dimension might lead to different results.

If urbanization does facilitate Negro voter registration, we should be able to see its effect most clearly in the region's largest urban complexes. When we compare the Negro registration rates of the 70 counties contained in the South's Standard Metropolitan Areas[21] with registration rates for nonmetropolitan counties, we find that more of the "metropolitan" counties have from 20 to 40 per cent of their voting-age Negroes registered than do the other counties. And many more of the nonmetropolitan counties have less than 20 per cent of their Negroes registered. Moreover, within the group of metropolitan counties, those with a population over 200,000 have slightly higher proportions of Negroes registered than do those with a population between 50,000 and 200,000. But none of these differences holds up when we compare metropolitan and nonmetropolitan counties containing approximately the same proportion of Negroes (Table 5–1). Thus, neither "urbanism" nor

TABLE 5–1.    *Median percentage of voting-age Negroes registered to vote in counties within standard metropolitan areas and all other counties, by level of Negro concentration*

| Percentage of Negroes in 1950 Population | Percentage of counties in SMA's of over 200,000 population | Percentage of counties in SMA's of less than 200,000 population | Percentage of counties not in SMA's |
|---|---|---|---|
| 0– 9% | 25.0%  (6) | 28.8% (11) | 37.8% (236) |
| 10–19 | 45.0   (11) | 30.0  (12) | 35.7  (133) |
| 20–29 | 30.0   (6) | 35.0   (6) | 32.2  (153) |
| 30–39 | 24.0   (6) | 23.8   (7) | 23.8  (142) |
| 40–49 | — | 15.0   (5) | 15.9  (110) |
| 50–59 | — | — | 12.0   (78) |
| 60–69 | — | — | 8.1   (50) |
| 70–79 | — | — | 5.8   (22) |
| 80–89 | — | — | 5.0    (4) |
| TOTAL COUNTIES | 29 | 41 | 928 |

"metropolitanism," as crudely defined by the census categories, appears to be independently related to high Negro voter registration.

The very low correlation between percentage of the labor force in manufacturing employment and Negro voter registration is explicable on other grounds. The word "manufacturing" conjures up images of the "New South"

---

[21] The Bureau of the Census defines Standard Metropolitan Area as a county or group of contiguous counties that contains at least one city of 50,000 inhabitants or more. The contiguous counties must be socially and economically integrated with the central city to be included in the SMA.

—with belching smokestacks, booming cities, and bulging payrolls. For the South as a whole this is a misleading picture. Although manufacturing in 1950 was associated with somewhat higher income for both Negroes and whites (the correlation between percentage in manufacturing and median income was +.19 for both races), manufacturing was not primarily an urban phenomenon (the correlation between percentage in manufacturing and percentage urban was +.08), nor was it associated with rapid population growth (the correlation with population increase between 1940 and 1950 is +.05). Manufacturing was negatively correlated with school years completed by both whites and Negroes (—.14 and —.05, respectively). This kind of low-wage industry centered in relatively stable, small towns is not very strongly associated with growing Negro voter registration. The recent industrialization of the region—electronics as opposed to home production of chenille bedspreads, for example—may be quite differently related to Negro participation. So few counties have this new type of industry that they tend to be hidden by the bedspreads in a county-by-county correlation.

Urbanization and industrialization are vastly overrated as facilitators of Negro voter registration. Urbanization and industrialization may provide necessary conditions for high levels of Negro political participation, but by themselves they are not sufficient to ensure such levels.

## Levels of white education

If, as we have argued, Negro registration rates in the South respond far more to the characteristics of the white community than to those of the Negro subcommunity, then Negro voter registration should be positively correlated with white educational levels. After all, racial prejudice and discrimination are most pronounced among people with little formal education.[22] Less resistance to Negro political participation and, therefore, more Negro voter registration could accordingly be expected in counties where whites are relatively well educated.

Just the opposite is the case for the South as a whole. The correlation between median school years completed by whites and Negro voter registration

[22] B. Bettelheim and M. Janowitz, The Dynamics of Prejudice (New York: Harper & Brothers, 1950); Herbert H. Hyman and Paul B. Sheatsley, "Attitudes Toward Desegregation," Scientific American, Vol. 195 (1956), pp. 35–39; Melvin M. Tumin, Desegregation: Resistance and Readiness (Princeton, N.J.: Princeton University Press, 1958), p. 195 and passim. James W. Vander Zanden, "Voting on Segregation Referenda," Public Opinion Quarterly, Vol. 25 (1961), pp. 92–105, finds the evidence in support of the relationship in voting on segregationist referenda in the South "inconsistent and even contradictory . . . this study seems to suggest that the socioeconomic factor may not play as simple or as critical a role as some of us doing research in this field have been prone to assign it." See also D. R. Matthews and J. W. Prothro, "Southern Racial Attitudes: Conflict, Awareness, and Political Change," Annals of the American Academy of Political and Social Science, Vol. 344 (1962), pp. 108–21.

is —.26, one of the largest negative correlations obtained in this study. When the average education of whites in a county increases, Negro voter registration in the county tends to decrease.

How can we account for this unexpected finding? In view of the surprising nature of the relationship, we might suspect that it is merely a reflection of some third variable which happens to be related both to Negro registration and to white education. If so, it should disappear when other factors are held constant. But the correlation holds up surprisingly well when other variables are controlled: only one of the other social and economic characteristics of southern counties reduces the correlation at all. That third variable is, once again, Negro concentration in the population. With Negro concentration in 1950 controlled, the partial correlation between white educational level and Negro registration is —.15; controlling for Negro concentration in 1900 produces a partial correlation of —.16. Although these are substantial reductions, the partial correlations are among the largest obtained after controlling for the extraordinarily potent factor of Negro concentration. The strong correlation (+.30) between Negro concentration and median school years completed by whites is almost as unexpected as the correlation between Negro registration and white education. The whites in the black-belt counties tend to be better educated—at least quantitatively—than do other white southerners. And, regardless of the percentage of Negroes in the population, fewer Negroes are registered in counties where whites have more education.

A second explanation for the negative relationship between white education and Negro registration might be that their relationship is curvilinear: at the lower educational levels, increases in white median school years might be associated with declining rates of Negro registration but, at higher educational levels, the relationship might be reversed. If this were the case, then the overall negative relationship would be a result of the generally low educational levels of the South. A few counties could not change the overall correlation. With only a few counties having a high level of white education, those few could have the highest rates of Negro registration without reversing the negative relationship between white education and Negro registration for the South as a whole. Figure 5–3 shows a curvilinear relationship, but it does not show high-education counties as highest in Negro registration.

As the number of school years completed by whites goes up through the primary and secondary grades, the proportion of voting-age Negroes registered declines.[23] In the very few counties in which the average white adult has completed high school or has received some higher education, the trend reverses and Negro registration rates begin to increase. But the reversal is not

[23] Eleven of the 28 counties in which the average white adult has completed less than seven years of schooling are French-Catholic parishes in Louisiana. Even if those parishes are eliminated, the trend shown in Figure 5–3 remains the same. The partial correlation between white school years and Negro registration, controlling for percentage Roman Catholic, is —.25.

sharp enough for the counties with the highest white education to reach as great a Negro registration as the counties with the lowest white education. Southern counties with extremely high white educational levels have only about average rates of Negro registration. What is impressive about Figure 5–3 is the near-uniformity with which an increase in white school years is associated with a decrease in Negro registration.

We cannot "explain away" our findings entirely, either by examining the correlation for hidden third variables or by examining the regularity of the association. So we must conclude that white education in southern counties is independently and negatively associated with Negro registration. Short of the highest levels, the higher the average education of whites in a county, the more actively and effectively they seem to enforce the traditional mores of the region against Negro participation in elections. An increase in average schooling for whites in the South seems to give them more of the skills they need to express effectively their anti-Negro sentiment. For example, the correlation between median school years completed by whites and the presence or absence of a White Citizens Council or similar organization is +.32. To *alter* white attitudes toward the Negro's place in southern politics seems to require considerably more formal education than the average southern white receives.

FIGURE 5–3. *Median percentage of voting-age Negroes registered to vote, by median school years completed by whites in county, in eleven southern states*

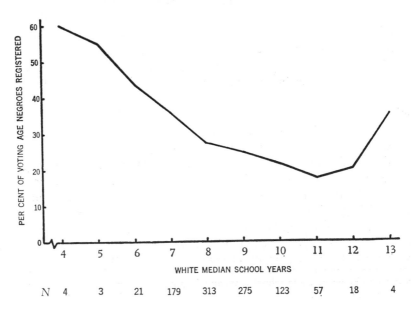

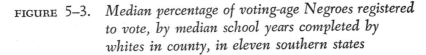

| N | 4 | 3 | 21 | 179 | 313 | 275 | 123 | 57 | 18 | 4 |

These findings and their explanations are completely contrary to what we would have expected from earlier studies and "common sense" interpretation. But the data cannot be denied, and they seem explicable only in terms of the interpretation advanced. To be sure, the negative correlation between white schooling and county rates of Negro registration is not large, once the proportion of Negroes in the population is taken into account. When a substantial positive correlation is expected, however, a modest negative relationship—or even the absence of any relationship—can pose large explanatory problems. Morever, because the correlation is based on all counties in the South rather than on a sample, we cannot dismiss it as a product of sampling error. Small in absolute terms but large in comparison with other correlates of Negro registration, it stands there demanding some explanation.

The explanation we have suggested only *appears* to negate the belief that education decreases prejudice. Education does reduce prejudice, even in the South. But anti-Negro sentiment decreases at an extremely slow rate among southern whites. The percentage in favor of integration, for example, varies between 0 and 3 per cent at different levels of schooling from none to high-school graduation. It reaches 8 per cent for those with some kind of technical training beyond high school, and 14 per cent for those with incomplete college training or with college degrees. Only at the level of postgraduate college training is there a marked increase—to 42 per cent—in the proportion of white integrationists.[24]

These survey findings from individuals thus support our findings and interpretation from aggregate county data. Average white education in southern counties is too low for the usual increases to have great consequence for white attitudes. Even in common-sense terms, one need only ask at what level in southern education will the dominant anti-Negro values be challenged. Certainly not until college, and not seriously in many of the region's colleges. Education may be the secular road to salvation in America, but it must come in large quantities to make any positive difference in the average southern county.

## White religious affiliation

A variety of studies suggest that religion plays some role—either as an independent or an intervening variable—in the racial politics of the South. Churchgoers have been found to be less tolerant than nonattenders,[25] and the South is a churchgoing region. Studies of Louisiana politics have found

[24] See Chapter Twelve for additional discussion of the relationship between formal education and white racial attitudes.
[25] Samuel A. Stouffer, *Communism, Conformity, and Civil Liberties* (Garden City, N.Y.: Doubleday and Co., 1955).

substantial political differences between the Catholic and Protestant sections of the state.[26] The correlation between white religious affiliation and Negro registration rates for the South as a whole therefore bears examination.

Negro registration rates are depressed as church membership among whites[27] increases (—.17), despite the fact that white membership in different churches has different functions. Baptist membership is negatively related to Negro registration (—.10), while Catholic membership is positively related (+.15). On a southwide basis, the percentage of Jews in the county's total church membership is not significantly associated with Negro registration.

Granted that Catholicism is positively related to Negro registration, we can partial out the influence of Catholicism in order to determine the correlation between non-Catholic white church membership and Negro registration. This partial correlation is, as expected, slightly greater (—.23) than the simple correlation. But the negative correlation between white church membership and Negro registration disappears when we hold Negro concentration constant. (The partial correlation is +.01.) Greater church membership among whites accordingly appears to be a reflection of other county attributes rather than an independent factor in relation to Negro registration.

The percentage of Roman Catholics in the white church population does seem to have some independent consequences for Negro political participation. The relationship between Catholicism and Negro voter registration does not disappear when Negro concentration is controlled. (The partial correlation is +.10.) The presence of Roman Catholics, then, seems to facilitate Negro voter registration on a southwide basis. Roman Catholic churches and priests presumably react less directly to other county attributes than do most Protestant churches and their ministers; in any case, Catholicism is independently and positively related to Negro voter registration.

The concentration of Catholic population in Louisiana and the small number of Catholics in most other parts of the South dictate caution, however, in accepting this explanation. For one thing, the distribution of Catholic percentages deviates so far from the assumption of normal distribution underlying correlation analysis that our southwide correlations may have been curiously and unpredictably affected. In the second place, the atypical political patterns of Louisiana—rather than Catholicism *per se*—may account for a large part of the correlation obtained.

26 Allan P. Sindler, *Huey Long's Louisiana* (Baltimore: The Johns Hopkins Press, 1956); V. O. Key, Jr., *op. cit.*, ch. 8; John H. Fenton and Kenneth N. Vines, "Negro Registration in Louisiana," *American Political Science Review*, Vol. 51 (1957), pp. 704–13.
27 The most recent attempt to compile county-by-county figures on church membership is reported in a census by the National Council of Churches of Christ, *Churches and Church Membership in the U.S.*, series C (1956). Negro churches are not included in this census, and the figures reported for many white churches appear to be incomplete.

# Negro versus white registration rates

We have assumed that our analysis is of Negro voter registration rather than of voter registration *in general*. But this assumption might be incorrect: although Negroes register to vote in the South at a much lower rate than whites, the registration rates of the two races could be highly correlated with one another, both responding to the same social and economic characteristics of southern counties. The data permit two tests of this possibility: (1) an examination of the relationship between Negro and white registration, and (2) a comparison of the relationships between county attributes and white registration with the relationships found between county attributes and Negro registration.

Negro registration does increase as white registration increases; the simple correlation is +.24. But when we examine the relationship of Negro to white registration for every level of white registration (see Figure 5–4), the correlation does not appear very impressive. The detailed relationships shown by the graph reveal that the lowest and the highest levels of white registration contribute most of the correlation between the registration rates of the two races. If both of the extreme points were eliminated, the curve would be virtually horizontal, indicating that Negro registration had no relationship at all to white registration. Only when white registration is extremely high

FIGURE 5–4.    *Median percentage of voting-age Negroes registered to vote, by percentage of whites registered in same county*

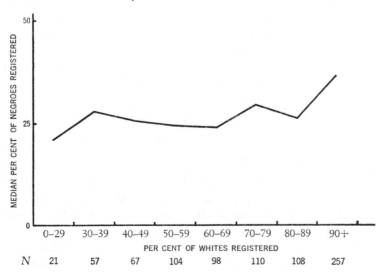

or extremely low is it associated with the rate of Negro registration. For the broad middle range of counties, with from 30 to 89 per cent of the whites registered—a group that contains over 70 per cent of all southern counties— Negro registration appears to be independent of white registration.

We also calculated the correlations between the percentage of eligible whites registered to vote and the same 20 social and economic factors we used in our effort to explain Negro registration. Although we chose these factors for their presumed relevance to Negro registration, the magnitude of the simple correlations suggests that they are as strongly related to white as to Negro registration. But when we compare these simple correlations for whites with those for Negroes, we find that the *direction* of the correlation is reversed for 15 of the 20 social and economic factors. Not one of the 20 variables is substantially and consistently related to *both* Negro and white rates of voter registration.

The reversal of relationships is so regular that social and economic attributes might appear to have opposite meanings for Negro and white registration. Closer inspection reveals, however, that the relationships are disparate rather than opposite.

The crucial variable for Negro registration is Negro concentration in the population, which not only furnishes the strongest simple correlation but is also the variable that most consistently accounts for other apparent "influences" on Negro registration. Indeed, Negro concentration has generally been cited as the critical factor in all dimensions of southern political behavior. Hence, one immediately suspects that all the variables that facilitate white registration must be positively correlated with concentration of Negro population, which would thereby stand as the dominant third factor for both Negro and white registration. This familiar interpretation would conveniently account for the striking discrepancy between correlates of white and Negro registration, but it is not supported by our findings. On the contrary, *Negro concentration has a negligible relationship to white voter registration.* Moreover, the small simple correlation of Negro concentration and white registration ($+.10$) becomes still smaller ($+.06$) when urbanism is controlled.

Although no single variable is as predictive of white registration as Negro concentration is of Negro registration, urbanism emerges as particularly significant. Percentage of population urban—which proved inconsequential in the analysis of Negro registration—furnishes one of the strongest negative correlations with white voter registration, a correlation that is not affected when Negro concentration is controlled. And we find the same relationship if, instead of percentage of population urban, we use Standard Metropolitan Areas as our index of urban-rural difference; white registration is consistently higher in rural than in urban counties. Other county characteristics associated with urbanization—such as high income and education levels for whites and Negroes—are similarly related to low white registration. Perhaps the rural white resident finds politics more meaningful in a one-party region, where personality plays such a prominent role in elections.[28] In any event, urban-rural differences are a key factor in variations in white voter registration.

Similar discrepancies are found in the relationships of white and Negro registration rates to the other social and economic characteristics of southern counties. Average white education, for example, manifested a strong negative association with Negro registration—an association that held up under various controls so well that it led to novel conclusions. White education is also negatively related to white registration, but the correlation is extremely small and it is reversed when percentage of population urban is controlled.

Without an extended consideration of white registration, then, we can conclude that our analysis does apply to Negro voter registration in particular rather than to voter registration in general. The social and economic characteristics of southern counties have widely different meanings for Negro and white registration.

## Conclusions

Political participation is shaped primarily by the personal characteristics of the individual. This view is widely held both by laymen and by professional students of political behavior. When we shift from the individual to the county as the unit of analysis, however, we find that community characteristics themselves have a powerful influence. Looking only at those Negroes with both low income and low education, for example, we find that 50 per cent in Piedmont County have voted, as compared with 49 per cent in Camellia, 25 per cent in Bright Leaf, and 9 per cent in Crayfish. (Those in Crayfish who have voted did so when they lived elsewhere.) Individual attributes are important, of course, but their importance is circumscribed or facilitated by the general characteristics of the places where the individuals live.

The most important county characteristic for Negro participation is the percentage of Negroes in the population. Whatever the attributes of individual Negroes, their overall proportion in the local population sets the bounds within which their participation will occur. Higher levels of Negro income and education are related to higher rates of political participation, for example, but only for the lucky few with income and educational advantages. White-collar employment for Negroes, on the other hand, has a multiplier effect: not only are those Negroes in white-collar employment more likely to be political participants, but their presence in an area also

---

[28] Urban counties in the South undoubtedly purge their registration lists with greater regularity than do rural counties. How much effect this may have on these correlations cannot be ascertained.

seems to lead other Negroes to participate. The kind of county in which Negroes win nonmenial jobs (above the required number of schoolteachers and morticians) is the sort of place where a Negro middle class has an opportunity to exert some political leadership. In negative terms, levels of white education and of farm tenancy also appear influential for rates of Negro political activity. White political participation, on the other hand, is quite differently associated with county characteristics. Contrary to the impression that whites participate most where Negroes are most prevalent, they actually

FIGURE 5–5.   *Rates of social and economic change in the South, 1940–1960*

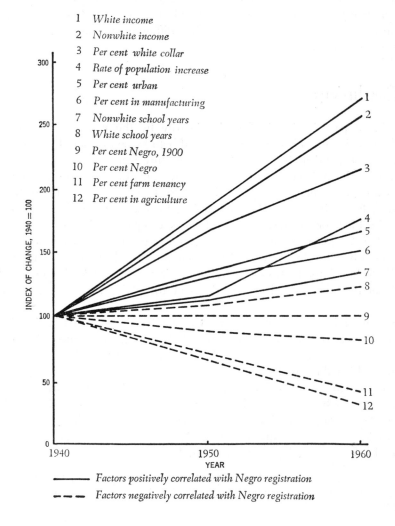

1   *White income*
2   *Nonwhite income*
3   *Per cent white collar*
4   *Rate of population increase*
5   *Per cent urban*
6   *Per cent in manufacturing*
7   *Nonwhite school years*
8   *White school years*
9   *Per cent Negro, 1900*
10   *Per cent Negro*
11   *Per cent farm tenancy*
12   *Per cent in agriculture*

——— *Factors positively correlated with Negro registration*
- - - *Factors negatively correlated with Negro registration*

participate most in rural areas, regardless of the number of Negroes in the locality.

The Negro registration rate is thus low, in rather large part, because of the social and economic characteristics of southern communities. These facts are not easily and quickly changed by law or political action. One cannot help but be impressed by the massive indications of stability in the situation —the extremely high negative correlation between percentage Negro in 1900 and Negro registration in 1958, the apparent failure of urbanization and industrialization to provide sufficiently favorable conditions for Negro political participation, the negative correlation between white educational levels and Negro registration, and so on.

At the same time, Negro registration has increased rapidly since 1944, and the social and economic factors we have considered indicate that this increase will continue. Figure 5–5 shows the trend since 1940 for the variables most strongly related to Negro voter registration.[29] *Every one of the variables positively associated with Negro registration is on the increase*—some have doubled in 20 years and all but one have increased by at least 50 per cent. Only one of the factors associated with low Negro registration—white school years completed—is also increasing, and a good many southern counties will soon reach the stage where this factor may tend to facilitate rather than hinder Negro political participation.[30] All the other factors negatively correlated with Negro registration (except, of course, percentage Negro in 1900) are declining rapidly. The South's social and economic structure may be the re- former's major barrier—but it may also be a long-run cause for hope.

---

[29] No trend data were available on religious affiliation. Median income figures, by race, were not available for 1940. In Figure 5–5 it is assumed that median income for both races increased at the same rate between 1940 and 1950 as between 1950 and 1960.

[30] If white school years completed continues to increase at the 1950–60 rate, the average southern white will have completed 11.4 years of schooling by 1970, and many southern counties will have average white school years completed of 12 years or more. Assuming that the relationship presented in Figure 5–5 continues to hold true, we may find that the effect of white education on Negro registration will gradually reverse itself.

*Chapter Six*

Chapter Six

# The Community Setting: Political Aspects

George Hopkins, Tom Johnson, Joe Barton, and Willy Clayton are all unusually well educated, middle-class Negroes with relatively high incomes and social standing in their respective communities. Yet only Hopkins (the young insurance agent in Piedmont County) and Johnson (the small businessman in Camellia County) are currently registered voters. Clayton (the social-studies teacher in Crayfish County) has never voted, and Barton (the relatively prosperous Negro farmer) has not voted since he moved to Bright Leaf County.

We can explain these contrasts partly in terms of the differences among Clayton, Barton, Johnson, and Hopkins as people and partly in terms of the social and economic differences among Crayfish, Bright Leaf, Camellia, and Piedmont counties. We can understand them still better if we consider the political characteristics of southern counties.

## Political systems of four southern communities

Willy Clayton is restrained from active political participation by the political system of Crayfish County no less than by its social and economic structure. Mississippi has the lowest proportion of Negro voters in the South, and its laws are designed to keep things that way.

The state has more demanding residence requirements, for example, than any other state in the Union: the prospective voter must have lived two years in the state and a full year both in the city or town and in the precinct where he hopes to vote.[1] Thirty-five states require a precinct residence of only

[1] Constance E. Smith, *Voting and Election Laws* (New York: Oceana Publications, 1960), p. 18.

a month or less, and only two other states (Maryland and New Hampshire) require as much as six months.

Until federal courts declared state poll taxes unconstitutional in 1966, Mississippi law imposed a poll tax of two dollars a year, the highest price for voting in the nation.[2] Moreover, the new voter could pay the tax during only eight weeks of the year, between December 1 and February 1, and he had to pay for the two preceding years as well as for the next two years. This is the season of the year when Mississippi sharecroppers are least likely to have cash and most likely to spend any money they do have on Christmas gifts for their children. Eight dollars is 20 per cent of the monthly income of the average Negro family in Crayfish County. The poll tax was collected by the sheriff, a public servant with whom few Crayfish Negroes would voluntarily seek contact.

Voters are actually registered by the clerk of the circuit court. If Willy Clayton had decided to register, he would have had to appear in person before this official—a wily politician who campaigned for the office by boasting that he was the man to maintain Crayfish's record of no Negro voters. Clayton would first have had to demonstrate that he had paid his poll tax before February 1, and then he would have faced a literacy test. If he passed, he would have moved on to more difficult obstacles. Applicants were required to "demonstrate to the county registrar a reasonable understanding of the duties and obligations of citizenship under a constitutional form of government."[3] Since Clayton is a social-studies teacher and the registrar of voters has never gone to college, let us assume that Clayton passed this test too. His final problem would have been to convince the registrar that he was of "good character." If he managed to do that, his name would have been published in the local paper for two weeks, according to state law, and any qualified Crayfish voter would have had the right to challenge his good character by filing an affidavit with the registrar within the next 14 days. It would then be up to Clayton to ascertain whether he had passed: applicants were not notified that they had become registered voters.

We have had to describe the registration process in Crayfish in hypothetical terms, because no Negro voter ever got beyond the first step. The registrar was ready to use any tactic to see that none did. "Our niggers is content, they are satisfied," he says. If a Negro tried to register, the registrar claims with zest, "I'd tell him that Mississippi has a $2.00 poll tax. With that $8.00, he

---

2 The Twenty-fourth Amendment banned the poll tax only as applied to the election of federal officials.

3 See U.S. Commission on Civil Rights, "Voting," *1961 Report,* Part I (Washington, D.C.: U.S. Government Printing Office, 1961), p. 31. In the summer of 1965, Mississippi voters, for the avowed purpose of keeping the "feds" from moving in, approved a constitutional amendment eliminating this requirement. Also eliminated were the requirements of "good moral character" and the ability to interpret any section of the U.S. Constitution.

could take $4.00 and buy a bottle of whiskey, and with the other $4.00 he could start the best damned crap game he's ever been in. He can't afford to vote!"

In a more sober vein, however, the registrar recognized that his office "has become important because of the political situation today." By "the political situation," he explains that he means that "the Supreme Court and NAACP are dictators to the South. We feel that eventually we must register some niggers, but I wouldn't register them unless forced to." When forced by court order to act, he planned to use "selective methods." Specifically, "I'll have leaders in each community suggest their least objectionable nigger and bring him in. I'll tell the whites the answers to the questions and go out and get a cup of coffee. When I come back they would have him ready."

This plan for highly "selective" registration is also a neat device for sharing with other white leaders the responsibility for Negro registration. The registrar himself is a petty politician (who explained with enthusiasm how he went about buying votes), but he is too crafty to assume sole responsibility for registering the first Negro voter in Crayfish history. He was in deadly earnest in his discussion of plans for resistance, with selective registration only as a last resort: a few weeks after the interview he assaulted a Student Non-violent Coordinating Committee worker who was trying to help Negroes to register.

Although Bright Leaf and Camellia counties lie in the black-belt tier of southern counties, both are in states of the Peripheral South. Piedmont County is in one of the less southern sections (geographically and culturally) of a Peripheral South state. Legal requirements for voter registration are not irksome in any of these states, and all had abolished the poll tax long before it was declared unconstitutional. State residence requirements are one year, as in most states in the nation, and county and precinct requirements are also normal, varying from 30 days to six months. Bright Leaf and Piedmont counties, unlike Camellia, do require a literacy test, but its administration seems reasonable or even lax. The registration process for Negroes in these counties is generally routine.

Camellia County has recently adopted the practice of mailing to registered voters cards that must be returned to keep registration current. Some liberal residents, assuming that Negro citizens are less likely to respond to such a request, regard this as a technique for decreasing the number of Negro voters. Even if they are correct, the technique is at least subtler than those employed in Crayfish County. When Tom Johnson, the shoe-shop proprietor in Camellia, was asked how he was treated when he registered, he replied, "Fine, Mrs. Wilson [the registrar] was the nicest old lady you ever did see."

All four of these counties are dominated by people who call themselves Democrats; no avowed Republican holds an elective public office in any of them. Nevertheless, the party systems of the counties are by no means identical. Piedmont County, for example, can be said to have a "modified" one-party system, in view of the respectable—albeit losing—vote for Republican candidates.[4] In most elections since 1888 Republican candidates for governor have received over 30 per cent of the Piedmont vote. Even in 1936, when Alf Landon offered little Republican appeal on the national ticket, the Republican candidate for governor received 32 per cent of the vote in Piedmont County. In the 1960 election Nixon received 43 per cent of the Piedmont vote as compared with 46 per cent for the Republican gubernatorial candidate. In 1964 Goldwater polled only 40 per cent of the vote, a weaker showing than most Republican candidates for state and local office made. Thus the Republicanism of Piedmont is not simply of the presidential variety.

In the other three counties the Republicans fare much worse in state and local contests. In 1960 only about 20 per cent of the Camellia and Bright Leaf voters supported the Republican candidate for governor in their states. In Crayfish County, Mississippi, no Republican candidate even appeared on the ballot. Camellia differs from Bright Leaf and Crayfish, however, in turning out a substantial Republican vote in presidential elections. Indeed, in 1956 and 1960 its Republican presidential vote was heavier than in Piedmont, reaching almost 50 per cent in both elections. In 1964 Goldwater carried the county easily, with 58 per cent of the votes. Whereas Piedmont County has a modified one-party system with a significant and indigenous Republicanism, Camellia has a one-party system marred only by defections to the Republicans in presidential voting. Bright Leaf appears to have a pure one-party system. Even Goldwater was unable to shake the hold of Democracy on its inhabitants —the Republican presidential candidate of 1964 attracted only 31 per cent of the vote.

While Crayfish's party system is in many ways the epitome of old-style one-partyism, any chance for local voters to demonstrate their racism produces wild deviations from normal patterns. Goldwater won 95 per cent of the votes in 1964, thus narrowly exceeding Dixiecrat Strom Thurmond's previous record of 93 per cent in 1948. Whether the 1964 defection will have more long-run consequences for the local party structure than the one-shot defection of 1948 is not yet clear. However, the voters' subjective identification with one party or the other is generally a better guide to the future than are election returns. The percentage of whites in each county who say they are either Republicans or Independents is: Crayfish, 3; Bright Leaf, 6; Camellia, 14; Piedmont, 32.

Like the whites, most Negroes in these counties who think in party terms regard themselves as Democrats. But a significant minority of the Negroes are so apolitical that they cannot place themselves either as Independents or as belonging to some party. This proportion of totally "apolitical" Negroes is

[4] This is according to the criteria of Austin Ranney and Willmoore Kendall, "The American Party Systems," *American Political Science Review*, Vol. 48 (1954), p. 483.

below 20 per cent in Piedmont and Camellia counties, but it is between a quarter and a third of all adult Negroes in Bright Leaf and Crayfish. The inability of most of these Negroes to think in partisan terms stems from severe informational and motivational deprivations, but it can also be viewed as a realistic response to the local situation. The "purest" one-party system, in Crayfish, is really a no-party system in organizational terms. The county has no semblance of Republican organization, and the Democratic organization exists mostly on paper. The Democratic executive committee of the county is required by law to administer the party's primary election, and that is all the party organization does in Crayfish. With no other responsibility in the primary, and no opposition in the general election, it has no need for precinct committees.

Crayfish voters think of the primary not as a party-conducted election but simply as an election for public office. Indeed, the few Republicans in the county vote in Democratic primaries with no questions asked. The redoubtable registrar of voters, for example, changed his registration to Republican in 1960 in the hope of becoming postmaster after a Nixon victory. When this plan failed, he proceeded to win office as clerk of court and registrar in the next Democratic primary. A few of his political rivals criticized his recent service as a delegate to the Republican state convention, but most voters recognized this charge as a red herring. The candidate was merely trying to get ahead in politics however he could; his temporary Republicanism had no more meaning in terms of his beliefs or practices than his Democratic affiliation. Another local politician, without changing his party registration, served as delegate to the Democratic state convention and as alternate delegate to the Republican state convention in the same year.

Bright Leaf has no Republican organization, but the Democrats are organized from the precinct level up. Party membership has enough meaning for participation in Democratic primaries to be restricted to registered Democrats. Camellia County has a Republican as well as a Democratic organization, but neither is very vigorous. One Republican leader said, "There are only postmaster Republicans in Camellia County." Even so, party affiliation is not regarded so casually as in Crayfish. The postmaster appointed by President Eisenhower, for example, is a former Democrat, but he had become an active Republican several years before his appointment. Camellia politics has a strong ideological flavor, but the conservative position is more actively represented by the local John Birch Society than by the Republicans. The Democratic organization sponsors rallies, conducts primaries, and engages in general election activity in presidential election years. But party posts are not considered prestigious or powerful, and elected officials pay little attention to the organization.

In Piedmont County both the Republicans and the Democrats are better organized. A leading local Democrat thinks the Republicans amounted to little in the past "because they used hacks too often" and because they were "mainly

a right-wing party." But around 1960 vigorous young leaders came forward
as representatives of respectable conservatism. The Young Republicans Club
has become highly attractive to conservative young voters, and the party is
increasingly active in general elections. The Democrats of Piedmont are much
more highly organized than those in the other counties, and party posts
are hotly contested by people recognized as real political leaders.

In Crayfish and Bright Leaf counties, Negroes do not attend party meetings
or hold party office, nor do they even dare to attend party rallies open to the
general public. A Bright Leaf Negro leader puts the point circumspectly:
"Negroes are not invited or encouraged to participate in political party organization here." Negroes do attend public rallies in Camellia County, but they
do not attend party meetings or hold party office. A professor at the predominantly white university who holds office on the county Democratic executive
committee recently tried, and failed, to get a Negro appointed to a party post.
(Only in recent years have white university personnel themselves held party
office.)

In marked contrast, Negroes in Piedmont County have been sending delegates to the county Democratic convention since the 1930's—well before
*Smith* v. *Allwright*. Negroes hold offices in both parties as well as in the local
government of Piedmont. In 1948 Negro and labor union elements in the
Democratic party joined forces to elect a county chairman favorable to both
groups. Since then Negroes have won a number of party rewards, such as
appointments to the state Democratic executive committee. The Republicans
have competed for Negro support through such devices as the nomination of
a Negro candidate for the state senate in 1956.

Where political parties do not bring similar interests together to compete
for public office and power, "functional equivalents" of parties tend to develop.[5] These functional equivalents differ considerably from place to place
in the South, but almost everywhere they take the form of factions within
the Democratic party.

Democratic factions in Crayfish are highly transient and personal. Each
election produces new alignments of voters, depending on who the relatives,
friends, neighbors, and fellow church members of the individual candidates
are. Local residents regard it as "dirty politics" for a candidate for one office
to show any interest in the outcome of other races. They see elections as
processes for awarding a series of separate prizes, and they feel that a candidate should be interested in only one jackpot at a time.

If any enduring factionalism exists in Crayfish, it is built around the numerous little hamlets where most county residents live. The population of

[5] See Gabriel A. Almond and James S. Coleman (eds.), *The Politics of the Developing
Areas* (Princeton, N.J.: Princeton University Press, 1960), p. 40; and R. L. Bowman
and G. R. Boynton, "Coalition as Party in a One-Party Southern Area: A Theoretical
and Case Analysis," *Midwest Journal of Political Science*, Vol. 8 (August 1964),
pp. 277–97.

Breedville is too small to dominate county politics, and the election of the five members of the county board of supervisors from separate districts is designed to preserve localism even in the unlikely event that Breedville should grow big. The attempt of some Breedville reformers to consolidate the white schools is the most controversial issue in Crayfish, but the friends-and-neighbors politics of the communities perpetuates the village schools.

Another political conflict centers on loyalty to the Democratic party. Local politicians who go along with the governor in his support for unpledged electors in presidential elections are called "regulars"; those who remain loyal to the national party are called "independents"! But this is an issue of little continuing importance. The white citizens of Crayfish are in agreement in their desire for industry and other money-making schemes and in their opposition to Negro rights. In this setting, the pursuit of office is the pursuit of personal rewards and little else.

Bright Leaf County also has multiple factions, but the greater heterogeneity of the county leads to a somewhat more structured pattern of competition. Because no one voluntarily moves into Crayfish, it is made up almost entirely of "old families." But Bright Leaf contains some "newer elements" who are identified with change. The county seat, Farmington, is more dominant in Bright Leaf County than Breedville is in Crayfish. And Farmington shows signs of an "old family–newer element" division. The "old family" crowd centers around several wealthy descendants of original settlers with banking and real estate interests. Most of the main-street merchants and professional men belong to this faction, by marriage if not by birth. The "newer element" includes the leaders of the expanding teachers college, local industries and businesses, and the newspaper.

A controversy over urban renewal in the early 1960's seems to have hardened these lines of division. The principal target of urban renewal was a Negro slum from which "old families" reaped a tidy profit in rent. A referendum on urban renewal was called for the same day as the election of mayor. The "newer element's" candidate for mayor favored urban renewal while the "old families'" candidate led the opposition. The bitterly fought contest ended in a narrow victory for urban renewal and an equally narrow victory for the mayoralty candidate who had opposed urban renewal. Time appears to be on the side of the "newer elements," however; when the new mayor's vote was needed to break a tie in the city council on a resolution to initiate urban renewal, he felt obliged to support the program. But the closeness of these contests suggests that a loose bifactionalism will continue to characterize Farmington politics for some time.

The Negro vote is not firmly identified with either of these factions, and the white politicians of Farmington still approach Negro voters in a clandestine manner. The Negro vote has grown to the point where it must be recognized, but the public recognition is still unfriendly. In 1960 a Negro was almost elected to the city council from a predominantly Negro district. Before the next municipal election the town fathers, in order to cut down the strength of the Negro vote, ruled that council members were to be elected at-large rather than on a district basis.[6]

Many "old family" people in Camellia County lament the loss of the good old days when public offices were passed from one leading family to another, with the officials serving without pay and without interference from other elements. One leader recalled that in his youth, "the substantial business element of the community ran Camellia County affairs free from the ordinary conception of politics and [motivated by a desire] for service to the community. About 15 to 18 years ago compensation became attached to the jobs, and the quality of leadership has dropped ever since." It was a system of cooptation and noblesse oblige.

The death of the old system was symbolized by the democratization of the choice of the annual Camellia Queen. Since the ante-bellum period the Camellia Queen had always been chosen discreetly by the leading families, and any genuine "old family" could claim several generations of queens. Shortly after the Second World War, however, "newer elements" demanded that the Camellia Queen be elected by the high-school students rather than named by the "old families." Since then, no "old family" member has reigned as queen; even a great-great-granddaughter of the territorial governor once had to settle for a position in the queen's court. The "old families" have preserved a shred of tradition by monopolizing the flower-bearer positions in the Camellia Queen coronation for their preschool youngsters. The honorific focus of the ceremony for Camellia "Society" has simply shifted to this lesser office.

While their children were rudely changing Camellia's happiest social event, the contractors, fuel-oil dealers, and automobile salesmen were pushing their way onto the city council and the county commission. In adult politics, too, the "old families" have adjusted their strategy to the necessities of wider public participation.

Camellia County politics has become too complex to be described in terms of "old families" versus "newer elements." The old families themselves have split into two fairly distinct factions, each of which has some support from "newer elements." Camellia County leaders, even as they deny the existence of local factions, tend to identify them. "There are no cliques and factions here," one leader said. "I don't like to play the factional battles myself. I did oppose M———'s group on integration and reapportionment." Each of Camellia's principal factions is based on real estate and financial interests, and those interests are tightly interwoven through family ties and generations of friendship and financial rewards. Each faction centers on a former governor,

---

[6] On the importance of election systems for Negro representation outside the South, see James Q. Wilson, *Negro Politics: The Search for Leadership* (Glencoe, Ill.: The Free Press, 1960), pp. 31–33.

a bank, a savings and loan association, a prominent law firm, and associated businesses.

The clash between these two factions is not confined to election day or to obvious economic self-interest. M———'s group consistently takes a moderate stand on racial issues and a relatively liberal view on almost all social and economic issues. The other "old family" faction is consistently reactionary on all issues. The battle lines are not as clearly drawn as when two political parties oppose each other, but, when active members of these two major factions talk politics, the meaning of "we" and "they" is clear.

The university and the Negroes make up the core of a small liberal faction in Camellia. Whenever a clear choice is presented, these liberals support the more progressive "old family" faction. They have recently been joined by the family controlling Capital City's third bank, the oldest in the area. The present generation of this family openly crusades for integration and other liberal causes to the point that their endorsement is feared as a liability. The more active members of this "third force" have recently formed a League for Better Government, a small group composed of a few integrationists from the business community, professors from the state university, and Negro activists primarily from the Negro university.

An old-style politician who has managed an uneasy coalition of poor white and Negro support could be called the "boss" of a fourth faction. Both in his personal style of life and in his stand on issues, the boss represents the lower classes of Camellia County. "He's a wild man," a spokesman for the reactionary faction said in a horrified tone. "Get one of those in and you are gone. He has Negro and labor support!" Most leaders of the progressive faction regard this "boss" with tolerance, and some have given him active support. The uncompromising liberalism of the League for Better Government represents a greater threat to the "boss'" control over his poverty-stricken followers: his base of support is growing shaky.

Urbania has already achieved the ideologically structured politics toward which Capital City seems to be moving. Comfortably dominated by business and industrial interests before the Second World War, it nevertheless harbored the seeds of distinct factional differences. Piedmont County's large industrial labor force was one of the most highly unionized in the South, and Negro insurance and banking firms were important elements in the county's economy. As early as 1935 some 150 Negro business leaders of Urbania met at their Tennis Club to organize the Urbania League for Negro Activities. In the 1940's representatives of the Southern School for Workers began to educate union members for political action.

The old consensus was challenged shortly after the war. White liberal and labor forces joined in a Citizens for Better Government (CBG) organization, which joined with the Urbania League for Negro Activities (ULNA) to form a potent coalition. In the late 1940's this coalition captured control of the county Democratic party organization, with 10 union members, 5 white liberals, and 2 Negroes winning 17 of the precinct chairmanships in Piedmont's 30 precincts. The coalition also elected liberal white businessmen as county chairman of the Democratic party and as mayor of Urbania.

Despite the temporary success of this labor-liberal-Negro coalition, its elements were never firmly united. Reactions to the Supreme Court's school desegregation decision of 1954 severely strained the coalition. Shortly after the decision, white racists formed a Political Education Committee to rally Urbania to the defense of segregation. This new organization made substantial gains among factory workers, and the union leaders lost much of their ability to "deliver" votes in support of coalition-endorsed, nonracist candidates. The liberal-labor-Negro coalition barely retained control of the party organization and the city government in 1956 and 1957, and in 1958 it lost control of the party. Nevertheless, it has managed to retain a sympathetic mayor throughout several changes of administration. Urbania is the only city in the four community study areas where the city officials responded to the racial protests in 1963 and 1964 by working openly and successfully to integrate privately owned businesses. Public facilities and employment were already desegregated, but the city went further and declared a policy of promoting employment without regard to race in private business as well.

The older businesses of Piedmont County have not been uniform in their opposition to the liberal-labor-Negro faction. Some of these businesses are national concerns producing for mass markets; hence they are especially sensitive to the racial opinions of people outside the South. Even so, many of them oppose the liberal economic policies of the postwar coalition in Urbania. Moreover, the city's merchants tend to align themselves with the conservative rural elements on both race and economics. Outside Urbania, Piedmont is similar to the other three counties: no Negro has been elected to county office, and no public schools outside Urbania are integrated.

## Community political systems and political participation: Problems of analysis

Crayfish, Bright Leaf, Camellia, and Piedmont counties are as different in their political characteristics as they are in their social and economic characteristics. To what extent do the distinctly political characteristics affect the rate of Negro political participation in different communities? This question is not easily answered. We could compare the rates of Negro voter registration in counties that have different legal requirements for voting, for example; but, if we discovered any differences, we could not safely attribute them to the legal requirements. They might stem from any or all of the social and economic attributes we analyzed in Chapter Five. By taking advantage of that analysis, however, we can consider the importance of political factors for Negro voter registration in the South free from any contamination by the social and economic factors we have already examined.

In computing the correlations between demographic characteristics and Negro registration rates, we obtained an equation—called a multiple regression equation—which represents the typical relationship between these 21 variables and Negro registration rates for all counties in the South. By entering the values of these social and economic attributes for each county into this equation, we obtain a "predicted" rate of Negro registration for every southern county. This predicted rate is the proportion of the county's voting-age Negroes who would be registered if the relationships between the county's socioeconomic structure and Negro registration corresponded exactly to those of the South as a whole. Some counties have just the level of Negro registration they "ought" to have; others have registration rates above or below the predicted level.

By examining the pattern of these deviations—called "residuals," in statistical parlance—we can control the effects of socioeconomic structure on Negro registration and thereby ascertain whether political and legal factors have any independent association with Negro registration and, if so, how much. A residual of 0 indicates that the rate of Negro voter registration is exactly what the county's social and economic attributes would lead one to expect; the positive or negative value of other residuals indicates whether the county's actual Negro registration is above or below the level expected from its socioeconomic characteristics. The larger the residual, the greater the need for other factors to explain the county's Negro registration rate.

This procedure enables us to control for variations based on social and economic characteristics. If a county has a small proportion of Negroes in its population, and if an unusually large number of them enjoy high incomes and good education, the county's predicted rate of Negro registration will be quite high, say, 40 per cent. Another county, with more Negroes and lower levels of Negro income and education, will have a low predicted rate, say, 15 per cent. Should 40 per cent of the Negroes actually be registered in both counties, the former would have a residual of 0 and the latter a residual of +.25. Despite their identical rates of Negro registration, we would say that the first county's rate of Negro registration could be explained entirely in terms of social and economic characteristics; in the second county we would expect to find some political factors that were not present in the first. We are concerned here, then, not with variations in Negro voter registration rates as such, but with those variations that we cannot account for by demographic analysis.

## State variations in Negro voter-registration rates

Perhaps the most significant political and legal fact about the South is that it is divided into 11 states. The rates of voter registration by adult Negroes vary widely from state to state.

The 250,000 Negroes estimated to be registered before *Smith* v. *Allwright* were unevenly distributed among the southern states (see Table 6–1). In

TABLE 6–1.   *Estimated percentage of voting-age Negroes registered to vote, 1940–1966, by state*

| STATE | YEAR | | | | | | | |
|---|---|---|---|---|---|---|---|---|
| | 1940 | 1947 | 1952 | 1956 | 1958 | 1960 | 1964 | 1966 |
| Mississippi | a | 1 | 4 | 5 | 5 | 6 | 7 | 14 |
| Alabama | a | 1 | 5 | 11 | 15 | 14 | 19 | 31 |
| South Carolina | a | 13 | 20 | 27 | 15 | b | 37 | 38 |
| Louisiana | a | 2 | 25 | 31 | 26 | 31 | 32 | 39 |
| Georgia | 2 | 20 | 23 | 27 | 26 | b | 27 | 46 |
| Arkansas | 3 | 21 | 27 | 36 | 33 | 38 | 40 | 54 |
| Florida | 3 | 13 | 33 | 32 | 31 | 39 | 51 | 62 |
| Virginia | 5 | 11 | 16 | 19 | 21 | 23 | 34 | 49 |
| Texas | 9 | 17 | 31 | 37 | 39 | 30 c | 58 | 59 |
| North Carolina | 10 | 14 | 18 | 24 | 32 | 38 | 47 | 49 |
| Tennessee | 16 | 25 | 27 | 29 | b | 48 c | 73 | 72 |

a Less than 0.5 per cent.
b No data.
c Incomplete data; the data for Tennessee are especially unreliable.
SOURCES: Same as for Table 1–1.

Mississippi, Alabama, South Carolina, and Louisiana, less than 0.5 per cent of the adult Negroes were thought to be registered to vote in general elections in 1940. At the other end of the continuum, in Tennessee, 16 per cent were registered. Negro registration increased rapidly after the death of the white primary but with conspicuous differences from state to state. The slowest increases occurred in the Deep South states of Mississippi and Alabama and in the three states—Texas, North Carolina, and Tennessee—which had the largest amount of Negro voting prior to *Smith* v. *Allwright*. In Arkansas and Florida, on the other hand, the proportion of Negroes registered increased much more quickly. By 1964 those states could be classed with Texas, North Carolina, and Tennessee. The uneven response to *Smith* v. *Allwright* is evident. The "Solid South" is a fiction, then, but the source of the variations is not so obvious.

Table 6–2 shows the 1958 registration rates, by county, *within* the 11

TABLE 6–2.   *Rates of Negro voter registration in the southern states, 1958*

| PERCENTAGE OF VOTING-AGE NEGROES REGISTERED TO VOTE | STATES (PERCENTAGE OF COUNTIES) | | | | | | | | | | | SOUTHWIDE PERCENTAGE OF COUNTIES |
| --- | --- | --- | --- | --- | --- | --- | --- | --- | --- | --- | --- | --- |
| | *Miss.* | *S.C.* | *Ala.* | *Va.* | *Ark.* | *Ga.* | *La.* | *N.C.* | *Texas* | *Fla.* | *Tenn.* | |
| 0–9 | 89% | 30% | 38% | 10% | 3% | 25% | 32% | 5% | 2% | 9% | 4% | 21% |
| 10–19 | 6 | 50 | 26 | 31 | 24 | 16 | 11 | 30 | 7 | 7 | 0 | 18 |
| 20–29 | 4 | 20 | 11 | 31 | 28 | 19 | 12 | 23 | 24 | 18 | 4 | 19 |
| 30–39 | 1 | 0 | 6 | 15 | 33 | 10 | 5 | 7 | 28 | 18 | 2 | 13 |
| 40–49 | 0 | 0 | 3 | 8 | 7 | 11 | 9 | 5 | 21 | 19 | 11 | 10 |
| 50–59 | 0 | 0 | 9 | 1 | 3 | 5 | 16 | 9 | 12 | 15 | 4 | 7 |
| 60–69 | 0 | 0 | 3 | 2 | 2 | 3 | 5 | 6 | 2 | 5 | 18 | 4 |
| 70–79 | 0 | 0 | 2 | 0 | 0 | 3 | 5 | 5 | 1 | 5 | 11 | 2 |
| 80–89 | 0 | 0 | 2 | 0 | 0 | 5 | 3 | 3 | 1 | 3 | 17 | 3 |
| 90 + | 0 | 0 | 0 | 2 | 0 | 3 | 2 | 7 | 2 | 1 | 29 | 3 |
| TOTAL | 100% | 100% | 100% | 100% | 100% | 100% | 100% | 100% | 100% | 100% | 100% | 100% |
| NUMBER OF COUNTIES ON WHICH FIGURES ARE BASED | 82 | 46 | 66 | 124 | 58 | 153 | 64 | 97 | 190 | 67 | 54 | 1,001 |
| UNWEIGHTED MEAN OF COUNTY PERCENTAGES | 3.4 | 12.5 | 20.5 | 24.1 | 27.6 | 30.4 | 31.2 | 36.0 | 36.8 | 39.1 | 72.3 | 30.4 |
| STANDARD DEVIATION | 6.6 | 7.8 | 20.3 | 15.6 | 11.2 | 25.6 | 26.9 | 26.5 | 15.6 | 21.0 | 25.1 | 24.3 |

SOURCE: U.S. Commission on Civil Rights, *1959 Report* (Washington, D.C.: U.S. Government Printing Office, 1959), and U.S. Commission on Civil Rights, "Voting," *1961 Report* (Washington, D.C.: U.S. Government Printing Office, 1961).

southern states and for the region as a whole. We can draw two general conclusions from this table. First, the range of Negro registration rates in the region was sizable. In most counties, the rate was very low—indeed, the most common (modal) situation was for less than 10 per cent of the voting-age Negroes to be registered. In a significant minority of cases, however, the level of Negro registration compared favorably with that of white southerners. Second, the southern states differed markedly not only when compared with one another on a statewide basis, but also when compared in terms of their internal distribution of Negro registration.

The greatest diversity in Negro registration rates was in Louisiana (standard deviation, 26.9),[7] North Carolina (26.5), Georgia (25.6), and Tennessee (25.1). In Louisiana, for example, the bottom third of the parishes had less than 10 per cent of their voting-age Negro population registered, while the top third had over 50 per cent registered. The diversity was almost as great in Georgia. In North Carolina, over 50 per cent of the counties had from 10 to 30 per cent of their adult Negroes on the voting lists, but there was a wide spread in both directions from this norm. Tennessee had an equally broad range, though with a higher norm than North Carolina.

Nothing like this diversity in Negro registration rates existed in Texas (standard deviation, 15.6), Virginia (15.6), Arkansas (11.2), South Carolina (7.8), or Mississippi (6.6). Whether this lack of variation resulted from social and economic homogeneity, from the characteristics of the state political system, or from some mixture of both is not now clear. What is clear, however, is that striking differences in the patterns of Negro registration existed from state to state.

In Table 6–3 we move from raw data to data that cancel out social and economic factors. Here the former Confederate states are ranked according to the average percentage of the voting-age Negro population registered to vote in their counties in 1958.[8] In Mississippi the average county had only about 3 per cent of its potential Negro electorate registered to vote. The average county in South Carolina had about 12 per cent. In Tennessee, on the other hand, the typical county had 72 per cent of the voting-age Negroes registered, a figure that is no doubt inflated by the state's casual approach to the niceties of electoral administration.

What accounts for these wide variations among the states? We have al-

[7] The standard deviation is a measure of the dispersion of values from the mean value—that is, of deviation from the norm. If the distribution of values being measured is "normal"—that is, if it approximates a bell-shaped curve—67 per cent of the cases fall within plus or minus one standard deviation from the mean. In any distribution, normal or otherwise, no less than 75 per cent of the cases fall within plus or minus two standard deviations from the mean.

[8] These figures differ slightly from those reported in Table 6–1 because they are unweighted means of county percentages.

TABLE 6–3.    *Mean percentage of voting-age Negroes registered to vote, by county, in southern states, compared to mean percentage predicted by twenty-one demographic variables, 1958*

| State | Actual mean percentage | Predicted mean percentage | Residual | Actual mean as percentage of predicted mean |
|---|---|---|---|---|
| Mississippi | 3.4% | 17.7% | − 14.3 | 19.2% |
| South Carolina | 12.5 | 19.4 | − 6.9 | 64.4 |
| Alabama | 20.5 | 26.8 | − 6.3 | 76.5 |
| Virginia | 24.1 | 34.3 | − 10.2 | 70.3 |
| Arkansas | 27.6 | 32.3 | − 4.7 | 85.4 |
| Georgia | 30.4 | 24.9 | + 5.5 | 122.1 |
| Louisiana | 31.2 | 31.2 | 0 | 100.0 |
| North Carolina | 36.0 | 32.8 | + 3.2 | 109.7 |
| Texas | 36.8 | 36.7 | + 0.1 | 100.3 |
| Florida | 39.1 | 32.6 | + 6.5 | 119.9 |
| Tennessee | 72.3 | 39.7 | + 32.6 | 182.1 |

ready shown that a part of the explanation lies in the difference in the social and economic structure of the states. Mississippi and South Carolina, for example, have a larger proportion of Negroes in their populations than the other southern states, and this has a depressing effect on Negro registration. But residual analysis reveals that differences in the social and economic characteristics of southern states offer only a partial explanation of their varying rates of Negro voter registration.

The second column of Table 6–3 gives the predicted Negro registration percentage for the average county within each of the southern states. Mississippi has the lowest and Tennessee the highest actual rates of Negro registration; on the basis of their social and economic attributes, they "ought" to have the lowest and highest rates. If this were a sufficient explanation, however, the predicted and the actual rates of registration should be the same. In two states—Louisiana and Texas—they very nearly are the same, but all the others have either more or fewer Negroes registered than expected. In Mississippi, for example, about 18 per cent of the voting-age Negroes ought to be registered if Mississippi counties responded to socioeconomic factors as other southern counties do; but, instead, only about 3 per cent are actually registered. The Negro registration rate is about 7 percentage points below the expected in South Carolina, 6 points below in Alabama, 10 points below in Virginia, and 5 points below in Arkansas. On the other hand, Tennessee

(+32.6 residual), Florida (+6.5), Georgia (+5.5), and North Carolina (+3.2) have more Negroes registered to vote than expected.

These state contrasts persist, accordingly, even after we control for the 21 social and economic factors examined earlier. Raw differences in registration rates show a wild variation—69 percentage points, for example, between Tennessee and Mississippi (column 1). But much of this difference clearly stems from the fact that Mississippi has so many more Negroes than Tennessee and is both more rural and less industrialized. When such factors are controlled, the difference of 69 points between the two states is reduced to 47 (column 3). Or, if we take less extreme cases and compare South Carolina with Florida, the raw difference of 27 points is reduced to a residual difference of 13. By the same token, residual difference may reveal that a small raw difference is more meaningful than it appears. Georgia counties, for example, have an average Negro registration rate 3 percentage points higher than Arkansas counties. But, if we allow for the social and economic attributes of these counties, we would expect the Arkansas average to be higher than Georgia's; hence, the raw difference of 3 points becomes a residual difference of 10 points.

The contrasts revealed by residual analysis demonstrate that the state political systems exert an independent influence on Negro voter registration. But to say that is not to say very much. What specific aspects of state politics account for these differences? We turn now to this problem.

## Legal requirements for voting

Around the turn of the century southern Bourbons, responding to the twin threats of the Negro vote and of populism, led a movement to restrict suffrage. They developed a "variety of ingenious contrivances to inconvenience the would-be voter."[9] Some of these contrivances survive to this day, despite the intervening rise and fall of the white primary, changing political attitudes and conditions, and the efforts of the United States Supreme Court. Just how effectively these electoral obstacles serve to disfranchise potential Negro voters is not known. Northerners discussing southern politics often cast these devices in "the role of chief villain."[10] Detailed analyses by Key and Ogden suggest that their impact on the turnout of *white* voters is fairly modest. "The chances are," Key writes, "that if other things remain equal (and they rarely do), elimination of the poll tax alone would increase voting in most southern states

[9] V. O. Key, Jr., *Southern Politics in State and Nation* (New York: Alfred A. Knopf, 1949), p. 531.
[10] *Ibid.*, p. 579.

by no more than 5 to 10 per cent of the potential number of white voters."[11] Our multiple regression analysis enables us to make a similar estimate for potential Negro voters, with the advantage of holding a large number of other things equal.

Five southern states—Alabama, Arkansas, Mississippi, Texas, and Virginia —levied poll taxes up to the time they were outlawed (1964 for national elections, 1966 for state and local elections). They varied in amount from Mississippi's two dollars to Arkansas' one dollar, and they had to be paid from one to nine months before election day. The tax was cumulative in Alabama, Mississippi, and Virginia; new voters were required to pay the tax for the preceding two or three years before they were enrolled. Most states exempted members of the armed forces, and some also exempted veterans, the elderly, the blind, the deaf or dumb, the maimed, Indians, and other miscellaneous categories of citizens.

All the southern states save Arkansas, Florida, Tennessee, and Texas require potential voters to pass literacy tests. But the formal requirements of the tests tell only part of the story: "Whether a person can register to vote depends on what the man down at the courthouse says, and he usually has the final say. It is how the tests are administered that matters."[12] In one North Carolina county, for example, the registrant is regarded as literate even if he requires help in reading the following words: *solemnly, affirm, support, Constitution, inconsistent, therewith, resident, township, precinct, ward, general, election,* and *registered.* In Crayfish County, on the other hand, the registrar of voters frankly tells researchers that the literacy test is administered so that no Negro can pass.

To what extent are differences in formal voting requirements—despite variations in their administration—related to differences in registration rates? Table 6–4 demonstrates that Negro registration varies with the stringency of formal voting requirements even when social and economic factors are controlled.

County registration rates (as of 1958) within the three states with both the poll tax and the literacy test are, on the average, 10.5 percentage points below the predicted level. Counties in the two states with neither a poll tax nor a literacy test have registration rates 18.1 percentage points higher than expected. The pattern is not perfect. South Carolina, with only a literacy test, has a lower residual than Alabama, which has both a fairly substantial poll tax and a literacy test. Texas has a small plus residual (+0.1) whereas Arkansas has a sizable negative one (−4.7); both are poll-tax states without a literacy requirement. Nonetheless, the tendency for the states with stringent formal voter requirements to have lower registration rates than those with

[11] *Ibid.*, p. 617. See also F. D. Ogden, *The Poll Tax in the South* (University, Ala.: University of Alabama Press, 1958), ch. 5.
[12] Key, *op. cit.*, p. 460.

TABLE 6–4. *State voter requirements and Negro voter-registration residuals, by county, 1958*

| Voter requirements | Mean county residual |
|---|---|
| **POLL TAX AND LITERARY TEST** | |
| Mississippi | − 14.3 |
| Virginia | − 10.2 |
| Alabama | − 6.3 |
| All counties in group | − 10.5 |
| **POLL TAX ONLY** | |
| Arkansas | − 4.7 |
| Texas | + 0.1 |
| All counties in group | − 1.0 |
| **LITERACY TEST ONLY** | |
| South Carolina | − 6.9 |
| Louisiana | 0 |
| North Carolina | + 3.2 |
| Georgia | + 5.5 |
| All counties in group | + 2.3 |
| **NEITHER LITERACY TEST NOR POLL TAX** | |
| Florida | + 6.5 |
| Tennessee | + 32.6 |
| All counties in group | + 18.1 |

more liberal requirements is impressive, even after controlling for 21 social and economic factors. If we could take into account the way these formal requirements are variously administered by the local officials within each state, the differences in Table 6–4 would undoubtedly be even greater.

A survey of county registration officials by the North Carolina Advisory Committee to the United States Commission on Civil Rights suggests the extremely wide variety of ways in which the same legal requirements are actually administered.[13] Some county registrars in North Carolina reported that they administered literacy tests which included such requirements as the taking of oral dictation, extensive reading aloud, and answering questions on the meaning of words and phrases; others settled for an ability to fill out an application form properly and to sign one's name. Several county registration officials reported that they did not enforce the constitutionally required literacy test at all. The following counties—all in the northeastern black-belt area of North Carolina—reported literacy tests that appeared to be unusually difficult or arbitrary.

[13] The returns of an Advisory Committee questionnaire mailed to county registrars are reported, in part, in "Voting and Voter Requirements in North Carolina" (mimeo.), June 4, 1961.

| County | County residual | Residual adjusted for state mean |
|---|---|---|
| Bertie | − 1.0 | − 4.2 |
| Camden | − 9.1 | − 13.3 |
| Currituck | − 15.1 | − 18.3 |
| Franklin | + 3.2 | 0 |
| Gates | − 22.1 | − 25.3 |
| Greene | − 6.1 | − 9.3 |
| Halifax | − 2.8 | − 6.0 |
| Northampton | + 0.7 | − 2.5 |
| Warren | + 1.8 | − 1.4 |
| MEAN | − 5.6 | − 8.9 |

The Negro registration rate of these counties is, on the average, more than 5 percentage points below the expected and almost 9 percentage points below that expected for North Carolina counties with the social and economic characteristics of these counties.

The North Carolina counties that do not administer literacy tests are all in the mountainous western part of the state. They and their residuals are:

| County | County residual | Residual adjusted for state mean |
|---|---|---|
| Catawba | + 23.5 | + 20.3 |
| Wilkes | + 32.6 | + 29.4 |
| Yancey | + 12.9 | + 9.7 |
| MEAN | + 23.0 | + 19.8 |

On the average, these counties have 23 percentage points more Negroes registered than predicted, and almost 20 percentage points more than the state average for counties with their social and economic characteristics.

Our community studies buttress this conclusion. The social and economic characteristics of Crayfish County, for example, are so depressed that only 12 per cent of its adult Negroes "ought" to be registered—that is, 12 per cent of the Crayfish Negroes would be registered if the relationship there between registration and county demographic characteristics were typical of that found in all southern counties. But the most blatantly anti-Negro procedures unearthed in this study are those of the registrar in Crayfish County, and it has *no* Negroes registered rather than 12 per cent. On the other hand, we would expect Piedmont County, on the basis of its demographic characteristics, to have a higher registration, 28 per cent. Registration in Piedmont is carried out by precinct registrars rather than by a central registrar for the entire county; some of the registrars are Negroes, and no registrar expresses any reservations about registering Negroes. The actual registration rate in Piedmont is twice as great as that predicted from demographic factors alone.

Crude as these data are, they suggest that both formal voter requirements and the manner in which they are administered are strongly related to variations in Negro voter registration. Part of this relationship stems from the tendency of counties with depressed social and economic characteristics to have stringent voting requirements and registrars who apply the requirements to the disadvantage of Negroes. But residual analysis demonstrates that the relationship holds up even when economic and social factors are taken into account. These positive findings call for a look at other political variables.

## The structure of competition: Party systems

The South differs from the rest of the United States in so many ways that it is tempting to assume that all the forms of its distinctiveness are functionally linked. Thus southerners register and vote in smaller proportions than do other Americans, and the South is the country's largest one-party region. Hence the one-party politics of the South must decrease voter participation. Much can be said for this interpretation. When the results of general elections are foreordained in favor of Democracy—and, despite changes in recent years, this is the most common situation for most offices in the South—general election campaigns are tepid affairs, party organizations make little if any effort to increase registration or to get out the vote, and the act of voting in general elections becomes little more than a ritual.

Furthermore, although the Democratic primaries may be hotly and regularly contested, this form of electoral competition seems less effective than partisan competition in stimulating political interest and activity. Contrary to a popular assumption, the turnout for primary elections in the South, where the primary may be the real election, is no greater than primary turnout in parts of the country where the real election comes later.[14] A sizable group of candidates running without party labels is harder to choose among, and the probable benefits to be gained from the election of one candidate rather than another are difficult to determine. Without the mental shorthand of party identification to structure the situation, the voter is presented with more vexing cognitive problems than he is in a partisan contest. Deciding where one's self-interest lies is more difficult, and the efforts or "costs" of voting are correspondingly increased. Democratic factions do organize get-out-the-vote efforts for their candidates. But these are transient affairs, relatively impotent even when compared to the inefficient efforts of local party organizations outside the South. All these characteristics of one-partyism have their greatest impact

[14] Key, *op. cit.*, ch. 23.

FIGURE 6–1.  *Party competition in the presidential election of 1956
and Negro voter registration rates by county*

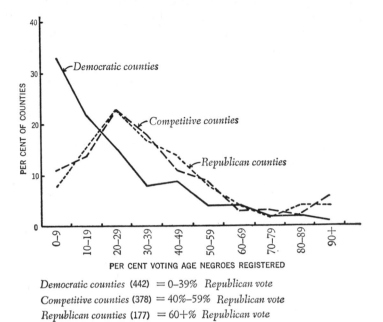

*Democratic counties* (442)  = 0–39% *Republican vote*
*Competitive counties* (378)  = 40%–59% *Republican vote*
*Republican counties* (177)  = 60+% *Republican vote*

on poorly educated, "have-not" groups in the southern electorate, among which
Negroes are the most conspicuous.[15]

When we apply this explanation to voter registration or general election
turnout, however, we find a dearth of supporting evidence. Lane, on the basis
of his survey of studies conducted in nonsouthern and European settings,
concludes that the relationship between the closeness of electoral contests and
voter turnout is small.[16] And recent research has demonstrated over and over
again that the acts of registration and voting satisfy needs of many citizens
which are entirely unrelated to politics, to say nothing of the nature of electoral contests. "Many of the motives which politicize a person are, in fact,
independent of the outcome of an election, and therefore independent of
whether the outcome is ever in doubt."[17]

Nonetheless, Figure 6–1 appears to support the earlier line of reasoning:
Negro voter registration increases in southern counties as party competition
increases. Counties in which Eisenhower polled less than 40 per cent of the

[15] *Ibid.*, ch. 14.
[16] Robert E. Lane, *Political Life* (Glencoe, Ill.: The Free Press, 1958), pp. 308–10. See
also James A. Robinson and William H. Standing, "Some Correlates of Voter Participation: The Case of Indiana," *Journal of Politics*, Vol. 22 (1960), pp. 96–111.
[17] Lane, *op. cit.*, p. 309.

vote for president in 1956 can safely be called Democratic. Relatively few Negroes tend to be registered in these counties, compared to the more competitive counties (those with 40 to 59 per cent for Eisenhower). But the rates of Negro registration are as high in heavily Republican counties (60 per cent and over for Eisenhower) as in the competitive counties. The difficulty with these findings, as with those cited by Lane, is that we do not know whether the differences result from competitive elections or from the tendency of presidential Republicanism to be strongest in areas where the social and economic inhibitions against Negro voting are most attenuated.

Table 6–5, which shows the mean residuals for Democratic, competitive,

TABLE 6–5.  *Party systems and Negro voter-registration residuals, by county, 1958*

| County party system | Mean residual | Number of counties |
|---|---|---|
| Democratic | − 0.9 | 442 |
| Competitive | + 1.3 | 378 |
| Republican | − 0.9 | 177 |

NOTE: Democratic counties are defined as those in which the Republican presidential vote in 1956 was from 0 to 39 per cent of the total vote. In competitive counties the Republicans polled 40 to 59 per cent; in Republican counties, 60 per cent and over.

and Republican counties, demonstrates that most of the tendency for Negro registration to increase with levels of competition in presidential voting is the result of the social and economic characteristics of the competitive counties. Both Republican and Democratic counties have slightly fewer Negroes registered than would be expected on the basis of their social and economic characteristics. The competitive counties have only 1 percentage point more Negroes registered than their social structure suggests. The existence or absence of partisan competition is associated with variations in Negro registration rates, then; but once we go beyond that simple covariation, we discover that the variations of both are largely accounted for by other factors.

## The structure of competition: Factional systems

Political competition in the South takes place largely within the Democratic party. And this kind of one-party politics seems to have a small inhibiting effect on Negro registration. But the structure of Democratic factionalism varies a good deal from one southern state to the next, and this may affect the meaning of voting to southern Negroes.

Repeatedly confronted with a choice between an incumbent like Senator Eastland and a challenger trying to beat the senior Senator from Mississippi at his own game, thousands of potential Negro voters may never have any incentive to try to register. Given a choice between Frank Porter Graham and Willis Smith, they might be expected to turn out in droves—as they did in the North Carolina senatorial primary of 1950. The southern Negro vote is "issue-oriented," and race is the issue. In some southern states, Negroes find all the candidates for public office unsatisfactory; in others, Negroes can usually distinguish one or more candidates as favorably disposed to Negro interests —despite the candidates' best efforts to avoid being labeled by whites as "Negro candidates"—and these candidates have some chance of winning. This normally seems to have been the case in Florida, Louisiana, North Carolina, Tennessee, and Texas, but rarely so elsewhere in the South.[18]

Southern states differ not only in the *kind* of choice offered to voters but also in the *number* of choices with which voters and potential voters are confronted. In some states, two fairly clear-cut factions battle it out on rather even terms, and these factions tend to persist from one election year to the next. In others, Democratic factionalism is more fluid and unstructured, the number of serious candidates tends to be larger, and one electoral contest has little relationship to the next. The extent to which the Democratic party divides into two party-like factions, or tends instead toward splintered factionalism, is suggested by the following figures on the percentage of the total vote won by the *two leading candidates* for governor in Democratic primaries between 1948 and 1960.[19]

| State | Median percentage |
|---|---|
| Virginia | 100% |
| Tennessee | 96 |
| Georgia | 95 |
| South Carolina | 90 |
| Arkansas | 82 |
| North Carolina | 78 |
| Texas | 69 |
| Florida | 61 |
| Louisiana | 59 |
| Alabama | 58 |
| Mississippi | 44 |

[18] This evaluation is made for the period before 1958, when the Civil Rights Commission reported the figures of Negro registration employed in this southwide county analysis.

[19] Primary election returns are from the initial primary (excluding runoffs); returns were compiled from Richard M. Scammon (ed.), *Southern Primaries '58* (Washington, D.C.: Governmental Affairs Institute, 1959); from various issues of the *Congressional Quarterly Almanac*, and *Congressional Quarterly Weekly Report*; legislative manuals and Reports of Secretaries of State; and the *New York Times*. Uncontested elections and contests involving incumbents in Arkansas and Texas—the only southern states in which governors may succeed themselves—were omitted in computing medians.

In Virginia, Tennessee, and Georgia, electoral battles appear to be dominated by one or two major factions that manage to attract virtually all the vote. In Texas, Florida, Louisiana (of the post-Long era), Alabama, and Mississippi, state politics follows the "every man for himself" style of fluid multifactionalism. The other states fall into an intermediate group; but with the two leading candidates capturing between 78 and 90 per cent of the vote, these states do not have extreme multifactionalism.

The small proportion of the total vote captured by the two leading candidates in the last five states on the list indicates that those states are clearly multifactional. But such a measure does not tell us whether the other states are bifactional or unifactional. To make this distinction, we need to look at the median percentage of the total vote polled by *the leading candidate* for governor in the *first* Democratic primary between 1948 and 1960.

| State | Median percentage |
|---|---|
| Virginia | 66% |
| South Carolina | 61 |
| Tennessee | 56 |
| Georgia | 49 |
| Arkansas | 48 |
| North Carolina | 47 |
| Texas | 40 |
| Florida | 35 |
| Alabama | 34 |
| Louisiana | 33 |
| Mississippi | 28 |

Factional struggles were most uneven in Virginia and South Carolina. During the 1950's these were not so much bifactional states as states in which one faction dominated without serious challenge. Four states (Tennessee, Georgia, Arkansas, and North Carolina) thus emerge as bifactional. The first measure showed the two leading candidates to dominate the first primary election, and the second measure showed that this predominant support was shared by two candidates rather than dominated by one.

From a logical point of view, the citizen should have less reason to vote where one dominant faction runs the show; there is no realistic choice to be made. Similarly, a voter of limited political interest and skill can determine where his self-interest lies in a bifactional state more easily than in a state characterized by fluid multifactionalism. Candidates can be identified as belonging to the Clements faction, or to the Talmadge, Faubus, or Kerr Scott faction, and these labels have at least some policy meaning.[20]

[20] In Louisiana the Long faction seems to have continuity, too, but the first primary often presents a number of "Long" and "anti-Long" candidates competing for the claim to speak for the faction.

We have thus identified two dimensions along which state factional systems may differ: the availability of candidates with differing racial views, and the number of Democratic factions with strength in gubernatorial primary elections. Both of these characteristics should be important for Negro registration. When we classify the 11 southern states according to these criteria and examine the mean county residuals of each type of state, we see that this is indeed the case (see Table 6–6). Looking first at the bottom row we see that

TABLE 6–6.  *The structure of factional competition in southern states, 1948–1960, and Negro voter-registration residuals[a]*

| Type of factionalism | Generally no major candidate favorable to Negroes | Generally one or more major candidates favorable to Negroes | ALL COUNTIES IN GROUP |
|---|---|---|---|
| One dominant faction | − 9.3 | | − 9.3 |
| Two competitive factions | + 2.7 | + 13.7 | + 7.3 |
| Multifactionalism | − 10.7 | + 1.4 | − 2.4 |
| ALL COUNTIES IN GROUP | − 4.9 | + 5.3 | |

[a] The numbers in the table are the mean residuals of counties in groups of states with the same type of factional system. The first figure in the first column, for example, indicates that the mean residual of all Virginia and South Carolina counties is −9.3.

in states that generally have no major gubernatorial candidate favorable to Negroes, county rates of Negro registration fall below what would be expected on the basis of their social and economic characteristics. And the rates are higher than predicted in states that generally have a major candidate who appears relatively favorable to Negroes. The difference along this dimension is about 10 percentage points. The righthand column of residuals reveals similar differences according to the number of factions. Negro registration is considerably higher in states where two factions structure electoral competition than in those where a single faction dominates or where many factions clamor for the voter's attention.[21]

When the two dimensions—the kind and the number of choices presented in a state's politics—are considered together, the lowest residuals are found in the multifactional states that usually have no candidates favorable to Negroes. Alabama and Mississippi are divided into many factions, but they are united in anti-Negro sentiments; their mean county residual is −9.3. Arkansas and Georgia have had bifactional Democratic politics, but the factions have been so similar in their racial policies that Negroes could not easily discern a sig-

[21] That the negative residual in the unifactional states is larger than in the multifactional states results from the fact that the former category includes no states that usually have candidates favorable to Negroes.

nificant difference; the mean residual of their counties is +2.7. Among the states that have offered candidates with discernible differences from the Negro point of view, Florida, Louisiana, and Texas have had multifactional politics in recent years. Taken together, they have a residual of +1.4. Finally, North Carolina and Tennessee have had both bifactional politics and perceptible differences between the factions on racial policy. This is the combination of characteristics most conducive to Negro registration; the mean county residual for these two states is +13.7.

The structure of Democratic factionalism thus appears to have a major impact on Negro voter registration.[22] Although this finding is based on data from every county in the South, the data are rather crude, because county factional systems are classified according to statewide indexes of racial policy and number of factions. But the finding is supported by more detailed knowledge of the four community-study counties and by aggregated survey data from 21 counties.

In local elections, Crayfish County has less well defined factions, and more of them, than any other community-study site; it also has the only negative residual measure of Negro voter registration among the four counties. Bright Leaf has somewhat more recognizable factions and a substantial positive residual. Camellia County has, at least occasionally, clear factional differences between a smaller number of groups, and it has a high positive residual. Piedmont most nearly approximates continuing bifactional competition in its dominant city; it has an extremely high positive residual.[23] In the counties where we can speak with confidence about local factions, then, we find in more extreme form the same relationship between number of factions and Negro registration that we found for all southern counties when we used statewide measures of factionalism.

Southwide survey data can be brought to bear on the other dimension of factionalism—the presence of candidates favorable to Negroes. In the 21 counties in which Negroes were interviewed, respondents were asked if white candidates for public office in the county did anything to get Negro votes. If Negro votes are actively solicited, we can assume that candidates relatively favorable to Negroes sometimes appear in local elections.

The approach of white candidates varies greatly. In some communities where Negroes are permitted to vote, they are treated strictly as objects of manipulation rather than as citizens to whom policy commitments must be

22 This is not to imply a single direction of causality: a more meaningful choice may lead more Negroes to register, the registration of more Negroes may lead candidates to take positions more favorable to Negroes, or both. So far as bifactional as opposed to unifactional or multifactional politics is concerned, however, one can conceive of the pattern of factionalism as the independent variable associated with Negro registration, but one can hardly imagine the registration rates of Negroes as the independent variable.

23 The residuals for Crayfish, Bright Leaf, Camellia, and Piedmont counties are, in ascending order, —12.1, +7.6, +28.5, +41.5.

made. A yard man in Florida, for example, reported that he had sold his vote for a high price—and then reneged on the deal. He readily explained the approach of white candidates to Negro voters, and his response to it:

> They buy Negroes out, for one thing. Why, I made $60.00 one day. A white guy asked me if I was going to vote for his man, and I said "yes," and he passed me a 20. I guess the two guys with him didn't want to be outdone so they passed me 20's too. But when I went to vote I voted for the man I wanted to.

A young Negro housewife in Texas reported that the same practice existed in her locality: "They try to bribe you and give you $15.00 at the polls to vote for them. It would be hard for a hungry man to refuse." The approach is sometimes more subtle, however. A 35-year-old truck driver in Virginia said, "One lady brought me five dollars for gas to take voters to the polls. I think she just wanted to buy my vote."

Simply buying votes does not, of course, imply that the candidate is under any obligation to the voter. On the contrary, it is the voter who is under obligation to the candidate; all the candidate does is come up with the money. We accordingly classify those counties where most Negroes report vote-buying as the only technique for winning Negro support as similar to those in which no effort is made to gain Negro support. In both kinds of county we infer from the nature of campaigns that candidates perceived as favorable to Negro interests do not usually appear on the ballot. This inference is supported both by the disdain that Negro respondents show for candidates who have bought their votes and by the pride with which they claim to have voted contrary to the "contract."

In other southern counties white efforts to capture Negro support take other forms. "Candidates give Negroes whiskey and have barbecues," a Tennessee coal loader reported. But he went on to say: "I told them [other Negroes] if they wanted to do that, go on and drink and eat and then vote like they wanted to. It's a secret ballot anyway." A Georgia sharecropper, commenting on open-handed white candidates in his locality, said, "They do all they can. Furnish you whiskey and cars before elections and bullets after the election." This lavish treatment, though it moves some Negroes to skepticism, still suggests that there are candidates who are trying to appear favorable toward Negroes. And in many cases white candidates make policy commitments to potential Negro supporters. The first comment of a chauffeur for a private family in North Carolina about the campaign efforts of local white candidates was simply, "They glad-hand you." Asked if they did anything else, he said "Set Martin Luther King free and promise you anything except turning you white."

We have classified counties of this sort as including candidates who seem favorable to Negroes. The average proportion of Negroes registered in such counties is about 11 percentage points higher than is expected from the social and economic structure of those counties. In counties where most Negroes report no campaign activity other than vote-buying, on the other hand, the average registration is about 9 percentage points lower than expected from the counties' social and economic structure. Thus three different forms of evidence —demographic data on all southern counties, community studies, and aggregated attitudinal data—all support the basic proposition of this section: regardless of the social and economic characteristics of southern counties, their rates of Negro voter registration go up as Negroes are presented with clearer choices, either in the form of bipolar factionalism or in the form of candidates favorable to Negro interests.

## Race organization

Southerners of both races have created a plethora of new racial organizations since *Smith* v. *Allwright* and *Brown* v. *Board of Education*. Scores of Negro voters leagues, civic leagues, community-betterment organizations, and ministerial alliances have been organized in local communities. The Southern Christian Leadership Conference, the Student Non-violent Coordinating Committee, and the Committee on Racial Equality have entered the lists along with the National Association for the Advancement of Colored People and the Urban League as instruments of Negro protest. Some of these national organizations have established local chapters in the South. Among the white majority, the White Citizens Councils, sometimes bearing different names in different areas but still dedicated to the defense of white supremacy, have sprung up; in recent years even the seemingly moribund Ku Klux Klan has shown signs of renewed vigor. Most of these racial organizations are involved in electoral politics, either quite directly and explicitly or, at a minimum, as a provider of cues in the confusing atmosphere of southern factional politics. These groups can be expected to have some impact on rates of Negro voter registration.

Table 6–7 shows the relationships between the extent of race organization in the counties and their Negro registration residuals.[24] Looking first at the marginal distributions at the far right and bottom of the table, we can readily see that extensive Negro organization is associated with a substantial surplus

[24] We have made strenuous efforts to ascertain—through correspondence and a systematic search of newspaper files—the location of all Negro and white race organizations and their local chapters. Our list is no doubt incomplete, but we are reasonably confident that the counties we think have such organizations do have them—at least on paper. We consulted the *New York Times* from January 1945 to February 1961, and the Southern Educational Reporting Service's "Facts on Film," Rolls 1–40, first supplement Rolls 1–3, second supplement Rolls 1–11, in a search for news about these organizations. We wrote letters of inquiry to known national and statewide organizations seeking the location of their local chapters. Finally, we consulted people we knew to be knowledgeable about the racial politics of specific states and localities.

TABLE 6–7.  *Mean Negro voter-registration residuals by extent of race organization in southern counties, 1958*

|  | White race organization in county | No white race organization in county | ALL COUNTIES |
|---|---|---|---|
| Local Negro organization and NAACP chapter | + 11.4  (14) | + 1.0  (10) | + 7.0  (24) |
| NAACP chapter only | + 0.8  (74) | − 0.3 (214) | − 0.01 (288) |
| No Negro organization, no data | − 10.5 (125) | + 0.4 (551) | − 1.6  (676) |
| ALL COUNTIES | − 5.5 (221) | + 0.3 (776) | |

NOTE: Too few counties have local Negro organizations but no NAACP chapters to permit computation of means. They have been included, however, in the means for "all counties." The numbers of counties on which means are based are in parentheses.

(7 percentage points) of Negro registered voters over the registration rate predicted by social and economic structure alone. Counties with white race organizations have about 5.5 percentage points fewer Negroes registered than predicted. Both types of race organization thus seem to be related to Negro registration rates to a fairly sizable extent.

The partial distributions in the center of the table are even more revealing. A local Negro organization, rather than an NAACP chapter, seems to have the greater impact on Negro registration. Most of these local organizations are explicitly political in orientation, whereas NAACP chapters are often little more than fund-raising agencies. Forty-three per cent of the counties with such local organizations have had at least one Negro public official, either elective or appointed, in recent years, whereas only 13 per cent of the counties with only NAACP chapters have had one or more Negro public officials. Only 0.3 per cent of the counties with no known Negro organizations have had a Negro appointed or elected to public office.

Negro registration does not seem to be inhibited by the existence of white race organizations, except in the areas with no Negro organizations at all; then the dampening effect seems to be substantial—more than 10 percentage points. In areas where both Negroes and whites are organized, the Negro registration rate is actually higher than in counties where only the Negroes are organized along racial lines. Under these circumstances, the formation of a white counter-organization may indicate that the Negro organization is particularly active. And the creation of a white race organization may actually have a boomerang effect, drawing the Negroes closer together in their own organizations than they might otherwise have been. So far as this kind of analysis can tell, local Negro political organizations seem to thrive on competition, white organizations on its absence. We shall examine the structure and functions of Negro political organizations later;[25] at this point we can say that their presence helps to account for a fair share of the variation in Negro voter-registration rates in the contemporary South, even after we have controlled for social and economic factors.

## Racial violence and intimidation

The South has had a violent history. Before the Civil War much of the region was thinly settled frontier country in which vigilantism and a "hell-of-a-fella'" tradition flourished.[26] The region's "peculiar institution"—slavery—was, by definition, based on force. A bloody civil war, fought largely on southern soil, followed by an anarchistic period of Reconstruction, served to reinforce this tradition of violence. The subsequent reestablishment of white supremacy and the disfranchisement of the Negro were achieved primarily by force, threats, and intimidation.

Constitutional and legal devices—such as the grandfather clause, poll tax, white primary, and legally enforced racial separation in other realms of life—generally followed the *de facto* realization of racial segregation and served to reinforce, maintain, and legitimize the arrangement. Most of these constitutional and legal defenses have now crumbled, a few of them voluntarily abandoned by the white South and more of them as a result of Supreme Court decisions. But even in the absence of these "legal" and "constitutional" barriers, many southern Negroes are reluctant to exercise their newly reestablished franchise and to participate fully in the political life of the region. Some of these nonvoting Negroes are undoubtedly and understandably afraid of possible violence or economic reprisal from a hostile white community.

We might expect Negroes living in areas marked by unusual racial violence to be particularly reluctant to try to register and vote. Unfortunately, reliable and complete data on the incidence of racial violence in southern counties are hard to come by. Most compilations of such incidents are based on newspaper accounts, which are probably adequate for the larger cities but spotty in their coverage of rural areas. Such data are confined to overt acts and rarely deal with threats or the subtler forms of intimidation. We shall use two such compilations in this analysis: the Tuskegee Institute's records of lynchings in the South between 1900 and 1931, and the Southern Regional Council's listing of acts of violence occurring between 1955 and 1960 in the wake of *Brown* v. *Board of Education*.[27]

25 See Chapter Eight.
26 W. J. Cash, *The Mind of the South* (New York: Vintage, 1960), p. 52.
27 The Tuskegee data are reported, by county, in Charles S. Johnson (ed.), *Statistical Atlas of Southern Counties* (Chapel Hill, N.C.: University of North Carolina Press, 1941). The reports on racial violence, 1955–59, may be found in *Intimidation, Re-*

Racial violence in the South was rather different during these two periods. Lynching was most common ". . . in the newer and more sparsely settled portions of the South, where cultural and economic institutions [were] least stable and officers of the law [were] farthest apart, poorest paid, and most dependent upon local sentiment."[28] Victims were almost invariably Negro and the cause of the mob action was an alleged crime by an individual Negro against a white person. In 1930, for example, the alleged reasons for that year's 21 lynchings were: murder (5), rape (8), attempted rape (2), robbery or theft (3), and bombing a house (1). No crime at all was alleged in the case of two lynchings.[29]

The new-style racial violence since the *Brown* decision tends to occur in urban rather than rural areas (Figure 6–2). Most recent violence has been triggered by collective efforts by Negroes to take advantage of their newly found legal rights. The targets of white violence and destruction are frequently institutions—churches, schools, temples—but they include white people who are presumably sympathetic to the Negro cause. (Of the 29 persons reported shot and wounded in racial incidents between 1955 and 1960, 11 were white. All 6 fatalities, however, were Negro.[30]) Counties with high rates of lynching in the early decades of this century have not been the areas with the most spectacular incidents of racial violence in recent years.

TABLE 6–8.   *Mean percentage of voting-age Negroes registered to vote in southern counties, by amount of racial violence*

| LYNCHING RATE, 1900–31 | AMOUNT OF RACIAL VIOLENCE, 1955–60 | | |
|---|---|---|---|
| | *None* | *Some* | TOTAL |
| Low | 15% (576) | 29% (80) | 16% (656) |
| High | 27% (216) | 7% (16) | 25% (232) |
| TOTAL | 18% (792) | 26% (96) | |

NOTE: A "low" lynching rate is less than 10 lynchings per 100,000 population in 1930. The numbers in parentheses are the total number of counties on which the percentages are based.

Table 6–8 presents the mean percentage of the voting-age Negro population registered to vote in southern counties, according to the rate of lynchings in those counties from 1900 to 1931 and to the amount of racial violence reported to have occurred in them from 1955 to 1960. The very few counties with both

---

*prisal, and Violence in the South's Racial Crisis,* published jointly in 1960 by American Friends Service Committee, Southeastern Office, High Point, N.C.; National Council of Churches of Christ, Department of Racial and Cultural Relations, New York; and Southern Regional Council, Atlanta, Georgia.
[28] A. F. Raper, *The Tragedy of Lynching* (Chapel Hill, N.C.: University of North Carolina Press, 1933), p. 1.
[29] *Ibid.,* p. 4.
[30] *Intimidation, Reprisal, and Violence in the South's Racial Crisis,* p. 15.

a history of lynching *and* recent racial violence have low rates of Negro regis-tration—about 7 per cent. The group of southern counties with the next lowest Negro registration rates are those with generally peaceful race relations, and the highest rates of Negro registration are found in counties with either heavy lynching in the past or present-day racial incidents, but not both.

This same rank order of counties is maintained when we control for 21 socioeconomic variables by examining Negro voter-registration residuals (see Table 6–9). The counties with both high lynching and high contemporary racial violence scores have about 11 percentage points fewer Negroes registered to vote than we would expect on the basis of the social and economic charac-teristics of the counties. Those with either some contemporary racial violence or a history of lynching have about 2 or 3 percentage points more registered Negroes than anticipated, whereas the counties with little or no violence have about the expected rate.

Apparently, to speculate a bit, race violence nowadays must be extremely massive in order to have a depressing effect on Negro voter registration. Save

FIGURE 6–2.  *Percentage of counties with high racial violence,*
*by percentage urban, 1950*

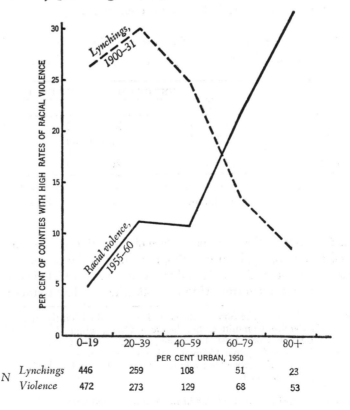

| | | 0–19 | 20–39 | 40–59 | 60–79 | 80+ |
|---|---|---|---|---|---|---|
| | | | | PER CENT URBAN, 1950 | | |
| N | Lynchings | 446 | 259 | 108 | 51 | 23 |
| | Violence | 472 | 273 | 129 | 68 | 53 |

TABLE 6-9. *Mean Negro voter-registration residuals of southern counties, by amount of racial violence*

| LYNCHING RATE, 1900–31 | AMOUNT OF RACIAL VIOLENCE, 1955–60 | | |
|---|---|---|---|
| | None | Some | TOTAL |
| Low | − 0.2 (575) | + 2.0 (80) | + 0.1 (655) |
| High | + 3.2 (216) | − 11.3 (16) | + 2.2 (232) |
| TOTAL | + 0.7 (791) | − 0.1 (96) | |

NOTE: A "low" lynching rate is less than 10 lynchings per 100,000 population in 1930. The numbers in parentheses are the total number of counties on which the percentages are based. No residual figure was obtained for one county in which the percentage of voting-age Negroes registered to vote was not known. Hence this table is based on one fewer case than is Table 6–8.

in the most violent 1 or 2 per cent of southern counties, racial violence seems to be more an indication of white weakness than of strength. Far lower rates of Negro registration are found in counties with little if any racial violence. Here Negro subordination may be so total that violence is not required to keep the Negro "in his place" and out of the polling booths. Racial violence, in itself, can be overestimated as an inhibition to Negro political participation. Save in a tiny fraction of southern counties, its effects, if any, seem to be to contribute to Negro militancy, solidarity, and political activity[31]—to say nothing of Justice Department investigations.

# The two souths

The 11 states of the old Confederacy have enough in common to make them America's most self-conscious region. Yet, without denying the distinctiveness of the South as a whole, every interpreter of the region discovers the "solid South" to be a fiction.

From time to time we have referred to the Deep South as different from the Peripheral South. The heart of the southern black belt and of the southern way of life is found in five contiguous states: Alabama, Georgia, Louisiana, Mississippi, and South Carolina. The six states of the Peripheral South— Arkansas, Florida, North Carolina, Tennessee, Texas, and Virginia—share memories of fellow membership in the Confederate States of America, but they are less distinctively southern. The average (mean) proportion of Negroes in the counties of the Deep South, for example, is 37 per cent, compared with 20 per cent for counties of the Peripheral South.

In political terms, too, the two subregions differ markedly; for example, the

[31] See Chapter Ten for a discussion of Negro *perceptions* of violence.

average county vote for the Dixiecratic candidate for president in 1948 was 57 per cent for Deep South counties but only 12 per cent for Peripheral South counties. The five states of the Deep South "seceded" from national preferences (along with Arizona) to vote for Barry Goldwater in 1964, while all six states of the Peripheral South stayed with the Union and L. B. J. These and other differences are sufficiently acute to justify a careful look at the two subregions.

In Chapter Three we discovered a peculiar bimodal distribution of southern Negroes along the Political-Participation Scale, with most falling either below or above the midpoint, in contrast to the normal distribution of southern whites. A bimodal distribution of this sort often indicates that two different populations have been combined in a single distribution. If we can identify the element that makes them different so that we can consider them as two groups, we may find that each forms a normal distribution, with each distribution concentrated toward a different end of the continuum. In other words, a bimodal distribution frequently conceals two underlying unimodal distributions. The South is recognized as the most distinctive and homogeneous political subculture in the United States, and opposition to political power for Negroes is one of its chief features. With these factors in mind, we attributed the peculiar (bimodal) pattern of political participation by southern Negroes to the extraordinary barriers to Negro voting thrown up in the South.

But the peculiar pattern of Negro participation in southern politics may be attributable to differences in the special subcultures of the Deep South and the Peripheral South. Plotting the distribution of participation separately for the Deep South and the Peripheral South, as in Figure 6–3, suggests important refinements in the interpretation. The bimodal distribution found for the entire South turns out to have resulted from the fantastically low levels of participation by Negroes of the Deep South. The political life of a majority of these Negroes (68 per cent) has never reached the level of voting; for most (53 per cent), the only form of political participation is in talking about public problems with their families or others in the community, and 15 per cent do not even talk about public problems. Most of the Deep South Negroes are thus concentrated toward the low end of the PPS.

Nevertheless, the distribution remains bimodal. Of those who have gone beyond mere talk, most have not stopped at voting but have also taken some part in campaigns or joined political groups. Six per cent have talked politics and voted without going further, whereas 19 per cent have also taken some part in campaigns and 7 per cent also belong to some political organization. Voting is more susceptible to discouragement by the political system of the Deep South than are other forms of participation. The interpretation advanced for the entire South thus appears to fit the Deep South particularly well.

The distribution of Negro participants in the Peripheral South is radically different. The unimodal form of the distribution resembles that of southern whites more than that of Deep South Negroes. A large majority (68 per cent) participate at the level of voting or beyond. The disappearance of the sharp dip at PPS Type III indicates that the Deep South's extreme inhibitions to Negro voting are not so potent in the Peripheral South. Negro participation falls far below that of whites even in the Peripheral South, but the inhibitions are not so severe as to produce the extreme picture of repression found for Deep South Negroes.

These findings support the conclusion that the political systems of the Deep South and the Peripheral South are functionally different for Negro participation. If the levels of participation by whites in the two subregions were also markedly different, our problem would be much broader. But no such contrast exists in levels of white participation. The two subregions differ only in regard to the political role of Negroes.

The personal characteristic most strongly related to variations in Negro participation is income. Therefore, the importance of political subregion for Negro political participation can be most severely tested by determining whether subregional differences remain when income is held constant. Table 6–10 demonstrates that, at every level of income, a greater percentage of Negroes in the Peripheral South than in the Deep South take part in politics. The higher rate of political participation by Negroes in the Peripheral South

FIGURE 6–3.   *Political Participation Scale types of southern Negroes, by subregion*

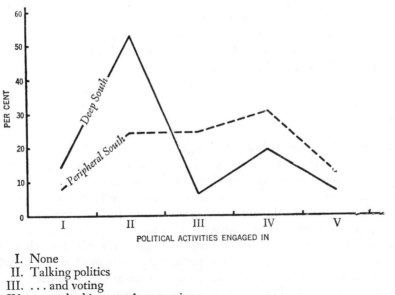

POLITICAL ACTIVITIES ENGAGED IN

    I. None
   II. Talking politics
  III. . . . and voting
   IV. . . . and taking part in campaigns
    V. . . . and holding office or belonging to political group.

TABLE 6–10.  *Negro political participation in the Deep South and Peripheral South, by level of income*

| FAMILY INCOME | PARTICIPATION BEYOND TALKING | | PARTICIPATION BEYOND VOTING | |
|---|---|---|---|---|
| | Deep South | Peripheral South | Deep South | Peripheral South |
| Below $1,000 | 33% | 56% | 28% | 30% |
| $1,000–2,999 | 28 | 57 | 23 | 39 |
| $3,000–4,999 | 33 | 82 | 21 | 50 |
| $5,000 + | 78 | 90 | 56 | 63 |

cannot be attributed simply to their better incomes, for even if the income levels of Negroes in both subregions were the same, sizable differences in participation would remain. Similar controls for other personal attributes (sex, age, education, occupation of respondent, and occupation of head of household) produce similar results.

We must add the political subregion in which a community is located to other political variables as an autonomous influence on Negro political participation. One community leader in Crayfish County mentioned to interviewers from the University of North Carolina that, "Up North where you fellas live, you've never had the problems we have down South." In the interest both of historical accuracy and of maintaining rapport, the interviewers hastened to explain that North Carolina had also been a part of the Confederacy. But perhaps the Crayfish resident was not so far wrong after all. From the perspective of the rest of the nation, the Peripheral South looks distinctively southern. From the perspective of Crayfish County, it looks almost as strange as the rest of the Union.

## Conclusions

The most important political and legal fact about the South is its division into 11 states. The counties of some states have far higher average rates of Negro voter registration than they "ought" to have on the basis of their social and economic characteristics, whereas others are far below the predicted levels. The range in the residuals between the highest and lowest states (Tennessee and Mississippi) amounts to almost 50 percentage points. No other political factor examined is nearly so significant. On the other hand, the meaning of these figures is not particularly clear until we probe salient features of the formal and informal political systems of the states.

Three such factors have a moderate relationship with Negro voter-registration rates: formal voter requirements (the range of residuals was 28.6

percentage points), state factional systems (24.4-percentage-point range), and the amount and kind of racial organization in the counties (21.9-percentage-point range). Two other political factors—the extent of partisan competition and the extent of racial violence in southern counties—have very small relationships with Negro voter-registration rates when we take into account the importance of social and economic factors.

In addition to these specific political factors, the inhibitions to Negro political participation that we have identified as peculiarly southern turn out to be most marked in the states of the Deep South. This subregion is so extreme that it is responsible for the basic distribution of Negro political participation that marks off the South so clearly from the rest of the United States. The Deep South and the Peripheral South can accordingly be described as different political subcultures.

The identification of different political cultures (or subcultures) is sometimes offered as an *explanation* of the differences implied by the concept. This makes political culture a most convenient residual variable—to it are attributed all differences that cannot otherwise be explained. We need not resort to such mysticism. The social, economic, and political factors inhibiting Negro political participation are simply much stronger in the Deep South than in the Peripheral South. Together they are strong enough to create a distinctiveness that does not disappear—under strict empirical testing—when socioeconomic variables are controlled. This distinctiveness may be labeled "political subculture," but the explanation of the distinctiveness must be in terms of the observable factors that make up the political subculture. In this chapter we have established the independent relationship of Negro political participation to formal voting requirements, state factional systems, and the amount and kind of county racial organizations. Partisan competition and racial violence are also components of southern political subcultures, but they contribute little to explaining Negro participation beyond what we can say on the basis of socioeconomic factors. Both the positive and the negative findings represent a start toward an *explanation* of behavior that is only *described* by talking about different political subcultures.

*Chapter Seven*

# Negro Leaders

As befits a social-studies teacher, Willy Clayton is one of the best-informed Negroes in Crayfish County, Mississippi. But when asked to name the "Negro leaders" in his community—"that is, people who have the most to say about the way things are run here"—his response was: "I can't think of anyone right now." Joe Barton, Tom Johnson, and George Hopkins experienced no difficulty in answering the same question. Each rattled off the names of well-known Negroes in Bright Leaf, Camellia, and Piedmont counties and then went on to tell our interviewer a little about the background and performance of each one. We suspect that Willy Clayton's response to the question was his typically guarded way of agreeing with one of his white neighbors who curtly dispensed with the same question about Negro leaders by saying: "There ain't none with any say."

A lack of competent Negro leadership is frequently cited as a major cause of Negro inactivity and impotence in southern politics. The development of able Negro leaders in local communities is widely thought to be a precondition for the attainment of political and social equality by the black masses of the region. Although our analysis of community social and political structure in the preceding chapters certainly does not "prove" this point, it does support the position with new and (at least to us!) persuasive evidence.

But so far our treatment of Negro leadership and its influence on mass participation has been based on gross characteristics of large aggregates of people. We have sought to present the "big picture" for the South as a whole. Of necessity, such large and abstract generalizations obscure the nuances and variety of political life. If local Negro leadership is as necessary as most students of the subject think it is, then a much more detailed examination of Negro leaders is in order. This is what we aim to provide in this chapter.

## Concepts of political leadership

Americans of all colors, regions, and persuasions have great faith in the efficacy of "leadership."[1] But social and political scientists are by no means agreed on who or what a "leader" is. Some of the most vitriolic arguments in the short history of these disciplines have raged over precisely this question. Some areas of agreement are gradually emerging from this conceptual chaos,[2] but the notion of leadership still remains treacherously vague and ambiguous.[3]

Perhaps the simplest and most straightforward way to view political leadership is to consider as political leaders only those persons in formal, governmental office. This "positional" approach of course ignores the fact that some nonofficeholders—the political "boss," the mayor's mistress, the mainstreet merchants, and so on—may have more influence over what the government does, and what it does not do, than the officials themselves. It overlooks, too, the fact that some public officials are more powerful and effective than others; even incumbents of the same position differ greatly in their influence.

Nonetheless, this approach to the study of political leadership has its value. No matter how much they may be influenced by others, no matter how little they actually initiate action, public officials must approve or acquiesce if communitywide plans and projects are to become legitimate and hence to stand a chance of being carried out. All public officials, according to this view, provide *at least* this modicum of political leadership. The authoritative and representative nature of governmental office provides incumbents with a political resource that no unofficial actor can possess.

In these terms very few southern communities can be said to have any Negro leadership. Only about 5 per cent of all southern counties had one or more Negroes in elective or appointive office from 1945 to 1960.[4] Negro officeholding is an almost exclusively urban phenomenon. Although the coefficient of correlation between the percentage of county population urban

[1] Gunnar Myrdal, *An American Dilemma* (New York: Harper & Brothers, 1944), ch. 33.

[2] See C. A. Gibb, "Leadership," ch. 24 in G. Lindzey (ed.), *Handbook of Social Psychology* (Cambridge, Mass.: Addison-Wesley Publishing Co., 1954), Vol. 2, pp. 877–920; W. Bell, R. J. Hill, and C. R. Wright, *Public Leadership* (San Francisco: Chandler Publishing Co., 1961); S. Verba, *Small Groups and Political Behavior: A Study of Leadership* (Princeton, N.J.: Princeton University Press, 1961); N. W. Polsby, *Community Power and Political Theory* (New Haven, Conn.: Yale University Press, 1963).

[3] This very lack of precision undoubtedly contributes to the utility of the concept in popular discourse, the "good guys" are "leaders," the "bad guys" are not.

[4] No complete listing of Negro public officials exists. We therefore sought to compile our own by consulting the *New York Times Index*, January 1945–February 1961, and the Southern Educational Reporting Service, "Facts on Film," Rolls 1–40 (May 1954–June 1958), first supplement, Rolls 1–13 (July 1958–June 1959), second supplement, Rolls 1–11 (July 1959–June 1960).

and the presence or absence of Negro public officials is only +.24, this seems to be the result of crudities in the census measure of "urban-ness" and of the fact that an urban setting is a necessary but not a sufficient condition for the emergence of this type of Negro leadership. Almost all communities in which Negroes serve as public officials are cities, but Negro officials emerge in only a small proportion of them.

Obviously, other factors help explain the success of Negroes in winning public offices. At first glance Negro concentration does not seem to be one of these—its correlation with Negro officeholding is only +.03. A more detailed examination shows that Negroes fail to win office *both* in counties where heavy concentrations of Negroes rouse white fears and repression *and* in areas with too few Negroes to give Negro candidates adequate support. This leaves a middle range of counties (having about 20 to 40 per cent Negro concentrations) with enough Negroes to give Negro candidates a meaningful bloc of votes but not so many as to stir whites to active countermeasures. Even under these most favorable of circumstances, less than 10 per cent of the counties could claim a Negro public official during the 15-year period we studied.

Further examination of the counties with Negro public officials suggests still other factors favorable to Negro officeholding: counties with Negro officials tend to be found in the Peripheral South, and to have electoral systems in which some public officials are chosen from relatively small geographical districts which roughly correspond to the boundaries of their Negro ghettos.[5] Thus, although the community preconditions for Negro officeholding are somewhat similar to those that encourage Negro voting, they are by no means identical.

Negro officeholding is so rare in the South that it is not a very satisfactory measure of Negro political leadership. So few Negroes qualify as "leaders" by this criterion that one is left with the misleading impression that southern Negroes are, save in a tiny fraction of communities, a leaderless mob.

Recognizing the lack of perfect congruity between officeholding and the actual exercise of influence, a number of researchers have identified leaders by means of a detailed examination of decision-making processes.[6] This is a fruitful approach but hardly feasible for a study in which leadership is only one facet of a larger problem. Even if this "policy-influence" approach had been physically and financially possible for this study, it would probably have suffered—like the positional approach—from the defect of being too restrictive.

[5] The statement about electoral systems and their relationship to residential patterns is based on our own community studies and knowledge of the counties in which Negro interviews were conducted. We do not, of course, have such detailed information about all southern counties.

[6] For the leading example of this approach, see R. A. Dahl, *Who Governs?* (New Haven, Conn.: Yale University Press, 1961).

Even in the large metropolitan areas of the South, few Negroes have been able to influence general public policy.[7]

In most southern communities, then, no Negro leaders can be found through either the positional or the policy-influence approach. Negroes neither hold office nor have a relatively great or direct influence on those who do hold office. Nevertheless, most Negroes in these communities *think* that they have leaders. And they are undoubtedly correct, for some leaders, by almost any definition of the term, are found in all groups.[8] The difficulty is that most Negro leaders in the South are influential only in the Negro subcommunity; they are denied both office and direct or substantial influence in the broader community. The criteria that have been most successfully applied in other studies are thus too demanding for this special population.

In view of these special difficulties, *we shall regard those people most frequently thought of as leaders by Negro citizens as being their leaders.*[9] Granted the reciprocal nature of leadership—in which the follower is as essential as the leader[10]—this appears the most satisfactory way of identifying a group of people who may be called Negro leaders in the South. Most of the people so designated do not hold public office and their influence over community decisions ranges from strongly negative to mildly positive. Nevertheless, they are the only "leaders" the Negroes have.

The only way to get more than superficial information on those Negro leaders is to talk to them. Even in the four community-study sites, the task of locating and interviewing everyone mentioned as a leader would have been virtually impossible. For purposes of comparison, we therefore attempted instead to interview the 10 Negroes most frequently named by all the citizens who were interviewed in the county.[11] Ties for tenth place occurred in Crayfish and Bright Leaf counties, and in these cases the cutoff point was adjusted

---

[7] Daniel C. Thompson, *The Negro Leadership Class* (Englewood Cliffs, N.J.: Prentice-Hall, 1963). Professor Thompson defines Negro leaders as those who try to influence policy, regardless of their actual influence: "The leader is one who for some period of time identifies overtly with the Negro's effort to achieve stated goals" (p. 5). Professor Thompson's study is of New Orleans, one of the more "liberal" cities in the South.

[8] See C. A. Gibb, *op. cit.*

[9] A more rigorous approach might be to identify as leaders those Negroes who exercise relatively great and direct influence over the decisions of the Negro community. But the "Negro community" and its "decisions" are neither official nor precisely identifiable.

[10] See Harold D. Lasswell and Abraham Kaplan, *Power and Society* (New Haven, Conn.: Yale University Press, 1950), p. 152.

[11] Both white and Negro nominations were counted for this purpose, with nominations weighted to give each race an influence equal to its proportion of the total population. In actual practice this procedure produced virtually the same group of "top" leaders as the use of Negro nominations only. It made one change in the Piedmont group (the man dropped was tenth on the Negro list and the man added was eleventh on the Negro list). It made no change in the Camellia group. It made one change in the Bright Leaf group (the man added was twelfth and the man dropped was in a five-way tie for ninth place on the Negro list). It made two additions to the Crayfish list (from seven men tied for twelfth place on the Negro list).

to the nearest breaking point (the number closest to ten). As a result, 11 "leaders" were selected from Bright Leaf and 12 from Crayfish. All the leaders selected in this manner were interviewed in Piedmont and Bright Leaf counties, 9 in Camellia, and 7 in Crayfish.[12]

We shall not put the word "leader" in quotation marks hereafter, but the crude operational definition of the term we are using here must not be forgotten. If "real" leaders are those with relatively direct and great influence on community decisions, only Piedmont County has any "real" Negro leaders, and even there they would not number as many as ten. If "real" Negro leaders are those who play a major role in decisions within the Negro community and in interracial contacts, then most of those on our lists are probably real leaders.[13]

But in no event should those named be regarded as making up the complete leadership structure of their community. In the first place, the selection of ten rather than more or fewer leaders was largely arbitrary, based on the fact that the number of nominations began to be small beyond that point and on the difficulty of locating and interviewing a larger number in each county. Theoretically, we might as logically have selected six or thirty leaders. Moreover, an increasing body of evidence suggests that a number of different power structures exist in the same community and that the overlap is not so great as is popularly believed.[14] Negro communities in the South may well have a more generalized leadership structure than does a city like New Haven, Connecticut, but this is a matter to be investigated, not assumed.

We were concerned with getting a more or less representative sample of Negro leaders, not with trying to discover the identity of all Negro leaders. If we had interviewed a different sample of citizens in each of these counties, we would probably not have come up with just the same set of leaders, especially in Bright Leaf and Crayfish, where "neighborhood notables" tend to be named. But we are confident that we would have come up with the names of similar kinds of people—that is, with a rough sample of those Negroes who were perceived as leaders.

[12] The poor response rate in Crayfish stemmed from miserable roads and little-known and virtually inaccessible leaders. In view of the great homogeneity of attitudes in Crayfish, a poor response rate there is less disturbing than it would have been in the other counties.

[13] Robert E. Agger and Daniel Goldrich found similar results from the two most common techniques for identifying leaders—participant observation, and nomination by a sample of the community's population. See "Community Power Structure and Partisanship," *American Sociological Review*, Vol. 23 (1958), pp. 383–92.

[14] See, for example, Nelson W. Polsby, "Three Problems in the Analysis of Community Power," *American Sociological Review*, Vol. 24 (1959), pp. 796–803; Benjamin Walter, "Political Decision-Making in North Carolina Cities," *PROD*, Vol. 3 (1960), pp. 18–21; and Dahl, *op cit.* A seminal study that presents a contrary view—and inspired much of the subsequent research in this field—is Floyd Hunter, *Community Power Structure* (Chapel Hill, N.C.: University of North Carolina Press, 1953).

## The social bases of leadership recruitment

Like national leaders,[15] Negroes named as community leaders in the South are a highly atypical group. Only 9 per cent of all the nominations go to women, for example, although they constitute a majority of the adult Negro population of the South.[16] When we couple this finding with the lower rate of mass participation by women than by men, we find that long-accepted notions about the peculiarly matriarchical character of the Negro subculture are again cast in doubt, at least in the political realm. But, then, matriarchy is said to be a characteristic only of working-class Negroes, and the occupations of those named as leaders indicate that they are overwhelmingly middle-class.

As Table 7–1 shows, a third of all references to Negro leaders in the South are to preachers or ministers, who far outstrip any other occupation in frequency of nomination. We can explain the preeminence of preachers among Negro leaders in a number of ways. In the first place they constitute one of the few professions that include Negro members in almost every southern community. Where potential leaders are extremely scarce, the mantle of leadership may fall to local preachers by default. Southerners are churchgoing people, and the church offers the only public gathering in which many Negro southerners find Negro points of view openly advocated.

The Negro minister is highly visible, then, and his professional role requires him to serve as a spokesman within the Negro community. The forensic and organizational skills developed in that role also equip Negro ministers to serve as spokesmen to the white community. Moreover, because they are not directly dependent on whites for their income as most southern Negroes are, any propensity to serve as an interracial spokesman is not inhibited by economic constraints. Indeed, the fact that he is "of the cloth" may ensure the Negro minister a modicum of respect, however condescending, from local whites.

Negro ministers differ greatly in their leadership roles. At one extreme is the part-time Methodist preacher in Crayfish County, who boasts that he is the only Negro ever permitted to attend the white Methodist church, a privilege that extends to the last pew on those Sundays when the bishop appears in Breedville. At another extreme is the Capital City grocer turned part-time preacher whose home and store were shot at by whites during his leadership of the local bus boycott. A different extreme along another di-

[15] D. R. Matthews, *The Social Background of Political Decision-Makers* (Garden City, N.Y.: Doubleday and Co., 1954).

[16] This finding contrasts sharply with that of Barth and Abu-Laban, who found 44 per cent of a Negro subcommunity power structure to be female. See Ernest A. T. Barth and Baha Abu-Laban, "Power Structure and the Negro Sub-Community," *American Sociological Review*, Vol. 24 (1959), pp. 69–76. It is supported, however, by Thompson, *op. cit.*, pp. 25–26.

TABLE 7–1.   *Occupational distribution of Negro leadership nominations in the South and in four community-study sites*

| Occupations of persons named as leaders | Crayfish County | Bright Leaf County | Camellia County | Piedmont County | Entire South |
|---|---|---|---|---|---|
| Preacher, minister | 8% | 10% | 63% | 12% | 34% |
| Lawyer | 0 | 15 | 0 | 7 | 6 |
| Doctor | 0 | 6 | 2 | 1 | 3 |
| College professor | 0 | 0 | 0 | 0 | 1 |
| Teacher, principal | 40 | 11 | 4 | 0 | 12 |
| College administrator | 0 | 0 | 8 | 2 | 3 |
| County agent | 0 | 4 | 0 | 0 | 1 |
| Business proprietor (general) | 4 | 20 | 18 | 1 | 11 |
| Mortician, funeral director | 3 | 6 | 2 | 1 | 9 |
| Banker, realtor, insurance | 0 | 11 | 0 | 65 | 3 |
| Farmer | 56 | 9 | 3 | 0 | 11 |
| TOTAL NOMINATIONS | 107 | 140 | 190 | 179 | 1,219 |

NOTE: Percentages do not total to 100 because some occupations were not ascertained and because some nominees have more than one occupation—farmer and preacher, for example.

mension is the Urbania minister with formal theological training who is active in the civil rights movement. Their claims to leadership differ with their personalities, with the nature of their training and of their congregations, and with the kinds of community in which they live. But preachers are the most obvious source of such leadership as Negroes have in most southern communities.

No other single occupational group receives anything close to the number of leadership nominations given to preachers. Granted the small number of Negro lawyers, doctors, and college professors in the South, however, the fact that these three professions receive 10 per cent of all nominations is impressive. Whereas many of the preachers in the South have simply "felt the call" and launched their careers without benefit of formal training, other professionals have had the benefit of formal training beyond the college level. Both the training and the job experience of lawyers develop political skills, and lawyers receive more nominations than doctors and college professors. Lawyers and doctors depend on a Negro clientele for their livelihood, and college professors enjoy some protection from local whites by virtue of job tenure and the sometimes fragile right of academic freedom.[17] For these professionals, political leadership does not mean loss of a job.

[17] Just how fragile academic freedom can be in the midst of racial crisis is suggested by C. Vann Woodward, "Unreported Crisis in the Southern Colleges," *Harper's* (October 1962), pp. 82–84.

Since schoolteachers represent the largest group of highly educated Negro professionals in the South, they might be expected to constitute the major base of Negro leadership. In most southern communities, however, they are extremely vulnerable to white pressures.[18] Despite their large numbers and unusual skills, they receive only 12 per cent of the Negro leadership nominations. A young housewife in rural Alabama explained why: "I just don't know no colored folks who do much leading around here," she said. "We got some teachers, but since Mr. White [a former Negro teacher] lost his job they don't have nothing to say about nothing."

Considered as a group, Negro businessmen are second only to preachers in being viewed as leaders by their fellow citizens, receiving almost a quarter of all nominations. Most Negro businessmen in the South operate on a small scale with scant profits—the fly-specked store with a privy out back is more typical than the glass-and-chrome store with employees' lounges. Nevertheless, whatever their varied training and skills, Negro businessmen get most of their income from other Negroes rather than from whites. Morticians and funeral directors are presented separately in Table 7–1 because death invokes a segregated set of activities in the South, requiring a Negro mortician in virtually every community. The southern way of death—in which whites will not embalm Negroes—guarantees Negro morticians an income that does not depend on white patronage, and they appear to have taken advantage of their position to offer services to the quick as well as to the dead. Despite the fact that teachers far outnumber morticians in the region, morticians receive almost the same number of leadership nominations.

Farmers seem to be regarded as leaders only where no more effective leaders can be found. They do not necessarily lack the skills necessary for effective leadership, but nothing in their occupation contributes positively to the development of such skills. On the contrary, farmers lead relatively isolated lives with little chance to develop broad contacts throughout the community. If these people are leaders at all, they are probably leaders of a rural neighborhood rather than of the community in a broader sense. Even so, farmers are mentioned in 11 per cent of the references to Negro leaders.

The poverty of leadership in Crayfish County is suggested by the fact that farmers are named in a majority of all Crayfish references to Negro leaders. Moreover, the proportion of "single-shot" leadership nominations in the county —nominations given to individuals who are named by no one else in the sample—is extraordinarily high. In Crayfish, 45 per cent of the people mentioned as leaders are named only once, compared with 29 per cent in Bright Leaf, 19 per cent in Camellia, and 6 per cent in Piedmont. The generality

18 For a report on the most vulnerable group of all, see James W. Prothro and Lewis Lipsitz, "Voting Rights of Negro Teachers in Four Mississippi Counties," Hearings before the U.S. Commission on Civil Rights, *Voting*, Vol. 1 (Washington, D.C.: U.S. Government Printing Office), held in Jackson, Mississippi, February 16–20, 1965, Exhibit 9, pp. 242–55.

and the clarity of perceived Negro leadership thus vary substantially and systematically from one county to the next.

Crayfish differs from the other counties not only in its heavy reliance on farmers for "leadership" but in its reliance on schoolteachers and principals. In view of the heavy restrictions on Negro teachers, the frequency with which teachers are named seems to reflect their status rather than their activities. The white lady who responded to the invitation to name Negro community leaders by saying, "There ain't none with any say," was probably correct.

Bright Leaf County is closer to the southwide pattern in the occupational distribution of its leadership nominations. It is like Crayfish, however, in giving a relatively small proportion of leadership nominations to preachers. In Crayfish the reason is that no Negro church has a full-time pastor. Except for itinerant preachers who conduct services once a month, the Negro ministry in Crayfish is made up of farmers or teachers who are only part-time preachers. Bright Leaf County has full-time ministers, but they have not led their parishioners in any militant demands for Negro rights. The white leaders of Bright Leaf have generally been paternalistic rather than harshly repressive, and Negroes have been content to bargain for bread-and-butter needs. Businessmen, lawyers, and doctors receive most of the leadership nominations in this setting.

Mass demonstrations and arrests have marked the race relations of Capital City, and preachers have furnished the most militant leadership. Organizational and inspirational rallies in support of the civil rights movement are held in the Negro churches, with the minister presiding, and the movement is imbued with revivalistic fervor. As a result, preachers overshadow every other group in Camellia County, receiving 63 per cent of all leadership nominations. The next largest number of nominations goes to businessmen, but most of these are accounted for by a grocer who is also a preacher, working in close collaboration with a Baptist minister who is the most widely acclaimed leader in the county. These two Baptists and the leading Methodist minister have been the principal organizers of boycotts, sit-ins, and demonstrations. Together they are mentioned in 46 per cent of all Camellia references to Negro leaders. When we note that the three most frequently named leaders in Crayfish receive 16 per cent, and in Bright Leaf 24 per cent, of all nominations, the concentration of nominations in Camellia is striking.

The Negro citizens of Piedmont County, however, are in even greater agreement than those of Camellia County on their top three leaders. Three business leaders—a bank president, an insurance company president, and an official of the insurance company—receive 56 per cent of all Piedmont references to Negro leaders. The leaders of these major financial institutions so far outrank other Urbania leaders that little room is left for the recognition of people in other occupations. Contrary to Frazier's argument that bourgeois Negroes withdraw from identification with the Negro masses,[19] Urbania's wealthy Negroes actively champion the goals of Urbania's Negro community. Although the bank president could have sent his children to a private school, for example, the court suit that brought about the desegregation of Urbania's school system was brought in the name of his child. One of Urbania's Negro leaders has been repeatedly elected to the city council and others have served in a variety of party and governmental positions, from the local to the national level. At least in Piedmont County, then, we would find a few Negroes who could be called leaders whether we employed the positional, policy-influence, or reputational approach.

In age, the most frequently named leaders in the communities we studied in detail are fairly similar to leaders identified in other community studies, with mean ages ranging from 51 in Camellia to 61 in Bright Leaf and Crayfish.[20] Taking the the mid-fifties as the dividing point between young and old leaders, Piedmont and Bright Leaf have almost equal numbers of young and old leaders, whereas Camellia and Crayfish are marked by an imbalance in the age distribution of their leaders. Seven of the nine most frequently named leaders in Camellia are young, compared with two out of seven in Crayfish. Recent racial protests in Camellia appear to have produced a new style of militant interracial contact in which the old leaders are less adept. Crayfish, on the other hand, has had no organized racial protests. The potential leaders among the young people tend to migrate, and the most visible Negro leaders are those whose status has made them the accustomed gatekeepers to the white community in a totally segregated system. These are people who have adjusted well to white dominance.

The educational level of Negro leaders in the two urban counties is quite high. All the leaders in Piedmont and all except two in Camellia have had some college education. Moreover, seven of the leaders in Piedmont and four in Camellia have pursued professional or academic work beyond the B.A. at nationally recognized universities, including Columbia, Harvard, Northwestern, Howard, Temple, North Carolina, Michigan, and Ohio State. Five of the Crayfish leaders have had some college training, but they all attended Negro colleges in Mississippi and only one received graduate training. The difficulty this man has with reading and writing suggests that the quality of training in Mississippi's Negro colleges is shockingly poor. Bright Leaf presents the greatest educational differences among Negro leaders: seven have had college training but four have a fourth-grade education or less, and two of these are functional illiterates.

---

[19] E. Franklin Frazier, *Black Bourgeoisie: The Rise of a New Middle Class in the United States* (Glencoe, Ill.: The Free Press, 1957).

[20] Our descriptions of the occupational and sex distributions of perceived leaders were based on data collected in our southwide sample survey. For attributes like age, on which we do not have data for the entire South, we shift to an exclusive reliance on interviews with the nominated leaders in the four community-study areas.

The poor education of leaders in the rural counties is accompanied by lack of geographical mobility and experience in other communities. Almost half of the leaders in the two rural counties have lived in those counties all their lives, as compared with a third in Camellia and none in Piedmont. The situation is particularly acute in Crayfish County, which loses potential leaders to other areas and attracts none from outside the state.

This brief picture of the social backgrounds of Negro leaders suggests several generalizations about the recruitment of Negro leadership in the South and the effects of different community structures on the process.

Like most other groups, southern Negroes look to those with relatively high prestige and status for leadership.[21] Perhaps 80 per cent of the Negroes nominated as leaders by our southwide sample hold white-collar jobs. A large majority of the leaders interviewed in Piedmont and Camellia counties were college graduates. Even in the two rural counties, the educational attainments of those looked to for leadership are extraordinary by local standards. The number of Negroes with these symbols of status—even in a community like Piedmont—is a small fraction of those found among whites; in rural communities, the number of Negroes with these qualifications is literally a handful. The socially defined base of political leadership for the Negro community is thus perilously small.

A second and equally important criterion narrows the choice of Negro leaders even further. The rank and file look to those members of the race who enjoy relative economic independence from whites for leadership, whenever they can be found. In Piedmont County, for example, 9 of the 10 leaders interviewed were relatively independent of local whites for their income; in Camellia, 6 out of 9; in Bright Leaf, 10 out of 11. Only in Crayfish County were a majority (4 out of 7) of the leaders interviewed highly vulnerable to pressures from white employers, and here the local Negroes had no other choice—almost no Crayfish Negroes enjoy freedom from white control.

Despite substantial and intriguing differences in detail from one community to the next (to which we shall return), *all* the leaders interviewed in Piedmont, Camellia, and Bright Leaf counties possessed either high status or economic independence from whites, and half of them possessed both. Only in Crayfish did we find any (2 out of 7) low-status, economically vulnerable Negroes among the leaders. Not one of Crayfish's most visible Negro spokesmen enjoyed both high occupational or educational status and relative invulnerability from white economic pressures. Some of the consequences of these and other community differences in Negro leadership recruitment will become apparent in the following section, as we shift attention from who the leaders are to how they behave and what they want.

21 Matthews, *op. cit.*, pp. 56–57.

## Leadership styles

In the traditional South the Negro leader is an essential but pathetic figure. He is "functional" because segregated communities cannot be maintained without some authoritative communication between the dominant and the subordinate populations. He is pitiful because all too often he cannot command the respect and confidence of the white leaders and at the same time retain that of the Negro masses. His source of influence in dealing with whites is not the power of his followers (which is virtually nonexistent), but the fact that ". . . in order to remain serviceable to the white community" he has to "maintain prestige among Negroes."[22] And this requires that he demonstrate some influence among the whites.

Thus the Negro leader's personal integrity and prestige are constantly at issue. Misperceptions or miscalculations by him or his white benefactors may cost him both, despite the best of intentions. And his intentions are not always the best: the near-monopoly of rewards controlled by the whites, plus habits instilled by the traditional leader's supine approach to his white sponsors, lead to frequent "sellouts." In Crayfish County, this is the only kind of Negro leadership that exists. The traditional "gatekeepers" still reign (but do not rule) supreme.

The typical Crayfish County leader takes much pride and satisfaction from his contact with whites and tends to confuse this contact with influence. One leader, a retired schoolteacher, says:

> I've built both of the [Negro] schools . . . yessir, I shine in asking the white folks to build these two schools. White people are very nice . . . very accommodating. They're helping me now to raise money for the church. And they are nice in helping me personally.

The elderly Negro undertaker reports "very cordial" relations with the white community and says "I talk with influential whites who recognize me as the spokesman for Breedville Negroes." A schoolteacher says that "whites confer with me and Negroes agree that I am a leader." That his fellow teacher, Willy Clayton, does not agree that he is a leader is, no doubt, of little importance to him. His kind of leadership depends first and foremost on his acceptance by influential whites.

The activities of Crayfish's traditional-style leaders are highly circumspect. The most they feel they can do is to encourage influential whites to help less fortunate Negroes (usually individuals but sometimes small groups) within the system of white dominance. The owner of a general store reports that he has "made loans and put up bail to get people released from jail" and that he has gotten "highway people out to grade roads." The mortician

[22] Thompson, op. cit., p. 63.

is still trying to get "fire plugs in the Negro community" of Breedville. Such efforts are the sum of civic action by Negro leaders in Crayfish. The leaders provide no challenge to the system of segregation; they try to bring about no major changes in the status of all Negroes. The retired school principal is reasonably frank about the limits of his leadership. "I have never done anything like speaking up for colored people," he says, "though I would if called on." So far he has heard no call—which is difficult to understand in view of the bitterness of the Crayfish Negroes. The elderly undertaker is more evasive about his lack of militancy. When asked by the lady reporter of the *Breedville Times* for his views on the integration problem, he replied, "That's my least worry, Miss."

Although Crayfish's Negro leaders are content with their own performance as leaders, they are extremely critical of one another. The two most favorable comments the seven leaders made about others were: "The other leaders are all right, as far as I know," and "They are fair—[I'm] not too certain about all of them." The second of these statements was made by a 73-year-old farmer, barely literate, who feels that the Negroes' life in Crayfish is "pretty fair" and that "Negroes may talk too much about race matters and rights." The most knowledgeable leader decribed his fellow notables as "semiliterate and not too courageous." The most common rating was the laconic "very poor."

Negro leadership in Crayfish is in no sense united. Not only do the leaders have little respect for one another; they do not even try to cooperate. This is, no doubt, partly the result of the ecology of Crayfish life: the county consists of many scattered hamlets, and the single town contains but a fraction of the total Negro population. But it is also partly a result of the nature of traditional Negro leadership. Each Negro leader has one or a few white sponsors, and this personal relationship is his main political resource. The pull of these "vertical" relationships with white notables is so strong that "horizontal" ties with other leaders are difficult to develop. Each traditional leader is an individual entrepreneur: he acts neither in concert nor in competition with other leaders. In truth, he hardly acts at all.

Bright Leaf County, on the other hand, is in a stage of transition; the traditional leaders are still there, but they have been joined by a different type altogether. Negroes are voting in Bright Leaf, and in increasing numbers. Some leaders have emerged on the basis of control over political resources—primarily votes—rather than on the basis of indispensability to the white leaders. As the political participation and power of Negroes increase, the leader's dependence on access to whites declines and his relationship to the Negro community becomes more central. This type of leadership, which for lack of a better name we shall call "moderate," still bears some similarities to the older style. Like the traditional leader, the moderate tends to be concerned with specific, concrete, and limited welfare-type objectives, but he is concerned with achieving these objectives for the entire Negro community and not just for a lucky few. His basic mode of operation is bargaining with whites, and the game is usually a very uneven one. But there are also important differences—the moderate leaders are not the white man's choice; they have emerged from and are responsive to the Negro community. They deal from a position of far greater strength than do the old-style leaders.

For example, when some of the younger Negroes of Farmington threatened to demonstrate against a drugstore because they could not get service at its lunch counter, the chief of police persuaded the store owner to institute "vertical integration." The stools at the lunch counter were removed, and both Negroes and whites are now served standing up. The Negro leaders of Bright Leaf were satisfied with this concession and chose not to complain that Negroes still could not sit down to eat in the company of whites. Most of the leaders in Piedmont or Camellia counties would not have accepted such a small concession. In fact, most public facilities in Urbania—whether privately or publicly owned—had been integrated well before the 1964 Civil Rights Act was passed.

At the same time, Bright Leaf's moderate-style leaders are far from being traditional "Uncle Toms." Whereas the mortician in Crayfish claims to have talked with influential whites to get fire protection for Negro houses, his counterpart in Bright Leaf is an active member of a Negro voters' league, contributes to the NAACP for the fight against segregation, and gives money to support registration and voting campaigns. These activities have an authentic ring of leadership, and they are typical of the responses of Bright Leaf leaders.

Efforts to increase Negro registration and voting seem to be the most common route to leadership in Bright Leaf; 9 of the 11 leaders who were interviewed mentioned that they took part in this effort. They also mentioned a number of other common activities—working for better school facilities, a playground and recreation progam, extended sewage facilities, better streets, and more employment for Negroes. All these activities seem to go together; eight of the leaders, for example, referred specifically to the effort to get a recreation center for Negroes as one of their claims to leadership. Leadership in Bright Leaf seems to rest on active involvement in a battery of efforts to improve the general lot of Negroes.

Although Negroes in Bright Leaf enjoy few advantages of income, education, and occupation over those in Crayfish, their leaders have much greater élan. The general feeling is that they have made significant progress since the Second World War. An elderly businessman who has lived through this change explained, "In politics, recently, Negro leaders have been effective. They have been able to secure commitments from candidates running for public office. The leadership is improving because of the younger group; before now it has not been too good." A young attorney sounds the same note of restrained optimism: "Because of increased registering and voting, Negro leaders have been effective in securing paved streets, better schools, and promises for improvements. Negro pressure on whites running for office is bringing about change. The quality of leadership leaves much to be desired, but it is improving." A real estate and insurance man who in the late 1950's was the first Negro candidate for public office in Bright Leaf since the turn of the century observed: "Now there is some unity and cohesion among Negro leaders."

Our informants were virtually unanimous in attributing these changes for the better to the rise to leadership of younger, better-educated men who enjoy relative independence from the whites—a lawyer, a doctor, and several younger businessmen. This is still a transitional stage, for, along with these well-trained younger men, the perceived Negro leaders include several semiliterate older men. But even they enjoy relative economic independence—at least compared to their counterparts in Crayfish.

Still a third style of Negro leadership has come into being in recent years— a leadership that is militantly concerned with symbolic "status" goals and prefers mass protest and civil disobedience over access to whites and political accommodation. The militant leader's base of power is his ability to sway the Negro masses and to symbolize their discontent; his relationships with white leaders are strained or nonexistent. As Wilson writes:

> It is often the case that the militant is at the greatest social distance from the influential whites who affect the course of events in the city most directly and surely. This is usually true either because the protester lacks status, or is considered to be "too radical," or occasionally because of a process of self-exile whereby he chooses not to approach, even up to the limits set for him, the larger community's influential persons.
>
> One of the immediate consequences of this distance from white decision-makers . . . is that the Negro protest leader sees the white "power structure" as an undifferentiated bloc of corporate and political leaders who act largely in unison toward agreed goals out of essentially identical motives. These goals, of course, are seen to be contrary to the interests of the Negroes. . . .
>
> Often, this perceived solidarity in the white leadership of the city proceeds to the point where it ceases being merely a unity and becomes instead a conspiracy.[23]

The militant leader speaks the language of combat. He is uninterested in, and very largely incapable of, compromise. Indeed, he owes his position as leader to disenchantment with the limited victories and gradualism of the moderates.

This style of leadership is most pronounced in Camellia County, where mass protests came early and resulted in the almost total rout of the college-based, moderate leaders by the militants. The most powerful Negroes in the county today all came into prominence as leaders of the bus boycott of the late 1950's. Almost all of them are young preachers with impressive oratorical and

[23] James Q. Wilson, *Negro Politics: The Search for Leadership* (Glencoe, Ill.: copyright © 1960 by The Free Press), pp. 226–27, reprinted by permission of the publisher. The entire discussion of leadership styles presented here is heavily influenced by this seminal work.

agitational abilities, if little or no theological training. Their program is simple and entirely unqualified. As one of them put it: "Segregation must go!" Implicit in this statement was another word: "Now!"

But even in Camellia a small legacy of moderate leadership still centers around the Negro college president and the football coach, who has a miraculous ability to build winning teams if no more stomach for racial controversy than his boss in the administration building on campus. The reluctance of these men to assume a militant posture is understandable—a public institution located in the state capital, the college is extremely vulnerable to political retaliation. Yet resentment of their unwillingness to assume militant leadership runs deep and is reinforced by class conflict within the Negro community. "The college crowd," according to Tom Johnson, enjoys a "cushion seat." A working-class respondent, after reluctantly naming the college president as a leader, added, by way of explanation: "He's got the position even if he ain't done nothing."

The result is that Negro leadership in Camellia County is fraught with bitter internal strife. "There is rivalry and jealousy," mused the college president, for the moment a thoroughly "academic" man. "A new type of leadership is evolving and no one gives up leadership willingly, even if he is old." The Baptist minister, who emerged from the bus boycott as the most popular leader in the county, thinks: "There is a lot of room for improvement [in the caliber of Camellia's Negro leadership]. Our leaders need to be more greatly committed to civic and community action. So many people who make good leaders are limited by jobs and contracts, such as college professors and schoolteachers. . . ." "No cohesion," one of the moderate leaders said. "Too much desire for self-recognition—no genuine concern for the people." From a different vantage point, one of the most popular leaders reached the same conclusion: "There is a great competition; 40 per cent of the leaders are straining for the 'top spot.' There is considerable envy and jealousy." The impressive fact about the Camellia comments is that *every leader* stressed dissension; the only difference is that the older leaders attributed dissension to demagoguery, and the newer leaders attributed it to competition. A leader near the "top spot" referred to both attributes: "There is jealousy between present and past leaders. There is also competition and envy among present leaders."

Militant "race men" are active in Piedmont County, too, but there the entrenched moderate-style leaders drawn from Urbania's large business community were flexible enough to adopt some of the militants' stance and rhetoric and to coopt many of them into their organization. Piedmont's Negro leaders are now more concerned with "status" goals and symbolic victories than they were a few years ago. Their demands are more insistent and extreme. This shift in style has certainly made their relationships with the white community and its leaders more difficult. But bargaining, compromise, and conciliation are still possible. Well-to-do businessmen and professional politicians make poor revolutionaries; such men still lead Urbania's Negro community. They are, as a group, characterized by self-confidence and high morale ("progress is exceptionally good"), mutual esteem ("Urbania has a very high quality of Negro leadership, probably the highest . . . in America"), cohesion, and continuity.

## Leadership goals

Negro leaders in southern communities have one basic aspiration: to promote better race relations. We asked each of the leaders to rate the race relations of his community on a 10-point scale or "ladder." We told him that the top of the ladder (marked 10) represented his idea of the most perfect race relations he could imagine and that the bottom of the ladder (marked 1) represented his idea of the worst possible race relations that he could imagine.[24] After locating his community in relation to his own conception of the best and worst extremes, he also indicated where he thought it had been five years ago and where he expected it to be five years from now. Table 7–2 presents the mean ratings for each county.

TABLE 7–2.    *Mean community race-relations ratings by Negro leaders*[a]

|  | Piedmont | Camellia | Bright Leaf | Crayfish |
|---|---|---|---|---|
| Five years ago | 4.1 | 2.2 | 4.5 | 4.9 |
| Today | 5.6 | 4.9 | 6.5 | 5.3 |
| Five years hence | 6.7 | 7.8 | 7.6 | 7.7 |
| LONG-RUN IMPROVEMENT[b] | 2.6 | 5.6 | 3.1 | 2.8 |

[a] Each leader rated his community on a scale ranging from 1 (worst race relations he could imagine) to 10 (best race relations he could imagine).
[b] The "long-run improvement" figures are derived by subtracting the rating for five years ago from the expected rating five years hence.

As rated by Negro leaders, Camellia County has the worst race relations, followed by Crayfish, Piedmont, and Bright Leaf. These evaluations are, of course, highly subjective, and they tell much more about the leaders of the counties than they do about the actual state of race relations. Camellia leaders see current race relations as poor, and they also have the worst recollections about the recent past. When we add to these views their high expectations for the near future, the incendiary possibilities noted earlier for Camellia appear

[24] The "self-anchoring" nature of this scale becomes more revealing when applied to the general public, especially for interracial comparisons. We discuss it more fully in Chapter Ten and Appendix C.

very real. Moreover, the rank-and-file Negroes in Camellia are not nearly so critical as their leaders. Although they have similar expectations for the next five years (with a 7.4 mean rating), they see the present and past conditions as much more favorable (6 and 4.8, respectively). Some of the difficulties of Camellia leaders may stem from this discontinuity in the way leaders and followers see their problems.

Crayfish leaders are less critical of their county's present and past race relations. Their rating of current conditions approaches the rating for Piedmont, and they think more favorably of their race relations five years ago than do the Negro leaders of any other county. This appears wildly unrealistic in view of the poverty and repression that so strongly mark Negro life in Crayfish. Its leaders clearly employ a less demanding standard of evaluation than do those of other counties. The comment of a retired schoolteacher that the county has had "no lynchings, no burnings" since he moved in from an adjacent county in 1929 indicates that Crayfish leaders have a more vivid feeling than most for what is involved in the "worst possible" race relations. Conversely, their limited horizons may make it difficult for them to picture how different things might be. The ratings of the community by Crayfish's rank-and-file Negroes, however, suggest a different explanation. The mass of Negroes have much more restricted experience in education and travel than their leaders have. Nevertheless, they rate past, present, and future race relations in their community lower than do the leaders or followers in any other community.[25]

As viewed by the mass of Negroes who endure life in Crayfish, its race relations are about as bad as they look to the outsider. And local residents see less advance in the last five years than the people or leaders in any of the other counties. Granted that the horizons of the mass of Negroes in Crayfish are even more limited than those of their leaders, this factor cannot account for the relatively high ratings the leaders give to their community's race relations. The explanation must lie instead in the special nature of Negro leaders in Crayfish and in their own relations with whites.

Crayfish is the only community-study county in which most Negro leaders were chosen almost solely because of their positions rather than because of overt activity in behalf of the Negro community. Their special positions ensure greater income for them than for the mass of Negroes, an income for which most are dependent on whites. Their positions also give them the honor of serving as "gatekeepers" between the Negro and white communities. Negro relationships with the white community are "very cordial," says the mortician, "I talk with whites." Only in Crayfish do Negro leaders evaluate relationships between the races in terms of their personal standing with whites. Extreme segregation may be hellish to the average Negro, but for the leaders it affords small increments of money or prestige that soften their criticism.

Piedmont leaders appreciate that their community's race relations are above

25 The mean ratings are: five years ago, 2.1; today, 2.7; five years hence, 5.5.

average, but they also realize that they have not approached the best possible relations. They see some gain over the past five years and expect more—but not spectacular—progress in the next five years. The ratings of the rank and file are close to those of the leaders,[26] except that they expect greater improvement in the near future. This set of views appears conducive to steady, soberly conceived pressure to attain Negro goals. The ratings of Bright Leaf County are similar to those of Piedmont, except that the values are higher. The same picture of steady progress emerges, and the rank and file do not differ greatly from their leaders. The most significant difference is that the newly successful leaders of Bright Leaf are even more optimistic than their followers about what can be accomplished in the near future.

Within their general concern over race relations, what are the more specific goals or ends of the Negro leaders? James Q. Wilson has identified two categories of goals pursued by Negro leaders in northern communities: *welfare goals*, which include tangible, "bread-and-butter" benefits for Negroes, such as better streets, jobs, or school facilities; and *status goals*, which include symbolic benefits, primarily in terms of the integration of Negroes into community life, with rewards allotted on the basis of individual merit rather than race.[27] In view of the longstanding commitment of southern political systems to segregation, the active pursuit of status goals by Negroes in the South can be expected to require great militancy. Nevertheless, status goals are pursued by Negro leaders in three of the community-study sites.

As Table 7–3 indicates, only in Crayfish do the leaders confine themselves

TABLE 7–3.    *Distribution of Negro leaders by goals with which concerned*

| Goals | Piedmont | Camellia | Bright Leaf | Crayfish |
|---|---|---|---|---|
| Status only | 8 | 5 | 0 | 0 |
| Status and welfare | 1 | 0 | 6 | 0 |
| Welfare only | 1 | 4 | 5 | 6 |
| None | 0 | 0 | 0 | 1 |
| TOTAL | 10 | 9 | 11 | 7 |

exclusively to welfare goals. The achievement of status goals, by their very nature, must be publicly visible, and a Negro leader in Crayfish would be foolhardy indeed to become publicly identified with the quest for equal status. Crayfish leaders state their objectives much more modestly: "helping people in difficulty with the sheriff," "getting people out of trouble," "employment for Negroes," "better fire protection," "would like to see Negroes voting."

Most of the ambitious leaders of Bright Leaf County describe a large num-

---

[26] The mean ratings are: five years ago, 4; today, 6; five years hence, 8.
[27] Wilson, *op. cit.*, p. 185.

ber of goals, ranging from such short-run objectives as greater Negro voter registration and better Negro school facilities to the long-run hope "to inspire and motivate people toward integration." In the small city of Farmington few status goals have been achieved, but the whites have at least been made aware that they exist. One of the leaders described his long-run objectives in terms of a recent experience: "I helped to lead a movement of Negroes to use the city swimming pool. They were denied, and the city closed the only swimming pool." In this situation, none of the leaders is concerned exclusively with status goals; five talk only of welfare objectives, and six talk of both welfare and status.

Whereas all the Bright Leaf leaders share a concern for welfare objectives, the Camellia leaders are seriously divided on objectives. Five emphasize status goals only, and four speak only of welfare goals. The division is basically between the college-based moderates and traditionalists on the one hand and the militants on the other. One of the former group seems to feel that the South's problem is primarily a "Negro problem." His objective is to "have Negroes come up to the standards of good citizens; improve honesty, morality, and law-abidingness among Negroes." One of the most militant (and popular) leaders is more concerned with requiring whites to observe the legalities. His short-run objective is simple: "Segregation must go!" Not only does tension exist between the goals of different leaders in Camellia, but the goals of the same leaders appear incompatible. The long-run objective of the leader whose first concern is to get rid of segregation—over bitter opposition from whites—is "to help build a society where people live together in love and harmony." The intransigence of local whites in defending segregation suggests that this leader will long be frustrated in his search for love and harmony.

The virtually exclusive focus of Piedmont leaders on status goals does not appear unrealistic. Their impressive welfare achievements and limited status victories permit them to think of fulfilling these trends "so that the Negro can become a full citizen." As one leader puts it: "An immediate objective is total school integration, then establishment of a merit system for employment at all levels—municipal, county, and statewide." His long-run objective is "total abandonment of segregation in Piedmont, statewide, and nationwide." The possibilities in Piedmont are less restricted than in the other three counties, and the objectives of its leaders are accordingly much more far-reaching.

In the South, Negroes are generally viewed as leaders only within the Negro community or as spokesmen for Negroes in demands on the broader community. Negroes do not, after all, take part in the highest levels of decision-making for most southern communities.[28] As a result of this exclusion and of the intense and singular needs of Negroes themselves, Negro leaders would not be expected to devote much attention to goals of the total community as

[28] This argument is made for Atlanta by Hunter, op. cit., pp. 138–39, and for New Orleans by Thompson, op. cit., p. 165.

distinct from the special goals of the Negro community. The welfare goals that dominate the concerns of Crayfish and Bright Leaf leaders are all geared to the needs of Negroes only, as are most of the status goals pursued in Piedmont and Camellia.

When we re-examine the goals in terms of a "communitywide" versus "Negro only" orientation, however, we find a striking difference between Piedmont and the other counties. Eight out of ten Negro leaders in Piedmont mention at least one communitywide goal, as compared with three out of nine in Camellia and none in Bright Leaf or Crayfish. The Negro leaders of Piedmont have economic and political ties with the total community that encourage an unusual sense of general community responsibility. The ability to think beyond racial gains alone is clearly revealed in such statements as this: "I want to improve conditions in Urbania for the colored and the white, and to make people feel that this is the kind of city they would like to live in 10 or 15 years from now." This community involvement is in extreme contrast to a common goal of Crayfish leaders—to help Negroes in trouble with the sheriff. The difference between Piedmont leaders and those in other counties demonstrates the ability of ethnic leaders to move beyond a race orientation when they are allowed to develop a vested interest in the larger community. The unavoidable preoccupation with racial deprivations in the other counties does not permit the luxury of statemanship.

## Conclusions: The quality of Negro leadership

In this chapter we have sought to describe the recruitment and behavior of Negro leaders in the South and to suggest some of the reasons why these differ from one community to the next. What do our findings imply about the quality of Negro leadership in the South?

Our analysis has identified three general types of Negro leaders in the South: *traditional* leaders, who seek ameliorative action from whites within the system of segregation; *moderates*, whose goal is to improve the welfare of all Negroes through gradual desegregation; and *militants*, who are dedicated to psychic victories and the immediate destruction of racial segregation. These distinctions are scarcely new. Where we may have pushed back the frontiers is in our finding that *Negro leaders who pursue these differing goals tend also to differ in their strategies and tactics, sources of influence, and recruitment patterns*. These relationships are summarized in Table 7–4.

These are abstract (or "ideal") types. Few real-life leaders are "pure" examples of any one type, and most communities contain more than one type of Negro leader. Some more or less "natural" progression from traditional to moderate to militant leadership seems to develop as southern communities modernize, yet remnants of the earlier type of leadership generally persist.

TABLE 7-4. *Types of Negro leaders in the South*

| | Traditional | Moderate | Militant |
|---|---|---|---|
| SOCIAL POSITION (*Relative*) | | | |
| a. Educational and occupational level | High or low | High | High or low |
| b. Economic independence from whites | Low | High | High |
| GOALS | Ameliorative action within segregated system; few beneficiaries | Improvement of welfare of all Negroes; gradual desegregation | Status goals; symbolic victories for all Negroes. Immediate destruction of segregation |
| STRATEGIES AND TACTICS | *Ad hoc*, covert, individual approaches to white leaders; ingratiation and supplication | Continuous, overt, organized efforts; legal attacks on segregation; bargaining | Mass protest movements; tend to be intermittent |
| SOURCES OF INFLUENCE | | | |
| a. With whites | Indispensability | Control over Negro votes and legal challenges | Fear of adverse publicity, boycotts, violence, federal intervention |
| b. With Negroes | Access and/or prestige | Political ability and performance | Agitational and forensic abilities |

Thus the most visible Negro leaders in the most backward county we have studied (Crayfish) are all of the traditional type. In Bright Leaf County, on the other hand, the leadership group contains both moderates and traditionals. All three types of leader have existed, at one time or another, in the two urban counties we studied in detail. But today in Piedmont County no traditional leader is sufficiently visible to show up in our rough sample, and the militants are less numerous and much less influential than in Camellia County. The fact that Negro militant leaders are most common in the less "liberal" or "advanced" of the two urban settings suggests that there is nothing inevitable about a change from moderate to militant styles as the modernization of the South progresses in the future.

But what does this tell us about the adequacy of Negro leadership? How good—or how bad—is local Negro leadership in the South today? In the last analysis, of course, the answer to this question depends on value judgments about which reasonable men can disagree. But social science can at least clarify what these differences of opinion are all about, even if it is unable to provide the ultimate answers.

Successful leaders realize two objectives: first, they instill morale among their followers and maintain wide consent to their rule; second, they are effective in attaining group goals.[29] Of course, these two tasks are related. High morale and acceptance of leadership are, to some extent, both a cause and a consequence of success in achieving group objectives. But these affective and instrumental dimensions of leadership can and do vary independently of one another, at least over the short run. Let us see what our data can tell us about these two aspects of leadership in the four communities we studied.

1. Looking at the *affective* aspect of leadership first, we can make some rough estimate of the morale of rank-and-file Negroes from their ratings of community race relations. The Piedmont and Bright Leaf county Negroes were most satisfied with local race relations (the mean rating was 6.4 in both communities), the Camellia residents next (mean, 5.4), and the Crayfish Negroes most discontent (mean, 2.7).

Negro leaders tend to be highly regarded by the Negro rank and file: over 80 per cent of the respondents in each community report that the leaders they have named are respected "a lot" by the Negro community. Any other answer to this question would have been surprising—respondents are most unlikely to name persons as leaders whom they do not regard as widely respected. And this respect does not necessarily imply respect for them *as leaders*—it may be more for the leaders' superior educational accomplishment or occupational position than for their performance in the civic realm. Thus the ratings of leadership quality made by leaders themselves probably reveal more about the general feelings of the Negro community toward the local leadership. Judged

29 See Verba, *op. cit.*, chs. 6–7.

by these standards, Crayfish leaders are least respected and Camellia leaders rank next to the bottom. The Negro leaders of Piedmont are most highly regarded, followed at a considerable distance by those of Bright Leaf.

Combining these various bits of information into a single ranking of the *affective adequacy* of Negro leadership in the four communities, we obtain the following ranking:

1. Piedmont
2. Bright Leaf
3. Camellia
4. Crayfish

2. Estimates of how adequate the leaders are in *attaining goals* are even more difficult to make. One factor does help us in this quest: the ultimate goal of all four Negro communities is the same—to attain complete racial equality. But how should a Negro community go about this? What intermediate goals can it and should it seek? How fast should the Negro community seek desegregation? And at what cost? Clearly, no single answer to these questions would be equally valid for all communities. A suitable strategy in one community might be entirely unrealistic or self-defeating in another. Nonetheless, we can specify some general preconditions for the attainment of this goal and then evaluate each community's leaders on that basis.

First, to pursue short-run or limited goals that conflict with the attainment of larger and longer-run objectives is scarcely rational strategy. Yet the leaders in Crayfish County, by seeking to ameliorate the more flagrant injustices of a segregated society on a case-by-case basis without at the same time challenging the system, are in fact functioning in a way that makes the county's existing order more bearable. They have not been very successful in this effort. But that does not undermine the point that traditional leadership contributes to the survival of a segregated society and fails to promote the long-run objectives of the vast majority of Crayfish's Negroes. The actions of the extreme militants in Camellia County are making the attainment of genuine racial equality more difficult in the long run, too. They have contributed to the rising racial tensions and hatreds that characterize the county. The escalation of racial conflict that the future seems to hold for Camellia County is most unlikely to lead to the biracial good society. The leaders of Piedmont County (basically moderates, but with some distinctly militant characteristics) and of Bright Leaf (a mixture of moderates and traditionals) have not yet had such a strongly negative impact on racial attitudes and feelings.

A group of Negro leaders for whom the local whites have respect and confidence (though not necessarily admiration) is probably another precondition for the peaceable reconciliation of racial controversies. The following percentage of the whites in each county report "a lot" of respect for local Negro leaders: Piedmont, 57 per cent; Bright Leaf, 50 per cent; Crayfish, 34 per cent;

Camellia, 18 per cent. Note that the "Uncle Tom-ism" of Crayfish's Negro leaders has *not* led to white respect and confidence and that the Negro leaders who have attained the most desegregation—in Piedmont—are those most highly regarded by local whites.[30] Even if the militants of Camellia County wanted to resolve some of their differences with the white community, the contempt in which they are held by local whites probably would preclude effective negotiations.

No leaders are likely to be very successful if they set out to achieve unattainable goals, or if their objectives diverge too far from those of the rank and file. In other words, the twin clichés that "politics is the art of the possible" and that "successful leaders are uncommon men with common ideas" are valid propositions.

The leaders of Piedmont County are by far the most socially and economically privileged group of leaders we have studied, and yet their feelings about the past and present of race relations are more nearly those of the Negro common man than is true in any other county. The correspondence in community ratings between leaders and rank and file is next closest in Bright Leaf. In Camellia the militant new leadership is much more critical of the recent past and present than is the ordinary Negro; in Crayfish the leaders are much more contented with their pathetic lot than is normal for the county. Moreover, the leaders in the last two counties are extraordinarily optimistic about the future. The average leader in Piedmont and Bright Leaf counties expects an improvement of 1.1 points on our community race-relations scale in the next five years. In Crayfish the leaders expect, on the average, an increase of 2.4 points; in Camellia they expect an improvement of 2.9! The leaders of Crayfish and Camellia counties thus seem to be both out of touch with their followers and hopelessly visionary about the rate of progress that can be expected in their respective communities.

So far as *goal attainment* is concerned, then, the Negro leaders of our four communities seem to rank in the same order of quality as they did along the affective dimension:

1. Piedmont
2. Bright Leaf
3. Camellia
4. Crayfish

These conclusions, drawn from the analysis of only four communities, cannot be applied to the South as a whole without extreme caution. But they suggest a general conclusion of some significance. Adequate Negro leadership does *not* automatically accompany expanding opportunities for its exercise. Camellia County is much more urban, industrialized, and racially "enlight-

---

[30] The direction of causality may be opposite to that suggested: the respect of whites may bring about effective Negro leadership and progress toward desegregation.

ened" than is Bright Leaf, and it has a far larger base of qualified potential leaders from which to choose. As the Bright Leaf example shows, relatively adequate Negro leadership can develop in a predominantly rural and hostile environment. No single type of leadership—traditional, moderate, or militant —is equally effective in all community settings. But, generally speaking, the traditional and militant leaders, when not forced to share their power with a significant number of moderates, are self-defeating. And the emergence of moderate[31] Negro leadership depends, in good measure, on the internal politics of the Negro community itself.

[31] Those Negro leaders whom most southern whites consider "moderate" are, by our definition, "traditional" leaders. Many southern Negro leaders who want to be considered "militant," and are so considered by whites, would be classified as "moderates" by our standards. The above statements should be interpreted in terms of our definitions.

Chapter Eight

# Negro Political Organizations

Political organization and political power tend to go together. Unorganized masses of people have little impact on government action. Few men, no matter how ambitious or talented, are able to achieve enduring political power without the support of an organized following. Indeed, organization and power are so closely associated in America that the terms are often used as if they were synonymous.

This is a mistake. Power has bases other than political organization—wealth, prestige, and knowledge are the most important.[1] But southern Negroes have few of these other resources to translate into political influence. Their greatest potential asset in politics is the vote. And for the votes of Negroes to have a substantial effect on southern politics, they must be pooled rather than chaotically distributed among alternative candidates and policies. To pool them requires organization. Political organization is the best way for "underdog" groups of all sorts—workers, farmers, immigrants, Negroes—to overcome their poverty in other political resources.

The Negroes of the South can rarely use existing political organizations to promote their interests. The state and local political parties, dominated by whites, are in business to win elections in a region where being clearly identified as "pro-Negro" is still political suicide. "Yankees" often express surprise on learning that Republican candidates in the South are as committed to segregation as are their Democratic opponents. If the region's Republicans are serious about winning elections, they must conform to local attitudes and prejudices. Other voluntary organizations that play a part in southern politics —farm groups, local chambers of commerce, trade or professional associations, unions, and the like—are even more difficult for Negroes to infiltrate. If

---

[1] See R. A. Dahl, *Who Governs?* (New Haven, Conn.: Yale University Press, 1961), chs. 19–23, for a discussion of different kinds of political resources.

Negroes are to organize for political purposes, they must create their own organizations.

And they have. Since *Smith* v. *Allwright* there has been a rapid growth of Negro associations in the South devoted to stimulating and directing Negro political activity.[2] These associations have taken a bewildering variety of forms and have developed at very different rates in different communities. They range in comprehensiveness and effectiveness from a handful of Negro organizations that compare favorably with the nineteenth-century political machines of the northern cities, to sporadic and confused organizations whose endorsement of a white candidate ensures his defeat.

We begin this chapter by examining the development of Negro political organizations in four different southern communities—Crayfish, Bright Leaf, Camellia, and Piedmont counties. This examination should give us an acquaintance with the wide range of organizational forms taken by Negro political groups in the South and an understanding of the conditions that must exist before Negro political organization can emerge. For, although Negroes must have organization to achieve political power, their chances of developing an effective organization depend heavily on the characteristics of the community in which the organization must operate.

## Negroes with no organizational support

Negroes in Crayfish County have no formal organization that could be described as even incidentally concerned with politics. The basic resource on which a political organization normally relies is the voting strength the organization can command. If an entire group is excluded from the franchise, it can hardly be expected to develop political organizations—unable to offer rewards or threats, it has nothing with which to bargain.[3] Any effort by Crayfish Negroes to establish a political organization would be taken as a revolutionary threat to the "closed society" of Crayfish County.[4] One elderly Negro leader, when asked about his organizational affiliations, proudly explained that he was a Mason, but he quickly added, "We never talk about voting and things like that at our meetings"!

In this atmosphere the few efforts Negroes have made toward political organizations have assumed the form of underground conspiracies. Early in the 1950's Crayfish members of the NAACP invited a Negro attorney from a

---

[2] For a description of this early period see A. Heard, *A Two-Party South?* (Chapel Hill, N.C.: University of North Carolina Press, 1952), ch. 14.

[3] Of course, it could pose threats outside the formal channels of politics—through mass boycotts or demonstrations, for example. The lack of militancy among Crayfish's Negro leaders and the extreme hostility of local whites make this tactic most unlikely.

[4] The phrase was coined by James W. Silver, *Mississippi: The Closed Society* (New York: Harcourt, Brace & World, 1964).

neighboring state to conduct classes on voter registration for Crayfish residents. The obstacles were monumental. Getting people to come to civic meetings is difficult enough when the meetings are well publicized, but these registration classes had to be kept secret from the whites! As a result, no sample registration forms could be secured, the site of the classes was changed from one meeting to the next, and the meetings were called at irregular intervals. Nevertheless, about 300 Negroes were trained over a three-year period.

Nothing could appear less blameworthy in most parts of the United States than classes for prospective voters. But in Crayfish County holding such classes was like trying to organize a new political party in the Soviet Union or trying to plan a jail break from Leavenworth. The training sessions ended when some whites learned about the classes from their Negro employees. The whites threatened to break up the meeting, and the visiting attorney escaped harm only when several domestics got help from the white housewives for whom they worked. Such incipient organization as the classes had inspired dissipated immediately. Indeed, the effort had probably been doomed from the outset. If Negroes could not openly conduct classes on registration procedures, they could hardly take advantage of the instruction they received. Prospective voters at that time had to pay a poll tax to the county sheriff, and in order to register they had to appear before the clerk of the criminal court; both officials would have assumed their roles as law enforcement officers if Negroes had approached them in their role as electoral officials.

Shortly after the Supreme Court declared state-enforced segregation in public schools unconstitutional in 1954, five Crayfish Negroes filed a petition with the school board seeking to get their children admitted to the white school. The action was ill organized—apparently a desperate gamble by a few individuals who entertained the wild hope that Supreme Court decisions might be respected even in Crayfish. They were quickly disabused of this notion. Crayfish whites, unaccustomed to formal demands from local Negroes, perceived the "threat" in highly unrealistic terms. They reacted as if they expected the Negro children to appear at the white school the next morning, without waiting for the school board to act on the petition, for court orders, for assignment to classrooms, or for any of the other procedures that would be required before the Negro children could transfer to the white school. The morning after the petition was filed, a number of heavily armed whites gathered around the school in automobiles. No Negro children appeared; nor have any appeared yet.

The show of force by whites seems ridiculous. No knowledgeable person should have expected Negro children to arrive at the school before any action had been taken on their petition. But if its purpose was to frighten the Negroes into withdrawing their petition, it was a well-conceived stratagem. Each of the Negro petitioners withdrew his name, claiming that he had been misled into signing what he thought was a request for the improvement of Negro schools.

This self-debasement was also functional: for the white community, because it permitted them to continue thinking that "our" Negroes prefer segregation, even though care must be taken to keep them from being duped by outsiders; for the Negroes, because they suffered no physical harm. Well after the incident had been settled, the chairman of the county school board was willing to be frank. "They claimed they thought they were just petitioning for better schools," he said, "but they knew damn well what they were petitioning for."

NAACP activity in Crayfish County is necessarily covert. Even suspicious attire may be taken as evidence of membership. The president of the county board of supervisors, for example, learned that the justice department was planning to file a suit against the Crayfish registrar because not a single Negro appeared on the voting lists. He decided that he knew "a good nigger" who could be allowed to register and drove out to talk with him about it one Sunday. The Negro, when summoned,[5] came out of his house wearing a suit and necktie. The county official asked where he was going "all dressed up" like that, and the erstwhile "good" Negro lost his chance for the franchise by saying that he was going to visit his sister in a neighboring state. "When I go to see my sister I don't get all dressed up," the official charged. He concluded that the Negro must have been planning to attend a district meeting of the NAACP.

What harm comes to a Negro who is discovered to be a member of the NAACP? No direct evidence was secured on this question. "There have been a few niggers killed here in Crayfish," the president of the board of supervisors reported, "but they weren't killed by *responsible* people." Most white leaders emphasized the lack of violence in Crayfish. Indeed, this emphasis was so strong and distinctive as to suggest that an absence of violence cannot be taken for granted in Crayfish as it can be, for the most part, in the other three communities. Whatever the sanctions, Negroes seem to regard the accusation of NAACP membership with great trepidation. The president of the board of supervisors, explaining his role as a true friend of the Negro, said, "A nigger came to me yesterday—he had been accused of belonging to the NAACP by a white man, and he was right tore up by it. He had attended a meeting, but when he discovered it was an NAACP meeting, he left. He had never told me a lie before, so I straightened it out. . . ."

Another futile effort to organize Crayfish Negroes occurred in 1961. A representative of the Student Non-violent Coordinating Committee held registration classes for Negroes, and this time the whites did not learn about the effort until the instructor appeared with two of his students before the registrar. As we reported earlier, the SNCC representative was clubbed with a pistol and arrested for disturbing the peace. The local Negroes did not succeed in register-

[5] Whites in Crayfish do not normally enter Negroes' homes; they call them out for conversation.

ing, and no more efforts in that direction were taken until after a federal registrar was sent to the county in 1965.

Efforts at Negro organization in Crayfish have thus been sporadic and unsuccessful. Moreover, they have depended on outside leadership. Even the church fails to furnish an organizational base for political action by Negroes in Crayfish. Only 4 per cent of the churchgoers there say that elections are discussed at church. The message of the Negro preacher in Crayfish deals with the heavenly life of another world, not with the hell of his present world.

## Intermediate stages of organization

Although Bright Leaf has no local chapter of the NAACP or of such protest organizations as CORE, its organizational life looks rich indeed when compared with that of Crayfish. Four organizations in Bright Leaf have encouraged Negro political activity: the Civic Association, the Benevolent Brothers, the Progressive Voters League, and the Bright Leaf County Progressive Council.

The Civic Association, founded in 1935, is the oldest of these organizations. It began, not as a political-action organization, but as an elite group of professionals and businessmen who could bargain with whites for services to the Negro community. Specifically, it was designed to perform the traditional "gate-keeping" function between the Negro and white communities. Ostensibly open to any Negro in Bright Leaf County, the Association was actually controlled by leading members of the Ministerial Alliance and by a few Negro professionals and businessmen who had contacts with the white community. Nevertheless, the organization was directed toward the needs of Negroes in general rather than simply toward the needs of the leaders.

The style of the Civic Association and the nature of white responses to it are suggested by the way in which the first Negro policeman was hired by the city of Farmington in 1951. Without fanfare, members of the Association asked the chief of police and the city council to hire a Negro policeman. The council delayed action until it learned of public reactions to Negro policemen in the state's largest city. On the basis of this report, the council appointed the first Negro to the police force. Most of the work of the Civic Association has been this sort of practical action for limited welfare gains. Although its leaders have always been interested in getting more Negroes registered to vote, they are careful not to threaten the whites with full-fledged Negro political organization. One Negro leader close to the Association commented:

> Only the Civic Association has any resemblance to a Negro political organization in Bright Leaf County, and it speaks for very few. The only effort at organizing Negro voters in the county has been haphazard. . . . The main organized concentration of leadership has been on action-welfare programs.

The Benevolent Brothers was founded a year after the Civic Association, but it has been concerned with problems of the Negro community only, and has not sought to serve as a link between the Negro and white communities. It is a benevolent, fraternal order made up of businessmen and quasi-professional Negroes who do not belong to the "inner circle" of the Civic Association. The fraternity trappings include a limited membership (25), a $25 initiation fee, weekly dues of $1, and a system of "blackballing" any prospective member who is unacceptable to a current member. In its early years, the Benevolent Brothers concentrated on giving to the poor at Christmas time and on fraternal activities. In the last ten years, however, the Brothers have actively campaigned to increase Negro voter registration. And in 1961 they successfully challenged the political leadership of the Civic Association. Eight leaders of the Association, without consulting other Negroes, had hand-picked their own president as nominee for the Farmington City Council. The Benevolent Brothers called a meeting of representatives of all Negro organizations and clubs, and this group endorsed a young attorney instead of the Civic Association leader. In the face of this communitywide decision, the Association acquiesced and agreed to support the attorney.

As a way of promoting the Negro's candidacy, representatives of all the Negro clubs in Farmington formed an organization called the Progressive Voters League. Registration increased markedly in the predominantly Negro ward, and victory seemed likely under Farmington's system of district election. At the last moment, however, two members of the Civic Association accepted bribes to lead small blocs of Negro voters to oppose the Negro candidate, and he was narrowly defeated.[6] The all-white city council responded to this near-victory by changing the electoral system to an at-large vote, which dims Negro prospects for success in the future. Nevertheless, the Progressive Voters League continues as an "umbrella organization" under which all Farmington Negroes can work together.

The Progressive Voters League is active only in Farmington. To encompass Negro groups from the entire county, a sister organization—the Bright Leaf Progressive Council—was also formed in 1961. The Progressive Council has pushed for such countywide goals as a bond issue to create an industrial school open to Negroes. Both the Voters League and the Progressive Council have been watched with sympathy by union leaders in Bright Leaf, who say that they supported the Negro candidate. It is unlikely that many rank-and-file white union members did, and no formal union-Negro coalition has developed. Even so, if the enthusiasm and activity of the 1961 campaign can be sustained, the old style of bargaining between whites and the leaders of the Civic Association will change. "Because of the rise of organizations among Negroes," one leader said, "whites are finding they will have to deal with more Negroes."

Camellia County has a more complete range of Negro organizations than

6 See the introduction to Part One for a more complete description of this incident.

Bright Leaf, but there has been no coordination among them. Between the Second World War and the outbreak of mass protest in Camellia in 1956, the Capital City Civic League tried to provide political leadership by sponsoring petitions to public officials, organizing rallies at which Negro voters could "meet the candidates," and even endorsing slates of white candidates. But individual political entrepreneurs in the Negro community made their own separate deals, selling small blocs of votes to the highest bidder. Today another, rather nebulous organization, the Progressive Voters Council, operates only at election time. One respondent suggested that it was merely a "paper" organization that served as a front for getting handouts from naïve white candidates. None of the Negro leaders bothered to mention it in talking about political activities in the county.

The Capital City Civic League has tried to operate as a genuine "uplift" organization, but it has failed to muster a strong following in the Negro community. Most of its officers have been from the staff of the Negro college, with which the mass of Negroes have little sense of identification. Militant protest has been unthinkable to the Civic League leaders, so its role has been restricted to negotiating with whites for welfare gains.

In 1956, however, Capital City Negroes suddenly entered—almost leaderless—into mass protest activity. Triggered by the arrest of college students who refused to observe the segregated seating practice on a city bus, a mass bus boycott developed. Behind this militant protest virtually the entire Negro community rallied. Lack of organization was a severe handicap during the early days of the boycott. Organization was essential, not only for the immediate and complicated task of directing car pools but for the formulation and communication of plans within the Negro community—and, ultimately, with the white community. The conservative Civic League leaders were discredited early in the negotiations, and at that point the League was doomed as an effective representative body. (Efforts have recently been made to revive it as a negotiating body concerned with welfare gains.) In the absence of any organization capable of speaking for the Negroes, the Negro community was represented at an initial meeting with the city manager by a nine-man committee from the Capital City Ministerial Alliance. But this special group was not representative of the Negro public. That same day, the Inter-Civic Council (ICC) was organized as an executive body to serve as a bargaining agent with the whites.

Despite efforts to subvert the ICC—by displaced Negro leaders as well as by whites—its militant stance evoked great enthusiasm from the Negro public. For the first time since Reconstruction, Capital City Negroes were making open demands on the white community. Negro ministers on the ICC held mass meetings in their churches and invested the protest movement with revivalistic fervor. Despite harassment of Negroes driving for the car pool— "they'd arrest you for driving too fast if you got over the speed limit and for obstructing traffic if you got under it"—the organizational effort was success-ful. Solid support of the boycott from the entire Negro community bolstered the prestige of the militant new leaders. But the success was restricted to the satisfaction of openly defying the white community and demonstrating that the Negro masses wholeheartedly supported the demands of their leaders. The demands themselves were not met; the city commission enacted an ordinance that authorized bus drivers to assign each passenger to a seat, on grounds of "safety" in distributing weight rather than on grounds of race. Only the bus between the Negro college and the Negro ghetto on the opposite side of town was actually integrated, and it has few white riders.

The ICC tried to channel the public enthusiasm it had evoked into greater political power, but with little success. It cooperated with the State Voters League in registration drives, and in 1957 the vice-president of the ICC an-nounced himself a candidate for the city commission. His candidacy, the first by a Negro in modern times, gave real impetus to the registration drive, and the election brought out a record number of voters for a local election in Capital City. White reaction to his candidacy was almost as intense as that of Negroes, and he was defeated by a two-to-one margin. This electoral effort marked the high-water mark politically for the ICC. The leaders have con-tinued to talk politics and have tried to "pressure" elected officials, but with little evidence of success.

Other organizations have had no better luck in attempting to win a share of political power for Capital City Negroes. In the face of adamant city officials staunchly opposed to any desegregation, and of a white electorate that votes almost solidly against any local candidate with a liberal position on racial questions, the races communicate through mass protest and lawsuits rather than through political action. A local chapter of the NAACP has been active in recent voter-registration efforts, but it has made its greatest advances in the courts. It initiated suits resulting in token desegregation of the schools and of facilities at the municipal airport. Capital City also has an active chapter of the Congress on Racial Equality (CORE), which cooperated with the NAACP in desegregating facilities at the airport. But these and other organizations suffer from lack of coordination. In the spring of 1964, for example, a "freedom march" on the state capitol failed even to approach expectations because CORE and the NAACP could not agree on the route of march!

Except for the momentary successes of the Inter-Civic Committee, then, Negro organizational efforts have had little positive effect on the politics of the area. Even the ICC has not been able to eliminate the individual dealings of Negro "ward heelers"[7] with white politicians and the consequent proliferation of slates "approved by Negroes." In 1964, an integrated League for Better

[7] This label has a special meaning in southern Negro communities: a "ward heeler" is an individual "wheeler-dealer" who sells votes to white candidates. He is in no sense a cog in a large and smoothly operating machine.

Government was organized by a few business and professional people, mostly professors, from the white and Negro community. When one of the candidates for the city commission received the League's endorsement, his long-time friends were incredulous at his refusal to repudiate the group. The endorsed candidate was soundly defeated. This group of "do-gooders" can hardly succeed where Negro efforts have failed. The charge made by one white leader about the NAACP applies even more to the League for Better Government: "The NAACP hasn't done the organizational job here it is capable of doing. There is too big a split between the college and the town. The NAACP is controlled by the college group, and they tend not to participate in the activities of the town and politics."

## Extensive and coordinated organization

Piedmont County has an even greater range of Negro organizations than Camellia. An NAACP chapter, various business-civic organizations, and labor unions appeared in Piedmont before 1954. Since then an NAACP youth group, the Student Non-violent Coordinating Committee, CORE, a Black Muslim temple, and special groups—such as those conducting spontaneous sit-ins—have added to the complex organizational structure of Urbania. But all these organizations, formal and informal, have been overshadowed by the Urbania League for Negro Activities (ULNA). Indeed, the activities of most of these other organizations are loosely coordinated by ULNA. The ULNA is far more than a Negro voting league; it is one of the most successful Negro efforts in any southern locality to combine elitist talents and mass support for the realization of broad political, economic, and social gains.

Urbania Negroes organized a formal voting league in 1935. The number of Negro voters in the city was already quite large by the standards of the time and the region. Negroes sent delegates to the Democratic county convention as early as 1932. Moreover, the Negro leaders enjoyed access to local party chieftains and to public officials as well. Why, then, was a general voter's league for Negroes established?

To begin with, all the public facilities of Urbania were segregated, as they were everywhere else in the South. Moreover, even in purely political terms, the registration of Negro voters was "selective," with the mass of Negroes excluded from registration. The Negro votes that were cast were not used to bargain effectively with white leaders for a fair share of governmental services. The casual visitor did not have to ascertain the skin color of the residents to know when he had entered the Negro section—unpaved streets, poor lighting, and other evidences of public neglect told him where he was. Despite the great need for political bargaining power on the part of the Negro community as a whole, unscrupulous Negro "ward heelers" sold small blocs of

Negro votes in each election. These political entrepreneurs generally exaggerated the number of votes they could deliver, and they often made no effort to deliver at all. Respectable Negro leaders were greatly concerned about this practice, because it reduced the chance of using the Negro vote as a resource in bargaining and because it gave the Negro community as a whole a reputation for dishonesty and irresponsibility.

A small group representing the Negro upper class met at their Tennis Club in 1935 to found the ULNA. Only successful businessmen and professional people attended the meeting. The first executive committee was composed of a local Negro insurance executive, the editor of the Negro newspaper, a professor, a leading minister, and a successful businessman. The leadership of the group has continued to be vested in the executive committee, and membership on this select committee is recognized as the reward for long and successful service to the Negro community. But the composition of the executive committee has been broadened to include representatives from all the major Negro organizations. By 1945, Negro labor union officials and other leaders from less prestigious groups had won seats. In this way the ULNA has avoided the danger of becoming an upper-class clique without direct ties to the Negro masses.

Membership in the ULNA was originally described as open to "all people in the county who can't sleep or eat in the leading local hotel." It is doubtful that membership was ever so wide as that statement suggested. Largely because of the work of the ULNA, the hotel integrated all its facilities in 1963. If the old, half-humorous description had been taken seriously, the organization would have had to disband, killed by its own success. But the ULNA is a thriving organization that will continue to push for a better break for the local Negro community in hiring, job training, and—of course—governmental services.

At present, membership in the ULNA is of two types, as formalized by Article III of the organization's 1958 constitution: (1) personal memberships are open to those citizens of Urbania "who affirm their interest in and subscribe to the purposes" of the organization, and (2) organizational memberships are open to representatives of each organization in Urbania which shall apply to, and be approved by, the executive committee of the ULNA. Included in the latter category are churches, parent-teacher associations, civic clubs, fraternal and political organizations, labor unions, faculties of educational institutions, business and professional associations, and other organizations of like purposes. Actually, even the mass rallies periodically called by the ULNA attract only four hundred to five hundred people; and the active hard core of the group does not total over one hundred. This number includes the 12 members of the executive committee, currently elected at large; the representatives from the various constitutent organizations; the organization workers, who comprise the block and precinct organizations; and other activists who regularly help in the many activities of the group.

The formal organizational structure of the ULNA is thus similar to that of the United States Chamber of Commerce, with both individual and organizational memberships. Such an all-encompassing structure is well geared to the aims of the organization. The founders of the ULNA felt that it could perform two immediate political functions. First, it could act as a centralizing and coordinating agency to maximize Negro registration and voting. Second, it could serve as a means for deciding which white candidate the Negro community could most profitably support. In other words, it was to create and direct a Negro bloc vote in order to reward friends and punish enemies. No longer would individual Negroes make deals on small blocs of Negro votes with individual white candidates. Once ULNA's political committee had decided on a slate, the members were to support the slate as a group. A sample ballot would be printed (in a Negro-owned and Negro-managed print shop), the "correct" candidates marked, and the endorsed slate distributed to Negro voters as they went to the polls.

In order to win mass support, the ULNA organized the Negro community block by block. Fortunately, the local Negro insurance company had a large field staff in the city that sold policies door to door and collected weekly payments. The overlap between the insurance salesmen and the ULNA's block workers was substantial. The use of such existing, nonpolitical structures as the basis for organized political activity is a common practice in the white community, especially in areas where political party organizations are weak.[8] Rarely, however, does a Negro sub-community have such a "natural" base for block-by-block organization.

By the beginning of the Second World War, the ULNA had expanded its operations substantially. It had led a movement to found a similar organization on a statewide basis. Although this movement had failed, it is impressive that a group with such initiative and ability had managed to develop in the South before the war. Within Piedmont, the ULNA had extended its efforts beyond politics by organizing economic, social, civic, and educational committees for special work and responsibility.

During the Second World War the organization continued to work for broad goals favorable to Negroes and by 1945 had won important gains. Streets had been paved, and the schools had been improved. Some extra police protection and better street lighting had been provided. The question of whether Negroes were to serve on juries was being considered. In addition, Negroes had won a more equitable distribution of federal relief funds and jobs, and the Urbania Police Department had hired Negro policemen.

ULNA representatives had gained access to the offices of public officials,

[8] See Alexander Heard, *The Costs of Democracy* (Chapel Hill, N.C.: University of North Carolina Press, 1960); and Eugene C. Lee, *The Politics of Nonpartisanship: A Study of California City Elections* (Berkeley, Calif.: University of California Press, 1960).

and either the executive committee or its representatives met with the mayor of Urbania fairly frequently to discuss the needs and problems of the Negroes in the community. This was an improvement over the earlier relationship, in which only a few important Negroes had enjoyed access to city offices. In 1948 the statewide importance of the ULNA was demonstrated when the recently elected governor of the state came to thank them, in person, for their support in the election.

After the war ULNA stepped up its activity in all areas of community life, especially politics. It continued to select a slate of favorable white candidates, and it began openly to support Negro candidates for local public office. It had endorsed some Negro candidates early in its history but with no hope of victory. The endorsements were a device to stimulate Negro registration before there were any sympathetic white candidates to support. Now the ULNA began to back candidates to win. This, plus the fact that white candidates for such high offices as mayor, governor, and the United States House of Representatives now came willingly (if still covertly) to the meetings of the executive committee to solicit its support, was an indication of growing strength. Bloc voting might prove self-defeating in the long run, as many whites and a few Negroes argued, but the Negro community had bloc-voted themselves some voice in local public decision-making nonetheless.

The leaders of the ULNA, like Negroes throughout the South, were historically inclined toward the Republican party. And yet they set about trying to win influence in the Democratic primaries. The Negro precinct chairmen served on the Democratic county executive committee *ex officio*. In 1948 these Negro chairmen, all of whom were leaders in the ULNA, cooperated with the Democratic precinct chairmen from predominantly white labor precincts to wrest control of the Urbania County Democratic Executive Committee from the powerful faction that had controlled it for years.

Although the ULNA failed to elect one of its members to the Urbania City Council in 1949, its votes helped elect a new mayor and several members of the council. Before the municipal election of 1951, a faction of the ULNA Executive Committee—led by the college professor who had been one of the founders of the ULNA and was to be the Negro candidate in 1951—argued that joining with white labor to back a common slate was not the best way to get a Negro elected to the city council. This faction felt that the time had come for a Negro to be elected to the city council and that "bullet" or "single shot" voting by Negroes was the only route to victory.[9] Only the influence of younger, more party-oriented members of the ULNA Executive Committee saved the coalition with white labor at that time.

[9] This "bullet" voting technique is a device for maximizing the advantage of the minority in an election in which more than one at-large vote is granted each voter. By voting for only one candidate, the minority group is able to increase the weight of its actual vote because the opposition presumably will vote for more than one candidate.

Unfortunately for the coalition, the white labor vote was harder to deliver than the labor leaders had anticipated, and the Negro candidate was defeated. This defeat was doubly disappointing to the Negroes, because they had thought their candidate was sure to win. The labor leaders came up with several explanations. A recent statewide election had engendered unusually strong racist feelings, they said; the strong advocacy of "don't let the Negroes take over the city government" by a newly developed committee of local whites had proved to be disruptive; and labor's victories in the prior municipal election had made the unions complacent. None of these reasons rang very true to Negroes. The whole affair looked like a "double-cross."

The next month, instead of accepting defeat with a philosophical "wait until next year," the ULNA held a mass meeting and reorganized itself. All positions on the ULNA Executive Committee were declared open for election. The current chairman managed to hold on to his position, but many of the faces were new. Only by increasing the membership of the Executive Committee to 25 was the chairman able to get an agreement on policies that would allow the Negro-labor coalition, and its strong support of the Democratic party, to continue.

In the municipal elections of 1953, a Negro was elected to the Urbania City Council for the first time in its history. The success was marred, however, by continuing conflict within the ULNA. The Executive Committee decided to back a candidate other than the college professor who had lost in 1951. The professor, rejecting the rejection, ran as an independent in the primary and was soundly beaten by the ULNA's candidate. Though factionalism continued in the ULNA, it did not again reach the point of an open break. The ULNA succeeded in getting its candidates elected in 1955, 1957, and 1959.

The school-segregation decision of 1954 proved very disruptive to the ULNA's relations with the white community. In May 1958, the friendly county Democratic chairman was defeated for reelection, and, in the same county convention at which he was defeated, only one Negro was selected as a delegate to the state convention. (In the past as many as 23 Negroes from Urbania had attended the state convention.) When the Piedmont County Young Democratic Club met in October, no members of the executive committee of the ULNA were invited. The ULNA leaders protested to the new Democratic county chairman, but he told them that the club was a private organization and could invite whomever it chose.

As it had in the past, the ULNA now closed its ranks. It set about recruiting new members and adopted a formal constitution. Several municipal bond elections were successfully carried in Urbania from 1945 to 1959, and impartial observers attributed the outcome to the Negro vote organized by the ULNA. These bond issues provided increased hospital, educational, and other public services of particular benefit to Negroes. One bond issue provided funds for building a fire station in the Negro community, and the ULNA was able to get it manned by Negro firemen. Negro deputy sheriffs, policemen, and election officials were employed for the first time. An integrated industrial school began to provide Negroes with training they had never been able to get before.

Thus even after the *Brown* decision greatly heightened local racial tensions, and thereby undercut the political effectiveness of the ULNA, the ULNA continued to serve as the bargaining representative of Urbania Negroes vis-à-vis the white community. Also the organization continued to value its coalition with labor and its ties with the local Democratic party—even when neither the party nor the rank and file of labor were particularly eager for Negro support.

The gubernatorial election of 1960 demonstrated that the ULNA could still direct the Negro vote toward its candidates. The ULNA experienced its most serious electoral split, however, in the municipal elections of 1961, when two of its long-time friends opposed each other in the mayoralty election. The former county Democratic chairman, who had headed the Negro-labor coalition and had often befriended the ULNA, ran against the incumbent, a man whom both the former chairman and the ULNA had supported for ten years. The ULNA Executive Committee met more than once to hear impassioned pleas for support from both sides. At last the committee abandoned the incumbent, though several members had serious misgivings. On election day, the Negro turnout was the lowest in years. Only 66 per cent of the total vote in the four heavily Negro precincts went to the ULNA-endorsed candidate. In other races in the same election, candidates endorsed by the ULNA received at least 80 per cent of the total vote in these precincts.

Apparently the break in the ULNA ranks had healed by the 1962 countywide election. The fact that an ULNA member was running for county commissioner helped rekindle the zest for battle. He led in the first primary but was defeated in the runoff. This campaign, though it ended in defeat, seemed to reestablish solidarity and confidence among the leaders and the Negro public. The wealthy, cosmopolitan, dignified chairman of the ULNA, according to his associates, spent 12 hours on election day driving voters to the polls. Later he said, speaking like the successful businessman he is, "The tremendous across-the-board team effort that hundreds of our people made in this campaign [is to be lauded]. It's an indication of growing community solidarity."

What gains have come from these years of labor by the ULNA? Perhaps the most significant is the respect that white community leaders have come to show for the organization. Sometimes this respect is grudging, but other times it is open and forthright. One white leader says, "The ULNA is the best race organization in the community and the most democratic."

Moreover, the ULNA has given the Negro public in Urbania a skillful and representative leadership structure on which it can depend. Its ability to organize a substantial Negro vote gives Negroes a loud enough voice to be heard in the Democratic party—the local majority party. Rising political strength has also brought welfare and status gains to Urbania Negroes. These gains, such as the desegregation of motels, hotels, and restaurants, cannot all be attributed directly to the ULNA. Many of them would probably have come anyway. But the ULNA hastened their coming by capitalizing on a relatively permissive environment and relatively strong Negro leadership and financial resources.

Other organizations, including the NAACP, CORE, fraternal and business organizations, youth groups at the college, and various special groups, have helped the ULNA to activate the Negro community. Often the NAACP and the ULNA have seemed to be one and the same organization in Urbania because of the widespread overlap in membership. For example, the chief counsel for the ULNA also directed the local NAACP legal redress committee. The two organizations cooperated closely in conducting voter-registration drives; the NAACP was always careful to remain nonpartisan, but it knew that the ULNA would channel most of the new registrants into the Democratic party. The legal approach to desegregation—long the policy of the NAACP—appealed to the business and professional men who dominate Urbania's Negro leadership. Negotiations, bargaining, and legal actions were techniques well fitted to their skills and general philosophy.

More militant organizations—CORE, for example—and student groups altered the techniques and pace of Negro efforts in Urbania. These groups, which relied on mass protest in the form of picketing, boycotts, and sit-ins, posed a threat to the ULNA leaders, who relied on less dramatic techniques. But the leaders adjusted to the new ways—not without some misgivings and tension—and brought the new groups into ULNA activities. In 1961, for example, cooperation between several groups led to the opening of sales positions in downtown Urbania stores to Negro applicants. In a neat division of labor, the youth groups furnished the pickets and the ULNA and NAACP handled the negotiations. All the groups used the threat of boycotts as their bargaining weapon. At the annual mass meeting of the ULNA in January 1962, speakers from the NAACP youth group at the college and from other, more militant groups appeared on the program. Later, in the drive to desegregate all Urbania facilities, the ULNA chairman promised the demonstrators that they would not languish in jail if arrested—the ULNA would come to their defense.

Even this comprehensive and coordinated program has not always met with success, however. Politically the ULNA has failed to get a Negro elected to the Piedmont County Commission. Urbania Negroes have occasionally been rebuffed by the very officials they helped elect to office; when the Mayor's Human Relations Committee recommended that the city-owned theater be integrated, the Urbania City Council refused to act. (After a siege of picketing, the theater was finally integrated.) The Urbania City School Board, even with a Negro member to prod the consciences of other members, moved slowly in desegregating the schools. Mass protest and an organized vote can be used only within the limits set by the dominant forces of the community. Even the most effective Negro organization must expect some setbacks in the South. But after each defeat, the Urbania League for Negro Activities has managed to inject new life and enthusiasm into the community and has re-organized for the next battle.

## Preconditions for effective Negro political organization: Situational factors

The four southern communities we studied in detail differ greatly in the development of Negro political organization. Good reasons can be found for this variation. In some communities, social, economic, and political factors tend to encourage—or at least not to inhibit—the growth of effective political organization. In others, these factors impose severe limits on the extent and effectiveness of Negro organization. These variables fall into two classes—those that are "external" to the Negro community and those that grow out of the Negro community itself. Let us look first at the "external" or situational variables.

### THE RACIAL ATTITUDES OF LOCAL WHITES

White attitudes about the proper "place" of the Negro help determine the success or failure of Negro efforts to organize. In Crayfish County, for ex-ample, the white community is solidly opposed to any relaxation of rigid segregation. Given a choice between "strict segregation, integration, or some-thing in between," every white Crayfish respondent except one said that he favored strict segregation. The exception was a young lady who had grown up in Los Angeles and who was living in Crayfish temporarily because her husband was driving a truck for a construction company.[10] Whites in the other counties are not unanimous in their dedication to rigid segregation: the proportion drops to 87 per cent in Bright Leaf, 65 per cent in Camellia, and 58 per cent in Piedmont. When we add Negro views to those of the whites, we find that a small majority of the total population of Piedmont rejects strict segregation.

More important, whites in Piedmont believe that Negro opinions *ought* to count in the community. On the proposition that "colored people ought to be allowed to vote," a majority of whites in Piedmont (69 per cent) and in Camellia (68 per cent) agree "quite a bit." Almost half the whites in

[10] The resident white interviewer, recognizing the heretical nature of this respondent's views, commented that "she wouldn't last long in Crayfish County."

Bright Leaf (49 per cent) but only 4 per cent of the Crayfish whites similarly endorse the principle of suffrage for Negroes. If we add those who agree "a little," white acceptance of the proposition becomes overwhelming in three of the counties: 90 per cent in Piedmont, 93 per cent in Camellia, and 82 per cent in Bright Leaf. But it reaches only 16 per cent in Crayfish! In the face of such determined opposition from those who control all the political and economic power, efforts to organize politically must assume the form of conspiracies.

White attitudes—either in themselves or as an index of other community factors—are not the only constraints on Negro efforts to organize. If they were, we would expect Camellia County to follow closely behind Piedmont in the scope and effectiveness of Negro political organization. Other situational factors, of varying importance and specificity, are suggested by a close examination of the four communities: the political style of white leaders, locally and statewide, in dealing with racial questions; the factional system peculiar to the community; the local electoral system; the relative homogeneity or heterogeneity of the community in nonracial terms; and the Civil War and Reconstruction experiences of the community. Added to public opinion on racial questions, these overlapping situational variables pretty much determine whether or not the Negro community can organize for political ends. And, taken together, they provide a reasonably clear and specific meaning to the ordinarily vague concept of "political culture."

## THE POLITICAL STYLE OF WHITE LEADERS

The white leaders in Crayfish openly espouse white supremacy. Only there can the leaders pretend that they have no "race problem." Crayfish Negroes are so browbeaten that the whites can sing the old refrain about having "good, happy niggers," and can repeat the old joke about the local Negro who finds life so miserable in the North that he wires his old "boss man" for money to return to the happy life on the farm. One of the leaders commented: "We have the best colored people in the world . . . our colored people are not giving us any trouble." And if they do give trouble, it is not reported. Merely from reading the *Breedville Weekly* one might conclude that no Negroes lived in Crayfish.

In Bright Leaf, the white leaders express paternalistic attitudes sometimes mixed with genuine benevolence. The response of the superintendent of schools to a question about relations with "the colored community" is illuminating:

Rather good, I think. There are some hotheads but a group of us are working to establish communication. I do what I can to show my love for them—get scholarships. Nigrahs come in the back door and stand—I tell them to have a seat, and suggest that they go out the front door—it's nearer. I call janitors in the schools "custodians." This is more than words and acts; they know I'll fight for them, for instance, give them money. The point is: treat them as humans, call them "Mister" and "Miss"; nothing special, just what human beings deserve.

The superintendent of schools is not typical of Bright Leaf's white leaders, most of whom hold more clearly anti-Negro stereotypes. But it is remarkable that we can find such a leader, who says that his prime objective is to prepare teachers for integration, in this community. This is not a transient, but an old and widely admired leader. The new high school in Farmington bears his name, and generations of graduates remember him with affection and respect.

Camellia County is more cosmopolitan and liberal than Bright Leaf, mainly because it is more urban and is the home of the state capitol and the state university. Although some Camellia whites, mostly from the university, have actively championed integration, the officials of Capital City have been virulently anti-Negro. Officeholders talk about the fine relations that existed with old-style Negro leaders before the bus boycott confronted them with the undeniable fact of mass Negro dissatisfaction. The chief of police, under whose direction the local police force has ruthlessly broken up demonstrations, says, "They want to be good, but the NAACP has caused friction—whites and colored are farther apart than in years. The college people and Negro preachers start things—they prey on younger niggers." The municipal judge, who has handed down stiff sentences to demonstrators, observes: "CORE is a Communist front, I'm convinced." Most Camellia leaders recognize that the two colleges in Capital City are the source of much racial agitation and regard them almost as alien institutions. They value the colleges as a source of entertainment (in the form of athletic events) and as a source of income, but they look on them with great suspicion. Crayfish's governing authorities can indulge themselves in the myth that neither Negroes nor whites in the community disapprove of the established system; Camellia's leaders are fighting against change, embittered by Negro defiance of segregation and infuriated by some white support of that defiance.

In Piedmont County the white leaders do not regard Negro demands as unreasonable in themselves. Although hard bargaining occurs and ill will exists, the right of the Negroes to work through the ULNA and other organizations is unquestioned. "The top leadership of Negroes is good, just top-flight," was the comment of the city manager.

LOCAL FACTIONAL AND ELECTORAL SYSTEMS

In a study of Negro leadership in northern cities, James Q. Wilson found that the structure and style of Negro politics reflected the general politics of the city in which the Negroes lived.[11] We may similarly expect the factional

[11] *Negro Politics: The Search for Leadership* (Glencoe, Ill.: The Free Press, 1960), pp. 52ff.

systems and the electoral systems of southern communities to help determine the nature and extent of Negro political organization.

Crayfish County has a purely personalized politics, with no identifiable factional structure. The Negro community has no factional structure and no politics of concern to the general community. Public officials are elected on a district basis. Normally this system tends to give Negroes a good chance of winning public office, because segregated housing concentrates the Negro population in a few districts where they may constitute a majority. With Negroes excluded from politics, however, Crayfish whites can keep an electoral system that results in heavy representation of the county's numerous hamlets. The emerging Negro political organization of Bright Leaf County is facilitated by the loose bifactionalism of the county, which provides a limited number of factions with which the Negroes can deal. Like Crayfish, Bright Leaf once elected public officials on a district basis, but this arrangement was dropped as soon as the Negroes organized to take advantage of it.

Camellia County's politics are conducted through white factions at least as recognizable as those in Bright Leaf. But the Negro factions are semi-atomistic and personalized. Accordingly, we must explain the rivalry among Negro leaders and their inability to create any enduring political organization with mass support in some other way than to say that they are simply a reflection of white factionalism. Camellia officials are elected at large, an arrangement that has denied recent Negro candidates any real chance of success. Piedmont has the most clear-cut system of factional competition, and the Negro community there has organized to win recognition and commitments from the enduring white factions. Many public officers are elected by district in Piedmont, and the system was not changed when Negroes began to win office: too many white politicians were indebted to the organized Negro vote.

### DIVERSITY OF INTERESTS

The white population of Crayfish is extremely homogeneous. Almost the entire population depends, in one way or another, on the farming, cattle, and dairy interests of the county. The only industry of any consequence is absentee-owned and serves simply to supplement the incomes of poorer whites by giving work to the white women in the county. In Bright Leaf, which is almost as homogeneous, farming interests dominate the county and a chamber of commerce viewpoint dominates Farmington. Competing interests have arisen in Farmington, however, as "newer elements" jostle "older elements" for advantage. Should this factionalism crystallize, the incipient Negro organization may be stimulated to greater activity. Camellia County is similarly dominated by business interests and "old families" that have grown rich with Capital City's growth. The general provincialism is mitigated by the presence of professionals in the colleges and the state government, but they are an ill organized and "alien" interest.

Only Piedmont has enough industries and unions to furnish economic as well as social heterogeneity. Union leaders, for example, negotiate with Negro leaders in seeking common candidates to support; in the other communities white laborers generally oppose candidates who are known to have Negro support.

LOCAL HISTORY

The history of each community is the final situational variable affecting political organizations. For example, a community that was the scene of long and bitter violence between labor and management as far back as the 1920's or 1930's might be expected to be organized politically along class lines to an unusual degree. In the South, the common experiences most important for a community's response to Negro political organizations are the Civil War and Reconstruction—or, more accurately, secondhand memories of "The War" and Reconstruction. These events have shaped all southern politics.

In Crayfish and Camellia counties, memories of that cataclysmic period are particularly bitter. The leading lawyer in Breedville (the only other lawyer is a drunk) delights in explaining how an outside land company exploited the corrupt legal system during Reconstruction by grabbing much of the land away from the people who had settled the Crayfish area. His delight appears to be enhanced by the violence used to drive the land company out and by the fact that he still gets an occasional fee from cases based on that period of confusion.

At the site of the state government, Camellia residents witnessed Negro and "carpetbag" control of the state government at first hand. A minor skirmish was fought near Capital City during the Civil War, and the townspeople stir up old memories every year in a formal celebration of the rout of the Yankees by a few old men and the brave young boys who were left in the university. At the turn of the century Camellia was still strictly a plantation county, with 80 per cent of its population made up of Negroes. Many "old family" leaders still act as if they were living in Crayfish rather than in a metropolitan area.

Bright Leaf residents have few exaggerated notions about an aristocratic past. The school superintendent explained,

> I call this a new town and a new community. Some nearby counties have pre-Civil War aristocracy; this county developed after the Civil War, and new leaders are recognized. Bright Leaf is a plebian county. It has no old aristocracy to fight.

He suggested that this lack of an ante-bellum history explains why Bright Leaf has better race relations than neighboring counties. Piedmont residents have favorable recollections of the Reconstruction. Before the Civil War the county was populated by poor farmers with few slaves, so the war itself produced no violent change in the way of life. Moreover, the end of the war and the presence of Union troops in the area triggered a local industrial revolution in textiles and tobacco. The development of successful industry rather than concern about the new status of Negroes thus dominated the Reconstruction period in Piedmont.

## Preconditions for effective Negro political organization: The Negro community

Favorable circumstances do not ensure effective Negro political organization, but they make it possible. The characteristics of the Negro community itself determine how well circumstances are exploited for political purposes. All the factors that we found in the preceding chapter to be conducive to high-quality leadership also tend to produce effective Negro organizations. More specifically, three factors seem to be particularly important for organizational effectiveness in the Negro communities examined: close ties between leaders and followers, organizational continuity, and organizational cohesion.

Most of the leaders of the Urbania League for Negro Activities won their positions through successful business, professional, or union activity *within* the Negro community. A few of the business leaders have Negro customers in a number of states. This economic relationship frees the ULNA leaders from dependence on whites; equally important, it demands that the leaders stay in close touch with the needs of ULNA members and nonmembers alike. In Camellia County the gap between leaders and followers is not so neatly bridged by economic ties; the largest pool of potential Negro leaders are employed by the college, and there is no economic incentive for them to remain in communication with the Negro masses. The "town-gown" division within the Negro community also tends to encourage leadership rivalry.

The continuity of the ULNA in Piedmont has resulted in experienced leaders and organizational prestige. The Inter-Civic Committee in Camellia was created to take over the direction of a single great effort—the bus boycott—and it has been unable to take on new functions. The Progressive Voters League in Bright Leaf grew out of the rivalry between two older organizations in the heat of an election campaign. This organization may be able to persist, but there are some indications that it may not survive for many other campaigns.

A high level of cohesion is necessary if political ambition and self-interest are to work for, rather than against, the racial cause. Southern whites traditionally assume that they can exploit individual Negroes, and it is easy for them to extend this assumption to politics. Moreover, many Negroes are highly vulnerable to economic inducements and threats. Urbania Negroes once competed for the largesse of white politicians seeking small blocs of Negro votes. Today such efforts are channeled through the ULNA, and Negro votes are "sold" for policy commitments, not for preelection payoffs. As we mentioned earlier, two Negro leaders in the Bright Leaf Civic Association, irritated because their candidate had been rejected by the Benevolent Brothers, were bribed to defect in a recent election. In Camellia County organizational rivalries produce competing slates of candidates endorsed by Negroes, with the result that white candidates refuse to place confidence in any Negro organization. One white politician explained that he was forced to rely on his personal organization:

> Three Negro groups were hauling to the polls on election day . . . and it was questionable as to whether they were getting them to vote correctly because they were handing out different lists even though CORE had distributed a list to the voters. I sent my own car with my name on the side and hauled Negro voters to the polls myself.

## Negro organization and the "bloc vote": The southwide picture

So far we have concentrated on the preconditions for effective political organization among the Negroes of the four communities we studied in detail. Now we want to shift our attention to the *effects* of political organization on the Negro vote *for the region as a whole*.

### EFFECTS ON VOTER REGISTRATION

In Chapter Six we analyzed data from all southern counties and discovered that extensive Negro organization is associated with a substantial (7-percentage-point) excess of registered Negro voters over what we would have predicted from the social and economic characteristics of southern counties. In a survey of the general population it is difficult to spot the organizational activity that produces this increment. Nevertheless, aggregate data from the 21 counties in our sample strongly support our earlier findings on the importance of Negro political organization.

Our interviewers came up with more accurate and detailed information on political and racial organizations in the survey counties than we could possibly obtain for all counties in the South.[12] We have used this information

---

12 Data were secured from each county in our sample on the presence or absence of these Negro political organizations: a biracial Human Relations Council; Negro religious, fraternal, or occupational groups active in politics; a county chapter of NAACP;

to classify the survey counties as low, medium, or high in Negro political organization. Again holding social and economic characteristics constant (through residual analysis), we find that the counties with low Negro political organization have an average (mean) residual of —5.2. This means that Negro registration in the counties with no Negro political organizations falls, on the average, some 5 percentage points below what we would expect from the generally depressed social and economic characteristics of those counties. The counties with a medium amount of Negro political organization have an average residual of —0.2, almost exactly what we would expect from their social and economic attributes alone. The counties with a high degree of Negro political organization, on the other hand, have an average residual of +16.7.

The relationship between Negro registration and organizational activity thus shows up more clearly when we confine our analysis to counties on which we have detailed information. In Chapter Six, when we were considering all southern counties, we found a difference of 9 percentage points that could be attributed to differences in organization. Now, from more refined data on a smaller number of counties, we find a difference of 22 percentage points.[13] The farther we pursue political factors, the more important they appear to be as an influence on Negro voter registration.

We can only expect to tease out faint residues of organizational activity from the southwide survey data. If Negro organizations are more active in politics than are white organizations, for example, we would expect more Negro voters to have registered initially as a result of outside encouragement rather than simply on their own initiative. Slight differences in the predicted direction do appear. When white voters are asked if there was "any special

---

a Negro Voters League. Counties with no such organizations are classified as low, those with some but not all types of organization are classified as medium, those with all four types of organization are classified as high in political organization.

This factual information on each county in the sample was secured by the interviewing staff through the procedure described in these instructions: "The following information is needed for *each county* in which interviews are conducted. . . . If you are interviewing in your home county, you may be able to fill it in yourself. If so, fill in the information but contact one of the five people in the county named below and go over it with him to see if he has anything to add: (1) any Negro in elective public office, (2) the editor of the Negro newspaper, if there is one, (3) the minister of the largest Negro church, (4) the Negro mortician with the largest business, (5) the principal of the largest Negro high school. For counties other than your residence, contact *two* of the persons named and get each of them to fill in the information on a separate form." This use of interviewers to secure factual information permits the combination of survey data with aggregate data of a sort that cannot be found in the census or other published sources. The potentialities of using interviewers to secure political facts on communities in addition to the opinions of individuals have not, to our knowledge, been exploited previously.

13 In the case of the southwide analysis, the difference is that found between counties with no Negro political organization and those with an NAACP chapter plus a local organization. For the survey counties, it is the difference in residuals between counties with no Negro political organization and those with the four types of organization mentioned above.

reason" why they first registered to vote, most say that there was no special reason or that they had simply come of age.[14] Only 1 per cent say that they were urged to register by a candidate, organization, or leader. Among Negroes, this trace of organizational activity is slightly more visible: 7 per cent of the Negro voters and 25 per cent of the Negroes who tried unsuccessfully to register say that they made the effort at the prompting of a candidate, organization, or leader.

### EFFECTS ON VOTER TURNOUT

Any successful political organization must be able to deliver the vote. Typically, the organization tries to increase turnout and crystallize sentiment in favor of a candidate most supporters of the organization would tend to vote for anyway. In view of the other indications of organizational effectiveness we turned up in the survey counties, we would expect to find greater turnout in counties with Negro political organizations. The findings reported in Table 8-1 completely confound this expectation. The percentages in the table

TABLE 8-1. *Percentage of Negro voters participating in all or most elections, by extent of Negro political organization*

| Type of electoral contest | No Negro organization | Some Negro organization | Four types of Negro organization |
|---|---|---|---|
| Presidential elections | 54% | 44% | 59% |
| Gubernatorial primary elections[a] | 46 | 28 | 44 |
| Gubernatorial general elections | 34 | 24 | 43 |
| Local or county elections | 46 | 35 | 39 |
| School board elections | 29 | 12 | 32 |
| N | 24 | 61 | 170 |

[a] Democratic primaries only.
NOTE: See footnote 12 for a description of the four types of Negro organization.

are based on voters only, and the small proportion of registered Negro voters in counties with no Negro organization are as regular in their turnout as the larger proportion in counties with a full range of Negro organizations. The success of Negro organizations in the South appears to lie in their getting greater numbers of Negroes registered, not in maximizing the turnout of those who are registered.

On closer inspection, the relationships reported in Table 8-1 appear to be curvilinear: regularity of turnout is relatively high among voters in counties with no organization and in those with high organization; it is low in the middle group of counties with incomplete organization. So we can say that

14 See Chapter Three.

the figures reflect two different phenomena—one motivational, the other organizational. In counties where Negroes have, through their own initiative, overcome barriers to voting, the voting lists include people with relatively high motivation. In counties with organizational support for Negro voting, people with only a mild commitment may be led to register and to vote. But a relatively strong organizational structure may be necessary to get these "extra" voters to the polls; such a structure is absent in the counties with an incomplete set of Negro organizations.

## EFFECTS ON VOTER PREFERENCES

Anti-Negro whites in the South frequently complain about the Negro bloc vote—and, of course, they denounce the candidate who seems to enjoy Negro support. The term "bloc voting" implies that the Negro vote is organized, that Negro voters self-consciously stick together, that bloc voting is somehow conspiratorial. But most Negroes may vote for the same candidate simply because the candidate ignores the race issue while his opponent devotes his campaign to denouncing Negroes and civil rights. No leadership, organization, or even communication between Negro voters would be necessary; a "bloc vote" might emerge as a result of similar but independent responses to the same stimuli. Basically, southern Negroes may tend to vote the same way because they all hurt in the same place. How much is the unity of the Negro vote in the South *self-conscious* "bloc voting"? How much is it merely the result of independent action by individuals with similar goals?

Indirect evidence on this question may be gained by examining the proportions of Negroes who admit that their votes would be influenced by the discovery that "most of the Negroes" or "the strongest white segregation leaders" in the area favor a particular candidate in an election.[15] As Tables 8–2 and 8–3 show, 63 per cent of southern Negroes say they would make up their own minds when Negro support for a candidate is suggested, but only 47 per cent say the same thing when segregationist support for a candidate is suggested.

Few people like to admit that they simply go along with the crowd; this may help account for the larger proportion of Negroes who say their vote would be influenced by a candidate's segregationist support than by his support from Negroes. But, among those who say they would be influenced, the direc-

---

[15] Respondents were not asked directly whom they would vote for in such a situation but were asked to "suppose that you . . . hadn't yet made up your mind who you would vote for." Then the discovery of Negro or segregationist support for a candidate occurs. "What difference would it make to you?" The open-ended form of this question and its highly permissive wording make it easy for respondents to say that such a discovery would make no difference or that "I'd make up my own mind." Given the widespread disapproval of bloc voting, we would expect Negroes to be reluctant to admit that it exists.

TABLE 8–2.  *Effect on respondent's vote of discovery that most Negroes support a candidate in a campaign in which respondent is uncertain of his preference*

| | WHITE | NEGRO | | |
| | | | | Counties with four types of |
| | | Counties with no | Counties with some | |
| | Southwide | Southwide | organization | organization | organization |
|---|---|---|---|---|---|
| Vote for | 1% | 31% | 22% | 23% | 40% |
| No difference, make up own mind | 78 | 63 | 71 | 72 | 55 |
| Not vote for | 18 | 0 | 0 | 0 | 0 |
| Other, don't know | 3 | 6 | 7 | 5 | 5 |
| TOTAL | 100% | 100% | 100% | 100% | 100% |
| N | 690 | 618 | 149 | 155 | 314 |

tion of influence is unanimously toward the Negro-supported candidate and almost as solidly against the segregationist-supported candidate.

The response of whites to the same questions is less clear-cut: 78 per cent deny that they would be influenced by the discovery that most Negroes supported a particular candidate, 18 per cent say they would vote against such a candidate, and 1 per cent say they would join the Negroes in voting for him. Support of a candidate by the strongest white segregation leaders would

TABLE 8–3.  *Effect on respondent's vote of discovery that white segregationists support a candidate in a campaign in which respondent is uncertain of his preference*

| | WHITE | NEGRO | | |
| | | | | Counties with four types of |
| | | Counties with no | Counties with some | |
| | Southwide | Southwide | organization | organization | organization |
|---|---|---|---|---|---|
| Vote for | 23% | 2% | 2% | 3% | 1% |
| No difference, make up own mind | 61 | 47 | 62 | 56 | 35 |
| Not vote for | 7 | 39 | 24 | 31 | 51 |
| Other, don't know | 9 | 12 | 12 | 10 | 13 |
| TOTAL | 100% | 100% | 100% | 100% | 100% |
| N | 688 | 618 | 149 | 155 | 314 |

be enough to induce support from 23 per cent of the whites and opposition from 7 per cent. Although the bloc vote by whites in campaigns involving racial issues is no doubt understated in these findings—and involves, even as stated, greater absolute numbers than the Negro bloc vote—the proportion of whites who deny being directly influenced by such issues is greater than the proportion of Negroes who deny it. And whereas almost all whites who admit to being influenced by Negro support say they would oppose the Negro-backed candidate, a fourth of those who would react to strong segregationist support would *oppose* the candidate so identified. As anticipated, then, Negroes are particularly sensitive to the "race issue" in politics, and they are virtually unanimous in their reactions to it.

Negro political organizations thus have a fertile field in which to work. Tables 8–2 and 8–3 suggest that they are already cultivating it. The proportion of Negroes who say they would vote for a candidate if he had the support of most other Negroes is almost twice as large in counties with all four kinds of Negro political organization as it is in counties with none or only some of these organizations. The proportion who say they would oppose a candidate supported by strong segregationists goes up from 24 per cent in counties with no Negro political organization, to 31 per cent where some such organizations exist, to 51 per cent where all four types of organization are found. Without attempting to unravel the causal factors in these strong relationships, we can conclude that a rational vote in terms of Negro interests is much more likely in counties that have a rich structure of Negro organizations.

Occasional comments suggest that political organization is directly responsible for at least some of these differences. A young wife employed as a cashier in Houston, which has a full assortment of Negro organizations, responded negatively when asked if Negro support for a candidate would influence her decision. But then she contradicted herself by saying, "The Harris Council of [Negro] Organizations endorse a candidate, and usually me and other people vote for him." Here the existence of a trusted organization helps individual voters to make up their minds. In a Columbia, South Carolina, slum, on the other hand, an elderly Negro lady spoke for a different generation. "I'm 105 years old," she claimed, "and have never voted and am not going to vote." [But just suppose you were voting?] "No, I wouldn't go along with no colored people." Negro organization may be necessary to a high level of Negro cohesion at the polls, but it is not sufficient in itself.

Negro political organizations must, if they are to survive, have an effect that is discernible at the polls. Aggregate county data demonstrate that Negro organizations achieve relatively high rates of voter registration in their counties. The data in Tables 8–2 and 8–3 also suggest that Negroes are more attuned to racial cues in counties with a wide range of Negro organizations. How much of this response is attributable to the work of these organizations is difficult to say.

Despite our fear that Negroes would be reluctant to talk about bloc voting, respondents were told, "In some places, you hear that Negroes get together and all vote for the same candidate." Then they were asked, "Have you ever heard about that happening here?" In the counties with no formal Negro organization, 3 per cent said yes; affirmative responses went up to 27 per cent in counties with an incomplete set of organizations and to 32 per cent in counties with a full array of organizations. Of course, not all Negroes are equally familiar with the organizational effort behind this cohesion in voting. An Arkansas maid who belongs to an organization but cannot remember its name describes the process vaguely, "Some person with influence calls a meeting and they all decide on the candidate they think is best." Piedmont residents are more aware of the organization behind the effort. One voter simply said, "Yes. The Urbania League for Negro Activities sponsors this." Another explained how, again naming the organization, "Well, this League for Negro Activities pass out leaflets."

White residents are not so well informed about these activities. Even when the analysis is confined to those who say that Negroes vote in their locality, white images of Negro bloc voting do not appear very realistic. In counties with a full set of Negro organizations, 38 per cent of the whites have heard that local Negroes vote together. But in counties with an incomplete array of organizations, only 16 per cent have heard of such activity, and the proportion goes up to 29 per cent in the counties with no Negro organization at all. The greater perception of bloc voting in areas with no organization to promote it than in counties with some such organizations suggests that, at least in the more repressive counties, this question triggered expressions of white fears rather than the facts of the situation.

But white candidates for public office cannot afford to be unrealistic. Their efforts to win Negro votes differ greatly with the extent of Negro political organization. As Table 8–4 indicates, only 11 per cent of the Negroes in counties with no Negro political organization report that white candidates do anything to get Negro votes, compared with 40 per cent where some Negro organizations are found and 52 per cent where a more complete set of organizations exists. Success in commanding the attention of candidates, a prerequisite for political influence, thus appears to be greatly increased by the presence of Negro political organizations.

The extent of bloc voting probably can be most clearly discerned from the voting preference of Negroes in gubernatorial primary elections. Even in a state like Alabama or Mississippi—where candidates often vie with each other to prove that they are the most extreme segregationists—some marginal differentiation can generally be detected. The 1964 inaugural address of Governor Paul Johnson of Mississippi, for example, revealed some uneasiness about that state's reputation as a "closed society."[16] In every state in our survey, a

16 James W. Silver, op. cit., p. xx.

TABLE 8–4.   *Negro respondents' perceptions of efforts of white*
*candidates to win Negro votes, by extent*
*of Negro political organization*

| White candidates' relation to Negro voters | No Negro organization | Some Negro organization | Four types of Negro organization | Negro southwide |
|---|---|---|---|---|
| Try to win support | 11% | 40% | 52% | 39% |
| Uncertain ("don't know") | 11 | 34 | 28 | 25 |
| Do not try to win support | 78 | 26 | 20 | 36 |
| TOTAL | 100% | 100% | 100% | 100% |
| N | 149 | 155 | 313 | 617 |

majority of the Negro voters reported that they voted for the gubernatorial candidate who would be judged least anti-Negro by outside observers. But the size of the majorities varied markedly with the extent of Negro political organization. In counties with no such organization, 60 per cent of the Negro voters supported the "pro-Negro" candidate, compared with 84 per cent in the middle group of counties and 88 per cent in those most organized.

In view of the common interest of Negroes in the race issue, majorities as great as 60 per cent may be expected without any organized bloc voting at all. Where organizations reinforce these common tendencies, cohesion in voting approaches the 90 per cent level. We cannot attribute all this increase in solidarity to organizational effort. To some extent, the differences we are discussing are differences between rural and urban counties. Although an urban environment may be a necessary condition to a rich Negro organizational structure, urban life in itself does not appear sufficient to explain differences of the magnitude that we found. Solidarity as great as that reported seems to represent the payoff that comes from organizational efforts.

An illustration of this payoff is provided by the performance of the ULNA in a recent gubernatorial primary. In order to nullify charges of Negro bloc voting between the first and second primary, the ULNA leaders decided to support a candidate in the first primary who was not the most liberal on either racial or economic policy. This strategem left the ULNA free, of course, to throw its entire strength behind the liberal in the runoff. As Table 8–5 demonstrates, the ULNA was able to deliver in the first primary an overwhelming majority of the vote in predominantly Negro precincts to a candidate who was not the "natural" choice of Negroes. While Negroes in other cities of the state were turning in solid votes for the liberal candidate, Urbania Negroes were equally solid for the choice of their organization. This is one of those rare cases in social science when an imputation of causal relations can be made without reservation. Where efficient leadership capitalizes on favorable con-

TABLE 8–5. *The ability to deliver the Negro vote in an "unnatural" direction: The vote in predominantly Negro precincts in a first gubernatorial primary in four Piedmont state urban areas*

| Racial stands of gubernatorial candidates | PREDOMINANTLY NEGRO PRECINCTS | | | |
|---|---|---|---|---|
| | Urbania | City X | City Y | City Z |
| Most pro-Negro | 207 | 4,209 | 2,352 | 2,209 |
| Moderate | 2,623 | 93 | 158 | 63 |
| Moderate | 79 | 103 | 66 | 44 |
| Most anti-Negro | 32 | 31 | 74 | 20 |

ditions for Negro organization, the results may be so dramatically effective that we must attribute them directly to organizational effort.

## The Negro church and politics

Negroes must create their own organizations before they can become a significant force in southern politics. But these organizations do not have to be *explicitly political*. All kinds of "nonpolitical" groups and organizations play an important part in the politics of the larger white community.[17] Why not in the Negro community, too?

The church—an almost totally segregated institution in the South—is the most likely "nonpolitical" agency to organize and direct Negro political activity in the region. Southern Negroes are a God-fearing, churchgoing people; 77 per cent of them report that they attend church with considerable regularity. Marx felt that capitalism contained "the seeds of its own destruction" because it brought workers physically together in factories and cities where they could be easily organized into a class-conscious, revolutionary proletariat. Southern whites, by teaching Negro slaves their religious practices but insisting that Sunday morning be segregated, may similarly have planted the seeds for the destruction of segregation. The church provided Negroes a common meeting ground, a corps of verbally skilled leaders who are economically independent of whites, and supernatural support for the overthrow of segregation. The fact that the most common occupation of Negro "leaders" in the South (as nominated by the Negro masses) was that of minister lends additional credence to this line of reasoning.

In order to examine this possibility, all our respondents who attended church were asked if election campaigns were ever discussed there. The most common response of both Negroes and whites was negative (see Table 8–6). But

[17] See D. B. Truman, *The Governmental Process* (New York: Alfred A. Knopf, 1962).

TABLE 8–6.   *Discussion of elections at church, as perceived by those who attend*

|                         | Negro | White |
|-------------------------|-------|-------|
| Elections discussed     | 35%   | 18%   |
| Elections not discussed | 54    | 63    |
| Don't know              | 10    | 18    |
| No answer               | 1     | 1     |
| TOTAL                   | 100%  | 100%  |
| N                       | 597   | 622   |

the minority who reported campaign discussions at church was twice as great among Negroes as among whites. And, despite the higher average education of whites, they were more likely than Negroes to say they did not know whether campaigns were discussed or not. Carrying the question of the church as a political organization a step farther, 5 per cent of the whites[18] and 18 per cent of the Negroes who attend say that their minister has said something about which candidate the members of the church ought to support. Almost a fifth of the Negroes who go to church thus receive direct clues as to how they should vote, and over a third hear some kind of discussion of elections.

The political nature of the Negro church in the South may be a result of compensatory activity by people who are excluded from open political participation. Or does it result from the high salience of politics for southern Negroes? If the former is the case, we would expect discussions of politics to be more frequently reported from counties where relatively few Negroes are registered to vote. Seventeen counties in our sample included enough Negro churchgoers to permit a test of this expectation. Among these seventeen, five rank extremely low in Negro voter registration (with 10 per cent or less of their eligible Negroes registered). All five of these counties also rank low (24 per cent or less) in the proportions of churchgoers who report discussions of politics at church. A reasonable amount of Negro political participation thus appears a necessary condition to a politicized church.

Discussions of elections at church seem to serve as an additional form of participation in areas where Negroes vote. Nor is the church a covert substitute for manifestly political organizations. In five counties with no Negro

18 Our interviews were conducted shortly after the 1960 presidential election, during which John F. Kennedy's Roman Catholicism was a matter of great concern in the overwhelmingly Protestant South and had a major impact on white voting in the region. See Philip E. Converse, *et al.*, "Stability and Change in 1960: A Reinstating Election," *American Political Science Review*, Vol. 55 (1961), p. 269; and Donald M. Freeman, "Religion and Southern Politics: A Study of the Political Behavior of Southern White Protestants" (Ph.D. dissertation, University of North Carolina, 1963).

political organization, the average proportion of Negro church attenders who report election discussions at church is 11 per cent. In five counties with some but not all four kinds of Negro political organization, the proportion reporting church discussions of elections goes up to 26 per cent. Finally, in seven counties with a high level of Negro political organization, the proportion reporting church discussions of elections reaches 50 per cent. When the Negro church gets into electoral politics, then, it is supplementing rather than substituting for more explicitly political organizations.

## Conclusions: Organization, bloc voting, and political payoffs

In this chapter we have argued that southern Negroes must *create* their *own* political organizations before they can become a significant force in southern politics. Their greatest political asset is the vote; they are very poor in other political resources. And, in order to maximize the impact of their votes on political decision making, they must organize those votes. This can be denounced as "bloc voting" by white southerners, and it generally is. But all political organizations seek a "bloc vote," and many white groups—the local chamber of commerce, the KKK, the country-club set, southern congressmen and senators, for example—often achieve a degree of unity in voting that rivals or surpasses that of Negroes. "You can talk all you want to about bloc voting," the political brains of the ULNA said, "but we learned it from you."

The opportunity of Negro communities to develop effective political organizations in the South depends, to a very large degree, on factors outside Negro control. Our survey of the development of Negro political organizations in Crayfish, Bright Leaf, Camellia, and Piedmont counties demonstrated this quite well. Favorable white attitudes and styles of political leadership; an electoral system in which the votes of Negroes are not submerged by those of whites; a white factional system that gives local politics enough structure so that Negroes have someone to bargain with; social heterogeneity and a community ethos that does not glorify the (largely mythical[19]) ante-bellum days—all these factors facilitate the development of Negro organization. The characteristics of the Negro community itself also shape organizational opportunities, primarily by facilitating or inhibiting close ties between Negro leaders and the masses and by facilitating or inhibiting organizational continuity and cohesion.

The effects of Negro political organization are difficult to judge, because the apparently more effective organizations tend to be found in areas where Negroes probably would be active and influential anyway. Nonetheless, our

[19] W. J. Cash, *The Mind of the South* (New York: Alfred A. Knopf, 1941).

analysis suggests that Negro organizations do have a substantial *independent* impact on the number of Negroes registered to vote and a smaller influence on the turnout of those Negroes who already are registered. And although, as Douglas Price has written, "Negro leaders have generally been unable to deliver the Negro vote except in the direction toward which Negroes were already inclined . . . ,"[20] we did detect some traces of influence beyond this point.

Most Negroes tend to vote the same way in most elections even when no organizational effort is made—after all, they all hurt in the same place. But the existence of an efficient and respected Negro political organization can increase the number of these votes, and it can also concentrate them in support of friends. This last gain is incremental—from perhaps 60 per cent of the Negroes voting the same way to a maximum of about 90 per cent—but it is a sizable increment. Thus although effective Negro political organizations require conditions that are not present in many—probably most—southern communities today, those that do exist stimulate a larger, more rational, and more concentrated Negro vote than would exist if there were no such organizations.

But a large and disciplined vote is not an end in itself. It is only a means of influencing government decisions and, through those decisions, of opening up an avenue to a better life for southern Negroes. A substantial organized vote is powerfully attractive to all politicians—be they northern or southern, white or black—but the governmental response to a sizable Negro bloc vote is not automatic. Indeed, the Negro vote appears to operate at a considerable discount. Negroes are a minority in almost all southern communities where organized voting is possible. They are highly visible. Where whites are so fearful and hostile toward Negroes that politicians run the risk of losing two white votes for every Negro vote gained, candidates are not likely to be *overtly* responsive to Negro wants and needs. Where the white vote is less predictably and less overwhelmingly anti-Negro, some ambitious politicians will try to build a biracial coalition of supporters. Even when this strategy works—as it has in Piedmont County, for example—the Negroes in the coalition are likely to receive a smaller "payoff" than their numbers merit. And such a coalition is very fragile—the white segment of the coalition may desert the first time someone cries "nigger." Because the Negroes can rarely win without white allies, especially in races in large geographical districts, they have to settle for considerably less than half a loaf or give up eating bread althogether.

Thus the returns of effective Negro political organization, judged in terms of government decisions favorable to the Negro community, may be slow in coming and modest when they arrive. We shall return to this broad problem in the concluding pages of this book.

20 H. Douglas Price, *The Negro and Southern Politics* (New York: New York University Press, 1957), p. 86.

*Chapter Nine*

# Mass Communications and Negro Political Participation

America, we are often told, is rapidly becoming a mass society. We have been so atomized, centralized, and propagandized that few regional, ethnic, or class differences in values, behavior, or life style remain. The spicy stew that once bubbled in the melting pot is now a bland purée. A major cause of this catastrophe—for those who take this view usually do so with alarm—is the mass media of communications: newspapers, magazines, television, radio, and the movies.

One sees signs of cultural homogenization on all sides. Even in America's most self-consciously "different" region, most things seem "standard American" rather than "southern." The statue in the courthouse square wears a different uniform, but most small towns in the South are highly reminiscent of their counterparts in Ohio or Nebraska. The stores on Main Street show the same goods at the same prices; the restaurants serve the same deep-fat-fried cuisine; identical juke boxes blare the same rock 'n roll by the same teen-age combos; the pretty girls look just as pretty in their made-in-New York dresses; American men wear identical suits everywhere. The cities—North and South—are interchangeable in appearance and suffer from identical problems: traffic snarls, urban decay, racial tension, smog, and crime. On this level at least, the South joined the Union long ago. The nation's network of mass communications seems to have brought about this cultural reconciliation.

Mass communications in the South are controlled from outside; they are aimed at a national rather than a regional audience. Television programing is dominated by three national networks and the advertisers of nationally marketed products. The content of southern newspapers is largely what comes in over the AP or UPI wires; mass-circulation magazines are not written in the

South for southern audiences. Southern radio stations depend almost entirely on nationally recorded entertainment and wire-service news "flashes" to fill in the blanks between commercials—a locally written and produced show is an event that broadcasters boast about at their Rotary meetings or before the FCC when time to renew the franchise comes around. The movies shown in the South are produced by nonsoutherners with an eye on the box offices of the world.

Local publishers, editors, broadcasters, and theater operators can to some extent tailor their output to satisfy local tastes and local prejudices. The selection, editing, and placement of news stories, the use of pictures and headlines, can substantially alter a message written in New York or Washington. Local television stations can refuse to broadcast Huntley-Brinkley news, the *Today* show, or David Susskind's *Open End* if these programs shock southern white sensibilities. Local theater operators do not rush to book movies on Negro themes into their popcorn palaces.

To make these comforting adjustments in the nationwide flow of words and other symbols is nothing more than common prudence: the local purveyors of mass communications are in business to make a profit, and antagonizing the people who count is not the way to riches. But pecuniary considerations also limit how much time and staff can be invested in making the package they sell locally palatable. Thus, even after the locals have chipped away the rougher edges of messages intended for national consumption, the mass media in the South still reflect standard, homogenized, American values and perspectives more than they do peculiarly southern preoccupations.

The national producers of symbols—the networks, the wire services, Hollywood, and the magazine publishers—are not renowned for their crusading tendencies. As V. O. Key persuasively argues, their major effect is probably to reinforce the *status quo*.[1] But it may be a national *status quo* that they reinforce, not a southern one. The mass media may try to avoid controversy, but the wickedness of racial segregation and the desirability of "one man, one vote" are scarcely controversial subjects among the vast bulk of Americans.[2] The national media reflect the common biases of their audience; the political and racial biases of white southerners are not common enough to carry much weight in a mass society.

If this line of speculation is correct, the mass media of communication may be one of the more powerful agencies of change in southern politics and race relations. This same nationally oriented communications network seems to have made the popular culture of the South "homogenized American." Can it not do the same to the *political* culture of the region? Specifically, will not the

[1] V. O. Key, Jr., *Public Opinion and American Democracy* (New York: Alfred A. Knopf, 1961), p. 395.
[2] At least not in the abstract. See James W. Prothro and Charles M. Grigg, "Fundamental Principles of Democracy: Bases of Agreement and Disagreement," *Journal of Politics*, Vol. 22 (1960), pp. 276–84.

media increase the political activities of southern Negroes by teaching them that political participation, *no matter what their white neighbors say*, is a normal, expected, and worthwhile activity in America? And will they not reduce southern white resistance to such a development by making whites more typically American and less "southern" in their racial attitudes and political orientation? If the mass media can destroy other regional, ethnic, and class differences in America, why can they not destroy the deviant political patterns of the South? In this chapter we shall essay an answer to these questions—with particular reference to how mass communications affect Negro political participation.[3]

We shall begin by looking at the actual content of the most politicized means of mass communications in the region—the newspaper. Communications are unlikely to have much effect if no one is listening. So we shall look next at how and how much southerners expose themselves to the flow of words and symbols carried by the media. Then we shall be in a position to try to determine the impact of mass communications on Negro political activity in the South.

## *The news southern style*

On Monday morning, May 13, 1963, the *Urbania Press* greeted the residents of Piedmont County with this black, eight-column headline on page one:

JFK SENDS TROOPS TO BASES NEAR BIRMINGHAM
FOLLOWING NEW OUTBREAK OF VIOLENCE IN CITY

*President Urges*
*Effort for Peace*

The *Capital City Bugle*, Camellia County's only daily newspaper, appeared that afternoon. Page one headlined an updated story on the same events:

U.S. TROOPS POISED
OUTSIDE BIRMINGHAM
50 HURT IN RIOTING

*JFK Challenged*
*by Gov. Wallace*

Hundreds of miles north, in Bright Leaf County, the *Farmington Daily Mirror* appeared the same afternoon. It headlined the same AP story with:

NEAR-NORMALCY IN BIRMINGHAM
AFTER RIOTS; TROOPS STAND BY

[3] The influence of the mass media of communications on white racial attitudes will be explored in Chapter Twelve.

The *Breedville Weekly* was not published in Crayfish County until the following Thursday afternoon. Its leading news story was:

DROUTH EASED SLIGHTLY
BY RAINS IN CRAYFISH

Thus did four southern newspapers react—or fail to react—to the 1963 "Mother's Day Riot" in Birmingham, Alabama.

The Birmingham riot was the first time during the racial revolution of the 1960's that American Negroes assumed the role of aggressors. Uncontrollable mobs of Negroes roamed the streets of an American city throwing rocks and bottles, breaking windows and setting fires, cursing and brawling among themselves and with policemen and white passers-by. Before then, most white Americans had become hardened to sporadic mob violence by white racists. But not many realized that Negro communities contained a violence-prone lunatic fringe, too, or that normally law-abiding Negroes could be goaded into violence. The passivity and nonviolence of American Negroes could never again be taken for granted, a fact that became ever more apparent as Negro rioting broke out in the black ghettos of New York, Chicago, Rochester, and other northern cities during the long hot summer of 1963. The "rules of the game" in race relations were permanently changed in Birmingham during the predawn hours of Mother's Day, 1963.

How and why did the riots occur?

During the spring of 1962 the Negro community of Birmingham, caught up in the spirit of the times, launched a "selective-buying" campaign against downtown stores as a protest against the segregation of public accommodations. In reprisal the three-man city commission—whose leading figure was Commissioner Eugene ("Bull") Connor, in charge of the police—voted to stop the distribution of free food to needy families (almost all of them Negro) until after the boycott had been ended.[4] Connor, who was running for governor at the time, was quoted as saying that he could solve Birmingham's racial problems with "two policemen and a dog" and that he would "sic" police dogs on Negroes who came downtown before the boycott was lifted.[5] His remarks did not lead to racial harmony in what was then widely considered to be the most segregated city in America. More united, determined, and bitter than ever before, the Negro community sustained the boycott and laid plans for additional protest activity in the future.

In early April 1963 a new drive began as hundreds of school children, aged 6 to 16, marched on City Hall, paraded in the streets, and picketed department stores. Four hundred and fifty of them were arrested the first day. As more demonstrations and more arrests took place over the next few days, tension mounted and the crowds of curious white and Negro onlookers became larger

[4] *Afro-American* (Baltimore), April 4, 1962.
[5] *Atlanta Inquirer*, April 14, 1962.

and more difficult to control. The demonstrators remained orderly, but pushing, shoving, name-calling, and fist fights began to break out among the bystanders.

"Bull" Connor's reaction to these threats to public order was to shoot high-pressure fire hoses at the Negro crowds and to unleash police dogs. ("Look at that dog go," Connor was quoted as saying admiringly as one animal lunged toward a Negro. "That's what we train them for—to enforce the law—just like we train our officers."[6])

Some Negroes began to taunt and hurl rocks at the police and firemen. One tried to stab a police dog and was knocked to the ground and beaten by six policemen. The daily crowds in the downtown area were now so large that traffic became hopelessly snarled as Birmingham ". . . turned into a teeming, surging mass of spectators and demonstrators."[7] In the midst of this incendiary situation the motel headquarters of the Negro protest movement and the home of its most prominent leader were bombed on the eve of Mother's Day. Before dawn the Negro rioting began. For four hours the Negro mob ran wild in an eight-block area in the Negro section of the city.

We can learn a good deal about the newspapers in our four southern communities by examining how they covered this story and how well they explained its causes and possible consequences to their readers.

The *Breedville Weekly* did not even try; it published not one word about the riots in either its news or editorial columns. This omission might be excused on the ground that it is a weekly paper circulating in an area in which a metropolitan daily newspaper is also available. But the paper does sometimes print editorials on developments outside the county, and large numbers of Crayfish residents read only the *Weekly* (see Table 9–3 on page 249). This time at least the *Breedville Weekly* totally failed to inform local residents about important (if distant) events with substantial local implications. It did nothing to dispel the vast ignorance of the world "outside" which characterizes the county.

All the news stories about the Birmingham riots that appeared in the *Urbania Press,* the *Capital City Bugle,* and the *Farmington Daily Mirror* came from Associated Press or United Press International wires. As a result, their riot stories were very similar—in some cases identical—and much the same as the reports that appeared in most other newspapers throughout the nation. They did differ, however, in which and how many of the wire-service stories they printed, in how the stories were headlined, and in the news photographs they printed.

The *Press* and the *Bugle* were the same size on May 13—18 pages—yet the Urbania daily printed twice as much about the riots as did the newspaper in Capital City. The lead story in the *Press,* a UPI dispatch from Washington, concentrated on the President's reaction to the crisis, the movement of federal

---

6 *Durham Morning Herald* (N.C.), April 8, 1963 (AP dispatch).
7 *Ibid.*

troops to military bases near Birmingham, and the return of Assistant Attorney General Burke Marshall to the smoldering city. Alabama Governor George Wallace's objection to the President's deployment of federal troops near Birmingham received little attention—less than one column-inch buried in the middle of a long story. A second story on page one, headed "Bombings Followed by Riots," described the events of the preceding Saturday and Sunday in Birmingham with an emphasis on the bombings and the ruthlessness and intransigence of Birmingham's white officials as proximate causes of the rioting. On the last page of the first section of the paper, a UPI correspondent described how "For 3 Hours, They Huddled in a Bomb-Torn Lobby," in an eye-witness account of the rioting. Among the incidents described was this one:

> . . . Mrs. Wyatt Tee Walker, wife of a top aide to Dr. Martin Luther King, Jr., moved in the wrong direction—toward her motel room. A trooper struck her on the forehead with the butt of his carbine.
>    The woman keeled over backward. Two Negro men grabbed and pulled her into the lobby and she was taken to the hospital with blood streaming down her face.

The *Press* ran three pictures about the story—one of the Reverend A. D. King's bombed home in Birmingham, another of several Negro homes burning early Sunday near the motel headquarters of the Negro protest movement, and a third of special officers armed with shotguns standing guard over the city after the rioting had ended.

The *Capital City Bugle* was much more interested in President Kennedy's threat to use federal troops in Birmingham than in what actually had happened there or why. It published no account of the events leading up to the riots comparable to the one in the *Press*, although the tail end of the long lead story did attempt a brief summary. The actions of the police before and during the riots received scant attention. The only picture the *Bugle* ran on the story showed a blood-smeared white police inspector, just hit in the head with a rock, being led to safety by two faithful Negroes.

The *Daily Mirror* in Farmington somehow succeeded in taking the excitement and significance out of the story altogether. Its headline on May 13 was bland. It ran no pictures of the riot—although it did print in this issue an entire page of pictures of the Verrazano-Narrows bridge under construction in New York. Its one and only news story on events in Birmingham concentrated on post-riot developments and made little effort to describe what had happened there or why.

The editorial comments on the riots—as limited as they were—give additional insight into the role of these newspapers in the region's racial crisis. The *Urbania Press* printed only one locally written editorial on the ugly episode. It appeared on the Monday after the riots and read, in its entirety:

### POLICE USE OF DOGS

Birmingham, Alabama, is not the only place police use dogs in efforts to break up mobs.

Tucked away well in the news story of the demonstrations put on Thursday night by Yale and Brown university students, was mention that Providence, R.I., police "used trained dogs to quell the disturbance" created by Brown students.

We hold no brief for police brutality, wherever and however exercised. But we ought to keep police methods in clear perspective and judge them accordingly.

After this meek "you're another" effort, the local editors let syndicated columnists explain and evaluate the events at Birmingham. The following day Joseph Alsop's column analyzed the riots and laid primary responsibility at the feet of "Bull" Connor and other "extremist" elements in Birmingham. Two days later Walter Lippmann praised the efforts of Assistant Attorney General Burke Marshall to reach an accommodation. He concluded:

These [Birmingham city] officials are morally responsible for the bombing which led to the rioting . . . there is no hope that reason and sanity and good will can prevail as long as the constituted authorities are opposed to accommodation.

The editors of the *Capital City Bugle* also left editorializing pretty much to their syndicated columnists. But while the *Press's* columnists range from moderates to mildly left-of-center, the *Bugle's* pundits are all conservative to reactionary in their views. Thus the first editorial comment on the riots to appear in the *Bugle* was in Holmes Alexander's column; it took the form of an allegorical discussion between President Kennedy and a psychiatrist:

"Well!" said the distinguished young statesman, "We've got a situation in Birmingham where police dogs are snapping at Negroes. That isn't a very good way to get the Negro vote, is it?"

"Perhaps not," Dr. Couchmaster agreed dryly.

"And the same way with those fire hoses. My brother and I like to hose people with oratory, and some of them seem to enjoy it, but nobody enjoys high-pressure water from fire hoses."

"You're beginning to think that the Negroes will wish you hadn't incited them to riot, is that it?"

"That's right," said the young statesman. . . .

"Instead of advancing racial rights by quiet statesmanship, you've made mob scenes almost a commonplace in this self-rule country . . ." [Dr. Couchmaster concluded].

On May 16, the *Bugle* reprinted an editorial from the Dallas, Texas, *Morning News* saying "events in Alabama show how the whole racial problem is wrought [sic] with hypocrisy, animosity and—most important—politics." Several days later another editorial was reprinted, this one from the Spokane, Washington, *Spokesman-Review*:

The determination of some Negro leaders to arouse mass demonstrations in Birmingham, Alabama, has put a severe strain upon local law enforcement officers. . . . Many [Negroes] have actually invited the shocking treatment dealt out by the officers. . . . Integration leaders like Martin Luther King are likely to lose much sympathetic support around the country if they persist in defying the local law in this manner.

Finally, on May 21, John Chamberlain commented on Birmingham in his column:

When a minority, whether racial or otherwise, is denied the use of public facilities that are open to everyone else, one can fully understand the gnawing sense of resentment and frustration that will grow out of the situation. Rights are rights. . . . But the question is: Can injustice ever be rectified by taking to the streets for a decision?

The *Farmington Daily Mirror* also followed a hands-off policy in its locally written editorials. The *Mirror* regularly prints John Chamberlain's column, including the one quoted above that appeared in the *Bugle*. The only other *Mirror* columnist to comment on Birmingham was James Marlow. Although he expressed some reservations about President Kennedy's constitutional authority to dispatch troops to Birmingham, he also gave the *Mirror*'s readers a little lecture that many of them needed. He wrote on May 14:

The racial disorders in Birmingham are only the latest evidence of Negroes' rapidly growing willingness to act by themselves against discrimination. Their actions now—in massive demonstrations, sit-ins, and most recently in riots in the Alabama city—have been building up as they got tired waiting for equal treatment. They've been waiting, except for a brief time in Reconstruction days, for 175 years. . . .

It was nine years ago this week—on May 17, 1954—that the Supreme Court outlawed segregation in public schools and opened the door to banning segregation in all public places. . . .

But that decision didn't say how fast desegregation of public schools should proceed. On May 31, 1955, the court gave its answer: with "all deliberate speed." What did that mean? Southern states interpreted it as meaning very slowly. It has been very slow. The Negroes are impatient, so impatient that some of them now condemn the NAACP for being too slow by relying too much on legal efforts to hasten the process. So some have resorted to direct action.

Several conclusions emerge from this brief look at the coverage of the Mother's Day riot in the newspapers of Piedmont, Camellia, Bright Leaf, and Crayfish counties.

The community that had already demonstrated the greatest capacity to grapple with race problems—Piedmont County—received the most adequate coverage of the riot in its newspaper; the communities with the most to learn from the riots received the least information and the fewest opinions. This deficit may have been overcome by the availability of other media in Crayfish, Bright Leaf, and Camellia counties, but the most politically relevant medium— the newspaper—did the worst job when a good job was most needed.

Second, the three newspapers that covered the riots at all relied almost entirely on the wire services and press syndicates for their news and commentary. In this respect, their treatment of the Birmingham riots was not at all unusual. A systematic content analysis of a sample of these newspapers[8] shows that 53 per cent of the news and editorial space of the *Urbania Press,* 49 per cent of the *Capital City Bugle,* and 55 per cent of the *Farmington Daily Mirror* came from these sources. (Only 7 per cent of the *Breedville Weekly's* news and editorial space was given over to material from the wire services and press syndicates.) This undoubtedly resulted in more thorough and sympathetic treatment of the Negro riots than otherwise would have been the case. Each of these newspapers had taken a "harder" line in covering Negro protest activity in their local communities than they did in covering the riots in Birmingham. News coverage of *local* racial conflict contains far more anti-Negro bias than do wire-service stories. Syndicated columnists also can and do take a more "national" and pro-Negro view of the racial revolution in the South than all but a handful of southern editors are likely to take. The heavy reliance of the small-town southern press on the wire services and syndicates may help account for the fact that the region's newspaper content on racial matters seems more enlightened than the opinions of its white audience.[9]

At the same time, our look at the coverage of the Mother's Day riots shows that southern editors can, within limits, "slant" their coverage of the news to fit their own—or their presumed audience's—preconceptions. The headlining, choice of stories, use of pictures, and selection of syndicated columnists affect the message of a newspaper. Certainly, of the three newspapers covering the riots the *Urbania Press* was the most favorable to the Negro cause. The editor of the *Capital City Bugle* did not write a word of text about the riots, but his states' rights, racist, and conservative leanings came through nonetheless. So did the essential dullness and fear of controversy of the *Farmington Daily Mirror.*

Concentrating on the coverage of an important news story can lead us to misjudge the performance of the newspapers in our four southern communities and to overlook political irrelevance of most of what appears in them. Our analysis of the newspapers in Piedmont, Camellia, Bright Leaf, and Crayfish counties shows that only about 25 to 30 per cent of their content is devoted to news and editorial matter (see Table 9–1). When we examine only that portion of the newspapers concerned with news and commentary, we find that

[8] See Appendix A for a description of this content analysis.
[9] See Roy E. Carter, Jr., "Segregation and the News: A Regional Content Analysis," *Journalism Quarterly* (Winter 1957), pp. 3–18, for a similar finding based on the content analysis of a representative sample of southern newspapers.

TABLE 9–1.   *Contents of leading newspapers in four southern communities (in percentage of total space)*

| TYPE OF CONTENT | Urbania Press | Capital City Bugle | Farmington Daily Mirror | Breedville Weekly |
|---|---|---|---|---|
| Advertisements | 53% | 51% | 46% | 64% |
| News and feature stories | 24 | 22 | 24 | 23 |
| Sports and hobbies | 7 | 8 | 6 | 1 |
| Comics, cartoons, crossword puzzle | 5 | 5 | 7 | 0 |
| Editorials, including letters to editor | 4 | 5 | 6 | 3 |
| Society news | 3 | 3 | 2 | 5 |
| Financial news | 3 | 0 | 2 | a |
| All others (fiction, humor, TV-radio listings, other calendar material, masthead and title) | 1 | 6 | 7 | 4 |
| TOTAL | 100% | 100% | 100% | 100% |
| N | 394 | 400 | 397 | 400 |

a Greater than 0, less than 0.5 per cent.

a great deal of it is not concerned with either politics or racial problems (see Table 9–2).

The *Breedville Weekly*, for example, was quite in character in failing to "cover" the Birmingham riots. The lion's share of the paper is devoted to advertisements (64.5 per cent), and the bulk of the news and editorial space (54 per cent) is devoted to "human interest" stories—the election of beauty queens, interviews with elderly inhabitants about their formulas for longevity, the first farmer to harvest his crop this season, and the like. The focus of the newspaper is heavily local—only a third of the news and editorial space of the paper is devoted to events occurring outside Crayfish County.

The three daily newspapers are much less local or regional in orientation— about half the news and editorial content of these papers concerns events outside the South. Even so, less than half of the news and editorial content of the *Farmington Daily Mirror* and *Capital City Bugle* is devoted to political or racial developments and problems. The *Urbania Press*, which devotes more of its news and editorial space to these subjects than the other papers do, still devotes about a third of this limited space to nonpolitical and nonracial subjects.

The sense of the newspapers' irrelevance must be particularly acute among Negroes. Although almost half of the residents of Crayfish County are Negro, only 4 per cent of the news and editorial space of the paper is devoted to stories with Negroes in them! The *Farmington Daily Mirror* carries more news about Negroes than any other paper examined, but it is carefully segregated

TABLE 9-2.   *News stories and editorials of the leading newspapers in four southern communities (in percentage of total news stories and editorials)*

| | Urbania Press (N = 108) | Capital City Bugle (N = 108) | Farmington Daily Mirror (N = 122) | Breedville Weekly (N = 104) |
|---|---|---|---|---|
| SUBJECT OF STORIES | | | | |
| Politics and government | 52% | 42% | 38% | 27% |
| Race relations | 2 | 2 | 4 | 1 |
| Politics, government, and race relations | 12 | 5 | 3 | 3 |
| Economic activity | 5 | 5 | 13 | 4 |
| Crime | 1 | 2 | 5 | 0 |
| Accidents and disasters | 2 | 4 | 3 | 1 |
| Public morals, health, and welfare | 1 | 2 | 6 | 3 |
| Science, inventions, and research | 1 | 4 | 1 | 0 |
| Education, arts, and culture (including popular culture) | 14 | 16 | 13 | 6 |
| General human interest | 9 | 18 | 13 | 54 |
| Other | 1 | 0 | 1 | 1 |
| TOTAL | 100% | 100% | 100% | 100% |
| LOCATION OF EVENTS IN STORIES | | | | |
| Local | 22% | 34% | 31% | 77% |
| State but not local | 22 | 8 | 19 | 10 |
| South, outside state | 12 | 6 | 4 | 3 |
| U.S.A., outside South | 31 | 38 | 34 | 7 |
| Foreign | 10 | 11 | 12 | 2 |
| Global (no geographical space specified) | 3 | 3 | 0 | 1 |
| TOTAL | 100% | 100% | 100% | 100% |
| RACE OF PRINCIPAL ACTORS IN STORIES[a] | | | | |
| White | 77% | 88% | 71% | 96% |
| Negro | 1 | 2 | 6 | 0 |
| Both | 19 | 8 | 19 | 4 |
| Other | 3 | 2 | 4 | 0 |
| TOTAL | 100% | 100% | 100% | 100% |

[a] Stories with no actors, or for which it was impossible to identify the actors' race, were omitted.

in a special daily column entitled "Colored News." Stories about Negroes in the *Capital City Bugle* are few, and they tend to be concerned with assault, theft, rape, lotteries, knifings, shootings, bootlegging in the Negro community, and the exploits of the Negro college's football team. The *Urbania Press*, faced with competition from a Negro weekly, makes little effort to cover the news of the Negro community, but it devotes more space than the other papers to the relationships between the two races in the area of its circulation.

The southern press—insofar as the newspapers examined here are representative—usually depicts a parochial and almost entirely white world in which politics and government are really not very important.

## The southern audience: Black and white

According to the "mass society" theory in its most naïve form, ". . . the messages of the media fall upon the just and unjust alike, as does the rain; from the relentless clamor of the media modern man has no escape."[10] In fact, the impact of the mass media is highly uneven, varying all the way from total saturation to complete aridity. Moreover, the attention paid to the different and competing media, and to the varying content of each medium, is highly selective. The results of communications research are virtually unanimous on how this selectivity usually works: people pay less attention to political news and serious commentary than to more titillating subjects, and they are more attentive to material that supports their preexisting attitudes than to that which challenges those attitudes.[11] Let us see if these tendencies prevail in the South today.

Sizable minorities of southerners pay little heed to some of the media (see Table 9–3). Almost a third of southern Negro adults fail to read a newspaper "more or less regularly," and well over half do not read magazines regularly. The electronic media are more popular; still, almost a third of southern Negroes are not a regular part of the TV audience, and over 20 per cent do not listen to the radio. This constraint on the brainwashing potentialities of the mass media[12] is somewhat less severe among southern whites, yet millions of them are still not reading, listening, or viewing as much as the publishers and broadcasters would like them to. Nonetheless, southerners who ignore one medium often rely heavily on another for their picture of the world "outside."

10 Key, *op. cit.*, p. 345.
11 *Ibid.*, p. 355. For useful summaries of the literature see J. T. Klapper, *The Effects of Mass Communications* (Glencoe, Ill.: The Free Press, 1960); and R. E. Lane, *Political Life* (Glencoe, Ill.: The Free Press, 1959).
12 The word-of-mouth spread of messages originally carried over the mass media may compensate for this lack of personal attention to a significant degree. See, for example, E. Katz and P. F. Lazarsfeld, *Personal Influence* (Glencoe, Ill.: The Free Press, 1955), for a study of "opinion leadership" and the two-step flow of mass communications.

TABLE 9–3. *Exposure of southern Negroes and whites to the mass media of communications*

| MEDIA | PERCENTAGE EXPOSING THEMSELVES "MORE OR LESS REGULARLY" | | NEGRO RATE AS PERCENTAGE OF WHITE RATE |
|---|---|---|---|
| | *Negro* (N = 618) | *White* (N = 694) | |
| Newspapers | 69% | 87% | 79% |
| Magazines | 45 | 67 | 67 |
| TV | 71 | 81 | 88 |
| Radio | 78 | 58 | 134 |

Less than half the Negroes in Crayfish County, for example, regularly read a newspaper; only about one fourth of them own TV sets. Yet almost 90 per cent—a figure considerably above the southwide norm for Negroes—are radio fans. Radio is much less popular among southern whites than among Negroes, but the whites tend to compensate by paying greater attention to the other media. As a result, few southerners of either race escape the media altogether (see Table 9–4). Only 4 per cent of the Negroes and 1 per cent of the whites report that they are not regularly exposed to any of the media; the most common pattern in both races is regular exposure to three or four different forms of mass communications.

Southern Negroes fall behind their white neighbors in media exposure. Almost all southern Negroes (96 per cent) who read the printed media also listen to radio or watch TV, but 22 per cent of the Negro adults expose themselves *only* to the electronic media. No doubt this is a reflection of the low levels of education and literacy among Negroes; but a consequence is that southern Negroes tend to be more attentive to the entertainment-oriented media than they are to those in which serious political communication is most likely.

TABLE 9–4. *Number of different media to which southern Negroes and whites are regularly exposed*

| NUMBER OF MEDIA | *Negro* | *White* |
|---|---|---|
| 0 | 4% | 1% |
| 1 | 10 | 7 |
| 2 | 18 | 19 |
| 3 | 27 | 42 |
| 4 | 41 | 31 |
| TOTAL | 100% | 100% |
| N | 618 | 694 |

The selectivity of audience attention within each communications medium may be politically more important than the choice among media. Newspapers provide the richest political fare of any media, but the contents of the *New York Times* are vastly different from those of the *Breedville Weekly* or the *Farmington Daily Mirror*. Television is primarily devoted to entertainment, but an exceptional viewer may confine his attention to half an hour a day with Walter Cronkite and *CBS News*. Our data permit only a rough and limited description of audience selectivity within the printed media. Even such a partial view provides some clues about how the southern audience selects messages from the vast stream of symbols aimed its way by all the communications media.

The newspaper-reading habits of the residents of Piedmont, Camellia, Bright Leaf, and Crayfish counties are revealing in several ways (see Table 9–5). The national "prestige papers"—the *New York Times, Wall Street Journal, Christian Science Monitor,* and the like—are very little read. Southerners tend to read *local* papers, although the table also reveals some interesting exceptions to this trend. Over 90 per cent of the newspapers read by both races in Piedmont County are locally edited and published; in Camellia, however, the comparable figure is only 60 per cent. The stridently reactionary stance of the *Capital City Bugle* appeals mightily to many white residents of the area; apparently it repels some, too. While Capital City is not within easy delivery range of any other city's newspaper, a quarter of the newspapers read by whites in Camellia County are dailies from other cities in the state; one out of every five newspapers read by the Negroes of the county is an "imported" daily.

Out-of-town papers are even more popular in Bright Leaf and Crayfish counties, but the explanation is different in each case. Bright Leaf is within the circulation area of the state capital's morning newspaper. The *Farmington Daily Mirror,* which has no discernible editorial policy and relies on the wire services as much as possible, is not likely to alienate anybody. It does bore or starve a good many Bright Leaf residents into subscribing to the competing paper. The *Breedville Weekly* in Crayfish County makes no pretense of covering anything but local news; the surprising thing is that more of the Crayfish population do not read out-of-town dailies, several of which are delivered in the county.

One out of every six Negro adults in the region (17 per cent) reads a newspaper especially written by and for Negroes. In most cases these papers— such as the Pittsburgh *Courier,* Baltimore *Afro-American,* or Chicago *Defender*—are published outside the South and enjoy national circulations. Urbania, however, supports a Negro weekly, the *Peripheral State News,* which one in three Negroes in the county reads with some regularity. Negro newspapers owe their existence, of course, to the failure of the regular press to meet the needs and to satisfy the interests of the black audience. Negro newspapers compensate for this neglect by concentrating on the struggle for civil

TABLE 9-5.  *Types of newspaper read, by race, in Piedmont, Camellia, Bright Leaf, and Crayfish counties*

| | Piedmont | | Camellia | | Bright Leaf | | Crayfish | |
|---|---|---|---|---|---|---|---|---|
| | Negro | White | Negro | White | Negro | White | Negro | White |
| TYPE OF NEWSPAPER | | | | | | | | |
| "Prestige"[a] | 2% | 6% | 2% | 12% | 0% | 4% | 0% | 0% |
| Dailies from nearby cities | 1 | 1 | 16 | 26 | 23 | 44 | 41 | 48 |
| Local | 62 | 91 | 62 | 59 | 60 | 50 | 32 | 44 |
| National or regional Negro | 3 | 0 | 18 | 0 | 15 | 0 | 14 | 0 |
| Local Negro | 29 | 0 | — | — | — | — | — | — |
| Other, miscellaneous, unclassifiable | 3 | 2 | 2 | 3 | 2 | 2 | 13 | 8 |
| TOTAL | 100% | 100% | 100% | 100% | 100% | 100% | 100% | 100% |
| Number of newspapers read | 164 | 138 | 73 | 102 | 52 | 114 | 37 | 71 |
| Percentage of adult sample reading newspapers | 87% | 92% | 60% | 94% | 48% | 85% | 48% | 73% |
| Mean number of newspapers read per population | 1.6 | 1.4 | 0.9 | 1.5 | 0.7 | 1.4 | 0.8 | 1.3 |
| Size of adult sample | 100 | 96 | 77 | 68 | 75 | 82 | 48 | 56 |

[a] *New York Times, New York Herald Tribune, Wall Street Journal, Christian Science Monitor, Kansas City Star, Louisville Courier-Journal.*

rights, the exploits of Negro heroes and celebrities, Negro social events, and other "race news." The racial and political views of these papers are congruent with those of their audience; the world as depicted by the Negro press revolves around the Negro and his problems. This scarcely can be said of the "white" newspapers of the region.

*Reader's Digest*, read "more or less regularly" by 25 per cent of the adults, is by far the most popular magazine in the white South. *Saturday Evening Post* (13 per cent), *Life* (12 per cent), *Look* (9 per cent), *Ladies' Home Journal* (8 per cent), and *McCall's* (8 per cent) are its closest competitors. These magazines are not totally devoid of political content, but they run heavily to pictures or to popular fiction and features. Only 8 per cent of all the magazines read by our white sample are strictly devoted to the coverage of public affairs. *Time* and *U.S. News and World Report*, the most popular of these, are not without their manifest weaknesses as guides to the world of politics (see Table 9–6).

TABLE 9–6.    *Types of magazines read by southern Negroes and whites (in percentage of all magazines read)*

| TYPE OF MAGAZINE | Negro | White |
|---|---|---|
| Negro (*Ebony, Jet, Tan,* etc.) | 38% | — |
| Low-brow (*Life, Look, Reader's Digest, Saturday Evening Post,* etc.) | 26 | 36% |
| Miscellaneous (church, TV, sports, children, gardening, trade, pulp, etc.) | 17 | 29 |
| Ladies' (*McCall's, Good Housekeeping, Redbook, Ladies' Home Journal,* etc.) | 7 | 15 |
| Farm (*Progressive Farmer, Farm and Ranch,* etc.) | 6 | 8 |
| News (*Time, Newsweek, U.S. News and World Report, Reporter,* etc.) | 6 | 8 |
| High-brow (*National Geographic Magazine, New Yorker, Harper's, Atlantic Monthly, Fortune,* etc.) | a | 4 |
| TOTAL | 100% | 100% |
| N | 601 | 1,194 |

a Less than 0.5 per cent, greater than 0.

Negro magazine readers have similarly low-brow, nonpolitical interests, but they often prefer to receive their entertaining fare from Negro sources: thus about one in every three southern Negroes reads at least one "Negro" magazine. *Ebony*, read by 22 per cent, is the single most popular magazine among southern Negroes. *Life* (14 per cent) and *Jet* (13 per cent) enjoy large leads in Negro readership over *Look* (5 per cent), *Reader's Digest* (4 per cent), *Time* (4 per cent), and *Saturday Evening Post* (2 per cent). Only 6 per cent of the magazines regularly read by southern Negroes are devoted primarily to news.

Thus the southern audience's selectivity both *within* and *between* media tends to bring the messages perceived into conformity with its preexisting attitudes and to reduce the effective political content of the media. The mass media may pay little attention to controversy and public affairs, but their audience pays even less. Can such shallow and seemingly nonpolitical attention to the mass media of communications affect basic political changes? The answer seems to be "yes"—at least so far as Negro political activity is concerned.

## The mass media and Negro political participation

The apparent impact of mass communications is much greater on southern Negroes than on southern whites (see Figure 9–1). Among those Negroes with no regular exposure to papers, magazines, radio, or TV, less than 20 per cent participate to the point of voting or beyond; among those who regularly expose themselves to all four media, 75 per cent are active at the level of voting or beyond. Such an overwhelming majority of whites have participated in politics,

FIGURE 9–1.  *Political participation in the South, by exposure to mass media and race.*

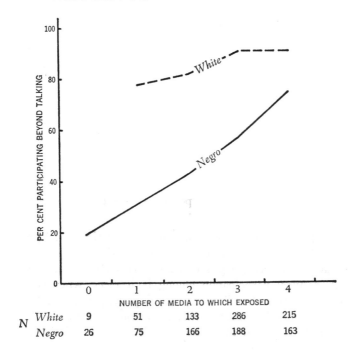

| | White | 9 | 51 | 133 | 286 | 215 |
| N | Negro | 26 | 75 | 166 | 188 | 163 |

at least to the extent of voting, that their participation varies much less with differences in media exposure than does that of Negroes. The racial gap in political participation narrows markedly only among those southerners regularly exposed to all four media. Even so, participation is as frequent among whites with minimum media exposure as it is among Negroes with maximum exposure.

The importance of the individual media for political participation varies quite a good deal, a point that Figure 9–1 does not reveal. Newspapers devote the largest share of their content to political news, and habitual newspaper readers are the most politically active segment of "The Great Audience": 83 per cent of the Negroes and 97 per cent of the whites who read three or more newspapers regularly are active to the point of voting or beyond (see Table 9–7). Failure to read a newspaper is, as we would expect, less of a deter-

TABLE 9–7.   *Percentage of Southerners politically active,[a] by race and exposure to mass communications media*

|  | Negro | | White | |
|---|---|---|---|---|
| **NUMBER OF NEWSPAPERS READ** | | | | |
| None | 33% | (191) | 79% | (90) |
| 1 | 57 | (221) | 89 | (307) |
| 2 | 62 | (141) | 89 | (224) |
| 3 or more | 83 | (64) | 97 | (73) |
| **NUMBER OF MAGAZINES READ** | | | | |
| None | 43% | (337) | 82% | (230) |
| 1 | 51 | (104) | 86 | (108) |
| 2 | 76 | (79) | 93 | (134) |
| 3 or more | 72 | (97) | 94 | (222) |
| **LISTENS TO RADIO?** | | | | |
| No | 41% | (135) | 90% | (289) |
| Yes | 56 | (483) | 88 | (405) |
| **WATCHES TELEVISION?** | | | | |
| No | 40% | (182) | 88% | (132) |
| Yes | 59 | (436) | 89 | (562) |

[a] PPS types III, IV, and V.

rent to white political participation than to Negro activity—79 per cent of the whites but only 33 per cent of the Negroes who do not regularly read newspapers are at least voters. Magazines are the medium next most strongly associated with political participation among both races, whereas the apparent effects of television and radio on political participation are only moderate among Negroes and altogether nonexistent among whites.

But are these statistical associations really "causal" relationships? That a communications diet consisting largely of headlines, sports, music, photographs, and TV comedies could "cause" such major differences in southern Negro political behavior seems almost incredible. We cannot know for certain whether this is what happens without a more rigorously experimental study than we have attempted here,[13] but at least the more obvious factors that might contribute to spurious correlations do not seem to be important in this instance.

In Chapter Four, for example, we found that the extent of one's formal education was highly predictive of political activity. Well-educated people are also those who tend to expose themselves to mass communications. Sixty-five per cent of the Negroes with some college education, for example, read newspapers and magazines, listen to the radio, and watch TV; only 32 per cent of those with grade-school education expose themselves regularly to all four media. Thus, the sharp increase in Negro activity associated with the consumption of mass communications may be the result of the higher educational levels of the regular consumers of communications rather than of anything learned from the media. Table 9–8 shows that this is true, to some extent, but it also shows that political participation rises sharply with media exposure even among Negroes with approximately the same amount of formal education. High-school-educated Negroes who expose themselves to all four media, for instance, participate at twice the rate of high-school-educated Negroes who pay attention to only one medium or to none at all.

A more severe test of any causal interpretation of these data is provided when we introduce statistical controls for income. We found in Chapter Four that income was even more strongly related to Negro participation than was education. Exposure to the mass media costs money. The relationship between Negroes' exposure to the media and the extent of their political activity might therefore be plausibly viewed as the result of a strong income-political participation relationship. But again Table 9–8 shows a strong tendency for media exposure and political activity to increase together even among Negroes with approximately the same income.

Finally, Negroes in urban areas and in the Peripheral South are more frequently members of "The Great Audience" than are Negroes living in rural areas or in the Deep South. Perhaps the positive association between media exposure and Negro participation is the result of the tendency for Negroes residing in less repressive environments to be more exposed to the media. Once again, the data in Table 9–8 show that this is not entirely the case.

We are not saying here that media exposure is *more* important than education, income, and subregion in explaining variations in Negro political participation. Each of these other factors also has an independent relationship to Negro political activity. Indeed, subregion of residence appears much more

[13] A model for such a study is C. I. Hovland, J. L. Janis, and H. H. Kelly, *Communication and Persuasion* (New Haven, Conn.: Yale University Press, 1953).

TABLE 9–8.  *Percentage of Negroes politically active,[a] by exposure to mass media, with controls for education, income, and subregion*

| | NUMBER OF MEDIA TO WHICH EXPOSED | | | Participation rate of highest-exposure group as percentage of rate of lowest-exposure group |
|---|---|---|---|---|
| | 0–1 | 2–3 | 4 | |
| EDUCATIONAL LEVEL | | | | |
| Some college | — (1) | 69% (16) | 81% (32) | 117% |
| High school | 33% (12) | 58 (90) | 69 (102) | 209 |
| Grade school or less | 29 (77) | 47 (171) | 54 (115) | 186 |
| ANNUAL HOUSEHOLD INCOME | | | | |
| $6,000+ | — (0) | — (8) | 89% (19) | — |
| $4,000–$5,999 | — (2) | 87% (23) | 84 (45) | 97% |
| $2,000–$3,999 | 41% (22) | 58 (65) | 63 (71) | 154 |
| Less than $2,000 | 25 (65) | 43 (178) | 50 (109) | 200 |
| SUBREGION | | | | |
| Peripheral South | | | | |
| Urban | 48% (25) | 73% (106) | 84% (116) | 175% |
| Rural | 30 (20) | 52 (48) | 60 (48) | 200 |
| Deep South | | | | |
| Urban | 33 (15) | 37 (43) | 46 (46) | 139 |
| Rural | 14 (28) | 33 (78) | 28 (40) | 200 |

[a] PPS types III, IV, and V. Percentages are omitted for all cells with less than 10 cases.

important than media exposure: Negroes in the Peripheral South with minimal media exposure are more likely to be active participants than are those in the Deep South with maximum exposure. What we are saying, then, is that exposure to the mass media makes *some* difference even when these other powerful influences are taken into account. Moreover, as close examination of the righthand column in Table 9–8 indicates, the effects of mass communications are proportionately greatest among Negroes who are *least* likely to be participants for other reasons. Participation rates seem most responsive to the mass media among poorly educated, impoverished, rural Negroes.

The *process* by which the mass communications media heighten political activity by southern Negroes is not clear. Exposure to the media definitely leads to increased political interest, greater factual knowledge about the political world, and enhanced feelings of political competence and power (see Table 9–9). But influence flows in the other direction, too: the more politically interested, informed, and self-confident Negroes expose themselves to the flow of facts and values in the communications media more than do those without these psychological attributes. Which is the chicken, which

TABLE 9–9.  *Exposure of southern Negroes to mass media and selected political attitudes and cognitions*

|  | NUMBER OF MEDIA TO WHICH EXPOSED | | |
| --- | --- | --- | --- |
|  | 0–1 (N = 90) | 2–3 (N = 278) | 4 (N = 248) |
| EXTENT OF POLITICAL INTEREST | | | |
| Great deal | 17% | 25% | 37% |
| Somewhat | 7 | 21 | 29 |
| Not much | 76 | 54 | 34 |
| TOTAL | 100% | 100% | 100% |
| LEVEL OF POLITICAL INFORMATION | | | |
| 6–7 (high) | 1% | 5% | 15% |
| 4–5 | 13 | 34 | 36 |
| 2–3 | 50 | 43 | 35 |
| 0–1 (low) | 36 | 18 | 14 |
| TOTAL | 100% | 100% | 100% |
| SENSE OF CIVIC COMPETENCE | | | |
| 3 (high) | 15% | 24% | 35% |
| 2 | 21 | 35 | 34 |
| 1 | 34 | 33 | 22 |
| 0 (low) | 30 | 8 | 9 |
| TOTAL | 100% | 100% | 100% |

the egg cannot be determined. Nonetheless, these political relevant psychological attributes and media exposure escalate together—political interest leads to media exposure, which leads to more interest, which leads to more exposure, and so on, in an inseparable chain.

Seventy-five per cent of the Negroes exposed to all four media are active in politics to the point of voting or beyond (see Figure 9–1), but only 66 per cent of this same group express any real interest in politics (see Table 9–9). *A "bonus" of politically unmotivated activists seems to go along with extensive consumption of mass communications.* On the other hand, 24 per cent of the adults with little exposure to the media have some interest in politics, but only about 15 per cent of this group are politically active. *Greater political motivation than activity seems to be associated with little media exposure.* Table 9–10 shows the same phenomenon at work: the mass media have an effect on Negro political participation over and above that which results from an increase in the political interest, knowledge, and sense of competence of individual Negroes.[14] The possible implications of this finding will be explored

[14] Reading down the columns of Table 9–10, one finds still greater variation by level of political interest, political information, and sense of civic competence when media exposure is held constant. The media thus appear to increase political participation principally *but not entirely* by contributing to political knowledge and attitudes.

TABLE 9–10. *Percentage of Negroes politically active, by exposure to mass media and selected political attitudes and cognitions*

| | NUMBER OF MEDIA TO WHICH EXPOSED | | | Participation rate of highest-exposure group as percentage of rate of lowest exposure group |
|---|---|---|---|---|
| | 0–1 | 2–3 | 4 | |
| **EXTENT OF POLITICAL INTEREST** | | | | |
| Great deal of interest | 60% (15) | 72% (69) | 81% (91) | 135% |
| Somewhat interested | — (6) | 63 (59) | 65 (72) | 103 |
| Not much interested | 24 (68) | 38 (150) | 42 (85) | 175 |
| **LEVEL OF POLITICAL INFORMATION** | | | | |
| 6–7 (high) | — (1) | 80% (15) | 94% (36) | 118% |
| 4–5 | 50% (12) | 57 (94) | 73 (90) | 146 |
| 2–3 | 33 (45) | 49 (119) | 52 (88) | 158 |
| 0–1 (low) | 16 (32) | 40 (48) | 32 (34) | 200 |
| **SENSE OF CIVIC COMPETENCE** | | | | |
| 3 (high) | 61% (13) | 64% (55) | 76% (72) | 125% |
| 2 | 26 (19) | 55 (89) | 69 (78) | 265 |
| 1 | 26 (31) | 52 (92) | 53 (64) | 204 |
| 0 (low) | 22 (27) | 29 (42) | 42 (36) | 191 |

NOTE: See footnote to Table 9–8.

at some length in the conclusion to this chapter. Before turning to that problem, let us examine the relationship between exposure to the Negro press and Negro political activity.

## The role of the Negro press

One out of every six Negro adults in the South reads a Negro newspaper; one out of every three reads a Negro magazine. What effects does exposure to this steady diet of "race" news, features, and exhortation have on Negro political participation?

Table 9–11 represents the beginning of an answer. Southern Negroes who read the Negro press are more active than those who do not. The difference in participation rates between those who read Negro newspapers and those who read only "white" newspapers, however, is relatively small compared to the difference between readers and nonreaders of any kind of paper. Negro magazine readers are much more active than those who read "white" non-

TABLE 9–11.   *Percentage of southern Negroes politically active, by exposure to Negro press*

| | Percentage PPS types III, IV, and V | N |
|---|---|---|
| TYPE OF NEWSPAPER EXPOSURE | | |
| Reads Negro newspapers | 71% | 104 |
| Reads only "white" newspapers | 60% | 322 |
| Reads neither | 33% | 191 |
| TYPE OF MAGAZINE EXPOSURE | | |
| Reads Negro magazines | 70% | 171 |
| Reads news magazines | 81% | 31 |
| Reads other magazines | 49% | 79 |
| Reads no magazines | 43% | 337 |

political journals or no magazines at all. They are somewhat less active than the tiny group of Negroes who read *Time, Newsweek, U.S. News and World Report,* or some other news magazine. With this one exception, regular ex-

TABLE 9–12.   *Percentage of southern Negroes politically active, by exposure to Negro press, controlling for education, income, and media exposure*

| | Reads Negro newspapers or magazines | | Reads only white newspapers and magazines | | Participation rate of those exposed to Negro press as percentage of rate of those exposed to white press only |
|---|---|---|---|---|---|
| EDUCATION | | | | | |
| Some college | 81% | (32) | 69% | (16) | 117% |
| High school | 75 | (112) | 50 | (80) | 150 |
| Grade school | 59 | (71) | 51 | (144) | 116 |
| ANNUAL HOUSEHOLD INCOME | | | | | |
| $6,000 and over | 93% | (14) | 85% | (13) | 109% |
| $4,000–$5,999 | 88 | (42) | 79 | (24) | 111 |
| $2,000–$3,999 | 69 | (80) | 50 | (54) | 138 |
| Under $1,999 | 57 | (75) | 46 | (149) | 124 |
| NUMBER OF MEDIA TO WHICH EXPOSED | | | | | |
| 1 | 50% | (10) | 41% | (34) | 122% |
| 2 | 50 | (16) | 55 | (97) | 91 |
| 3 | 67 | (60) | 46 | (63) | 146 |
| 4 | 76 | (131) | 63 | (46) | 121 |

NOTE: See footnote to Table 9–8.

posure to the Negro press is associated with incrementally higher rates of political activity than is readership of the "white" press.

Again tricky problems of interpretation remain: Do the contents of the Negro media bring about these higher rates of political activity, or is the self-selected audience such that they would be more active than the non-readers anyway? The Negro media are printed; semi-literate Negroes are not likely to be among the audience. The Negro press is especially attentive to the activities and accomplishments of the Negro middle class; most of its readers can afford the time and money required to read it in addition to the white media. As a result of these and other factors, the reader of the Negro press is typically of a class in which he would be politically active whether he read the Negro media or not. But, as Table 9–12 shows, the readers of the Negro press are more active than Negroes who read only the "white" press even with educational and income levels and the extent of their exposure to the general media controlled.

The same kind of mechanisms seem to account for this finding as for the relationship between exposure to the general media and Negro political activity. The readers of the Negro press are more politically interested and informed than are those Negroes who read only the "white" press. But this alone does not account for the first group's higher participation: those who read the Negro press participate in politics at a higher level than do equally interested and informed Negroes who read only the "white" press (see Table 9–13). Exposure to the Negro press does, then, seem to contribute

TABLE 9–13.  *Percentage of southern Negroes politically active, by exposure to Negro press, with controls for political interest and information*

| | Reads Negro newspapers or magazines | Reads only white newspapers and magazines | Participation rate of those exposed to Negro press as percentage of rate of those exposed to white press only |
|---|---|---|---|
| POLITICAL INTEREST | | | |
| Great deal | 88% (78) | 74% (72) | 119% |
| Somewhat | 74 (73) | 55 (40) | 135 |
| Not much | 44 (64) | 39 (128) | 113 |
| POLITICAL INFORMATION | | | |
| 6–7 (high) | 91% (44) | 88% (8) | 104% |
| 4–5 | 76 (86) | 54 (90) | 141 |
| 2–3 | 58 (66) | 50 (109) | 116 |
| 0–1 (low) | 42 (19) | 45 (33) | 93 |

NOTE: See footnote to Table 9–8.

toward even higher levels of political activity than does exposure to the "white" media.

## Conclusions: Mass communications, "modernization," and Negro political participation

The central theme of this chapter has been a paradox. The mass media of communications—our "picture of the world" outside our own personal experience[15]—contain little explicitly political content. The southern audience, and especially its Negro component, pays less attention to the meager political messages of the media than to the media's more frivolous content. Yet this highly selective exposure to the flow of largely apolitical messages does seem to produce political activity by southern Negroes. How can this be true? What explains this curious set of findings?

The basic explanation seems to be provided by the concept of "modernization."[16] Two clues suggest the importance of this concept. First, the more apathetic, undereducated, impoverished, and rural Negroes are the ones whose rate of political participation seems most responsive to media exposure. Second, although exposure to mass communications does increase the political interest, knowledge, and sense of competence of Southern Negroes, it seems to increase their rate of political activity even more. In other words, *exposure to the mass media increases both political motivation and politically unmotivated activity in politics.* These two empirical findings suggest that mass communications are contributing to the "modernization" of the South, especially the South of the lower-class and rural Negro, and that the acceptance of the modern ethos implies political participation whether one is politically motivated and knowledgeable or not.

The American South is still far from being a "mass society," an atomized agglomeration of people cut loose from their cultural roots and stable social controls and thus easily exploitable through the mass media of communications. Such a society, if it exists at all, is an outcome of urbanization and industrialization; it is "modernization" carried to an ultimate and pathological stage. But much of the South is not yet even "modern" or urban or industrial. The rural and small-town South is still, to quite a large degree, a "traditional" society: one of "status" rather than of "contract," of "Gemeinschaft" rather than of "Gesselschaft," of "ascription" rather than of "achievement," of "locals"

[15] This image was first popularized by Walter Lippmann in his classic *Public Opinion* (New York: Macmillan, 1922).

[16] D. Lerner, *The Passing of Traditional Society: Modernizing the Middle East* (Glencoe, Ill.: The Free Press, 1958), chs. 1–3. This entire book has influenced our thinking in this section.

rather than of "cosmopolitans."[17] These dichotomous distinctions are, of course, really shorthand for continua: no real-world community, no actual social relationship, is entirely one or the other. Within the same community some aspects of social life may be more modern than others. Thus, the distinction between a "traditional" and a "modern" society is admittedly gross, but it is an important one to make if we are to understand today's changing world.

The rural and small-town Negro in the American South still leads a life that is more nearly comparable to that of the Indian in rural Mexico or the peasant in the Middle East than it is to that of an upper-middle-class professional in New York City or Los Angeles. The rural southern Negro is born into an inferior caste, a stigma from which there is no escape short of a segregated grave. He works the land with his hands and body; mechanization comes in the form of a mule, if he is lucky. His family—which tends to be large, in the pre-industrial pattern—lives in an unpainted shack with few of what most other Americans consider necessities. Chances are that he is illiterate or nearly so. The rhythm of nature—of sunrise and sunset, the passing of the seasons—punctuate a life routine very much like that of his father, and his father's father. Traditional people everywhere are characterized by a reverence for the past, a passive acceptance of the present, and a fatalism about the future. Their mental horizons do not extend far beyond the physical one; they know no other way of life. Modern societies, on the other hand, are characterized by high individual aspirations, geographical and social mobility, and a faith in rationality rather than custom. Lerner comments in describing modernization in the Near East:

> People come to see the social future as manipulable rather than ordained and their personal prospects in terms of achievement rather than heritage. Rationality is purposive: ways of thinking and acting are instruments of intention (not articles of faith); men succeed or fail by the test of what they accomplish (not what they worship). So, whereas traditional man tended to reject innovation by saying "It has never been thus," the contemporary Westerner is more likely to ask "Does it work?" and try the new way without further ado.
> The psychic gap between these two postures is vast.[18]

The mass media of communications subvert traditional ways—despite, indeed, probably because of, the poverty of their explicitly political content. The most hackneyed situation comedy or detective story on TV paints a glamorized picture of a way of life quite different from that known by the tradition-bound southern Negro. The world of the daytime "soap opera" is a thoroughly modern world. The prominence of Negro entertainers on the *Ed Sullivan Show* teaches a lesson about individual aspirations and achievement; the way

[17] These very similar distinctions are associated with the works of Henry Maine, Ferdinand Tonnies, Ralph Linton, Max Weber, Talcott Parson, and Robert K. Merton.
[18] Lerner, *op. cit.*, pp. 48–49.

these performers are treated by the inarticulate Irishman in charge carries a message about human dignity and equality. The world of popular music, so important in radio programing, is dominated by Negro musicians. The heroes of the sports pages, since Joe Louis and Jackie Robinson, are just about as often Negro as white. The barely literate, tradition-bound southern Negro is not likely to read the *New York Times* or even, except inadvertently, listen to radio or TV newscasts. But, as we have seen, almost all southern Negroes do expose themselves to the entertainment provided by the media.

Exposure to the media is associated with the acceptance of modern attitudes (see Table 9–14). There *are* alternatives to the traditional mode of life; indi-

TABLE 9–14.   *Exposure to mass media and attitudes toward change of southern Negroes*

| ATTITUDE TOWARD CHANGE | NUMBER OF MEDIA TO WHICH EXPOSED | | |
|---|---|---|---|
| | 0–1 | 2–3 | 4 |
| 1–2 (most favorable) | 11% | 17% | 27% |
| 3–4 | 16 | 35 | 41 |
| 5–6 (least favorable) | 73 | 48 | 32 |
| TOTAL | 100% | 100% | 100% |
| N | 75 | 245 | 222 |

NOTE: The construction of the scale on attitude toward change is explained in Chapter Ten.

vidual circumstances *can* be improved through individual effort and initiative; politics *is* one way of trying to improve one's lot in life. Even those who fail to read the last of these morals from the media often seem to carry away another notion: political participation is a "good thing"—it is expected of modern Americans regardless of their motivations or the potential payoffs. Thus, once an awareness of alternatives develops, once tradition-bound people develop the ability to visualize themselves living in a different society,[19] the process of modernization has begun. Thanks in part to the media, this is what is still happening to the rural and working-class Negro in the South. And with modernization goes political participation, in the American South as well as in the rest of the "underdeveloped" world.

[19] The critical importance of vicarious experience and empathy in the process of modernization is argued by Lerner, *op. cit.*

Chapter Ten

# Psychological Factors and Negro Participation

Minnie Smith and Jane West live a few blocks from each other in the Negro ghetto of Farmington, the county seat of Bright Leaf County. Both women were born a few miles away, Mrs. Smith 51 and Mrs. West 49 years ago. Both attended the same segregated school; Minnie dropped out after five years of schooling, Jane after six. Both ladies married; neither had children. Mr. West died a few years ago. Mr. and Mrs. Smith both work in Farmington's tobacco-processing plants during the brief harvest season, making no more than $2,000 between them. They are unemployed the rest of the year. Mrs. West does the same sort of work and "enjoys" the same per-capita income as the Smiths—about $1,000 a year.

But Minnie Smith is a political activist while Jane West is not. Mrs. Smith talks about "politics, living conditions, housing, and labor unions . . . who we gonna vote for . . ." with her friends, family, and co-workers (when she is able to work at all). She has talked to the Negro leaders in Farmington about the "conditions of [our] streets, schools, housing, [and] about a [Negro] swimming pool . . . and different things we think should be improved." She first registered to vote in 1943 because, as she said, ". . . I just got interested in politics," and has voted fairly regularly since then, especially in Democratic primaries for governor and in presidential elections. She views herself as a "strong" Democrat and voted for Kennedy in 1960. She has taken part in political campaigns—at least to the extent of buying tickets and talking to others in attempts to influence their vote. She teaches Sunday School at her church and belongs to the AFL-CIO, tobacco workers union, the women's auxiliary of her husband's lodge, and the NAACP. She is thus classified as a Type V on our Political Participation Scale.

Jane West talks to no one about politics and has never voted or even tried to register—although she says that she has wanted to vote and expects to some day. She has never participated in a political campaign in any way and belongs to no voluntary organization or group save her church. She is a Type I on our Political Participation Scale—that is, she takes no part in politics whatsoever.

Obviously a southern Negro's social and economic characteristics and the nature of the community in which he or she lives do not entirely determine how and how much he or she participates in the political process. Rather, people may react quite differently to identical circumstances. Thus, in order to describe and explain Negro participation we must consider the perceptions and attitudes of southern Negroes as well as the world "outside."

Even if Minnie Smith and Jane West had reacted in the same way to the nearly identical worlds in which they live, this fact by itself would tell us nothing about why and how they translated the external world into political participation or the lack of it. Poverty and low participation tend to go hand in hand, for example. But how and why are the objective facts of low income and severe deprivation converted into political inaction? Only by examining the psychological characteristics of our subjects can we answer this question.

We cannot, of course, achieve as much depth or detail in this quest as we would like. The human psyche is marvelously complex; psychologists and psychiatrists have made slow progress in studying it, either through the clinical analysis of individuals or through controlled laboratory experiments. The sample survey is a ponderous tool for such a delicate operation. We are concerned in this book with millions of minds represented by a sample of persons each interviewed for an hour or so. We can offer only a superficial and partial picture of the psychological attributes of southern Negroes and how these attributes are related to political participation. But the startling political differences between Minnie Smith and Jane West—who *as individuals* are almost identical and who also live in the same *community*—require some examination of psychological factors.

## Political interest

Political activity is not free of cost—at a minimum, it takes time. Accordingly some interest in politics is essential to political participation. Since the costs of participation for southern Negroes are often unusually high, unusually high interest may be essential to Negro political participation.

On several counts, Negroes might be expected to show little interest in politics. Few Negroes rank high in education, occupational prestige, or income, all of which tend to promote interest. The political interest of other newly enfranchised groups—women, for example—tends to be rather low during the early years of their enfranchisement. Participation breeds interest, but the opportunity to participate is new for most southern Negroes—nonexistent for others. Finally, political interest seems to increase when citizens are confronted with hotly contested campaigns between candidates who stand for meaningful alternatives; the one-party system and the segregationist position of an overwhelming majority of southern politicians may kill Negro political interest before it is born.

On the other hand, southern Negroes might be stimulated into political interest by their deprivation at the hands of local government and by their hope of relief from the national government. The political interest of other minority groups in the United States and elsewhere tends to be unusually high. Minority groups have more to gain—and lose—from politics. Many southern Negroes believe, as one of them said in Camellia County, that the "ballot box is [the] greatest means of achieving something."

The facts lend at least some support to both lines of argument (see Table 10–1). Half of the Negro sample reported that they were "not much"

TABLE 10–1.  *Political interest of southern Negroes and whites*

| SELF-RATING OF POLITICAL INTEREST | Negro | White |
|---|---|---|
| Great deal | 28% | 28% |
| Somewhat | 22 | 39 |
| Not much | 49 | 33 |
| Don't know, no answer | 1 | a |
| TOTAL | 100% | 100% |
| N | 618 | 694 |

a Greater than 0, less than 0.5 per cent.

interested in politics, while only a third of the white sample indicated an equal lack of interest. But 28 per cent of the Negroes said they were a "great deal" interested, the same proportion as among the whites. When one recalls the vast educational, status, and income gap between the two races in the South, this finding is startling.

Southern whites and Negroes thus differ only modestly in political interest. Since they differ vastly in political participation, the *relationship* between political interest and political participation must be different for the two races.

Indeed it is, as Figure 10–1 makes clear. The figure shows the political participation of both races at different levels of political interest. (Here we are defining participation as activity beyond mere talk, but the basic findings would be the same if we defined participation as talking politics or as activity

FIGURE 10–1.   *Political interest and participation of southerners,
by race*

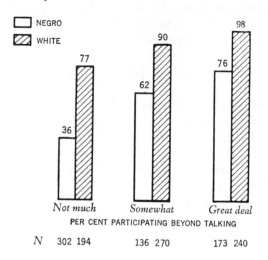

N    302 194     136 270     173 240

beyond voting.[1]) First, whites participate more at every level of political interest. The same amount of interest, concern, and attention results in much more political participation. Second, participation depends more on personal interest in politics among Negroes than among whites. Three fourths of the whites without much interest in politics at least reach the point of voting, but only about a third of the Negroes without interest reach that point. The relatively high costs of voting for southern Negroes most strongly affect those who are only slightly involved and poorly motivated. Keen interest is necessary to overcome the restraints.

The correspondence between political interest and political participation is not perfect. If it were, everyone with interest would take part at least to the extent of voting, and no one without interest would bother to vote. In fact, however, a vast majority (78 per cent) of the whites who confess a lack of interest are counted among the voters of the South. This is in contrast to only 36 per cent for Negroes without interest and 70 per cent for Negroes who are interested. *If southern Negroes could translate their existing level of political interest into participation in the same fashion as whites do, there*

[1] The most stringent definition of participation—as activity including officeholding or political-group membership—would show more Negroes as participants among those with any political interest. But relatively small numbers are involved here for both races.

*would be a 19–20-percentage-point increase in the proportion of Negroes who vote or who participate beyond voting!*

The picture differs, however, from one southern community to the next. The situations in Piedmont, Camellia, Bright Leaf, and Crayfish counties are presented in Table 10–2. In Piedmont County—the most urban and least

TABLE 10–2. *Relationships between political interest and participation among southern Negroes, by community*

| | PIEDMONT | | | | CAMELLIA | | |
| | | Non- | | | | Non- | |
| | Participant | participant | TOTAL | | Participant | participant | TOTAL |
|---|---|---|---|---|---|---|---|
| Interested | 60% | 9% | 69% | | 36% | 9% | 45% |
| Not interested | 20% | 11% | 31% | | 35% | 20% | 55% |
| TOTAL | 80% | 20% | 100% | | 71% | 29% | 100% |
| | | | (100) | | | | (77) |

| | BRIGHT LEAF | | | | CRAYFISH | | |
| | | Non- | | | | Non- | |
| | Participant | participant | TOTAL | | Participant | participant | TOTAL |
|---|---|---|---|---|---|---|---|
| Interested | 29% | 28% | 57% | | 14.5% | 12.5% | 27% |
| Not interested | 11% | 32% | 43% | | 23 % | 50 % | 73% |
| TOTAL | 40% | 60% | 100% | | 37.5% | 62.5% | 100% |
| | | | (75) | | | | (48) |

NOTE: Participants = PPS types III, IV, and V—voting and above. "Interested" = self-rating of "great deal" or "somewhat" interested in politics.

repressive of the four communities—the Negroes are just about as likely to be interested in politics as are whites (71 per cent of the whites and 69 per cent of the Negroes are interested), and the *relationship between political interest and political activity* is about the same for the two races. Nine per cent of the Negroes are interested nonparticipants as contrasted with 5 per cent of the whites; 20 per cent of both races participate in politics though they are not interested in it.

In the other three counties, however, the picture is very different from that found in Piedmont. The proportion of interested participants goes down sharply: Piedmont, 60 per cent; Camellia, 36 per cent; Bright Leaf, 29 per cent; and Crayfish, 14.5 per cent. The number of uninterested nonparticipants goes up just as sharply: Piedmont, 11 per cent; Camellia, 20 per cent; Bright Leaf, 32 per cent; Crayfish, 50 per cent.

The proportion of interested but inactive Negroes is the same in Camellia as in Piedmont, 9 per cent. In Bright Leaf this group numbers 28 per cent of the total—apparently most of these Negroes have been overtly or covertly discouraged from finding a normal outlet for their political concern but have not been frightened into total uninterest. A reduction in the real or imagined barriers to participation would probably prompt most of these latent activists to become real ones. Recent organizational efforts in Bright Leaf suggest that an increase in the proportion of interested nonparticipants may represent an early stage in the politicization of the Negro citizenry. Crayfish has not reached this stage. The barriers to Negro participation are far greater than in Bright Leaf, and the proportion of interested nonparticipants is not much greater in Crayfish than in Piedmont or Camellia. Apparently the threat of white hostility to Negro participation is so great in Crayfish that few Negroes can maintain political interest in the face of it, and most lapse into uninterested inactivity.

A major reason why more whites than Negroes take part in southern politics is that so many uninterested whites still participate. Among Negroes more uninterested participants are found in the two urban communities—Piedmont and Camellia—and in the most repressive Deep South county—Crayfish—than in Bright Leaf. Even those who do participate in Crayfish do not admit to much political interest—and, as we saw in Chapter Three, they participate in covert ways, such as giving money or joining the NAACP, rather than openly by voting. In the far less terrifying environment of Bright Leaf County few uninterested Negroes participate at all, while in Piedmont and Camellia the pattern of uninterested voting approximates that found in the white community.

Why do the uninterested bother to participate? Table 10–3 suggests one

TABLE 10–3. *Percentage of southern Negroes participating in politics, by political interest and political activity of spouse*

| Political interest of respondent | Spouse has voted | Spouse has not voted |
|---|---|---|
| Interested | 90% (125) | 52% (110) |
| Not interested | 72% (60) | 20% (153) |

NOTE: The entry in each cell represents the percentage of respondents with the two characteristics indicated who qualify as participants (PPS type III, IV, or V). Thus the first entry in the first column indicates that, among those Negroes who are interested in politics and whose spouses have voted, 90 per cent are participants.

major reason—social pressure from one's family, friends, and peers. Even when the level of interest of respondents is held constant, life with a spouse who is a voter greatly increases the probability of participation. Among Negroes who are personally uninterested in politics, for example, 72 per cent of those who are married to voters are also participants themselves; this compares with

20 per cent for uninterested Negroes who are married to nonvoters. The difference is not quite so staggering among those who are personally interested, but it is still great: 90 per cent of those married to voters are participants, while 52 per cent of those married to nonvoters participate.

Political interest continues to make a difference when the voting experience of the spouse is held constant, but the differences are not so great. We can see this most readily by looking at the rates of participation when the two variables are in conflict: 72 per cent of the politically uninterested who are married to voters are participants; 52 per cent of the politically interested who are married to nonvoters are participants. These findings do not mean that the pressures toward participation that come from living with a voter necessarily outweigh political interest as a causal factor. For one thing, the presence of one voter in a family signifies that the entire family lives in an area where it is possible for Negroes to vote. But the findings do permit an answer to the question that prompted them: the citizen—white or Negro—will tend to vote, even though he may be personally uninterested in politics, if he lives in an environment in which voting is expected and encouraged. The great gap between Negro and white rates of participation can thus be explained in large part by the fact that voting is expected of whites, regardless of their interest. When the family environment and the community setting of Negroes produce similar expectations, they also participate, even when they are personally uninterested in participation.

## Ignorance and information

Some information about politics and government would seem to be a precondition for political participation. To "talk politics" without either imparting or learning a trace of factual information is virtually impossible—there would be nothing to talk about, to gossip or gripe about, or to evaluate. The act of voting presupposes that the elector *knows* when it is election day, that he *knows* how to get registered, that he *knows* where his polling place is, that he *knows* how to mark a ballot, and so on. More demanding forms of participation require far more elaborate and accurate cognitive maps of the political world. If this common-sense argument is valid, then southern Negroes —no less than other people—require more than motivation in order to participate; they must also possess accurate and relevant factual information. The low participation rates of southern Negroes may be more a matter of ignorance than of uninterest.

We administered a simple political-information test to each respondent as part of our interview. The questions, along with the percentages of Negroes and whites who answered them correctly, are given in the following table.

|  | PERCENTAGE ANSWERING CORRECTLY | |
| --- | --- | --- |
|  | Negro | White |
| 1. Do you happen to remember whether Franklin Roosevelt was a Republican or Democrat? [Which?] | 57% | 87% |
| 2. Who is the governor of [this state] now? | 68 | 90 |
| 3. About how long a term does the governor serve? | 65 | 67 |
| 4. What is the county seat of [this] county? | 65 | 89 |
| 5. About how many years does a United States Senator serve? | 8 | 20 |
| 6. Do you happen to know about how many members there are on the United States Supreme Court? | 8 | 21 |
| 7. What were the last two states to come into the United States? | 35 | 79 |

The results of this quiz do not add to the South's renown for political erudition. From 10 to 20 per cent of the whites did not know that F.D.R. was a Democrat, the name of their state governor, the location of their county seat, or that Hawaii and Alaska had just been admitted to the Union. Eighty per cent did not know that United States Senators—those stalwart supporters of the southern way—serve for six-year terms or that Earl Warren is only one of nine partners in crime on the Supreme Court. But the pool of politically relevant information possessed by southern Negroes is even shallower and substantially so. The average number of questions answered correctly by Negroes was 3.1; the average white respondent knew the answer to 4.6 questions. Nine per cent of the Negroes could not answer a single one of the seven questions correctly; only 1 per cent of the whites were equally ignorant.

Is political information positively associated with participation, as our original hypothesis suggests? Does the information gap between whites and Negroes help account for their different degrees of involvement in political life? Figure 10–2 gives the beginning of our answer to both questions. Political participation does increase with political information for both races. But the relationship between a person's knowledge and his participation is radically different depending on whether he is Negro or white. Almost all whites participate in politics at least to the point of voting, be they ignorant or well informed. Information level is far more important in accounting for differences in Negro participation. Ninety per cent of the highly informed Negroes have voted or engaged in higher levels of participation, as compared with only 35 per cent of those with low scores on our quiz. When participation is defined as taking part in campaigns or holding a political office or group membership (as in the lower figure), racial differences are greatly reduced. Indeed, such participation is more frequent among highly informed Negroes than among highly informed whites.

We must not conclude on the basis of Figure 10–2 alone that to bombard the South with civics books would increase Negro political activity there. For one thing, a person's political interest and how much political information he has tend to be highly correlated. The more interested a person is in politics, the more likely he is to acquire political information. The politically ignorant tend to be the politically uninterested, and vice versa. Thus both the motivation to participate and the cognitive equipment to do so tend to be found in the same persons. Perhaps politically informed Negroes participate more than the ignorant simply because greater interest leads to more information.

Figure 10–3 tells us that the relationship between information and participation is not merely a reflection of differences in political interest. It shows the percentage of whites and Negroes who participate at least to the extent of voting, by level of both interest and information. Interested and informed whites participate a little more than those who are uninterested and uninformed. The differences are quite small, however, because most whites participate to this extent regardless of their personal attributes. For Negroes, on the other hand, interest and information each seem strongly related to participation, even after controls are introduced for the other. The "greatly

FIGURE 10–2. *Political information and participation of southerners, by race*

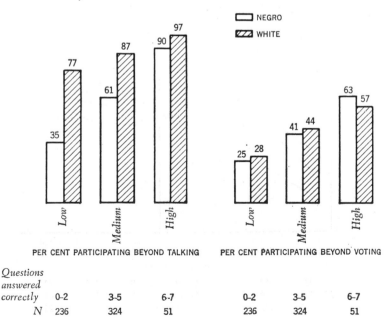

| | PER CENT PARTICIPATING BEYOND TALKING | | | PER CENT PARTICIPATING BEYOND VOTING | | |
|---|---|---|---|---|---|---|
| Questions answered correctly | 0-2 | 3-5 | 6-7 | 0-2 | 3-5 | 6-7 |
| N | 236 | 324 | 51 | 236 | 324 | 51 |

interested" Negroes participate at a rate about 15 percentage points higher than those with "some interest," after we have controlled for the extent of their factual knowledge. The gap between those with "some" and "not much" interest is slightly larger. But the increase in participation as knowledge increases among Negroes with the same amount of interest is also large. Fifty-eight per cent of the greatly interested Negroes with low information scores participate beyond talking, as compared with 97 per cent of those who are greatly interested and well informed. The same pattern holds for Negroes with "some" or "not much" interest. Their participation goes up sharply as their politically relevant knowledge grows, regardless of their level of political interest.

Thus, for the political participation of southern Negroes, the richness and accuracy of their cognitive maps of the political world are no less important than their motivation. This does not mean necessarily that greater factual knowledge *causes* higher rates of participation. Participation results in heightened political knowledge as well as the other way around. Democratic politics is, to some extent, an exercise in mass education. The depressing political ignorance of southern Negroes is, therefore, not merely the result of their inferior formal schooling but also of their long exclusion from political life. As Negroes receive more and better formal education, their interest and participation in politics will increase; as they carry out their roles as active citizens, they will learn more about the political world; and that in turn will

FIGURE 10–3.   *Political participation of southern Negroes and whites, by information and interest*

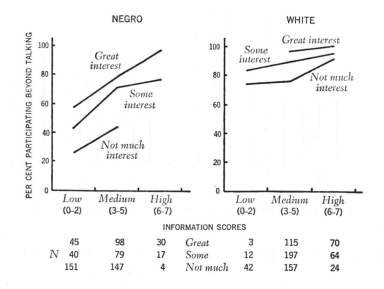

lead to more interest. The "cycle" of poverty exists not just in economics but in the cognitive and political life of southern Negroes as well. Negroes will have little chance to rise permanently above their present status as "second-class citizens" until this cycle of ignorance and inactivity has been broken. But once it has been broken, participation, interest, and knowledge will further the development of one another. The vicious circle will become benign.

## Sense of civic competence

Toward the middle of our interviews, we presented each respondent with a series of hypothetical problems and asked him what, if anything, he would do about them. The first problem went as follows:

First, let's *imagine* you have a child going to a school where there is nobody to help the children across the street. The crossing is dangerous, and one day a child is hit by a car. You think that somebody should be put there to help the children. Do you think you would do anything about it, or figure that there wasn't much you could do?

[*If you would do anything*] What would you do? [*If necessary*] Would you talk to somebody about getting something done?

[*If you would talk to somebody*] Who is that—that is, what does he do, or what's his position? Is he a Negro or a white person?

In Farmington, Minnie Smith responded to this problem with characteristic assurance: "I could do something about it," she said, and then went on to describe how she would visit the white chairman of the board of aldermen about "getting someone put there." Jane West was less sure of herself: "I'd try to do something about it—because I love children," she said. She would "notify the police"—who would presumably already know of the accident— and talk to "anyone who had some children." (A follow-up question about the race of those she would talk to revealed that "anyone" to Mrs. West meant "any Negro.")

Although Jane West's response to this hypothetical tragedy seems mild and tentative, it is far more positive than that of some other Negro respondents. "I'd figure it wouldn't be much I could do," a retired housewife in Crayfish County replied, "especially if the child is hit by a white person." An unemployed laborer in rural Louisiana was bitter in his response: "If it was so that I was in a community where people had rights, I would do something about it."

Obviously, Minnie Smith *believes* she would have some influence, and she knows at least one place to go in an effort to keep such an accident from occurring again. Jane West is less certain that she can alter the situation or about how to proceed in an attempt to do so. The responses of the Negro lady in Crayfish County and the unemployed man in Louisiana would be little different if the South had won the Civil War.

Do these feelings of influence or powerlessness make any difference? Gabriel Almond and Sidney Verba argue, in their study of political attitudes in five western democracies,[2] that attitudes about one's ability to affect politics and government are crucial to the operation of democratic political systems. Citizens who believe that they can influence government decisions are more satisfied and loyal than those who do not. Moreover, they are likely to be more active as well, for "if an individual believes he has influence, he is more likely to attempt to use it." Almond and Verba call this belief in the efficacy of one's own political action *subjective civic competence*. It consists of (1) a belief that public officials can be and are influenced by ordinary citizens, (2) some knowledge about how to proceed in making this influence felt, and (3) sufficient self-confidence to try to put this knowledge to work at appropriate times and places.[3]

Of course, a *sense* of competence and *actual influence* are not the same thing. Even if Minnie Smith actually did visit the chairman of the board of aldermen to complain about a dangerous school crossing in Farmington, she probably would not alter the situation significantly, if at all. Jane West's redundant call to the police and discussions with Negro parents seem even less likely to solve anything. And perhaps the elderly lady in Crayfish County was wrong in assuming that the white county fathers were so callous that they would do nothing about a traffic accident involving a Negro child. People can and do grossly exaggerate or underestimate their "real" political competence.

Nonetheless, Almond and Verba argue, subjective civic competence cannot be totally divorced from objective reality. They found that subjectively incompetent citizens tended to be politically inactive and tended to be overlooked in the scuffle of democratic politics. Thus feelings of incompetence lead to "real" incompetence. The subjectively competent citizen, on the other hand, tends to be politically active, and government is far more likely to respond to the wants and needs of activists. Occasional rewards for political activity reinforce the individual's sense of competence, which helped to stimu-

[2] *The Civic Culture* (Princeton, N.J.: Princeton University Press, 1963), p. 182.
[3] They distinguish between subjective "citizen" competence—a feeling that one can shape general government policy—from subjective "subject" competence—a belief that one can shape the implementation of policy by government officials. *Ibid.*, p. 215ff. Our hypothetical problem about the dangerous school crossing concerns administration more than general policy, so that, in their terminology, we are primarily concerned with feelings of competence as a "subject" rather than as a "citizen." Yet these two concepts are clearly related to one another, as Almond and Verba demonstrate, and objective situations in which ordinary southern Negroes can, in fact, affect basic and general policy are so infrequent that all the hypothetical problems contained in our interview are of the more limited, administrative sort. It should be noted that Almond and Verba's analysis appeared after our interviews had been taken.

late his activity in the first place. The sense of civic competence or incompetence tends to become self-fulfilling.

The objective facts about the Negroes' position in southern politics suggest that most southern Negroes would have a very low sense of civic competence. Their political activity has been discouraged for generations; the benefits they have derived from government have been few. To maintain a personal sense of civic competence would seem difficult when attempts to influence government are doomed to failure. Although the opportunities for Negroes to participate in politics are growing, and although in some areas Negroes possess substantial "real" influence on government decision-makers, a survival of the sense of civic incompetence among Negroes might depress participation long after their political opportunities had improved.

Is this, in fact, the case in the South today? Let us return to our hypothetical story about the dangerous school crossing.

When we classify all the responses to the school-crossing story according to the probability that each respondent would take some action, we find little difference between Negroes and whites—about 85 per cent of both races probably would take some kind of action (see Table 10–4). The Negroes, as

TABLE 10–4.   *Probability of action in the dangerous school-crossing situation, by race*

| PROBABILITY OF ACTION | *Negro* | *White* |
|---|---|---|
| *Definitely would take action* ("I'd do something," "Yes, I would," "I'd talk to somebody," etc. Follow-up action specified.) | 57% | 51% |
| *Probably would take action* ("Yes, if in my power," "I'd try to do something," "I believe I would," etc. Follow-up action specified.) | 28 | 36 |
| *Probably would take no action* ("There ought to be something done," "I don't know whether there is much I can do," etc. No follow-up action indicated.) | 4 | 6 |
| *Definitely would take no action* ("There wouldn't be much I could do," "I wouldn't know what to do," etc. No follow-up action indicated.) | 10 | 6 |
| Don't know, no answer, refusal | 1 | 1 |
| TOTAL | 100% | 100% |
| N | 618 | 694 |

we have observed before, are a little more often found at the extremes ("definitely would" or "definitely would not") than are the whites. These differences are small enough, however, to be entirely the result of sampling error and the imprecisions of coding free-answer responses.

Although the proportion of Negroes and whites who say that they would do something about the dangerous school crossing is virtually the same, the *way* the two races would go about bringing influence to bear is rather different (see Table 10–5). Half of the persons whom whites say they would talk to

TABLE 10–5.   *Persons approached in effort to change dangerous school-crossing situation, by race*

| PERSONS RESPONDENT WOULD TALK TO | Negro | White |
|---|---|---|
| Private "influentials" | 8% | 1% |
| Friends and relatives | 8 | 3 |
| School officials | 33 | 49 |
| Police officials | 22 | 22 |
| Other public officials | 18 | 16 |
| Miscellaneous | 11 | 9 |
| TOTAL | 100% | 100% |
| Number of persons talked to | 800 | 1,056 |
| Number of contacts per respondent | 1.3 | 1.5 |

are school officials, and 85 per cent of those they would approach are public officials of some sort. The Negroes were more reluctant to approach public officials directly and far more likely to attempt to change the situation by approaching private persons thought to have some influence—ministers, lawyers, friends, neighbors, or relatives. One out of every five or six contacts suggested by Negroes would be of this type; only one out of every 25 contacts proposed by whites would be with friends, neighbors, relatives, and other perceived private "influentials"—this despite the fact that whites on the average proposed to talk to more persons about the problem than the Negroes did.

Thus Negroes undoubtedly and understandably tend to feel less competent to approach government officials than whites do. They are more likely to choose an indirect approach to governmental decision-makers through perceived influentials and intermediaries, or to content themselves with discussions with their immediate friends and neighbors, who are unlikely to have any effect on governmental policy or its administration. Thus the southern Negroes' level of subjective civic competence is lower than that of whites. In view of the Negroes' historic position in the South, however, this deficiency in subjective competence is surprisingly small. Given the infrequency with which southern Negroes have succeeded in influencing government policy or its administration, they are surprisingly self-confident and subjectively competent.

Nonetheless, some Negroes feel far more competent than others about their ability to influence government. Is Negro political participation encouraged by these feelings of competence, as the Almond and Verba analysis suggests it should be?

In order to examine this possibility, we combined the Negro responses to two additional hypothetical problems—one concerning a close friend in trouble with the police and the other about a family who are unemployed and hungry[4] —with the responses to the school-crossing problem. Then we counted the number of times each Negro said that he definitely would take action. Political participation increases significantly as the Negroes' subjective civic competence increases: 70 per cent of the Negroes who say they would act in all three instances participate at least to the extent of voting; 58 per cent of those who would definitely act in two cases, and 48 per cent of those who would act once, participate at the level of voting or beyond. The really large difference, however, is between those who say they would not take action in any of these situations and those who say they would—only 31 per cent of those who would not act have ever voted or participated politically to a greater degree. Subjective competence clearly plays a part in accounting for Negro activity and inactivity in politics.

The sense of civic competence is, as we might expect, rather closely related to both political interest and political information. The more interested a person is in politics and the better informed he is about politics, the more likely he is to take action when a specific problem arises. This conclusion raises the possibility that the association between subjective competence and participation is merely the result of one or both of these other powerful vari-

[4] See Appendix C.

FIGURE 10–4.   *Relationship between subjective civic competence and political participation of southern Negroes, by political information and interest*

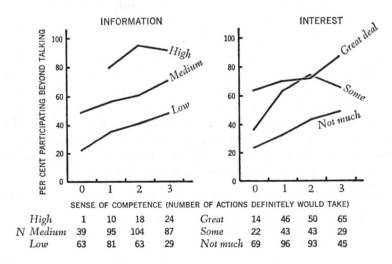

| | | | | | | | | |
|---|---|---|---|---|---|---|---|---|
| *High* | 1 | 10 | 18 | 24 | *Great* | 14 | 46 | 50 | 65 |
| N *Medium* | 39 | 95 | 104 | 87 | *Some* | 22 | 43 | 43 | 29 |
| *Low* | 63 | 81 | 63 | 29 | *Not much* | 69 | 96 | 93 | 45 |

ables. In fact, however, we find that political competence is still strongly associated with participation after we control for the effects of information and interest (see Figure 10–4). Among those with a relatively low level of political information, for example, the proportion who participate beyond talking increases from 22 to 48 per cent as we go from those with lowest to highest sense of civic competence. The increase in participation with increasing sense of competence is less dramatic but still clear at the other levels of political information: at the medium-information level, the increase is from 49 to 71 per cent; at the high-information level, from 80 to 91 per cent. We find the same general picture when we examine the relationships between our measure of civic competence and participation within groups of Negroes with the same amount of political interest. Thus while sense of civic competence is related to both political information and interest, it has a discernible impact on Negro participation which is independent of these two important variables.

Our data, of course, will not tell us whether the subjective sense of competence produces participation or whether participation produces subjective competence. They do demonstrate, however, that these two characteristics are found together.

## Party identification

"The ideal of the Independent citizen, attentive to politics, concerned with the course of government, who weighs the rival appeals of a campaign and reaches a judgment unswayed by partisan prejudice . . ."[5] is so popular in America that we often overlook the role of political parties as reference groups. The evidence shows conclusively, nonetheless, that most Americans develop an emotional identification with a political party early in life.[6] Once formed, this party attachment tends to survive and grow stronger from one election to the next throughout a normal lifetime.[7]

Party identification has a number of consequences. Usually formed while the individual's knowledge of the political world is rudimentary, it serves as a screen through which he perceives most subsequent political stimuli. It helps him to organize and evaluate political reality. This selectivity comes in very handy in making electoral decisions, for example, for the number and complexity of factors to be weighed in making a "rational" voting choice are almost without limit. Partisanship provides a short cut to, and an approximation of, "rational" political choice for those whose time, interest, information, and

[5] Angus Campbell, et al., The American Voter (New York: John Wiley and Sons, 1960), p. 143.
[6] Herbert Hyman, Political Socialization (Glencoe, Ill.: The Free Press, 1959); Fred I. Greenstein, Children and Politics (New Haven: Yale University Press, 1965), pp. 64ff.
[7] Campbell, op. cit., chs. 6–7.

analytic powers are limited.[8] Emotional attachment to one of the parties also encourages political involvement. The minority of Americans who remain true Independents, "far from being more attentive, interested, and informed," according to the Survey Research Center's presidential election studies, tend to ". . . have somewhat poorer knowledge of the [campaign] issues, their image of the candidates is fainter, their interest in the campaign is less, their concern over the outcome is relatively slight. . . ."[9]

One plausible reason for the low rate of political activity among southern Negroes might be lack of party identification. Party identification is generally learned within the family in which one is born. If a parent has never voted, and if he is not at all sure that his child will ever have the opportunity to do so, then party identification may not be passed on from one generation to the next. Besides, which party is the southern Negro to adopt for his own? The party of Lincoln is also the party of Goldwater and his "southern strategy"; the party of the poor is also the party of white supremacy in the South. For these or other reasons, southern Negroes may be less inclined than whites to develop emotional attachments to political parties.

This line of speculation seems to be partly true—but mostly false—in the South today. When asked if they "usually think of themselves as a Republican, a Democrat, an Independent, or what?" and then further asked to rate the strength of their identification, our Negro and white samples indicated the following degrees of partisan attachment:[10]

|  | Negro | White |
|---|---|---|
| Strong partisans | 31% | 37% |
| Weak partisans | 30 | 38 |
| Leaners | 12 | 12 |
| Independents | 5 | 7 |
| Apoliticals | 22 | 6 |
| TOTAL | 100% | 100% |
| N | 618 | 694 |

Partisan attachments are found among 75 per cent of the whites and 61 per cent of the Negroes. This disparity results almost entirely from the fact that one in five Negroes, but only one in 20 whites, was unable to locate himself along the partisan continuum at all. Such people are not so much unpartisan as altogether "apolitical," and four or five times as many Negroes as whites fall into this category. But among those Negroes who are to some extent

[8] See Anthony Downs, An Economic Theory of Democracy (New York: Harper & Brothers, 1957), ch. 3, for a discussion of the difficulties of rational voting and methods for reducing the "costs" involved.
[9] Campbell, op. cit., p. 143.
[10] The exact wording of the question may be found in Appendix B.

TABLE 10–6.  *Strength of party identification and political participation, by race*

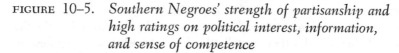

| STRENGTH OF PARTY IDENTIFICATION | PERCENTAGE PPS III, IV, AND V | | Negro rate as percentage of white rate |
| --- | --- | --- | --- |
| | Negro | White | |
| Strong partisans | 77% (193) | 98% (256) | 79% |
| Weak partisans | 54% (183) | 88% (266) | 61% |
| Leaners | 58% (71) | 84% (85) | 69% |
| Independents | 48% (33) | 85% (48) | 57% |
| Apoliticals | 17% (138) | 46% (39) | 37% |

politicized, the strength of partisan attachment is virtually the same as among whites. Under the circumstances, this is perhaps more remarkable than the heavy excess of "apoliticals" among the Negroes.

As strength of party identification increases, so does political activity in both

FIGURE 10–5.  *Southern Negroes' strength of partisanship and high ratings on political interest, information, and sense of competence*

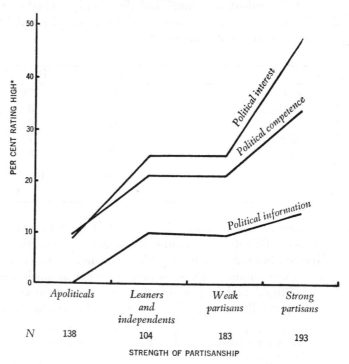

\* High = "Great deal" of interest; 3 on political competence score; 6 or 7 information questions correct.

races (see Table 10–6). Again we find the now familiar subsidiary patterns: Negroes participate substantially less than whites at the same levels of party identification, and political participation varies much more with partisanship among Negroes than it does among whites. Moreover, the mechanisms by which party identification leads to political activity are about what we would have guessed from earlier studies. The more partisan a southern Negro is, the greater his political interest and sense of political competence are likely to be (see Figure 10–5). The partisans are also better informed about the political world than Independents or apoliticals are, but here the apparent effects of party identification are much more modest.

Party identification, however, does more than increase political activity by heightening individual interest, competence, and information. It has a rather sizable *independent* influence on Negro political participation (see Table 10–7). If a southern Negro is highly interested in and unusually well informed about politics, then a strong sense of partisanship seems to produce very little additional participation. Such Negroes are participating at a rate roughly comparable to that of southern whites anyhow. On the other hand,

TABLE 10–7.   *Percentage of southern Negroes politically active, by strength of party identification and political interest, information, and competence*

| STRENGTH OF PARTY IDENTIFICATION | EXTENT OF POLITICAL INTEREST | | |
|---|---|---|---|
| | *Great deal* | *Somewhat* | *Not much* |
| Strong partisans | 85% (93) | 77% (44) | 63% (57) |
| Weak partisans | 67 (45) | 66 (47) | 42 (90) |
| Leaners and independents | 81 (26) | 64 (25) | 37 (52) |
| Apoliticals | 25 (12) | 24 (21) | 15 (104) |
| | LEVELS OF POLITICAL INFORMATION | | |
| | *High (6–7)* | *Medium (3–5)* | *Low (0–2)* |
| Strong partisans | 100% (26) | 79% (123) | 58% (43) |
| Weak partisans | 75 (16) | 56 (108) | 45 (58) |
| Leaners and independents | 90 (10) | 60 (55) | 38 (39) |
| Apoliticals | — (0) | 18 (39) | 16 (97) |
| | SENSE OF POLITICAL COMPETENCE | | |
| | *High (3)* | *Medium (1–2)* | *Low (0)* |
| Strong partisans | 85% (66) | 79% (104) | 48% (23) |
| Weak partisans | 67 (39) | 54 (113) | 39 (31) |
| Leaners and independents | 64 (22) | 55 (73) | 33 (9) |
| Apoliticals | 15 (13) | 18 (83) | 17 (42) |

NOTE: Politically active = PPS types III, IV, or V.

if a Negro is not very interested or well informed—which is true of the bulk of southern Negroes—then partisanship is strongly associated with participation. Party identification seems to have its greatest impact, so far as participation is concerned, among the less politicized but still not subjectively incompetent Negroes.

So far we have discussed party identification without regard to its content.[11] And yet a person may think of himself as a strong Republican, for example, without having a very good notion of why, or of what the party is like. A southern white may see the Democratic party as a bulwark of white supremacy, whereas his Negro tenant down the road may have a very different image of the same party. The richness and detail of a voter's picture of the party system are, therefore, somewhat different from the strength of the emotional attachment to one of the contenders.

When we examine the mental pictures southerners have of the political parties, we find—in keeping with the relationship of general political information to participation—that the more southern Negroes know about the parties, the more likely they are to participate in political life.

| Number of things "liked" or "disliked" about either political party | Percentage PPS types III, IV, or V |
|---|---|
| None | 33% |
| 1 | 50 |
| 2 | 62 |
| 3 | 69 |
| 4 | 73 |
| 5+ | 75 |

Since knowledge about political parties goes up sharply with partisanship—despite cynical talk to the contrary—cognitive richness may, in fact, account for the positive association between party identification and political participation. As Table 10–8 indicates, this is not the case. Strong party identification leads to increased political participation *particularly* among those who know little about the parties. Those who are well informed about the parties tend to participate at rather high levels whether they are partisans or not.

Thus party identification is an additional psychological attribute of southern Negroes that helps account for the extent of their political participation. Its special explanatory power is a function of *when* it is normally learned in the life cycle and *upon whom* it has its greatest effects. Normally, it is among the first attitudes learned in the process of political socialization. It therefore approximates a "cause," coloring everything else we learn about the political

[11] A more complete discussion of the concept of "party image" and its relationship to party identification may be found in Chapter Twelve.

TABLE 10–8. *Percentage of southern Negroes politically active, by strength of party identification and richness of party image*

| STRENGTH OF PARTY IDENTIFICATION | RICHNESS OF PARTY IMAGE | | |
|---|---|---|---|
| | *Strong (4+)* | *Medium (2–3)* | *Weak (0–1)* |
| Strong partisans | 79% (61) | 82% (85) | 67% (46) |
| Weak partisans | 63% (27) | 57% (76) | 49% (79) |
| Leaners and independents | 81% (21) | 64% (33) | 39% (49) |
| Apoliticals | — (2) | 0 (13) | 20% (123) |

NOTE: Each entry is the percentage of southern Negroes with the indicated combination of characteristics who have participated in politics beyond the level of talking.

world. Its effects on political participation tend to be greatest among the least well informed and interested citizens, and this is of great significance, too. If southern Negroes are ever to approximate the participation rates of southern whites, relatively apathetic and ignorant Negroes must be made to participate *as the ignorant and apathetic whites are already doing.*[12] Our political parties, viewed as reference groups, may prove to be one of the major instruments for bringing this change about.

# Sense of deprivation

By objective standards, a vast majority of southern Negroes are "deprived." If one assumes that a family income of $3,000 a year is required to buy the basic necessities of life, then over 70 per cent of all southern Negro families are poverty-stricken. If four years of high school is the minimum amount of education an American must have in order to live a happy and productive life, then about the same proportion of southern Negroes are grossly unprepared for existence in this technological age. If a stable family life, a decent home, adequate police protection, and so on, are prerequisites of tolerable living, then the existence of millions of southern Negroes is intolerable. Most important of all, if one assumes that all men need to be treated with fairness and dignity, that all men desire to be judged on the basis of individual merit, then virtually all Negroes in the South are "deprived."

But the *sense of deprivation*—the feeling of being capriciously denied one's due—is not the same thing as these objective facts. Anthropologists have demonstrated how pliable human nature is. The squalid huts, illiteracy, malnutrition, and disease of primitive life may strike us as extreme forms of deprivation. But the natives usually know no other way, and, when they do,

[12] For a classic statement see Walter Lippmann, *The Phantom Public* (New York: Harcourt, Brace & World, 1925).

they often reject "progress" for what we would consider to be a backward way of life. Economists tell us that middle- and upper-income groups in the United States have the severest unsatisfied cravings for goods and services—the commodities advertised in the *New Yorker* appeal to them rather than to the poor tenant farmer in Alabama who does not even see the Sears Roebuck catalog. Some well-off but not rich Americans may *feel* more deprived, in this one area of life, than many poor people. The *sense* of deprivation thus depends on one's standards and with whom one compares oneself. It is a relative, subjective matter; it may bear little relationship to objective facts.

This piece of folk-psychology is, of course, very comforting to many white southerners. "I think the nigger is happier like he is," a linesman with a Georgia power company said. "That is the way he wants to [live]." A construction worker in rural Louisiana agreed. "In the past," he said, "the Negro had his life, he went to town on Saturday, went to Levee Street, and laid out all night, and he was happy." Logically and psychologically, these men could be correct; centuries of subordination may have led southern Negroes to accept ignorance, poverty, and social subordination without feeling any subjective *sense* of deprivation.

Although this is possible, no one really knows whether it is true. Southern segregationists have stoutly maintained that the region's Negroes are a happy and contented lot; integrationists have argued from the objective facts that southern Negroes must be miserable. Neither position is based on systematically collected facts about the feelings of Negroes. Our interviews offer clues on this critical question.

Our respondents, both white and Negro, were asked to describe to our interviewers "the very best way that Negroes and white people could live in the same place together" and its opposite, "the very worst kind of race relations you could imagine a community having."[13] Once each had defined these extremes at length, he was handed a picture of a ladder and told, to quote from the interview schedule:

> Here is a picture of a ladder. Suppose we say that at the *top* of the ladder [*point to top*] is the *very* best, the really perfect kind of race relations you have just described. At the bottom is the *very worst* kind of race relations.
>
> Where on this ladder [*move finger rapidly up and down ladder*] would you put [*name of this local community*]? That is, where you are living now?

The ratings the respondents then gave—each supplying his own standard of judgment—reflect their own sense of the "goodness" or "badness" of race relations without regard to how they defined their racial ideals.

Most whites, as expected, feel quite good about race relations in their home

---

[13] The self-anchoring scale is described and explained in F. P. Kilpatrick and Hadley Cantril, "Self-Anchoring Scaling, a Measure of Individuals' Unique Reality Worlds," *Journal of Individual Psychology*, Vol. 16 (1960).

FIGURE 10–6.    *Ratings of race relations in home communities today, by race*

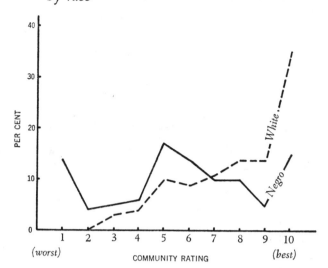

towns; the modal rating—chosen by over a third of all southern whites—is that the actual race relations are the very best imaginable! (See Figure 10–6.) Some whites are less sanguine, but for conflicting reasons. A butcher in Cray-fish County, who defined the best form of race relations as "the niggers as slaves and the white people as their masters," felt that race relations warranted only a rating of 8; a retired Army officer in Arkansas who believed that the ideal would be "to treat the Negro as just another citizen" rated his com-munity as only a 3 by his scale of values.

Negroes take a far dimmer view of community race relations; their modal rating was 5, exactly half that of the whites. The Negro ratings vary more widely, however, than do those of whites. About 15 per cent of the Negroes agree with the whites that present-day race relations are the best imaginable, a clear indication that segregation has, in fact, had a substantial impact on Negro standards and aspirations. These Negroes apparently do not know or want anything "better," by objective standards, than the kind of racial arrange-ments they have always known. And given the almost frightening conflict in Negro and white racial ideals,[14] the Negro ratings are surprisingly high. Only about a fourth of the Negroes give southern race relations the miserable ratings that the objective facts would seem to dictate. On the whole, Negroes feel less deprived than one would expect on the basis of their objective situ-ation. This lowering of the Negroes' level of aspirations is a major consequence of segregation that no one—regardless of his racial views—can afford to overlook.

[14] See Chapter Twelve.

FIGURE 10–7.    *Political participation of southerners, by rating of community race relations today*

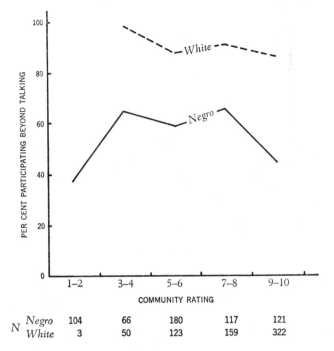

| N | | 1–2 | 3–4 | 5–6 | 7–8 | 9–10 |
|---|---|---|---|---|---|---|
| | Negro | 104 | 66 | 180 | 117 | 121 |
| | White | 3 | 50 | 123 | 159 | 322 |

But this triumph of segregation has been far from complete. Almost all Negroes feel some deprivation, and a minority feel acutely deprived by the local system of race relations. What difference does this make for the extent of their participation in the political system?

As Figure 10–7 indicates, sense of satisfaction or dissatisfaction with local race relations makes much more difference for the rates of political participation of Negroes than for those of whites. When participation is defined as activity at the level of voting or beyond, almost all southern whites qualify as participants, regardless of their variations in terms of other attributes. Nevertheless, a small difference in rates of participation can be discerned between those whites least and most satisfied with their local race relations: the proportion of participants drops from 98 per cent among the few whites who rate the system quite low (3 or 4 on the ladder) to 86 per cent among the many whites who rate the system quite high (9 or 10).[15] This difference hardly means that dissatisfaction with race relations is itself a factor that leads whites to participate. It probably reflects the fact that the few whites who are suffi-

[15] Although this difference is small, it is slightly too large to be dismissed as a product of sampling error.

ciently detached and unprovincial to be critical of their communities are also the kind of alert and informed citizens who participate in public affairs.

The Negroes who are least satisfied with their community's race relations, on the other hand, are least likely to be political participants. Among those who think the system of race relations in their locality is about as bad as any they can imagine (ratings of 1 or 2), only 38 per cent have ever voted or taken a more active part in the political process. Surprisingly, however, the one other group that approaches the low level of participation of those least satisfied is made up of those who are most satisfied with their community's race relations (ratings of 9 or 10). Only 44 per cent of them have ever gone beyond the talking stage in political participation. Participation is lowest at the two extremes—among those either highly dissatisfied or highly satisfied. It is significantly higher among those between the two extremes, with the proportion of participants ranging from 59 to 66 per cent.

Before we accept and try to account for this peculiar finding, we must recognize that we have been talking about Negro ratings of race relations without regard to the "self-anchoring" nature of the rating scale. What is the best possible situation for an integrationist would presumably be the worst possible situation for a segregationist. The few Negro segregationists in the South may accordingly account for the small proportion of participants among those who rate their community race relations as the best possible. To test this possibility, we must reexamine the relationship between political participation and the rating of the local system of race relations, but this time with the Negroes who favor integration separated from those who do not. As Figure 10–8 shows, the curvilinear relationship between sense of deprivation and political participation holds up strongly for the vast majority of Negroes who prefer integration. On the other hand, very few of those who favor segregation or "something in between" participate, regardless of their feelings of deprivation or contentment. They have—grudgingly and partially in some cases and without question in others—accepted a system with little room for political activity by Negroes, and they play the inactive part the system assigns to them.

In evaluating these findings, we must keep in mind that we are dealing with the way individuals rank their own community's race relations in terms of their personal view of the worst and best relations that any community might have. The ratings thus may reflect the "objective" characteristics of their home communities as much as the subjective evaluations and feelings of individuals. If this is so, an exclusively psychological interpretation of these ratings would be an error. But this proves not to be the case; the "objective" characteristics of communities seem to have almost nothing to do with the ratings respondents give them. If we take white agreement with the statement that "colored people ought to be allowed to vote" as a measure of community permissiveness, some of the most repressive counties tend to be rated very highly by local Negroes, while some of the most permissive counties are rated as nearly the worst of all possible worlds. The Kendall's coefficient of rank correlation between community permissiveness and Negro ratings of the same communities is a microscopic .03! These community ratings, then, tell us much about the individuals who make them but almost nothing about the objective characteristics of the individual's home town.

How can we account for the unexpected fact that the most contented southern Negroes tend to participate at a low level? The most plausible remaining possibility is that the 20 per cent of the Negro population who rate their community as 9 or 10 just do not know any better. Their horizons are so limited that they are not aware of how bad their situation is, and the same ignorance explains their failure to participate in the political process. Less than 1 per cent of those rating the race relations of their home community as 9 or 10 got a high score on our political-information test, compared to 10 per cent of the Negro population as a whole. Only 2 per cent of them have been to college, whereas 12 per cent of them have had no formal education whatsoever. Those who think their community is nearly the worst of all possible worlds (1 or 2 ratings) have similarly poverty-stricken cognitive structures—only 6 per cent scored "high" on our political-information test, 7 per cent attended college, and 13 per cent have not attended school for a day in their lives. Ignorance, then, helps explain why both the most contented and the most alienated Negroes participate least in the region's politics. Those who know—

FIGURE 10–8.    *Political participation of southern Negroes, by rating of race relations in home community and by race relations ideal*

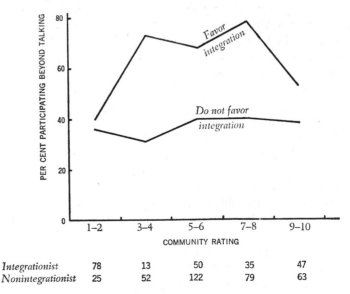

| N | | 1–2 | 3–4 | 5–6 | 7–8 | 9–10 |
|---|---|-----|-----|-----|-----|------|
| | *Integrationist* | 78 | 13 | 50 | 35 | 47 |
| | *Nonintegrationist* | 25 | 52 | 122 | 79 | 63 |

or are at least able to imagine—something better or worse than their own existence also have the cognitive equipment needed to be active citizens in the American polity.

If all this is true, then a Negro's rating of his home community's race relations depends in large part on the richness and accuracy of his cognitive map of the world. We already have found this to be a determinant of Negro participation rates. Does this mean, then, that our measure of sense of deprivation is really a measure of the respondents' knowledge? If it is, the sense of deprivation's curvilinear relationship to participation would disappear altogether when level of information is controlled (see Figure 10–9). The sense of deprivation or well-being tapped by Negro ratings of local race relations makes no significant difference to participation among the highly informed Negroes —they participate at a relatively high level regardless of their community rating. But, of course, very few highly informed Negroes give their communities an extremely high rating (1 per cent) or an extremely low one (11 per cent). Among the large majority of Negroes who are not well informed, however, the moderately satisfied Negro participates more than either the

FIGURE 10–9. *Negroes' community rating and political participation, by political information*

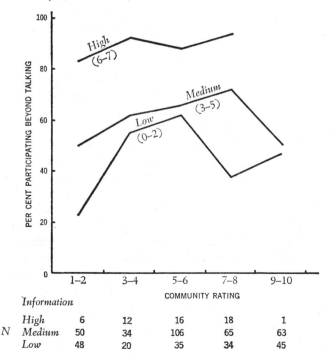

| Information | | 1–2 | 3–4 | 5–6 | 7–8 | 9–10 |
|---|---|---|---|---|---|---|
| | High | 6 | 12 | 16 | 18 | 1 |
| N | Medium | 50 | 34 | 106 | 65 | 63 |
| | Low | 48 | 20 | 35 | 34 | 45 |

alienated or the contented. Thus, although the sense of deprivation and political information are closely associated variables, both have independent effects on Negro political participation.

So far we have examined the effects of a sense of deprivation or satisfaction on Negro participation, using the respondents' own ideals and aspirations as our measuring instrument. And yet, as we argued earlier, the sense of deprivation is a relative matter. Whether one feels better off than others may be more important than how he evaluates his own position in comparison with some vaguely conceived and abstract ideal.

Our interview asked each respondent not only to rate his own community's race relations on a 10-point, self-anchored scale, but also to rate race relations in six other communities—New York, Little Rock, Chicago, Atlanta, "a small town in Mississippi," and "a small city in Ohio." The percentage of the Negro voting-age population who felt that their community's race relations were "better," according to their own standards, than those places was as follows:[16]

| | |
|---|---|
| New York | 26% |
| Chicago | 39% |
| A small city in Ohio | 52% |
| Atlanta | 68% |
| Little Rock | 73% |
| A small town in Mississippi | 87% |

A fourth of the southern Negroes feel better off than the residents of Harlem, and about four out of ten feel better off than the Negroes of Chicago's South Side. In every other comparison, the Negroes tended to feel relatively well off —especially when compared to other southern Negroes. Table 10–9 shows that this sense of *relative* well-being is definitely and positively related to Negro participation rates. In every comparison except for New York, those Negroes who feel relatively well off, so far as race relations are concerned, participate more than those who feel relatively deprived. This is particularly true for comparisons with southern communities. Those who feel better off than Negroes in Atlanta, Little Rock, and rural Mississippi participate much more than those who do not. Southern Negroes who feel they are better off than Negroes in New York are a small and deviant group—made up heavily of undereducated rural residents—and they participate much less than those who rate their home communities as worse than New York in race relations. On the other hand, it is at least conceivable that most southern Negroes do live in communities with "better" race relations than those of Atlanta, and most objective observers would probably agree that most southern communities are "better" than Little Rock or Mississippi. Thus a completely unrealistic sense of relative well-being does not have the consequences for participation

[16] Little Rock, Atlanta, and Mississippi respondents were omitted on comparisons involving these three localities.

TABLE 10–9. *Relative race relations ratings and political participation of southern Negroes*

| REFERENCE COMMUNITY | PERCENTAGE PARTICIPATING BEYOND TALKING | | |
|---|---|---|---|
| | Home community better than reference community | Home community worse than reference community | Percentage-point difference |
| New York | 46% (71) | 60% (383) | − 14 |
| Chicago | 60% (131) | 55% (319) | + 5 |
| A small city in Ohio | 59% (185) | 56% (233) | + 3 |
| Atlanta | 61% (312) | 48% (122) | + 13 |
| Little Rock | 62% (334) | 42% (99) | + 20 |
| A small town in Mississippi | 61% (416) | 43% (44) | + 18 |

that a sense of relative well-being partially based on objective facts appears to have.

A sense of relative deprivation or well-being may result not only from comparing one's lot with that of others, but also from expectations about the future. The comforting belief that history is on one's side excuses much present-day unpleasantness, as the communist nations have amply demonstrated. And a man with forebodings about the future may feel "deprived" even though his present level of satisfaction would otherwise be quite high.

Again, our series of questions on community race relations permits us to examine these possibilities for southern Negroes. In addition to giving us current ratings and comparisons with other communities, our respondents also estimated where they expect their community to be on the scale five years from now. Table 10–10 shows the relationships between current ratings, expectations for the future, and participation rates. Regardless of how they evaluate their community today, those who expect improved race relations in the future participate substantially more than those who expect deterioration or no change. The least active Negroes are those who currently believe that local race relations are poor and who expect no change for the better. Almost

TABLE 10–10. *Percentage of southern Negroes participating beyond talking, by current rating of community race relations and expectations for change in the next five years*

| CURRENT RATING | EXPECTATIONS DURING NEXT FIVE YEARS | | |
|---|---|---|---|
| | Improvement | No change | Deterioration |
| Low (1–3) | 44% (113) | 28% (14) | — (1) |
| Medium (4–7) | 65% (243) | 47% (15) | 50% (12) |
| High (8–10) | 64% (67) | 50% (70) | 31% (32) |

as politically passive, however, are those who now are pleased with local race relations but anticipate future deterioration. The most active Negroes, as we would expect from the analysis below, are those who rate their community as only fair but who expect discernible progress during the next five years. If anything, these future expectations appear to be more predictive of Negro participation rates than does relative deprivation based on comparisons with other communities today.

## Sense of racial inferiority

The central fact of an American Negro's existence is the color of his skin. For centuries this inescapable badge has meant social, economic, and political inferiority—especially in the South.[17]

The psychological consequences of this brutal experience may take a variety of forms. As a compensatory device, Negroes might turn the white man's racism upside down and adopt a doctrine of black supremacy. After all, the white man is ultimately responsible for the painful injustice that Negroes experience every day. To conclude from this that whites are morally inferior beings would not be difficult. Or Negroes might accept the whites' evaluation of the Negro race. Most Negroes are poor, undereducated, and unskilled; the whites' racist arguments are constantly reinforced by the apparent facts of segregated life. A deep sense of racial inferiority and personal insecurity would be another quite normal reaction to generations of systematic degradation. A third possible psychological outcome of the Negroes' segregated existence would be the rejection of racism in all its various forms. But for Negroes to maintain a faith in an egalitarian ethos seems most unlikely and difficult, given the conditions under which they live.

Whatever the psychological consequences of subordination, the Negro's attitude toward his own race must help determine what part, if any, he plays in southern politics. For this reason, our interview contained a series of questions asking both Negroes and whites to compare their race with the other and to tell us which "was smarter," "behaved better," "was more dependable," and "tried to get ahead more."[18] A rating of whites as superior on any of these qualities was counted as +1; Negro superiority was counted as −1; and a response indicating no difference between the races was counted as 0. When we sum the ratings for each respondent, we obtain a score ranging from +4 (whites superior in all four respects) through 0 (no difference between the two races) to −4 (Negroes superior in all respects).

The distribution of these racial stereotype scores for the two races (Figure

---

[17] S. M. Elkins, *Slavery: A Problem in American Institutional and Intellectual Life* (Chicago: University of Chicago Press, 1959).
[18] See Appendix B.

10–10) clearly demonstrates Negro belief in the similarity of the two races. The distribution of Negro scores approximates a normal-distribution curve with the mode near the point of no difference between the races. "People are people," a middle-aged Negro working in a Western Electric plant in North Carolina said. "Scrape us or paint us and nobody would know who's who." A Negro coed at Virginia State College agreed: "I can't think of anything worse than judging people not for what they are but because of color. To me this is ignorance . . . the exterior of a person doesn't tell me anything, but it's what's inside that counts."

Obviously, southern Negroes did not learn these egalitarian sentiments from their white neighbors. The overwhelming majority of the whites were convinced of their own racial superiority—56 per cent rated whites as superior in all four respects—intelligence, behavior, dependability, and ambition. Only 4 per cent could, on balance, see no difference between the two races, and less than 1 per cent rated Negroes as slightly better than whites. Even those whites who occasionally answered that Negroes were superior in some respect often did so for double-edged or trivial reasons. A Louisiana housewife argued that Negroes were more ambitious than whites because "they're trying to push our children out of our schools so theirs can get a better education." An elderly, retired nurse in Texas felt that Negroes "behave better" because "you don't see niggers in halters and shorts on the streets." A housewife in North Carolina could not quite bring herself to believe that Negroes were intellectually equal

FIGURE 10–10. *Racial stereotypes, southern Negroes and whites*

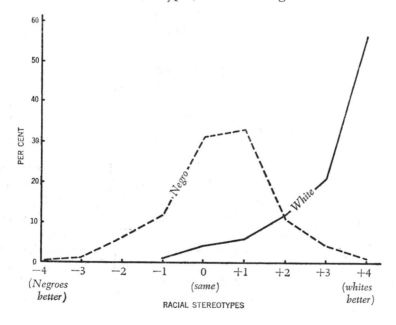

to whites, "but," she said, "there are some smart ones, like nigger Powell and Weaver in Washington"—at best a backhanded compliment for a United States Congressman and a Cabinet official.

Although southern Negroes tend to be relatively free of racial bias—particularly when compared with whites—they are not all willing to conclude that "people are people." Those Negroes with racial stereotypes more often possess a sense of racial inferiority than of superiority. A full 60 per cent of the Negroes, for example, feel that whites try harder to get ahead than Negroes do. A 22-year-old college senior tried to explain why. "Because they [whites] have more advantages to start with," she said, "so it doesn't take much to encourage them. They start out with something, not at the bottom." A senior at North Carolina A. and T. College agreed that "most Negroes accept mediocrity" because of the high probability of failure if they seek more ambitious goals. An old lady in Alabama, a farm laborer with a third-grade education, argued just the opposite. "Course with them on top, trying to hold us down," she said, "we got to try harder." A postgraduate student in Florida elaborated on these sentiments. Negroes try to get ahead more, he argued, "because . . . the white man has made him feel incompetent. . . . He has to excel to even rate since he is black."

Negroes are most likely to feel superior to whites in intelligence—about a quarter of the sample said that Negroes were smarter than whites (compared with 60 per cent who said they were the same and about 10 per cent who said whites were superior). In Florida a retired brickmaker without a day of formal schooling summed up the main reason for his feeling that way:

> It look like the colored one is smarter because he was awful far back in the beginning and now he have slowly crept right up on them so the colored one must be a little smarter or the white folks woulda still been way ahead.

A student in a teachers' college in North Carolina was less sure about progress in the past but confident about the future. "When we get the chance," he said, "we will equal and pass them *and they know it*." Finally, an unemployed truck driver in South Carolina provided the ultimate reason for Negroes' being smarter than whites. "Why," he said, "they don't even know how to clean and cook for themselves, you know they can't be smart!"

Do these feelings of racial equality and inequality have any consequences for the rate at which Negroes participate in politics? Table 10–11 shows the relevant data. Neither a belief in white superiority nor a belief in Negro superiority is consistently related to participation at the level of voting. Thus, at first, these attitudes appear to have no effect on the rate of Negro participation. When we consider higher levels of participation, however, racial attitudes do appear relevant to participation. Feelings of racial inferiority or superiority affect only the higher and more demanding forms of participation. Only 33 per cent of Negroes with strongly pro-white (or anti-Negro) racial stereotypes

TABLE 10–11.   *Racial stereotypes of Negroes and political participation,
by level of activity*

| | LEVEL OF POLITICAL ACTIVITY | | | |
| RACIAL STEREOTYPE | Ever voted or beyond (PPS III–V) | Ever campaigned or beyond (PPS IV–V) | Belong to political group or hold office (PPS V) | N |
|---|---|---|---|---|
| Strongly pro-white (+3, +4) | 58% | 33% | 3% | 33 |
| Slightly pro-white (+1, +2) | 50% | 33% | 8% | 251 |
| No difference (0) | 54% | 35% | 13% | 180 |
| Slightly pro-Negro (−1, −2) | 64% | 49% | 16% | 99 |
| Strongly pro-Negro (−3, −4) | 60% | 50% | 20% | 10 |

have ever campaigned or participated at a more demanding level than voting,
and a mere 3 per cent have reached the highest level of participation. Fifty
per cent of those with strongly pro-Negro stereotypes have reached the level
of campaign participation, and 20 per cent are active at the highest level.
Participation at the level of campaigning or beyond almost doubles as the
Negro stereotypes shift from racial inferiority to superiority, while participation at the highest level increases sevenfold.

When we introduce controls for political information, the magnitude of this
relationship is not reduced (see Figure 10–11). Indeed, the sense of racial
inferiority is one of the few variables we have uncovered that drastically affects
the rate of participation of highly informed Negroes: those with pro-white

FIGURE 10–11.   *Negro political participation and racial stereotypes,
by information and interest*

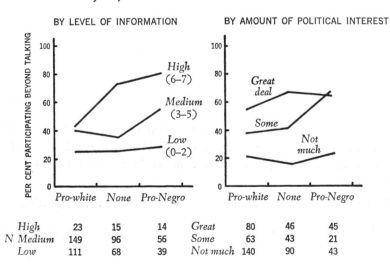

| | BY LEVEL OF INFORMATION | | | | BY AMOUNT OF POLITICAL INTEREST | | |
|---|---|---|---|---|---|---|---|
| | Pro-white | None | Pro-Negro | | Pro-white | None | Pro-Negro |
| High | 23 | 15 | 14 | Great | 80 | 46 | 45 |
| N Medium | 149 | 96 | 56 | Some | 63 | 43 | 21 |
| Low | 111 | 68 | 39 | Not much | 140 | 90 | 43 |

stereotypes participate at only about *half* the rate of those who feel that Negroes are at least the equal of whites. A sense of racial superiority, however, apparently has much less impact on those moderately informed and virtually none on those with little or no factual information about government and politics. The combination of high factual information *and* racial self-confidence is almost explosive—80 per cent of this small group have participated in campaigns or have taken an even more active role in the political process.

When we examine the relationship between racial feelings and participation, with political interest held constant (see Figure 10–11 again), the results are less dramatic. Although feelings of racial adequacy still result in some increase in participation within each category of interest, the differences are small. Controlling for political interest tends to reduce the relationship of racial stereotype to political participation to the point of insignificance.

Thus the southern Negro's evaluation of the worth of his own race may not only affect the goals he seeks through politics; it may also affect the level of his participation. Racial pride and confidence—especially when combined with a high level of cognitive sophistication—lead to high levels of participation by Negroes in the South. Feelings of racial inadequacy do not seem appreciably to reduce Negro voting rates, but they do diminish the frequency with which Negroes participate beyond the voting stage. A sense of racial inferiority is largely incompatible with high levels of political activism.

## Resistance to social change

The South is the closest approximation to a traditional society that we have in the United States today. It is America's own "underdeveloped area," bound by a reverence for history and custom and built on the base of a near-peasantry. In other societies—ranging from the Soviet Union to Brazil to Uganda to Viet Nam—the rural peasant's resistance to change is the chief barrier to rapid modernization. Might the southern Negro—America's closest equivalent to a rural peasantry—display the same deep-seated resistance to change as the rural peasant does elsewhere? And might this, in turn, help explain the low rate of Negro participation in southern politics?

In order to answer these questions, we tried to measure the underlying attitudes of southerners toward change. We asked each respondent to indicate whether he agreed or disagreed "quite a bit" or "a little" with the following statements:

   1. If you start trying to change things very much, you usually make them worse.
   2. If something grows up over a long time, there will always be much wisdom in it.

FIGURE 10–12.  *Attitudes of southern Negroes and whites toward change*

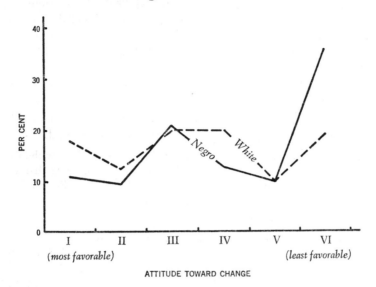

3. It's better to stick by what you have than to be trying new things you don't really know about.

4. We must respect the work of our forefathers and not think that we know better than they did.

5. A man doesn't really get to have much wisdom until he's well along in years.

Each of these items, taken from a larger measure of "classical conservatism" developed by Herbert McClosky,[19] taps the individual's commitment to the ways of the past. We can predict the response to any one of the statements from the responses to the others with sufficient consistency for us to combine the battery of items into a scale or measure of a single dimension of attitudes— what we call "resistance to social change."[20]

Southern Negroes tend to be much more resistant than do southern whites to the abstract idea of change (Figure 10–12). More than a third of the Negroes—as compared to only 19 per cent of the whites—scored at the most resistant end of the scale. One of these, a 105-year-old washerwoman in South Carolina, provides a classic (if extreme) example of the attitudes of this group. Approached by our interviewer, the old lady began by saying, "I don't talk to

[19] Herbert McClosky, "Conservatism and Personality," *American Political Science Review*, Vol. 52 (1958), pp. 27–45. We are indebted to Professor McClosky for giving us the exact wording of the statements used in the scale that he discusses in his article.

[20] See Appendix C.

nobody but my white people; I don't want nobody coming around here bothering me about nothing." Asked for her opinion of the NAACP, she said that she disagreed with it and then volunteered, "I think we ought to stay in our place; that's how I was raised, in slavery." Her opinion of the worst possible race relations was "when the colored people start to trying to be like the white people." For her the South has been headed steadily downhill since the Emancipation Proclamation.

Most southern Negroes who are psychologically resistant to change are not senile ex-slaves. Neither is resistance to change the automatic result of advanced years and inadequate schooling. For example, a 64-year-old Negro farmer in Florida, with only one year of formal education, said:

> I really enjoy gitting to see how many more things we can do now than we us'ta. How many advantages and privileges these young people have that we didn't have, and how if they use these opportunities and use 'em right, just how many more doors will be open to them. Just wonders!

To this man change is a delight, not an agony. But fewer Negroes are like him than are like the old washerwoman in South Carolina.

The finding that a larger proportion of southern Negroes than of whites are emotionally resistant to the idea of change is not just another irony in the strange life of America's underdeveloped area. As Figure 10–13 indicates, these attitudes have consequences for political participation. Both Negroes and whites who favor change participate in politics more than those who resist

FIGURE 10–13.   *Attitudes of southern Negroes and whites toward change and political participation*

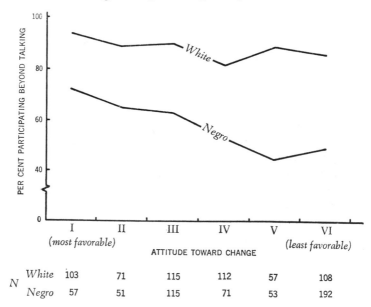

change. This difference is understandably greater for Negroes than for whites—72 per cent of the Negroes most favorably inclined toward change have at least voted, and only 49 per cent of those predisposed toward the *status quo,* or "the good old days," have participated to that degree. The Negro traditionalists reject the hazards of change for the folk wisdom of a past that gave them no legitimate political role; most of them abstain from participating in the politics of the contemporary South.

As with the other psychological variables we have examined in this chapter, attitude toward change is related to political interest and political information. Only 3 per cent of the Negroes most resistant to change received a high score on our information test, whereas 22 per cent of those most predisposed toward change were highly informed. Sixty-one per cent of the extreme resisters but only 42 per cent of the extreme innovators rated themselves as "not much interested" in politics. Given the strength and direction of these relationships, we must, if we are to draw causal inferences, show that the relationship between resistance to change and nonparticipation persists even when the effects of political interest and information are statistically controlled. Figure 10–14 shows that the relationship does persist. The percentage of those who have ever voted, or who have participated to an even greater extent, increases from 72 to 92 per cent among the greatly interested Negroes as their attitudes toward change move from unfavorable to favorable. Predispositions toward

FIGURE 10–14. *Attitudes of southern Negroes toward change and political participation, controlling for political information and interest*

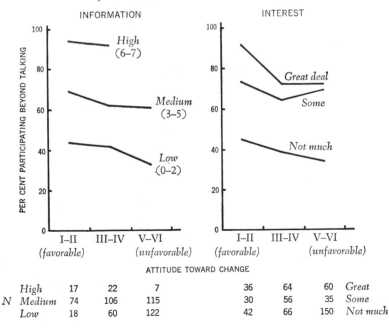

| | | (favorable) | | | (favorable) | | | |
|---|---|---|---|---|---|---|---|---|
| | High | 17 | 22 | 7 | | 36 | 64 | 60 | Great |
| N | Medium | 74 | 106 | 115 | | 30 | 56 | 35 | Some |
| | Low | 18 | 60 | 122 | | 42 | 66 | 150 | Not much |

change do not make as great a difference in any other interest or information category, but the impact they do have is all in the predicted direction. Tradition-bound Negroes, fearing the risks of change, tend not to participate in southern politics.

In the Declaration of Independence, Thomas Jefferson said, ". . . all experience hath shewn, that mankind are more disposed to suffer, while evils are sufferable, than to right themselves by abolishing the forms to which they are accustomed." The preference for the ways of the past among a third of the South's adult Negroes supports Jefferson's proposition. But a fifth of the Negroes are located at the opposite extreme, eager for change; for an increasing number, the evils of accustomed forms no longer appear sufferable.

## Intimidation and fear

Snarling police dogs straining at their leashes—mobs running wild in the streets—beatings, shootings, kidnapings, bombings—cross-burnings by a resurgent Ku Klux Klan—these and other forms of racial violence have dominated the headlines from the South in recent years. The casual reader of the press might conclude that southerners—both white and Negro—are living in a reign of terror like the one that followed the French Revolution of 1789. But most southerners—Negro and white—have neither taken part in nor personally observed these incidents; for most, the daily round of life goes on much as before, despite the sickening film clips shown almost every night on the TV news.

Nonetheless, the period since *Brown* v. *Board of Education* has been one of the most violent in the region's history. Although most of the violence has served no purpose other than catharsis, some of it was calculated to frighten Negroes from active protest or participation. And regardless of white motives, a likely consequence of any racial violence is the intimidation of some southern Negroes.

In Chapter Six we analyzed this question on a *community* basis, examining Negro voter-registration rates for counties that had experienced different levels and types of racial violence. We found that Negro registration was lowest in the small number of counties with extremely high rates of racial violence *and* in those with relatively peaceful race relations. We found that the counties with some but not an extraordinary amount of racial violence have the highest rates of Negro voter registration. Save in the small number of extremely violent counties, then, racial violence seemed to be more an indication of white weakness than of strength and to be greatly overestimated as an inhibition to Negro participation.

But these tentative conclusions were based on the analysis of county data; they tell us little about the feelings and behavior of individuals. In this chapter our unit of analysis has shifted from the community to the individual. How many southern Negroes feel intimidated? How much and in what ways does this feeling affect Negro political participation?

We learn little by asking someone outright if he is afraid. We must draw inferences from questions that spare the respondent the embarrassment of such an admission. But we are fairly safe in assuming that only those who are aware of racial violence or intimidation in their vicinity are likely to be very frightened about their own survival and well-being. So we asked the Negro respondents these questions:

> Have you ever heard of anything happening to Negroes around here who have voted or taken some part in politics or public affairs? [If yes:] could you tell me about it—what happened? [When? Why? Where?]

Sixteen per cent of the adult Negroes mentioned at least once such incident in their area.[21]

TABLE 10–12. *Types of Negro activity "causing" racial incidents, as recalled by Negro respondents remembering such an incident*

| Type of activity | Percentage of all incidents |
|---|---|
| Tried to register or vote | 33% |
| Registered or voted | 5 |
| | |
| Joined NAACP or other group | 4 |
| Led registration or voting drives | 6 |
| Other political leadership | 4 |
| Ran for public office | 4 |
| | |
| Engaged in protest activity | 13 |
| Led protest activity | 10 |
| | |
| No activity mentioned | 12 |
| Other | 4 |
| Refusal, no answer | 5 |
| | |
| TOTAL | 100% |
| N | 98 |

The most common type of Negro activity to trigger the racial incidents our respondents described were efforts to register or vote—over one third of their stories concerned this rudimentary level of participation (see Table 10–12).

21 A few Negroes may have been so fearful that they failed to give a truthful answer to the question. But only one refused to answer the question outright, and only three responded with a "don't know." The response rate for this particular question was one of the highest we obtained from over a hundred questions. Few respondents seemed to feel so threatened by the question that it affected their replies.

The next most frequent cause of racial violence was participating in (13 per cent) or leading (10 per cent) various forms of protest. A wide range of other activities accounted for the remainder of the incidents.

TABLE 10–13. *What happened to Negroes involved in racial incidents, as recalled by Negro respondents remembering such an incident*

| What happened to Negro | Percentage of all things mentioned |
|---|---|
| General threats | 4% |
| Harassment by law enforcement officer, etc. | 12 |
| Economic sanctions employed | 46 |
| Told to leave town or county | 1 |
| Violence explicitly threatened | 4 |
| Violence employed | 29 |
| Other | 4 |
| TOTAL | 100% |
| N | 112 |

One third of the racial incidents involved violence or the threat of violence (see Table 10–13). Outside Houston, for example, a Negro longshoreman said:

> You remember the incident that happened out here when the whites hanged that man to a tree and carved KKK on him. This is how they feel. They think they can get away with it. Well, they picked the wrong fellow. It should have been me. Now the younger of us have gotten tired and they are showing the world that they are tired of being second class in first class America. That's all. I'm talking too much!

More common—in almost half the incidents reported—was the use of economic sanctions against Negro activists. In Bright Leaf County, for example, "Some [people] were put out doors and lost jobs here in Farmington because they tried to vote. . . ." In rural Louisiana, a farmer

> . . . was boycotted. They wouldn't gin his cotton or sell him any gas and he was refused a chance to buy anything in some stores until the [federal] government stepped in, and all that was because he attempted to vote. He wasn't alone, but they took revenge on him.

Some Negroes in the same county expected far worse—"It is said that if you tried [to vote] you wouldn't get away from the place alive." No doubt this was the impression the hostile whites in the community hoped to convey by using less extreme sanctions. Harassment by policemen and other public officials was also frequently reported. In Capital City, for example, one of the leaders of the Negro bus boycott ". . . was always getting tickets for speeding and running stop signs when he wasn't doing nothing," and ordinary Negroes "were gitting in jail for just walking around town toting signs." The street lights were turned off outside the church of one of the militant ministers leading the movement, and vandals broke the church windows and burned a cross on the church lawn. Threatening telephone calls (". . . and you know there is no way to trace them, so they say . . ."), cross-burnings (". . . the other night the KKK burned . . . a cross on my neighbor's yard. . . ."), the destruction of churches ("Some white boys burned down our church Sunday morning before day-[break]"), legal harassment (". . . he has had a lot of trouble with the city about his signs and stuff. After all the years the [gas] station has been there, the signs weren't too close to the street until now"), and other forms of intimidation were reported by respondents in many southern communities.

And yet the difference in participation rates between Negroes who have heard such stories and those who have not is small. Fifty-four per cent of the Negroes who have not heard these frightening tales qualify as participants beyond the level of talking politics, but 51 per cent of those who are aware of these scare tactics also have participated to the same extent. Indeed, those aware of racial violence in their immediate area have almost twice the proportion (17 per cent) of extreme activists (PPS Type V) in their midst as do those who have not heard about it (9 per cent), Southern Negroes may be frightened at various times and places, but fright does not seem, on a south-wide basis, to dampen their efforts to participate in politics.

What factors help explain the slight effect of intimidation on Negro political participation?

Ironically, one factor is the relatively low level of political interest and information of southern Negroes. Only 14 per cent of those Negroes who are "not much interested" in politics and public affairs have ever heard these scare stories, whereas 20 per cent of those with a great deal of interest have. Only 13 per cent of those Negroes who scored extremely low on our political-information test (no questions or only one answered correctly) have heard of racial incidents, whereas 27 per cent of the highly informed (6 or 7 questions answered correctly) are aware of them in their immediate area. Thus the scare stories are more often heard by those whose motivation and cognitive equipment are sufficient for them to participate in the political process. Those most easily dissuaded from participation are less likely to be aware of racial incidents. Some southern Negroes are just too poor, ignorant, and apathetic to be easily frightened.

Even when the relatively uninterested and politically ignorant Negroes are made aware of racial incidents, the likelihood of their participating is not greatly affected. Table 10-14 shows the frequency of political participation by Negroes who are aware and by those who are unaware of local racial incidents, with their level of political interest and information held constant. Among the Negroes with "not much" interest, those who have heard the scare stories participate a little less than those who have not heard them. The same is true of the less well informed. Awareness of local racial incidents seems to have

TABLE 10–14.  *Percentage of Negroes participating to the extent of voting or beyond who have and have not heard "scare stories," with political interest and information controlled*

|  | Have heard scare stories | Have not heard scare stories |
|---|---|---|
| POLITICAL INTEREST |  |  |
| Great deal | 75% (35) | 57% (139) |
| Somewhat | 63% (19) | 64% (116) |
| Not much | 31% (42) | 37% (260) |
| POLITICAL-INFORMA-TION SCORES[a] |  |  |
| High 6–7 | 93% (14) | 90% (38) |
| 4–5 | 66% (35) | 64% (160) |
| 2–3 | 32% (34) | 50% (217) |
| Low 0–1 | 27% (15) | 31% (98) |

[a] Number of questions answered correctly.

the opposite effect among well-informed and highly motivated Negroes—as it clearly did for the Texas longshoreman quoted above. Yet the percentage-point differences in Table 10–14 are so small and the number of cases so few that most of these findings might result wholly from sampling error.

The nature of the Negro activity that led to white reprisals offers a final explanation for the lack of a significant relationship between awareness of racial incidents and Negro participation. As the data in Table 10–12 indicate, a wide variety of Negro activities are capable of triggering an ugly racial incident. The most common "cause" of racial intimidation was reported to be efforts to register or vote. This is a very different stimulus of violence or intimidation from other kinds of Negro "agitation," such as organizing or taking part in a sit-in, bus boycott, or picket line. In the first case, Negroes are merely trying to exercise a constitutional right; in the second, they are taking the initiative and are challenging the white community in fashions other than through the normal processes of government. Attempts to join the NAACP, or to lead a voter-registration drive or other Negro political activity, or to run for public office fall between these two extremes. While comparable activities are routine for white citizens, such activities represent a much higher level of participation than merely trying to use the franchise. The "causes" of the incidents described by our respondents (classified into these three types) and the rates of participation of the respondents aware of each are presented in Table 10–15.

First of all, Negroes who are aware of local racial incidents flowing from Negro protest movements are *much* more politically active than those who have heard about other types of incidents or who are unaware of them alto-

TABLE 10–15.   *Political participation of southern Negroes who have and have not heard "scare stories," by content of scare stories heard*

| NATURE OF STORY RESPONDENT HEARD | PERCENTAGE OF RESPONDENTS HEARING TYPE OF STORY WHO ARE | | | |
|---|---|---|---|---|
| | PPS *types* III, IV, *and* V | PPS *types* IV *and* V | PPS *type* V | N |
| Have heard no scare stories | 54% | 36% | 9% | 516 |
| Story concerned Negro registration or voting | 30% | 19% | 8% | 37 |
| Story concerned Negro joining group, providing political leadership, or running for office | 45% | 28% | 11% | 18 |
| Story concerned Negro engaged in or leading protest movement | 87% | 61% | 17% | 23 |

gether. A whopping 87 per cent of them have taken part in politics to the point of voting or beyond, compared to 54 per cent of those who have not heard about these incidents. Just as those Negroes who initiated the protest movement are not intimidated, neither are those who have heard about the sometimes violent consequences of protest activity. Although we cannot be absolutely certain—because those who have heard of violence and intimidation resulting from protest activities probably would have been quite politically active anyhow—this form of racial "intimidation" seems to reinforce Negro determination to act rather than diminish it. For example, a lumber grader in Capital City—the scene of bitter and prolonged protest activity—was asked if there was any special reason for his not having voted. Here is his reply:

> Well, I hadn't given much thought 'til here lately. You know, you can live in a place where everything is at a standstill, nobody doing nothing, and you will be in a rut with them. But there ain't nothing that's keeping us from it, so the next time they be voting, I'll be there, too. I been thinking 'bout it seriously here of late. This is all our problem, and if some is going to jail, the least I could do is vote.

An electrician in the same town, talking about the sit-ins, put it another way: "My people have probably gotten tired of sitting and waiting for Santa Claus and another Abraham Lincoln. They are coming to the front now. And now is the time!" Another unintimidated resident of Capital City said calmly, "What's mine I want, and if I have to spat to get it then I don't mind." Many hundreds of miles away, an unemployed porter in Texas suggested that the fruits of violence may be bitter:

> I go along with them [the sit-inners] because I feel if we wait longer it will take longer. So they should make white people wake up to the fact that we are citizens and deserve to be treated that way. Why, all kinds of people can come

to this country and receive better treatment than us. You know, even Russians
. . . they can eat in these stores—we can't. Yet we go and die in the war to be
treated this way. To hell with America if this is what it gives! White people are
fakes. They are selfish and want everything for themselves.

While the stories of protest are scarcely "intimidating" to today's Negroes,
the older-style violence does seem to be related to relatively low rates of Negro
participation. Only 30 per cent of the Negroes telling us about racial incidents
concerning voting or registration and 45 per cent of those who are aware of
incidents about joining groups or seeking to provide political leadership have
ever voted or participated in politics beyond that point. Fifty-four per cent of
those who have heard no scare stories have been that politically active. Here
again, though, the Negroes hearing such stories probably come from parts of
the South where inhibitions other than fear are compelling. (Our analysis of
aggregate data in Chapter Six supports this interpretation.) And when we look
at the incidence of high levels of political activity by Negroes (PPS Type V
in Table 10–15), we see that awareness of local racial incidents seems to
encourage rather than discourage this high level of commitment.

To sum up: most Negroes are unaware of specific racial incidents in their
localities. In most cases, this is because there has been none, but in some cases
there are incidents that the low interest and information of most Negroes keep
them from becoming aware of. To the extent that racial incidents and violence
do inhibit political participation, these effects are confined to the least interested and informed segment of the Negro community and to incidents that
are sparked by Negro efforts to exercise the franchise or to provide organization
and leadership. These incidents tend to occur where Negro participation would
be quite low on other grounds; we should not confuse a relationship with a
cause. But those Negroes who are aware of the violence and unpleasantness
surrounding the protest movement are so much more participant than other
Negroes that awareness of this kind of incident in the locality probably can
be said to encourage participation that would not otherwise occur.

Negroes participate in politics much less than whites do, but the analysis
here and in Chapter Six suggests that intimidation and fear are not major
causes. In the long run, efforts at intimidation may well lead to more Negro
participation than would have occurred if the white community had refrained
from violence altogether.

## Conclusions

Minnie Smith and Jane West, the demographically matched pair of Negroes
in Bright Leaf County who participate in politics at such different rates,
probably will never read these pages. It is just as well. Despite their prominence in this chapter, both of them would probably find it a crashing bore.

But these two middle-aged women serve as a constant reminder that similarities in personal characteristics and community environment do not automatically and directly produce similarities in behavior. To trace all the intricate linkages between "outside" objective factors to the psychological attributes of individuals and then to show how these in turn produce differences in political participation is a more ambitious task than our data permit. Thus in this chapter we have concentrated on the last part of the causal chain, the relationship between the attitudes and cognitions of southern Negroes and their political participation.

We examined eight psychological characteristics of southern Negroes—interest in politics, the amount of politically relevant information they have at their command, sense of civic competence, party identification, sense of deprivation, attitudes toward social and political change, feelings about the inferiority or superiority of the Negro race, and awareness of efforts at intimidation by local whites (which we assumed to be a precondition for feelings of intimidation and fear). We found each of these attributes to be related to the participation of southern Negroes in the political process. To say—on balance—which of these psychological characteristics is the most important is difficult. No single measure does full justice to the complexities of the relationships between the Negroes' feelings, predispositions, and cognitions and their activity—or inactivity—in the world of politics. A rough approximation is provided, however, by the following coefficients of contingency, which indicate the extent of association between psychological characteristic and participation by scores ranging from 0 (absolutely no association) to 1 (the characteristic completely predicts PPS).[22]

|  | Coefficient of contingency (Tschuprow's "T") |
|---|---|
| Strength of partisanship | .29 |
| Political interest | .28 |
| Political information | .24 |
| Sense of civic competence | .17 |
| Sense of deprivation | .12 |
| Attitude toward change | .12 |
| Sense of racial inferiority or superiority | .08 |
| Awareness of local racial incidents | .04 |

Political partisanship, interest, and information prove to be the three most important variables for Negro participation, followed by the sense of civic

[22] For a discussion of Tschuprow's coefficient, see G. U. Yale and M. G. Kendall, *An Introduction to the Theory of Statistics* (New York: Hafner Publishing Co., 1950), p. 54ff.

competence. This is understandable, for these four are measures of explicitly political attitudes and cognitions, whereas the other psychological dimensions examined are more generalized in nature. Nonetheless, these general attitudes and beliefs tend also to be associated with participation—especially the Negroes' sense of deprivation and attitudes toward change. The sense of racial inferiority or superiority (because it seems to affect participation only at high levels) and awareness of racial incidents (because it has opposite and to some degree self-canceling effects) have the smallest overall relationships to political participation.

These attitudes tend to be related to one another as well as to political participation, as Table 10–16 shows. Party identification, political interest, and

TABLE 10–16.  *Interrelationships of the psychological characteristics of southern Negroes*

| | COEFFICIENT OF CONTINGENCY (*Tschuprow's "T"*) | | | | | | |
|---|---|---|---|---|---|---|---|
| | Strength of party identification | Political interest | Political information | Sense of civic competence | Sense of deprivation | Attitude toward change | Sense of racial inferiority or superiority |
| Political interest | .22 | | | | | | |
| Political information | .16 | .22 | | | | | |
| Sense of civic competence | .14 | .16 | .20 | | | | |
| Sense of deprivation | .08 | .11 | .13 | .07 | | | |
| Attitude toward change | .14 | .18 | .16 | .11 | .05 | | |
| Sense of racial inferiority or superiority | .01 | .09 | .05 | .12 | .02 | .06 | |
| Awareness of local intimidation | .07 | .06 | .01 | .09 | .02 | .01 | .08 |

information are almost as closely related to one another as they are separately to participation. When controls are introduced for the effects of each on the other, all three of these variables prove to be of about equal importance as predictors of participation among southern Negroes. The sense of civic competence is also significantly related to political information, interest, and partisanship. The effects of sense of competence on participation are not merely the result of this fact, however, as we demonstrated earlier in the chapter. The measures of more generalized attitudes tend to be far more independent of one another than the political characteristics are, but they tend to be noticeably

FIGURE 10–15. *Eight psychological variables and Negro political participation*

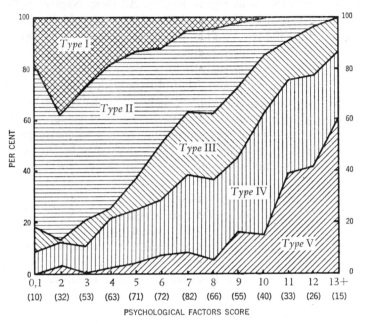

related to partisanship, political interest, information, and competence. Much of the impact that these generalized feelings of deprivation, resistance to change, racial inferiority, and fear (and their opposites) have upon political participation probably comes from their influence on the more specifically political characteristics of the Negro psyche. Be that as it may, the politically relevant psychological characteristics of southern Negroes are *both* more closely related to one another and to political participation than are the other attitudes and cognitions examined in this chapter.

If "objective" influences on political participation are mediated through Negro attitudes and cognitions, then we should expect the psychological characteristics examined in this chapter, when taken together, to explain most of the variation in Negro political participation we have found to exist in the South. In order to examine this possibility, we prepared an overall index of psychological readiness for participation. We used all eight psychological factors discussed in this chapter and assigned each dimension an equal weight.[23] This gives us a rough overall measure of psychological predisposition toward political participation ranging from a score of 0 (no factors conducive to participation) to 16 (all factors conducive to participation). When we plot

[23] See Appendix C.

the distribution of PPS scores by the strength of the psychological forces encouraging participation, we can see the tremendous power of these eight psychological variables (as in Figure 10–15). All those Negroes with a score of 11 or more have voted or have participated at an even higher level; almost half of them are PPS Type V's. Those Negroes with one or no psychological characteristic associated with participation are almost all Type I's and II's. Very few southern Negroes participate in politics without participant attitudes and adequate cognitive equipment. Most of those with psychological characteristics strongly motivating and equipping them for an active role in politics are already participating in politics at least to the extent of voting.

Thus, in order substantially to increase the amount of Negro participation in southern politics, Negro attitudes and cognitions must be altered. This is a far more difficult and time-consuming task than altering the formal political system or social structure, although these "objective" and "external" factors have a profound effect on Negro attitudes. Change in the Negroes' objective status may not quickly change the psychological characteristics instilled by decades of subordination. Segregation's greatest triumph has been its impact on Negro minds. For some the scars are permanent; nothing short of death will eliminate their crippled psyches from the political scene. For the others the scars will respond but slowly to the salve of objective equality.

# Chapter Eleven

# Negro Political Participation: A Summary View and a Causal Analysis

Some critics damn social scientists for explaining human behavior so dispassionately and rigorously that they take all the mystery out of the universal game of speculating about the human condition. Others condemn them for failing to explain anything important about the unfathomable and unique qualities of the human being.

As a product of social research, this book is a target for both charges. With some regret, we submit that they are equally ill founded. We would prefer to agree with the first criticism, but the current state of political research does not permit the luxury of being damned for too much success. The most thorough research has explained only a small part of the fascinating variation in human behavior. We can dismiss the charge of total failure without reluctance. In this chapter we shall try to support both these assertions.

A well-established approach in social research is to examine the relationship of each of a series of variables to the phenomenon to be explained. For example, we have examined the importance of such individual attributes as sex, age, and education for Negro political participation. But what appears to be a causal relationship may actually be spurious, a mere reflection of some underlying factor related to both the variables in the original relationship. When we discovered that Negroes with high income take a more active part in politics than Negroes with low income, for example, we were not satisfied with the independence of the relationship until we discovered that it held true when other factors, such as education and occupation, were also taken into account.

Two features of our approach permit a more general consideration of the factors explaining Negro civic activity.

First, we have employed a generalized concept of political participation. Rather than separate efforts to explain differences in the frequency of talking politics, voting, taking part in campaigns, belonging to political organizations, and holding public office, we have combined all these activities into a single political-participation scale. This concentration on a single dependent variable enables us to take a more generalized view of the independent variables as well.

The second distinctive feature of our approach is that we have tried to bring several different classes of data to bear upon a single problem. At the individual level, we have examined the importance of social and economic characteristics and of attitudes and cognitions. Although some of these measures of individual attributes represent innovations (for example, the specification of the motivational and cognitive dimensions of education rather than the conventional reliance on school years completed), for the most part they are the conventional variables of survey research. But we have also tried to recognize that the characteristics of the communities where southern Negroes live may influence political participation. At the community level, we have been concerned with both political and socioeconomic attributes.

We have found that all four classes of factors—community socioeconomic structure, individual socioeconomic attributes, community political system, and individual attitudes and cognitions—have some explanatory power. Must we leave these as disjointed explanations, with their relative importance and their interrelationships undetermined? To some extent, we must. We cannot duplicate the depth of insight afforded by our four community studies for every county in which we conducted interviews. The style and quality of Negro leaders, for example, are significant factors about which we have information only in the depth-study areas. Nevertheless, by using county data from the United States Census and similar sources, and by aggregating individual responses from the people we interviewed, we can develop crude indicators of a number of socioeconomic and political attributes of all the counties included in our survey.

We propose in this chapter to tie together—as best we can—the different classes of variables we have introduced, to assess their combined importance, to determine the relative importance of each, and to identify the sequence of influence (the chain of causality) represented by these variables. Initially, such a combination of individual and community attributes may appear comparable to adding apples and oranges; on second thought, however, it appears perfectly legitimate. We are trying to explain variations in the level of political activity of *individuals*. For this purpose, individual characteristics like level of education or amount of political interest can clearly be related to the level of participation of the same individuals. In addition, we shall view the characteristics of southern counties—such as the percentage of population Negro or the number of Negro political organizations—as characteristics of every Negro living in the county. Community characteristics thus become individual characteristics as well, and we are able to relate the variations in political activity by individual Negroes throughout the South to these personal-community characteristics. This assumes that, for each Negro, the nature of the community where he lives (represented by such measures as the percentage of Negroes in the county) is one of his personal characteristics. This kind of personal characteristic differs from purely individual attributes (such as a person's number of years of schooling), but both deserve consideration. Which kind of characteristic is more important is an empirical question. That both *are* important for individual participation can hardly be denied in view of the findings in the preceding chapters.

The statistical device through which we tie these variables together is multiple correlation and regression analysis. In Chapter Three, we used simple correlations to examine the association between two variables, and partial correlations to measure the remaining association between the two when the contribution of a third variable was taken into account. Now, in order to determine the overall strength of association between Negro participation and four different classes of variable, we must compute multiple correlations. Like the coefficient of simple correlation, $r$, used in Chapter Five, the coefficient of multiple correlation $R$ can vary from 0 (no association between the independent variables and the dependent variable) to 1 (the independent variables perfectly predict the dependent variable).

How large must a correlation be before we accept the association it measures as significant? In a strictly statistical sense, the amount of variance in the dependent variable "explained" by variations in the independent variables is the value of $R$ squared ($R^2$). If $R = .90$, then 81 per cent of the variance in the dependent variable is explained by variations in the values of the independent variables—clearly a significant association. But such high correlations are rarely found in the social sciences. What about an $R$ of .33? Is it "significant"? The answer depends on one's expectations, or on his view of social realities, and on *what* is being explained.

An $R$ of .33 can be said to account for about 11 per cent of the variance in the phenomenon under study. If one expects to explain *all* its variance, then an explanation of little more than one tenth is not very significant. But if we recognize the multiple nature of causation, the complexity of social phenomena, and the difficulties in developing accurate measures of fine differences among people, an $R$ of .33 may be regarded as highly significant. It means that the researcher has identified one measurable set of many complex influences on human behavior. More refined measures of the same variables might well produce a higher correlation, but—as measured by the values used to derive the correlation—the phenomena represented by the values are clearly linked in a meaningful way.

A baby may displace only one tenth of the water in a large tub, but we do not conclude from this that the baby is either nonexistent or unimportant.

Moreover, the baby may leave a ring in the tub as an undeniable reminder that it was there. Our search is for such "rings in the tub"—for traces of important phenomena that *help* to account for the variation in individual human behavior. To expect an explanation of all such variation from a few crude measures of selected attributes is to adopt a simplified view of social realities.

In addition to one's theoretical expectations, the evaluation of the significance of a correlation will depend on what is being explained. If one is trying to account for variations in the *average* behavior of large numbers of individuals in different areas—for instance, the percentage of adult Negroes registered to vote in different counties—then somewhat higher correlations can be expected than if one were trying to account for variations in the behavior of all individuals. In the former case, the use of an average figure for an entire area eliminates the need to account for individual variation from the central tendency. Thus, relating all the social and economic characteristics we considered in Chapter Five to the percentage of Negroes registered to vote in southern counties, we get a multiple correlation coefficient of .53. When we add the political attributes of the counties discussed in Chapter Six to the equation, the $R$ goes up to .70.[1] This is an unusually high correlation for social research, accounting for about half the county-to-county variation in the proportion of adult Negroes on the registration books.

Our present objective is to account for variations in the level of political participation of southern Negroes *as individuals*. All the idiosyncratic, unmeasured, and unmeasurable variations in human behavior are included in this task; hence, we can expect a lower correlation. Anything approaching a correlation of .4 would have undoubted significance. In an analogous problem, that of explaining the partisan preferences of white voters in Erie County, Ohio, a classic study of voting behavior found a correlation of "approximately .5" between socioeconomic characteristics and partisan preference. On the basis of that strong a correlation, the authors concluded that "social characteristics determine political preference."[2] Although the exclusive reliance of that study upon social and economic attributes has been criticized, no one has denied that the association found was of impressive significance.

Throughout this book we have conceived of political participation as consisting of any public expression of political interest or preference. This has been operationally defined as talking about politics, voting, taking part in political campaigns, belonging to political organizations, and holding public or party office. We found that all these activities represent different forms or dimensions of the same kind of behavior, and we have felt safe in labeling

[1] For a detailed presentation of this analysis, see our articles, "Social and Economic Factors and Negro Voter Registration in the South," *American Political Science Review*, Vol. 57 (1963), pp. 24—44, and "Political Factors and Negro Voter Registration in the South," *ibid.*, Vol. 57 (1963), pp. 355—67.

[2] Paul F. Lazarsfeld, Bernard Berelson, and Hazel Gaudet, *The People's Choice* (New York: Columbia University Press, 1948), 2nd ed., p. 27.

that behavior "political participation." Other forms of participation might be added—writing letters to public officials or to the newspaper, for example—but the forms we have chosen represent one valid way of ranking people according to the extent of their political activity. What we have been trying to explain, then, are the rankings of individuals on our five-point Political Participation Scale.

In Chapter Two we said that we viewed political participation as a product of two levels of variables, those representing individual attributes and those representing community attributes. Moreover, we divided each level of variables into two classes, those representing factors with a proximate or immediate impact on participation and those representing factors with a less immediate or distal impact. This produces the following fourfold classification:

|  | Distal factors | Immediate factors |
|---|---|---|
| Individual level | Socioeconomic attributes | Attitudes and cognitions |
| Community level | Socioeconomic structure | Political system |

With 10 to 17 different variables in each class,[3] the multiple correlation co-

[3] The variables employed in each class are: *Community (county) socioeconomic structure:* percentage of population nonwhite, percentage of farms operated by tenants, percentage of labor force in agriculture, population density, median age of whites, percentage of white labor force in white-collar occupations, percentage of Negroes who are male, median Negro income, percentage of whites favoring strict segregation, percentage of whites who agree that "colored people are all alike," mean score of whites on attitude-toward-change scale, mean score of whites on racial stereotype scale, percentage of Negroes favoring strict segregation, percentage of Negroes who agree that "white people are all alike," mean score of Negroes on attitude-toward-change scale, mean score of Negroes on racial stereotype scale. *Community (county) political system:* location in Deep or Peripheral South, difficulty of legal voter requirements, percentage of votes Republican in 1960 presidential election, degree of party competitiveness, factional structure of Democratic party in state, percentage of Negroes who perceive white candidates as seeking Negro votes, Negro race organizations, white race organizations, percentage of Negroes who have heard scare stories about registration or voting, percentage of votes Dixiecratic in 1948 presidential election, percentage of Negroes higher than PPS Type II, percentage of whites who favor Negro voting "quite a bit," percentage of Negroes with a "great deal" or "some" interest in politics, mean score of Negroes on political-information test, mean score of Negroes on intensity of party identification, mean number of things liked or disliked by Negroes about political parties, mean score of Negroes on sense of civic competence. *Individual socioeconomic attributes:* sex, age, education, income, occupation (of respondent and head of respondent's household), geographic mobility, class identification, number of mass media to which exposed, number of nonpolitical-group memberships. *Individual attitudes and cognitions:* political interest, political information, strength of party identification, number of things liked or disliked about political parties, sense of civic competence, knowledge of scare stories about Negro registration or voting, attitude on segregation-integration, score on attitude-toward-change scale, score on racial stereotype scale, response to statement that "white people are all alike."

efficients and the amount of variance they explain follow, in ascending order of magnitude:

| Class of variables | R | $R^2$ |
|---|---|---|
| Community socioeconomic structure | .43 | 18% |
| Community political system | .44 | 19% |
| Individual socioeconomic attributes | .52 | 27% |
| Individual attitudes and cognitions | .58 | 34% |

All four classes of variable contribute significantly to the variation in the level of political activity of southern Negroes, but the magnitude of the correlations varies considerably. The explanatory power of individual attitudes and cognitions—as we have measured—is roughly twice as great as that of either class of community-level variables. Individual social and economic characteristics are also more predictive of individual participation than are community characteristics, but the difference is not so great as for individual attitudes and cognitions.

These findings fit the explanatory model we outlined in Chapter Two and suggest that other factors tend to work *through* their effects on the opinions and knowledge of individuals. If this is true, then the combined explanatory power of all four classes of variable should not be much greater than that found for the single class of attitudes and cognitions. Additional statistical manipulation is required to test this idea. In the process of computing R, we obtained multiple regression equations for each of the four classes of independent variable. Each regression equation gives us a predicted PPS score for every individual, telling us what his level of political activity would be if he responded typically to the class of variables included in the equation. We thus get four predicted scores for each individual, one for each of the four classes of variable. By treating these four *predicted* scores as independent variables and computing their multiple correlation with the actual scores, we get a measure of the combined association of the four classes of variable with level of political participation. This multiple correlation coefficient is .63, a degree of association that statistically explains 40 per cent of the variance in Negro PPS scores.

This is the largest correlation with individual variations in political activity that we have found, but it adds only six percentage points to the explanatory power of a single class of variables—individual attitudes and cognitions. Although other factors are important for understanding Negro political participation, then, they are important mostly because they affect the political attitudes and knowledge of individual citizens. The simple correlations of each set of predicted PPS scores with each other set are all positive and relatively strong.

|  | Individual socioeconomic attributes | Community socioeconomic structure | Community political system |
|---|---|---|---|
| Individual attitudes and cognitions | + .64 | + .41 | + .43 |
| Individual socioeconomic attributes |  | + .32 | + .34 |
| Community socioeconomic structure |  |  | + .95 |

The predicted PPS scores that we get using any of these classes of variables is fairly close to what we would get by using another. Predictions from individual socioeconomic attributes are closest to those from individual attitudes and cognitions. This is what we would expect, because the latter are most closely related to actual political participation and the former have the second-strongest relationship. Predictions from either class of variable at the individual level are less strongly related to those from the community-level variables. Although community characteristics explain much less of the variance in individual participation than do individual characteristics, the predictions from the two classes of community-level variables are virtually identical.

Figure 11–1 reproduces the model with which we began in Chapter Two, but this time with the empirical findings to support it. Overall, our four classes of variable are highly predictive of individual political participation $(R = .63)$, and they are, in varying degrees, related to each other. The Beta weights for the four classes of variable are included in each box. These values tell us the relative contribution of each of these classes of variables to the overall association with political participation—the higher the value of the beta weights, the greater the contribution of that class of variable to the multiple correlation. As we surmised from differences in the magnitudes of the multiple correlation coefficients, community socioeconomic structure makes the smallest contribution $(\beta = .110)$, community political system the next smallest $(\beta = .349)$, individual socioeconomic attributes a much greater contribution $(\beta = .428)$, and individual attitudes and cognitions the greatest of all $(\beta = .580)$.

The direction of causality in influences on Negro political participation, as we have measured them, thus appears clear. All four classes of variable are related to the level of political activity of southern Negroes. For the most part, however, community factors appear important because they tend to shape the individual attributes that more directly and successfully account for differences in participation.

But these inferences about the direction of causality can be refined and tested through a more sophisticated statistical technique, causal model analysis.

FIGURE 11-1.

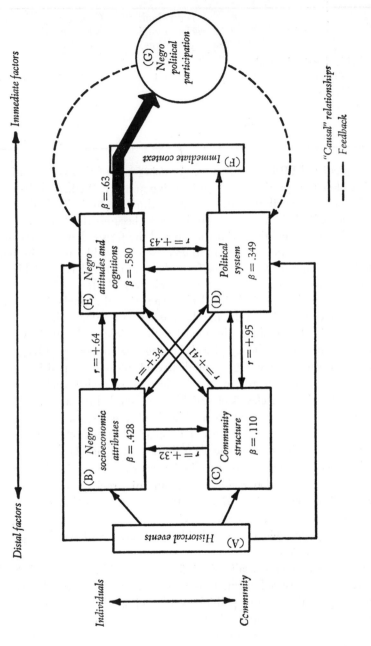

Distal factors ⟵⟶ Immediate factors

Individuals ⟵⟶ Community

(A) Historical events

(B) Negro socioeconomic attributes  β = .428

(C) Community structure  β = .110

(D) Political system  β = .349

(E) Negro attitudes and cognitions  β = .580

(F) Immediate context

(G) Negro political participation

β = .63

r = +.43

r = +.64

r = +.34

r = +.41

r = +.95

r = +.32

——— "Causal" relationships
- - - - Feedback

Developed most fully by Hubert M. Blalock,[4] this technique permits answers to two crucial questions: Are all the possible causal paths indicated by arrows in Figure 11–1 actually operative? What is the direction of causation in each set of relationships? Through the technique of causal model analysis, we are able to reduce the number of operative causal paths to seven.

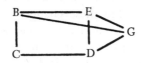

Adding a path coefficient analysis (a technique developed by Raymond Boudon[5]) to this reduced set of relationships, we further eliminate the paths between B and G and between D and G. Through the combination of these two techniques we can thus greatly simplify the model presented in Figure 11–1. The statistical analysis of our empirical findings supports the interpretation we have offered on theoretical grounds.[6] The direction of causation and the number of operative paths of direct causal relationships are as follows:

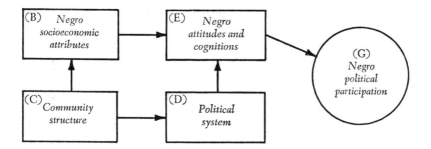

Only two developmental sequences are operative, one from C to D to E to G, the other from C to B to E to G. Community structure (by which we mean the community's social and economic characteristics) is thus seen to have *direct* effects on social and economic attributes of individual southern Negroes and on the community political system, but *not* on Negro attitudes and cognitions *or* on Negro political participation. Individual socioeconomic attributes and

[4] *Causal Inferences in Nonexperimental Research* (Chapel Hill, N.C.: University of North Carolina Press, 1964). Also see Herbert A. Simon, "Spurious Correlations: A Causal Interpretation," *Journal of the American Statistical Association*, Vol. 49 (1954), pp. 467–79.

[5] "A Method of Linear Causal Analysis: Dependence Analysis," *American Sociological Review*, Vol. 30 (1965), pp. 365–74.

[6] We are indebted to Charles F. Cnudde for calling our attention to the applicability of the Blalock and Boudon techniques to our findings and for his kindness in performing the statistical analysis. For details on the procedures involved, see his article, with Donald J. McCrone, "The Linkage Between Constituency Attitudes and Congressional Voting Behavior: A Causal Model," *American Political Science Review*, Vol. 60 (1966), pp. 66–72.

the political system have direct effects *only* on attitudes and cognitions. *All effects on political participation are interpreted by Negro attitudes and cognitions.*

The policy implications of these findings are of considerable significance. Legal changes in the political system—such as those stemming from the Voting Rights Act of 1965—can increase Negro political activity. But any increases are likely to be small unless or until these changes in the legal climate lead to such changes in Negro attitudes and cognitions as greater interest, partisanship, information about the parties, and general political information. The associations among all these classes of variables are great enough, however, to suggest that a real change in one is likely to have some impact on all the others.

Another conclusion to be drawn from our findings is that we have a long way to go before we are in danger of explaining all the mysterious variations in human behavior. The overall explanatory power of our model is sufficient to account for about 40 per cent of the variance in the political activities of Negroes throughout the South. Unmeasured historical events and factors in the immediate context of political activity—boxes A and E in the diagram—may account for some of this unexplained variance. We suspect that more of it is attributable to two limitations in the classes of variables we have measured: (1) the measures used are often crude indicators of the factors for which they stand; (2) some of the factors that could be included in depth community studies—such as quality of local leadership—could not be included at all in a southwide survey. To account for 40 per cent of the variance in a form of political behavior does not take all the mystery out of that aspect of human life; but it does significantly reduce the area of mystery.

Part Three

Part Three

# The Impact of Negro Political
# Participation on Southern Politics

So far we have sought to describe Negro participation in southern politics in the 1960's and to explain why Negroes do not participate more than they do. If participation were merely a matter of voting, and if the gap between white and Negro voting rates were merely the result of whipcracking white election officials, our problem would have been relatively simple. But we have argued that active citizenship in American democracy calls for far more than just voting—talking politics, taking part in political campaigns, joining political groups, and holding party or public offices are also ways to engage in the political process. And far from a single explanation of the Negro's low participation— such as the poll tax, the discriminatory administration of electoral laws, or violence and intimidation—we have discerned a host of mutually reinforcing factors that tend to discourage Negro political participation in the region. Individual and community characteristics—social, economic, political, and psychological—all conspire to reduce Negro political activity in the South.

But the situation is changing. A mere projection of past trends into the future would lead to the conclusion that Negro participation will increase. Our analysis of the multitudinous causal factors now shaping Negro participation strongly reinforces this conclusion and suggests at least some of the conditions that must be met before southern Negroes can become full-fledged actors on the political stage. We can, therefore, expect steady and substantial increase in Negro voting and other forms of political participation in the South in the years ahead.

What are the likely consequences of such a revolutionary change in the political culture and practices of the region? Southern politics since Reconstruction has been organized to eliminate— or at least to reduce to a bearable minimum—the political influence of Negroes. What will happen to these political patterns when Negro voices can no longer be ignored? And can we assume that increased Negro participation will end racial segregation, now more *de facto* than *de jure* but still very real? Can Negroes— once they participate in adequate numbers and with sufficient unity and skill—vote themselves equality in other realms of life? If not, what then happens to America's backward yet rapidly developing South?

The answers to these and similar questions are of compelling interest not just to professional students of political systems (although the theoretically inclined can learn from them much about political systems in the process of change), not just to southerners (although their dreams of a prosperous and progressive "New South" depend largely on the answers), but to all Americans and inhabitants of the free world. The future shape of the entire American political system and America's ability to provide enlightened world leadership will depend in part on the answers to these questions.

The answers cannot be definitive. Nonetheless, in Part Three we shall offer the best answers we can. Our focus shifts from an attempt to explain Negro political participation to an examination of the probable consequences of that participation. Negro participation becomes—in the language of social science—an independent rather than a dependent variable; our interest shifts from the past and the present to the present and the future.

The first questions to be asked about the increasingly biracial politics of the new South are: What does the newcomer to the political system want? What demands will Negroes make? How and how soon do they expect to achieve their political goals? We shall consider these and related questions in Chapter Twelve.

If Negroes are to be content with political and peaceable efforts to achieve their goals, then their wants and needs must be translated into governmental policy. Political parties are the basic institution through which this translation process is brought about: in Chapter Thirteen we shall examine the Democratic and Republican parties as mechanisms for Negro self-improvement via political action.

If southern Negroes fail to achieve what they consider to be their legitimate and long overdue goals through regular political channels, then we can expect them to resort to less "traditional" and "legitimate" tactics. As every reader of these pages knows, the advent of the sit-ins, freedom rides, mass boycotts, and demonstrations in 1960 marked the beginning of this process. In Chapter Fourteen we shall examine the principal participants in the Negro protest movement, Negro college students. These students are not only today's protesters, they are also tomorrow's political leaders—in Chapter Fifteen we shall examine what we can expect from them in this future role. Finally, in Chapter Sixteen we shall try to sum up the politics of desegregation that faces the South in the critical years to come.

Chapter Twelve

# The Crisis of Southern Politics

On September 15, 1964, the people of Tuskegee, Alabama, trooped quietly to the polls to vote in a city election. Otherwise life went on much as before in the run-down and sleepy-looking little town in the midst of Alabama's black belt. But by nightfall it was apparent that a momentous event had occurred that day in Tuskegee: among the men the voters had elected to the city council were the Reverend K. L. Buford and Dr. S. H. Smith. Both were Negroes—the first members of their race to be elected to public office in the state of Alabama since Reconstruction.[1]

The Tuskegee story is too long and involved to repeat here.[2] If Booker T. Washington had not established Tuskegee Institute there in 1881, if the Supreme Court of the United States had not outlawed an outrageous racial gerrymander of the city in 1960, if the United States Congress had not passed the Civil Rights Act of 1957, if the United States Justice Department had not intervened to ensure that local Negroes were given a reasonable chance to become registered voters, the outcome of the 1964 municipal election would have been very different. The complex of events and forces that resulted in a Negro majority among the town's voters is not likely to occur frequently in the South.

Even so, the Tuskegee municipal election of 1964 is a symbol of revolutionary change. Politics is no longer just a white man's game in the South. Throughout most of the region, politics is now biracial. It has been that way in Piedmont County for decades and in Camellia County for years; Negroes

[1] *New York Times*, September 16, 1964; *Birmingham News* (Alabama), September 16, 1964. Four additional Negroes were elected to county office on November 4 of the same year. See Bernard Taper, "Reporter at Large: A Break with Tradition," *New Yorker*, July 24, 1965, pp. 58ff., for a description of subsequent events.
[2] Much of the history and background of the Tuskegee story may be found in Bernard Taper, *Gomillion versus Lightfoot* (New York: McGraw-Hill, 1962).

331

in Bright Leaf County are becoming a political force to be reckoned with. Only in Crayfish County, and other counties like it, do the old rules of southern politics still hold. This, too, will change in time. In the new southern politics Negroes have political power, and their power is growing. In this and subsequent chapters we shall try to determine what this seemingly irreversible change means for the future of the South.

## What Negroes want

The basic fact about the new southern politics is that most southern Negroes desperately want something that most southern whites are adamantly unwilling to give—equality. Philosophers have argued endlessly about the meaning of the word, but to southern Negroes equality has a clear and simple meaning. They want to be treated as men, not as Negroes. They want a world, as one Negro college student from Virginia put it, in which "race is just about as important as eye color," a world in which a "human being is a human being regardless of race or color." This vision is widely shared. When asked if they prefer "integration, strict segregation, or something in between," 65 per cent of southern Negroes chose integration.

Southern whites, on the other hand, just as strongly want strict segregation; 64 per cent of them chose this alternative when presented with the same question.[3] When we present the distribution of these preferences graphically, as in Figure 12–1, the magnitude of the Negro-white conflict in the South emerges dramatically. On the question of segregation—which is the pivot around which all else revolves in the South—the southern population is divided into two hostile groups, with solid support for segregation by whites and for integration by Negroes.

Perhaps the most startling aspect of this awesome division is that Negroes support integration as solidly as whites support segregation. For three and a half centuries they have been treated as inherently inferior beings. All this time, they have been under great pressure to accept dominant white values. And they have done so in most areas—from cosmetics to religion. But not many have succumbed to the white image of proper race relations.

This sharp racial division would not be so frightening if these conflicting opinions were not so deeply felt and intensely held by both races. On most policy questions, a sizable portion of the citizenry has no opinion; this is especially true in a region of relatively low education such as the South. But on this question only 1 per cent of the whites and 4 per cent of the Negroes gave a "don't know" response. In addition, people who don't much care tend to choose "in between" rather than extreme responses to survey questions. Despite

[3] In order to facilitate interviewing, we reversed the alternatives for white respondents to read "strict segregation, integration, or something in between."

the fact that our question used the term *"strict* segregation," only 28 per cent of the whites and 14 per cent of the Negroes took the "in between" position.

But we need not rely solely on these inferences to judge the intensity with which southerners—both Negro and white—hold their incompatible racial views. Let our respondents speak for themselves. "They 'minds me of a rattle-snake," a 78-year-old Negro farmer in Camellia County said, referring to his white neighbors. "Sometimes you can get by one, then again you bound to get struck." A Negro man in Capital City was more vehement and explicit: "The Lord needs to kill every last one of them." "It's not but one way for them [Negroes and whites] to live together and get along," a Negro yardman living hundreds of miles away said, "and that's for the Old Jim Crow race to die out." "I couldn't imagine that," a Negro watchman in Piedmont County said, when asked to describe the best race relations possible, " 'cause white folks would kill us before they'd let that happen."

Hatred flows both ways. A white dairyman in Crayfish County defined his ideal of race relations as, "Back to slavery! That would put them [Negroes] where low-down white trash from the North couldn't make them believe they are better than southern white people." A truck driver in rural Georgia expressed his ideal just as starkly: "Give all the whites a shotgun!"

These attitudes, fears, and hatreds are not new. But in the past the awesome gap between Negro and white aspirations could safely be ignored—the white man ran the South in his own way, and the rest of the nation was not dis-

FIGURE 12–1.   *Southerners' preferences on integration-segregation*

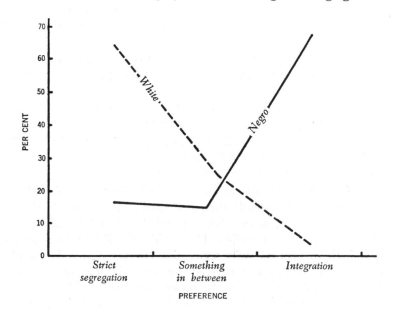

PREFERENCE

posed to do anything about it. The politically effective part of the South—the white part—was united on racial policy and Negroes could do little about it—except to move North. Now the situation is very different. Increasingly, the southern Negro is armed with the vote; he enjoys at least some political power; his attitudes and aspirations count. The political future of the South will be dominated by a deep and bitter division along racial lines on the major problem of the region.

Leaders of each race thus have a minimum of maneuverability on racial issues. On most other issues, the predominance of moderate opinions and of popular indifference affords a cushion of ambiguity that permits leaders to act. They can work out compromises without knowing for certain what the popular response will be—or that any response at all will follow. In the South today the white leader who contemplates a tentative step toward accommodating Negro demands can expect to be labeled a "nigger-lover"; the Negro who cooperates with white leaders can expect to be labeled an "Uncle Tom." Indeed, we seriously wonder whether a viable political system in the South will be possible, granted the extreme polarization of opinion, without one race being dominated by the other.

This situation is more severe in some parts of the South than in others. In Figure 12–2 the race-relations preferences of Negroes and whites are presented for the four communities we studied in detail. In Piedmont and Camellia counties, the conflict between the two races is severe. In the upper South county, 86 per cent of the Negroes want integration while 63 per cent of the whites prefer strict segregation; in Camellia County, the whites are somewhat more likely to be segregationists (67 per cent), but a somewhat smaller proportion of the Negroes (68 per cent) are committed to integration than in Piedmont. In both counties, however, fairly sizable minorities of whites are "moderates" (22 per cent in Piedmont and 24 per cent in Camellia) and a small but significant number are integrationists (15 per cent in Piedmont and 9 per cent in Camellia). One out of every three white adults in Piedmont is not a segregationist; in Camellia County one third of the Negroes are not integrationists. Both communities, then, have at least some middle ground; the consensus *within* each race is not monolithic.

The two rural counties we studied differ from Piedmont and Camellia and from each other as well. The Bright Leaf County Negroes are less committed to the goal of integration than the Negroes in the other communities—only a third of them chose this alternative while half said they preferred race relations as they were. Apparently the paternalism of the whites in the county has resulted in a more contented Negro population than is found in either of the urban counties or in Crayfish. Thus, while the Bright Leaf whites are overwhelmingly in favor of strict segregation (87 per cent), the conflict between white and Negro preferences is relatively mild. The figures for Crayfish, on the other hand, show almost complete consensus *within* each race and almost complete discord *between* them: only 8 per cent of the Negroes and

2 per cent of the whites fail to go along with the majority of their own race. The middle ground of opinion has disappeared. The potential for racial conflict in this situation is almost absolute. The accommodation of such a vast conflict through democratic political processes seems virtually impossible.

But perhaps we are overstressing the potential for racial conflict in these communities and in the South as a whole. Gunnar Myrdal, in his *An*

FIGURE 12–2.    *Southerners' preferences on integration-segregation, by community*

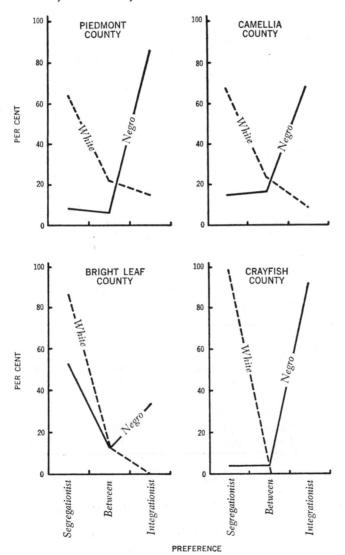

*American Dilemma,*[4] placed heavy stress on a tension-reducing mechanism, called "the rank order of discriminations," which we have not yet considered. White people, "nearly unanimously" according to Myrdal, rate some types of racial discrimination above others, with the bar against intermarriage and sexual relations between Negro males and white females at the top, and discrimination in the courts, by the police, or in routine economic transactions near the bottom. And, Myrdal says, "The Negroes' own rank order is just about parallel, but inverse, to that of the white man."[5] Thus the areas of life in which Negroes most want desegregation are the areas in which white men are most likely to give in to their demands, and vice versa. Obviously the effect of this happy congruence is greatly to reduce the conflict stemming from the South's clashing racial attitudes.

But Myrdal's theory was based, as he was the first to point out, on unsystematic impressions. And a very great deal has happened to American race relations since Myrdal wrote his classic. Can we count on the "rank order of discriminations" to reduce the politico-racial tensions in the South today and in the future?

We can explore this question by looking at how Negroes and whites define and describe "the very best way that Negroes and white people could live in the same place together," and its opposite, the worst possible arrangement of a biracial community. The frequency with which Negroes and whites mentioned specific realms of life in answering this open-ended question provides a measure of the value they attach to each; these figures are presented in Table 12–1. In Table 12–2 the percentage of whites favoring strict segregation and

TABLE 12–1.  *Percentage of whites and Negroes mentioning specific areas of life in describing best possible and worst possible race relations*

|  | White | Negro |
|---|---|---|
| Public schools | 60% | 9% |
| Housing and residential patterns | 55 | 13 |
| Sex and marriage | 52 | 14 |
| Churches and religion | 36 | 6 |
| Public accommodations | 32 | 5 |
| Personal relationships | 30 | 13 |
| Jobs and employment | 12 | 8 |

of Negroes favoring rapid integration of these same areas of social life are juxtaposed.

The first thing to notice in Table 12–1 is that very few Negroes, as com-

[4] (New York: Harper, 1964), ch. 3, part 4.
[5] *Ibid.,* p. 61.

TABLE 12-2. *Percentage of whites and Negroes mentioning specific areas of life favoring strict segregation and rapid integration of area mentioned*

|  | Whites favoring strict segregation | Negroes favoring rapid integration |
|---|---|---|
| Sex and marriage | 98% | 1% |
| Churches and religion | 92 | 50 |
| Housing and residential patterns | 85 | 13 |
| Public schools | 83 | 34 |
| Public accommodations | 75 | 53 |
| Personal relations | 65 | 55 |
| Jobs and employment | 44 | 45 |

pared to whites, mentioned specific areas of community living. This cannot be dismissed merely as the reflection of lower levels of education among Negroes; these same Negro respondents proved as voluble and articulate as whites in responding to other open-ended questions about subjects of less emotional import to them at other points in the interview.[6] Rather, the Negroes tended not to refer to concrete areas of life in describing their pictures of the best (and worst) of all racial arrangements because they wanted equality in all of them. Unlike the whites, they felt little need to specify, qualify, or explain. Thus, for example, a junior at Florida A. and M. University said:

> I would say an ideal situation would be for Negroes and whites to repress the idea of skin coloration to such an extent that one neighbor would be regarded with the same esteem as any other; become Mary, the next door neighbor, not Mary, the white neighbor or vice versa. Period, amen, amen.

Negroes tend to think about segregation and desegregation in these global terms rather than in any rank order of preferences.

The whites, on the other hand, seem to have been considerably more anxious about the possible desegregation of some areas of life than others. At the time of our interviews, the desegregation of the public schools was uppermost in their minds—six out of every ten white respondents volunteered some comment about what the racial composition of the schools should be. Eighty-five per cent of those mentioning the matter were opposed to even token desegregation. "What puzzles me is that they are so dirty . . . ," a housewife in Texas said. "I wish they could change and be more like we are. Of course I wouldn't want a child like that, all dirty and filthy, in school with my children." A brick mason in Arkansas made another popular argument—"They [Negroes] don't want to have schools together any more than we do." And a college professor in Capital City, who was among the small minority of whites who

[6] For examples see the material in Chapter Thirteen on "party images."

favored token desegregation of the schools, explained why he was reluctant to go beyond that point. "I'd say I was for complete integration," he reported, "but I know what a financial strain it would put on me to send my children to private schools. . . . I think under present [conditions] the intellectual loss to my children [resulting from wholesale desegregation] would be too great."

Almost as many whites—55 per cent—mentioned housing and residential patterns as mentioned the schools, and the opposition to "mixing" in this realm was equally strong. "Put a high fence around them," a 35-year-old man in Little Rock said. "I don't want them anywhere around. . . . They need to have separate schools, separate neighborhoods, and separate everything!" In rural Georgia a young man with a high-school education defined his ideal of race relations as "Just like it is—separate schools, housing, separate social life. Can you imagine living close to a nigger juke joint?"

But the young wife of a labor-union official in Florida, an avowed integrationist, was able to see Negroes as something more than an undifferentiated mass. "I wouldn't want my children going to school or church or anywhere with 'trash' whether they were white or colored," she said. "I wouldn't care if they [Negroes] lived next door to me if they lived the same as I did—clean, and kept their properties up, etc. . . . They should be able to live in a social class that they are able to afford." Very few southern whites are able to draw such elementary distinctions about Negroes.

Over half (52 per cent) of the whites were worried about intermarriage and sexual relations across race lines—and 98 per cent of these were steadfastly against it. "I know a Negro man over here," a white dairy farmer in Crayfish County said, "who is living with his daughter and having a child every year for 'The Welfare' to take care of—now you know white people don't do things like that. The worst thing would be intermarriage." A middleaged housewife in Arkansas said: "I just can't feature my daughter and son dancing with niggers even if Mrs. Roosevelt did." Another housewife, this one in Georgia, was convinced that intermarriage "would bring on a war between the Negroes and white people." An elderly lady in a neighboring state disagreed:

> Some people are scared to death [that] their children will marry niggers but any white boy or girl that's that big a fool—there's no use worrying about. If they have to go to a school together, it doesn't necessarily follow they'll marry! That's silly. People ordinarily marry people with similar backgrounds and those that go overboard—let 'em!

Interestingly enough, sexual relations and intermarriage were the areas of life most often mentioned by Negroes, too—although only 14 per cent of them did so. Almost all Negroes mentioning the matter did so to express resentment at the white males' traditional access to Negro females and to deny their interest in intermarriage. A college sophomore in North Carolina said: "Most people think when you integrate a community you want intermarriage, and this isn't so." "When I say integration," a 45-year-old Negro carpenter in Texas explained, "I mean equal opportunity for jobs, [equal access to] public places, tax-supported places, not necessarily social contact."

The sexual exploitation of Negro women by white men rankled some of the older Negroes. One of them, a farmer in Georgia, defined the worst possible race relations as ". . . the white man sneaking around the colored women. . . ." A Negro housewife in Alabama, who would no doubt be classified by the educational authorities as functionally illiterate, gave our interviewer a little lesson in southern semantics: "When white folks say 'mix' they mean some white man having him a colored woman. That's all 'mix' means to them."

Very few Negroes—only about 1 per cent of those mentioning the issue—agreed with the freshman at Bethune-Cookman College who said that integration inevitably involved intermarriage ". . . because marriage produces the families and families make the communities."

No other areas of life concerned the whites quite so much as the public schools, housing and residential patterns, and sex and marriage. However, about one third of the whites did mention churches or religion, public accommodations, and personal relationships and racial etiquette. They expressed overwhelming disapproval of moves to integrate the region's churches (92 per cent) or public places (75 per cent), or to do away with traditional modes of treating Negroes in personal relationships (65 per cent). Very few whites mentioned jobs and employment practices at all—apparently this is not a highly salient issue for them. Moreover, this is the only area of life in which a majority of the whites who do think about it favor some policy other than strict segregation.

We see, then, that Myrdal's insight about a "rank order of discriminations" holds only partially true. True, intermarriage and racially integrated housing are highly salient issues among southern whites, and very few southern Negroes are inclined to push rapidly for either one. Equal job opportunities for Negroes do not seem to worry white southerners—indeed, most of them seem to favor the idea. But the conflict potential in all other realms of life is still exceedingly high. In these areas, as can be seen in Table 12–2, large majorities of whites still oppose what most Negroes want very badly. The "rank order of discriminations" may have eliminated some troublesome problems from the political arena for the time being, but the organization of most of the social life in the South still remains at issue. And the willingness of southern Negroes to postpone efforts at integrating some areas of life is solely a matter of expediency, of political tactics. In the long run, they insist that southern whites become colorblind.

## Farewell to Uncle Tom

Although a large majority of southern Negroes are deeply committed to the goal of racial integration, about one in every three Negroes is not. Sixteen per cent of the Negroes interviewed indicated a preference for "strict segregation" and another 15 per cent for "something in between" strict segregation and integration. This is a significant minority of opinion. Perhaps this group may be able to convert other Negroes to a less militant racial stance in the future. Perhaps, in league with the tiny group of moderate and integrationist whites, they will be able to bridge the gap between white and Negro majorities.

Even the most casual examination of these Negroes rules out this possibility. Table 12–3 compares the social and economic characteristics of the Negroes

TABLE 12–3.  *Social characteristics of southern Negroes preferring strict segregation, integration, and "something in between"*

| RESPONDENT CHARACTERISTICS | RACIAL PREFERENCE | | |
|---|---|---|---|
| | *Segregation* (N = 94) | *In between* (N = 89) | *Integration* (N = 400) |
| Blue-collar occupation | 99% | 91% | 87% |
| Grade-school education or less | 88 | 53 | 51 |
| Income less than $2,000 a year | 86 | 56 | 48 |
| Female | 71 | 69 | 56 |
| Grew up on farm | 71 | 51 | 57 |
| Over 60 years of age | 34 | 22 | 23 |
| Never been outside of South | 45 | 38 | 35 |
| Lives in Deep South | 46 | 48 | 38 |

NOTE: The numbers indicate the percentage of Negroes with a given racial attitude who possess the characteristics listed in the lefthand column. Thus 99 per cent of the Negro segregationists have blue-collar occupations.

who are not integrationists with the characteristics of those who are. The Negro "Uncle Toms"[7] and, to a lesser degree, the Negroes who are "in between" prove to be a miserable lot, ill equipped to provide the kind of leadership needed to ameliorate the South's politico-racial cleavage. Almost all of them are blue-collar workers with a grade-school education at best and with a family income of less than $2,000 a year. They tend also, in disproportionate num-

[7] A logical possibility is that some Negroes who prefer segregation are not "Uncle Toms" but believers in black supremacy of the type espoused by the Black Muslims. An examination of the Negro respondents favoring segregation, however, reveals so few potential black nationalists that this group can safely be assumed to consist almost entirely of old-style "Uncle Toms."

341 THE CRISIS OF SOUTHERN POLITICS

bers, to be elderly women with rural backgrounds and limited exposure to the patterns of life outside the American South. The proportion of them to be found in the Deep South is slightly larger than on the edges of the region, but the harshness of Negro life in the Deep South apparently has produced very little "payoff" in more frequent Negro acquiescence to white supremacy. The southwide resistance to white preferences in race relations is the more impressive in view of the great differences between the Deep South and the Peripheral South in Negro political participation and in white attitudes.

A look at the political and psychological characteristics of Negroes not committed to racial integration underscores this picture of ignorance, poverty, and apathy (see Table 12–4). Seventy per cent of the Negro segregationists (as

TABLE 12–4. *Political and psychological characteristics of southern Negroes preferring strict segregation, integration, and "something in between"*

| RESPONDENT CHARACTERISTICS | RACIAL PREFERENCE | | |
|---|---|---|---|
| | Segregation (N = 94) | In between (N = 89) | Integration (N = 400) |
| Has never voted | 80% | 69% | 50% |
| Not much interested in politics | 70 | 56 | 41 |
| Poorly informed about politics (0–2 correct) | 62 | 47 | 28 |
| Highly resistant to idea of change (Types V–VI) | 68 | 46 | 40 |
| Not much interested in other Negroes | 23 | 8 | 5 |
| Has participated beyond voting (PPS types IV–V) | 19 | 25 | 45 |

NOTE: See note to Table 12–3.

compared to 41 per cent of the integrationists) are "not much interested" in politics; 80 per cent (compared to 50 per cent of the integrationists) have never voted. Negro Uncle Toms are very poorly informed about public affairs —62 per cent as compared to 47 and 28 per cent of the uncommitted Negroes and integrationists answered fewer than three questions correctly on our information test. They tend to be relatively resistant to the idea of change and relatively unconcerned about the fate of other members of their own race.

Segregationist sentiment among Negroes cannot be expected to have political importance. The politically active segment of the Negro population in the South is far more devoted to integration than is the total Negro population. If we consider the racial views of only politically active Negroes (PPS types III, IV, and V), we find 78 per cent (as compared to 65 per cent for the total

Negro population) devoted to integration; thus the effective gap between white and Negro opinions is actually greater than that indicated in Figure 12–1. Negro segregationists are not likely to become political activists in the future because their social, economic, and psychological characteristics seem largely incompatible with this role. Even fewer possess the training, interest, and skills needed for political leadership.

Moreover, the Uncle Tom is rapidly disappearing from the southern scene. Between 1961 and 1964, the proportion of voting-age Negroes preferring "strict segregation" to "integration" or "something in between" was cut in half; the percentage dropped from 16 to 8. During the same period, those favoring desegregation increased from 65 to 71 per cent; those preferring "something in between," from 15 to 18 per cent.[8]

The few Negro segregationists who remain are pathetic survivors of an era that has gone and will never return. So far as their direct and personal influence on the future of southern politics is concerned, they might as well not be there. At least one of them, a 78-year-old Negro woman in Capital City, realizes it. After reporting that she personally favored segregation she remarked, by way of clarification:

> I don't think I'll be in this world long so I'd just as soon it stayed like it is, for peace's sake. But the world can't wait for me to die, so let the young folks go on fight for their rights. . . . Well, I guess *all* us old ones better die so we can't teach and influence the young ones with what used to be. Then God's word [will] come to pass. He said he would raise up a nation that would obey and that men would study war no more. And if we old ones, whites more than black, was to stop influencing the young ones, then God's word *would* come about.

## Influences on white racial attitudes

If centuries of slavery and segregation have convinced only a pathetic minority of Negro southerners that they should accept inferior status, today's milder forms of suppression cannot be expected to accomplish the task. Indeed, southern Negroes will, in all probability, become even more militantly dedicated to racial equality in the future. Thus, only a substantial change in white attitudes can narrow the frightening gap between the objectives of the two races. But, as a Negro laborer in Arkansas said, ". . . when a person has gone so long thinking he is superior, it's pretty hard for them to change. . . ." Will these changes occur? And, if so, will they occur soon enough to diminish the

[8] The 1964 figures were collected by the Survey Research Center of the University of Michigan in its presidential election study of that year. The question wording in 1964 was identical to ours of 1961 save for the substitution of "desegregation" for "integration" as one of the three options provided the respondent. Although a meaningful distinction can be drawn between "integration" and "desegregation," few respondents are likely to have drawn such a fine distinction.

South's politico-racial crisis? By identifying the characteristics of white strict segregationists, moderates (those who say they favor "something in between"), and integrationists, and by considering the prospects for an increase or decrease in the incidence of these characteristics, we should be able to estimate the possibility of these changes occurring.

Numerous studies have shown that racial prejudice and discrimination tend to be related to low levels of formal education. If southern segregationist sentiments are linked to the low educational levels of the region, then a continued increase in the average schooling of southerners could be expected to lead to a basic modification of attitudes. The impact of education on racial attitudes is clearly demonstrated by the findings in Table 12–5. The propor-

TABLE 12–5.    *Level of education and racial attitudes of white southerners*

| AMOUNT OF SCHOOLING | RACIAL ATTITUDE | | | | | |
|---|---|---|---|---|---|---|
| | Strict segrega-tion | In between | Integra-tion | Don't know, refusal, no answer | TOTAL | N |
| 0–6 years | 89% | 9 | 0 | 2 | 100% | 91 |
| Junior high school | 75% | 19 | 3 | 3 | 100% | 114 |
| Incomplete high school | 70% | 26 | 1 | 3 | 100% | 95 |
| Complete high school | 66% | 30 | 3 | 1 | 100% | 152 |
| Complete high school plus other (non-college) training | 54% | 36 | 8 | 2 | 100% | 61 |
| Some college | 50% | 36 | 14 | 0 | 100% | 108 |
| Complete college | 41% | 45 | 14 | 0 | 100% | 49 |
| College and post-graduate training | 11% | 47 | 42 | 0 | 100% | 19 |

tion of whites who are strict segregationists decreases with every increase in formal education. Whites with no more than grammar-school education are *eight times* as likely as those with postgraduate college training to be strict segregationists. But a careful examination of the findings suggests that they provide no basis for expecting large-scale change in southern attitudes within the near future. The combined number of moderates and integrationists does not exceed the number of strict segregationists within any education level below completion of college—and only 8 per cent of the southern whites have a college degree. Although the proportion of college graduates in the region will certainly continue to increase, it will not soon move from 8 per cent to a majority of the population. Education decreases dedication to strict segregation, but extremely high levels of education are apparently necessary to produce actual acceptance of integration. Even among those whose formal education terminated with a college degree, only 14 per cent favor integration. To find substantial support for integration, we must look to those with graduate-school training—and these "eggheads" constitute not quite 3 per cent of the white adults of the South.[9]

We would be going too far if we were to assume that a majority of southern whites would have to hold college degrees before increased education could significantly modify southern racial patterns.[10] More modest increases in the general level of education in the South might have some effect. The whites with incomplete college training are evenly divided between strict segregation-ists and those with moderate or integrationist views. Such a division, even though it includes only a small portion of integrationists, could certainly be expected to produce a different pattern of politics. With more and more whites going beyond high school, then, the size of the strict segregationist majority can be expected to decrease.

TABLE 12–6.  *Number of mass media channels exposed to, and the racial attitudes of white southerners*

| NUMBER OF DIFFERENT MEDIA EXPOSED TO REGULARLY | RACIAL ATTITUDE | | | | |
|---|---|---|---|---|---|
| | *Strict segregation* | *In between* | *Integra-tion* | TOTAL | N |
| 0–1 | 88% | 12 | 0 | 100% | 57 |
| 2 | 80% | 16 | 4 | 100% | 132 |
| 3 | 59% | 32 | 9 | 100% | 279 |
| 4 | 58% | 36 | 6 | 100% | 213 |

In addition to formal schooling, the informal education that comes from exposure to different racial ideas and customs may be a potential source of change. The white South's most important window on the world outside is provided by the mass media of communications. We described the contents of, and the southern audience for, the media in Chapter Nine, where we found that mass media tend to encourage political participation by southern Negroes. Do the same communications also encourage southern whites to accept standard American racial values rather than their more repressive regional variant?

Table 12–6 suggests that the answer is yes, but that the effects of the media are limited. As we see in Table 12–6, the proportion of southern whites who are "strict segregationists" declines from 88 per cent to 58 per cent as

[9] Of this 3 per cent, almost half grew up outside the South.
[10] The relationship between higher education and integrationist attitudes probably is as much the result of differential recruitment into colleges and universities as of changed attitudes flowing from what the students learn while attending them. If so, the rela-tionship between having a college education and possessing pro-Negro attitudes would be substantially reduced if more than half the southern whites were to attend college. We have assumed that the association is not *entirely* the result of selective recruitment.

regular exposure to the media increases from little or none to a good deal. On the other hand, the mass media do not seem so effective in producing full-fledged integrationists as does higher education; heavy media exposure is associated with growing racial moderation, not acceptance of the Negro position. And, of course, sizable majorities of southern whites still prefer strict segregation regardless of how much they read newspapers and magazines or listen to TV and radio.

Even this much impact by the media on southern racial attitudes is, in fact, an exaggeration. The better-educated tend to expose themselves more to mass communications than do other whites; they also tend to have more liberal racial attitudes. When the relationship between mass-media exposure and white racial attitudes is examined with education controlled, the apparent impact of the media is further reduced (see Table 12–7). Formal education clearly has a greater impact on white racial attitudes than do mass communications.

Actual experience with different racial outlooks and customs, as distinct from the largely vicarious experience of the media, may have a greater impact on southern whites. As southerners share in the increasing mobility of all Americans, will their exposure to integrated public facilities elsewhere weaken or reinforce their dedication to the peculiar institutions of the South? White southerners who have been outside the South are much more likely than those who have never left the region to believe in integration or moderate segregation. Indeed, not a single integrationist was found among respondents who have never been outside the South. And the farther the individual has been from the South, the more likely he is to have attitudes atypical for the region. Geographical mobility presumably means exposure to different customs, and such exposure apparently modifies the values of southerners. The more foreign the exposure, the more likely the modification.

Either of two possibilities might render these inferences invalid. First, travel may be associated with some other characteristic, such as high education, in such a way that education rather than travel would turn out to be the real source of the link between travel and nonsegregationist views. Second, self-selection may lie behind the apparent effect of travel; those who hold southern views least strongly may be most inclined to travel outside the region.

An examination of the relationship between formal schooling and travel reveals that people with more education are, as suspected, much more widely traveled than those with less education. But this does not necessarily mean that travel itself has no independent influence on racial attitudes. When we make our comparisons between people with the same amount of education, as in Table 12–8, the strength of the relationship between travel and racial attitudes decreases but by no means disappears. At every level of education, those who have been outside the South are less likely to be strict segregationists than those who have never left the region.

TABLE 12–7. *Exposure to the mass media of communications, and racial attitudes of white southerners, with education controlled*

| RACIAL ATTITUDE | NUMBER OF MEDIA | | | | | | | | | | | |
|---|---|---|---|---|---|---|---|---|---|---|---|---|
| | 0–1 | | | 2 | | | 3 | | | 4 | | |
| | EDUCATION | | | | | | | | | | | |
| | Low | Medium | High | Low | Medium | High | Low | Medium | High | Low | Medium | High |
| Strict segregation | 90% | 85% | — | 91% | 74% | 60% | 75% | 63% | 39% | 80% | 62% | 44% |
| In between | 10 | 15 | — | 9 | 24 | 20 | 22 | 32 | 40 | 17 | 34 | 45 |
| Integration | 0 | 0 | — | 0 | 2 | 20 | 3 | 5 | 21 | 3 | 4 | 11 |
| TOTAL | 100% | 100% | — | 100% | 100% | 100% | 100% | 100% | 100% | 100% | 100% | 100% |
| N | 41 | 13 | 2 | 58 | 54 | 20 | 71 | 125 | 83 | 30 | 111 | 71 |

NOTE: Low education = grade school or less; medium education = some high school; high education = some college training.

TABLE 12–8. *Geographical mobility and racial attitudes of white southerners, with education controlled*

FARTHEST PLACE RESPONDENT HAS BEEN

EDUCATION

| RACIAL ATTITUDE | Outside North America | | | Outside U.S.A. | | | Outside South | | | Within South | | |
|---|---|---|---|---|---|---|---|---|---|---|---|---|
| | Low | Medium | High | Low | Medium | High | Low | Medium | High | Low | Medium | High |
| Strict segregation | 71% | 54% | 35% | 57% | 46% | 45% | 72% | 60% | 46% | 89% | 86% | 57% |
| In between | 22 | 38 | 41 | 29 | 42 | 45 | 25 | 35 | 36 | 8 | 14 | 43 |
| Integration | 5 | 8 | 24 | 5 | 8 | 10 | 1 | 4 | 18 | 0 | 0 | 0 |
| Don't know, refusal, no answer | 2 | 0 | 0 | 9 | 4 | 0 | 2 | 1 | 0 | 3 | 0 | 0 |
| TOTAL | 100% | 100% | 100% | 100% | 100% | 100% | 100% | 100% | 100% | 100% | 100% | 100% |
| N | 41 | 39 | 58 | 21 | 24 | 31 | 119 | 106 | 72 | 117 | 43 | 14 |

NOTE: Low education = grade school or less; medium education = some high school; high education = some college training.

Although Table 12–8 shows that geographical mobility has an independent effect on racial attitudes when education is "partialed out," it also reinforces our confidence in the role of formal education itself. The difference between those with high and low education is greater, regardless of the amount of their travel, than the difference between the well-traveled and the nontraveled, regardless of the amount of their education. Moreover, the nature of the response to travel varies according to the level of one's education. At every level of education, greater mobility means a decrease in strict-segregationist views, but only for those with high education is much of the shift to integrationist beliefs. For those at the low or medium level of education the shift is to a moderate position between strict segregation and integration. Increasing white education holds out the prospect of a decrease in segregationist attitudes, and the increasing mobility of white southerners reinforces and adds to that prospect. Again, however, the prospect is for an increase in moderate views rather than for an early conversion to integrationist values.

The relationship between geographical mobility and racial attitudes does not disappear when we control for the important third variable, education. But what about the self-selection problem—the possibility that those with nonsegregationist values choose to travel rather than that those who travel modify their values? A simple test of this possibility seems to be offered by the fact that involuntary travel in the armed services has been a common experience for the present generation of adult American males. If travel while in the armed services modifies racial sentiments, we can fairly safely reject the possibility that our findings are a result of the self-selection process. Again the data support the inference that exposure to nonsouthern customs has an independent effect on racial attitudes: the percentage of veterans favoring integration increases from 0 to 7 to 11 as the locus of service shifts from the South only to the United States outside the South to the world beyond the United States.

But the effect of travel in the service is confined to increasing the proportion of integrationists at the expense of the proportion of moderates. The proportion of strict segregationists among southern veterans is the same regardless of where they served. Travel in the service is less important than the fact of service itself for the percentage favoring strict segregation. Only 55 per cent of all white veterans in the South favor strict segregation, as compared with 63 per cent of all adult white males and 65 per cent of all adult white females in the region.

We conclude not only that self-selection does not account for all the effect of travel on racial attitudes but also that military service itself—a largely non-voluntary act—may decrease dedication to racial inequality.

We have identified four factors—education, mass communications, geographical mobility, and armed service experience—that appear to decrease segregationist sentiment. Increasing numbers of southern whites have been exposed to all these experiences, and more of all four—certainly of the first three—may reasonably be expected in the future. Granted the great importance of formal education, and the fact that each new generation receives more schooling, we may expect young white southerners to be less committed than their elders to segregation. Moreover, studies of other populations have consistently found that conservatism—in the same sense of accepting ethnic and other group norms—increases with age. But the relationship between age and the racial attitudes of white southerners does not correspond to these expectations. If the young adults of the South represent the hope of the future, they may be the hope of the strict segregationists rather than of anyone else.

Rather than a steady increase in segregationist sentiment with advancing years, the proportion of strict segregationists declines as we move from the youngest white southern citizens through those in their thirties and forties. Only with the 50-year-old group does the percentage begin to ascend, reaching a high point with those in their sixties and seventies. The percentage of strict segregationists within each age group of southern whites is:[11]

| | |
|---|---|
| 21–29 | 65% |
| 30–39 | 61% |
| 40–49 | 62% |
| 50–59 | 66% |
| 60–69 | 71% |
| 70+ | 74% |

The great commitment of the very old to segregation is, of course, in keeping with expectations created by the normally conservative effect of aging. But the greater adherence to strict segregation of the very young than of those in their thirties and forties deserves examination. It is the more impressive in view of the fact that more people have a high level of education in the youngest group than in any other. Because of their greater schooling, an equal proportion of strict segregationists among the very young would have been mildly surprising; the slightly greater proportion that was found therefore has more meaning than the size of the difference would suggest. When we hold education constant and confine the comparison of age groups to people with the same amount of education, the youngest southern whites include more segregationists than the middle-age groups at every level of education. Indeed, within the low- and medium-education categories, the largest percentage of strict segregationists is found in the 21-to-29 age group, and, within the high-

---

11 We eliminated the 18-to-20-year-olds in our sample from this analysis, because all of them came from a single Deep South state, Georgia. The voting age is 21 elsewhere in the region. Hence persons under 21 are not included in our sample for the other states.

education category, only those over 60 years of age include more strict segregationists than the very young.

Why do more restrictive racial views turn up among the very young than among those in early middle age? Three factors contribute to the difference: more southern whites in their thirties and forties were brought up outside the South, more of them have served in the armed forces, and more have been exposed by travel to nonsouthern customs. Another factor may be the *nature* of the greater education to which the youngest age group has been exposed. These people were between the ages of 14 and 22 at the time of the Supreme Court's school-desegregation decision in 1954. Since the "black Monday" of that decision, white youths in the South may have been subjected to a more concentrated indoctrination in the merits of segregation.

Nevertheless, we need not agree with the middle-aged Negro maid in Urbania who concluded that "the way those white folks hate us, it's going to take God to change them." For between 1961 and 1964[12]—and without divine intervention—the distribution of white racial attitudes changed in small but hope-inspiring ways. The proportion of adult whites preferring "strict segregation" declined from 64 to 51 per cent; whereas the proportion of moderates increased from 28 to 39 per cent, and of integrationists, from 7 to 9 per cent.[13] These shifts did little to narrow the awesome gap between Negro and white ideals, because Negro militancy and commitment to integrationist goals increased during the same period.[14] But they do demonstrate that change is possible.

The above analysis suggests that future changes in white racial attitudes, though perhaps modest, should continue in the direction of eventual reconciliation.

[12] See footnote 8.

[13] Herbert H. Hyman and Paul B. Sheatsley, "Attitudes Toward Desegregation," *Scientific American*, Vol. 221 (1964), pp. 16–23, report, on the basis of longitudinal studies conducted by the NORC, significant increases in integrationist attitudes among both northern and southern whites since 1942. Their operational definition of the South includes Delaware, the District of Columbia, Kentucky, Maryland, Oklahoma, and West Virginia, which are not included in our definition; hence their results are not directly comparable with ours. However, the magnitude of the 20-year increases in integrationist sentiment found within their extended definition of the region is a good sign.

[14] Changes in Negro racial attitudes were as follows:

| Respondent's preference | 1961 | 1964 |
|---|---|---|
| Strict segregation | 16% | 8% |
| In between | 15 | 18 |
| Integration (desegregation) | 65 | 71 |
| Don't know, etc. | 4 | 3 |
| TOTAL | 100% | 100% |
| N | 615 | 918 |

# *"Living together as strangers"*[15]

The prospects for major changes in white racial attitudes seem to be fairly good only if we take a long-range view. But Negro leaders have made it abundantly clear that they are unwilling to wait for slow processes gradually to erode segregation. "We want our freedom *now*; we want it *all*; we want it *here*." The words are those of the Reverend Martin Luther King; the sentiments they express are shared by most black southerners. The South must somehow ameliorate—if not "solve"—its racial problems *before* the millennium has arrived, *before* the hearts and minds of most white men have been won to the cause of equality.

If this sort of accommodation is to be made, southerners must first realize the depth and extent of their differences. Knowledge of the conflicting views that divide southerners along racial lines seems a necessary if not sufficient condition for coping with these differences through democratic political processes.

How well aware are white and Negro southerners of the differences that divide the races on the question of segregation? Most nonsoutherners would probably assume that neither race could exist in the midst of such strongly divergent opinions without being aware of their existence. And they might be joined by social scientists: survey data have revealed a reasonable measure of success among citizens who were asked to estimate the position of various groups on questions that divide the groups less sharply and about which they have less intense opinions.

But other findings leave open the possibility that southerners might actually be ill informed about their differences. In the first place, communication crosses caste lines in a highly imperfect fashion; hence, one or both races may receive inaccurate impressions of the preferences of the other. In the second place, selective perception, through which an individual's perceptions of the views of others are influenced by his own values, may lead to a distortion of the information that is communicated. These are mutually reinforcing phenomena in public opinion, and southern race relations is a ripe field for the operation of both.

Table 12–9 indicates that, regardless of the overwhelming preference of Negroes for integration and of whites for strict segregation, neither group can correctly estimate the views of the other. Although both races are misinformed, the estimates of whites are much more inaccurate than those of Negroes. Only 22 per cent of the whites recognize that most Negroes favor integration, but 47 per cent of the Negroes recognize that most whites favor segregation. The greater inaccuracy of whites can also be seen by comparing the proportion of

[15] This is the title of an editorial in the Norfolk, Virginia, *Pilot*, September 26, 1962, stimulated by an earlier report of our findings.

TABLE 12–9.　*Southern white and Negro estimates of the other race's attitudes on segregation and integration*

| ESTIMATED NUMBER OF WHITE STRICT SEGRE- GATIONISTS OR OF NEGRO INTEGRATIONISTS | *Negro estimates of white opinion* | *White estimates of Negro opinion* |
|---|---|---|
| All | 21% | 4% |
| Most | 26 | 18 |
| About half | 21 | 21 |
| Less than half | 20 | 39 |
| Practically none | 0 | 1 |
| Don't know, refusal, no members of other race in area | 12 | 17 |
| TOTAL | 100% | 100% |
| N | 615 | 685 |

whites who say that "less than half" or "practically none" of the Negroes prefer integration with the proportion of Negroes who perceive equally small numbers of whites as favoring segregation. Such grossly inaccurate estimates occur among whites at twice the rate at which they occur among Negroes. The greater frequency of "don't know" responses among whites than among Negroes is a more direct expression of the relative lack of information among whites.

The great inaccuracy of whites in estimating the views of Negroes is not surprising. Inaccurate information about the views of the subordinate group may be considered one of the prices the superordinate group must pay for a repressive social system. Or, rather than viewing misinformation as a liability, one could say that the communication process permits the dominant group the luxury of ignorance about the wishes of those who are dominated. The percentage of Negroes who favor integration actually exceeds the percentage of whites who favor strict segregation. But the communication of Negro views is blocked in various ways. In almost all forms of activity in the South, Negroes are required by law to behave in conformity to segregationist values, whatever their opinions. Negroes in some localities may be afraid to express their dissatisfactions. In some cases, behavioral conformity may not be enough; white employers may elicit assurances from their Negro employees that they prefer segregation. Although the pressures from the dominant white majority have not succeeded in molding Negro opinions, then, they have succeeded in inducing many Negroes to refrain from expressing those opinions—or even to express contrary opinions—in contacts with local whites.

Southern Negroes, on the other hand, live under a system of segregation that is a constant institutional reminder of the segregationist beliefs of the white majority. Local police and judges stand ready to correct any misperceptions on which Negroes begin to act. How, then, can we explain the fact that only a minority of southern Negroes—albeit a very large minority—recognize that most southern whites favor strict segregation? The answer must lie in selective perception. Their personal preference for integration must lead southern Negroes to underestimate the degree of white hostility to integration, despite the conspicuous evidence to the contrary.

Selective perception characterizes whites as well, as Table 12–10 demon-

TABLE 12–10. *Percentage of southern whites and Negroes aware of other race's attitudes on segregation and integration, by racial attitude*

| RESPONDENT'S RACIAL ATTITUDE | Negro awareness of white opinion | White awareness of Negro opinion |
|---|---|---|
| Strict segregation | 53%  (94) | 18%  (443) |
| Something in between | 44    (89) | 25    (194) |
| Integration | 48    (400) | 50     (44) |

NOTE: The percentages in the first column indicate the portion of Negroes with a given racial attitude who say that "all" or "most" whites favor strict segregation; the second-column percentages indicate the proportion of whites with a given racial attitude who say that "all" or "most" Negroes favor integration.

strates. White integrationists are three times more likely than segregationists and twice as likely as those in between to perceive correctly the portion of Negroes favoring integration. White integrationists are better able to perceive Negro preferences, not necessarily because they are better informed but because they hold the same preferences.

The opinions of Negroes similarly tend to influence their estimates of the other race's preferences, although to a less extreme degree. Over half the Negro segregationists recognize that all or most whites also prefer segregation, whereas somewhat less than half of the Negro integrationists make such an accurate estimate. But this contrast (53 per cent to 47.5 per cent) is not nearly so great as that between white integrationists and white segregationists (50 per cent to 18 per cent). Just as the pattern of communication in the South leaves the superordinate group as a whole less informed about the other race's aspirations, so does it permit them greater freedom to project their own views to others.

From the Negro's vantage point, however, the preferences of whites are less ambiguous. The harsh realities of segregation set bounds that usually leave little room for selective perception; the more severe the repression, the more narrow the limits of misperception. Thus the Negroes in Piedmont County— the least segregated and most "liberal" of the counties we studied in detail—

have the *least* accurate picture of white attitudes in their area; only 43 per cent realize that most local whites prefer segregation. In Bright Leaf and Crayfish, these figures are 53 and 58 per cent, respectively. And in Camellia County, which has a long, bitter, and largely abortive experience in racial protest, 73 per cent of the Negroes are realistically aware of the structure of white attitudes.

Although each race in the South is surprisingly ignorant of the other's point of view, the failure of southern whites to realize how discontented their Negro neighbors are is a more serious stumbling block to racial accommodation. Even in the midst of sit-ins, boycotts, and freedom rides, a majority of southern whites did not realize in 1961 that Negroes were bitterly unhappy about segregation. Let us examine the 22 per cent of southern whites who did recognize deep-seated Negro resentment then. Are their characteristics such as to suggest early recognition by other whites of the nature of Negro demands?

To begin with, we must face the possibility that correct information on Negro attitudes is simply one manifestation of a generally superior level of information. When we analyze the results of our political-information test with the racial views of the respondents held constant, we find that general political information has no relation to awareness of Negro racial attitudes.[16] Among the strict segregationists, those who are ignorant of Negro preferences actually have slightly higher information scores than those who are aware of Negro attitudes. Among the moderates, the difference is reversed, but in both cases the differences are minute. Although we may expect modern modes of mass communication to raise the general information level of southern whites, then, such an improvement will apparently have no direct effect on white perceptions of Negro attitudes.[17]

When we look at the level of formal schooling rather than at the level of political information, the sense of stability in white misperceptions is even stronger. Table 12–11 reveals that, with white racial views held constant, more education makes no contribution at all to greater white awareness of Negro attitudes. Indeed, for strict segregationists there is a slight decrease in awareness as education goes up, and for moderates, a fairly sizable decrease. The assumption that white perceptions of Negro demands might be changed more quickly than white attitudes gets no support from these findings.

If white ignorance of Negro attitudes does not stem directly from lack of information or education, perhaps it results simply from lack of contact with

16 The mean number of questions answered correctly by each group of southern whites was: strict segregationists aware of Negro attitudes, 4.4; strict segregationists unaware, 4.5; moderates aware, 5.2; moderates unaware, 4.9; integrationists aware, 5.3. Too few integrationists were unaware to permit computing a mean score for this group.

17 Although exposure to the mass media of communications does tend to weaken white commitment to segregation, it does *not* contribute to an awareness of Negro views. The percentage of whites "aware" of Negro racial attitudes varies thus according to the number of media they are regularly exposed to: none or 1, 23 per cent; 2, 17 per cent; 3, 25 per cent; 4, 21 per cent.

TABLE 12-11.   *Percentage of white southerners aware[a] of Negro racial attitudes, by racial attitude and education*

| WHITE RACIAL ATTITUDES | WHITE EDUCATION | | |
|---|---|---|---|
| | Low | Medium | High |
| Strict segregation | 29% | 29% | 27% |
| In between | 45 | 41 | 37 |
| Integration | [b] | [b] | 89 |
| N | 173 | 134 | 111 |

[a] The view that "all" or "most" Negroes favor integration is counted as "aware"; the view that "less than half" or "practically none" favor integration is scored as incorrect. Other responses—"about half," "don't know"—and failures to respond are excluded from this and subsequent tabulations related to white awareness of Negro racial attitudes.

[b] Too few cases for percentaging.

Negroes. The most common form of close contact between whites and Negroes in the South is in an employer-employee relationship, but contact with Negroes as employees is associated with a lower level of awareness of Negro attitudes when we compare whites with the same racial attitudes. Because the employer-employee relationship places the Negro in the familiar role of subordination, such white contact with Negro employees seems to reinforce inaccurate views of Negro attitudes.

Contact with Negroes as fellow shoppers is probably the type of association in the contemporary South most nearly akin to contact in the use of integrated public facilities. But, again, whites with a given racial attitude are less likely to be aware of Negro attitudes if they report contacts with Negroes as fellow shoppers than if they report no such contacts.[18]

Like education and information, contact with Negroes does not contribute directly to white awareness of Negro attitudes. The effect of travel and of military service on white awareness, when preference is controlled, is similarly nonexistent or unimpressive. Ironically, each of these factors *does* contribute directly to more moderate or integrationist sentiment. Contrary to our expectations, white misperceptions of Negro preferences may be harder to change than white attitudes themselves.

The general conditions under which whites may become aware of Negro attitudes are suggested by the contrast in awareness between whites in the Deep South and whites in the Peripheral South. This is the only variable we have examined in this chapter that serves, in clear independence of white

18 For a more detailed analysis of the importance of different kinds of contact on racial attitudes, see John Orbell, "Social Protest and Social Structure: Southern Negro College Student Participation in the Protest Movement" (Ph.D. dissertation, University of North Carolina, 1965).

preferences, to increase awareness of Negro preferences. Among strict segregationists, 32 per cent in the Peripheral South compared to 22 per cent in the
Deep South realize that Negroes prefer integration (see Table 12–12). And

TABLE 12–12.  *Percentage of white southerners aware of Negro racial
attitudes, by racial attitude and subregion of residence*

| RACIAL ATTITUDES OF WHITES | SUBREGION OF RESPONDENTS' RESIDENCE | |
| --- | --- | --- |
|  | *Deep South* | *Peripheral South* |
| Strict segregation | 22% | 32% |
| In between | 31 | 42 |
| Integration | — | 88 |
| N | 105 | 315 |

the difference between moderates in the two subregions is slightly greater.
The Peripheral South contains a much larger proportion of moderates and
integrationists than the Deep South does, but these are differences between
people with the same personal preferences.

The greater ability of whites in the Peripheral South to recognize the preference of most Negroes for integration appears to be supported by three factors,
all of which are important for the future race relations and politics of the
region.

First, more of the Negroes in the Peripheral South than in the Deep South
actually do prefer integration. The difference is not great (68 per cent to
60 per cent), but it is large enough for us to say that the actual situation in the
Peripheral South should call forth more white estimates that most Negroes
prefer integration. Despite this difference, the fact remains that most Negroes,
even in the Deep South, are integrationists.

A second factor underlying the subregional difference in awareness is that
Negroes in the Peripheral South are more articulate about their opinions.
With more Negroes voting, sometimes supported by active and efficient political organizations, and with public and private expressions of discontent
over segregation, the muting effects of the Deep South's pressures for conformity are decreased. Even whites who are appalled at Negro demands may
be forced at least to recognize that the demands exist.

Finally, the whites in the Peripheral South are not nearly so close to consensus on segregation as are those in the Deep South. With a large minority
of fellow whites rejecting strict segregation, even the strongest segregationist
may be forced to recognize that Negroes must also reject segregation.

Thus, in a county like Crayfish, the local whites are almost entirely ignorant
of Negro racial attitudes—only 8 per cent of the whites there realize that most

of the local Negroes are integrationists! In Camellia County, which actually contains a smaller proportion of Negro integrationists than Crayfish but where the Negroes are more aggressive, articulate, and active, and where they have the support of a minority of whites, 28 per cent of the whites have a reasonably accurate picture of Negro aspirations and goals. In Piedmont County, where white integrationists and moderates are more numerous than in Camellia and where the Negroes are more effectively organized, 38 per cent of the whites are adequately aware of Negro attitudes. But only in Bright Leaf County, of those we studied in detail, did a majority (63 per cent) of the whites correctly assess Negro attitudes, and there only because a majority of the Negroes preferred what the whites wanted them to—segregation.

Despite all the southern whites' talk about understanding "our niggers," and all the southern Negroes' stories about knowing "our white folks," the two races truly are "living together as strangers." *This situation is getting worse, not better.* In 1961, 22 per cent of southern whites had a reasonably accurate view of predominant Negro racial attitudes: over three years later they could do no better. Indeed, they did a little bit worse (21 per cent). In the meantime, however, a burst of optimism seems to have swept the Negro communities of the South. In 1961, 21 per cent of the Negroes believed that "all" southern whites favored "strict segregation"; in 1964, only 4 per cent of them did. In 1961, 26 per cent of the Negroes interviewed said that "most" southern whites were segregationists; three years later 14 per cent of them did. As southern Negroes gain power and concessions in the region, as the federal government intervenes in the racial struggle more and more strenuously on their behalf, they too fall prey to the selective perception and wishful thinking which in harsher days were almost impossible—except for white people.

So long as this mutual underestimation of the seriousness of the conflict persists, the new biracial brand of southern politics promises to be a dangerous version of blind man's bluff.

## Expectations for the future

What, then, does the future hold for race relations and politics in the South?

Paradoxically, Negro and white southerners more nearly agree on this question than on any other we have examined in this chapter. Each respondent in our survey was asked to locate the race relations in his community on a ten-step ladder, with the "very best" kind of race relations he could imagine represented by 10 and the "very worst" by 1. Having rated present race relations, he was then asked where on the ladder he would have put the race relations of his community "five years ago" and where he expected it to be "five years from now."

The results are presented in Figure 12–3. The strict segregationist majority among the southern whites has the most idyllic image of the past and the greatest sense of doom for the future. White integrationists, on the other hand, join the Negroes in low ratings of southern race relations for the past and present and in high expectations for the future. White moderates occupy a position between the extreme segregationist whites and the Negroes at every point in time, being more satisfied with the past and present than Negroes and more optimistic about the future than strict segregationist whites.

Because these ratings are based on a scale in which each respondent defines his own "best" and "worst" race relations, they are impressive testimony to one form of consensus that characterizes all southern groups—agreement that the South is moving from segregation toward integration. Only a small minority of whites join the vast majority of Negroes in approving of the change. But, in view of the degree to which personal preference conditions estimates of the other race's views on segregation, consensus on the direction of movement, whether defined as progress or as retrogression, represents no mean achievement. White segregationists may blame the course of events on "outside agitation" or an unfriendly national government, but they at least recognize where events are leading.

FIGURE 12–3.   *Mean ratings of race relations by Negroes and white "strict segregationists," "moderates," and "integrationists"*

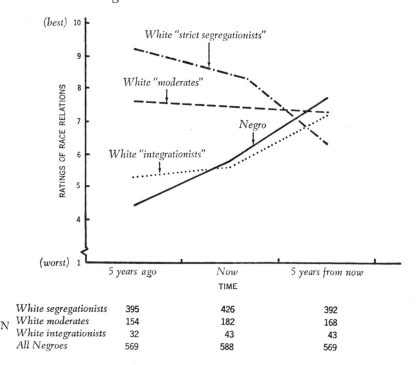

|  | 5 years ago | Now | 5 years from now |
|---|---|---|---|
| White segregationists | 395 | 426 | 392 |
| White moderates | 154 | 182 | 168 |
| White integrationists | 32 | 43 | 43 |
| All Negroes | 569 | 588 | 569 |

Nonetheless, our data on the expectations of southerners provide more than a little cause for concern: for while both races anticipate the same *direction* of change, the *rates* of change they expect are largely incompatible. Notice in Figure 12–3 that, on the average, southerners—*regardless of their race or attitudes toward segregation*—expect race relations in their communities five years from now to be around 7 on our 10-point scale. Given the clashing standards by which these judgments were made, this is an impossibility. Most Negroes expect the South to take a breathtaking leap toward racial equality— exactly half of the Negro integrationists, for example, expect their communities to deserve near perfect ratings (9 or 10) in five years! The whites, on the other hand, tend to view the drift toward desegregation as a gradual process. Although white segregationists expect more rapid desegregation than either the white integrationists or moderates, still over a fourth of them expect to rate race relations at 9 or 10 in five years. Unless these expectations are revised in the light of events, some large group of southerners is certain to be deeply disappointed. Perhaps, as some wag put it, the "revolution of rising expectations" throughout the world might better be called the "revolution of rising frustrations." At any rate, one seems to be leading to the other in the American South.

In the past, southern Negroes have borne the brunt of frustrated expectations: they have accepted glacial progress toward "first-class citizenship" with amazing grace and docility. But the new mood of militancy and impatience penetrates deeply into the Negro community today. As a Negro maid in South Carolina said, "Colored people refuse to be pushed around now." They have learned that southern whites are frightened. "They sho is skeered if they ain't got a police with a big gun to protect 'em," a railroad laborer in Capital City commented.

Negroes have developed a new confidence in themselves. The wife of a common laborer said, that, in the event of a race riot in Houston, "There would be more dead whites than Negroes. Because, you see, Negroes are tired."[19] Negroes can no longer be expected to accept frustration of their hopes and dreams without protest of an extremely disruptive and potentially violent sort. And the tolerance of southern whites for rapid integration has not been seriously tested since Reconstruction. The history of that period does little to quiet our fears of a possible racial explosion.

Again, we find major differences in the patterns of expectations *within* the region. In Piedmont County, for example, the expectations of the two races seem to be reasonably realistic and fairly compatible (see Figure 12–4). The Negroes feel that they have improved their lot more substantially during the last five years (+2.3 points) than those in the other three communities we studied; they expect this improvement to continue at a slower rate (+1.7)

19 See William Brink and Louis Harris, *The Negro Revolution in America* (New York: Simon and Schuster, 1964), especially Chapter 4 on the new mood of militancy and self-confidence. Almost a quarter of their national sample expect violence, and over half believe that Negroes would win such a showdown. *Ibid.*, pp. 73–74.

during the next five years. The whites in Piedmont anticipate a deterioration, from their point of view, in race relations, but they do not expect this change to be disastrous: indeed, they expect less deterioration during the next five years than do the whites in any of the other communities.

In Camellia, on the other hand, the Negroes expect a great leap forward (+2.1) from a situation that has improved very little during the last five years (+0.5). The whites in Camellia expect what they view as deterioration in race relations to continue at about the same rate as before (−1.5 during the next five years as contrasted to −1.1 during the last five).

Negroes in Bright Leaf are more contented with their position than any other group of Negroes, and they expect only modest rates of improvement in the future. On the average, the whites of the county seem psychologically prepared for the amount of change the local Negroes are likely to demand— the whites, on the average, expect a deterioration of −2.8 points in the next five years.

FIGURE 12–4. *Mean ratings, race relations by Negroes and whites, by community*

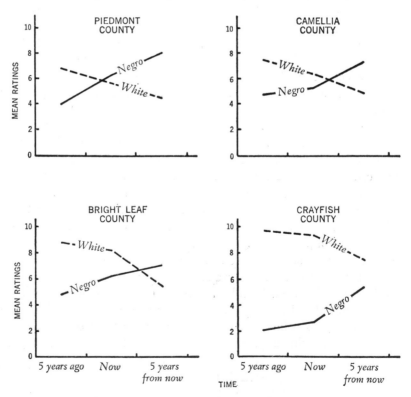

If the expectations of the residents of Camellia County cause apprehension, those of the Negroes and whites in Crayfish County must be viewed with genuine alarm. The gap between the two races' satisfaction with race relations is very large and neither has sensed any major change during the last five years. But the Negroes are anticipating great improvement in the future whereas the whites expect only moderate deterioration. Given the stark cleavage in their attitudes toward segregation outlined in Figure 12–2 and the lack of realism and compatibility of expectations presented in Figure 12–4, effective biracial political democracy in Crayfish County is almost impossible to conceive in the near future.

While Piedmont and Bright Leaf counties, for different reasons, seem to have the best chance to survive the racial revolution in a reasonably democratic fashion, all four communities face a troubled future. How can communities so sharply divided, and characterized by such high levels of tension and frustration, be expected to resolve their racial problems in a peaceful and democratic fashion?

## Conclusions: Politics without consensus

We have found, so far in this chapter, that Negroes and whites are dangerously divided on the major issue of southern politics—racial segregation. Although southern Negroes are not likely to demand rapid desegregation of a few areas about which whites are particularly adamant (for example, housing and marriage), and although whites are not deeply committed to continued segregation of economic or political life, the preferences of the two races still are very largely incompatible.

In the past, this cleavage did not pose a threat to democratic politics in the South, since Negroes had no political power. Democracy was for whites only. Now that Negroes are becoming politically active and powerful in the region, the system is being placed under very great strain. If men must "agree on fundamentals" before they "safely can afford to bicker"—as much democratic political theory suggests[20]—then the increasingly biracial politics of the South will be stormy indeed in the years ahead. Such a deeply felt and basic conflict may be impossible to resolve without resort to such massive violence that a "new Reconstruction" will inevitably follow—for federal troops are the only realistic alternative to political accommodation.

The short-run chances for narrowing the gap between Negro and white preferences in the South are poor. Negroes cannot be expected to abandon their demands for equality now. Although the white southerners' commitment

[20] See, for example, Ernest S. Griffith, John Plamenatz, and J. Roland Pennock, "Cultural Prerequisites to a Successfully Functioning Democracy: A Symposium," *American Political Science Review*, Vol. 50 (1956), pp. 101–37.

to total segregation is weakening, this is far too gradual a process to satisfy the region's Negro citizens. Neither racial group has an accurate picture of the attitudes and feelings of the other; southern whites in particular are shockingly unaware of their differences with their Negro neighbors. And, while both races agree that the South is moving toward desegregation, Negroes are anticipating a much faster rate of change than are the whites.

Granted all this, what are the chances for maintaining a democratic political system in the South? Can such an awesome and basic conflict be resolved through political accommodation? Or is a racial explosion followed by massive and forceful federal intervention inevitable?

Certainly the facts presented so far provide little cause for optimism. And yet some grounds may be found for hope that such a tragedy can be avoided.

### CONFLICTING VALUES AND GOALS

At the same time that most southerners are deeply committed to segregation if they are white or integration if they are Negro, they also cherish other values and goals. "I'm not a segregationist; I'm not an integrationist," a white laborer in deepest Georgia said, "but I'm in favor of obeying court orders." The manager of a supermarket on the edge of the Negro district in Winston-Salem went even further:

> Let the court make laws and then people abide by the laws. You can't fight [them]. I say if you don't like the law, get the law changed, but don't try to fight laws. This thing of integration is coming, so it's no use fighting it.

The fear of violence leads some, like a house painter in Capital City who cannot imagine peaceable integration, to an opposite conclusion. The best form of race relations, he said, was "the old traditional way. That's the only answer. Of course there are injustices in the traditional way . . . [but] . . . *peaceful injustice is better than violence.*" The same abhorrence of violence runs through the responses of most Negroes as well. A Negro nurse's aide in Farmington expressed a common viewpoint when she said that she favored integration, "but I don't like fighting and carrying on."

A desire for law and order is not the only value most Negroes and whites in the former Confederate states hold in common. Like other Americans, for instance, they want more and better jobs and housing, higher incomes, a better education for their children. These other goals can, and from time to time do, conflict with the southern whites' belief in segregation. When southern whites have had to choose between desegregated schools or none at all, they overwhelmingly have chosen the former. When manufacturing concerns in the region must choose between a lucrative defense contract and a continuation of discriminatory hiring practices, most southern businessmen opt for the contract and the cash. Nor is racial integration the sole, or the absolute, value for southern Negroes. At times they must choose between racially integrated schools and the safety or happiness of their own children, between better housing now or integrated housing at some distant future date, and so on and on.

Neither race can always have the racial policy it prefers *and* other things it badly wants and needs. Thus the multiple values and multiple goals of southerners result in a gap between what they prefer in race relations and what they will bear. "You asked me what I favor," a white Arkansas housewife who believed in segregation said, "not what I will accept graciously; not what I thought was 'right.'" The desire of each race for values other than segregation or integration serves to dampen the effects of their conflict on racial policy. Inflexible insistence on maximizing one value at the expense of all others is not a rational mode of behavior.[21] However, ordinary southerners—white or Negro—cannot be expected always to behave rationally in such an emotion-cloaked area as race relations.

## CONSENSUS ON DEMOCRATIC IDEALS

Southerners believe in political democracy. They have been taught much the same political ideals as Americans above the Mason-Dixon Line. They believe that "democracy is the best form of government," that basic governmental decisions should be made by the vote of a comprehensive electorate, that the majority should rule, and that minorities have rights. They believe not only that the American political system is "democratic," but that our political institutions are the most perfect expression of democratic ideals ever realized. On the abstract level, they substantially agree on basic values and principles, on the "rules of the game." Myrdal placed great stress on this point 20 years ago. The "American Dilemma," as he saw it, was the clash between the high ideals Americans profess and how they actually behaved when confronted by the presence of a large Negro minority. Once Americans came to realize the logical inconsistencies between their Fourth of July oratory and reality, the "Negro problem" would be well on the way to solution.

Subsequent events have led us to assign far less importance to the overwhelming agreement of Americans with the abstract principles of the Declaration of Independence and the Preamble to the Constitution of the United States. The average man can, more or less indefinitely, "hold these truths to be self-evident" but fail to see their relevance to concrete, practical problems. Thus most southerners experience no difficulty in being convinced democrats and convinced racists at the same time. Nor do other Americans feel any inconsistency when they proclaim a belief in "free speech" but oppose renting

[21] For an examination of the gap between what southerners want and what they will bear, and the role of conflicting goals in producing this gap, see Melvin M. Tumin, *Desegregation: Resistance and Readiness* (Princeton, N.J.: Princeton University Press, 1958), especially the summary, ch. 12.

the local auditorium to a group of socialists or atheists for a public meeting. The consensus on fundamental principles largely disappears as one descends from the cloudy heights of rhetoric to the mundane level of day-to-day living.[22]

### LEADERSHIP AND MASS INDIFFERENCE

Yet American politics—and its southern variant—has been a reasonable approximation of democracy *without* any very meaningful consensus on the mass level. Just how and why this should be so is not entirely clear. But recent research suggests at least two factors that may help explain this apparent paradox.[23]

First, the most active and influential members of the political system seem to have a more thoroughgoing and genuine dedication to democratic principles and procedures than do their followers. They are more aware of the logical implications of the democratic creed and more likely to feel bound by these implications in their daily lives. They are also more aware that men are "creature[s] of many values and desires which simultaneously seek satisfaction —[and that] . . . what one does to satisfy any one of these desires will affect one's ability to satisfy the others as well."[24] Although our study does not provide systematic data on either point, we believe that both generalizations are true for the leaders of the two races in the South today. This does not mean that the Negro and white leaders of the South agree on the question of segregation—far from it—but that they are more aware of the necessity to seek political accommodation for their conflicting views than is the average southerner and more agreed on the general procedures to be followed in seeking this resolution.

But for these elite perspectives to have substantial effects, a second factor is necessary—the masses of the citizens must be relatively indifferent to the outcome of leadership negotiations. On most issues, most of the time, this is the case—the rank-and-file citizens accept the decisions arrived at by their leaders without even trying to render an independent judgment on them, or even being aware that decisions have been made. Thus the lack of political concern of most citizens provides an element of "slack" within which leaders are relatively free to make decisions and to adjust conflicts. On the race issue in the South, however, this benign apathy scarcely exists among whites or Negroes. And both the political indifference of Negroes induced by centuries of subordination and the legal and extralegal barriers to Negro participation are dis-

[22] Cf. James W. Prothro and Charles M. Grigg, "Fundamental Principles of Democracy: Bases of Agreement and Disagreement," *Journal of Politics*, Vol. 22 (1960), pp. 276–84.

[23] Ibid.; Robert A. Dahl, *Who Governs? Democracy and Power in an American City* (New Haven, Conn.: Yale University Press, 1961), especially ch. 28; Herbert McClosky, "Consensus and Ideology in American Politics," *American Political Science Review*, Vol. 58 (1964), pp. 361–82.

[24] Tumin, *op. cit.*, p. 199.

appearing. So is the "slack" in the political system. Under these conditions, the democratizing and ameliorating consequences of leadership are substantially reduced from what they are under normal circumstances.

## DIFFERENTIAL RATES OF GROWTH IN NEGRO POWER

The growth in Negro political power will be quite uneven in different places in the South. In some communities—Piedmont County, for example—Negroes have already entered the political system en masse, and the political problem of reconciling their views with those of the white majority has already arrived. In others, Negroes are virtually powerless; their attitudes have yet to become politically significant. The frightening lack of consensus in Crayfish County, for example, will become politically relevant only as Negroes become enfranchised and politically organized.

The differential rates at which Negroes achieve political power may therefore tend to soften future political conflict. Negroes may achieve the political power which their numbers merit first in areas where the reconciliation of Negro and white social attitudes is most possible and last in areas where the chasm between the goals of the two races is now unbridgeable.

But as the evidence for Piedmont and Camellia counties indicates, Negroes can achieve substantial political power in the face of great white hostility. In these communities the lack of consensus on racial policy—while less than it would be if Negroes in Crayfish County were suddenly to become politically powerful—is still severe. And, as the Tuskegee example with which this chapter began indicates, federal intervention can greatly speed up the process by which Negroes achieve political power *despite* local white opposition and nearly total conflict on racial policy.

Finally, the view that Negroes will achieve political power only slowly in areas most divided over racial policy assumes that the gap between Negroes and whites somehow will be reduced during the period of delay. This means, in effect, that white racial attitudes will somehow be changed—otherwise the anticipated lag would serve no purpose.

## WHITE RACIAL ATTITUDES AND THE FUTURE
## OF DEMOCRACY IN THE SOUTH

The mechanisms that conceivably might soften the conflict of southern Negroes and whites over segregation—the existence of conflicting goals, consensus on democratic ideals, the impact of leadership, and the differential rates of growth in Negro power—seem unlikely to be enough, by themselves, to ensure the avoidance of a racial holocaust and the preservation of political democracy in the South. Only a significant change in white racial attitudes, awareness, and expectations can do that.

This does not mean that all white southerners must become wholehearted advocates of racial integration. It does mean that the present consensus of white southerners on racial policies must be weakened. A fairly sizable minority of white moderates and integrationists, when joined with a larger group of Negro political activists, create a political atmosphere in which white politicians can "give in" to pressures from the federal government and bargain and compromise with Negro spokesmen without committing political suicide in the process.

This kind of race politics already exists in much of the Peripheral South, where there are appreciably more white moderates and where even the strict segregationists are more likely to be aware of Negro preferences. Despite the fact that a majority of the white citizens—and politicians—strongly prefer segregation, genuine accommodations are being made democratically. The Negro activists believe that the rate of change is too slow, and a majority of the whites feel that it is being made in the wrong direction. So far, however, both would prefer to live with these frustrations than face the dimly recognized alternative.

In the Deep South, neither the critical minority of white moderates nor the large bloc of Negro voters is yet in being. But if the Deep South is to join the Union, these groups must develop sufficiently to make the accommodation of deep racial conflict politically feasible.

The major thrust of our analysis is that the forces of change within the South, as well as pressures from outside, are working in that direction.

Chapter Thirteen

# Southern Negroes and the Political Parties

In the 1964 presidential election, Mississippi was the most Republican state in the Union. Given a choice between Democrat Lyndon B. Johnson—the first southerner to become president in modern times—and Barry Goldwater, the voters in the most "southern" state in the country chose the Republican candidate by a margin of nine to one. In Alabama, Goldwater polled almost 70 per cent of the vote, running against a slate of unpledged Democratic electors; no electors pledged to the Johnson-Humphrey ticket were even on the ballot. The Arizona conservative won in South Carolina (59 per cent) and Louisiana (57 per cent) by margins usually considered to be landslides. Even Georgia, which never before had been carried by a Republican, gave 54 per cent of its vote to Republican Goldwater. In every other southern state save the Democratic candidate's home state of Texas, the vote was close. All this in the face of the greatest Democratic landslide in history! Lyndon Johnson ran much more strongly in traditionally Republican Maine and Vermont than he did in *any* of the former Confederate states.

The 1964 presidential campaign and election were among the most extraordinary in American history.[1] It would be unwise to assume that the political patterns of that year will persist. But mass defections of southerners to the Republican party in presidential elections is nothing new. Florida, Tennessee, Texas, and Virginia went for Eisenhower in both 1952 and 1956. In the latter contest, Eisenhower actually polled a majority of the votes cast in the South. Richard Nixon's strong showing in 1960—he received more votes than Eisenhower, though he carried only Florida, Tennessee, and Virginia—suggests that this was not merely a tribute to a popular war hero. In presidential elections the Republicans have demonstrated impressive and growing strength in

[1] T. H. White, *The Making of the President—1964* (New York: Atheneum, 1965).

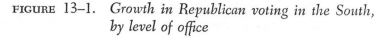

FIGURE 13–1.   *Growth in Republican voting in the South, by level of office*

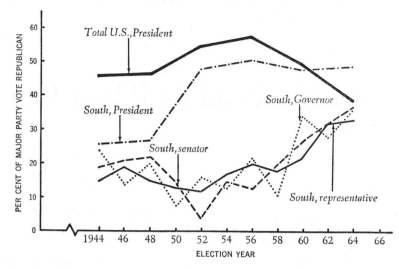

the South over the last 20 years, regardless of changing candidates and issues.[2] In state, local, and congressional elections Republican gains have been more modest (see Figure 13–1). On these lower levels of politics, despite occasional and well-publicized exceptions, the vast bulk of the South remains a Democratic area.

What kind of party system is this? What does the future hold for the politics of the South? And what effect will these changes have on the southern Negroes' struggle for equality?

## The one-party system and Negro political power

Historically, the one-party system was a defense against the threats to white supremacy that the South experienced during the post-Reconstruction and Populist eras. Combined with the white primary, the one-party system barred Negroes from participating in the real election decision—the Democratic primary—without apparent conflict with the Fifteenth Amendment. The South presented a united front to the rest of the nation, at least on racial matters. A solid bloc of southern states held a virtual veto over the selection of presi-

[2] See, on the growth of Republicanism in the South: A. Heard, *A Two-Party South?* (Chapel Hill, N.C.: University of North Carolina Press, 1952); D. S. Strong, *The 1952 Presidential Election in the South* (University, Ala.: University of Alabama, Bureau of Public Administration, 1955); *Urban Republicanism in the South* (University Ala.: University of Alabama, Bureau of Public Administration, 1960); A. Sindler (ed.), *Change in the Contemporary South* (Durham, N.C.: Duke University Press, 1963), articles by R. J. Steamer, D. S. Strong, and P. E. Converse.

dential candidates by Democratic National Conventions, and their electoral votes seemed essential to success in the election itself. Southern senators, by united action, were able to filibuster to death all threatening legislation. Southern congressmen, assured of longer tenure than their northern colleagues by their region's lack of vigorous partisan competition, fell heir to positions of power in Congress more or less automatically through the operation of the seniority system.

The South has changed since the one-party system was first perfected. The white primary is dead, along with virtually all the other "legal" barriers to Negro participation in the South. Millions of Negroes have migrated from the South to the large metropolitan areas of the North and have begun to vote. Thanks largely to the New Deal, the vast majority of these emigrants abandoned the party of Lincoln for that of F.D.R.—but not so irrevocably that northern Democrat politicians could afford to be insensitive to their wants and needs. Truman, Kennedy, and Johnson proved that the solid support of the South was unnecessary for Democratic presidential victory—indeed, it seems unlikely that any of these men would have gone to the White House if their program had been entirely satisfactory to the South or repugnant to northern Negroes. The national Democratic Party is firmly committed to the ardent pursuit of Negro voters wherever they may be. This strategy is, of course, highly unsatisfactory to the party's southern wing.

Even under these changed circumstances, the southern one-party system remains a device for limiting the political power of southern Negroes in state and local affairs.[3] In the southern one-party system, Democratic primaries (the "real" elections) typically are contests among several self-selected candidates running on an every-man-for-himself basis. There is little continuity in candidates or issues from one year to the next, and even less connection between contests for different offices—say, lieutenant governor and county sheriff—being decided at the same time. This type of free-wheeling, individualistic, and unstructured politics presents the voters with a far more difficult task than does a partisan contest. The alternatives of policy and personnel have not been reduced and simplified by party processes. There are no party labels to tell the voters who the "good guys" are.

> It is conceivable that in a world of perfectly informed and ideally involved voters the simplification functions of parties would be superfluous. In the real world, where citizens are parents, home-owners, job-holders, television viewers, and baseball fans, as well as voters, some procedure for facilitating political perception and evaluation seems essential.[4]

This procedure the one-party system of the South fails to provide.

[3] The classic analysis of one-party politics and its consequences is V. O. Key, Jr., *Southern Politics* (New York: Alfred A. Knopf, 1949). See especially ch. 14 for a discussion of the consequences of one-partyism.

[4] F. I. Greenstein, *The American Party System and the American People* (Englewood Cliffs, N.J.: Prentice-Hall, 1964), p. 73. Ch. 5 of this volume contains a systematic summary of the point of view presented there.

Thus, by reducing the effectiveness of the vote as a means of advancing one's own interests, the one-party system favors those who can get what they want without assistance from government. It favors those best equipped through education, interest, and experience to make sense out of ambiguous and fluid political situations. It favors those with political resources other than the vote—money, status, and knowledge—over those whose only leverage on the government comes from their massed voting power. In short, it favors the "haves" over the "have nots." And the largest "have not" group in the South— the group that has the most to gain from governmental activity—is the Negroes. They are still the principal losers under the South's system of one-party politics. And that, of course, is just what the founders of the system intended.

Thus the Negroes' stake in the future organization of southern politics is substantial. They stand to gain more than anyone else from the development of a genuine two-party system in the South. But is this what the future holds?

The present structure of southern politics—massive "Presidential Republicanism" combined with Democratic dominance of state, local, and congressional politics—could conceivably continue more or less indefinitely. The contrary view that Republican presidential voting inevitably must "filter down" to state, local, and congressional races until a genuine two-party system emerges at all levels of politics is, after all, merely a plausible hypothesis. The world can be a pretty implausible place, especially when race and politics mix. The heavy Republican vote for president in recent years may have been the result of the appeals of particular candidates and transitory issues that have left few permanent marks on the body politic. Once Eisenhower, Korea, the Catholic issue, and Goldwater have passed from the scene, the straying Democrats may return, chastened but still welcome, to the tolerant ranks of Democracy.

In this chapter we shall examine these possibilities—relying primarily on our interviews with random samples of Negroes and whites conducted a few months after the 1960 presidential election and similar interviews conducted by the Survey Research Center, University of Michigan, during and after the Johnson-Goldwater battle of 1964.

## Party identification

"Belonging" to a political party in America is a casual affair. There is no universally accepted way of determining who is a Democrat and who is a Republican. The most useful approach is to define as Democrats or Republicans those who *think* of themselves as Democrats or Republicans. Rather than slicing the electorate in two, we can think of the electorate as ranging along a continuum: from those most strongly identified with the Democratic party; through decreasing states of emotional commitment to those who identify with neither party; and then, in gradually increasing degrees, to those who identify strongly with the Republican party.[5]

Southern whites and Negroes are arranged along such a continuum in Table 13–1. Despite heavy defections to the Republicans in recent presidential

TABLE  13–1.  *Party identification of southerners, 1961 and 1964, by race*

| PARTY IDENTIFICATION | WHITE | | NEGRO | |
|---|---|---|---|---|
| | *1961* | *1964* | *1961* | *1964* |
| Strong Democrat | 29% | 35% | 28% | 53% |
| Weak Democrat | 32 | 29 | 23 | 23 |
| Independent, closer to Democrats | 7 | 6 | 8 | 2 |
| Independent | 7 | 8 | 5 | 9 |
| Independent, closer to Republicans | 5 | 6 | 4 | 1.5 |
| Weak Republican | 6 | 7 | 7 | 1.5 |
| Strong Republican | 8 | 7 | 3 | 1 |
| Apolitical | 5 | 1 | 20 | 7 |
| Other, minor party | a | a | 0 | 0 |
| Don't know, refusal, no answer | 1 | a | 2 | 2 |
| TOTAL | 100% | 99%[b] | 100% | 100% |
| N | 694 | 288 | 618 | 198 |

[a] Greater than 0, less than 0.5 per cent.
[b] The second column does not add to 100 because of rounding.

elections, southerners are still very heavily Democratic in their party identification. In early 1961, a little over 60 per cent of the southern whites thought of themselves as either "strong" or "not so strong" Democrats, compared to about 14 per cent who thought of themselves as Republican in some degree. Southern Negroes showed equal disdain for the party of Lincoln (and Earl Warren). Only about 10 per cent of the voting-age Negroes called themselves strong or weak Republicans, while slightly over half considered themselves Democrats.[6] The small differences in party preferences between Negroes and

[5] This approach has been pioneered by the Survey Research Center. See A. Campbell, et al., *The American Voter* (New York: John Wiley and Sons, 1960), ch. 6. The legal definition of party membership is official party registration. This definition contains many anomalies [see E. E. Schattschneider, *Party Government* (New York: Holt, Rinehart and Winston, 1942), pp. 53–61] and is difficult to apply in the South, because not all states have formal voter-registration systems and most Negroes are not registered to vote.

[6] In early 1961, 78 per cent of southern whites who said they were registered to vote were registered as Democrats. Eighty-three per cent of southern Negro voters were so registered. For additional details on party registration, see our "Southern Images of Political Parties: An Analysis of White and Negro Attitudes," *Journal of Politics*, Vol. 26 (1964), pp. 89–91. This article was reprinted in A. Leiserson (ed.), *The American South in the 1960's* (New York: Frederick A. Praeger, 1964).

whites result primarily from the fact that 20 per cent of the Negroes were unable to classify themselves along the partisan continuum, whereas only 5 per cent of the whites were equally "apolitical." When these respondents—for whom politics has almost no psychological reality anyway—are ignored, the differences between the two races in the distribution of party identification are almost entirely eliminated.

*Almost four years later—at the very time Goldwater was capturing 49 per cent of Dixie's popular vote—the proportion of whites thinking of themselves as Democrats seems to have increased from 61 to 64 per cent!* In addition, Negro Republicanism was pretty well wiped out by the Goldwater campaign; the 10 per cent of southern Negroes identifying with the Republican party in 1961 had shrunk to 2.5 per cent by 1964. The number of Negro "apoliticals" declined sharply during the same three or four years, too, from about 20 per cent to 7 per cent. The percentage of the region's Negroes identifying with the Democrat party jumped from 51 per cent in 1961 to 76 per cent in 1964.

Thus we find a large majority of all southerners, regardless of race, identified with the Democratic party. This consensus between southern Negroes and whites is amazing, even to those hardened to the vagaries of American politics. The sharpest and most divisive conflict in American politics exists between those same southern Negroes and whites. About 70 per cent of the white Democrats believe in "strict segregation" of the races, a belief that is concurred in by only about 14 per cent of their Negro fellow Democrats (see Figure 13–2). Or, to look at it the other way, only 6 per cent of the white Democrats

FIGURE 13–2.    *Relationships between party identification and other attitudes of southerners, by race*

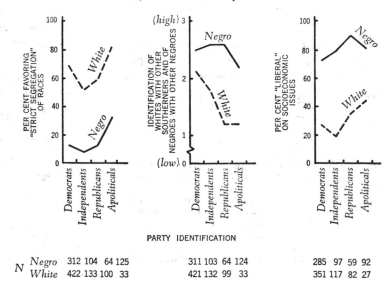

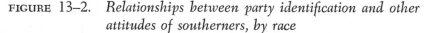

| | | | | | | | | | | | |
|---|---|---|---|---|---|---|---|---|---|---|---|
| N | Negro | 312 | 104 | 64 | 125 | 311 | 103 | 64 | 124 | 285 | 97 | 59 | 92 |
| | White | 422 | 133 | 100 | 33 | 421 | 132 | 99 | 33 | 351 | 117 | 82 | 27 |

agree with the nearly 80 per cent of Negro Democrats who say that integration is desirable. A majority of whites in the South prefer strict segregation, but the size of the majority depends on their party identification. Next to the white "apoliticals," the white Democrats are the most segregationist group in the electorate, while the Negro Democrats are as strongly in favor of racial integration as are other Negroes.

The anomaly is underscored by other findings. Among whites, identification with the Democratic party is positively associated with identification with the South as a region.[7] Indeed, white Democrats are almost twice as likely as white Republicans to "feel close to" other southerners. Negroes, regardless of party identification, feel much closer to Negroes than to other people. Indeed, they are even more self-conscious about their "Negro-ness" than whites are about their "southern-ness." Thus the southern Negroes' overwhelming identification with the Democratic party is not a result of indifference to the fortunes of their own race.

Perhaps we can account for this massive political miscegenation on the basis of perceived common interest in "bread-and-butter" social-welfare issues. The data summarized in Figure 13–2 do not seem to support this possibility. In both races, the Republicans are, on the average, a little more "liberal" than the Democrats. But these differences are small enough to suggest that party identification is not strongly and consistently linked with social-welfare liberalism among either whites or Negroes in the South. Southern Negroes, regardless of their party identification, tend to be "liberal"; southern whites, regardless of their party identification, tend to be more conservative. The Negroes are so much more liberal than the whites that the most conservative partisan grouping of Negroes contains twice the proportion of liberals as the most liberal partisan grouping of whites. Perhaps nowhere is the cliché about bedfellows in politics more true than in the South today.

Party identification usually represents a standing decision—*ceteris paribus*— to support the party's candidates. This is true in the South as well as in the rest of the country (see Figure 13–3). But if the correspondence between party identification and voting were perfect, the recent history of the South would have to be rewritten. In fact, it is not perfect. In 1960 Kennedy failed to gain the votes of 10 per cent of the white strong Democrats, and over a third of the ballots cast by white weak Democrats went to Nixon. While Nixon managed to hold the support of almost all the strong Republicans and white not-so-strong Republicans, Kennedy made heavy inroads into the less strongly partisan Negro Republicans. And in 1964, Barry Goldwater and his "southern strategy" temporarily reduced the predictive power of party identification to zero for southern Negroes by driving virtually all southern Negroes, *including the Republicans*, into voting for L.B.J.

Under more normal circumstances, however, defections among strong par-

[7] See Appendix C for the construction of all indices used in this passage and in Figure 13–2.

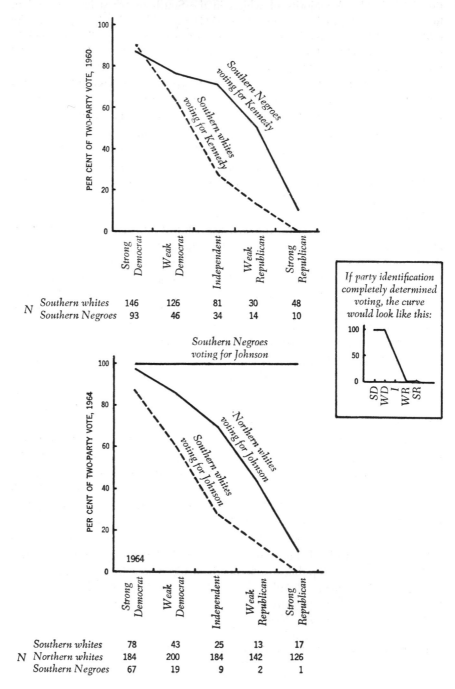

FIGURE 13–3. *Party identification and presidential voting
in 1960 and 1964*

Southern Negroes voting for Kennedy

Southern whites voting for Kennedy

PER CENT OF TWO-PARTY VOTE, 1960

| | Strong Democrat | Weak Democrat | Independent | Weak Republican | Strong Republican |
|---|---|---|---|---|---|
| N Southern whites | 146 | 126 | 81 | 30 | 48 |
| Southern Negroes | 93 | 46 | 34 | 14 | 10 |

If party identification
completely determined
voting, the curve
would look like this:

Southern Negroes
voting for Johnson

Northern whites
voting for Johnson

Southern whites
voting for Johnson

PER CENT OF TWO-PARTY VOTE, 1964

1964

| | Strong Democrat | Weak Democrat | Independent | Weak Republican | Strong Republican |
|---|---|---|---|---|---|
| Southern whites | 78 | 43 | 25 | 13 | 17 |
| N Northern whites | 184 | 200 | 184 | 142 | 126 |
| Southern Negroes | 67 | 19 | 9 | 2 | 1 |

tisans—be they white or Negro, Democrat or Republican—are few. Most of those who vote contrary to their party identification are relatively lukewarm partisans. Even so, *southern whites consistently vote less Democratic than do southern Negroes or northern whites with the same direction and strength of party identification.* Thus the political behavior of southern whites has been characterized, at one and the same time, by stable party identification and rising Republican voting. How this is possible, and what permanent effects this touch of political schizophrenia may have on the region's party system, still remain to be explained. The concept of "party image" is central to an understanding of both these problems.

## *The concept of "party image"*

American political parties speak with many voices. The national Democratic and Republican parties are loose confederations of state and local organizations, and they are normally divided into competing "wings" and "factions" at each level of government. The understandable tendency for all these party groups to avoid clear-cut or extreme policy stands contributes to the confusion. Confronted with this ambiguity, voters can have quite different pictures of what the parties are like. Thus, for example, a white mail-carrier in rural Georgia said, while trying to define the differences between the Democratic and Republican parties: "I think if you'd put them in a sack and shake them up you wouldn't know which . . . jump[ed] out first." A retired carpenter near by disagreed. "They's a difference, Lawd, yes. The main difference is the Republicans believe in a lot of hard harsh things and the Democrats in good living, good jobs, and good times."

Others were less certain. A 70-year-old dowager in Florida said, "The name [Republican] offends my sensibilities but actually in some ways it is more like the old Democratic party I once believed in." In Little Rock, Arkansas, a 60-year-old woman also was puzzled: "I was always raised a Democrat. I used to think Republicans made depressions, but Eisenhower didn't make one. But I don't believe he was a real Republican." "The Republicans freed the niggers, didn't they?" asked a Virginia farmer defiantly. "And they uphold the nigger." But recent events—among them four civil rights acts passed by Democratic congresses, a Democratic president who ordered troops to protect a Negro student at "Ole Miss," and a Republican candidate who based his campaign for the presidency on a covert appeal to racial prejudice—may have shaken even this article of faith.

Southern Negroes seem just as perplexed for sometimes opposite reasons. "The southern Democrats fight civil rights," according to a Negro college student in North Carolina. A Negro sharecropper in Georgia looked at the parties differently. He was a Republican until ". . . President Roosevelt brought us out, the Negro out in the world. I figured I should be what my daddy was. [But] President Roosevelt did a miracle, put bread in our mouths. Hoover put money in his own pocket and nobody else's." A Negro brick-maker in Florida said that he liked the Republican party ". . . because I am an old man and I believe in old things. And to my weak judgment the Republicans always did more for the colored people than the Democratic people." But another elderly Negro, this one a Democrat in Tennessee, said, ". . . I know they say the Republicans freed the slaves . . . [but] to me they are not free yet."

These mental pictures of party—vague, often confused and contradictory—we shall call "party images." Party image is not the same thing as party identification. Although the two concepts obviously are related, two people may identify with the same party but have different mental pictures of it and evaluate these pictures in different ways. Party identification is no doubt the more basic and less changeful of the two—the evidence is overwhelming that it is formed early in life and does not easily or often change.[8] But, while party image is not so deeply rooted or so stable as party identification, it is likely to be less ephemeral than voter attitudes toward the issues and candidates of specific campaigns.[9]

Perhaps the seemingly impossible Democratic coalition of southern Negroes and white segregationists, and the large deficit of Democratic presidential voters as compared to Democratic party identifiers, are explained by the different pictures of the parties that southerners carry around in their heads. And perhaps, too, these images will reveal things about the political future of the region that exclusive attention to party voting or party identification will not.[10]

## Southern images of the political parties

When asked early in 1961 if there was "anything in particular you like" or "don't like" about the political parties, about a third of both races (31 per cent of the whites, 33 per cent of the Negroes) could not mention a single thing

[8] H. Hyman, *Political Socialization* (Glencoe, Ill.: The Free Press, 1959); H. McClosky and H. E. Dahlgren, "Primary Group Influence on Party Loyalty," *American Political Science Review*, Vol. 53 (1959), pp. 757–76; F. I. Greenstein, *Children and Politics* (New Haven, Conn.: Yale University Press, 1965).

[9] Because most studies of attitudes toward political parties are carried out during election campaigns, they exaggerate the respondents' comments on transient and particular issues and personalities. For a study of relatively stable images of political parties, data such as ours, collected during a noncampaign period, offer distinct advantages. Even though attitudes toward specific issues and party leaders are an important component of party images, they can be built into the overall concept of the party as an enduring organization. Although the Survey Research Center does not specifically use the concept of party images, its analysis of perceptions of parties and party attitudes is similar. See Campbell *et al., op. cit.*, chs. 3–4.

[10] For an illustration of how exclusive concentration on either party *voting* or party *identification* can lead to seemingly contradictory results, see D. S. Strong, "Durable Republicanism in the South," and P. E. Converse, "A Major Political Realignment in the South?" in A. Sindler, *op. cit.*, pp. 174–94, 195–222.

they liked or disliked about either one.[11] Almost four years later, a different sample was asked the same series of questions in the midst of the Johnson-Goldwater presidential campaign. During this peak period of political concern, 18 per cent of the whites and 21 per cent of the Negroes still were unable to name or evaluate any attribute of either party. For this sizable minority of southerners, party politics either does not exist or is entirely devoid of content. They perceive the chief links between the mass of the people and their government dimly if at all. One would ordinarily assume—on the bases of their lower educational and status levels and their systematic exclusion from the political arena for over half a century—that this cognitively deprived group would consist primarily of Negroes. It does not. Negroes as a group have as fully developed images of the two parties as do southern whites, despite these handicaps. Their party images, however, are by no means identical to those of their white neighbors.

In 1961 both races had essentially favorable attitudes toward the Democratic party. The white respondents liked almost twice as many things as they disliked about the Democrats and disliked almost twice as many things as they liked about the Republican party. The Negroes were even more favorably inclined toward the Democratic party: they mentioned more than six favorable attitudes toward the Democrats for every unfavorable reference, and they took a somewhat dimmer view of the GOP than did the whites. Let us examine the content of these attitudes.

The most popular aspect of the Democratic party among white southerners was that the party is good to (or better for) the common people and the workingman (see Figure 13–4). Twenty-seven per cent of the white respondents with any image of the parties mentioned this as something they liked about the Democratic party; a very few of the whites—less than 2.5 per cent and mostly Republican—saw the party as being "too good to" or "bad for" the workers and common man. Thus the Democratic party was viewed and praised as the champion of the little man. Almost as many whites—19 per cent of those with party images—said that "conditions are good (or better) under the Democrats," and that the Democratic party brings higher wages, more jobs, and the like. Less than 1 per cent of the whites disagreed, and those who did disagree were more than 70 per cent Republican. These two points, plus traditional support for the party—"I'm just a Democrat," "I've always been a Democrat," views expressed by 24 per cent of the whites—dominate the southern whites' favorable images of the Democratic party.

The party's perceived liberalism and its dedication to social-welfare policies and government spending were much more controversial aspects of the Democratic image. Eleven per cent of the whites approved of this liberalism, 18 per cent complained that the party was too liberal, and less than 1 per cent said

[11] The questions were numbers 72–75 in the Negro Adult Questionnaire and 61–64 in the White. See Appendix B. The questions used by the SRC in 1964 were identical.

FIGURE 13–4. *Party images of southerners, by race, 1961*

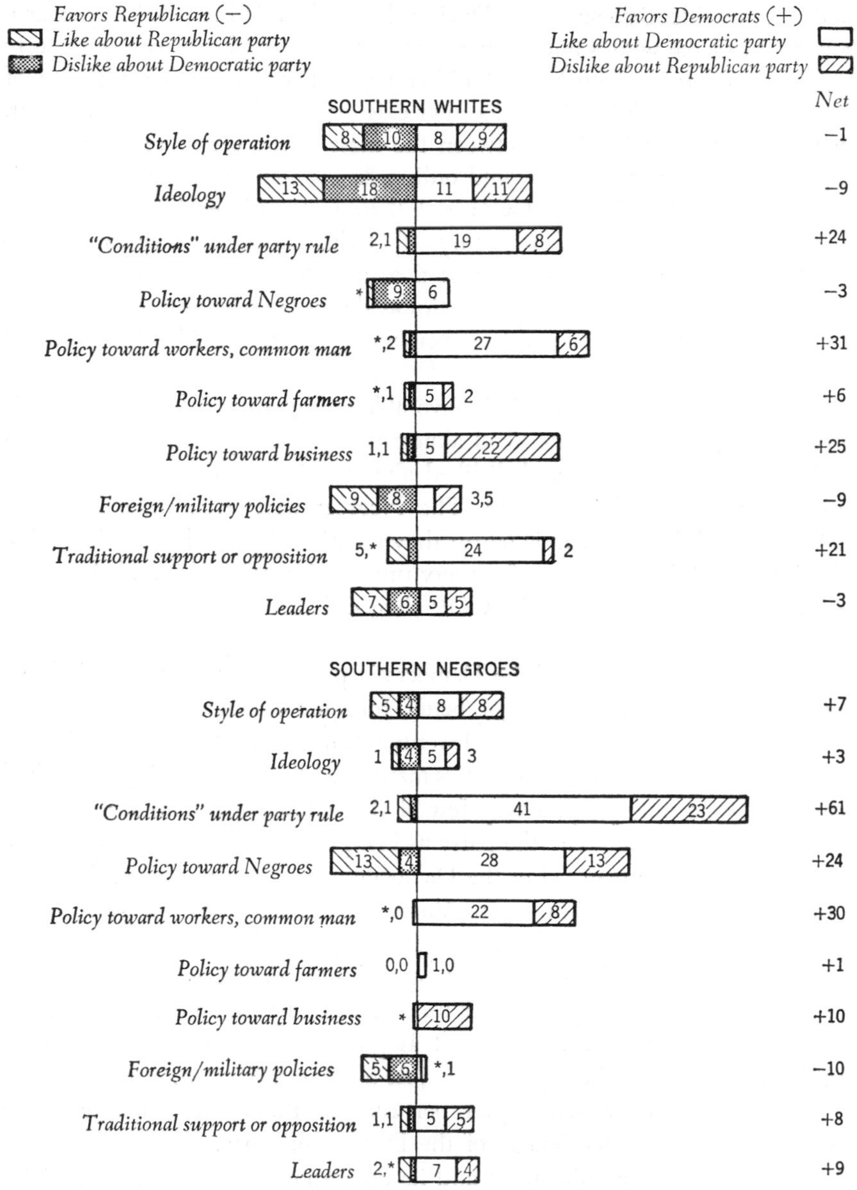

Favors Republican (−)
Like about Republican party
Dislike about Democratic party

Favors Democrats (+)
Like about Democratic party
Dislike about Republican party

SOUTHERN WHITES

| | | Net |
|---|---|---|
| Style of operation | 8  10  8  9 | −1 |
| Ideology | 13  18  11  11 | −9 |
| "Conditions" under party rule | 2,1  19  8 | +24 |
| Policy toward Negroes | *  9  6 | −3 |
| Policy toward workers, common man | *,2  27  6 | +31 |
| Policy toward farmers | *,1  5  2 | +6 |
| Policy toward business | 1,1  5  22 | +25 |
| Foreign/military policies | 9  8  3,5 | −9 |
| Traditional support or opposition | 5,*  24  2 | +21 |
| Leaders | 7  6  5  5 | −3 |

SOUTHERN NEGROES

| | | Net |
|---|---|---|
| Style of operation | 5  4  8  8 | +7 |
| Ideology | 1  4  5  3 | +3 |
| "Conditions" under party rule | 2,1  41  23 | +61 |
| Policy toward Negroes | 13  4  28  13 | +24 |
| Policy toward workers, common man | *,0  22  8 | +30 |
| Policy toward farmers | 0,0  1,0 | +1 |
| Policy toward business | *  10 | +10 |
| Foreign/military policies | 5  6  *,1 | −10 |
| Traditional support or opposition | 1,1  5  5 | +8 |
| Leaders | 2,*  7  4 | +9 |

NOTE: Numbers are percent of all those with party images.
* = 70.0 < 0.5%.

the party was too conservative. The net loss of party popularity as a result of the Democrats' association with economic liberalism is thus substantial.

The "style" of the Democratic party—the way in which it runs the government and manages its own internal affairs—was also more frequently a negative (10 per cent) than a positive (8 per cent) factor. Here the Independents seemed to be most impressed with the view that the Democrats were inefficient, dishonest, and undignified. Democratic leaders—the ones most frequently mentioned were recent Presidents, and almost all were national rather than regional or local figures—were a little more often disliked (6 per cent) than liked (5 per cent). Democratic foreign policy also was, on balance, a source of unpopularity among the few whites mentioning it at all.

But the most negative element in the Democratic image among white southerners was that it was "too good to Negroes"; 9 per cent of the whites with party images mentioned that they disliked this facet of the party, and not one volunteered that he approved of the party's racial policies. Moreover, this was the element most disliked by strong Democrats, and it was the second most unpopular aspect of the party among weak Democrats.

The Negro image of the Democratic party in 1961 had many similarities to that of the whites, along with significant differences. Forty-one per cent of the Negroes agreed with the whites that "conditions are good" under the Democrats. Not much of an argument was possible on this point among Negro southerners; Negro Republicans no less than Democrats believed it to be true. Negroes mentioned that the party was "good to workers" almost as often as did whites (22 per cent compared to 27 per cent). The overwhelming view was that the party was "good to Negroes"; 28 per cent mentioned this belief while only 4 per cent (mostly Independents and Republicans) disagreed. The whites who mentioned the party's racial policies agreed that Democrats were pro-Negro, but they unanimously deplored rather than applauded the fact.

A second major difference between the two races is that the Negro image of the Democratic party was far less ambivalent than that of the southern whites. The Negroes liked almost everything about the party as they saw it. Only in two categories of issues—foreign policy and relationships with big business —was the Negro image predominantly negative, and in neither case was the number of respondents mentioning the point large or the surplus of dislikes over likes substantial.

The attitudes of southern whites toward the Republican party in 1961 mirrored in neat reversal their views of the Democratic party. The same grounds for liking and disliking were mentioned, with each party seen as good where the other was bad. Because their net view of the Democrats was favorable, their net view of the Republicans emerges as quite unfavorable. The most frequently mentioned factor in 1961 was the charge that the Republicans were "too good to big business" (21 per cent). Associated dislikes

—that conditions are bad under the Republicans (8 per cent), that the Republican party is bad for workers (6 per cent) and farmers (7 per cent), and that it is too conservative (6 per cent)—round out this image of the Republican party as favorable to big business and opposed to the "common man." As would be expected, Democrats brought up most of these negative points.

Some elements of a political party's image—such as its general ideology—will repel some voters but attract others. So long as more voters are attracted than are repelled, the party gains from that element of its overall image. But other elements—such as corruption—will not have the quality of both attraction and repulsion; merely to hold this image is to dislike the party. Unfortunately for the Republicans in the South, several unfavorable elements in their image approach the second category—hardly anyone favors bad "conditions," favoritism toward big business, and unfavorable treatment of workers and farmers.

On the other hand, all the favorable elements in the Republican party's image were weakened by some unfavorable reactions to the same elements. The conservatism of the party on social-welfare questions provoked more favorable comment (13 per cent) than any other feature, but others cited the same features as one of the most objectionable aspects of Republicanism (11 per cent). Favorable comments on the foreign-military policies of the Republicans (9 per cent) more clearly outweigh unfavorable reaction (5 per cent) on the same point. This was the second most emphasized attraction of the Republican party for the white population as a whole, and it was also the factor most emphasized by those Democrats able to express any liking for the Republican party. Republican leaders are liked (7 per cent) more than they are disliked (5 per cent), but their style of operation received more unfavorable (9 per cent) than favorable (8 per cent) comment.

Southern Negroes took an even more unfavorable view of the Republican party in 1961 than southern whites did (see Figure 13-4). Lower levels of education are generally associated with reluctance to criticize, but 39 per cent of the Negro respondents (as great a proportion as among the whites) offered criticisms of the Republican party.[12] These criticisms almost completely overshadow their favorable comments. The best thing about the Republican party as seen by the southern Negro in 1961 was its policy toward Negroes. But even here the ratio of favorable to unfavorable comment was much smaller than for the Democratic party. Only one aspect of the Republican party—its foreign-military policies—gave it a clear net advantage among southern Negroes, and only 6 per cent of them mentioned foreign policy at all. The "party of Lincoln" was seen as the party of depression, big-business favoritism,

[12] This finding offers reassurance on the troublesome problem of "response set." Granted their lower educational levels, southern Negroes might be thought to be disposed toward positive rather than negative comment in general.

and mistreatment of workers. A 34-year-old Negro maid put a common perception of party differences this way:

> In my opinion the Republicans want everything for themselves and the other rich
> folks. The Democrats will help the poor folks and make them rich ones get up
> off . . . theirs to help, too. You know, if Eisenhower hadn't got out of that seat
> all of us would have been on the breadline.

In view of the South's political distinctiveness, the terms "Democratic party"
and "Republican party" might have a meaning for southerners different from
their meaning for other Americans. In praising the Democratic party,
southerners might have in mind a distinctly southern organization associated
with moonlight, magnolias, states' rights, and white supremacy. In disdaining
the Republican party, southerners might be reacting to an "outside" institution
associated with "The War" and venal carpetbaggers.

But this is not the case. Southern citizens clearly think of political parties
in national rather than regional or local terms. Not one respondent, when
asked to comment on the Democratic and Republican parties, requested the
interviewer to clarify what level of party organization he had in mind. Moreover, when we compare the images of the parties held by southerners with
those held by nonsoutherners, we discover that they are very similar.[13] Nonsouthern whites favored the Democratic party's liberalism and better treatment
of the common man more than southern whites did and tended to be more
critical of the Republican party's conservatism and pro-business bias. Neither
party received much criticism from northerners for being pro-Negro. Northern
Negroes cited traditional approval of the party more often, and service to
Negroes much less often, than did southern Negroes as a reason for liking
the Democrats. There was less unanimity in the North that "conditions" are
better under Democratic than Republican rule. But none of these differences
between northern and southern party images was large.

Not only is the *content* of northern and southern images very similar, but
so, too, is the pro-Democratic *direction* of party likes and dislikes. Table 13–2
summarizes the ratio of likes and dislikes of both parties by section and
race in 1961 and 1964. These ratios are virtually identical in both North
and South. The sole exception is that southern whites—especially in 1961—
were much more critical of the Republican party than were northern whites.
Otherwise, the overall pictures of the two parties are much the same above
and below the Mason-Dixon Line. The attitudinal differences between
southerners and nonsoutherners are much less acute than are the differences
between the party system of the South and the rest of the country. Political

[13] The data on attitudes toward parties of nonsoutherners used for comparative purposes
here are from the 1960 presidential election study of the Survey Research Center. We
give a complete report on the North-South comparisons in our "The Concept of
Party Image and Its Importance for the Southern Electorate," in K. Jennings and H.
Ziegler (eds.), *The Electoral Process* (Englewood Cliffs, N.J.: Prentice-Hall, 1966).

TABLE  13–2.   *Attitudes toward the Democratic and Republican parties:*
*ratio of likes to dislikes, 1961 and 1964,*
*by section and race*

|  | DEMOCRATIC PARTY | | REPUBLICAN PARTY | |
| --- | --- | --- | --- | --- |
| SECTION AND RACE | *1961* | *1964* | *1961* | *1964* |
| Southern whites | 1.7 | 1.2 | 0.6 | 0.8 |
| Northern whites | 1.6 | 1.4 | 1.2 | 0.9 |
| Southern Negroes | 6.2 | 13.3 | 0.4 | 0.1 |
| Northern Negroes | 5.8 | 13.2 | 0.5 | 0.2 |

NOTE: The data on 1961 northern attitudes are from the University of Michigan Survey Research Center's 1960 Presidential Study. All 1964 data are from the Center's Survey of that year.

institutions tend to become self-perpetuating, assuming new functions when they have met those for which they originally developed.[14] This may be what has happened to the one-party systems of most southern states. But now that southern attitudes are very similar to those that undergird two-party politics elsewhere in the country, the party systems of the South may be ripe for change.

# Changing party images: 1960–1964

"The campaign of 1964," Theodore H. White wrote in his *The Making of the President—1964*, "was that rare thing in American political history, a campaign based on issues. War and peace, the nature and role of government, the quality of life—all were discussed in a campaign that will leave its mark behind in American life for generations."[15]

Maybe so. But up to this point the evidence that the campaign had a lasting impact on southern politics is mixed. Barry Goldwater did poll a lot of votes in the South—but so did Hoover, Eisenhower, and Nixon. And so did J. Strom Thurmond as the Dixiecratic candidate in 1948. As we saw above, the effect of the Goldwater campaign on the party identification of southern whites was either negligible or negative. The Republican campaign of 1964, coupled with the heat and horror of "the Negro Revolution," apparently drove almost all southern Negroes out of the Republican party. But so few southern Negroes were Republicans before Goldwater that this was not a startling development, at least in quantitative terms. Perhaps Senator Goldwater and his "southern strategy" *did* alter southern images of the two political parties.

[14] See, for example, V. O. Key, Jr., *American State Politics: An Introduction* (New York: Alfred A. Knopf, 1956), p. 195, footnote 18.
[15] T. H. White, *op. cit.*, p. 294.

An analysis of interviews taken during the 1964 campaign by the Survey Research Center of the University of Michigan permits us to see how much southern party images were changed by the Johnson-Goldwater contest. To make it easier to summarize the rich detail of these interviews and to compare them with those taken in 1961, we devised an "index of party image" by counting each favorable attitude toward the Democratic party or unfavorable attitude toward the Republican party as +1 and by counting each unfavorable Democratic or favorable Republican reference as —1. Because we coded as many as four "likes" and four "dislikes" for each party, the index of party attitudes for each respondent ranges from +8 (most pro-Democratic) to —8 (most pro-Republican).[16] The results are shown in Table 13–3.

TABLE 13–3.  *Changes in party images, 1961–1964, by race*

| INDEX OF PARTY IMAGE | SOUTHERN NEGROES | | SOUTHERN WHITES | |
|---|---|---|---|---|
| | *1961* | *1964* | *1961* | *1964* |
| Strongly pro-Democratic (+3 and up) | 24% | 52% | 23% | 23% |
| Mildly pro-Democratic (+1 or +2) | 52 | 42 | 39 | 29 |
| Neutral (0) | 14 | 3 | 11 | 11 |
| Mildly pro-Republican (—1 or —2) | 8 | 3 | 18 | 19 |
| Strongly pro-Republican (—3 down) | 2 | 0 | 9 | 18 |
| TOTAL | 100% | 100% | 100% | 100% |
| N | 415 | 157 | 479 | 236 |

NOTE: Percentages are of those persons with party images.

The most obvious finding is that the party images of southerners changed sharply between early 1961 and late 1964. The proportion of southern Negroes with strongly pro-Democratic images more than doubled, from 24 to 52 per cent. By 1964, 94 per cent of the southern Negroes with party images had generally favorable attitudes toward the Democratic party whereas only 3 per cent had pro-Republican images. But 1964 was not an unmitigated Republican disaster in the South. Although the Republicans were unable to shake the overwhelming emotional identification of southern whites with the Democratic party, they did gain a great deal of ground in altering party images

---

[16] Up to five "likes" or "dislikes" were coded by the SRC in 1964, so the theoretical maximum and minimum scores for that year were ±10. This difference in coding procedures might have affected the comparability of the 1961 and 1964 data by inflating the value of extremist respondents in the latter year, except for the fact that so few respondents mentioned more than four "likes" or "dislikes." Only one white and one Negro respondent obtained a (net) party-image score higher than ±8.

among the whites. The proportion of southern whites with strongly pro-Republican party images doubled between 1961 and 1964, from 9 to 18 per cent. The number of southern whites with pro-Democratic images declined from 62 to 52 per cent over the same four-year period. Most of these gains, it should be noted, seem to have come at the expense of mildly favorable images of the Democratic party; the proportion of the southern whites with strongly pro-Democratic images remained at 23 per cent from shortly after the election of President Kennedy through the Johnson-Goldwater campaign.

The increase in pro-Democratic images of southern Negroes was not merely the result of growing Democratic party identification. When we look at the changes in Negro party images, with party identification controlled (Table 13–4), we see a rather steady increase of about 10 percentage points in the

TABLE 13–4. *Changes in southern party images, 1961–1964, by race and party identification*

| RACE AND PARTY IDENTIFICATION | PERCENTAGE WITH PRO-DEMOCRATIC IMAGES | | MEAN PARTY-IMAGE SCORE | | N | |
|---|---|---|---|---|---|---|
| | *1961* | *1964* | *1961* | *1964* | *1961* | *1964* |
| NEGRO | | | | | | |
| Strong Democrats | 86% | 96% | + 2.2 | + 3.4 | 152 | 98 |
| Weak Democrats | 84 | 92 | + 1.8 | + 2.8 | 115 | 37 |
| Independents | 77 | 93 | + 1.4 | + 2.3 | 74 | 15 |
| Republicans | 27 | a | − 0.4 | a | 44 | 3 |
| WHITE | | | | | | |
| Strong Democrats | 87% | 80% | + 2.3 | + 2.2 | 175 | 96 |
| Weak Democrats | 71 | 52 | + 1.0 | + 0.4 | 145 | 65 |
| Independents | 40 | 24 | − 0.6 | − 1.3 | 73 | 41 |
| Republicans | 13 | 3 | − 1.4 | − 2.8 | 77 | 35 |

a Too few cases to compute percentages or mean.

proportion of Negroes with pro-Democratic images, be they strong Democrats, weak Democrats, Independents, or Republicans.

Although southern whites showed no significant changes in party identification during the same period, their party images did shift toward the Republicans. The drop-off in the proportion of southern whites with pro-Democratic images was most acute among the weak Democrats (19 percentage points) and Independents (16 percentage points). Among the strong Democrats, the Democrats fared better, with a loss of 7 percentage points. Only 13 per cent of the Republicans had held pro-Democratic images in 1961; this minority had shrunk to a miniscule 3 per cent by 1964. These changes in party image help to account for the shift of southern whites to Republican voting in recent presidential elections. For an understanding of changes in voting behavior,

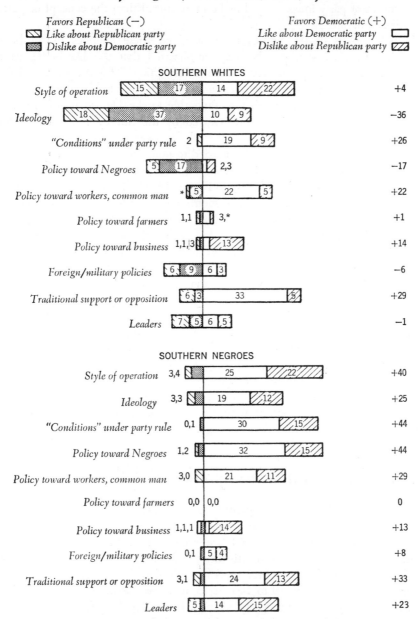

FIGURE 13–5. *Party images of southerners, 1964, by race*

*Favors Republican (−)*
⬒ *Like about Republican party*
▨ *Dislike about Democratic party*

*Favors Democratic (+)*
*Like about Democratic party* ▭
*Dislike about Republican party* ▨

**SOUTHERN WHITES**

| | |
|---|---|
| *Style of operation* 15 17 14 22 | +4 |
| *Ideology* 18 37 10 9 | −36 |
| *"Conditions" under party rule* 2 19 9 | +26 |
| *Policy toward Negroes* 5 17 2,3 | −17 |
| *Policy toward workers, common man* * 5 22 5 | +22 |
| *Policy toward farmers* 1,1 3,* | +1 |
| *Policy toward business* 1,1,3 13 | +14 |
| *Foreign/military policies* 6 9 6 3 | −6 |
| *Traditional support or opposition* 6 3 33 5 | +29 |
| *Leaders* 7 5 6 5 | −1 |

**SOUTHERN NEGROES**

| | |
|---|---|
| *Style of operation* 3,4 25 22 | +40 |
| *Ideology* 3,3 19 12 | +25 |
| *"Conditions" under party rule* 0,1 30 15 | +44 |
| *Policy toward Negroes* 1,2 32 15 | +44 |
| *Policy toward workers, common man* 3,0 21 11 | +29 |
| *Policy toward farmers* 0,0 0,0 | 0 |
| *Policy toward business* 1,1,1 14 | +13 |
| *Foreign/military policies* 0,1 5 4 | +8 |
| *Traditional support or opposition* 3,1 24 13 | +33 |
| *Leaders* 5 14 15 | +23 |

NOTE: Numbers are percent of all those with party images.
* = 70.0 < 0.5%.

the concept of party image may thus be more useful than the concept of party identification.

Which aspects of the parties brought about these changes in southern attitudes? In 1961 southern Negroes emphasized that the Democrats were the better of the two parties for economic "conditions," for Negroes, and for the workingman. By comparison, the comments of southern Negroes on other aspects of the parties—although also favorable to the Democrats—were few. In 1964 the southern Negroes interviewed by the Survey Research Center felt even more strongly than before that the Democrats were better for their race and its problems, but they also tended to praise the Democrats and damn the Republicans more often than before because of their style, ideology, foreign and military policies, and leaders (see Figure 13–5). There was also a sharp increase in the number of Negroes mentioning "tradition" as a reason for favoring the Democrats. The national Democratic party's record on civil rights was the major cause of the increasingly favorable attitudes of southern Negroes toward the party, but this civil rights record resulted in *generalized approval* of the party and its ways, not just an improved image in the civil rights field.

The major shifts in party images among whites were more focused. The number of southern whites who said they disliked the Democratic party because it was "too liberal" increased from 18 to 37 per cent; the proportion specifically mentioning that the Democratic party was too pro-Negro for their taste increased from 9 to 17 per cent. A slight growth also appeared in generalized disapproval of the party's handling of "gut and group" issues—policies toward workers, farmers, and business. But everywhere else the party either held its own or slightly improved its position among the mass of white southerners. The growing white discontent with the Democratic party, then, seems restricted to the areas of race and ideology.

## Party images, party identification, and the vote

Do changes in images of the political parties help explain the recent voting behavior of southerners? The relationships between party images and presidential voting for 1960 and 1964 are presented in Figure 13–6. Clearly, southerners' perceptions of and attitudes toward the parties are closely linked to their presidential voting preferences (with the obvious exception of the Negroes in 1964). From 70 to 100 per cent of both white and Negro voters voted in each year for the party about which they had favorable images. A comparison of Figure 13–6 with Figure 13–3 indicates that party-image scores were, at least for these two elections, more predictive of presidential voting than was party identification. Note, for example, that the difference in voting behavior between Negroes and whites with the same party identification is large in both 1960 and 1964, but that the difference in the way

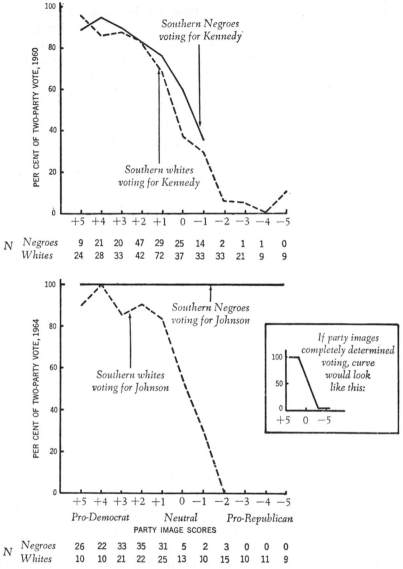

FIGURE 13–6. *Party images and presidential voting in 1960 and 1964*

Negroes and whites with the same party-image scores voted in either year is much smaller.

But we must offer several caveats. First, we do not know whether party images "cause" partisan voting or vice versa; all we know is that the people who vote for a presidential candidate tend to have a favorable image of the party that nominated him. These favorable perceptions of party could quite possibly have developed *after* the decision to vote for the candidate had been made on some other grounds. But regardless of which is cause and which effect, *a vote for a presidential candidate seems to leave favorable stereotypes of his party which survive beyond the duration of the campaign and election.* Since we are interested in the impact of recent elections and events on the

TABLE 13–5.   *Percentage of southern Negroes and whites voting Democratic in presidential elections, 1960 and 1964, by party identification and party images*

| | WHITE | | NEGRO | |
|---|---|---|---|---|
| YEAR AND PARTY IDENTIFICATION | Pro-Democratic images | Neutral or Pro-Republican images | Pro-Democratic images | Neutral or Pro-Republican images |
| *1960* | | | | |
| Strong Democrat | 94% (113) | 72% (18) | 90% (69) | 85% (13) |
| Weak Democrat | 75 (65) | 30 (27) | 87 (32) | 62 (8) |
| Independent | 38 (13) | 13 (38) | 70 (20) | 50 (8) |
| Republican | 12 (8) | 4 (55) | 50 (4) | 8 (13) |
| *1964* | | | | |
| Strong Democrat | 94% (63) | 54% (13) | | |
| Weak Democrat | 81 (21) | 33 (5) | | |
| Independent | 67 (3) | 11 (18) | | |
| Republican | — | 4 (26) | | |

NOTE: All Negroes in 1964 sample voted Democratic. Percentages are of two-party vote.

southern party system, rather than in explaining the voters' choices, this is all we want and need to know.

A second point to keep in mind in interpreting these data on party images and the vote is that, most of the time, a person's party images are congruent with his party identification: those who think of themselves as Democrats or Republicans usually view the party with which they identify more favorably than they view its electoral opponent (see Table 13–4, for example). Yet under the special circumstances of the contemporary South, this correspondence is by no means perfect. And, as Table 13–5 shows, the relationship between party images and the vote is *not* just the result of the close correlation between party images and party identification. When we look at the relationship between party images and presidential voting while holding party identification constant, we still find a strong relationship between party images and the vote. Ninety-four per cent of the white strong Democrats in 1960, for example, voted for Kennedy if they also had favorable images of the Democratic party. Only 72 per cent of the same group who had neutral or pro-Republican images stuck with J.F.K. If we look at the white weak Democrats in 1960, we see that 75 per cent of those with pro-Democratic images voted for Kennedy while only 30 per cent of those *without* pro-Democratic images did! We can see the same tendency among the Negroes in 1960, although in a much less extreme form.

Perhaps the most interesting comparisons suggested by Table 13–5 are between the whites in the two different election years. The strong Democrats with pro-Democratic images voted overwhelmingly for both Kennedy and Johnson. The weak Democrats with pro-Democratic images were less unanimous, but they were still heavily Democratic in both years (75 per cent in 1960; 81 per cent in 1964). The Democratic identifiers without pro-Democratic party images, however, show clear signs of having broken away from the party in their presidential voting as well as in their party perceptions. In 1960 most defectors were weak Democrats without pro-Democratic images. By 1964, however, even the *strong* Democrats with neutral or pro-Republican party images seemed to be drifting away from the party. Although 54 per cent of them still voted for Johnson, this was 40 percentage points below the Democratic vote of the strong Democrats with pro-Democratic party images.[17]

# Conclusions: The prospects for two-party politics in the South

What, then, are the prospects for the development of a real two-party system in the South? Were the heavy votes for Republican presidential candidates in recent years merely the result of such transitory factors as the nature of the candidates and the issues? Or is the South experiencing a more basic change, a shift in party loyalties and voting habits?

## THE FUTURE OF THE NEGRO VOTE

First, the Democratic bias of Negro southerners is so overwhelming that few of them are likely to shift permanently to the Republican camp in the foreseeable future. Not only are they heavily and increasingly Democratic in their party identification, but their images of the parties are extraordinarily favorable to the Democrats and hostile to the GOP. And those southern

---

[17] The index of party image counts each expression of party attitude equally. In fact, some party attitudes are more closely related to presidential voting than others. See D. R. Matthews and J. W. Prothro, *op. cit.*, pp. 100–4.

Negroes who have voted in recent presidential elections voted even more heavily Democratic than their party identifications and images require. As more southern Negroes vote in the future, they can be expected to swell the Democratic ranks under normal circumstances—a fact that has not escaped the attention of the Kennedy and Johnson administrations' civil rights strategists.[18] On the other hand, southern Negroes are peculiarly sensitive to a single issue—civil rights—and this makes them much less "safe" for the Democrats in individual elections than they otherwise would be. The aspect of the Democratic party image that apparently lost the Democrats more Negro votes than any other in 1960 was the belief—confined to a very few Negroes— that they were not so pro-civil rights as the Republicans.[19] The significant shift to Eisenhower in 1956 was caused by the belief that neither Stevenson nor the Democratic party was sound, from the Negro viewpoint, on the race issue.[20]

Yet the Negro Democrats who voted Republican in either 1956 or 1960 have retained their favorable attitudes toward the Democratic party despite their defections (see Table 13–7). Only if the Republican party is somehow able to improve its image among southern Negroes will these occasional defections solidify into Republican identification and a "normal" Republican vote. Given the nomination of Goldwater in 1964, the congruence of the Negroes' pro-Democratic views on civil rights with their other attitudes about the parties, and the Republican party's increasing voting strength among white southerners, the GOP does not seem likely to capture much continuing Negro support. A more likely alternative would be growing Negro Independence. A faint trend in this direction is discernible among those few Negroes who have ever changed their party identification (see Table 13–6), but even these new Negro Independents are far more favorably inclined toward the Democratic than the Republican party.

### SOUTHERN WHITES AND PARTISANSHIP: STABILITY AND CHANGE

The partisan future of southern whites is much more problematical. Although the South seems irrevocably committed to two-party politics in presidential elections, the vast majority of southern whites retain their emotional identification with the Democratic party even though some of them have not supported its presidential candidate for a decade or more. This has seriously inhibited Republican gains in state and local politics and the growth of two-partyism at all levels of the ballot.

Only about 15 per cent of the white respondents in 1961 reported ever having changed their party identification. Of those who have changed, about

[18] See L. E. Lomax, "The Kennedys Move in on Dixie," *Harper's*, May 1962, pp. 27–33.
[19] Matthews and Prothro, *op. cit.*, p. 103, table 6.
[20] See H. L. Moon, "The Negro Vote in the Presidential Election of 1956," *The Journal of Negro Education*, Vol. 26 (1957), pp. 219–30.

TABLE 13–6.   *Changes in party identification of southerners, by race, and mean party-image scores of changers*

| PATTERN OF CHANGE IN IDENTIFICATION | WHITE | | NEGRO | |
|---|---|---|---|---|
| | Percentage | Mean Score | Percentage | Mean Score |
| Republican to Democrat | 17% | + 1.7 | 42% | + 2.0 |
| Democrat to Republican to Democrat | 15 | + 0.8 | 0 | — |
| Republican to Independent | 11 | − 0.6 | 11 | + 0.4 |
| Independent to Republican to Independent | 1 | a | 0 | — |
| Republican to Apolitical | 0 | — | 1 | a |
| Democrat to Apolitical | 2 | a | 6 | + 1.0 |
| Independent to Democrat to Independent | 1 | a | 0 | — |
| Democrat to Independent | 39 | − 1.1 | 21 | + 1.9 |
| Republican to Democrat to Republican | 0 | — | 1 | a |
| Democrat to Republican | 14 | − 1.6 | 18 | − 0.1 |
| TOTAL | 100% | | 100% | |
| N | 100 | | 81 | |

a Too few cases for computing mean.
NOTE: Based on 1961 data; too few cases in 1964 to permit analysis.

14 per cent changed from Democratic to Republican and 17 per cent from Republican to Democratic (see Table 13–6). Another 15 per cent of the whites have wavered—starting out their political lives as Democrats, switching to the Republicans, and then switching back to the Democrats. The small net effects of these changes among southern whites are in sharp contrast to the massive shifts in party identification that some have read into recent presidential election returns. Among those who have changed from a party identification to self-classification as Independents or Apoliticals, on the other hand, the Democrats are the heavy losers. If this net movement from Democratic to Independent is viewed as a transitional stage en route to identification with the Republicans, then the long-run prospects for the Republican party appear brighter. This, in fact, would seem likely to be the case among the whites. The whites who have changed from Democratic to Independent have a mean party-image score of −1.1, almost as pro-Republican a score as those who have been Republicans all their lives (mean score, −1.4). Even the white Republicans who have changed to Independent are more favorably inclined toward the GOP than toward the Democrats.

Remember, however, that these are changes in party identification that have occurred over the *entire lifetime* of the respondents. The very small percentage of southerners who have ever changed their party identification means that the net movement would make only small and slow changes in the overwhelmingly pro-Democratic distribution of southern party loyalties. On this level, the Republican tide is sweeping over Dixie at glacial speed.

But a southerner's *party identification* does not tell us how he evaluates the parties today. Party identification is not easily changed. *Attitudes toward the parties* are more volatile than party identification, even though they are less transitory than reactions to the events and personalities of specific campaigns. Thus "party images" *are* changing within the white electorate of the South—and changing toward a more favorable view of the GOP. A majority of southern whites still view the Democratic party as the better of the two parties, but the gap is narrowing and negative images of the Democratic party and positive attitudes toward the Republican party have grown at a lively pace in recent years—especially when compared to the stability of party identification.

Those southern voters with the least favorable attitudes toward the Democrats, or the most favorable attitudes toward the Republicans, are the most likely to vote Republican *regardless of their party identification*. Table 13–7 gives the mean party-image scores of Democratic identifiers by their presidential vote in 1956 and 1960. Among whites, those who voted for both Stevenson and Kennedy have the most favorable image of the Democratic party. Those who broke away from the Democratic party in 1956 to vote for Eisenhower and then returned to the fold with Kennedy in 1960 have almost as favorable an image of their own party, a fact which suggests that many southerners agree with the lady quoted earlier who said that Ike was not a "real" Republican. A vote for Nixon by a white Democrat who supported Stevenson is associated with a low pro-Democratic party-image score,[21] while those who voted for both Eisenhower and Nixon actually have a slightly more favorable image of the Republican party than they do of the one with which they identify. The white Democrats who voted for Goldwater in 1964 have even more pro-

---

[21] P. F. Converse, *et al.*, "Stability and Change in 1960: A Reinstating Election," *American Political Science Review*, Vol. 55 (1961), pp. 269–80, stress the impact of Kennedy's Catholicism on the 1960 voting, especially in the South. But the low party-image scores of white Democrats for Nixon suggest that anti-Catholicism was not the only factor in the wholesale desertion of the Democratic party in favor of a man who clearly was a "real" Republican. Converse *et al.*, *op. cit.*, have shown that the more frequently a southern Protestant attended church, the more seriously he took the threat from Rome and the more likely he was to vote for Nixon over Kennedy. Our data show some tendency for images of the Democratic party to become less favorable as church attendance becomes more regular. These relationships may reflect an enduring suspicion among churchgoing Protestants toward the role of minority religious groups in the Democratic party, a suspicion that was merely heightened during the 1960 campaign. Or they may represent nothing more than the lingering effects of the singular importance of religion in the 1960 campaign, in which case the relevance of Protestant church attendance for party image may gradually diminish.

TABLE 13–7. *Mean party-image scores of white and Negro southern Democrats, by presidential vote in 1956 and 1960*

| | | MEAN PARTY-IMAGE SCORES | |
|---|---|---|---|
| *1956 vote* | *1960 vote* | *White* | *Negro* |
| Stevenson | Kennedy | + 2.1 (108) | + 2.2 (65) |
| Eisenhower | Kennedy | + 2.0 (45) | + 1.9 (39) |
| Stevenson | Nixon | + 1.1 (14) | + 2.2 (4) |
| Eisenhower | Nixon | − 0.5 (31) | + 0.2 (39) |

NOTE: The numbers in parentheses are cases on which the means were computed. "Strong" and "weak" Democrats were considered as Democrats.

Republican images—their mean score was −0.6, while the Democrats who voted for LBJ had a mean score of +2.2.

Thus the wholesale defections of white Democrats to the Republican party in recent presidential elections have left lasting marks. These dissident Democrats have party-image scores usually associated with Independent or Republican status. Figure 13–7 gives the proportion of southern whites with Democratic, Republican, or Independent party *identifications* for each party-*image* score. The odds in favor of being an Independent or Republican go up very sharply between the party-image scores of 0 and −1. The average Democrat for Goldwater, as well as the average Democrat who voted Republican in both 1956 and 1960, is already in this critical range. But will these people in fact change their party identifications to bring them into congruence with

FIGURE 13–7. *Mean party-image scores of white Democrats, by presidential vote, 1956–1964, compared with relationships between party images and party identification*

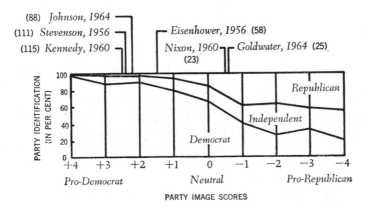

their party images? An examination of the causes of their disenchantment may provide some clues.

### CIVIL RIGHTS, ECONOMIC CONSERVATISM, AND WHITE DISENCHANTMENT

Defections from a "normal" vote—that is, a vote for the candidates nominated by the party with which a voter is psychologically identified—are usually caused by the voter's attitudes toward the candidates and the issues of particular campaigns. Generally speaking, these candidates and issues change from one campaign to the next. Stevenson's eloquence and "indecisiveness"— Kennedy's youth and Catholicism—Eisenhower's warm grin and distinguished war record—Nixon's "hatchet-man" reputation—Goldwater's penchant for naïve ideological "solutions" to complex problems—Johnson's extraordinary legislative ability and "wheeler-dealer" past—all may have influenced many voters in recent presidential elections. Although these short-run factors may cause large defections in particular races, they are unlikely to bring about major and permanent change in party identifications. They are too transitory and idiosyncratic to have such lasting effects.

However, the failure of large numbers of southern whites to vote for the presidential candidates of their party in recent years does not seem to have been just the result of personalities or temporary issues. Rather, the major causes of southern disenchantment seem to have been much the same in every election during the last 20 years—the national Democrats' championing of civil rights for Negroes and their advocacy of an active role for the federal government in the economic life of the country. The relative importance of these two issues in affecting the votes, images, and loyalties of southern whites may be the key to the puzzling future of southern politics.

Table 13–8 shows the percentage of southern white Democrats who voted for Kennedy in 1960, by their racial and economic attitudes and by the strength of their identification with the Democratic party. The first conclusion we can draw from these data is that strength of party identification was much more predictive of the vote in 1960 than were the voters' attitudes on either or both of these policy issues: the weak Democrats defected more heavily to the Republicans than the strong Democrats regardless of where they stood on racial or economic matters. Although less influential than party identification, economic conservatism was a more important cause of Democratic defections in 1960 than was belief in white supremacy. The Democratic segregationists stood almost as firmly behind Kennedy as did moderates and integrationists with the same economic viewpoints and the same strength of party loyalty. The economic conservatives, however, voted consistently more heavily for Nixon than did the liberals, even with party identification and racial views held constant.

The party-image scores of the white Democrats followed much the same

TABLE 13–8.    *Party images and presidential vote in 1960 by white Democrats, by strength of party identification and racial and economic views*

| | RACIAL VIEWS | | | |
| --- | --- | --- | --- | --- |
| | STRONG DEMOCRATS | | WEAK DEMOCRATS | |
| ECONOMIC VIEWS | Racial moderates and inte-grationists | Strict segre-gationists | Racial moderates and inte-grationists | Strict segre-gationists |
| PERCENTAGE VOTING DEMOCRATIC | | | | |
| Liberals (I, II) | 100%  (5) | 93%  (27) | 67%  (6) | 67%  (15) |
| Moderates (III, IV) | 89%  (28) | 98%  (40) | 68%  (19) | 59%  (29) |
| Conservatives (V) | 62%  (8) | 79%  (14) | 50%  (18) | 47%  (15) |
| PERCENTAGE WITH PRO-DEMOCRATIC IMAGES | | | | |
| Liberals (I, II) | 100%  (5) | 92%  (39) | 67%  (6) | 67%  (21) |
| Moderates (III, IV) | 81%  (31) | 94%  (47) | 85%  (20) | 64%  (44) |
| Conservatives (V) | 70%  (10) | 67%  (15) | 74%  (19) | 71%  (17) |

NOTE: Voting percentages are of the two-party vote; party-image score percentages are of all those with party images.

pattern as the vote. The economic conservatives among the Democratic identi-fiers had the least favorable images of the party; the difference between the party-image scores of the segregationists and the racial moderates or inte-grationists was small; the strong and weak Democrats differed sharply in their party image, regardless of their attitudes on social and economic issues. This indicates, of course, that these economic attitudes and party loyalties affected *relatively stable attitudes toward the parties* as well as toward the particular candidates and issues of 1960.

With both of the national political parties scrambling for the Negro vote in 1960, the segregation issue was effectively neutralized. On the whole, white southerners perceived the Republican party as equally unsound on this issue as the Democratic party. Thus most southern segregationists—despite vicious fights every four years at the Democratic National Convention over the party's platform and presidential nominee[22]—preferred to remain in the Democratic fold, except for those who happened to be quite conservative in matters of economic policy. By no means all of them were.

The "conservatism" of southern Democrats is exaggerated.[23] As the only significant party in the region, the Democrats of the South include virtually the entire range of economic and political belief found in the rest of the

[22] See A. Sindler, "The Unsolid South," in A. Westin (ed.), *The Uses of Power* (New York: Harcourt, Brace & World, 1962), pp. 229–83.
[23] V. O. Key, Jr., *Public Opinion and American Democracy* (New York: Alfred A. Knopf, 1961), pp. 101–5.

country. The region's public officials have tended to come from near the conservative end of this spectrum—partly because the unstructured nature of the region's politics favors the *status quo*, partly because the bulk of the region's working class have black skins and do not vote.[24] But on the mass level, a populistic brand of liberalism on "gut issues" is by no means uncommon (see Table 13–9). When the overwhelmingly liberal economic atti-

TABLE 13–9.    *Relationship between economic and racial views of white Democrats, by strength of party identification, 1961*

| Liberalism-Conservatism scores | Percentage in group | Percentage of group for "strict segregation" | N |
|---|---|---|---|
| STRONG DEMOCRATS | | | |
| 1. (Most liberal) | 9% | 93% | 15 |
| 2. | 23 | 85% | 39 |
| 3. | 30 | 53% | 51 |
| 4. | 22 | 76% | 37 |
| 5. (Most conservative) | 16 | 59% | 27 |
| TOTAL | 100% | | 169 |
| WEAK DEMOCRATS | | | |
| 1. (Most liberal) | 8% | 86% | 14 |
| 2. | 15 | 75% | 28 |
| 3. | 29 | 67% | 54 |
| 4. | 21 | 68% | 38 |
| 5. (Most conservative) | 27 | 49% | 49 |
| TOTAL | 100% | | 183 |

tudes of the southern Negroes are added to the attitudes of the white electorate, the differences in economic attitudes between North and South largely disappear.

Moreover, economic conservatism and racial prejudice do *not* tend to go together in the South. Among white Democrats in the South, in fact, economic liberals are much more likely to be strict segregationists than are avowed opponents of "the welfare state" (see Table 13–9). This has meant that those Democrats most likely to be repelled by the national party's vigorous championing of Negro rights were also most likely to be attracted by the Democratic party's concern for "the little man." Thus we find that white voters who explicitly complained that the Democratic party was "too good to Negroes" in 1961

[24] Additional factors contributing to the "unrepresentativeness" of southern congressmen's voting records are presented in G. Robert Boynton, "Southern Conservatism: Constituency Opinion and Congressional Voting," *Public Opinion Quarterly*, Vol. 29 (1965), pp. 259–69.

actually voted six percentage points more heavily for John F. Kennedy than did the southern whites who made no such criticism of the party![25]

The Goldwater campaign of 1964 represented an ill-conceived attempt to break this paradox. Goldwater's covert appeals to racial prejudice had the desired effect in the South (see Table 13–10). The proportion of strongly

TABLE 13–10.  *Party images and presidential voting of white Democrats in 1960 and 1964, by strength of party identification and racial attitudes*

| RESPONDENTS' RACIAL ATTITUDES | STRONG DEMOCRATS | | WEAK DEMOCRATS | |
|---|---|---|---|---|
| | *1960* | *1964* | *1960* | *1964* |
| PERCENTAGE VOTING DEMOCRATIC | | | | |
| Strict segregationist | 93% (89) | 81% (42) | 64% (55) | 54% (26) |
| Moderate or integrationist | 86% (42) | 94% (36) | 59% (37) | 71% (17) |
| PERCENTAGE WITH PRO-DEMOCRATIC IMAGES | | | | |
| Strict segregationist | 90% (125) | 73% (49) | 69% (94) | 46% (41) |
| Moderate or integrationist | 80% (50) | 88% (48) | 75% (51) | 62% (24) |

Democratic segrationists voting Democratic dropped from 93 per cent to 81 per cent between the elections of 1960 and 1964. The spurt in Republican voting among less partisan Democrats committed to segregation was almost as dramatic: 64 per cent voted for Kennedy, only 54 per cent for Johnson. Even so, *Lyndon Johnson managed to win majority support from the region's white segregationists with a great deal to spare.*

The election of 1964 and the racial crisis of the early 1960's seem to have had a greater impact on the party images of the region's segregationists than on their votes.[26] Perhaps this means that the Goldwater campaign—although a Republican disaster nationally—sowed seeds that future Republican candidates will be able to harvest. But the Republicans cannot count on the alleged economic conservatism of southern segregationists to bring about this realignment. In order to capture the support of most southern segregationists, the Republican party will have to appeal to racism. But the election of 1964 proved conclusively that the Republicans cannot win a national election that way.

If the Republicans should nominate another Goldwater in 1968, they undoubtedly would score massive and probably permanent gains in the South.

[25] Matthews and Prothro, *op. cit.,* p. 102, table 5.
[26] Remember, however, that the 1964 interviews were taken during the presidential campaign and hence probably reflect the transitory issues and personalities of the campaign more than do the interviews taken some months after the 1960 presidential elections.

But they probably would reduce themselves to permanent insignificance in national politics. The southern white segregationsts are such a deviant group that no national political party can afford to appeal to them *on the basis of their racial attitudes* and hope to survive. It might be poetic justice if the adherents to the dying cause of white supremacy were, by embracing Republicanism, to destroy the party of Lincoln. But this is scarcely the way to build a two-party system in the South, or preserve one for the nation.

If, as is far more likely, the Republicans nominate presidential candidates in the future who are as strongly and openly dedicated to the cause of civil rights as the Democratic candidates are, then the *status quo ante* Goldwater will be restored. Even under these familiar circumstances, history seems to be on the Republicans' side. The number and proportion of southern whites with favorable images of the Republican party, especially those who are economic conservatives, will probably continue to increase in the future.[27] Because party images are closely associated with voting, Republican votes should grow as well. In time, these favorable images should lead to changes in party identification and party registration; for party image, identification, and registration are normally consistent with one another. Nothing short of massive shifts in party identification and registration in favor of the Republicans will lead to a real two-party system, with healthy partisan competition at all levels of the ballot. But this realignment could be a very slow process, its rate depending on such things as the rate of social and economic change, the skill of Democratic leaders in using their present control over state and local governments to protect their electoral position, and other largely unpredictable events.

### NEGRO POLITICAL ACTIVITY AND THE DEMOCRATIC COALITION

One predictable—and ironic—inhibition to the development of two-party politics in the South may be the growing Negro vote. The Democratic party will be the almost exclusive beneficiary of the growth in Negro voting in the region. The new Negro voters will cancel out a good deal of the anticipated losses among southern whites—unless they speed the flight of southern whites from the party of their forefathers.

Some signs suggest that this political form of "blockbusting" may already have begun. Figure 13–8 plots the proportion of white southerners identified with the Democratic party and voting for Kennedy in 1960, *by the level of political activity of the Negroes in their local communities.* In those communities where the Negroes were relatively inactive in 1960, the level of Democratic party identification and of Democratic presidential voting were both very high among whites. Few white Democrats voted for Nixon in these

---

[27] In addition to the evidence presented in this chapter, see Matthews and Prothro, "The Concept of Party Image," in Jennings and Ziegler, *op. cit.* We there present evidence that the demographic correlates of pro-Republican party images are on the increase in the South, while the demographic correlates of pro-Democratic party images are on the decline.

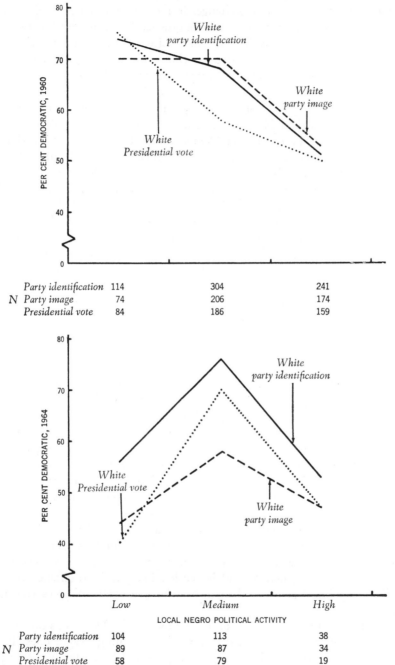

FIGURE 13–8. *Local Negro political activity and white Democratic voting, images, and identification, 1960–1964*

PER CENT DEMOCRATIC, 1960

White
party identification

White
party image

White
Presidential vote

|  | | | |
|---|---|---|---|
| Party identification | 114 | 304 | 241 |
| N Party image | 74 | 206 | 174 |
| Presidential vote | 84 | 186 | 159 |

PER CENT DEMOCRATIC, 1964

White
party identification

White
Presidential vote

White
party image

Low  Medium  High

LOCAL NEGRO POLITICAL ACTIVITY

|  | | | |
|---|---|---|---|
| Party identification | 104 | 113 | 38 |
| N Party image | 89 | 87 | 34 |
| Presidential vote | 58 | 79 | 19 |

racially backward areas. But in communities with moderate Negro political activity, a sizable number of white Democrats voted Republican in 1960 *without* making corresponding changes in their party loyalties or party images. This was the sort of setting where incongruence between white party identification and presidential voting was most often found. Finally, where local Negroes were just about as active as whites, the whites' party identification and presidential voting tend to converge once again—*but at about 25 percentage points lower in Democratic strength than in the racially repressive areas!*

Southern voting patterns were wildly different in 1964. Goldwater polled many more votes than Nixon had in areas of little Negro political activity. He also made heavy inroads on Democratic party identification and Democratic party images in these same areas. Nonetheless, about a third of the white voters in areas of low Negro activity who voted for Goldwater retained their Democratic party identification throughout the campaign. In areas of high Negro political activity, on the other hand, Goldwater polled almost as large a proportion of the white votes, and fewer of these voters clung to their emotional identification with the Democratic party. Thus in both of these very different presidential elections, high Negro political activity on the community level was associated with relatively high Republican voting *supported by equally Republican party loyalties and party attitudes.*

Although the Republicans were able to poll many votes in areas where local Negroes were not especially active in politics, they were less successful in changing basic party loyalties and attitudes in those areas than they were in communities where Negro political power is a factor to contend with. Southern Republicanism in areas of active Negro involvement in politics is much more than mere "Presidential Republicanism" or a transitory reaction to fleeting events. Growing Negro political power is related to genuine party realignment.

We must not read too much into these figures, however. Our data are on different communities at the same point in time, and the same neat patterns will not necessarily occur over a period of time within a single community. Even if they do, this movement toward congruence between presidential voting and party identification is not necessarily the result of Negroes' driving whites out of the Democratic party, like the first Negro family moving into an all-white neighborhood. Rather, the same community conditions—urbanization and industrialization, for example—that facilitate Negro political activity also probably encourage Republican party identification among southern whites. Certainly, the whites living in areas of heavy Negro political participation are less segregationist—and hence less likely to be frightened by growing Negro political activity—than those who live where Negroes vote rarely if at all.

Nonetheless, the figures serve to remind us that the Democrats undoubtedly will lose some white supporters as a result of gaining Negro ones. Politics everywhere is a matter of balancing such gains and losses; rarely does a party attract one group without repelling at least some members of another. How much white support can the Democrats lose and still show a net gain from the anticipated influx of Negro Democrats?

If we take the 1960 presidential vote as an example, and assume that Negroes will vote Democratic in at least as large proportions in future elections as they did then, we can compute the proportion of white voters the Democrats will have to hold in order to carry the South at different levels of Negro voting turnout.[28] This is what the picture looks like:

| Percentage of Negroes voting | Percentage of white voters also needed to win a majority of the popular votes in the South |
|---|---|
| 30% | 46  % |
| 40 | 44 |
| 50 | 42.5 |
| 60 | 41 |
| 70 | 40 |

Every 10-per-cent increase in Negro voter turnout means that the Democrats can sacrifice one and one half to two percentage points of their white vote and still poll a majority of all popular votes. But at almost every conceivable level of Negro turnout, the Democrats will have to poll a little over 40 per cent of the white votes in the South in order to win. Or to look at these figures in a different way, thanks to the growing Negro vote and its overwhelming Democratic bias, the Democrats can afford to lose up to one third of their normal white identifiers to the Republicans and still carry the South—by a hair. Can they do it?

The combination of southern whites and Negroes in the same party is a potentially explosive alliance. But our analysis suggests a number of things that contribute to the stability of this arrangement.

First, about one third of each race has no image of the Democratic party, and a large number of the others have only the most rudimentary image. This widespread ignorance eases the coexistence of clashing racial groups within the same party.

[28] This hypothetical analysis is of *popular* votes only and not electoral votes. Because the presidential strength of the Republican party is not evenly distributed throughout the South, the Democrats could carry the region in *popular* votes but not win the electoral votes of all the southern states. In order to carry all southern states, the Democrats would have to poll considerably more than 50 per cent of the region's popular vote.

These calculations assume that 88 per cent of those Negroes who do vote will vote Democratic (which is the percentage Kennedy would have received in 1960 if all Negroes who had ever voted actually had) and that the rate of white turnout remains the same as in 1960 even while Negro turnout increases.

Second, the amorphous nature of American parties permits the two races to perceive the same party somewhat differently. The whites do not identify with the Democrats on the state and local levels, whereas the Negroes identify on the national level—neither set of respondents made such neat distinctions, and both sets responded to our questions primarily in national terms. But the southern wing of the party no doubt seems more important to some whites than to most Negroes.

Third, the white strong Democrats include a large share of those whites who are most likely to be repelled by the party on racial grounds. Because these southern-oriented whites view identification with the Democratic party as a reaffirmation of their faith in the southern way of life, they cannot easily break away from the party even when it may be, in fact, undermining southern traditions.

Fourth, most southern Negroes and whites agree that the Democratic party is superior to the Republican party. True, on racial matters they are sharply divided. But on domestic issues most Negroes and many whites in the South agree that the Democratic party is the party of prosperity, jobs, and government spending. Most southern whites and virtually all the Negroes approve of this kind of party. And neither race is particularly happy about the alternative, the Republican party, which finds itself unable to win national elections when it appeals to racially inspired white discontent with the Democratic party.

" 'Course neither party likes us much," a 74-year-old Negro Democrat said, "but we here and they have to do something." So far, the Democrats have done enough to please most southern Negroes without alienating too many whites. Thus a 71-year-old white Democrat, a strict segregationist, remembers, "When I was little the Republicans was called Radicals, and they weren't much thought of in the neighborhood." The Democrats have held onto enough support from this unlikely coalition to dim the short-run prospects of the Republicans. Yet the average age of this pair of respondents is 72, and their average schooling is six years. As they and their political memories fade from the southern scene, the Republicans can anticipate a brighter future.

In all likelihood, however, genuine two-party politics will come to the South too late to be of much help in the "Negro revolution." Southern Negroes probably will have to seek advancement within the confused and shifting context of a predominantly one-party system (in state and local politics) combined with substantial "Presidential Republicanism." How this, and other related factors, affect the Negroes' ability to achieve racial equality through political activity is the subject of the concluding chapter of this book.

Chapter Fourteen

# Negro Students and the Protest Movement

On Monday, February 1, 1960, four Negro teen-agers walked into a five-and-ten-cent store in Greensboro, North Carolina, sat down at the lunch counter, and ordered a cup of coffee.[1] When they were refused—local custom permitted Negroes to purchase merchandise in the store but not to eat there—they continued to sit at the counter, silently waiting for service. For a while everyone tried to ignore them. Then the Negro cooks came out of the kitchen and urged the boys to return to their dormitories at North Carolina Agricultural and Technical College, where they were freshmen. The well-dressed youngsters sat on silently until the store closed for the day. Thus began the "sit-ins," a movement that was to plunge the South into turmoil for many months and revolutionize the pace and tactics of Negro civil rights activities in the United States from that day onward.

On Tuesday the four freshmen, joined by about 20 new recruits from A. and T., returned to the same lunch counter. Again they were refused service. Wednesday and Thursday they returned, their numbers swelled by students from Bennett College (a Negro institution near by) and a few white girls from the Woman's College of the University of North Carolina, also located in Greensboro. By Friday, white teen-agers had begun to taunt and heckle the silent demonstrators.

Saturday morning the store was jammed with Negroes and whites, mostly young people. The Negroes continued to sit while "the white boys waved Confederate flags, chanted, and cursed."[2] In midafternoon, the manager of

[1] This description is drawn from Daniel H. Pollitt, "Dime Store Demonstrations: Events and Legal Problems of the First Sixty Days," *Duke Law Journal*, Vol. 1960 (1960), pp. 315–65; and Virgil C. Stroud, *In Quest of Freedom* (Dallas, Texas: Royal Publishing Co., 1963). Professor Stroud is a member of the faculty at North Carolina A. and T. College.

[2] Pollitt, *op. cit.*, p. 318.

the store received an anonymous bomb threat and police emptied the store. When it opened again on Monday morning, the lunch counter was closed. Thus ended—temporarily—the Greensboro demonstration.

But by then Negro students were demonstrating in Winston-Salem, Durham, Charlotte, and other North Carolina cities. From this base, the sit-ins rapidly spread into other areas. On February 11, students from Hampton Institute in Virginia sat in at the local Woolworth's. The next day student demonstrations took place in Rock Hill, South Carolina, and Deland, Florida. Students from Fisk University and Tennessee A. and I. began demonstrating in Nashville on February 13. Demonstrations broke out at Montgomery, Alabama, on February 25. By March 5 they had spread to Houston, Texas. Five days later sit-ins were staged in Little Rock, Arkansas, and on March 15 in Atlanta, Georgia. The sit-in movement reached Baton Rouge, Louisiana, on March 28 and Jackson, Mississippi, on April 11. Within a year and a half after the initial Greensboro sit-in, demonstrations had been held in over a hundred cities and towns in every southern and border state, as well as in Illinois, Nevada, and Ohio. At least 70,000 Negroes and their white sympathizers had taken part in them.[3]

Begun as a protest against segregated lunch counters in variety stores, the movement rapidly expanded its targets to include all types of public accommodations—parks, swimming pools, theaters, restaurants, churches, transportation facilities, museums, art galleries, laundromats, beaches, and courtrooms. The systematic boycott of segregated business establishments by the Negro community became the standard—and persuasive—weapon of the movement. Roused Negro youths demonstrated even to protest discrimination in employment practices and voter registration.

All this required organization and liaison with the adult Negro community and its established leaders. The first Greensboro demonstrators sought and got assistance from the then little-known, New York-based Congress on Racial Equality (CORE). Martin Luther King and the youth leaders of the NAACP were on the scene in Greensboro before the first week of protest had ended.[4] These groups continued to provide aid and comfort to the movement from then on. But the students retained the initiative. In April the Student Nonviolent Coordinating Committee (SNCC, pronounced "snick") announced that the students intended to stay free of the control of adult leaders and organizations.

The reaction of the white South to these developments was overwhelmingly hostile. Most lunchroom proprietors continued to refuse service to Negroes. Public officials warned against participating in the demonstrations, a rash of

[3] These estimates were made by the authoritative Southern Regional Council, "The Student Protest Movement: A Recapitulation," September 1961, p. 3 (mimeo.).
[4] Louis E. Lomax, *The Negro Revolt* (New York: Harper & Brothers, 1962), pp. 122–23.

new anti-trespass laws and ordinances were passed, and older statutes were vigorously enforced. An estimated 3,600 students and their supporters had been arrested by September 1961.[5] A number of Negro students and faculty members—at least 141 students and 58 professors—were dismissed by their colleges and universities for taking part in the movement. Hundreds of students voluntarily withdrew from college to protest these expulsions.

In a number of places, the demonstrators were met with open violence. During the first few weeks of protest, for example, rioting broke out in a Chattanooga store when "whites, mostly students, began throwing flower pots, dishes, bric-a-brac, and other merchandise" at the Negroes sitting at the lunch counter.[6] One white youth found a bullwhip in the store and proceeded to use it on a Negro. In Houston, three masked white men grabbed a young Negro, flogged him with a chain, carved "KKK" on his chest, and hung him by his knees from a nearby tree. Two days after the first Montgomery sit-in, a marauding band of whites attacked a Negro woman with miniature baseball bats concealed in brown paper bags. In several places demonstrating students were barely saved from white mobs by the police, who sometimes had to threaten the use of tear gas and fire hoses. When the police were less alert or less dedicated, the students were beaten.

Throughout all these trials, the students were—with amazingly few exceptions—true to their doctrine of nonviolence. They sat at counters and walked picket lines in silence, neither responding to insults nor expressing outrage at how they were being treated. They neither struck back when assaulted nor resisted arrest. Rarely has this nation seen such a display of courage and self-sacrifice.

## Prelude to protest

Historians will no doubt trace the beginnings of the Negro protest movement to a day earlier than February 1, 1960. The four freshmen at North Carolina A. and T. did not just stumble upon a new approach to desegregation. And their act of "spontaneous rebellion"[7] would not have grown rapidly into a mass movement if conditions had not been ripe.

Most of the Negro youngsters who took part in the protests of 1960 and 1961 were born during the early years of the Second World War. The war and its aftermath reshaped the world in which they grew up. In the first place, the war had exposed many southern Negroes to nonsegregated societies for the first time. When these veterans returned to the South, many brought home

[5] Southern Regional Council, op. cit., p. 3.
[6] Pollitt, op. cit., p. 332. The other examples of violence also are drawn from this article.
[7] Southern Regional Council, op. cit., p. 1.

with them a new image of themselves, new hopes and aspirations, and the belief that, having risked their lives in the defense of their country, they deserved nothing less than first-class citizenship. They soon learned that these hopes and dreams were unfounded.

At the same time, the wartime and postwar boom benefited Negroes economically. To be sure, they did not improve their economic position relative to that of whites; rather, they stayed at the bottom of the heap while the entire heap lurched upward. Nonetheless, Negroes began to enjoy goods and services they had never had before; fewer of them lived in abject poverty. Men with empty stomachs rarely rebel; people without purchasing power do not launch economic boycotts of business establishments that do not treat them fairly. Thus the wartime and postwar improvements in the Negro's economic position left him with the same sense of *relative* deprivation as before, but with more economic resources to do something about it.

Finally, the war and postwar boom hastened the Negro flight from the rural South to cities in the South, North, and West, for that is where the jobs were. Life in an urban ghetto is rather different from life on a farm. The informal restraints on aggressiveness toward whites are very largely gone. So, too, are most personal relationships with white people—save the highly impersonal and segmentalized contacts of city dwellers in general. Viewed from the ghetto, whites could easily be thought of as "The Man"—a faceless, collective enemy.

The psychological impact of the Supreme Court's school-desegregation decision on the Negro subculture is hard to overestimate. The Negro journalist Louis Lomax has written:

> It would be impossible for a white person to understand what happened within black breasts on that Monday [May 17, 1954, when *Brown* v. *Board of Education* was handed down by the Court]. An ardent segregationist has called it "Black Monday." He was so right, but for reasons other than the ones he advances: that was the day we won; the day we took the white man's laws and won our case before an all-white Supreme Court with a Negro lawyer, Thurgood Marshall, as our chief counsel. And we were proud.[8]

The *Brown* decision, hailed as the second Emancipation Proclamation, raised Negro expectations to new heights. But these expectations were to be ground down by the vehemence and ingenuity of southern resistance. The four freshmen at A. and T. had been in grammar school on the day the decision was announced. More than five years later, on the day they began their silent vigil at the Woolworth lunch counter in Greensboro, considerably less than 1 per cent of all Negro students in the South were attending desegregated schools.[9]

This slow progress toward racial equality provoked a growing disillusion-

---

[8] Lomax, *op. cit.*, pp. 73–74.
[9] *Status of School Segregation-Desegregation in the Southern and Border States* (Nashville, Tenn.: Southern Education Reporting Service, 1960).

ment with traditional attacks on segregation and with the established leadership of the Negro community. Until then the battle for civil rights had taken place very largely inside the courtroom. Over the years the NAACP had won an impressive string of legal victories. But how much difference had they made to the average Negro? Seemingly, very little. In local communities the struggle had been led by middle-class Negroes—the only ones with enough status and skill to bargain with what more and more Negroes came to call the "white power structure." At best the results of these endless conferences, committees, and councils were modest. Most Negroes found them imperceptible.

As the Negro masses grew more militant and demanding, the established Negro leaders were caught in a crossfire of conflicting demands. On the one hand, their position as leaders depended on their access to and acceptance by the white community leaders. This, in turn, depended on their having a reputation for "reasonableness" among the whites. On the other hand, if the Negro leaders failed to reflect the growing militancy of their followers, they would lose their influence over the Negro rank and file. Paralyzed by this dilemma, many leaders began to lose the respect and confidence of both Negroes and whites.

The time was ripe for rebellion—rebellion against white domination and segregation, against legalism, against gradual reform through governmental action, against established Negro organizations and leaders.

The first indication of what was to come had occurred in Montgomery, Alabama, in 1955.[10] One day in December, a middle-aged Negro woman named Mrs. Rosa Parks refused to move to the back of a bus. For this insubordination Mrs. Parks was arrested. Within 24 hours a mass boycott of the busses had been organized by an *ad hoc* committee of Negro ministers. One member of this committee was a young Baptist minister named Martin Luther King, Jr. King emerged from the long and bitter boycott as the most eloquent and respected voice that southern Negroes had had for a very long time. King was a militant devotee of direct mass action and civil disobedience. But he also was deeply devoted to a concept of nonviolence that he had learned from Gandhi and from Christian theology. King's ideas—expressed with boldness and emotion—had a profound effect on the Negro community. Undoubtedly they influenced the thinking of the young demonstrators who, a few years later, were to seize the initiative from their elders. The Southern Christian Leadership Conference (SCLC), a loose confederation of ministers organized around King, was another important by-product of the Montgomery boycott.

The next major revolt occurred not in the South but in Wichita, Kansas. In August 1958, what apparently was the first organized "sit-in" was held there.[11] The next week the movement spread to Oklahoma City. Several lunch counters were desegregated, and demonstrations continued to be staged in this

10 Lomax, *op. cit.*, ch. 8.
11 Southern Regional Council, "The Student Protest Movement, Winter, 1960," February 25, 1960, pp. 2–5 (mimeo.).

border city through 1960 and 1961. Although the sit-ins spread from Oklahoma City to a few other cities in the state—Enid, Tulsa, and Stillwater—they went no farther. A 1959 Miami, Florida, sit-in was a completely unrelated enterprise organized and directed by CORE, which had had experience in direct-action techniques while trying to desegregate housing projects in the North. In any event, the Miami sit-in was brief and abortive.

Thus the four freshmen at North Carolina A. and T. were not the first protesters. But they managed to do something that no one else had been able to do—they drew hundreds and thousands of college students into active protest. They managed to create a region-wide "movement" from what had been scattered and sporadic protests. And they managed to commit this movement to the use of direct, highly provocative tactics in its struggle for freedom and equality. This is more than enough to ensure that February 1, 1960, will go down as a major turning point in the history of the South.

## The extent of student participation

Throughout most of the world—Europe, Asia, Latin America, and Africa—university students are a major political force. Strikes, boycotts, rioting, and picketing by students are almost commonplace and have been known to topple governments, force basic changes in public policy, and make and break political careers. By comparison, American college students have been politically passive.

But the four youngsters from North Carolina A. and T. changed all that, at least for Negro students in the South. "If we leave it to the adults," an 18-year-old freshman in Atlanta said, referring to his longing for racial equality, "nothing will become of it." A junior in North Carolina went even further. "You know," he said, "the adults still feel the white man can do no wrong." In Mississippi a freshman girl concluded that "most adults have given up hope or just don't care." Only the young, many Negro students seem to have decided, could bring about a radical change in racial patterns. And they were "tired of sitting back and waiting on the older folks." "Waiting is forever," a sophomore in New Orleans said. "You gotta do something."

During the first year of the protests almost a quarter (24 per cent[12]) of the Negro students in the South took some part in the sit-in movement. From 1 to 2 per cent participated in the more controversial and violent freedom rides.

[12] This and subsequent figures on the attitudes and behavior of Negro college students are based on interviews with a random sample of southern Negro students enrolled in accredited, predominantly Negro institutions of higher learning in the 11 states of the South. The sample is described in Appendix A.

No doubt students tended to exaggerate the extent of their activity in the protest movement, just as some adults falsely claim they voted in the last election or took part in other praiseworthy activities. The 24 per cent figure is therefore probably a bit high.

Eighty-five per cent of all Negro students enrolled in predominantly Negro colleges and universities in the South approved of these activities, whereas only 5 per cent were opposed to them (See Table 14–1). Student enthusiasm

TABLE 14–1.   *Feelings of Negro college students about sit-ins and freedom rides*

| Feelings | Sit-ins | Freedom rides |
|---|---|---|
| Strongly approve | 53% | 49% |
| Approve | 32 | 35 |
| Neutral | 4 | 5 |
| Disapprove | 4 | 3 |
| Strongly disapprove | 1 | 1 |
| Uncodeable response | 2 | 3 |
| Don't know, no answer, refusal | 4 | 4 |
| TOTAL | 100% | 100% |
| N | 264 | 264 |

for the protest movement was extraordinary: "It's a new social revolution." "It's the most remarkable movement since the emancipation of the slaves." "This is the day of the *New* Negro." "I think they are just wonderful."

The most common form of student participation was sitting-in at counters or waiting rooms, and kneeling-in, lying-in, or standing-in at other public facilities. Sixty-five per cent of the students active in the movement took part in at least one of these activities. This amounts to about 16 per cent of *all* Negro college students in the South—an extraordinarily high percentage of any group to participate in an invariably unpleasant and potentially danger-ous activity of dubious legality[13] (See Table 14–2). Twenty-nine per cent of the active students engaged in picketing, and 23 per cent took part in mass demonstrations and marches. Only 3 per cent of the activists claimed that they had taken part in the freedom rides.

The student participants in these protest demonstrations were very matter of fact about them. One sit-inner in Florida said, "There were some [whites]

[13] At the time these protest activities began, they seemed clearly contrary to prevailing legal concepts of property rights and local ordinances regarding trespassing and disturbing the peace. Subsequent Supreme Court decisions [*Burton* v. *Wilmington Parking Authority*, 365 U.S. 715 (1961); *Lombard* v. *Louisiana*, 373 U.S. 267 (1963)] and the passage of the 1964 Civil Rights Act greatly narrowed the area of racial discrimination permissible by "private" agencies. In *Bell* v. *Maryland*, 378 U.S. 226; *Barr* v. *Columbia*, 378 U.S. 146; *Barrie* v. *Columbia*, 378 U.S. 347; *Robinson* v. *Florida*, 378 U.S. 153; and *Griffin* v. *Maryland*, 378 U.S. 130, all decided on June 22, 1964, the Court reversed convictions for trespass or disturbing the peace without deciding the constitutional issue of whether an individual can practice discrimination in his place of public accommodation with the support of state police and courts to enforce the practice.

TABLE 14–2.   *What students who participated in the protest movement did, 1960–1962*

| Activity | Percentage of students participating in movement who engaged in activity | Percentage of all Negro students who engaged in activity |
|---|---|---|
| Sat in at counter, waiting room, etc. | 60% | 15% |
| Picketed | 29 | 7 |
| Took part in mass demonstrations, marches, etc. | 23 | 6 |
| Led or organized Negro protest activities | 11 | 3 |
| Wade-in, kneel-in, stand-in | 5 | 1 |
| Rode on freedom bus, train, etc. | 3 | 1 |
| Donated money | 2 | a |
| N | 65 | 264 |

a Greater than 0, less than 0.5 per cent.
NOTE: Percentages do not total 100 because some students engaged in more than one activity.

who wouldn't eat with us, but they didn't say anything to us; they just quietly left. . . ." Even those who encountered more overt opposition tended to describe their experiences with almost clinical detachment. "Well," a sophomore at Southern University said, "we were at a lunch counter—the Greyhound Bus station in New Orleans—and we just sat in. Then we were thrown out. . . . I was one of the 77 jailed." A freedom rider from Tennessee described his participation in this bloody phase of the protests by saying, "We rode to Alabama. I was put out of the city." Another sit-in participant described his experiences without emotion:

> We were met by the police . . . [the] student drivers were given tickets for illegal parking. We were burned on our arms with cigarettes, pushed around, and had doors closed in our faces.

Only rarely do signs of outrage or indignation come through. One freshman from Louisiana complained of the treatment she received at the hands of the police: "I don't think there are any words to describe how dirty the policemen were." Another youngster was shocked by the signs of white hatred:

> Nothing happened except the way the manager acted and the expression of hatred on his face. They placed racks of clothes . . . to block Negroes from seats. I also noticed the expression on the white people's faces. . . . At one store they piled groceries and things on the counter and roped off seats. Nothing happened except the looks we got and the pushing. I don't think I'll ever forget that

experience because before I had never conceived of people hating anyone because of his color. Before it was secondhand to me, but this was firsthand experience.

One out of every 6 demonstrators was arrested; one of every 20 was thrown in jail. About 1 in every 10 reported having been pushed, jostled, or spat upon; the same proportion were either clubbed, beaten, gassed, or burned; another 8 per cent were run out of town (See Table 14–3). Only 11 per cent of the

TABLE 14–3.    *What happened to students who participated in the protest movement, 1960–1962*

| What happened | Percentage of students participating in movement | Percentage of all Negro students |
|---|---|---|
| Arrested | 15% | 4% |
| Nothing | 11 | 3 |
| Pushed, jostled, spat at | 11 | 3 |
| Called names | 8 | 2 |
| Clubbed, beaten, gassed, burned | 8 | 2 |
| Jailed | 6 | 2 |
| Threatened | 6 | 2 |
| Water or food spilled on | 2 | a |
| N | 65 | 264 |

a Greater than 0, less than 0.5 per cent.
NOTE: Percentages do not total 100 because some students reported more than one of these experiences.

protesters reported that nothing untoward had happened to them.

Although student support of the demonstrations was almost unanimous, a majority of the students at predominantly Negro institutions in the South did not actively take part in the protest between 1960 and 1962. The most popular reason given for their failure to participate was their geographical separation from the scene of active protests or a general lack of opportunity (see Table 14–4). "There was no place to go, I suppose," one inactive student in Texas said. "Where I live we had no problem." Smaller numbers pleaded conflicting school or job commitments. "The football coach said not to," one student athlete in Tennessee said. "He didn't want us to get arrested and miss any games or practice. He said we had scholarships to play football, not sit in." A North Carolina student confessed that she ". . . didn't want to have a jail record. One day I'm going to look for a job and this might be held against me." Seven per cent of the reasons volunteered had to do with personal unsuitability, on grounds ranging from "I wouldn't have had the nerve" to "I'm not a non-violent person. I would have found it hard not to go to the aid of someone who was hurt, and this would not help the movement." Very few of the non-

TABLE 14–4.   *Reasons given by Negro students for not participating in the protest movement, 1960–1962*

| Reason for nonparticipation | Percentage of total reasons |
| --- | --- |
| No special reason, don't know | 24% |
| Geographical separation | 21 |
| Lack of opportunity (general) | 12 |
| Conflicting school and job commitments | 10 |
| Fear of consequences—loss of job, expelled from school, etc. | 8 |
| Don't believe in them | 8 |
| Personally unsuited for, fear of experience | 7 |
| Have not been asked to, didn't know how to | 6 |
| Opposition of parents and teachers | 4 |
| TOTAL | 100% |
| N | 210 |

participants mentioned opposition from parents ("Mom told me—if I went, try to keep from getting in trouble") or teachers ("They told us we should decide which is more important—education or sit-ins").

But these "explanations" of inactivity, in the face of what must have been substantial social pressure from activist fellow students, should be interpreted with care. The human ability to rationalize comfortable inaction knows few bounds. So let us examine the participants in the protest movement to see if we can infer, from what we know about their personal characteristics, attitudes, and life situations, why some Negro students in the South actively engaged in protest activities while others did not.

## Who were the protesters?

The students who poured out of their classrooms into the stores and streets to protest against segregation in 1960 and 1961 were not entirely "typical" Negro college students. Rather, they differed from their schoolmates in a number of identifiable ways. These differences are of some interest in and of themselves. But, more important, they provide clues as to *why* some students were active in the protest movement while others were not. Who, then, were the protesters?

Given the substantial physical risks involved in active protest, one might expect the protesters to be almost entirely young men. In fact, the student protesters were almost as often girls as boys: 48 per cent of the students who personally took part in the sit-ins and freedom rides were female. If the sex ratio in Negro colleges was the same as in white institutions—where female students are almost invariably outnumbered, often by two or three to one—

this would mean that a larger proportion of the girl students took part in the demonstrations than of the boys. But, in fact, well over half (57 per cent) of the Negro students enrolled in predominantly Negro institutions at the height of the sit-ins were women—a fact that no doubt reflects the special importance of women in the Negro subculture.

If we divide all the students in our sample into three groups according to the extent of their involvement in the protest movement—those who personally took part in the sit-ins and freedom rides (25 per cent), those who belonged to protest organizations but did not themselves take part in the protests and demonstrations (14 per cent), and those who neither belonged to protest organizations nor took part in the protests (61 per cent)—and examine the proportion of each sex at each level of participation, we find 30 per cent of the male students and 21 per cent of the female students at the most active level and 12 per cent of the men and 17 per cent of the women at the second level of involvement. Thus if participation is defined as personal and direct participation in the protests, the male students were a little more likely to be activists than were the female students. If membership in protest organizations is considered an indication of protest activity, the women students were just about as active as the men. Regardless of which view we adopt, we find that the large gap in participation rates between adult Negro males and females reported in Chapter Four just did not exist among the student protesters.

A good deal more important than sex differences in accounting for participation in the protests was the nature of the communities in which the young students were raised (See Table 14–5). The more urban the students' early environment, the more likely they were to have been active in the movement. A third of the students raised in large cities personally took part in the protests, but only 15 per cent of those raised on farms joined the demonstrations and picket lines. Three-fourths of the farm boys and girls were completely inactive —that is, they neither took part in the demonstrations nor belonged to a protest group. The active protesters also came, in disproportionate numbers, from areas of moderate concentrations of Negroes. The students raised in areas with very few Negroes (less than 20 per cent of the total population) or large numbers of them (over 40 per cent) were less likely to become involved.

Both of these findings might lead us to assume that the protesters came disproportionately from the Peripheral South. But this would be an error—the students from the Deep South probably were a little more active, personally, than those from the more liberal states on the edge of the region. Almost twice the proportion of students from the Peripheral as from the Deep South joined protest groups and stopped their activity at that point, whereas the students from the Deep South more often tended to be either high-level participants (27 per cent) or totally inactive (63 per cent). But these differences are small indeed. The safer conclusion is that the students in the two subregions took part in the protests at essentially the same rate. Given the greater opposition

TABLE 14–5.   *Home-community background of Negro students and their participation in the protest movement*

| | LEVEL OF PARTICIPATION | | | | |
| | Active in protests | Belong to protest group | Neither | TOTAL | N |
|---|---|---|---|---|---|
| **KIND OF COMMUNITY STUDENT GREW UP IN** | | | | | |
| Farm | 15% | 10 | 75 | 100% | 59 |
| Town | 18% | 25 | 57 | 100% | 57 |
| Small city | 30% | 7 | 63 | 100% | 81 |
| Large city | 33% | 18 | 49 | 100% | 67 |
| **PERCENTAGE OF NEGROES IN COUNTY WHERE STUDENT GREW UP** | | | | | |
| 0–19% | 21% | 18 | 61 | 100% | 28 |
| 29–39% | 32% | 12 | 56 | 100% | 116 |
| 40–59% | 17% | 19 | 64 | 100% | 81 |
| 60%+ | 19% | 10 | 71 | 100% | 31 |
| **SUBREGION OF STUDENT'S HOME** | | | | | |
| Deep South | 27% | 10 | 63 | 100% | 128 |
| Peripheral South | 22% | 19 | 59 | 100% | 134 |

to the protests in the Deep South, and the far lower levels of adult Negro participation there, this in itself is surprising.

The largest single demographic difference between the students who joined the protest movement and those who did not is their social class (see Table 14–6). The higher the social and economic status of the Negro student, the more likely he was to become an active member of the movement. Over half of the students from families with an annual income of over $6,000 personally participated in the demonstrations or belonged to protest groups, but only 6 per cent of the students from families with an income of less than $2,000 were that active! If we use the occupation of the head of the student's family as an index of status, the same class differences in participation appear.

What, then, does this brief demographic portrait of the Negro protester add up to? *All* Negro college students are extremely fortunate youngsters; very few Negroes have their educational opportunities, and educational achievement is even more highly valued in the Negro subculture than in white America. But even within this select group the protesting students were especially blessed. They tended to come from areas with enough Negroes to create a genuine "Negro problem" but not so many as to result in extreme repression by whites; they tended to come from cities where race relations were, relatively

TABLE 14-6.   *Social class of Negro students and the extent of their participation in the protest movement*

| | EXTENT OF PARTICIPATION | | | | |
| | *Active personally* | *Belonged to protest group* | *Neither* | TOTAL | N |
|---|---|---|---|---|---|
| ANNUAL INCOME OF FAMILY | | | | | |
| Under $2,000 | 3% | 3 | 94 | 100% | 30 |
| $2,000-$3,999 | 26% | 9 | 65 | 100% | 69 |
| $4,000-$5,999 | 19% | 21 | 60 | 100% | 68 |
| $6,000+ | 34% | 19 | 47 | 100% | 76 |
| OCCUPATIONAL CATEGORY OF HEAD OF STUDENT'S FAMILY | | | | | |
| White-collar | 32% | 20 | 48 | 100% | 62 |
| Blue-collar | 25% | 15 | 60 | 100% | 146 |
| Farmer | 14% | 8 | 78 | 100% | 37 |
| Housewife | 18% | 0 | 82 | 100% | 11 |

speaking, more benign than in the countryside; and they tended far more often than the average Negro student to come from middle-class homes.

"Revolutionary movements seem to originate," Crane Brinton has written in the *Anatomy of Revolution*, "in the discontents of not unprosperous people who feel restraint, cramp, annoyance rather than . . . crushing oppression."[14] A demographic picture of the student protesters suggests that this was the case for the sit-in movement as well. But Brinton's argument is based as much on the psychological attributes of revolutionaries as on their social positions. Let us look at the psychological characteristics of the protesters before we conclude that his analysis holds.

## The psychology of protest

Negro college students were on the whole much more discontented with race relations in the South of the early 1960's than were the adult Negroes of the region. When asked to rate southern race relations on our self-anchoring "ladder," the average student chose a value of 4.5 as compared to the 5.8 rating made by the average Negro adult a few months earlier (see Figure 14-1). Moreover, the students were much more nearly united in their judgments than were the adults. Almost a third of the adults thought southern race relations

[14] (Englewood Cliffs, N.J.: Prentice-Hall, 1952), p. 278.

FIGURE  14–1.   *Ratings of current race relations by Negro*
*students and adults*

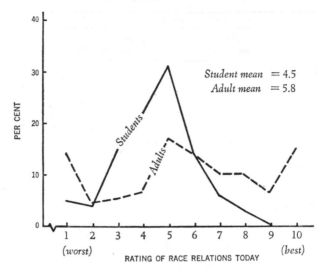

*Student mean* $= 4.5$
*Adult mean* $= 5.8$

were good (rating them 8, 9, or 10), although 15 per cent thought they were
as bad as they could imagine (rating them 1). Less than 5 per cent of the
students were found at either of these extremes. The overwhelming student
view, using their own standards of judgment, was that race relations in the
South were bad but could be worse.

These student evaluations definitely were associated with participation in
the protest movement: the students with the greatest sense of discontent tended
to be more active in the protest than were the relatively contented (see
Table 14–7). Almost a third (32 per cent) of the students who rated the

TABLE  14–7.   *Extent of student participation in the protest movement,*
*by their ratings of race relations*

| LEVEL OF PARTICIPATION IN THE PROTEST MOVEMENTS | RATINGS OF CURRENT RACE RELATIONS IN THE SOUTH | | | |
|---|---|---|---|---|
| | *(Worst)* 1 or 2 | 3 or 4 | 5 or 6 | *(Best)* 7 or 8 |
| Active personally | 32% | 26% | 25% | 8% |
| Belonged to protest group but not active personally | 12 | 11 | 17 | 16 |
| Neither active personally nor member of protest organization | 56 | 63 | 58 | 76 |
| TOTAL | 100% | 100% | 100% | 100% |
| N | 25 | 96 | 118 | 25 |

South as either 1 or 2 on the race-relations ladder took an active part in the protest. Only 26 per cent of those who rated the region at 3 or 4, 25 per cent who rated it 5 or 6, and only 8 per cent of those who rated it at 7 or 8 were equally involved in demonstrations. Or, to look at the table in a different way, 56 per cent of those students who thought race relations were very bad failed to take any part in the movement, whereas 76 per cent of those who thought race relations were reasonably good neither joined protest groups nor took part in the demonstrations.

TABLE 14–8.   *Percentage of Negro students agreeing with statements indicating racial hostility, pessimism, and despair, by extent of their participation in protest movement*

| | LEVEL OF STUDENT PARTICIPATION IN PROTESTS | | |
| --- | --- | --- | --- |
| STATEMENT | Active in protests (N = 65) | Belong to protest group but not active (N = 38) | Neither (N = 161) |
| All white people are prejudiced against Negroes. | 6% | 3% | 22% |
| In spite of what some people say, when Negroes are arrested in the South they do receive fair treatment. | 26 | 39 | 20 |
| I have seen so much unfairness to Negroes that I don't believe you can ever change the attitudes of white people in the South. | 5 | 8 | 16 |
| The southern Negro does have a chance to make something of himself. | 98 | 97 | 96 |
| All white people are alike. | 2 | 0 | 6 |

These figures by themselves might seem to suggest that the major motivating forces behind the sit-ins and freedom rides were anger, hatred of and hostility toward whites, and alienation from a white-dominated world in which it was the students' misfortune to have been born with a dark skin. This, however, is not the case.

Examine Table 14–8. It contains a set of statements about white people in the South and their treatment of Negroes, along with the percentage of the active protesters, inactive members of protest organizations, and nonparticipant students who agreed with each statement. Only 6 per cent of the participants in the sit-ins and freedom rides agreed that "all white people are prejudiced

against Negroes," whereas 22 per cent of the inert students believed this statement to be true! Although the difference in attitude between the students with
varying degrees of involvement in the protests is smaller for the other statements, the more active students consistently are more tolerant, understanding,
and optimistic about white people and segregation than are the inactive
students.

The same conclusion is supported when we examine the students' estimates
of white opinions on racial questions. Seventy-seven per cent of the Negro
students who correctly perceived that "all" or "most" southern whites favored
"strict segregation" were totally inactive in the protest movement, whereas
those who underestimated the extent of white opposition to Negro demands
were far more actively involved (see Table 14–9). The student protesters

TABLE 14–9.   *Negro student perceptions of white support for strict
segregation and extent of their participation
in protest movement*

| LEVEL OF PARTICIPATION IN THE PROTEST MOVEMENT | STUDENTS' PERCEPTIONS OF PROPORTION OF WHITES IN SOUTH FAVORING "STRICT SEGREGATION" | | |
| | All or most | About half | Less than half |
| --- | --- | --- | --- |
| Active personally | 13% | 26% | 33% |
| Belonged to protest group but not active personally | 10 | 27 | 7 |
| Neither active personally nor member of protest organization | 77 | 47 | 60 |
| TOTAL | 100% | 100% | 100% |
| N | 82 | 85 | 96 |

apparently were not "the children of despair"[15] but of hope and optimism.

The students who actively participated in the protest movement during its
early stages felt relatively fortunate when comparing their lot to that of other
Negroes in the South. Thus, for example, we find that those students who
believed that race relations were better in their home towns than in the South
as a whole participated more actively in the protests than those who felt that
they had been raised in communities with relatively poor race relations (see
Table 14–10). This conclusion presents an apparent paradox. At the beginning of this section we argued that the students who were most discontented
with southern race relations tended to participate most heavily in the protest
movement. Now we find that the active students felt a greater sense of relative
advantage than did the inactive ones! But these attitudes need not be in

[15] *Ibid.*, p. 278.

TABLE 14–10.    *Negro students' sense of relative advantage and deprivation and the extent of their participation in the protest movement*

| LEVEL OF PARTICIPATION IN THE PROTEST MOVEMENT | STUDENT BELIEF ABOUT RACE RELATIONS | | |
|---|---|---|---|
| | *Better in home community than in South as a whole* | *Same in home community as in South as a whole* | *Worse in home community than in South as a whole* |
| Active personally | 33% | 23% | 15% |
| Belonged to protest group but not active personally | 13 | 16 | 15 |
| Neither active personally nor member of protest organization | 54 | 61 | 70 |
| TOTAL | 100% | 100% | 100% |
| N | 115 | 62 | 87 |

conflict: quite different standards seem to have been used in arriving at these two judgments. *Compared with other Negroes*, the student protesters felt relatively fortunate. But *judged by absolute standards*—what they felt they deserved as *men*—they felt shabbily treated indeed.

Another psychological characteristic of the active student protesters was their superior factual knowledge of the world outside the South and the Negro ghetto. When we gave the students in our sample a shortened version of the political-information test administered to the adult sample, the protesting students answered more questions correctly (an average of 2.3 out of 4) than the inactive students (1.9). The active protesters read more newspapers (an average of 2.5) than the inactive members of protest groups (2.3) or the totally uninvolved (1.9). The same was true of magazines: the protesters on the average read 3.3 magazines regularly; the nonactive members, 2.8; and the inactive students, 2.7. The protesting students also watched TV and listened to the radio more than the inactive students did. Frequent personal contacts with whites in a variety of circumstances was also positively associated with active participation in the demonstrations. So, too, was travel outside the South. Without a superior acquaintance with the world at large, the Negro youngsters might have remained content with their lot as the most privileged members of a large group of "second-class citizens." But with this knowledge came new standards and reference groups that apparently made this once comfortable status increasingly unbearable.[16]

[16] Ruth Searles and J. Allen Williams, Jr., in "Negro College Students' Participation in Sit-ins," *Social Forces*, Vol. 40 (1962), pp. 215–19, developed the notion of the shifting reference groups of the Negro protesters. Our analysis has been substantially influenced by their thinking.

Thus a psychological analysis of the early student protesters does not reveal a portrait of bitter, alienated, and deprived agitators or "beatniks." Rather, the Negro activists tended to be unusually optimistic about race relations and tolerant of whites. They not only *were* better off, objectively speaking, than other Negroes but *felt* better off. At the same time, they were far better informed than other Negroes about the nonsegregated world outside the South. This resulted in a sense of relative deprivation when they compared their chances with those of middle-class whites and the values professed by the white community. Thus the active protesters felt deprived by "white" or general American standards of judgment at the same time that they felt relatively advantaged by Negro standards. This distinctive combination of conflicting feelings may well be, as Brinton argues, a precondition for all rebellions. At least they seem to have touched off the student protests of the early 1960's.

## The college community and student protest activity

Despite overwhelming student approval of the objectives and methods of the protest movement, the extent of protest activity varied a great deal from one college campus to another. (See Figure 14–2.) In 20 out of the 30 institutions in which we held interviews, more than 80 per cent of the students approved of the resort to direct action; in all 30 schools a clear majority of the students favored the protest movement. Yet in six colleges, not one student in the sample personally took part in the demonstrations or belonged to a protest

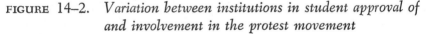

FIGURE 14–2.    *Variation between institutions in student approval of and involvement in the protest movement*

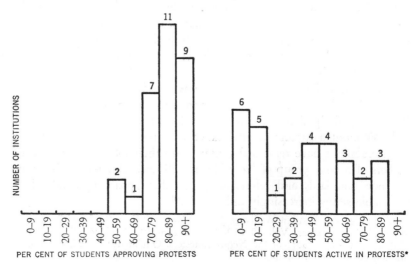

organization; in five more institutions, less than 20 per cent of the sample had done either of these things.

Moral approval is private and cheap; active involvement in a political movement requires a willingness to pay costs and run risks, which for the student protest movement were unusually high. Even so, we would expect to find a positive association between student attitudes at a college and the same students' rate of participation in the protests. The actual Pearsonian coefficient of correlation between student support for and participation in the protests, by college, is $+.51$. This is a respectably high figure; but it means that only 25 per cent ($r^2$) of the variation in protest activity from college to college is "explained" by student attitudes. Being a student in some Negro colleges must have made it easy to translate favorable attitudes into action, whereas being a student in other colleges must have made it hard.

Negro colleges differ in a number of ways that may help account for the variations in student protest activity. Eighteen of the colleges in our sample, for example, were state institutions; 12 were private. Although both types of institution depend in large part on white acceptance and financial support, the public colleges are far more vulnerable to pressures from the white community. Financial dependence on private philanthropy (largely northern) differs greatly from financial dependence on a southern state legislature enraged by the "irresponsible" and "revolutionary" activities of "ungrateful" Negro students. The movement threatened more than just the financial support of state schools; many white politicians reacted to the demonstrations by threatening to fire college administrators and professors, to expel students, even to close the Negro schools altogether if the students did not stop forthwith. In some cases these threats were carried out. Understandably, therefore, many administrators of state-supported Negro colleges did everything they could to discourage student participation in the protests. Even without cues from administrators, many students would hesitate to engage in activities that they felt threatened the survival of their *alma mater*.

The Negro colleges vary in size—most are rather small, but a few rival white institutions in size and complexity. Protest activity might be expected to flourish in the larger, more impersonal institutions in which it is harder for administrators to put pressure on individual students. Or we might expect the contrary: the closer personal ties of the small college might make it easier to mobilize student predispositions into group action. In either event, we might reasonably expect the size of the Negro school to affect the rate of student participation in the sit-ins and freedom rides.

Finally, the Negro colleges differ in that elusive attribute called academic "quality." True, no Negro institution in the South rates very well when compared with its white counterparts. Even so, the Negro schools do differ significantly in the quality of education they provide. A superior education—relatively speaking—should lead to the greater knowledge and awareness of alternatives to segregation that we earlier found associated with protest activity.

In order to test this speculation, we constructed a scale of academic quality based on such generally accepted indicators as the student-teacher ratio, the proportion of the faculty holding Ph.D. degrees, the number of books in the library, and the dollars spent each year per student.[17]

TABLE 14–11.  *Characteristics of Negro college and student attitudes toward and participation in the protest movement*

| | N | Percentage of students favoring demonstrations | Percentage of students participating in demonstrations[a] | Percentage of students favoring demonstrations who participated[a] |
|---|---|---|---|---|
| **QUALITY OF INSTITUTION** | | | | |
| Type I (best) | 37 | 95% | 54% | 57% |
| Type II | 53 | 91 | 55 | 60 |
| Type III | 61 | 80 | 38 | 48 |
| Type IV (worst) | 75 | 77 | 21 | 27 |
| **CONTROL OF INSTITUTION** | | | | |
| Private | 94 | 91 | 53 | 58 |
| Public | 170 | 79 | 31 | 39 |
| **NUMBER OF STUDENTS IN INSTITUTION** | | | | |
| Fewer than 1,00 | 115 | 87 | 43 | 49 |
| 1,000–2,499 | 80 | 84 | 36 | 43 |
| 2,500+ | 69 | 77 | 36 | 47 |
| **NEGRO CONCENTRATION IN COUNTY CONTAINING COLLEGE** | | | | |
| 0%–19% | 58 | 95 | 60 | 63 |
| 20%–39% | 104 | 83 | 44 | 53 |
| 40%+ | 102 | 77 | 22 | 29 |
| **SIZE OF CITY OR TOWN IN WHICH COLLEGE LOCATED** | | | | |
| 100,000+ | 109 | 89 | 50 | 56 |
| 10,000–99,999 | 100 | 78 | 40 | 51 |
| Less than 10,000 | 55 | 82 | 17 | 21 |

[a] Personally active or belonging to protest organization.

In Table 14–11, we can see that all three of these characteristics—institutional control, size, and quality—were related to the student attitudes toward and activity in the protest movement. The proportion of students *favoring* the sit-ins varied from 95 per cent at the best Negro colleges to 77 per cent at the poorest, from 91 per cent in private institutions to 79 per cent in public schools,

[17] See Appendix C for the construction of this scale of academic quality.

and from 87 per cent in the smallest colleges to 77 per cent in the largest colleges. These differences in attitudes are relatively small, however, compared to the differences in *participation rates* at these same types of school. Fifty-four per cent of the students at the best colleges either took part in the demonstrations personally or belonged to a protest organization, while only 21 per cent of the students at the poorest institutions were that active. Fifty-three per cent of the students at private colleges were involved in the movement, compared to only 31 per cent at public colleges and universities. The size of the institution seemed to make the least difference in the rate of student participation—43 per cent of the students at the smallest and 36 per cent of the students at the largest colleges either took part in the demonstrations or belonged to one of the protesting organizations.

Finally, note that these same three characteristics of the Negro colleges are related to the proportion of the favorably inclined students who became activists. The mobilization of latent support into active involvement was much more complete at the better, private institutions and slightly more effective in the smaller schools.

The Negro colleges differ not only in their size, quality, and sponsorship but also in the nature of the communities in which they are located. A number are in small, black-belt towns; others are in urban areas with a relatively small Negro population. One would expect more active white hostility to the sit-ins and freedom rides in the first type of setting than in the second. As we can see by referring again to Table 14–11, student protest activities varied according to the size of the place in which the college was located and the proportion of Negroes in its population. Sixty per cent of the students at colleges located in counties with populations containing less than 20 per cent Negroes—and hence characterized by more enlightened white racial attitudes—became protesters; only 22 per cent of the students at colleges in places with populations containing 40 per cent or more Negroes took part. The difference between the most urban and the most rural schools was just about as large.

This entire picture is complicated by the fact that all these characteristics of the colleges and their communities are closely related to one another.[18]

[18] The extent of the association between each of these variables can be seen from the matrix of coefficients of association ($Q$) below:

|  | Academic quality | Public-private control | Percentage Negro | Size of town |
|---|---|---|---|---|
| Public-private control | — .75 | — | — | — |
| Percentage Negro in county | 0 | + .72 | — | — |
| Size of college town | + .10 | — .68 | — .91 | — |
| Size of college | — .29 | + .95 | + .52 | — .39 |

Variables must be dichotomized in computing $Q$, and the values obtained vary somewhat according to how this is done. The above coefficients should therefore be considered as approximate.

Generally speaking, the better colleges tend to be privately controlled, relatively small and located in larger cities with relatively low Negro concentrations compared to the countryside; the poorer institutions tend to be relatively large, public, and rural. When we examine the associations between each of these five characteristics and student protest activity, controlling for all the other factors, two variables emerge with substantial and independent impact on student participation in the protests: the quality of the school, and the degree of Negro concentration in the county in which the school is located (see Table 14–12).

TABLE 14–12.   *Quality of college, Negro concentration in county containing college, and student attitudes toward and participation in the protest movement*

| COLLEGE CHARACTERISTICS | | Percentage of students favoring the demonstrations | Percentage of students participating in movement | Percentage favoring demonstrations who participated | N |
|---|---|---|---|---|---|
| *Quality* | *Percentage Negro in county* | | | | |
| Good | Low | 94% | 69% | 73% | 52 |
| Good | High | 92 | 33 | 36 | 36 |
| Poor | Low | 88 | 41 | 47 | 111 |
| Poor | High | 73 | 14 | 20 | 62 |

NOTE: "Good" quality = types I and II; "poor" quality = types III and IV. Low Negro concentration = 0–39 per cent Negro; high Negro concentration = 40 per cent and above. Participation in movement = personally active or belonging to protest organization.

Can we conclude that variations in student protest among the Negro colleges are largely the result of the quality of education the students received, modified by the varying degrees of white hostility and resistance they faced in their college communities? This certainly is a plausible interpretation of the data introduced so far, but it overlooks one very important factor—the selective recruitment of students. Earlier we found substantial class differences in the level of student protest activity, and the higher-quality schools attract more high-status students than do the inferior schools. These middle-class Negro youngsters may have *come* to college with the attitudes and cognitions that we found to be associated with active protest.

This is true—up to a point. But the kind of school the Negro youths attend still makes a large difference in their participation in the protest movement *after we have controlled for their social class* (see Table 14–13). The low-status students who attended the better institutions were just about as active in the protests as were their more fortunate fellow students. In the relatively inferior schools, the high-income students participated much more than the majority of students who were not so well off. But even under these circum-

TABLE 14–13.   *Family income and percentage of students participating in the protest movement, controlling for characteristics of college*

| COLLEGE CHARACTERISTICS | | FAMILY INCOME | |
|---|---|---|---|
| Quality | Percentage Negro in county | Less than $5,000 | More than $5,000 |
| Good | Low | 65% (17) | 71% (35) |
| Good | High | 35 (17) | 32 (19) |
| Poor | Low | 32 (57) | 54 (52) |
| Poor | High | 9 (45) | 26 (19) |

NOTE: See note to Table 14–12.

stances, the quality of the school and the degree of Negro concentration in the college community were more predictive of student participation in the protests than was the income of the student's family.

The inter-institutional variations in protest activity by students do not, then, appear to be solely the result of selective recruitment. Rather, they seem to flow primarily from the differing quality of the educational experience itself, modified by community differences in white resistance, actual or anticipated.

## The protester as student

So far we have tried to explain student participation in the protests of 1961 and 1962 without examining our subjects' most central role—that of student. We have found that the active protesters tended to come in disproportionate numbers from middle-class families and urban places where race relations were relatively benign; that they tended to be relatively optimistic, tolerant of whites, and well informed; and that they tended to be students at the better Negro colleges located in communities where white hostility to the protests was likely to be relatively mild. But what kind of *students* were they? And were their characteristics *as students* related to the extent of their activity in the protest movement?

The answer to the last question is definitely "yes." As Table 14–14 shows, the frequency with which Negro students took part in the protests increased moderately from the freshman to the sophomore year. A much sharper increase took place between the second and third year. When we examine the seniors, we find that an impressive 45 per cent of them had personally participated in either the sit-ins or the freedom rides. Four freshmen may have begun the student protest movement, but it was the older, more advanced students who flocked to the movement in disproportionate numbers.

TABLE 14–14.   *College class and academic major of students and the extent of their participation in the protest movement*

| | Personally active | Belonged to protest organization | Neither | TOTAL | N |
|---|---|---|---|---|---|
| COLLEGE CLASS | | | | | |
| Freshman | 14% | 10 | 76 | 100% | 99 |
| Sophomore | 18% | 16 | 66 | 100% | 68 |
| Junior | 38% | 19 | 43 | 100% | 47 |
| Senior | 45% | 11 | 44 | 100% | 47 |
| ACADEMIC MAJOR | | | | | |
| Humanities | 46% | 8 | 46 | 100% | 26 |
| Physical sciences | 35% | 20 | 45 | 100% | 49 |
| Social sciences | 28% | 20 | 52 | 100% | 50 |
| Vocational (misc.) | 19% | 12 | 69 | 100% | 45 |
| Education | 12% | 11 | 77 | 100% | 73 |
| Business administration | 11% | 11 | 78 | 100% | 18 |

A tempting conclusion is that the educational efforts of the colleges had something to do with this—that the increase in participation among upper-classmen was the result of their having attended more lectures, read more books, and taken part in more dormitory bull sessions than the younger students—in a word, that they were more fully educated. Americans of all colors have great faith in the power of education to shape opinions and behavior and to "solve" problems, but research on the effects of formal education scarcely justifies such extreme faith.[19] Before we conclude that the college-class differences in participation result from the added education of the upper-classmen, we must dismiss a number of alternative explanations.

First, the underclassmen seemingly had a shorter period of time than the juniors and seniors in which to join the movement; the lower rate of participation among freshmen and sophomores may reflect this fact. But the freshmen could have become active in the movement before going to college—thousands of Negro high-school students did. And the movement had been under way for only about two years at the time of our interviews. Thus the sophomores, juniors, and seniors all had had the same length of time to become active *while in college*, but the frequency with which they did so was very different.

The sharp jump upward in participation between the second and third years suggests still another possibility. The Negro junior colleges all ranked rather

[19] Thus V. O. Key, Jr., in *Public Opinion and American Democracy* (New York: Alfred A. Knopf, 1961), p. 343, concludes: "In the largest sense the educational system is a great mechanism for conserving the values, the institutions, the practices of the political order. . . . Yet the educational process does not completely embalm the political system. From it there come the political innovators as well as the conservers."

low on our scale of academic quality, and students at low-quality schools tended to be less active in the movement. The differences in participation between college classes may be merely a reflection of the fact that a disproportionate number of the upperclassmen in our sample were attending high-quality, four-year institutions. This tendency certainly does exist—the students at the poorer schools were rather heavily concentrated in the freshman and sophomore years, while the superior Negro institutions had a better balance among the four college classes. But even after we control for type of college, we find that the upperclassmen participated a great deal more than the freshmen and sophomores (see Table 14–15).

TABLE 14–15.  *College class, academic major, and student participation in the protest movement, controlling for type of college attended*

|  | TYPE OF COLLEGE | | | |
|---|---|---|---|---|
|  | Good-quality, low percentage Negro | Good-quality, high percentage Negro | Poor-quality, low percentage Negro | Poor-quality, high percentage Negro |
| COLLEGE CLASS |  |  |  |  |
| Juniors and seniors | 85% (26) | 67% (9) | 55% (38) | 29% (24) |
| Freshmen and sophomores | 54% (26) | 21% (28) | 34% (73) | 5% (40) |
| ACADEMIC MAJOR |  |  |  |  |
| Arts and sciences | 76% (33) | 50% (18) | 60% (48) | 8% (24) |
| Vocational | 58% (19) | 16% (19) | 27% (63) | 18% (38) |

NOTE: Percentages are of students with the indicated attributes who were personally active or who belonged to protest organizations. Thus the first entry means that 85 per cent of the juniors and seniors at good-quality schools in counties with a relatively low proportion of Negroes were participants.

Greater learning apparently does lead to greater participation. And the second academic difference between the protesting and the inactive students substantially reinforces this conclusion: *the subjects that the Negro students were studying in college were strongly related to the extent of their activities in the protest movement* (see Table 14–14). The most active students were majoring in the humanities; 46 per cent of them were personally active in the protests. The physicists, chemists, biologists, and natural scientists generally were just about as active. Students of the social sciences were the third most likely group to become involved. Participation dropped off sharply among the large majority of students engaged in vocational studies, especially education and business administration.

How can we explain these differences in participation? Both the subject matter of these disciplines and the self-selection of students into them are probably relevant. First, the largest group of vocationally oriented students—the education majors—were preparing themselves to enter a highly segregated profession. This aspect of teaching may discourage the Negro students who are most deeply dedicated to racial integration from majoring in the field, and it may attract those who are most willing to accept segregation. And looking forward to a teaching career—almost always, because of certification requirements, in the state where they are attending college—the education majors may have wanted to avoid an involvement of which their future white employers would not approve. We saw in earlier chapters that once these youths become schoolteachers they will find it difficult, if not impossible, to play a militant role in the racial politics of southern communities. Apparently most education majors accept this restraint while they are still training for the job. Indeed, to follow any strictly vocational line of study in college—such as business administration or nursing—is to prepare oneself to succeed within the confines of the existing social and economic system.

The students who choose to study one of the sciences or the humanities, on the other hand, probably have a greater interest in learning as an end in itself. In the process of their studies—particularly if they are humanists or social scientists—they become thoroughly committed to the universalistic value system of the western world that is so at odds with southern racial realities. To exaggerate a bit, the arts and sciences students are preparing themselves to judge—and perhaps change—the world rather than to rise within it. The vocational student is characterized by less exalted and more materialistic aspirations.

But, again, more mundane factors may account for differences in participation rates. The "impractical" arts and sciences attract higher-status students at all institutions—the poor boy struggling to get through college is more likely to view education as a means of occupational advancement than of acquiring "conspicuous culture." And the academically superior colleges (which tend to be private and expensive) put more stress on education in the arts and sciences than do the poorer, public institutions with their more job-oriented, lower-status clientele. These social class and college biases might account for the differences we have found in participation by field of study—but they do not. When the quality of the college is controlled, the sharp differences in participation by the students' field of study remain little changed (see Table 14–15).

Thus the more and the better the education the Negro college student enjoyed, and the more this education was concerned with the liberal arts and pure sciences, the more likely he was to become an activist in the protest movement. We cannot, of course, "prove" the ultimate "causes" of action. To "control" for all the effects of all other variables is statistically impossible, and to imagine what all these other variables are is intellectually impossible.

But formal education does appear to have played a major role in triggering the student protest movement. The *quantity, quality,* and *content* of the Negro youths' education were *all* strongly related to the extent of their protest activities. These relationships cannot easily be explained away on other grounds.

Optimism, tolerance, factual knowledge, and rejection of Negro reference groups and values in favor of universalistic and "white" standards characterized the original protesters; these characteristics seem to have resulted, in large part, from their formal schooling. In this case at least, education seems to have played the dynamic role Americans like to assign to it. Whether the action it helped to inspire contributed to a "solution" of a "problem"—another role Americans typically assign to education—is an entirely different matter.

## The impact of the sit-ins

The concrete results of the sit-ins were impressive—at least by the attenuated standards usually employed in measuring racial progress in the South. By September 1961 the authoritative Southern Regional Council reported that at least one establishment had desegregated its eating facilities in each of 76 cities in the old South. A majority of these successes, however, emerged in three states on the periphery of the region (Florida, North Carolina, and Virginia) and, except in Atlanta and Savannah, Georgia, not one establishment in the Deep South had given in to the protests.[20] Nonetheless, even in some cities in the Deep South people began to realize that the integration of public accommodations was inevitable. "We've been watching these freedom rides and boycotts in other cities," the mayor of Macon, Georgia, is quoted as saying in 1962, "and we're getting the picture. Even Robert E. Lee had to surrender, didn't he?"[21]

But the thousands of students who spearheaded the demonstrations were not really interested in coffee and hamburgers.[22] They were interested in achieving racial equality in the South and in achieving it quickly. It could not be achieved by applying sporadic pressure to a handful of businessmen. But the publicity the demonstrations had generated might turn the trick, and the students knew it. The protests were, in the words of one student in North Carolina, "a way to indicate our dissatisfaction with the way we are treated" and to make "the white people wake up and think about what is happening." The students were well suited to the role. They were, as a Florida sophomore put it,

> . . . sort of "select." They are not the type of Negro that whites usually judge us by. Usually they judge us by the very low class type of Negro, and by the demonstrations they get a chance to see Negroes who are different.

[20] Southern Regional Council, op. cit., pp. 14–15.
[21] Wall Street Journal, February 6, 1962.
[22] A professor of the four freshmen at North Carolina A. and T. quotes one of the original protesters as saying, "We didn't want to set the world on fire—all we wanted was to eat." (Stroud, op. cit., p. 18.) This may have been true for the original four protesters, but it certainly was not true for the thousands of other students who later joined the movement.

The demonstrations also were a concrete way of proving the urgency and intensity of the young Negroes' demands—"We are striving for equality *and will stop at nothing* to get it!" The demonstrations were, in sum, a classic example of propaganda of the deed. We must judge the efficacy of the sit-ins and the freedom rides primarily by their effect on public opinion.

### THE IMPACT ON SOUTHERN WHITE OPINION

The contrast between the dignity and courage of the young Negro protesters and the ugly and sometimes violent behavior of their white tormentors was not easy to overlook, especially when the same awful scenes were reported day after day on the nation's TV screens and front pages. Even the Virginia *Richmond News Leader*, which prides itself on being the authentic voice of southern traditionalism, was moved to say:

> Here were the colored students, in coats, white shirts, ties, and one of them was reading Goethe and one was taking notes from a biology text. And here, on the sidewalk outside, was a gang of white boys come to heckle, a ragtail rabble, slackjawed, black-jacketed, grinning fit to kill, and some of them, God save the mark, were waving the proud and honored flag of the Southern States in the last war fought by gentlemen: Eheu! It gives one pause.[23]

And, after the police in Birmingham and Montgomery failed to protect the freedom riders, the *Atlanta Constitution* wrote:

> The point is not to judge the beaten, but to take a look at the beaters. . . . Either a community is going to believe in civilization or it is going to revert to the jungle. . . . To blame the violence on the demonstrators is sophistry of the most hurtful order. These people who go barnstorming across the South in busses are curious. . . .
>
> But this is not the point of what happened in Alabama. Any man in this free country has the right to demonstrate and assemble and make a fool of himself if he pleases without getting hurt. If the police, representing the people, refuse to intervene when a man—any man—is being beaten to the pavement of an American city, then this is not a noble land at all. It is a jungle. But this is a noble land. And it is time for the decent people in it to muzzle the jackals.[24]

Nonetheless, rank-and-file southern whites remained overwhelmingly opposed to the students and their demonstrations. At the time of our interviews with adults—the sit-ins had been under way for about a year, and the freedom rides were just beginning—only 7 per cent of the voting-age whites approved of the demonstrations, and almost all of these had been convinced integrationists before the protests began (see Table 14–16).[25] The sit-ins had the

[23] February 22, 1960.

[24] May 22, 1961. For an analysis of the dubious propaganda value of the freedom rides, see the Southern Regional Council, *The Freedom Ride*, May 1961 (mimeo.).

[25] Only a longitudinal study could demonstrate this point conclusively. Given the evidence on the stability of white racial attitudes presented throughout this book, however, this seems to be a safe assumption to make in analyzing these data.

TABLE 14–16.    *Attitudes of southern whites toward the sit-ins,*
*by their racial attitudes*

| ATTITUDE TOWARD SIT-INS | RACIAL ATTITUDES | | | |
|---|---|---|---|---|
| | *White segregationists* | *White moderates* | *White integrationists* | *All whites* |
| Strongly approve | a | 1% | 18% | 1% |
| Approve | 1% | 16 | 16 | 6 |
| Neutral, no attitude toward, uncodeable responses | 7 | 23 | 34 | 13 |
| Disapprove | 63 | 53 | 32 | 59 |
| Strongly disapprove | 24 | 5 | — | 17 |
| Have not heard of sit-ins | 5 | 2 | — | 4 |
| TOTAL | 100% | 100% | 100% | 100% |
| N | 443 | 192 | 44 | 694 |

a Greater than 0, less than 0.5 per cent.
NOTE: "Don't know's" on racial attitude are included in percentages for "all whites."

immediate effect of alienating the Negro's friends while solidifying the opposition of his enemies.

Only 17 per cent of the white moderates and 34 per cent of the avowed integrationists approved of the demonstrations early in 1961. Almost 90 per cent of the segregationists clearly opposed them—about a quarter of these, bitterly so. "They think it's time to rule the world," a retired police chief in South Carolina said caustically. "They say the proprietor should close up," an elderly housewife in Montgomery remarked, "but I'd get me a bat and I'd run them out. I wouldn't close up." A middle-aged butcher in Crayfish County was even more extreme: "I think white people ought to take them out and horsewhip the black so-and-so's."

Even the vast numbers of white southerners who were repelled by these violent sentiments—and the actions they had triggered—felt that the demonstrators were morally and legally wrong. "Those are privately owned concerns," a college graduate in Capital City said. "They [the Negroes] have no business going in there and making a fuss." A secretary in a south Georgia town felt ". . . they are going about this in the wrong way. They are wrong. Even in a public place you should wait until you are invited. The Negro in the South has never been invited. They are disobeying the ethical code." "After all," a Florida real estate salesman said, ". . . they *do* have facilities where they can eat. It's not a question of their being hungry."

To miss the point of these dramatic events so completely requires powerful psychological defenses. White southerners—especially the segregationists and the moderates—apparently had such defenses. The major one was the belief that the sit-ins were the result of "outside agitation" rather than of genuine discontent over racial conditions; about half the explanations offered for the sit-ins by white segregationists and moderates and over a third of those offered by white integrationists were along these lines (see Table 14–17).

TABLE 14–17. *Causes of sit-ins as seen by southern whites, by their racial attitudes (in percentage of all "causes" mentioned)*

| CAUSES OF SIT-INS | RACIAL ATTITUDES | | | |
| --- | --- | --- | --- | --- |
| | *White segregationists* | *White moderates* | *White integrationists* | *All whites* |
| "Outside" agitation | 53% | 47% | 37% | 50% |
| "Inside" agitation | 19 | 23 | 21 | 20 |
| Agitation, general and unspecified | 16 | 9 | 7 | 13 |
| Spontaneous movement | 11 | 18 | 33 | 15 |
| Other, unclassifiable | 1 | 3 | 2 | 2 |
| TOTAL | 100% | 100% | 100% | 100% |
| N | 434 | 218 | 54 | 706 |

Ironically—in view of the fact that Negro discontent with the NAACP and its legalistic strategy contributed to the demonstrations—the NAACP was seen as the moving force behind the sit-ins. "I think they are paid by this big organization," a clerk in Florida said, "I can't think of it [pause] NAACP—which Nixon is president of." Most other southerners did not confuse the 1960 Republican candidate for president with Roy Wilkins, but over a quarter of them falsely perceived the NAACP as the instigator of the movement. A somewhat smaller number (14 per cent) tended to blame the whole thing on the communists. "Khrushchev is behind all communist action in this country," a housewife in Crayfish County explained. "He says our downfall will have to be from within and this integration [movement] is promoted directly by him."

Next to the NAACP and the communists, northerners were the favorite culprits. The ideas of a semiskilled worker in rural Georgia were fairly typical:

> They get started from the North; the Yankees come down here and get them started. They don't want to live with 'em, and they think if they can get us to a' mixing they [the Negroes] will like the climate here and they can send all their niggers down here to live.

"On TV," the wife of a white laborer in Montgomery said, "Negroes can be on and the whites put their arms around them. These Negroes think around here that they can do the same thing." A salesman in Arkansas was convinced that the entire movement was started by Negro entertainers in the North: "You know that tall thin Negro singer with the soft voice? He was the starter of the whole movement. He sponsored the first one and has put in much of the money." White entertainers also got their lumps. "That Dave Garroway," a housewife in Mississippi said, "I used to like him until he talked like he did about the Negroes. [We] ought to put about six in a house with him and let them stay about a week, bet he'd change his mind—after smelling them and really finding out how unclean they are in thoughts and their bodies." Finally, a retired policeman in Florida suggested why so many southern racists could not believe that the sit-ins were a genuine Negro movement. "There's never been a nigger born," he said, "with sense enough to administrate such a thing."

When asked to speculate on the motivation of the demonstrators, most southern whites again displayed their defensiveness by assigning dubious motives to the youngsters who were risking life and limb at the local drugstore (see Table 14–18). Most segregationists and moderates chalked the whole

TABLE 14–18.   *Major motivation ascribed to sit-inners by whites, by their racial attitudes*

| MOTIVATION OF SIT-INNERS | RACIAL ATTITUDES | | | |
|---|---|---|---|---|
| | *White segregationists* | *White moderates* | *White integrationists* | *All whites* |
| Desire for social equality | 12% | 21% | 37% | 16% |
| Demand for legal rights | 7 | 17 | 27 | 11 |
| Youthful exuberance | 25 | 21 | 11 | 23 |
| Paid to do it | 11 | 4 | — | 8 |
| Ignorance, don't know better, duped | 25 | 17 | 7 | 22 |
| Communism | 5 | 2 | — | 4 |
| Love of race, etc. | 5 | 8 | 9 | 6 |
| Other, unclassifiable | 10 | 10 | 9 | 10 |
| TOTAL | 100% | 100% | 100% | 100% |
| N | 353 | 169 | 44 | 576 |

NOTE: "Don't know's" on racial attitude are included in percentages for "all whites."

thing off to youthful exuberance ("Well, I think some do it for excitement"), a desire for publicity ("They want their names in the papers and need attention"), or immaturity and ignorance ("They're just crazy and ignorant people"). A sizable minority of white southerners were convinced that the protesters were being paid—"It's the best money for easy work." Still others felt that participation in the protests was merely the result of inborn cussedness: "Some agitators has trouble in their blood. They are just like dope addicts—until they get something started they aren't happy." Only about a fourth of the whites—almost all of them integrationists and moderates—felt that the demonstrating students were motivated by a desire for equality or moral rights.

Thus apparently the sit-ins did not convert many white southerners to the rightness of the Negro cause. Even after five years of sit-ins most white southerners were unaware of the depth of Negro discontent in the region, as we saw in Chapter Twelve. This frightening ignorance probably would have been even greater had it not been for the protests. But this heightened awareness of Negro discontent was purchased at the price of increased bitterness, tension, and defensiveness among the whites of the South.

### THE IMPACT ON SOUTHERN NEGRO OPINION

The protests were so dramatic and so well publicized that very few Negroes in the South were untouched by them. After a year of demonstrations, only 14 per cent of the Negro adults in the South had never heard of the sit-ins, and those who had heard of them overwhelmingly approved of them (see Table 14–19). This was true even though many adult Negroes felt—quite

TABLE 14–19.   *Attitudes of adult southern Negroes toward the sit-ins*

| Attitude toward sit-ins | Negro adults |
|---|---|
| Strongly approve | 30% |
| Approve | 22 |
| Neutral, no attitude toward, uncodeable response | 12 |
| Disapprove | 19 |
| Strongly disapprove | 3 |
| Have not heard of sit-ins | 14 |
| TOTAL | 100% |
| N | 618 |

accurately—that the "revolt" was almost as much against them and their leadership as against the dominant whites. "My idea is this," a middle-aged laundress in Piedmont County said. "We older people didn't have the guts to do it, but the young people didn't care even if they died." A white-collar worker in North Carolina agreed. "We are too complacent and slow for the young people," he said. "It's the greatest!" a laborer's wife said in Florida. "I tell you, they have courage I never dreamed of."

A new mood of impatience and militancy was sparked in Negro adults by the sight of their youngsters being heckled and beaten up by white people. A fifty-ish unemployed porter in Texas said:

> I go along with them [the protesters] because I feel if we wait longer it will take longer. So they should make white people wake up to the fact that we are

citizens and deserve to be treated that way. Why, all kinds of people can come to this country and receive better treatment than us. You know, even Russians— and whites pretend they hate them. But they can eat in these stores—we can't. Yet we go and die in the war to be treated this way. To hell with America if this is what it gives! White people are fakes. They are selfish and want everything for themselves.

An electrician in Capital City expressed the new mood in less extreme language. "My people have gotten tired of sitting around and waiting for Santa Claus and another Abraham Lincoln," he said in trying to explain the origins of protest activity. "They are coming to the front. And *now* is the time!"

Even the few Negroes who opposed the demonstrations often expressed admiration for the breathtaking boldness of the younger generation. "I don't like that much," a 78-year-old wife of a tenant farmer in Florida said about the tactics of the protesters. "I don't understand it much, I reckon. I don't see why—but you know, I ain't even in the same generation with them children. There is two or three generations 'twixt us, so they don't think like I do. I ain't never been skeered of white peoples, but I sure couldn't do like these children."

And some Negroes opposed the sit-ins only because they wanted something more. A semiliterate painter in Capital City spoke to this point:

We get things. Now just like we got policemans, we get colored bus drivers but they don't drive nowhere but to [slang name of Negro district] and up to the [Negro] school and some of our people is so happy 'til they busting shirt buttons. So the white people do no more cause we is satisfied. It'll be the same way with the sit-ins. They work out something somewhere and some of our folks will just get so glad they can set down by white folks 'til in the end what we got won't be worth the nights them poor people spent in jail.

The solution, as this man saw it, was a more broadly based mass movement:

What I'm driving at is, why should them few little freedom riders and sit-inners be the ones that get pushed around and put in jail and everything while all the rest of us colored folks sit back and wait to enjoy the good part? I think something orta be done but it just don't look like the sit-in is what that is. Look like to me it orta be something all of us work at. Then it would mean more to everybody.

This frustrated activist was soon to have his wish. The sit-ins, by arousing new feelings of racial pride, self-confidence, and impatience with moderation in the Negro population, provided the necessary conditions for the mass protests that followed. This was, perhaps, the most important consequence of the sit-ins.

### THE IMPACT ON NORTHERN OPINION

The protest movement, when viewed as a propaganda or educational campaign, was not aimed exclusively at a southern audience. The sit-ins, freedom rides, and other forms of mass demonstrations sought to catch the attention of the nation and the world—and they did. They made "the Negro problem," which northern whites preferred to forget, the number-one domestic problem of the country. And certainly the protest movement was far more favorably received in the North than in the former Confederate states. Sympathy and support for the protesters poured into the South—in the form of volunteers, money, and sympathetic treatment in the mass media. The federal government responded to this new concern by taking a more aggressive stance in dealing with civil rights violations in the South. Finally, in the wake of the Birmingham riots of 1963, President Kennedy proposed a new civil rights act that was to become law after his death in a far tougher form than he or most political observers had thought possible. All these developments can be traced back to the day in Greensboro, North Carolina, when four young Negroes sat down at the lunch counter in Woolworth's.

But as the mood and tactics of the movement spread northward and into such areas of interracial contact as housing, employment, and schools, some whites in the North became concerned and fearful. Responsible men began talking of a "white backlash." By 1963 a nationwide survey conducted by Louis Harris for *Newsweek* magazine found that most northern whites favored racial equality in the abstract but felt strongly that the Negroes were moving too far too fast. They were also opposed to the direct-action tactics of Negro protests.[26] The attitudinal gap between southern and nonsouthern whites on the race problem was still wide, but the gap between black and white, regardless of section, was beginning to look even wider.

[26] William Brink and Louis Harris, *The Negro Revolution in America* (New York: Simon and Schuster, 1964), ch. 9, especially pp. 144–45.

Chapter Fifteen

# College Students and the New Negro Leadership

Every college commencement speaker worthy of his stipend tells his audience, at some point in his address, that they are the future leaders of their community, state, and nation. No one takes this prediction too seriously. Interpreted literally, it is patently false; not all leaders are college-educated, and most college graduates do not become leaders. But taken loosely and metaphorically—which is the way commencement speakers talk—these tired old words contain an important truth. In America a disproportionate share of our leaders emerge from the minority who have been exposed to higher education.[1]

The disproportionate chance for leadership enjoyed by the college-educated is far greater among southern Negroes than among other Americans. True, the Negro college student's chances of becoming a leader of the total community—from president of the local chamber of commerce to President of the United States—are just about nil. But the chance that he will be called on to perform as a leader of other Negroes is very high.

The reasons are obvious. Prestige is generally a prerequisite of leadership; the college-educated southern Negro belongs to an elite far more exclusive and exalted in his community than the elite to which the white college graduate belongs. And successful leadership of any style—traditional, moderate, or militant—demands skills that are in very short supply in the Negro community. The highly educated more often have these skills than do ordinary Negroes. We saw in Chapter Seven, for example, that over 70 per cent of the Negro leaders in Piedmont and Camellia counties, almost half of those in Bright Leaf, and almost a third of those in Crayfish were college graduates.

[1] See Donald R. Matthews, *The Social Background of Political Decision-Makers* (New York: Random House, 1954).

443

Given the few Negro college graduates in these communities—especially in the two rural ones—the proportion of leaders drawn from among them was exceedingly high.

The students at Negro colleges in the South today will probably comprise a sizable portion of the future Negro leadership of the region. Of course, this cadre can and will be supplemented by Negroes without college training and by Negro southerners attending colleges in the North or racially integrated institutions in the South, and by college-educated migrants from the North. And yet, again as we saw in Chapter Seven, those Negroes who do become leaders without benefit of college training tend to be inferior ones. The number of southern Negroes trained in integrated southern colleges, or in the North, and the number of college-educated northern Negroes who migrate South, are insignificantly small.

We cannot assume merely because of the apparent lack of other desirable alternatives that today's Negro college students *will in fact* meet the future leadership needs of the race. For one thing, today's students have gone through the unique experience of the protest movement. Because no previous student generation has had this traumatic experience, no one knows how—if at all— it will affect their behavior as adults. Perhaps their experience as protesters will make this generation of college students particularly eager and qualified to accept the responsibilities of leadership. Perhaps it will not. Their hyperactivity in the protest movement may indicate that they reject normal political processes and routine modes of participation in community and political affairs. The attitudes that prompted them to revolt may be so at odds with those of the mass of southern Negroes that few of them will become leaders, even if they should want to. The normal restraints of adulthood—a regular job, a family, a home to be paid for—may make the only mode of participation they know— direct action and civil disobedience—no longer practical. And, above all, they may not even stay in the South. If they do become leaders in disproportionate numbers, it may be in Chicago, New York, or Los Angeles rather than in the former Confederate states where they grew up and went to college.

So let us examine our sample of Negro college students to see, if we can, whether they are likely to become leaders of southern Negro communities and, if so, what sort of leaders they are likely to be.

## Today's protesters: Tomorrow's leaders?

Today's Negro college students possess in abundance what may be the most important single prerequisite for political leadership—as a group they are very much interested in politics and public affairs (see Table 15-1). Only 15 per cent of them report "not much" interest in politics, compared to almost 50 per cent of the Negro adults in the South who rate themselves that way. More-

TABLE 15–1.   *Political interest and activity of Negro college students compared to that of Negro adults*

|  | Students (N = 264) | College-educated Negro adults (N = 49) | All Negro adults (N = 618) |
|---|---|---|---|
| POLITICAL INTEREST (SELF-RATING) | | | |
| Great deal | 34% | 49% | 28% |
| Somewhat | 51 | 37 | 22 |
| Not much | 15 | 14 | 49 |
| Don't know, no answer | a | 0 | 1 |
| TOTAL | 100% | 100% | 100% |
| POLITICAL ACTIVITIES EVER ENGAGED IN | | | |
| Talk about public problems | 99% | 98% | 87% |
| Voted in election | 15 | 76 | 41 |
| Took part in political campaign | 63 | 53 | 35 |
| Belong to political or racial group | 31 | 33 | 11 |

a Greater than 0, less than 0.5 per cent.
NOTE: These political activities are not arranged in a cumulative scale in this table because most students are not of voting age.

over, their *actual participation* in public life has *not* been confined just to the picket lines. Compared to Negro adults, they are far more likely to have talked to others about public affairs (99 to 87 per cent), to have taken at least a small part in political campaigning (63 to 35 per cent), and to belong to a political or racial organization (31 to 11 per cent). Only in voting do the adults display greater participation than the college students, and this because most of the students (63 per cent) are not of voting age or have not been of voting age long enough to have had the opportunity to vote. Almost half of the students who had had an opportunity to vote had done so; 99 per cent of those not yet of voting age wanted and expected to do so.

Table 15–1 also compares the political interest and activities of the college students with those of college-educated adults. Here we see that today's students are a little less interested in public affairs than are adults with some college education. The rates of overt political participation are about the same —again, with the obvious exception of voting. This does not mean that today's students are necessarily less concerned about politics than yesterday's, for political activity and interest normally increase with age up to the mid-fifties or beyond. We should expect today's Negro college students, then, to increase their political activity as they advance in age until it surpasses that of previous generations of college men and women in the Negro communities of the

South. After all, while they were still in their teens and early twenties, they launched a powerful new political movement and at the same time equaled and sometimes surpassed their equally well educated elders in other, more routine forms of political participation.

A second prerequisite for Negro leadership is an interest in and an identification with other members of the race. Without these sentiments a man cannot reasonably be expected to run the risks and pay the costs of Negro leadership in the South today, or to play the role satisfactorily if he inexplicably should be cast in it. A vast majority of the Negro students have these essential attitudes (see Table 15–2). Identification with other Negroes is

TABLE 15–2. *Student identification with Negroes compared to that of adults*

|  | Students (N = 264) | College-educated adults (N = 49) | All Negro adults (N = 618) |
|---|---|---|---|
| **FEELING ABOUT NEGROES IN GENERAL** | | | |
| Feel pretty close | 89% | 90% | 88% |
| Not closer than to others | 11 | 10 | 12 |
| TOTAL | 100% | 100% | 100% |
| **EXTENT OF INTEREST IN OTHER NEGROES** | | | |
| Good deal | 82% | 90% | 77% |
| Some | 17 | 10 | 13 |
| Not much | 1 | 0 | 10 |
| TOTAL | 100% | 100% | 100% |

so strong among Negro southerners that no significant difference exists in its frequency among students and adults—about 9 out of 10 Negroes feel "pretty close" to others regardless of their generation or level of schooling. The college students are more *interested* in the fate of other Negroes than the adults in general, but a little less interested than their college-educated elders. Student interest in other Negroes, in all probability, will increase with age in the same fashion as more generalized political interest does.

So far, then, the current generation of Negro college students appears to offer prime candidates for political leadership. With but few exceptions, they already possess the political interest, record of political activity, and identification with other Negroes that adult leadership seems to require. And, if research on the political consequences of aging is a reliable guide, we should expect all these attributes to increase in strength and frequency as the students grow into adult roles. The present generation of college students in the Negro colleges is probably far better equipped by interest and inclination for the challenges of leadership than were previous generations of Negro students.

But *where* are they likely to provide this leadership? When asked where they would most *like* to live, 48 per cent of the students said somewhere outside the South, 22 per cent said somewhere in the South, and the rest could not say. Two cities—New York and Los Angeles—appealed to this group of youngsters more than any other place. Chicago, Washington, D.C., Detroit, Boston, San Francisco–Oakland, and Seattle were also among their favorite locations. Except for Atlanta and Miami, which ranked fifth and sixth in desirability, the South was not viewed as a very good place to live by many of the students.

But dreams are cheap. Thus only 60 per cent of the students who want to live outside the region expect to do so. The *expectations* of the students are summarized in Table 15–3. A full third of the students—50 per cent of

TABLE 15–3.   *Where Negro students expect to live after college*

| LOCATION | Percentage of all students | Percentage of all students with reasonably clear residential expectations |
|---|---|---|
| Place where student grew up | 21% | 30% |
| State in which student grew up | 11 | 15 |
| Outside native state, but in South | 3 | 5 |
| Outside South, but in U.S.A. | 33 | 48 |
| Outside U.S.A. | 1 | 2 |
| Don't know | 31 | — |
| TOTAL | 100% | 100% |
| N | 264 | 182 |

those with reasonably clear residential expectations—*expect* to live outside the region. Over 40 per cent of those who expect to move out of the region think they will live on the Pacific Coast (see Table 15–4)—mostly in Los Angeles and southern California, but also in San Francisco, Oakland, Seattle, and other West Coast cities. A quarter of these students plan to move to the Northeast—mostly to New York, but also in appreciable numbers to Washington, D.C., Philadelphia, and the Boston area. Fourteen per cent look to the Midwest—especially the industrial cities of Chicago, Detroit, and Cleveland—as their future homes. Very few expect to migrate to the border or mountain states. If most of these plans and expectations are realized, up to half of these potential leaders will be lost to the region where the struggle for racial equality is most severe and where their potential political talents are most badly needed.

TABLE 15–4.    *Regions in which Negro students expecting to live outside South expect to live*

| LOCATION | |
|---|---|
| Pacific Coast | 41% |
| Northeastern states | 24 |
| Midwest | 14 |
| Border states | 7 |
| Mountain states | 1 |
| Outside South, unspecified | 10 |
| Abroad | 3 |
| TOTAL | 100% |
| N | 91 |

Admittedly, statements of intention are not perfect predictors of behavior. The students' expectations contain more than a little wishful thinking. The proportion expecting to migrate, for example, declines rather sharply as graduation and the hard realities of "life" approach. Fifty-eight per cent of the freshmen with clear residential expectations, 48 per cent of the sophomores, 53 per cent of the juniors, and only 38 per cent of the seniors in our sample expected to live outside the former Confederacy.

On the other hand, plans and expectations may change in the other direction, too. For example, every Negro college student in our sample who expects to live in the South also expects to fill a professional or technical job; only 49 per cent of the college-educated southern Negroes fill such jobs today. Without a drastic improvement in the occupational opportunities for Negroes in the region, a very large number of youngsters are going to be disappointed. What will happen to these students who are trained for and expect to fill better jobs than they are able to find in the South? Many of them will emigrate—especially since only half the students who expect to live in the South really prefer to live there. These facts suggest a good deal more movement out of the South than the students presently expect. Thus, though we cannot predict the exact rate of emigration, the students will probably leave the South at a rate—perhaps one out of every two, three, or four—far in excess of the Negro rank and file.

But more than a college education, favorable political and racial attitudes, and a willingness to remain in the region are necessary before a Negro is likely to become a leader in the South. In Chapter Seven, we found that virtually all Negro leaders are men. Unless this strong preference for males as leaders should change—and nothing suggests that it will—the 57 per cent of the college students who are women are not very likely to become leaders. We also found in Chapter Seven that Negro leaders tend to come predominantly from a few white-collar occupations—ministers, doctors, lawyers, businessmen, and the like—which command high prestige in the Negro community *and* which provide relative economic independence from whites. All the students expecting to remain in the South plan to hold white-collar jobs, but 68 per cent of them expect to become schoolteachers, a group so vulnerable to white economic pressure that few of them can be expected to become effective leaders.

At the time of our interviews, approximately 61,250 southern Negroes were enrolled in accredited, predominantly Negro institutions of higher learning in the former Confederate states. If we subtract those who definitely expect to move out of the region, all women, and all who expect to become school-teachers from this total pool of potential leadership, only about 7,900—13 per cent—are left with much chance of becoming southern leaders.[2] Of course, not all these will become available for adult leadership roles each year—perhaps only about a third, or 2,650, will. This is a pathetically small number from which to choose the leaders of almost 10 million people living in thousands of communities in 11 states.

# Why the flight from the South?

Everyone knows of the massive emigration of Negroes from the South since the First World War. In 1910 about 85 per cent of all American Negroes lived in the 11 states of the former Confederacy; 50 years later only about 50 per cent were still there. Such a great trek scarcely could go unnoticed. But both scholarly and popular attention has been directed primarily to the knotty problems that this vast migration has created for northern cities. Much less thought has been given to its consequences for the region from which the migrants fled.

Those who have paid some attention to this matter generally have con-cluded that the South is better off without these millions of Negroes. For one thing, the relatively backward economy of the South could not absorb all this Negro manpower; the great migration was partly a response to the hard fact of labor shortages in the North combined with a labor surplus in the South. And many assume that a decrease in the concentration of Negroes in the southern states will quiet white fears of black domination and ease the transition to racial justice.

[2] This is how we calculated this estimate: at the time of our interviews, there were 72,558 students enrolled in accredited, predominantly Negro institutions of higher learning in the 11 states of the former Confederacy. In the process of finding respond-ents to be interviewed as part of our sample, we found that 0.88 per cent of those approached were not Negroes, 5 per cent were not residents of the South, and 9.7 per cent had dropped out of college. Altogether 15.59 per cent of the original 72,558 total enrollment were dropped from our sample, leaving 61,248 students in the universe of southern Negroes actually enrolled in predominantly Negro institutions. Our sample of this universe consists of 264 interviews. Thus each respondent "stands for" 232 students.

But even after we concede these points (and the second one is subject to qualification),[3] the allegedly benign effects of Negro emigration for the South are cast in an entirely new light when we consider its effects on the region's Negro leadership. The South will probably lose from a third to a half of its most highly trained potential leaders as a result of emigration. The present critical shortage of Negro leaders in the region is not likely to be mitigated under these conditions; in fact, the shortage may become more acute in the years ahead. Without leadership in adequate quantity and quality, the Negro masses will not participate in politics as frequently or as effectively as they otherwise would.[4] The flight from the South by educated Negro youths may prove to be a major—perhaps *the* major—deterrent to the southern Negroes' full and expeditious realization of racial and political equality.

Why then do the students expect to leave? Why the flight from the South?

Their motivations are both distressingly obvious and distressingly obscure. The large northern and western cities are no racial paradise, a fact that a vast majority of the students planning to move there give every indication of realizing.[5] At the same time, the racial problems of these cities are less severe—and life in them is less constraining for a Negro[6]—than is true in the South. This, too, is clearly perceived by the students, *even by those who expect to remain in the region.* New York was rated as 7.7, Chicago as 6.9, and "a small city in Ohio" as 5.7 on our race-relations ladder by the students expecting to stay in the South. The same group rated Atlanta as 5.1, the South as a whole as 4.8, Little Rock as 3.9, and "a small town in Mississippi" as 2.3. Given these attitudes, the important question may not be why so many students intend to migrate but why so many of them do not. The racial attitudes of the students do not provide a satisfactory answer to either question.

If we look at the likelihood of migration as a function of racial attitudes, we notice at once that differences in racial attitudes make little difference for migration plans (see Table 15-5). About half of all students with clear residential expectations plan to leave the South, and this is just about the proportion found at every level of attitude that includes a reasonably large number of students. Thus, about 80 per cent of the students who rated race relations in the South as 1 or 2 on our race-relations ladder, 64 per cent of

---

[3] See Chapter Five.

[4] See Chapters Six and Seven.

[5] For example, the students who plan to move north do not differ appreciably from those who plan to remain in the region in the way they rate the race relations of northern cities. The mean ratings are:

|  | Expect to live in South | Expect to live outside South |
|---|---|---|
| New York | 7.7 | 7.7 |
| Chicago | 6.9 | 6.8 |
| A small city in Ohio | 5.7 | 6.2 |

[6] The psychological effects of moving north are often explored in Negro fiction. See, for example, Ralph Ellison, *The Invisible Man* (New York: Random House, 1952).

TABLE 15-5.  *Percentage of Negro college students expecting to live outside South, by their racial attitudes*

| ATTITUDE | Percentage | N |
|---|---|---|
| RATING OF SOUTH'S RACE RELATIONS TODAY | | |
| 1 or 2 (very poor) | 79% | 14 |
| 3 or 4 | 45 | 67 |
| 5 or 6 | 51 | 81 |
| 7 or 8 (good) | 45 | 20 |
| RACIAL STEREOTYPES | | |
| Pro-Negro | 64% | 22 |
| None | 53 | 49 |
| Pro-white | 46 | 105 |
| IDENTIFICATION WITH OTHER NEGROES | | |
| 0 (little or no) | — | 1 |
| 1 | 61% | 18 |
| 2 | 38 | 26 |
| 3 (strong) | 50 | 137 |
| PREFERENCE ON RACIAL POLICY | | |
| Segregation | — | 2 |
| Moderate | 47% | 15 |
| Integration | 51 | 164 |

NOTE: Percentages are based only on the total number of students with clear residential expectations.

those with pro-Negro racial stereotypes, and 61 per cent of those with little emotional identification with other Negroes expect to leave the South. But only a tiny minority of Negro students possess any one of these attitudes and feelings. Students who view themselves as racial "moderates" rather than as integrationists are a little more likely to plan to remain in the South—but almost all the students view themselves as integrationists. Students who displayed severe frustrations over segregation or hostility toward whites are much more likely to plan to migrate than those who do not—but again only a handful of students display such strong feelings of injustice, frustration, and hostility (see Table 15-6).

These data, then, do suggest that some highly atypical attitudes are associated with expectations of emigration. But they tell us little about the vast majority of the students who do not have these attitudes, and about half of the "typical" students with clear residential plans expect to move out of the region. For most students, racial attitudes and feelings do not seem to have very much, if anything, to do with whether they intend to migrate.

The students' opportunities to move, and their chances of making a respectable living where they now live, *do* have a great deal to do with their ex-

TABLE 15–6.   *Negro students' attitudes toward whites and segregation,
and their residential expectations*

| STATEMENT | Percentage of those agreeing with statement who expect to live outside South | N |
|---|---|---|
| All white people in the South are prejudiced against Negroes | 52% | 27 |
| In spite of what some people say, when Negroes are arrested in the South they do receive fair treatment. | 41 | 46 |
| I have seen so much unfairness to Negroes that I don't believe you can ever change the attitudes of white people in the South. | 58 | 19 |
| The southern Negro does have a chance to make something of himself. | 50 | 175 |
| All white people are alike. | 72 | 7 |

pectations of mobility. This becomes clear if we look at the personal background and characteristics of the students who expect to leave the South (Table 15–7). First, over 60 per cent of the men but only about 40 per cent of the women expect to migrate. A young man can more easily strike out alone for a new and strange city in the North or West and, lacking adequate economic opportunities at home, he is more obliged to do so. Most of the girls are oriented toward the roles of wife and mother; they tend not to separate from their parental family until they form one of their own. Thus the male's greater ease of mobility and his occupational preoccupations seem to encourage thoughts of emigration.

The nature of the students' home community has an uneven but revealing relationship to their expectations about migration. Those who grew up in large cities and those who grew up on farms are less inclined to leave the South than are those from towns or small cities. Those from the two extremes —large cities and farms—probably have similar migration plans for opposite reasons. Negro students from metropolitan areas enjoy better occupational opportunities and, even if race relations are no better in the metropolis, its greater size and impersonality tend to insulate the Negro community from daily degradation. Compared with their big-city cousins, a slightly larger proportion of the farm boys and girls expect to migrate. But despite poor occupational prospects and unpleasant race relations, fewer of these students than students from towns and small cities expect to leave the South. Their more limited horizons and their greater commitment to the parental family probably account for their tendency to assume that their future lies in the South.

Race relations in the home community also have a peculiar relationship

TABLE 15–7.  *Personal background and characteristics of students and their residential expectations*

| CHARACTERISTIC | Percentage expecting to live outside South | N |
|---|---|---|
| SEX | | |
| Male | 61% | 72 |
| Female | 43 | 100 |
| TYPE OF COMMUNITY IN WHICH STUDENT GREW UP | | |
| Farm | 45% | 40 |
| Town | 56 | 39 |
| Small city | 58 | 57 |
| Large city | 39 | 46 |
| PERCENTAGE NEGRO IN COUNTY IN WHICH STUDENT GREW UP | | |
| 0%–19% | 63% | 19 |
| 20%–39% | 48 | 77 |
| 40%–59% | 53 | 70 |
| 60%+ | 61 | 23 |
| OCCUPATION STUDENT EXPECTS TO FOLLOW | | |
| Engineer | 80% | 5 |
| Physician, dentist | 75 | 8 |
| Social or welfare worker | 60 | 15 |
| Accountant | 50 | 8 |
| Professor | 47 | 17 |
| Lawyer | 40 | 5 |
| Schoolteacher | 33 | 91 |
| Other professional and technical | 75 | 16 |
| All lower occupations | 100 | 11 |

to migration plans. In general, students who plan to leave the South rate their home towns slightly better on our race-relations ladder (an average of 4.9) than do those who expect to remain in the South (4.7). From an objective point of view, the percentage of Negroes in the home counties of students may be taken as a rough indicator of the state of race relations (as in Table 15–7), with the places having the greater numbers of Negroes being the most repressive. No central tendency exists in the relationship between migration plans and the proportion of Negroes in the home counties. On the contrary, students from counties at the two extremes—with the lowest and highest concentrations of Negroes—most frequently plan to migrate. The relative restiveness of those from places with the fewest Negroes probably

reflects a greater awareness of the possibilities for migration; the same restiveness among students from places with the greatest concentrations of Negroes
probably stems from a more desperate need to "escape."

The final characteristic that is related to emigration expectations in
Table 15–7 is the most powerful explanatory factor of all—the students' expected occupations. Eighty per cent of the prospective engineers expect to live
outside the South; 75 per cent of the physicians and dentists; and 60 per cent
of the welfare workers. On the other hand, only 33 per cent of those who
expect to become schoolteachers, 40 per cent of those who want to become
lawyers, and 47 per cent of those who want to become college professors
plan to leave the region. Although the number of cases on which these percentages are based is perilously small, these large differences seem to be the
result of varying occupational opportunities in the North and South.

Certainly the Negro engineer, physician, dentist, or welfare worker can
expect a professionally more satisfying or economically more remunerative
life outside the South than in it. There are just more, and better, opportunities for them outside the region. The geographical mobility of the prospective
schoolteachers, on the other hand, is severely limited by the heavy female
representation in the profession and by state variations in teacher-certification
requirements. Besides, professional opportunities are plentiful for them in
the South. The fledgling college professors labor under similar constraints—
until very recently their professional opportunities outside predominantly
Negro colleges have been slight,[7] and most of the Negro colleges are in the
South. Lawyers, regardless of their color or region, are not characterized by
much geographical mobility. In the practice of law the advantages of having
an established "name" and personal contacts are well known. At least in the
short run, one's home town is the best place to hang out a lawyer's shingle.

Finally, the small number of students who do not expect to fill professional,
technical, or managerial occupations *without exception* expect to leave the
region. If a student's chances for a reasonably prestigious, satisfying, and
remunerative career in the job of his choice seem good, he tends to stay in
the South. If not, he tends to join the steady outflow of Negroes headed
toward the North and West.

Of course, we cannot be certain that a student formed his occupational
plans *before* he formed his residential plans. Perhaps many students decide
to leave the region and then pick a profession or occupation they can follow
outside the South. But the lack of strong correlations between racial feelings
and attitudes and plans to migrate, combined with the substantial association

[7] See the *New York Times*, April 14, 1963, for a report on the lack of Negro professors
at nonsouthern colleges and universities. During the last several years, however, the
competition among northern colleges for the services of qualified Negro professors has
become vigorous.

between expected occupation and expected residence, argue the other way—that the occupational aspirations of students more often determine their feelings about migration than vice versa.

If this is true, then the region may have a better chance than is often assumed of retaining a larger share of its highly trained Negro manpower. Greater occupational opportunities for college-educated Negroes should have such an effect even before the racial millennium arrives. After all, southern Negroes are *southerners*, and the region has a powerful hold on its own. Given a better occupational chance, many more Negro students would stay at "home," despite all its imperfections.

## Internal migration and variations in future leadership potentials

So far in our examination of today's Negro college students as potential leaders in the South we have viewed the region as a unit. To leave the analysis at this point would be very misleading. The college students who plan to remain in the South will not distribute themselves evenly throughout the region or automatically appear where their leadership skills are most needed. When we consider the effects of probable future migration *within* the region along with the consequences of massive emigration, the shortage of educated Negroes to fill future leadership roles approaches absolute and disastrous proportions in large parts of the South.

Table 15–8 compares the subregions within the South where the students

TABLE 15–8.   *Effects of migration on distribution of all college students and potential leaders within South*

| RESIDENCE | Deep South | Peripheral South | TOTAL | N |
|---|---|---|---|---|
| All students' pre-college homes | 49% | 51 | 100% | 257 |
| Expected home of students remaining in South | 52% | 48 | 100 | 89 |
| Expected home of potential leaders remaining in South | 36% | 64 | 100 | 19 |

lived before going to college with the regions within the South where they expect to live after leaving school. Although all areas of the South will lose large numbers of college-educated youths to the North and West, those who expect to remain in the region after college probably will be distributed about 50-50 between the Deep and the Peripheral South. This represents a small net shift in favor of the Deep South. A slightly larger proportion of the students from the Peripheral South expect to move out of the region (38 per cent) than is true among students from the Deep South (32 per cent). As a result, a little over half the students who plan to remain in the region after college expect to live in the Deep South, while a little less than half the students initially came from this subregion. So far, the combined effects of anticipated emigration and internal movement on the geographical distribution of the remaining college-educated Negroes in the region does not seem very significant.

But the most likely future leaders—men who do not expect to migrate, who plan to follow high-status occupations, and who should be economically independent of whites—present a different picture. Sixty-four per cent of these "potential leaders" who have clear residential expectations intend to live on the periphery of the region; not one of them plans to live in either Mississippi or Alabama. Thus the parts of the South that now have the most qualified Negro leaders stand to gain still more, while the areas with the greatest shortage of trained leaders face continued or even heightened poverty in this basic political resource.

We find the same picture of the rich becoming richer as the poor become poorer when we look at the type of place in which the students expect to live after college (see Table 15–9). Only about 15 per cent of the students brought

TABLE 15–9.   *Type of place student grew up in and expectations of geographical mobility*

| | EXPECTED RESIDENCE | | | | |
| TYPE OF PLACE STUDENT GREW UP IN | *Where student grew up* | *Not original home but in South* | *Outside South* | TOTAL | N |
|---|---|---|---|---|---|
| Farm | 15% | 40 | 45 | 100% | 40 |
| Town | 13% | 31 | 56 | 100% | 39 |
| Small city | 32% | 10 | 58 | 100% | 57 |
| Large city | 54% | 7 | 39 | 100% | 46 |

up on farms or in small towns expect to return to them, whereas 32 per cent of those raised in small cities and 54 per cent of those who grew up in large cities (that is, with populations over 100,000) expect to return "home." This might present no problem, especially in light of the trend toward urbanization of the entire southern Negro population, if a minority of urban-born students migrated into small towns and rural areas as adults. But, with very few exceptions, urban Negro students who plan to migrate expect to move out of the South altogether. If native sons do not return to the more rural areas, they are not replaced, and the countryside is gradually denuded of its most promising and well trained potential leaders. This process is almost as much the result of rural and small-town Negroes' moving to the cities *within* the South as it is of their desertion of the South for the delights of New York or Los Angeles ghettos.

The devastating effects of this process on the leadership potential of the rural and small-town South are suggested by Table 15–10. Eighty-five per

TABLE 15–10.   *Where potential Negro leaders expect to live in South*

| TYPE OF PLACE STUDENT EXPECTS TO LIVE | SUBREGION OF EXPECTED RESIDENCE | | | |
|---|---|---|---|---|
| | *Deep South* | *Peripheral South* | TOTAL | N |
| Standard metropolitan area | 26% | 21% | 47% | 9 |
| City, but not SMA | 5 | 32 | 37% | 7 |
| No city mentioned | 5 | 11 | 16% | 3 |
| TOTAL | 36%  (7) | 64%  (12) | 100% | 19 |

NOTE: The small number of cases in this table makes the percentages more suggestive than definitive. Fifteen of the potential Negro leaders had no clear residential expectations and were omitted from the table.

cent of the "potential leaders" expect to live in cities; almost 50 per cent expect to live within the region's few metropolitan areas. At most, 15 per cent of the potential leaders expect to live in small towns or rural areas, which currently contain about half of the region's Negro population. Sharp differences appear between the Peripheral and Deep South in this respect. Almost all the potential leaders who expect to live in the Deep South plan to live in metropolitan areas. The smaller cities, towns, and rural areas of the Deep South have no attraction for potential leaders. In the Peripheral South, on the other hand, the smaller cities as well as the metropolitan areas seem to attract a goodly number of potential leaders. If the students' expectations of geographical mobility—both within and from the South—are reasonably reliable guides, the current college generation can be expected to produce almost no qualified leaders for the rural and small-town Deep South or for rural areas in the Peripheral South.

## What kind of leadership will today's students provide?

For large parts of the South, the most likely answer to this question seems to be "none at all." But whatever qualified, indigenous Negro leadership emerges in the South of the future will probably be furnished by the young people now enrolled in the predominantly Negro colleges in the region. Let us shift our attention from the *amount* of leadership we can expect from this group to the *kind* of leader some of them are likely to become.

To predict leadership performance 10 or 20 years ahead on the basis of the skills and orientations young people have as students is, of course, extraordinarily hazardous. Leadership is a relationship between people; it is situational, not a trait that adheres to a person at all times and places. Who becomes a leader and how well he performs in the role depend, in large measure, on circumstance; the same person may be a highly successful leader in some settings and a failure in others.

Moreover, people change as they mature, accept new roles, and enter new phases of life. The students' very lack of adult responsibilities, for example, undoubtedly was an important reason why they took the lead in the protest movement. The college radical who becomes the pillar of the local chamber of commerce and the undergraduate atheist who ends up as a deacon in the Presbyterian Church are too commonplace for us to assume that student orientations are fixed for life. Of course, change does not, in every case, mean growing conservatism. A very conventional and academically undistinguished student at Harvard College named Franklin D. Roosevelt became one of the greatest leaders of the underprivileged in American history.

These caveats should not be forgotten. But if we are so foolhardy as to try to anticipate the future, we must grasp at whatever straws we can find. The characteristics and attitudes of today's Negro college students are one clue to the future. If we constantly keep in mind that these attributes are not immutable, and if we apply what we know about the effects of maturation on behavior, we may learn something about the future of Negro politics in the South by examining the rising Negro elite as it is now.

Given the fact that the cream of Negro youth seems more intent than the less skilled and less well educated on migrating out of the region, one might reasonably assume that, *within* the college student population, the "better" students would be more likely to migrate than the average students. If anything, the reverse seems more likely—students who plan to remain in the region are slightly better academically than southern Negro students as a whole (see Table 15–11). Seniors, students with "A" or "B" academic averages, and students at higher-quality institutions make up a slightly larger proportion of those expecting to stay in the region than they do of all Negro college students. The main reason for this tendency is that women tend to be somewhat "better" students than men—at least insofar as these indexes of academic quality are concerned—and more women than men expect to remain in the region.

Thus, when we eliminate the girls and prospective schoolteachers and focus on the 13 per cent of the students most likely to become southern leaders, we find that both their grade averages and the quality of the schools they attend fall below the average for all Negro students. Majors in the social and

TABLE 15–11.    *Academic characteristics of potential southern leaders,
all students expecting to remain in the South,
and all students*

|  | Potential southern leaders (N = 34) | Students expecting to remain in South (N = 91) | All students (N = 264) |
|---|---|---|---|
| **COLLEGE YEAR** | | | |
| Freshman | 32% | 33% | 38% |
| Sophomore | 26 | 25 | 26 |
| Junior | 18 | 19 | 18 |
| Senior | 24 | 23 | 18 |
| **TOTAL** | 100% | 100% | 100% |
| | | | |
| **GRADE AVERAGE** | | | |
| "A's" and "B's" | 29% | 37% | 31% |
| "C's" and "D's" | 71 | 63 | 69 |
| **TOTAL** | 100% | 100% | 100% |
| | | | |
| **QUALITY OF COLLEGE** | | | |
| Better (types I and II) | 29% | 37% | 34% |
| Poorer (types III and IV) | 71 | 63 | 66 |
| **TOTAL** | 100% | 100% | 100% |
| | | | |
| **ACADEMIC MAJOR** | | | |
| Humanities | 0% | 9% | 10% |
| Social sciences | 26 | 19 | 19 |
| Physical sciences | 24 | 14 | 19 |
| Education | 6 | 38 | 28 |
| Business administration | 12 | 6 | 7 |
| Other vocational | 32 | 14 | 17 |
| **TOTAL** | 100% | 100% | 100% |

physical sciences and in vocational subjects are more numerous among these
potential southern leaders than among all those students who expect to remain
in the region. Students specializing in the humanities and education—predominantly girls—are scarcely represented at all. But these changes merely tend
to bring the potential southern leader group more nearly back into line with the
students as a whole. Qualitatively, if not quantitatively, the South seems likely
to hold its own among the Negro college students: the students expecting
to live in the South, and thus comprising the pool of most likely Negro

leaders for the future, are neither much smarter nor dumber, better nor more poorly trained, than those who plan to flee to the North and West.

The present generation of Negro students is overwhelmingly committed to the goal of racial equality: 94 per cent of the potential southern leaders and 89 per cent of all the students prefer racial integration to strict segregation or "something in between" (see Table 15–12). A commitment to integration is far more common among students than among adult Negroes,

TABLE 15–12.   *Comparison of Negro student and Negro adult attitudes toward segregation and their estimates of the opinions of others*

|  | Potential southern leaders (N = 34) | All students (N = 264) | College-educated adults (N = 44) | All Adults (N = 618) |
|---|---|---|---|---|
| RESPONDENT'S RACIAL PREFERENCE |  |  |  |  |
| Strict segregation | 0% | 1% | 0% | 15% |
| In between | 6 | 9 | 8 | 14 |
| Integration | 94 | 89 | 92 | 65 |
| Don't know, etc. | 0 | 1 | 0 | 6 |
| TOTAL | 100% | 100% | 100% | 100% |
| RESPONDENT'S ESTIMATE OF NUMBER OF NEGROES PREFERRING INTEGRATION |  |  |  |  |
| All or most | 88% | 70% | 63% | 57% |
| About half | 9 | 21 | 14 | 17 |
| Less than half | 3 | 8 | 23 | 15 |
| Don't know, etc. | 0 | 1 | 0 | 11 |
| TOTAL | 100% | 100% | 100% | 100% |
| RESPONDENT'S ESTIMATE OF NUMBER OF WHITES PREFERRING "STRICT SEGREGATION" |  |  |  |  |
| All or most | 27% | 31% | 37% | 47% |
| About half | 41 | 32 | 24 | 21 |
| Less than half | 32 | 37 | 35 | 20 |
| Don't know, etc. | 0 | [a] | 4 | 12 |
| TOTAL | 100% | 100% | 100% | 100% |

[a] Greater than 0, less than 0.5 per cent.

only 65 per cent of whom chose integration when confronted with the same alternatives. But this seems to be the result of educational rather than generational differences; college-educated adults are just as strongly in favor of desegregation as are students. In all probability, then, tomorrow's Negro leaders in the South will possess the same general goal as today's leaders. To date, neither black nationalism nor white supremacy has made discernible progress among the students.

The current attitudes of the students suggest, however, that they may push a good deal faster to realize the goal of integration and that they may expect substantial progress in a shorter period of time than do most Negro adults. In the first place, the group of potential southern leaders perceive the Negroes in the region as more solidly in back of racial integration than do other Negroes: 88 per cent of the potential leaders believe that "all or most" Negroes in the South favor integration, compared to 70 per cent of all students, 63 per cent of the college-educated adults, and 57 per cent of all Negro adults.

Although the potential leaders' perceptions more accurately reflect reality in this instance, the same group grossly underestimates the extent of white hostility they are likely to face. Only 27 per cent of the most likely southern leaders believed that "all or most" whites favor strict segregation, compared to 31 per cent of all students, 37 per cent of the college-educated adults, and 47 per cent of all adults. This relative lack of realism may result from youthful optimism and exuberance; it may well change as experience reveals the limits of the possible. As of now, however, the young potential leaders tend to underestimate the dimensions of the problems they are likely to face in the future.

Somewhat the same picture emerges when we examine student expectations about the rate of change in southern race relations. As can be seen in Table 15–13, the college students—both the potential leaders and the others—consider race relations in the South to be a good deal worse than do adults, even the college-educated ones. But they also feel that the situation has improved sharply during the last five years, and they expect this rate of improvement to increase noticeably during the next five years. The Negro adults are in a sanguine mood, too. But the students expect southern race relations to merit a rating five years from now that is more than three times what it was five years ago, whereas the college-educated adults expect only a two-to-one improvement. The less well educated adults expect even less racial progress. Again, adult experience may dampen these hopes, but as of now the future Negro leaders of the South seem likely to be characterized by impatience and demands for much faster realization of racial equality.

Some appreciation of the potential consequences of leadership by Negroes who are not college-educated emerges from Table 15–14. Both the students and adults were asked whether they agreed or disagreed with a series of statements indicating hostility toward white people and bitterness about segregation in the South. Very few of the college-educated—present-day or former

TABLE 15–13.    *Comparison of Negro student and Negro adult ratings of race relations in the South, five years ago, today, and five years from now*

| TIME OF RATING | MEAN RATING | | | |
| --- | --- | --- | --- | --- |
| | Potential southern leaders (N = 34) | All students (N = 264) | College-educated adults (N = 49) | All adults (N = 618) |
| Five years ago | 2.3 | 2.7 | 3.9 | 4.4 |
| Today | 4.4 | 4.5 | 5.4 | 5.8 |
| Five years from now | 7.2 | 7.5 | 7.8 | 7.7 |
| Change from 5 years ago | + 2.1 | + 1.8 | + 1.5 | + 1.4 |
| Expected change, next 5 years | + 2.8 | + 3.0 | + 2.4 | + 1.9 |
| Total change over 10-year period | + 4.9 | + 4.8 | + 3.9 | + 3.3 |

TABLE 15–14.    *Comparison of student and adult attitudes toward whites and segregation*

| STATEMENT | PERCENTAGE AGREEING WITH STATEMENT | | | |
| --- | --- | --- | --- | --- |
| | Potential southern leaders (N = 34) | All students (N = 264) | College-educated adults (N = 49) | All adults (N = 618) |
| All white people in the South are prejudiced against Negroes. | 12% | 16% | 16% | 51% |
| In spite of what some people say, when Negroes are arrested in the South, they do receive fair treatment. | 29 | 25 | 16 | 29 |
| I have seen so much unfairness to Negroes that I don't believe you can ever change the attitudes of white people in the South. | 12 | 12 | 12 | 45 |
| The southern Negro does have a chance to make something of himself. | 91 | 97 | 96 | 90 |
| All white people are alike. | 3 | 4 | 2 | 30 |

students—displayed signs of bitterness and hatred, whereas rank-and-file Negroes displayed a good deal of both. If the students' high hopes for the future are not realized, they may abandon their relatively tolerant and forbearing attitude toward whites. If not, those students who have achieved leadership positions may be superseded by less well educated leaders who are willing to appeal to the mass hatreds that are already there.

As we suggested in Chapter Thirteen, adult Negroes in the region seem to accept the Democratic party as the best means of making their growing electoral

TABLE 15–15.    *Comparison of student and adult party identification and party images*

| | Potential southern leaders (N = 34) | All students (N = 264) | College-educated adults (N = 49) | All adults (N = 618) |
|---|---|---|---|---|
| PARTY IDENTIFICATION | | | | |
| Democratic | 24% | 50% | 64% | 51% |
| Independent, leaning Democratic | 26 | 17 | 6 | 8 |
| Independent | 15 | 10 | 8 | 5 |
| Independent, leaning Republican | 12 | 5 | 8 | 4 |
| Republican | 21 | 11 | 14 | 10 |
| Apolitical, don't know | 2 | 7 | 0 | 22 |
| TOTAL | 100% | 100% | 100% | 100% |
| | | | | |
| PARTY IMAGE | | | | |
| Pro-Democratic | 57% | 75% | 72% | 77% |
| Neutral | 26 | 10 | 13 | 14 |
| Pro-Republican | 17 | 15 | 15 | 9 |
| TOTAL | 100% | 100% | 100% | 100% |

NOTE: Those without party images were omitted from the percentages in the bottom half of the table.

power effective. Indeed, this commitment to Democracy is so much stronger among southern Negroes than among southern whites that some Negro intellectuals have argued that Negroes are sacrificing their bargaining power. Politicians, so this line of argument goes, tend to reward unwavering affection with studious neglect; a wandering eye and a wayward heart with ardent pursuit. The most likely southern leaders among today's Negro college students cannot be charged with ignoring this injunction (see Table 15–15). Only 24 per cent of the potential leaders think of themselves as Democrats, and

21 per cent identify with the GOP. The comparable figures for all Negro students are 50 per cent Democratic and 11 per cent Republican; among college-educated adults, 64 per cent Democratic and 14 per cent Republican; and among all Negro adults, 51 per cent Democratic and 10 per cent Republican. Party identification tends to grow stronger as one matures—the relatively large proportion of Independents among the students should diminish over the years. But at least a sizable minority of these youthful independents "lean" Republican. And although the potential leaders' image of the Republican party is not appreciably more favorable than that of other Negroes, their image of the Democratic party is *much* less favorable.

The lesser commitment of these Negro college students to the Democrats is not a reflection of traditional Negro Republicanism. The college students—and especially the potential leaders—are highly experimental and irreverent toward traditional ways, including the post–New Deal tradition of Negro support for the Democratic party (see Table 15–16). Except for civil rights,

TABLE 15–16.    *Comparison of student and adult attitudes toward socioeconomic "liberalism" and toward idea of social change*

|  | Potential southern leaders (N = 34) | All students (N = 264) | College-educated adults (N = 49) | All adults (N = 618) |
|---|---|---|---|---|
| SOCIOECONOMIC "LIBERALISM" |  |  |  |  |
| Liberal (types I and II) | 3% | 11% | 68% | 12% |
| Moderate (type III) | 21 | 23 | 15 | 10 |
| Conservative (types IV and V) | 76 | 66 | 17 | 78 |
| TOTAL | 100% | 100% | 100% | 100% |
| ATTITUDES TOWARD CHANGE |  |  |  |  |
| Most favorable (types I and II) | 67% | 61% | 45% | 20% |
| In between (types III and IV) | 30 | 36 | 38 | 35 |
| Most unfavorable (types V and VI) | 3 | 3 | 17 | 45 |
| TOTAL | 100% | 100% | 100% | 100% |

they tend to be highly conservative on social and economic questions.

These interviews were taken before the Goldwater campaign of 1964. The Republicans' "Southern strategy" of 1964 may have nipped the party's chances for significant gains among the Negro leadership class in the South by prematurely conceding the Negro vote to the Democrats. But the Democrats can take relatively little comfort from this—the future Negro leaders of the region are far less clearly in their corner than are the Negro rank and file.

Such, then, would seem to be the most likely contours of future Negro leadership in the South—at least to the extent that today's college students will provide this leadership. No doubt this prospect appears threatening to most southern whites, few of whom welcome any growth in Negro aggressiveness, impatience, and militancy. But the alternatives to leadership supplied by local, college-educated Negroes are even more horrifying from the typical southern white man's point of view.

## Alternatives to a college-educated political elite

If the rising Negro elite of college-educated youngsters does not provide the bulk of Negro leadership in the South, who will? There seem to be two major alternatives:

1. Negroes who have not had the benefit of a college education, may take over the lion's share of Negro leadership in the South by default, especially in the region's rural areas and small towns. In Chapter Seven we saw that such poorly educated leaders tended to be either traditional "Uncle Toms" or extreme militants. For rather different reasons, neither type of leadership is likely to achieve the goals of their Negro followers under present conditions.

The Uncle Toms are so dependent on the white community, both economically and politically, that they cannot produce the results their followers demand in a time of high racial tension such as will exist in the South for years to come. This ineffectiveness leads to a loss of legitimacy, which leads to greater ineffectiveness, and so on, as one Uncle Tom after the next is ground to nothingness between the conflicting goals of the white and black worlds. Where this happens, Negro demands go unmet and racial frustrations and hatreds grow unchecked. In the long run, a racial holocaust is the logical outcome of continued "leadership" by these quaint survivals of a way of life long dead.

Many of the militant Negroes who have risen from the masses without benefit of higher education have done so by exploiting race and class hatreds. They lack the most important source of prestige and legitimacy in the Negro community—education—and they tend to make up for that lack through their forensic and agitational skills. This does not mean that all militants are unprincipled demagogues or that all college-educated Negroes are racial statesmen. It does mean, however, that the poorly educated Negro leader is more likely to appeal to the latent racial hatreds of the black masses than is a better-educated leader.[8] He is less likely to seek the negotiated settlement of issues, too—partly because negotiation is inconsistent with the "hard line" that has

---

[8] It is significant here to note that the Black Muslims are an almost exclusively lower-class movement. See Eric Lincoln, The Black Muslims in America (Boston: Beacon Press, 1961).

got him where he is, and partly because he is less skillful at bargaining than better-educated Negroes.

Neither the traditional nor the extremely militant leader, then, is likely to provide the type of Negro leadership required if the South is to solve its racial problems short of violence. And, of course, violence is no solution.

2. The second alternative to southern Negro college students as a source of future leadership is provided by the outside world. When Negroes in Crayfish County, Mississippi, decided that they wanted to vote and were unable to find local leaders able or willing to help them do so, they looked outside the county for help—first to a Negro lawyer from a neighboring state and then to the young SNCC worker whose story we told at the beginning of this book. Where local leadership is nonexistent, the "outsider" is the only recourse for a Negro community demanding concessions that the white community is unwilling to give. This imported leadership may take many forms —SNCC or CORE workers, college students from the North, Martin Luther King, or federal law enforcement officials—but it is the functional equivalent of effective, indigenous leadership. These outsiders know how to organize people for political or social action, they are financially supported from outside the area, they are not permanent members of the community. The sanctions generally used by whites to stifle Negro initiative—loss of employment, ostracism, harassment—do not work against them. Only violence, and the threat of it, remains. Given the mood of the rest of the country, and the political realities of national politics, violence aimed at outsiders merely conjures up still more intervention.

Outsiders are a poor substitute for indigenous Negro leaders. Their presence reinforces the whites' feelings of persecution and self-delusions about "their" Negroes' being a contented lot who would gladly return to their prior state of happy subservience if they were only left alone. Outside intervention is a new and different form of paternalism. The southern Negroes' shriveled self-respect and self-confidence are better served by doing things for themselves, on their own initiative. Without intimate knowledge of local ways, the outsider can create problems that otherwise would not exist—and then self-righteously return home, leaving the local Negroes holding the bag.

But in most of the rural and small-town South, what are the alternatives? Today rural and small-town Negroes want justice and equality as much as their urban brethren do; without leadership they can achieve neither. But their most skillful potential leaders—college-educated, middle-class Negroes— have deserted them, or shortly will. Those who remain—mostly schoolteachers —will be in no position to exert the kind of aggressive leadership that the unsatisfied wants of the masses require. Where these conditions hold—and outside the cities they are the most common conditions—there is no alternative to the outsider. Those who resent him the most have no one to blame for his presence but themselves.

Chapter Sixteen

# Conclusions: The Politics of Desegregation

A few weeks after the passage of the Voting Rights Act of 1965, Georgia's junior United States Senator Herman Talmadge addressed a meeting of the Hungry Club, a Negro civic organization in Atlanta. To this affluent and influential audience of business and professional men (the name of the club refers to the condition of the members' minds rather than to the condition of their stomachs) the son and political heir of one of the South's best-known racial demagogues insisted that race was no longer a factor in Georgia politics. Qualified Negroes, Talmadge said, should be appointed without delay to positions of responsibility in federal, state, and local government. "Young Hummon's" speech was a smash—just like the talks on "the Negro peril" he had given at small-town filling stations a few years earlier.

In the question-and-answer period after the Hungry Club speech, a Negro businessman asked Senator Talmadge: "Why didn't you make such a speech five or six years ago?" To loud and prolonged laughter, the senator replied, "You didn't ask me."[1]

Both the senator and his audience knew the underlying meaning of this exchange. Five or six years ago—before the Negro vote became a significant force in Georgia politics, before the Supreme Court struck down the state's "county unit" system of Democratic nominations, which had grossly magnified the power of rural areas—Talmadge probably would not have accepted an invitation from a Negro group; or he would have delivered a very different speech. Five or six years ago, it would never have occurred to the Hungry Club to invite him as a speaker.

• • •

[1] In our description of this incident we lean heavily on Ralph McGill, "Talmadge Embodies Georgia Change," *Raleigh News and Observer* (N.C.), January 1, 1966.

On December 18, 1965, Walter B. Jones of Greenville defeated four other candidates in a special Democratic primary for the vacant seat in the United States House of Representatives from the First Congressional District of North Carolina. This was expected—Jones had been running for the post for four years, and the death of the incumbent Congressman (Herbert Bonner) seemed finally to have cleared the way. What was surprising about the primary was not that Jones won, but that Mrs. Sarah E. Small of Williamston came in second. She was the state's first Negro congressional candidate since the turn of the century.

Mrs. Small—who had no prior political experience or reputation and almost no funds or organization—polled 6,000 votes in North Carolina's most traditionally "southern" congressional district, running far ahead of several respected white politicians. Jones's campaign workers reduced the vote for the other white candidates by arguing that white voters in the sprawling, thinly populated district had better close ranks behind front-running Jones or else face the possibility of a runoff against the Negro candidate. At the least Mrs. Small's campaign, following hot on the heels of a sharp increase in Negro registration, was impressive enough to make Jones's appeal credible to quite a number of white voters.

The "threat" proved to be more than a little exaggerated—Jones polled four votes to every one for Mrs. Small. But Jones was not elected yet, and the race issue was to give him cause for concern from an entirely new direction.

In the general election, heretofore only a formality in the solidly Democratic First, an unknown college professor named John East filed against Jones and began running against President Lyndon Baines Johnson, the national Democratic party, and civil rights legislation. Suddenly, Jones, the "white hope" in the primary, emerged as a dupe of the wild-eyed integrationists in Washington! Alarming reports filtered in from the boondocks about Professor East's rapidly growing support in an area in which bona fide registered Republicans are in exceedingly short supply. Mr. Jones, an experienced politician not given to panic, kept on shaking hands, eating barbecued chicken, and talking about tobacco prices until election day. He won by 7,456 votes, the narrowest general-election margin in the memory of even the most ancient courthouse hangers-on. As Congressman-elect Jones left for Washington, Mrs. Small and Professor East both publicly vowed to do better next time.[2] They probably will.

•    •    •

On January 22, 1966, the Alabama State Democratic Committee met at the Dinkler-Tutweiler Hotel in Birmingham. This group of "Democrats" had refused to support Lyndon Johnson over Senator Barry Goldwater two years before because Johnson supported civil rights legislation. But in 1966 they

[2] *Raleigh News and Observer* (N.C.), December 19, 1965.

voted by secret ballot to strike the "white supremacy" slogan from the party's emblem on the ballot.

"I never thought," one out-voted member of the committee shouted in the turmoil following the vote, "we'd substitute black supremacy for white supremacy in Alabama. The white race is supreme in this world by the mandate of God Almighty!" The majority of the committee, however, was less impressed by divine intent than by the fact that over 150,000 Negroes were registered to vote in Alabama.[3]

Less than four months later, on May 3, 1966, Alabama voters overwhelmingly endorsed white supremacy, Mrs. Lurleen Wallace, and the anti-Negro activities of Governor George Wallace, who was constitutionally barred from seeking reelection and for whom Mrs. Wallace was a "stand-in" candidate.

Mrs. Wallace polled over 400,000 votes, running far ahead of Attorney General Richmond Flowers, the only gubernatorial candidate openly to appeal to Alabama's new Negro voters. Over 150,000 Negroes voted; Flowers got slightly under 145,000 votes.

More revealing than Mrs. Wallace's victory was the defeat of Walter Calhoun, Negro candidate for sheriff in Wilcox County, Alabama. No Negroes had voted in Wilcox before the passage of the Voting Rights Act of 1965, but with the aid of federal registrars 3,691 had registered before the 1966 primary. Because the total white population of voting age was less than 2,600, Mr. Calhoun's chances looked good. But Lummie Jenkins, the white sheriff, who had held the office for 27 years, defeated his challenger—3,460 to 2,738. Jenkins's 1966 campaign was novel in one respect: he shook hands with Negroes for the first time in his life. The sheriff reminded Negroes that he had "never mistreated them." When he needed to arrest a Negro, the sheriff rarely went out and brought in the suspect. "I just send out word to the niggers and they generally come on in," he explained. With a solid bloc vote from whites, this campaign theme added enough Negro votes to keep Sheriff Jenkins in office.

The Negro director of a Wilcox County affiliate of the Southern Christian Leadership Conference admitted that the sheriff had no reputation for brutality, but, he argued, "A lot of Negroes were afraid to vote with all of those white people working in the polling places as election officials. They were afraid they might lose their jobs, or something." This local SCLC leader added: "We learned a lot about how to campaign this time, and next time it won't be so new and we'll win." Flushed with victory, the sheriff had different expectations: "This was something new to them [the Negroes] and a lot of them voted, but next time most of them won't bother."[4]

• • •

[3] *New York Times,* January 23, 1966.
[4] *New York Times,* May 4, 1966.

The old order changes, however slowly. The growing numbers of Negro voters in the South seem to be a catalyst.

But in what direction is the South changing? How fast? How much does the growing Negro vote have to do with these changes? These are the questions we tried to examine in Part Three of this book. We are now ready to sum up and to hazard some general conclusions about the new southern politics. We can also face the question: What payoffs can southern Negroes expect from their growing vote?

## Escalating political tension and peaceful coexistence

One characteristic of the new southern politics (as described in Chapter Twelve) will be a heightening of political conflict and tension. Despite some changes in white attitudes in recent years, southern Negroes and whites remain deeply divided on the major issue of the region—racial segregation. This division is not likely to disappear in the near future.

In the past the practical difficulties of running a democratic political system under conditions of extreme conflict were "solved" by the simple expedient of disfranchising the weaker of the two clashing groups—by creating a mixed system of democracy for whites and autocracy for Negroes. The question now facing the South is whether its democratic procedures will continue to function—like its drinking fountains, busses, and toilets—now that the "white only" signs have come down. Since political systems are more complex than mechanical ones, the answer is not obvious.

As southern Negroes reenter the political system in massive numbers, their racial attitudes and expectations suddenly become politically relevant—as Senator Talmadge's appearance at the Hungry Club made clear. Their political visibility can in turn trigger a white counter-reaction, or "backlash," as in the First Congressional District of North Carolina or, even more clearly, in Alabama. Negro demands and white reactions could escalate to the point where democratic procedures would break down.

In Chapter Twelve we isolated some mechanisms that tend to reduce this danger. Both sides to the dispute tend to underestimate the seriousness of the cleavage, to believe that they have more supporters among the members of the other race than they actually have. These misperceptions—although scarcely comforting on other grounds—may tend, at least temporarily, to reduce the sense of conflict. The multiple values and multiple goals of southerners, Negro and white, result in a gap between what they prefer in race relations and what they will bear. Southern whites, for example, want better jobs, better schools, and many other things, not just segregation. They may have to sacrifice one objective for others. And, while southern Negroes want full racial equality, they are too realistic to start off by demanding the badges of social equality—such as intermarriage—about which whites are most sensitive. Negro political power, in the absence of massive federal activity to the contrary, will tend to grow more slowly in areas where white hostility is most intense. Finally, the leaders of both races in the region seem to have a more thoroughgoing commitment to democratic principles and procedures than the rank and file and a greater willingness to try to ameliorate racial strife.

Nonetheless, we must recognize the extreme difficulties of conducting biracial democratic politics in the South so long as most whites remain dedicated to racial segregation. Bargaining and compromises between leaders of the two races become extremely difficult when the rank and file hold diametrically opposite views.

Just how far the tensions between Negroes and whites will escalate toward chaos and massive violence is not now clear. This will depend ultimately on whether southerners find a rate of racial change that is fast enough to satisfy most Negroes but slow enough not to frighten most whites into panicky countermeasures. Pressures from the national government seem to be expanding the capacity of whites in most parts of the South to accept changes they would have found unthinkable a generation ago. By the time the Peripheral South becomes like the rest of the United States, the Deep South will probably be like the Peripheral South of old. Unlike the Republic of South Africa, the Deep South has no real choice.

## Southern party systems in flux

The most direct and immediate effect of growing Negro voting on southern party systems will be the addition of a large number of new Democrats to the region's electorate. No matter what measure of partisanship one examines— party voting, party registration, party identification, or party images—southern Negroes prove to be a far more Democratic group than their white neighbors. Indeed, they are probably the most overwhelmingly Democratic group in the nation.

But politics is a matter of balancing gains and losses. The net effects of increased Negro voting in the region are less certain and less favorable to the Democrats. The very actions that have given the Democrats such commanding support among Negroes have alienated many southern whites. Curiously, at least to those unfamiliar with the vagaries of the region's politics, the massive disenchantment of southern whites with the Democratic party has *not* yet led to corresponding, permanent gains for the Republicans. As we saw in Chapter Thirteen, a large majority of southern whites, including many who have not voted for a Democratic presidential candidate for years, still think of themselves as Democrats. And until these disaffected southern whites switch their party identification and party registration, the Republicans will

474 THE IMPACT ON SOUTHERN POLITICS

be severely handicapped in their efforts to win state and local offices. Republican gains are being made at these lower levels, but they are far less spectacular than those scored by recent GOP presidential candidates.

One or two more presidential campaigns like that of 1964, in which the Republicans appealed explicitly to the racial prejudices of the white South, and an abrupt and thoroughgoing party realignment might well be brought about. But Senator Goldwater seems to have proved conclusively that his party cannot follow this strategy and win national elections, too.[5]

The odds are, therefore, that southern white segregationists will be left without influential champions in *either* national party. The Republicans, to be sure, may try to appeal to southern segregationists by references to "states' rights," "decentralization," and "conservatism"—vague slogans that can be variously interpreted in New York and Mississippi. But the South's segregationists tend to be economic "liberals"[6] for whom the Democrats have a powerful pocketbook appeal. The presidential Republicans may already have done about as much damage as they can to the anomalous Democratic coalition by appealing to the alleged "conservatism" of the white South—for the South is not an especially "conservative" region.

This means—especially when we remember that the Democrats will receive the support of almost all the new Negro voters—that two-partyism (or its approximation)[7] will come to the South far more slowly than is generally expected. In the short run, southern politics will be characterized by vigorous party competition in presidential politics and Democratic dominance at other levels of the ballot.

This has to do only with the "normal" vote of southerners, however. In fact, both Negro and white southerners are unusually issue-oriented voters, and both are preoccupied by a single issue—race. The injection of racial controversies into particular campaigns can result in sharp but temporary divergences from the norm. This merely underscores the fact that the structure of party politics in the South is likely to remain unusually complex, confusing, and changeful in the years ahead. For while racial controversy can subvert old-style Democratic dominance, it also stands athwart all efforts to organize southern politics along seemingly more "rational" lines.

[5] See P. E. Converse, A. R. Clausen, and W. E. Miller, "Electoral Myth and Reality: The 1964 Election," *American Political Science Review,* Vol. 59 (June 1965), pp. 321–36.

[6] We use the label here in the sense in which it is used in everyday political discourse. Relatively few of these people possess a coherent liberal *ideology*. Rather, they have a general bias in favor of government activity and spending. See A. Campbell, *et al., The American Voter* (New York: John Wiley and Sons, 1960), ch. 9.

[7] Only half of the American states have pure two-party systems by one reasonable, if arbitrary, definition. See A. Ranney, "Parties in State Politics," ch. 3 in H. Jacob and K. Vines (eds.), *Politics in the American States: A Comparative Analysis* (Boston: Little, Brown, 1965). Some system between pure one-partyism and pure two-partyism is therefore a quite probable outcome of partisan change in the South.

We are not at all sure, moreover, that a party system that aligned all Negroes, economic liberals, and integrationists against all white segregationists and economic conservatives would be particularly "rational." The costs of being on the losing side in such a system are dangerously high; such starkly polarized politics would heighten the political tensions in the South, which already are severe. The politics of race and the politics of class now divide the southern electorate in somewhat different ways; the noncongruence of these political cleavages tends to dampen and moderate the effects of both. The South desperately needs bridges between those who are dedicated to racial equality (mostly Negroes) and those who are fighting bitterly to preserve the racial *status quo* (mostly whites). The Democratic party is presently the most venerable and viable organization that contains large numbers of both. Common class interests tend to hold these people together despite their racial differences.

This, it seems to us, is the beginning of a "rational" and desirable party system for the South, one in which class-based issues are more important than racial ones. It is the upper-middle-class, economically conservative, racially moderate whites who need to be driven from the Democratic party into the Republican, not the region's segregationists. Then, and only then, will a politics of class prevail over a politics of race in the South as in the rest of the nation.[8] This kind of party realignment will not be built in a day.

## Mass action and civil disobedience

Southern Negroes have perfected and popularized a set of direct-action techniques—sit-ins, lie-ins, wade-ins, massive street demonstrations, community-wide boycotts, and civil disobedience in a seemingly endless variety of forms—that were almost unknown in America until the student protest movement of the early 1960's. Originally employed during Negro efforts to desegregate public accommodations in the South, these techniques have been less frequently used in the region since the Civil Rights Act of 1964 declared the segregation of public facilities illegal. Direct-action techniques may be harder to apply to the remaining (more important and subtle) areas of racial segregation. And yet the South has not seen the last of them.

An entire generation of future leaders has cut its teeth on the racial protests. The militant and sacrificial style of the Negro protesters, their willingness to defy established law if it seems unjust, and their faith in the efficacy of the bold and provocative gesture will accompany a good many of them into full-fledged adulthood and positions of political responsibility. The same phenom-

[8] For an argument that a politics of class is more functional for democracy than politics organized on other lines, see R. A. Alford, *Party and Society: The Anglo-American Democracies* (Chicago: Rand McNally & Co., 1963), chs. 10–11.

enon has been noted, in a more extreme form, among the rising leaders in developing nations:

> Memories of past conflicts often condition current behavior. Individuals brought up in a political system in which there have been coups, assassinations, political arrests, and underground movements will not readily adopt a political style emphasizing peaceful and rational discussion. Violent nationalist movements . . . do not generally produce a bargaining, pragmatic style of leadership.[9]

The early student protesters we described in Chapter Fourteen were an unusually optimistic, privileged, and tolerant group of Negro youngsters, about as far from an embittered, alienated group of professional radicals as one can imagine. But their first venture into politics was as militant protesters against blatant injustice. Eventually, they won. Such a generation is unlikely to abandon militant, direct action altogether, even under drastically altered circumstances.

American government is a complex, multitiered structure in which major decisions can be made at a number of different levels. A minority of political opinion at one level (say, the county) can sometimes be transformed into a majority by having the same problem decided at a higher level (say, the state). If, however, the problem is decided at the national level, the statewide majority may become part of a nationwide minority, and the county minority may find itself part of a national majority. Under these conditions, both sides in American political controversies try to get differences settled at the level of decision-making most favorable to their preferences. The losers typically try to get the controversy reconsidered at a more favorable level of the government.[10]

In the years ahead, southern Negroes are going to be trying, often for the first time in this century, to convert their votes into favorable public policies in southern states and localities. Almost everywhere they are going to be in a minority; finding enough like-minded whites to form a winning biracial coalition will often be difficult. The Negroes' best chance of winning, therefore, will often be to try to convert local or state issues and problems into national ones. For on a nationwide basis southern Negro demands are often favored by a clear majority, or at least by majorities in the large, northern swing states that dominate presidential elections.

Changing a local or state controversy into a national one usually requires enlarging the size of the public;[11] this in turn requires extensive publicity and appeals to the dominant values of the society at large. As the history of the

---

[9] J. La Palombara and M. Weiner, "Political Parties and Political Development: Observations from a Comparative Survey," *Items*, Vol. 20 (March 1966), pp. 3–4.

[10] An excellent example of this process is provided by C. Silverman, *The Little Rock Story* (Inter-University Case Program, No. 41, rev. 1959).

[11] D. B. Truman, *The Governmental Process* (New York: Alfred A. Knopf, 1962), was the first to develop the importance of this point. See pp. 225, 247, 355–62, 380ff., 422–23, 433, and 463ff.

sit-in movement demonstrates, the southern Negro's greatest success in winning national support has come through massive, direct-action techniques and civil disobedience. It is possible for southern Negroes to engage in these practices so often that they will lose majority support in the North, at which point the tactic will become self-defeating.[12] But until that time, we can expect continued mass protest activity by southern Negroes.

The amount and character of Negro protest activity in the South of the future will depend on how successful southern Negroes are in satisfying their demands through more normal political processes. We shall return to this question later on. But one thing seems reasonably sure: if neither normal political activity nor direct-action tactics succeed in satisfying Negro demands within a reasonable length of time, then racial violence followed by forcible federal intervention will come. The anomic, leaderless, and largely self-defeating rioting in the Watts area of Los Angeles in 1965 might seem a bland and gentle prelude compared with what *could* happen in the South.

## Translating votes into public policy

Political pundits have assumed that the vote will automatically give southern Negroes influence over public policy commensurate with their numbers. Once Negroes are voting in substantial numbers, the argument goes, southern state and local officials will either respond to Negro demands or suffer at the polls. Negroes will then be able to use their political leverage to force governments to eliminate segregation in other realms of life. Hence the special significance of the vote to southern Negroes.

Attractive as this argument is, it is much too simple. The linkages between mass attitudes, as expressed in elections, and public policy are exceedingly complex and little understood. The best research we have suggests that the translation of votes into power, and power into policy, is by no means automatic, and that public officials and political leaders have far more freedom of maneuver in dealing with their constituents than had been initially realized.[13] The governmental response to Negro votes, then, may not be at all automatic in the South or anywhere else. The experience of northern Negroes—who have been voting in large numbers for many decades and yet are still distinctly "second-class citizens"—is not very comforting to those who would place pri-

---

[12] See, for example, W. Brink and L. Harris, *The Negro Revolution in America* (New York: Simon and Shuster, 1964), for northern white attitudes toward the Negro protests of the early 1960's.

[13] See, for example, L. A. Dexter, "The Representative and His District," *Human Organization*, Vol. 16 (1947), pp. 2–13; V. O. Key, Jr., *Public Opinion and American Democracy*, (New York: Alfred A. Knopf, 1961), ch. 21; W. E. Miller and D. Stokes, "Constituency Influence in Congress," *American Political Science Review*, Vol. 57 (1963), 45–56.

mary reliance on the vote as the "solution" to the Negro problem in the South.

## THE VOTE AS A POLITICAL RESOURCE

A number of resources can be translated into political power—votes, money, prestige, information, skill, organization, and so on.[14] Individuals and groups possess varying amounts of these resources. The amount of *potential* political power they have is *not* directly determined by the amount of *any one resource* they have. Rather, it depends on how much of *all* these resources they control. (In the typical case there is likely to be a good deal of dispersion, with those having a great deal of one resource not having much of the others.) People's actual power depends, further, not just on the level of their total resources but also on whether they choose to expend these resources to further their political goals. The local millionaire, for example, may have a tremendous power *potential* because he is wealthy, but little actual power because he is more interested in chasing nubile blondes and buying yachts than in seeking political influence. It is therefore possible for individuals and groups with limited political resources who invest them heavily in politics to be more influential than those with vast power potential but no inclination to use their resources for political purposes. In the usual case, the proportion of all political resources actually used for political purposes tends to be small. The result is a great deal of "slack" (or unexpended resources) in the political system.

Southern Negroes have but one political resource in abundance—votes. Southern whites, most of whom still oppose the Negro's political objectives, tend to have the lion's share of *all* political resources, including votes. The competition between the two groups for control over public policy will tend to be very uneven unless southern whites fail to use their overwhelmingly superior resources for political ends. No doubt there has been a great deal of "slack" in the utilization of political resources by southern whites in the past. But the more threatened they feel by evidence of rising Negro political power in the future, the more their disproportionate resources will be invested in politics and the less "slack" there will be. Racial inequalities in political resources other than the vote, then, probably will result in southern Negroes' receiving less influence over policy than their proportionate share of the electorate would seem to dictate.

Even the vote itself has limitations as a political resource for southern Negroes. They are in a minority almost everywhere in the South. (In the relatively few communities where Negroes are potentially a clear majority of the electorate, white resistance to Negro voting tends to be most vehement, and the barriers to the effective use of the ballot, once achieved, are likely to be greatest.) In order to win, southern Negroes generally have to enter into

[14] This discussion of political resources and their relationship to power follows R. A. Dahl, *Who Governs?* (New Haven: Yale University Press, 1961), chs. 19–28.

coalitions with at least some white politicians and voters. In situations characterized by an overwhelming white consensus in favor of segregation, biracial coalition-building is almost impossible. A good many Negroes in the South may finally win the right to vote only to find themselves in a more or less permanent political minority.

Where a significant minority of moderate and integrationist whites is in being—as in Peripheral South cities like Urbania—Negro-white political coalitions are easier to arrange. But opponents of biracial coalitions need merely take steps to increase the salience of the racial issue to the electorate at large, and the Negro-white coalition usually dissolves. In view of the corrosive effects of the racial issue and the lack of other stable political structures in one-party systems, Negroes in the South may have to rely primarily on joining *ad hoc* coalitions on an issue-by-issue basis. On many state, local, and "style" issues,[15] for example, the Negroes' most likely allies are the economically conservative but racially moderate middle classes; in presidential politics and on class issues, however, they may receive greater benefits from highly volatile, "populistic" coalitions with heavily segregationist white workers.

Such a complex and fluid political situation, characterized by high tension levels and limited "slack," places heavy demands on political leaders. For one thing, bargaining and negotiations between white and Negro leaders must be almost continuous and call for highly developed political skills. In the second place, followers may become confused by rapidly shifting strategies and alliances. They must be given clear cues and constant guidance lest they inadvertently throw their votes away. All these things southern Negro leaders must be able to do, and do well, before the Negro vote can have a major impact on public policy, *even in areas where biracial coalitions are formed.* The desperate shortage of capable Negro leaders (see Chapter Seven) and the possibility that this shortage will become even more severe in the future (see Chapter Fifteen) not only affect how often Negroes go to the polls, but how effectively they use their votes once they get there.

## TYPES OF NEGRO GOALS

Southern Negroes seem to have a better chance of achieving some types of racial objectives than others by way of the ballot box. Other modes of attack —litigation, demonstrations, and federal intervention—are likely to be more fruitful than the vote in grappling with many kinds of civil rights problems.

First, Negro votes are an effective resource in altering segregationist practices when *the costs of abandoning segregation are relatively low for the white community.* For example, police brutality tends to decline and, to a lesser extent, the entire administration of justice tends to improve after southern

---

[15] The distinction between "style" and "class" (or "position") issues is from B. Berelson, P. F. Lazarsfeld, and W. N. McPhee, *Voting* (Chicago: University of Chicago Press, 1954), pp. 194ff.

Negroes become active members of the electorate.[16] The psychic and monetary costs of such reforms for whites are modest. Where, on the other hand, the white community perceives the costs of abandoning segregation as high—such as in the areas of housing or school desegregation—the Negro vote seems to have little impact. The coefficient of correlation between the proportion of the Negro adult population registered to vote and the existence of desegregated schools, by county, in 1958 was +.03! Change in this area tends to be brought about through litigation and federal action. Negro political muscle demonstrated at the local polls seems entirely irrelevant.

A second factor that affects the ability of the Negro vote to bring about desegregation is the *visibility of the issue to the white community*. If the benefits of the reform are confined to the Negro ghetto, and if the change can be brought about without a great deal of publicity, then the Negro vote seems to carry more punch. Negro policemen, for example, have been hired in many southern communities and assigned to responsibilities in Negro residential areas with scarcely any publicity or controversy. Hiring Negro firemen, however, tends to be much more difficult. Either Negro and white firemen must share the same living quarters or else the community must build a new firehouse. And a new firehouse takes money, often a bond issue. So hiring Negro firemen is both more costly and more visible, and hence harder to achieve.

Third, the power of the Negro vote increases to *the extent that whites perceive the issue as involving matters of fairness and impartiality*. One of the greatest resources of Negroes in their struggle for equality is the obvious congruence of many of their demands with the "democratic" and "good government" ethos. Reforms that can be justified by simple and clear appeals to the whites' sense of fair play and impartiality have a relatively good chance of being adopted. Thus nondiscrimination in public hiring practices is far easier to achieve than a policy of compensatory opportunities that seems, on its face, to discriminate in favor of Negroes. Police brutality and discrimination in electoral administration are obviously unfair, and very few white southerners are prepared to defend either practice as inherently desirable.

Finally, the vote can help southern Negroes to achieve racial equality only in the *public sector of community life*. Even a responsive government is of little help in altering injustice in areas where the government has no legal authority or informal influence. As the more blatant, legal, "southern" forms

16 In this section we rely heavily on W. R. Keech, "The Negro Vote as a Political Resource: The Case of Durham" (Unpublished Dissertation, University of Wisconsin, 1966). See also U. S. Commission on Civil Rights, *1961 Report*, Vol. I, "Voting," (Washington, D.C.: U.S. Government Printing Office, 1961), part III, pp. 143–99; H. S. Whitaker, "A New Day: The Effects of Negro Enfranchisement in Selected Mississippi Counties" (Unpublished Dissertation, Florida State University, 1965); A. Sindler, "Protest Against the Political Status of the Negro," *Annals*, Vol. 357 (1965), pp. 48–54.

of segregation are replaced by more subtle, *de facto*, "northern" forms, the vote as a weapon in the civil rights struggle will become less and less potent.

## THE VALUE OF THE VOTE

This is not to argue that the vote is of little or no value to southern Negroes. It is to argue, however, that the concrete benefits to be derived from the franchise—under the conditions that prevail in the South—have often been exaggerated.

To be sure, much of the extravagant talk about the vote being *the* key that will unlock the door to racial equality for southern Negroes should be discounted as political hyperbole. It is dangerous talk nonetheless. Statements to this effect by responsible public officials, from the President of the United States on down, and by scores of prominent Negro leaders, just might be taken at face value. The result might be to lull nonsoutherners into thinking that the southern Negroes' struggle for equality has been won when the tide of battle has merely begun to shift, to lead southern Negroes to expect miracles from the vote and to become deeply embittered when the miracles fail to materialize, and to lead southern whites to panic at the prospect of a "black domination" of the region that will never come. The vote for southern Negroes is a necessary but not a sufficient condition for racial progress in the South. So are continued pressures from the non-South and realism and understanding from Negro and white southerners.

The concrete, measurable payoffs from Negro voting in the South will *not* be revolutionary. But these are not the only reasons for valuing the franchise. The effects of taking part in the process of self-government *on the participant* —on his self-esteem and his sense of civic responsibility—must not be ignored. One middle-aged Negro interviewed in the course of this study was asked why he so deeply wanted to vote. He replied simply: "To be a man." This is reason enough to justify all the efforts and sacrifices that have been made to reenfranchise the Negroes of the South. Race will remain a serious problem in the South until southerners—Negro as well as white—accept the moral worth of Negroes as a matter of course. The vote and its exercise by southern Negroes will help both groups move toward this new day.

# Epilogue

On Thanksgiving Day in 1965 the white residents of Crayfish County could find few reasons to give thanks. God might still favor keeping Negroes "in their place," but higher powers in Washington clearly had other ideas. And for the moment those powers had the upper hand.

A few days before, three federal registrars of voters had arrived in Crayfish, set up headquarters in the basement of the Breedville post office, and announced that they were there to register Negroes as voters under the provisions of the Voting Rights Act of 1965.

These representatives of the national government were met with cold hostility, but no one actually attacked them. None of the federal registrars was a Mississippian, but none was a "Yankee"—all were from nearby states.

Political realities had changed drastically since the pistol-whipping of the SNCC representative four years earlier. In an effort to ward off federal intervention, the state legislature had relaxed its stringent requirements for voter registration. Jim Rock, the intransigent registrar of voters, had died of a heart attack. His replacement, a 26-year-old college graduate, was ready to accept the new southern politics.

Breedville and Crayfish County had accepted outside authority, but only with resentment and uncertainty. They seemed less confident than before that "we have the happiest niggers in the world," all committed to second-class citizenship. This uncertainty was heightened when 1,300 Negroes manfully trooped in to register, asserting their rights as American citizens for the first time in their lives.

Among these new voters, some 200 were courageous enough to go to the courthouse (rather than to the post office) and register with the new county registrar. The symbolism of registering at the county courthouse, where the SNCC worker had been assaulted four years earlier, made the extra effort worth while. But the rest of the Crayfish Negroes were content to register at the federal post office.

Formally accepting the inevitability of nondiscrimination, the county school authorities have signed a statement of compliance with civil rights statutes. Legally, no school in Crayfish is segregated; parents are free to choose the school their children will attend. Yet by the end of the 1965–66 school year, no Negro parent had chosen to send a child to the all-white school. (Needless to say, no white parent had chosen the Negro school for his child either.)

Crayfish Negroes have thus moved only a small distance out of "their place." They have made no more effort to integrate Breedville's restaurants or dilapidated movie house than they have to integrate the schools. As to how many will actually exercise their newly won franchise, local leaders are uncertain. One white leader estimates that the Negro vote will "not be too heavy unless the federal government gets in the act like it did on registration." The Negroes, he said, retain "deep-seated misgiving about going to the courthouse or other regular polling places," as well they might. If the new registrants come to vote in groups, he feels, perhaps as many as half of them will actually vote. How many of these will lose their jobs the next day is problematical.

The white politicians do not know what to do about the newly registered citizens of their county. As our informant put it, "They obviously can't go out hell-bent seeking colored votes." Nonetheless, they have made some covert appeals—the road supervisors have graveled some driveways, and roads that had been neglected for years have been repaired. Perhaps the day has come when such officials can no longer say they do not "give a damn about a nigger road."

•   •   •

The "civil rights revolution" has not had revolutionary consequences for Bright Leaf County. Negro voting and Negro demands on the government both continue to increase—and without the aid of federal registrars. But what is stunning in Crayfish is taken for granted in Bright Leaf. Negro demands are modest (by non-Crayfish standards), and white responses are relatively moderate and realistic.

Token desegregation of the Farmington schools was achieved without great fanfare in 1962 when two Negro boys entered the white high school. The rural schools of Bright Leaf were integrated in 1965. By 1966, only half a dozen Negro pupils were in Farmington's white schools. All of Farmington's restaurants are now integrated, and, as a prominent white leader comments, "The whites just accept it. There's been no real trouble." The more expensive restaurants still have few Negro customers, but the lunch counter at the five-and-ten-cent store on Main Street does a thriving business with both Negroes and whites. After an early period of "vertical integration," the lunch stools have been returned to their places at the counter.

In April of 1966 local chapters of the SCLC and NAACP (neither organization yet exists in Crayfish) held meetings to plan further integration of the schools and new voting drives. These meetings were reported in colorless fashion along with social events and church meetings in a regular column the Farmington *Daily Mirror* now calls "Community Notes." (A few years ago, the same column was entitled "Colored Community Notes.") But the outcome of these meetings made the front page. A committee from the two Negro organizations presented the City Council and the County Commission with a list of grievances and demands. The demands included the employment of Negroes as deputy sheriffs, as bank tellers, and as firemen; "total" integration of cemeteries; "total" integration of schools, including faculty and staff; the abandonment of the county's "freedom of choice" plan of school desegregation for the assignment of children to integrated schools; and the establishment of a county good-neighbor commission that would be "truly representative" of the community. The old-style Negro leadership has obviously lost out to more militant, younger leaders.

White leaders of Farmington received these demands with equanimity "We hired Negro policemen quite a few years ago," one of them said. "We found qualified people, so we did this fairly easily." His explanation of successful desegregation in terms of the availability of competent personnel—with no ideological references to the "southern way of life"—seems typical of Bright Leaf County.

Not all the white people of Bright Leaf County, of course, have taken these developments in stride. The Ku Klux Klan has been revived in the county, but it has made little headway. During early 1966, for example, a handful of Klan members marched down the main street of Farmington in full regalia. The chief of police, noting that they had no parade permit, told the group to disperse and leave town. One Klansman alleges that the chief was overly zealous in breaking up the demonstration and brought suit against the policemen, charging brutality! The local court dismissed the suit.

Life in Bright Leaf today might be summarized as follows: whites do not treat Negroes with much respect, but they do not totally ignore them or viciously suppress them. Negroes are not really happy with their situation, but they are not so displeased as to engage in strong protest activity.

Negro demands can be expected to increase. Since the national political system supports these demands and Bright Leaf whites are realistic in their response, the local system may manage to combine change with stability.

•    •    •

Richard Jones is a tall, muscular, handsome man in his mid-forties. A basketball player in his undergraduate days at Tuskegee Institute, he went on to graduate work at the University of Illinois, where he took his Ph.D. in psychology. In 1950, when he received his degree, northern universities were not clamoring for Negro Ph.D.'s as they are now; so he returned south to accept a position at the Peripheral State Agricultural and Mechanical College in Camellia County.

Professor Jones has been chairman of the Department of Psychology there for several years. But as he prepared for the first meeting with his class on race relations in the spring semester of 1966, he felt an unusually keen sense of anticipation. This time he was scheduled to teach the course at A. and M.'s sister institution, Peripheral State University, formerly a segregated white institution but now with a small group of Negro students. For the first time in the history of P. S. U., a Negro professor would be charged with instructing and judging a class of white students—in a course on race relations!

Five years earlier, Professor Jones could not sit at the front of a Capital City bus. Now he was to stand at the front of a class of white students. Others might have expected trouble, but Jones was accustomed to the ways of Capital City. He had been on the P. S. U. campus many times without ever experiencing any unpleasantness. And the *Capital City Bugle,* which had predicted (and implicitly encouraged) violence five years ago, had now accepted the inevitable. Partly because it was under new ownership and partly because of the force of events, the *Bugle* confined itself to a factual article about Professor Jones's appointment as an exchange professor.

Demand for the course was so great that admission was limited to seniors and juniors who were psychology majors. Of the 48 students who qualified, only two were nonsoutherners and most were from traditionally segregationist communities. Their professor's only complaint about their performance was that there was a complete absence of any racist sentiment in class discussions. He was also struck by their total ignorance of what life is like for Negroes in the South. Among the students the only complaint was that his exams were too tough. It sounds like a typical class.

Five years before he took over his class of white college students, Professor Jones explained to us one of the many difficulties a Negro parent faces in the South. On a Saturday afternoon drive with his seven-year-old daughter, he passed one of Capital City's numerous small parks, this one in a "better" white neighborhood. His daughter noticed a set of swings and asked her father to stop and let her play. A militant champion of civil rights but also concerned to protect his child from unpleasantness, he declined. Childlike, she persisted. "But why not, Daddy? We aren't in a hurry!" He commented to us, "One of the worst problems is that you have to lie to your children and appear to be unkind to them." Unwilling to tell his daughter that she could *never* play in the park because of her color, he replied, "Another time, Honey, another time we will." He was not trying to be prophetic, but another time has indeed come to Camellia County.

Change has been great, but it should not be exaggerated. The Jones girl is too old to play on the park swings today, but she does like to swim. Unfortunately, Capital City closed its public swimming pools rather than integrate them. And she is too old to be sheltered and puzzled by evasive remarks about "another time." Her father is taking part in a suit to get the swimming pools reopened immediately. He thinks they will be open before she is too old to take advantage of them.

Politics in Camellia County has perhaps changed less than race relations. The Negro leaders who emerged as a result of the bus boycott are still in power. One of them, a highly militant minister, has been promoted by his church and no longer has much time to devote to political affairs. The others find that the militant rhetoric of the early 1960's is no longer called for. "If you have a problem [of racial injustice] all you have to do is pick up the phone and call [United States Attorney General] Katzenbach."

Professor Jones hopes to breathe some new life into the Negro political community soon. He has just announced his candidacy for the Democratic Executive Committee of the county. In the chaotic factionalism of Camellia— the white politicians remain as divided as always—he just might make it. It looks as if A. and M. College—so badly routed after the bus boycotts—will once again be represented among the Negro leadership of the county, and by a professional student of race relations at that.

● ● ●

The ugliness of Urbania makes a vivid impression on even the casual visitor. Approaching 100,000 in population, it is a dirty, smelly city. The congested business district is particularly offensive. One recent visitor, searching the skyline for some break in the drabness, quickly found it in the dominating structure of the city. On the highest elevation in the business district, a hand-some contemporary structure of twelve stories stands above the rest of the buildings. It dominates them in its excellent architecture no less than in its height.

On closer inspection, the visitor discovered that the building was the central office of the Upper State Insurance Company. The approach was across a podium with planters, reflecting pools, and fountains. As the visitor entered the glass-walled main floor, he was struck by the fact that the receptionist was a Negro. He concluded that the insurance company must be unusually progressive to employ a Negro for such a conspicuous position.

The visitor's guide in his tour of the building was also a Negro, but he was not surprised by that. He had often observed Negroes in this role in the South. When he was escorted to the top floor, he found the view depressing. From the highest point in Urbania, the squalor of much of the city, especially the Negro section, was apparent.

As the visitor passed the office of the company's vice-president, he noticed that even this high-ranking official was a Negro. Amazed to find a Negro as a major official in what was obviously one of the leading business establishments of the area, he asked his guide about the racial policies of the company. She replied that the company had been founded and developed by Negroes; all the high-ranking officers and virtually all the employees were Negroes.

This kind of experience could hardly be reproduced anywhere else, north or south. Urbania's visitor had stumbled upon a major insurance company and one of the largest Negro business enterprises in the world. The impressive physical setting suggested that he must be in the midst of Urbania's "power elite." If we recognize that elites are not homogeneous, this conclusion is correct. The Upper State Insurance Company does not dominate the politics of Urbania but it does play a significant role.

Urbania's finest business building was dedicated in the spring of 1966. About 5,000 people were present for the major address, delivered by the Vice-President of the United States. In addition to foreign diplomats and a number of national leaders, the Governor of Upper State, both its senators, and several of its representatives were present for Vice-President Humphrey's address. Referring to the slogan of die-hard southern segregationists—"The South will rise again"—he pointed to the tallest building on Urbania's skyline and added, "Well, it is rising, but not in the way these people meant."

## APPENDIX A

# Data Collection Procedures

In this book we have drawn on a large volume and a wide variety of data. The methods used in collecting data of this sort have a profound effect on their quality and accuracy. In this appendix, therefore, we shall describe in detail the procedures we followed.

## Southwide sample survey of Negro and white opinions

Our most important single source of data was a southwide sample survey of the opinions of Negro and white adults conducted in the spring of 1961.

### DEVELOPMENT OF QUESTIONNAIRES

During the early summer of 1960 we prepared two draft questionnaires, one for Negro respondents and another for whites. Later that summer the questionnaires were pretested on about 200 respondents in one urban and one rural community in North Carolina by a trained staff of white and Negro interviewers from the Institute for Research in Social Science at the University of North Carolina. Preliminary analysis of these interviews and consultations with other scholars led us to revise our questionnaires substantially. We had the revised versions pretested in February 1961 in a Florida city by the interviewers from the Survey Research Center of the University of Michigan, who were to conduct the actual survey. The authors and representatives of the Field Section of SRC took part in this pretest. We revised the questionnaires once again on the basis of this experience and in response to advice from the Field Section of SRC.

The interview schedules used in this survey appear in Appendix B. We prepared the Negro interview schedule first and followed it as closely as possible in preparing the interview schedule for whites. The questions addressed to whites might have been quite different if the white respondents had not been essentially a "control group" for a study of southern Negroes.

THE SAMPLE

The individuals interviewed in this survey are a representative cross section of citizens of voting age (18 and over in Georgia; 21 and over elsewhere) living in private households in the 11 states of the former Confederacy: Alabama, Arkansas, Florida, Georgia, Louisiana, Mississippi, North Carolina, South Carolina, Tennessee, Texas, and Virginia.

Since the bulk of the analysis was to consist of Negro-white comparisons, we sampled Negroes at about three times their actual proportion of the region's population. The result was two samples of approximately equal size; the Negro sample contains 618 interviews, the white sample contains 694. (We could, by dropping the supplementary Negro interviews, merge these two sets of interviews into a single sample of southern adults without regard to race. We have not done so in the course of this book; consequently the interviews may be thought of as two separate samples.) In determining whether respondents were "Negro" or "white," the interviewers used the vague "social" definition of race employed by all southerners in their daily lives.

As is customary in survey research, residents of military establishments, hospitals, religious and educational institutions, logging and lumber camps, penal institutions, hotels, and large rooming houses were excluded because of the serious practical difficulties of sampling and interviewing such persons and because a large proportion of them are legally or otherwise disfranchised.

Both the Negro and white samples were drawn by the Survey Research Center through its regular procedures.[1] The SRC employs stratified, multistage, probability sampling techniques rather than a simple random sample. The sampling for our study required the following procedures:

1. Grouping the counties of the South into relatively homogeneous strata on the basis of subregion, population concentration, and degree of industrialization. From each of the resulting 18 strata, one Primary Sampling Unit (PSU, a county or group of counties) was selected.
2. Within each of the 18 PSU's, a number of cities, towns, and rural areas were randomly selected.
3. Within each city, town, or rural area, blocks or similar small areas (segments) were randomly selected.
4. Within each segment, dwelling units were randomly selected. One adult

[1] These have been fully described in A. Campbell, G. Gurin, and W. E. Miller, *The Voter Decides* (Evanston, Ill.: Row, Peterson and Company, 1954), Appendix F.

was interviewed in each dwelling unit. The respondent was designated by an objective procedure of selection,[2] and no substitutions were allowed.

This sampling procedure gives a close approximation of a random sample and, because of the geographical clustering of respondents, keeps interviewing costs at a practical level. Departures from pure random sampling, however, make tests of statistical significance that are based on the assumption of pure random sampling—such as chi-square—inappropriate.

## INTERVIEWING

The interviews were conducted between March and June, 1961, by professional interviewers. Interviews with the sample of southern whites were conducted by the SRC's regular field staff, undoubtedly one of the best in the world. All interviews with Negro respondents were conducted by specially recruited, SRC-trained Negro interviewers. The nature of our study demanded that we use a segregated interviewer force, despite very heavy costs in money, time, and administrative problems.[3] "Most survey research is conducted (1) with questions that have an affective quality that is not conducive to extreme reactions; (2) in communities with only a normal level of tension; (3) with respondents who, while perhaps hesitant to express themselves because of a variety of psychological and social factors, need not be fearful of physical coercion if they give the "wrong" responses; and (4) within language and status bounds that permit a relative ease of communication."[4] We could assume the existence of none of these conditions for our study. On the contrary, we were virtually certain that white interviewers would seriously bias the responses of southern Negro respondents, particularly in rural areas.

Since interviewers must have enough education to fill out forms, conduct correspondence, and carry out other "middle-class" activities, we may have eliminated racial bias without getting rid of class bias. In order to minimize this risk, we eliminated prospective Negro interviewers whose manner and appearance were too "middle class." And, at the very least, the same class bias existed in the interviewing of the white sample, since the SRC's white interviewers were middle-class persons, too.

A more serious problem was that SRC's regular interviewers were likely to be more skillful than the inexperienced, *ad hoc* Negro interviewers. We took several steps to reduce this gap. Negro applicants were thoroughly screened and personally interviewed; each attended a four-day training session con-

[2] See L. Kish, "A Procedure for Objective Respondent Selection Within the Household," *Journal of the American Statistical Association*, Vol. 44 (1949), pp. 380–87.
[3] For a detailed description, see M. Axelrod, D. R. Matthews, and J. W. Prothro, "Recruitment for Survey Research on Race Problems in the South," *Public Opinion Quarterly*, Vol. 26 (Summer 1962), pp. 254–62.
[4] *Ibid.*, p. 255.

ducted by the SRC with the authors in attendance. This training included intensive instruction and practice in using our questionnaire. Finally, we kept the Negro field staff as small as possible (16, all residing in one of the 18 PSU's), and we spread the interviews over as long a period as possible in order to maximize the number of interviews conducted by each new Negro interviewer. In interviewing, as in other activities, the quality of performance increases with practice.

Detailed examination of the interviews suggests that the Negro interviewers obtained a level of response from respondents beyond what even the most skillful and experienced white interviewer could have obtained; in other respects, their performance was not significantly lower in quality than that of the white Survey Research Center professionals.

It is never possible to interview every individual in a sample. Since those who are missed are unlikely to be a random assortment of persons, this failure may result in error. We directed our interviewers to "call back" at least three times if the potential respondent was not available for interviewing at the first visit. Our field staff obtained the following highly satisfactory response rates:

|  | *Negro* | *White* | *Total* |
|---|---|---|---|
| Completed interviews | 87% | 84% | 85% |
| Noninterviews | 13% | 16% | 15% |
| Not at home | 6 | 4 | 5 |
| Refusal | 3 | 8 | 6 |
| Other | 4 | 4 | 4 |
| TOTAL | 100% | 100% | 100% |

Despite our worst fears—reinforced by the forebodings of some professional colleagues who argued that a sample survey on race and politics could not be carried out in the South during the early 1960's—not one interviewer was insulted, threatened, or "run out of town."

CODING

By early June 1961 the interviewing had been completed and the questionnaires had been edited and shipped to Chapel Hill. We spent the summer preparing Negro and white codebooks (which again were made as nearly identical as possible), hiring and training coders (advanced graduate students in political science and sociology), and coding the responses for punching on IBM cards. Seven highly trained and intelligent coders were employed for three months. This job was completed on September 15, 1961.

ERROR AND ACCURACY

Properly conducted sample surveys yield useful estimates but they do not provide exact values. Errors may arise from many sources: asking the "wrong" questions, poor wording of the questions, interviewer bias and mistakes in recording, nonresponse, coding inaccuracy, and so forth. We have already mentioned our efforts to minimize such errors. But one final and inescapable source of error must still be discussed—sampling.

Sample statistics reflect the random variations that arise from contact with only a fraction of the population. The proportion of individuals in a sample having a given attribute will usually be somewhat larger or smaller than the value that would have been obtained if the whole population had been interviewed. Fortunately, the size of this sampling error can be calculated from the characteristics of the sample.

The computations of sampling error reported below indicate the range on either side of the sample estimate within which the population value can be expected to lie 95 times in 100 chances. For example, our survey estimate that 86.5 per cent of the white respondents in the South had voted at least once is subject to a sampling error of about 2.6 percentage points. In order to achieve a 95 per cent "level of confidence" we must double this "standard error." Our original finding accordingly boils down to this: in at least 95 samples out of 100, between 81.3 and 91.7 per cent of the adult whites in the South would be found to have voted at least once. The chances are 5 in 100 that the percentage would fall outside this range.

To compute sampling errors for every statistic derived from a survey would be far too costly. These errors show enough regularity to permit the computation of average sampling errors for various divisions among respondents and for different numbers of interviews. Using the data from this study, the SRC Sampling Section computed the sampling error presented in Table A–1. Note that our sampling error varies from a low of 3.8 to a high of 12.6, depending

TABLE A–1.   *Approximate sampling error[a] of percentages (expressed in percentage points)*

| REPORTED PERCENTAGES | NUMBER OF INTERVIEWS | | | | | |
|---|---|---|---|---|---|---|
| | 700 | 500 | 400 | 300 | 200 | 100 |
| 50 | 8.6 | 8.9 | 9.1 | 9.6 | 10.4 | 12.6 |
| 30 or 70 | 7.9 | 8.1 | 8.4 | 8.8 | 9.6 | 11.6 |
| 20 or 80 | 6.8 | 7.1 | 7.3 | 7.6 | 8.4 | 10.1 |
| 10 or 90 | 5.2 | 5.3 | 5.6 | 5.8 | 6.2 | 7.6 |
| 5 or 95 | 3.8 | 3.9 | 4.2 | 4.3 | 4.7 | 6.2 |

[a] The figures in this table represent *two* standard errors. Hence, for most items the chances are 95 in 100 that the value being estimated lies within a range equal to the reported percentages, plus or minus the sampling error. The values are based on the average of computations of individual sampling errors carried out on our data, and allow for departures from simple random sampling in the survey design. The sampling error does not measure the total error involved in specific survey estimates, since it does not include nonresponse and reporting errors.

on the number of cases on which the sample estimate is based and the percentage of the population estimated to have a given attribute. The sampling errors in the table are *average* errors in both the *Negro* and the *white* samples.

Differences between survey estimates are often of greater interest than the level of the estimates. These may be differences between groups contained in

TABLE A–2.   *Approximate sampling error*[a] *of differences (in percentage points)*

|  | 700 | 500 | 300 | 200 | 100 |
|---|---|---|---|---|---|
| FOR PERCENTAGES FROM 35 PER CENT TO 65 PER CENT |
| 700 | 11.1 | 11.6 | 11.8 | 12.4 | 14.0 |
| 500 |  | 11.3 | 11.9 | 12.5 | 14.1 |
| 300 |  |  | 12.3 | 13.0 | 14.6 |
| 200 |  |  |  | 13.4 | 15.1 |
| 100 |  |  |  |  | 16.2 |
| FOR PERCENTAGES AROUND 20 PER CENT AND 80 PER CENT |
| 700 | 9.6 | 9.8 | 10.2 | 10.8 | 12.5 |
| 500 |  | 10.0 | 10.4 | 11.0 | 12.7 |
| 300 |  |  | 10.8 | 11.3 | 13.0 |
| 200 |  |  |  | 11.8 | 13.4 |
| 100 |  |  |  |  | 14.8 |
| FOR PERCENTAGES AROUND 10 PER CENT AND 90 PER CENT |
| 700 | 7.4 | 7.4 | 7.8 | 8.1 | 9.2 |
| 500 |  | 7.5 | 7.9 | 8.1 | 9.2 |
| 300 |  |  | 8.3 | 8.5 | 9.6 |
| 200 |  |  |  | 8.7 | 9.8 |
| 100 |  |  |  |  | 10.7 |
| FOR PERCENTAGES AROUND 5 PER CENT AND 95 PER CENT |
| 700 | 5.3 | 5.4 | 5.7 | 6.0 | 7.2 |
| 500 |  | 5.5 | 5.7 | 6.1 | 7.3 |
| 300 |  |  | 6.0 | 6.3 | 7.5 |
| 200 |  |  |  | 6.6 | 7.8 |
| 100 |  |  |  |  | 8.7 |

[a] The values shown are the differences required for significance (two standard errors) in comparisons of percentages derived from two different subgroups of the current survey. Average values are given for each cell.

the same survey (e.g., between white-collar and blue-collar Negroes) or differences between groups contained in different samples (e.g., between Negro and white blue-collar workers). Table A–2 contains these calculations for our data. When the N's for the two groups being compared are 200 and 500 and the proportions are around 20 per cent, the approximate sampling error is 11 percentage points. For this example, then, only differences in proportions greater than 11 percentage points between the two groups are likely to be significant 95 times out of 100.

# Sample surveys of Negro and white opinions in four southern communities

In order to examine the relationships between community-based political variables and Negro political participation, we conducted four community studies in "Piedmont," "Camellia," "Bright Leaf," and "Crayfish" counties. The main body of systematic data on these four counties consists of interviews with representative samples of Negro and white citizens of voting age.

We used the standard questionnaires for Negro and white adults in the eight samples in these counties. Three of the counties—Camellia, Bright Leaf, and Crayfish—were single county PSU's in the SRC's southern sample. A relatively few additional interviews, when added to those taken as part of the southwide sample, resulted in representative samples of Negroes and whites in each county. These additional interviews were conducted at the same time as the southwide survey, by the same interviewers. The response rates reported on p. 492 include these additional interviews.

Piedmont County was not included in the SRC's southwide sample; the sampling and interviewing in this county were handled separately. The Research Triangle Institute of North Carolina drew two area probability samples of the county designed to yield approximately 100 white and 100 Negro respondents. Graduate students at the University of North Carolina, after receiving the same training as the new Negro interviewers, conducted the interviews with white respondents. One Negro interviewer administered all the interviews with Negro respondents. The response rates were as follows:

|  | Negro |  | White |  |
|---|---|---|---|---|
| Completed interviews | 91% |  | 84% |  |
| Noninterviews | 9% |  | 16% |  |
| Respondent not at home |  | 5 |  | 6 |
| Refusal |  | 2 |  | 10 |
| Other |  | 2 |  | — |
| TOTAL | 100% |  | 100% |  |

The supplementary interviews used in the community studies were coded at the same time as the southwide sample.

These county samples were small:

| County | Negro respondents | White respondents |
|---|---|---|
| Piedmont | 100 | 96 |
| Camellia | 77 | 68 |
| Bright Leaf | 75 | 82 |
| Crayfish | 48 | 56 |

The more homogeneous the population, the less the need for a large sample—if each member of a population were the same as all the others, a sample of one would suffice. For this reason, our samples in Crayfish and Bright Leaf are much smaller than in Piedmont and Camellia.

In general, however, sampling error is inversely proportional to the square root of the sample size. Thus the sampling error of an estimate based on 100 cases is almost 2.5 times as large as that of an estimate based on 600 cases; the sampling error of an estimate based on 50 cases is almost 3.5 times as large. The small size of these county samples, then, prohibits extensive analysis internal to these eight samples. Further, it suggests that differences between these samples must be two or three times as large as those listed in Table A–2 before they can be considered statistically significant.

## Negro college student survey

Southern Negro college students were among the most prominent actors in the "Negro revolution" of the early 1960's. Since only a few of them fell within our southwide sample, we conducted a separate southwide survey of Negro college student opinion during 1962. In the fall of 1961 we modified the standard interview for Negro adults for use with a student population. We added a few new questions of particular relevance to the students.

The persons interviewed in this survey are a representative cross section of Negro students from southern homes working toward degrees at accredited, predominantly Negro institutions of higher learning in the 11 states of the former Confederacy. The survey population included part-time as well as full-time students, graduate students as well as undergraduates, and students living away from campus as well as those on campus; it excluded the handful of Negroes in "integrated" institutions of higher learning in the region. Non-Negroes and nonsoutherners attending these institutions who appeared in the sample were not interviewed. (This exclusion of individuals who do not qualify as members of the sample population is common—e.g., election surveys normally exclude aliens who appear in samples of voting-age populations.)

The sample of students was drawn by the authors. We selected 340 student names from the colleges' lists of degree candidates in the following way: starting at random, we counted N names down a list of all Negro college students in the region and added the next ten names to the sample; then we skipped N names and took the next ten; and so on. (So long as the exact enrollment of the college or university was known, it was not necessary even to know the actual names of the students. In a few cases, interviewers merely received the sample number of the students to be interviewed.) The clustering in this sample design reduced the number of institutions at which interviews were conducted to 30, a manageable number. On the other hand, by departing from pure random sampling, sampling error was increased.

The Negro field staff of 1961 was reactivated to conduct the student interviews. Travel costs—the 30 institutions in our student sample were not all in or near the PSU's in which our Negro interviewers lived—required that this staff be supplemented by eight new interviewers recruited from the student bodies of institutions represented in the sample. A special four-day interviewer training session was held for these new interviewers immediately before they began work in January 1962.

The results of this survey were as follows:

|  | Percentage | Number |
|---|---|---|
| Completed interviews | 84 | 264 |
| Noninterviews | 16 | 52 |
|   No longer in school | 10 | 33 |
|   In school but not interviewed | 6 | 19 |

Interviews were completed during the winter, coded during April by essentially the same staff that had coded the adult interviews, and punched and verified on IBM cards by early summer of 1962.

We have computed no special tables of sampling error for this survey; the values in Tables A–1 and A–2 may be used for purposes of *roughly estimating* the size of sampling error. The student sample is actually less clustered than the two adult ones.

## Aggregate county data

Thirty-four demographic and political attributes of all counties in the South were collected during the summer of 1960 from the United States Census and other sources too numerous to list here.[5] Graduate student assistants recorded, coded, and verified these data. As in all other coding operations for this study, a minimum number of highly trained coders was employed.

[5] A copy of this list of sources is available from the authors on request.

# Content analysis of newspapers in four southern communities

The content analysis of the leading local newspapers in Piedmont, Camellia, Bright Leaf, and Crayfish counties was based on a pure random sample. All issues of each paper between May 13, 1963, and May 13, 1964, were collected, and the total number of pages in all issues during the year was counted. Each page was viewed as consisting of spatially defined segments (1/16 of the page) called "Basic Sampling Units." Basic Sampling Units were then chosen at random for each newspaper. (We are indebted to Dean Wayne Danielson of the University of North Carolina School of Journalism for allowing us to use his computer program, which draws samples of newspaper content in this fashion.)

The number of Basic Sampling Units chosen for each paper was:

|  | Total number of BSU's | Number of BSU's containing news and editorial material |
| --- | --- | --- |
| Urbania Press | 394 | 108 |
| Capital City Bugle | 400 | 108 |
| Farmington Daily Mirror | 397 | 122 |
| Breedville Weekly | 400 | 104 |

The content of these BSU's was coded by two trained and experienced coders using code categories developed by the authors. After the original coding, each coded a sample of the BSU's originally coded by the other. The reliability coefficient of their work (which is the number of category assignments on which both coders agreed, divided by the sum of all category assignments made by both coders) ranged from 91.8 per cent for the *Capital City Bugle* to 82.4 per cent for the *Breedville Weekly*. The mean coefficient of reliability for all four newspapers was 86.9 per cent.

# APPENDIX B

# The Questionnaires

The interview schedule designed for use with Negro adults in the South was modified for use with the samples of white adults and of Negro college students. In the presentation of the questionnaire that follows, these modifications can be identified by reference to the three columns of question numbers. If a number appears in all three columns opposite a question, that question was asked of all three samples. A number in only one or two columns means the question was asked only of the samples identified at the column top.

One consistent modification is not identified. In view of the affect-laden quality of different pronunciations of the word "Negro" among southern whites, the term "colored people" was substituted for every use of the word "Negro" in adapting the Negro questionnaire for use with the white sample. Unless some other change was also made in the question, we have not reprinted it as different in the white questionnaire.

[A] *Negro Student*   [B] *White Adult*   [C] *Negro Adult*

COMMUNITY AND CIVIC PARTICIPATION STUDY

I am helping a group of people at the University of North Carolina who are studying public opinion on community and civic participation. I'm mainly interested in questions like this, for example:

| [A] | [B] | [C] | |
|-----|-----|-----|---|
| 1 | 1 | 1 | When you talk with your friends, do you ever talk about public problems—that is, what's happening in the country or in this community? |

499

[A] *Negro Student*  [B] *White Adult*  [C] *Negro Adult*

| [A] | [B] | [C] | |
|---|---|---|---|
| la | la | la | (*if "yes"*) What public problems do you talk about? [Anything else?] |
| 2 | 2 | 2 | Do you ever talk about public problems with any of the following people? |
| 2a | 2a | 2a | Your family? |
| 2b | 2b | 2b | (*if "yes"*) What public problems do you talk about? |
|  | 2c | 2c | People where you work? |
| 2c |  |  | Your fellow students? |
| 2d | 2d | 2d | (*if "yes"*) What public problems do you talk about with them? |
|  |  | 2e | Are these people Negroes or whites? |
| 2e |  | 2f | Negro community leaders—such as club or church leaders? |
|  | 2e |  | Community leaders such as club or church leaders? |
| 2f | 2f | 2g | (*if "yes"*) What public problems do you talk about with them? |
| 3 |  | 3 | Do you ever talk about public problems with any white people? |
|  | 3 |  | Do you ever talk about public problems with any colored people? |
|  |  | 3a | (*if "yes"*) Who are they? |

    \_\_\_\_\_ any R [respondent] works for
    \_\_\_\_\_ others where R works
    \_\_\_\_\_ friends
    \_\_\_\_\_ white community leaders
    \_\_\_\_\_ white government officials
    \_\_\_\_\_ other (*write in*)

**3a** (*if "yes"*) Who are they?
    \_\_\_\_\_ any who work for R
    \_\_\_\_\_ others where R works
    \_\_\_\_\_ friends
    \_\_\_\_\_ Negro leaders
    \_\_\_\_\_ Negro government officials
    \_\_\_\_\_ other (*write in*)

**3a** (*if "yes"*) Who are they?
    \_\_\_\_\_ any R works for
    \_\_\_\_\_ others where R works
    \_\_\_\_\_ friends
    \_\_\_\_\_ white community leaders
    \_\_\_\_\_ white government officials
    \_\_\_\_\_ other college students
    \_\_\_\_\_ other (*write in*)

| [A] | [B] | [C] | |
|---|---|---|---|
| 3b | 3b | 3b | What public problems do you talk about? |
| 4 | 4 | 4 | Do you ever talk about public problems with government |

[A] *Negro Student*   [B] *White Adult*   [C] *Negro Adult*

| [A] | [B] | [C] | |
|---|---|---|---|
| | | | officials or people in politics, I mean Democratic or Republican leaders? |
| 4a | 4a | 4a | (*if "yes"*) What problems do you talk about? Anything else? |
| 4b | | 4b | Is this person [Are these people] white or Negro? |
| | 5 | 5 | Have you ever held an office in a political party or been elected or appointed to a government job? |
| | 5a | 5a | (*if "yes"*) What office or job was that? |
| 5 | 6 | 6 | Have you ever given any money or bought tickets or anything to help someone who was trying to win an election? |
| 6 | 7 | 7 | Have you ever gone to any political meetings, rallies, barbecues, fish fries, or things like that in connection with an election? |
| 7 | 8 | 8 | Have you ever done any work to help a candidate in his campaign? |
| 8 | 9 | 9 | Have you ever talked to people to try to get them to vote for or against any candidate? |
| 9 | 10 | 10 | Generally speaking, how interested are you in politics—a great deal, somewhat, or not much at all? |
| 10 | | | How about your parents, how interested are they in politics—a great deal, somewhat, or not much at all? |
| | 11 | 11 | Do you belong to any clubs or groups like these? (*show card 1*) |

\_\_\_\_\_ labor union [like AFL-CIO or a carpenters' union]

\_\_\_\_\_ political club or group [like Young Democrats, Young Republicans, or a political organization]

\_\_\_\_\_ organizations concerned with race relations [like Human Relations Council, NAACP, voters' leagues]

\_\_\_\_\_ fraternal organizations or lodges [like the Masons, Knights of Pythias, or Knights of Columbus]

\_\_\_\_\_ PTA [that is, Parent-Teachers Association]

\_\_\_\_\_ business, professional, or civic groups [like the Kiwanis or Lions clubs]

\_\_\_\_\_ farm group [like Farm Bureau]

\_\_\_\_\_ a church or church-connected group

\_\_\_\_\_ other

\_\_\_\_\_ none

| | 11a | 11a | (if "yes" to any of above) Which is that? |
| 11 | | | Do you belong to any club or group like these? (*show card 1*) |

YES   NO

\_\_\_\_\_ \_\_\_\_\_ NAACP [the National Association for the Advancement of Colored People]

[A] *Negro Student*    [B] *White Adult*    [C] *Negro Adult*

[A]    [B]    [C]

_____ _____ CORE [Congress on Racial Equality]
_____ _____ Southern Christian Leadership Conference
_____ _____ Urban League
_____ _____ "Muslims" [the Nation of Islam in America]
_____ _____ SNCC [Student Non-violent Coordinating Committee]
_____ _____ A Negro voters league
_____ _____ Any other group concerned with race relations or politics (specify)

|  |  |  |  |
|---|---|---|---|
|  | 12 | 12 | Does anyone in your family living here with you belong to any groups like these on the list? |
|  | 12a | 12a | (*if "yes"*) Who is that? Which clubs? |
| 12 |  | 13 | Now, thinking of the NAACP (the National Association for the Advancement of Colored People), do you generally agree with what it does, or do you generally disagree? |
| 12a |  | 13a | (*if "disagree"*) Why do you disagree? |
| 13 |  |  | How about CORE (the Congress on Racial Equality), do you generally agree with what it does, or do you generally disagree? |
| 13a |  |  | (*if "disagree"*) Why do you disagree? |
| 14 |  |  | How about the Southern Christian Leadership Conference (SCLC), do you generally agree with what it does, or do you generally disagree? |
| 14a |  |  | (*if "disagree"*) Why do you disagree? |
| 15 |  |  | How about the Urban League, do you generally agree with what it does, or do you generally disagree? |
| 15a |  |  | (*if "disagree"*) Why do you disagree? |
| 16 |  |  | How about the Muslims (The Lost-Found Nation of Islam in America), do you generally agree with what it does, or do you generally disagree? |
| 16a |  |  | (*if "disagree"*) Why do you disagree? |
| 17 |  |  | How about the Student Non-violent Coordinating Committee, do you generally agree with what it does, or do you generally disagree? |
| 17a |  |  | (*if "disagree"*) Why do you disagree? |
| 18 | 13 | 14 | What is your religious preference? |
| 19 | 14 | 15 | Would you say you go to church services regularly, often, seldom, or never? |
|  | 14a | 15a | (*if ever attends*) Are problems of race relations—that is, how white people and Negroes get along—ever discussed at your church? |
|  | 14b | 15b | Would you say your minister believes that religion or the Bible favors segregation or integration? |
|  | 14c | 15c | Are election campaigns ever discussed at your church? |

[A] *Negro Student*   [B] *White Adult*   [C] *Negro Adult*

| [A] | [B] | [C] | |
|---|---|---|---|
| | 14d | 15d | (*if "yes"*) Does your minister ever say anything about which candidate the members of the church ought to vote for? |
| 20 | 15 | 16 | Are there any newspapers that you read more or less regularly? |
| 20a | 15a | 16a | (*if "yes"*) Which ones? |
| 21 | 16 | 17 | Are there any magazines that you read more or less regularly? |
| 21a | 16a | 17a | (*if "yes"*) Which ones? |
| 22 | 17 | 18 | Do you listen to the radio more or less regularly? |
| 23 | 18 | 19 | How about TV, do you watch fairly regularly? |
| | | | Now, I would like to describe some things that sometimes happen to people. Then I'll ask you: If you were faced with this problem, would you do anything about it or would you not bother with it? |
| | 19 | 20 | First, let's imagine you have a child going to a school where there is nobody to help the children get across the street. The crossing is dangerous, and one day a child is hit by a car. You think that somebody should be put there to help the children. Do you think you would do anything about it, or figure that there wasn't much you could do? |
| | 19a | 20a | (*if would do anything*) What would you do? |
| | 19b | 20b | (*if necessary*) Would you talk to somebody about getting something done? |
| | 19c | 20c | (*if would talk to somebody*) Who is that—that is, what does he do, or what's his position? |
| | | 20d | Is he a Negro or a white person? |
| 24 | | 21 | Let's say you have a close friend who gets in trouble somehow with the police. You feel he hasn't done anything wrong. Would you try to do anything about it, or would you stay out of it? |
| 24a | | 21a | Would you talk to anybody about it? (*probe*—Who is that, or what does he do, or what's his position?) |
| 24b | | 21b | (*if would talk to somebody*) Is he a Negro or a white person? |
| 25 | | 22 | What if you aren't treated right at some white store. Would you do anything about it, or would you figure there wasn't much you could do? |
| 25a | | 22a | Would you talk to anybody about it? (*probe*—Who is that, or what does he do, or what's his position?) |
| 25b | | 22b | (*if would talk to somebody*) Is he a Negro or a white person? |
| | | 23 | What if some friends of yours needed help pretty bad. The man is out of work and the children are hungry. Would |

[A] *Negro Student*　　[B] *White Adult*　　[C] *Negro Adult*

| [A] | [B] | [C] | |
|---|---|---|---|
| | | | you do anything about it, or would you figure there wasn't much you could do? |
| | | 23a | Would you talk to anybody about it? (*probe*—Who is that, or what does he do, or what's his position?) |
| | | 23b | (*if would talk to somebody*) Is he a Negro or a white person? |
| | | 24 | What if you decided that the white school closest to where you live is much better than the Negro school. Would you want your children to go there, even if they were among the first few Negroes to attend the school? |
| | | 24a | Would you do anything about it, or would you figure there wasn't much you could do? |
| | | 24b | Would you talk to anybody about it? (*probe*—Who is that, or what does he do, or what's his position?) |
| | | 24c | (*if would talk to somebody*) Is he a Negro or a white person? |
| 26 | | | Suppose that you are married and have small children. Then you decided that the white school closest to where you live is much better than the Negro school. Would you want your children to go there, even if they were among the first few Negroes to attend the school? |
| 26a | | | Would you do anything about it, or would you figure there wasn't much you could do? |
| 26b | | | Would you talk to anybody about it? (*probe*—Who is that, or what does he do, or what's his position?) |
| 26c | | | (*if would talk to somebody*) Is he a Negro or a white person? |
| | 20 | | Now suppose you usually have lunch at a drugstore that is near where you work or shop (in town). One day when you walk in to eat, you see a couple of colored people eating there. Would you just go ahead and eat there like always, walk out, or just what would you do? |
| | 20a | | Would you talk to anybody about it? (*probe*—Who is that, or what does he do, or what's his position?) |
| | 21 | | What if you had children going to a school and the court ruled the school had to admit a few colored children. Would you have your children keep going to school there? |
| | 21a | | Do you think you would do anything about it, or would you not bother about it? |
| | 21b | | (*if would do anything*) (*if necessary*) Would you talk to somebody about getting something done? |
| | 21c | | (*if would talk to somebody*) Who is that—that is, what does he do, or what's his position? |
| | 25 | | Who would you say are the three most important Negro |

[A] *Negro Student*   [B] *White Adult*   [C] *Negro Adult*

| [A] | [B] | [C] | |
|---|---|---|---|
| | | | leaders in this community—that is, people who have the most say about the way things are run here? |
| | | 25a | *(each leader, in turn)* What does he do? |
| | | 25b | How much would you say *(first, second, third leader)* is respected by the Negro community as a whole—a lot, some, or not much? |
| | | 25c | How much would you say *(first, second, third leader)* is respected by the white community as a whole—a lot, some, or not much? |
| | | 25d | Have you ever talked with any of these important people you just mentioned about some problem you were interested in? |
| | | 25e | *(if "yes")* Which ones? |
| | | 26 | Who would you say are the three white people who have the most say about the way things are run here? |
| | | 26a | *(each leader, in turn)* What does he do? |
| | | 26b | Do you know how much *(first, second, third leader)* is respected by the Negro community as a whole—a lot, some, or not much? |
| | | 26c | How much would you say *(first, second, third leader)* is respected by the white community as a whole—a lot, some, or not much? |
| | 22 | | Who would you say are the three most important leaders in this community—that is, people who have the most say about the way things are run here? |
| | 22a | | *(each leader, in turn)* What does he do? |
| | 22b | | How much would you say *(first, second, third leader)* is respected by the white community as a whole—a lot, some, or not much? |
| | 22c | | How much would you say *(first, second, third leader)* is respected by the colored community as a whole—a lot, some, or not much? |
| | 22d | | Have you ever talked with any of these important people you just mentioned about some problem you were interested in? |
| | 22e | | *(if "yes")* Which ones? |
| | 23 | | Who would you say are the three colored people who have the most say about the way things are run here? |
| | 23a | | *(each leader, in turn)* What does he do? |
| | 23b | | Do you know how much *(first, second, third leader)* is respected by the white community as a whole—a lot, some, or not much? |
| | 23c | | How much would you say *(first, second, third leader)* is |

[A] *Negro Student*   [B] *White Adult*   [C] *Negro Adult*

| [A] | [B] | [C] | |
|-----|-----|-----|---|
| | | | respected by the colored community as a whole—a lot, some, or not much? |
| 27 | | | How much do you respect the Negro leaders in the town or place where you grew up—a lot, some, or not much? |
| 28 | | | What about the other Negro youths there, how much do you think they respect the Negro leaders? |
| 29 | | | What about the Negro adults where you grew up, how much do you think they respect the Negro leaders? |
| 30 | | | Now, how do you feel about the white leaders in the town or place where you grew up—do you respect them a lot, some, or not much? |
| 31 | | | What about the other Negro youths there, how much do you think they respect the white leaders? |
| 32 | | | What about the Negro adults where you grew up, how much do you think they respect the white leaders? |
| 33 | 24 | 27 | Have you ever heard of the sit-in movement—that is, some of the young Negroes going into stores, and sitting down at lunch counters, and refusing to leave until they are served? |
| 33a | 24a | 27a | (if "*yes*") What is your feeling about this? |
| | 24b | 27b | Why do you suppose these young people decide to join the sit-in demonstrations once they are started? |
| | 24c | 27c | How do you suppose these sit-in demonstrations get started? |
| 33b | | | Have you taken part in the sit-in demonstrations? |
| 33c | | | (if "*no*") Is there any special reason why you haven't taken part? |
| 33d | | | (if "*yes*") In what way? How? What happened? |
| 33e | | | Compared with other students active in the sit-ins, would you say that you have been very active, fairly active, or not very active? |
| 33f | | | How did others you are in contact with feel about your participation in the sit-ins? Take your parents, for example, how did they feel about it? |
| 33g | | | What about your close friends? |
| 33h | | | What about your professors? |
| 33i | | | And what about the school administration? |
| 34 | | | Have you heard of the freedom rides—that is, some young Negroes riding busses, trains, and airplanes and using waiting-rooms and rest-rooms previously reserved for whites only? |
| 34a | | | (if "*yes*") What is your feeling about this? |
| 34b | | | Have you taken part in the freedom rides? |
| 34c | | | (if "*no*") Is there any special reason why you haven't taken part? |
| 34d | | | (if "*yes*") In what way? How? What happened? |

[A] *Negro Student*   [B] *White Adult*   [C] *Negro Adult*

| [A] | [B] | [C] | |
|-----|-----|-----|---|
| 34e | | | Compared with other students active in the freedom rides, would you say that you have been very active, fairly active, or not very active? |
| 34f | | | How did others you are in contact with feel about your participation in the freedom rides? Take your parents, for example, how did they feel about it? |
| 34g | | | What about your close friends? |
| 34h | | | What about your professors? |
| 34i | | | And what about the school administration? |
| 35 | | | Why do you suppose that young people decide to join the sit-in demonstrations and freedom rides once they are started? |
| 36 | | | How do you suppose these demonstrations get started? |
| 37 | 25 | 28 | Do you know whether either of your parents ever voted in any elections, or don't you remember? |
| 37a | 25a | 28a | (*if either parent voted*) Does your father usually vote Democratic or Republican? |
| 37b | 25b | 28b | And how about your mother? |
| 38 | 26 | 29 | (*if married*) Has your husband [wife] ever voted? |
| | 27 | 30 | What about you? Have you ever voted? |

IF NEVER VOTED

| | | | |
|-----|-----|-----|---|
| | 28 | 31 | Have you ever wanted to vote? |
| | 29 | 32 | Is there any special reason why you haven't voted? |
| | 30 | 33 | Do you think you will ever vote? |
| | 31 | 34 | As you may have heard, some states have a special kind of tax called a poll tax. What about here in _____ [state]? Do you happen to know whether there is a poll tax here? |
| | 31a | 34a | (*if "yes"*) Have you ever paid the poll tax here in _____ [state]? |
| | 31b | 34b | (*if "no"*) Is there any special reason why you haven't? [Any reason at all?] |
| | 32 | 35 | Have you ever tried to register so that you could vote? |
| | 33 | 36 | (*if "yes," tried to register*) When was that? [Any other time?] |
| | 34 | 37 | Where was that? |
| | 35 | 38 | (*ask following questions about most recent or only time*) Was there any special reason why you tried to register at that time? |
| | 36 | 39 | Did anybody tell you that you ought to register, or was it entirely your own idea? |
| | | 39a | (*if told to*) Who was that? |
| | | 39b | Was he a Negro or a white person? |
| | | 39c | Was this somebody you knew? |
| | | 39d | (*if "yes"*) How do you know him? |

[A] *Negro Student*  [B] *White Adult*  [C] *Negro Adult*

| [A] | [B] | [C] | |
|---|---|---|---|
| | | 39e | Was he speaking for some organization? |
| | | 39f | (*if "yes"*) What organization |
| | 37 | 40 | When you tried to register, did the registration official see if you could read and write or if you could understand the Constitution, or anything like that? |
| | 37a | 40a | (*if "yes"*) Would you tell me about that as best you can remember? |
| | 38 | 41 | Did you get registered? |
| | 38b | 41a | (*if "yes"*) Do you remember whether you registered as a Democrat, Republican, or Independent? Which? |
| | 38a | 41b | (*if "no"*) What happened? |
| | 39 | 42 | Would you say that getting registered was something you felt was an important step in your life, or that it didn't really make much difference? |
| | | 43 | How did they treat you when you tried to register? |

IF HAS VOTED

| [A] | [B] | [C] | |
|---|---|---|---|
| | 40 | 44 | When did you register for the first time? |
| | 41 | 45 | Was there any special reason why you registered at that time? |
| | 42 | 46 | Was that here in _____ [county]? |
| | 42a | 46a | (*if "no"*) Where was it? |
| | 43 | 47 | Do you remember whether you registered as a Democrat, a Republican, or Independent? |
| | 44 | 48 | Are you still registered that way? |
| | 44a | 48a | (*if "no"*) How are you registered now? |
| | | 49 | How did they treat you when you registered? |
| | 45 | 50 | Did anyone tell you that you ought to register, or was it your own idea? |
| | | 50a | (*if told to*) Who was that? |
| | | 50b | Was he a Negro or a white person? |
| | | 50c | Was this somebody you knew? |
| | | 50d | (*if "yes"*) How did you know him? |
| | | 50e | Was he speaking for some organization? |
| | | 50f | (*if "yes"*) What organization? |
| | 46 | 51 | Would you say that getting registered was something you felt was an important step in your life, or that it didn't really make much difference? |
| | 47 | 52 | When you went to register, did the registration official see if you could read and write or if you could understand the Constitution, or anything like that? |
| | 47a | 53 | (*if "yes"*) Would you tell me about that as best you can remember? |
| | 48 | 54 | Are you now registered to vote in _____ [county]? |

[A] *Negro Student*   [B] *White Adult*   [C] *Negro Adult*

| [A] | [B] | [C] | |
|-----|-----|-----|---|
| | 48a | 54a | *(if "no")* Why not now? |
| | 49 | 55 | Last fall, you remember that Nixon ran against Kennedy for president. How much interest would you say you had in that presidential election—a great deal, quite a lot, not very much, or none at all? |
| | 50 | 56 | In the elections for president since you have been old enough to vote, would you say you have voted in all of them, most of them, some of them, or none of them? |
| | 50a | 57a | *(if ever voted for president)* Do you remember for sure whether or not you voted in the Kennedy-Nixon election last fall? |
| | 50b | 57b | *(if "yes")* Which one did you vote for? |
| | 51a | 58a | In 1956 you remember that Eisenhower ran against Stevenson. Do you remember for sure whether or not you voted in that election? |
| | 51b | 58b | *(if voted)* Which one did you vote for? |
| | 52a | 59a | In 1952 you remember that Eisenhower ran against Stevenson for the first time. Do you remember for sure whether or not you voted in that election? |
| | 52b | 59b | *(if voted)* Which one did you vote for? |
| | 53 | 60 | Since you have been old enough to vote, about how often would you say you have voted in Democratic primaries for governor—all of them, most of them, some of them, or none of them? |
| | 53a | 60a | *(if ever voted in democratic primary)* In the last Democratic primary for governor, _____ ran against _____. Do you remember for sure whether or not you voted in that primary? |
| | 53b | 60b | *(if voted)* Which one did you vote for? |
| | 54 | 61 | What about the elections for governor in November when a Republican runs against a Democrat. Have you voted in all of them, most of them, some of them, or none of them? |
| | 55 | 62 | What about elections for school board members. Have you voted in all of them, most of them, some of them, or none of them? |
| | 56 | 63 | What about elections for local or county office, like sheriff or mayor. How often have you voted in them? |
| | | 64 | When was the last time you voted? |
| | | 65 | Did anybody talk to you about voting that time, or was it entirely your own idea? |
| | | 65a | *(if not own idea)* Who was that? |
| | | 65b | Was he a Negro or a white person? |
| | | 65c | Was that somebody you knew? |

[A] *Negro Student*   [B] *White Adult*   [C] *Negro Adult*

| [A] | [B] | [C] | |
|-----|-----|-----|--|
|     |     | 65d | *(if "yes")* How did you know him? |
|     |     | 65e | Was he speaking for some organization? |
|     |     | 65f | *(if "yes")* What organization? |

ALL RESPONDENTS

|     | 57  |     | What about the colored people around here—do any of them vote? |
|-----|-----|-----|--|
|     | 57a | 66  | In some places, you hear that Negroes get together and all vote for the same candidate. Have you ever heard about that happening here? |
|     | 57b | 67  | Do white candidates do anything to get Negro votes? |
|     | 57c | 67a | *(if "yes")* What is that? |
|     | 57d | 67b | Sometimes you hear that Negro votes can be bought. Does that ever happen around here? |
|     |     | 68  | Have you ever heard of anything happening to Negroes around here who have voted or taken some other part in politics or public affairs? |
|     |     | 68a | *(if "yes")* Could you tell me about it—what happened? [When? Why? Where?] |
|     |     | 69  | Suppose that you planned to vote in an election but hadn't yet made up your mind who you would vote for. Then you found out that most of the Negroes in this area favored one of the candidates. What difference would it make to you? |
|     |     | 70  | Now, suppose that you planned to vote in an election but hadn't yet made up your mind who you would vote for. Then you found out that the strongest white segregation leaders in this area favored one of the candidates. What difference would it make to you? |
|     | 58  |     | Suppose that you planned to vote in an election but hadn't yet made up your mind who you would vote for. Then you found out that the colored leaders in this area favored one of the candidates. What difference would it make to you? |
|     | 59  |     | Now, suppose that you planned to vote in an election but hadn't yet made up your mind who you would vote for. Then you found out that the strongest segregation leaders in this area favored one of the candidates. What difference would it make to you? |
| 39  |     |     | What about you? Have you ever voted, or aren't you of voting age? |
| 40  |     |     | *(if not of voting age)* Do you want to vote when you become of voting age? |
| 41  |     |     | Do you think you will ever vote? |
| 42  |     |     | *(if "no," but of voting age)* Have you ever wanted to vote? |
| 43  |     |     | Is there any special reason why you haven't voted? |
| 44  |     |     | *(if "yes," has voted)* Last fall you remember that Nixon |

[A] *Negro Student*   [B] *White Adult*   [C] *Negro Adult*

| [A] | [B] | [C] | |
|-----|-----|-----|---|
| | | | ran against Kennedy for president. How much interest would you say you had in that presidential election—a great deal, quite a lot, not very much, or none at all? |
| 45 | | | Do you remember for sure whether or not you voted in the Kennedy-Nixon election last fall? |
| 45a | | | (*if "yes"*) Which one did you vote for? |
| 46 | | | Have you ever heard of anything happening to Negroes who have voted or taken some other part in politics or public affairs where you grew up? |
| 46a | | | (*if "yes"*) Could you tell me about it—what happened? [When? Why? Where?] |
| 47 | 60 | 71 | Do you think there are any important differences between what the two parties stand for, or do you think they are about the same? |
| 48 | 61 | 72 | I'd like to ask you what you think are the good and bad points about the Democratic and Republican parties. Is there anything in particular that you like about the Democratic Party? [What is that?] |
| 49 | 62 | 73 | Is there anything in particular that you don't like about the Democratic Party? [What is that] |
| 50 | 63 | 74 | Is there anything in particular that you like about the Republican Party? [What is that?] |
| 51 | 64 | 75 | Is there anything in particular that you don't like about the Republican Party? [What is that?] |
| 52 | 65 | 76 | Generally speaking, do you usually think of yourself as a Republican, a Democrat, an Independent, or what? |
| 52a | 66a | 76a | (*if Democrat*) Would you call yourself a strong Democrat or a not very strong Democrat? |
| 52b | 66b | 76b | Was there ever a time when you thought of yourself as a Republican rather than a Democrat? |
| 52c | 66c | 76c | (*if "yes"*) When did you change from Republican to Democrat? |
| 53a | 67a | 77a | (*if Republican*) Would you call yourself a strong Republican or a not very strong Republican? |
| 53b | 67b | 77b | Was there ever a time when you thought of yourself as a Democrat rather than a Republican? |
| 53c | 67c | 77c | (*if "yes"*) When did you change from Democrat to Republican? |
| 54a | 68a | 78a | (*if Independent, other, "don't know"*) Do you think of yourself as closer to the Republican or Democratic Party? |
| 54b | 68b | 78b | Was there ever a time when you thought of yourself as a Democrat or a Republican? |
| 54c | 68c | 78c | (*if "yes"*) Which party was that? |
| 54d | 68d | 78d | When did you change? |

[A] *Negro Student*    [B] *White Adult*    [C] *Negro Adult*

| [A] | [B] | [C] | |
|---|---|---|---|
| | | 79 | There's quite a bit of talk these days about segregation and integration, and it is important to know how Negroes really feel about these questions. In general, how many of the Negroes in this area would you say are in favor of integration—all of them, most of them, about half, or less than half of them? |
| | | 80 | What about you? Are you in favor of integration, strict segregation, or something in between? |
| | | 81 | Now, how about the white people? How many would you say are in favor of strict segregation of the races—all of them, most of them, about half, or less than half of them? |
| | | 82 | Have you ever known a white person well enough that you would talk to him as a friend? |
| | | 82a | (*if "yes"*) How did you come to think of this person as a friend? |
| | | 83 | Do you often come into contact with white people like |

YES    NO

| [A] | [B] | [C] | |
|---|---|---|---|
| | | 83a | _____ _____ people you work for? |
| | | 83b | _____ _____ other people in your work? |
| | | 83c | _____ _____ people who live near by? |
| | | 83d | _____ _____ people where you shop or trade? |
| | 69 | | There's quite a bit of talk these days about segregation and integration, and it is important to know how people in the South really feel about these questions. In general, how many of the white people in this area would you say are in favor of strict segregation of the races—all of them, most of them, about half of them, or less than half of them? |
| | 70 | | What about you? Are you in favor of strict segregation, integration, or something in between? |
| | 71 | | How about the colored people? How many of them would you say are in favor of integration—all of them, most of them, about half, or less than half of them? |
| | 72 | | Have you ever known a colored person well enough that you would talk to him as a friend? |
| | 72a | | (*if "yes"*) How did you come to think of this person as a friend? |
| | 73 | | Do you often come into contact with colored people like |

YES    NO

| [A] | [B] | [C] | |
|---|---|---|---|
| | 73a | | _____ _____ people who work for you? |
| | 73b | | _____ _____ other people in your work? |
| | 73c | | _____ _____ people who live near by? |
| | 73d | | _____ _____ people where you shop or trade? |
| 55 | | | Now, what are your feelings about the Communist party— |

[A] *Negro Student*    [B] *White Adult*    [C] *Negro Adult*

| [A] | [B] | [C] | |
|-----|-----|-----|---|
| | | | Is there anything in particular that you like about the Communist party? [What is that?] |
| 56 | | | Is there anything in particular that you don't like about the Communist party? [What is that?] |
| 57 | | | There's quite a bit of talk these days about segregation and integration, and it is important to know how Negroes really feel about these questions. In general, how many of the Negroes in the South would you say are in favor of integration—all of them, most of them, about half, or less than half of them? |
| 58 | | | What about you? Are you in favor of integration, strict segregation, or something in between? |
| 59 | | | Now, how about the white people? How many would you say are in favor of strict segregation of the races—all of them, most of them, about half, or less than half of them? |
| 60 | | | Have you ever known a white person well enough that you would talk to him as a friend? |
| 60a | | | (*if "yes"*) How did you come to think of this person as a friend? |
| 61 | | | Do you often come into contact with white people like |
| | | | YES    NO |
| 61a | | | \_\_\_\_\_ \_\_\_\_\_ students or teachers? |
| 61b | | | \_\_\_\_\_ \_\_\_\_\_ people you work for? |
| 61c | | | \_\_\_\_\_ \_\_\_\_\_ other people in your work? |
| 61d | | | \_\_\_\_\_ \_\_\_\_\_ people who live near by? |
| 61e | | | \_\_\_\_\_ \_\_\_\_\_ people where you shop or trade? |
| 62 | 74 | 84 | On the whole, do you think white people are smarter than Negroes, Negroes are smarter than white people, or that they are about the same? |
| 63 | 75 | 85 | In general, do you think white people behave better than Negroes, Negroes behave better than white people, or that they are about the same? |
| 64 | 76 | 86 | By and large, do you think white people are more dependable than Negroes, Negroes are more dependable than white people, or that they are about the same? |
| 65 | 77 | 87 | On the whole, do you think white people try to get ahead more than Negroes, Negroes try to get ahead more than white people, or that they are about the same? |
| 66 | 78 | 88 | Here in the South, as in many parts of the world, different races of people are living together in the same communities. Now I would like for you to think about the very best way that Negroes and white people could live in the same place together. In other words, what would be the very best kind of race relations, the most perfect, you could imagine? Take your |

[A] *Negro Student*　[B] *White Adult*　[C] *Negro Adult*

| [A] | [B] | [C] | |
|---|---|---|---|
| | | | time in answering—such things are not easy to put into words. [Anything else? *(if refers only to schools)* Anything besides schools?] |
| 67 | 79 | 89 | Now, taking the other side of the picture, what would be the very worst kind of race relations you could imagine a community having? *(use "Anything else?" probes)* |
| | 80 | 90 | *(hand the ladder, card 2, to respondent)* Here is a picture of a ladder. Suppose we say that at the *top* of the ladder *(point to the top)* is the *very best*, the really perfect, kind of race relations you have just described. At the very bottom is the *very worst* kind of race relations. |

| | |
|---|---|
| 10 | *(very best)* |
| 9 | |
| 8 | |
| 7 | |
| 6 | |
| 5 | |
| 4 | |
| 3 | |
| 2 | |
| 1 | *(very worst)* |

| [A] | [B] | [C] | |
|---|---|---|---|
| | | | Where on this ladder *(move finger rapidly up and down ladder)* would you put _____ [local community]—that is, where you are living now? *(circle step number on R's card)* |
| | 81 | 91 | Now think of race relations here in _____ [local community] five years ago. Where on this ladder would you put the race relations of _____ [local community] five years ago? |
| | 82 | 92 | Thinking now of future race relations here in _____ [local community], where on the ladder do you expect the race relations of _____ [local community] to be five years from now? |
| | 83 | 93 | Now, let's think about some other places. Where on the ladder would you put the race relations of |
| | | | *(Indicate comments, if any.)* |
| | 83a | 93a | _____ New York? |
| | 83b | 93b | _____ Little Rock? |
| | 83c | 93c | _____ Chicago? |

[A] *Negro Student*   [B] *White Adult*   [C] *Negro Adult*

| [A] | [B] | [C] | |
|---|---|---|---|
| | 83d | 93d | _____ Atlanta? |
| | 83e | 93e | _____ a small town in Mississippi? |
| | 83f | 93f | _____ a small city in Ohio? |
| 68 | | | Where on this ladder (*move finger rapidly up and down ladder*) would you put the South today—that is, the South as a whole right now? (*circle step number on R's card*) |
| 69 | | | Now think of race relations in the South five years ago. Where on this ladder would you put the race relations of the South as a whole five years ago? |
| 70 | | | Thinking now of future race relations in the South, where on the ladder do you expect the race relations of the South as a whole to be five years from now? |
| 71 | | | Now, let's think about some specific places. Where on the ladder would you put the race relations of (*Indicate comments, if any.*) |
| 71a | | | _____ the town or place where you grew up? |
| 71b | | | _____ New York? |
| 71c | | | _____ Little Rock? |
| 71d | | | _____ Chicago? |
| 71e | | | _____ Atlanta? |
| 71f | | | _____ a small town in Mississippi? |
| 71g | | | _____ a small city in Ohio? |
| | | | Now I'd like to read some of the kinds of things people tell me when I interview them and ask you whether you agree or disagree with them. I'll read them one at a time and you just (*hand R card 3*) tell me the letter in front of the answer that's closest to how you feel, "A" if you agree quite a bit, "B" if you agree a little, "C" if you disagree a little, "D" if you disagree quite a bit. |
| | 84 | | Colored people ought to be allowed to vote. |
| 72 | 86 | 94 | In spite of what some people say, the condition of the average man is getting worse, not better. |
| 73 | 85 | 95 | These days a person doesn't really know whom he can count on. |
| 74 | 87 | 96 | Sometimes I think people ought not to bring children into the world, the way things look for the future. |
| 75 | 88 | 97 | Nowadays a person has to live pretty much for today and let tomorrow take care of itself. |
| 76 | 89 | 98 | There's not much use in people like me voting because all the candidates are usually against what I want. |
| 77 | 91 | 99 | The government should leave things like electric power and housing for private businessmen to handle. |
| 78 | 90 | 100 | The government in Washington ought to see to it that everybody who wants to work can find a job. |

[A] *Negro Student*　　[B] *White Adult*　　[C] *Negro Adult*

| [A] | [B] | [C] | |
|---|---|---|---|
| 79 | 92 | 101 | If cities and towns around the country need help to build more schools, the government in Washington ought to give them the money they need. |
| 80 | 93 | 102 | The government ought to help people get doctors and hospital care at low cost. |
| 81 | | 103 | All white people in the South are prejudiced against Negroes. |
| 82 | | 104 | In spite of what some people say, when Negroes are arrested in the South they do receive fair treatment. |
| 83 | | 105 | I have seen so much unfairness to Negroes that I don't believe you can ever change the attitudes of white people in the South. |
| 84 | | 106 | The southern Negro does have a chance to make something of himself. |
| 85 | 96 | 107 | If you start trying to change things very much, you usually make them worse. |
| 86 | 97 | 108 | If something grows up over a long time, there will always be much wisdom in it. |
| 87 | 98 | 109 | It's better to stick by what you have than to be trying new things you don't really know about. |
| 88 | 99 | 110 | We must respect the work of our forefathers and not think that we know better than they did. |
| 89 | 100 | 111 | A man doesn't really get to have much wisdom until he's well along in years. |
| 90 | | 112 | All white people are alike. |
| | 94 | | Colored people are all alike. |
| | 95 | | Demonstrations to protest integration of schools are a good idea, even if a few people have to get hurt. |
| 91 | 101 | 113 | Now, I'd like to ask you a few questions that you may or may not be able to answer. Do you happen to recall whether President Franklin Roosevelt was a Republican or a Democrat? [Which?] |
| | 102 | 114 | Who is the governor of _____ [this state] now? |
| | 103 | 115 | About how long a term does the governor serve? |
| | 104 | 116 | What's the county seat of _____ County [county R lives in]? |
| 92 | 105 | 117 | About how many years does a United States Senator serve? |
| 93 | 106 | 118 | Do you happen to know about how many members there are on the United States Supreme Court? How many? |
| 94 | 107 | 119 | What were the last two states to come into the United States? |

This finishes the regular part of the interview. Now we need to ask a few more questions about you so that we can compare the answers of people in different age groups, men with women, people in different jobs, and so on.

[A] *Negro Student*   [B] *White Adult*   [C] *Negro Adult*

| [A] | [B] | [C] | BACKGROUND INFORMATION |
|---|---|---|---|
| | 1 | 1 | How long have you lived in _____ County? |
| | 1a | 1a | (*unless "all my life"*) Where did you grow up? |
| | 2 | 2 | Were you brought up mostly on a farm, in a town, in a small city, or in a large city? |
| | 3 | 3 | What's the biggest city or town you have ever been in? |
| | 4 | 4 | What is the farthest place from here that you have been in? |
| | 5 | 5 | Are you married, single, divorced, separated, or widowed? |
| | 6 | 6 | How many children are there under 18 years old in this family? |
| | 7 | 7 | What age is the youngest child? |
| 1 | | | What is your age? |
| 2 | | | Where did you grow up? |
| 3 | | | Were you brought up mostly on a farm, in a town, in a small city, or in a large city? |
| 4 | | | Do you still think of this place where you grew up as your home? |
| 4a | | | (*if "no"*) What is your home now? |
| 5 | | | What's the biggest city or town you have ever been in? |
| 6 | | | What is the farthest place from your home that you have been in? |
| 7 | | | Are you married, single, divorced, separated, or widowed? |
| 8 | | | What year of college are you in? |
| 9 | | | What is your major field of study? |
| 9a | | | (*if major not yet chosen*) Probable major field of study? |
| 10 | | | About what has been your grade average in college so far? |
| | 8 | 8 | How many grades of school did you finish? |
| | 8a | 8a | (*if 11–12 years*) Have you had any schooling other than high school? |
| | 8b | 8b | (*if "yes"*) What other schooling have you had? |
| | 8c | 8c | (*if attended college*) Do you have a college degree? |
| 11 | 9 | 9 | Were you [or spouse] ever in the armed services of the United States? |
| 11a | 9a | 9a | (*if "yes"*) Which one of you was that? |
| 11b | 9b | 9b | Where did you [spouse] serve? |
| 12 | | | Where do you expect to live when you leave college? |
| 13 | | | Where would you most like to live? |
| 14 | | | Assuming that you live where you expect to, do you think you will be active in political or race relations problems? |
| 14a | | | (*if "yes"*) What do you think you will do in connection with these problems? |
| 15 | | | What occupation do you expect to follow? (*if needed*) I mean, what kind of work do you expect to do? |
| 16 | | | What kind of work would you most like to do? |

[A] *Negro Student*   [B] *White Adult*   [C] *Negro Adult*

| [A] | [B] | [C] | |
|---|---|---|---|

IF R NOT HEAD OF HOUSEHOLD

    10    10    (If R is head of household, skip to question 20; if R is not head) What is your occupation? (*if needed*) I mean, what kind of work do you do? (*be specific*)

    10a    10a    (*if housewife, skip to question 15*) Do you work for yourself, for someone else, or for a company?

    10b    10b    (*if R is unemployed*) What kind of work do you usually do? (*be specific*)

    10c    10c    Do you work for yourself, for someone else, or for a company?

    10d    10d    (if R is retired) What kind of work did you do before you retired? (*be specific*)

    10e    10e    Did you work for yourself, for someone else, or for a company?

    11    11    (*if R is* [was] *not a farmer, skip to question 15; if R is* [was] *a farmer continue*) Do [Did] you own the farm, manage it, rent it, farm it on shares, or are [were] you paid to work on it?

    12    12    How much land do [did] you farm? _____ (number of acres)

    13    13    About how much do [did] you farm, full-time or just part of the time?

    14    14    What kind of farming do [did] you do?

    15    15    What is [head's] occupation—that is, what does he [she] do? (*be specific*)

    15a    15a    (*if housewife, skip to question 25*) Does he [she] work for himself, for someone else, or for a company?

    15b    15b    (if head is unemployed) What kind of work does he usually do? (*be specific*)

    15c    15c    Does he work for himself, for someone else, or for a company?

    15d    15d    (*if head is retired*) What kind of work did he do before he retired? (*be specific*)

    15e    15e    Did he work for himself, for someone else, or for a company?

    16    16    (*if head is* [was] *not a farmer, skip to question 25; if head is* [was] *a farmer*) Does [Did] he own the farm, manage it, rent it, farm it on shares, or is [was] he paid to work on it?

    17    17    How much land does [did] he farm? _____ (number of acres)

    18    18    About how much does [did] he farm, full-time or just part of the time?

[A] *Negro Student*   [B] *White Adult*   [C] *Negro Adult*

| [A] | [B] | [C] | |
|---|---|---|---|
| | 19 | 19 | What kind of farming does [did] he do? (*Skip to question 25.*) |

IF R IS HEAD OF HOUSEHOLD

| | 20 | 20 | What is your occupation? (*if needed*) I mean, what kind of work do you do? (*be specific*) |
|---|---|---|---|
| | 20a | 20a | (*if housewife, skip to question 25*) Do you work for yourself, for someone else, or for a company? |
| | 20b | 20b | (*if R is unemployed*) What kind of work do you usually do? (*be specific*) |
| | 20c | 20c | Do you work for yourself, for someone else, or for a company? |
| | 20d | 20d | (*if R is retired*) What kind of work did you do before you retired? (*be specific*) |
| | 20e | 20e | Did you work for yourself, for someone else, or for a company? |
| | 21 | 21 | (*if R is [was] not a farmer, skip to question 25; if R is [was] a farmer*) Do [Did] you own the farm, manage it, rent it, farm it on shares, or are [were] you paid to work on it? |
| | 22 | 22 | How much land do [did] you farm? _____ (number of acres) |
| | 23 | 23 | About how much do [did] you farm, full-time or just part of the time? |
| | 24 | 24 | What kind of farming do [did] you do? (*Continue with question 25.*) |

OCCUPATION OF HEAD OF STUDENTS' HOUSEHOLD

| 17 | | | Was your father, mother, or someone else the head of the household in which you grew up? |
|---|---|---|---|
| 18 | | | What is his [her] occupation—that is, what does he [she] do? |
| 18a | | | (*if housewife, skip to question 23*) Does he [she] work for himself [herself], for someone else, or for a company? |
| 18b | | | (*if head is unemployed*) What kind of work does he [she] usually do? |
| 18c | | | Does he [she] work for himself [herself], for someone else, or for a company? |
| 18d | | | (*if head is retired*) What kind of work did he [she] do before he [she] retired? |
| 18e | | | Did he [she] work for himself [herself], for someone else, or for a company? |
| 19 | | | (*if head is [was] not a farmer, skip to question 23; if head is [was] a farmer continue*) Does [Did] he [she] own the |

[A] *Negro Student*   [B] *White Adult*   [C] *Negro Adult*

| [A] | [B] | [C] | |
|-----|-----|-----|---|
| | | | farm, manage it, rent it, farm it on shares, or is [was] he [she] paid to work on it? |
| 20 | | | How much land does [did] he [she] farm? |
| 21 | | | About how much does [did] he [she] farm, full-time or just part of the time? |
| 22 | | | What kind of farming does [did] he [she] do? |

ALL RESPONDENTS

| [A] | [B] | [C] | |
|-----|-----|-----|---|
| 23 | 25 | 25 | There's quite a bit of talk these days about different social classes. Most people say they belong either to the middle class or to the working class. Do you ever think of yourself as being in one of these classes? |
| 23a | 25a | 25a | (*if "yes"*) Which one? |
| 23b | 25b | 25b | (*if "no"*) Well, if you had to make a choice, would you call yourself middle class or working class? |
| 24 | | 26 | Some Negroes feel they have a lot in common with other Negroes, but others we talk to don't feel this way so much. How about you? Would you say you feel pretty close to Negroes in general or that you don't feel much closer to them than you do to other people? |
| 25 | | 27 | How much interest would you say you have in how Negroes as a whole are getting along in this country? Do you have a good deal of interest in it, some interest, or not much interest at all? |
| | 26 | | Some people in the South feel they have a lot in common with other southerners; but others we talk to don't feel this way so much. How about you? Would you say you feel pretty close to southerners in general or that you don't feel much closer to them than you do to other people? |
| | 27 | | How much interest would you say you have in how southerners as a whole are getting along in this country? Do you have a good deal of interest in it, some interest, or not much interest at all? |
| 26 | 28 | 28 | And now would you tell me how much income your family made altogether during the last year, 1961. I mean before taxes, including the income of everyone in the family? (Hand R card 4) Just call off the letter on this card in front of the correct amount. |

A. under $1,000          F. $5,000–$5,999
B. $1,000–$1,999        G. $6,000–$7,499
C. $2,000–$2,999        H. $7,500–$9,999
D. $3,000–$3,999         I. $10,000–$14,999
E. $4,000–$4,999         J. $15,000 and over

Thank you very much.

[A] *Negro Student*    [B] *White Adult*    [C] *Negro Adult*

| [A] | [B] | [C] | |
|-----|-----|-----|---|
| | | | BY OBSERVATION |
| 1 | 1 | 1 | R's sex |
| 2 | | | R's residence |
| | | | _____ dormitory |
| | | | _____ student boarding house |
| | | | _____ other private residence |
| | | | _____ fraternity or sorority house |
| | | | _____ with own family |
| | | | _____ other (write in) |
| | 2 | 2 | Characteristics of R's residential area |
| | 2a | 2a | racial composition |
| | | | _____ virtually all white |
| | | | _____ mixed |
| | | | _____ virtually all Negro |
| | 2b | 2b | location |
| | | | _____ open country |
| | | | _____ rural, nonfarm |
| | | | _____ suburban fringe |
| | | | _____ city or town |
| | 3 | | Pronunciation of "Negro" |
| | | | _____ Negro |
| | | | _____ Nigger |
| | | | _____ other (Neegra, Nigro, Nigra, etc.) |
| | | | _____ avoidance of "Negro," (exclusive use of "colored people") |
| | | | _____ avoidance of "Negro," use of other terms (write in) |
| 3 | | 3 | R's skin color |

*very light* — — — — — — — — — — — *very dark*

# APPENDIX C

# Scales and Indexes

We have used a number of statistical measures of social, psychological, and political phenomena in this book. In this appendix we discuss the construction of these measures, in the order in which they appear in the text.

### POLITICAL PARTICIPATION SCALE

The PPS is a Guttman-type, cumulative scale of political participation constructed, for white respondents, from questions 1, 2a, 2c, 2e, 3, 4, 9 on political discussions; 27 on voting; 6, 7, 8 on campaign participation; and 5, 5a, 11, 11a on officeholding and political memberships. The comparable questions for Negro respondents are 1, 2a, 2c, 2f, 3, 4, 9; 30; 6, 7, 8; and 5, 5a, 11, 11a.

Respondents were dichotomized into those who had ever engaged in any of these activities and those who had not. The percentages of the Negro and white southwide samples with positive responses on each item were as follows:

|  | Negro | White |
|---|---|---|
| Talked politics | 86.9% | 88.5% |
| Voted | 41.3 | 85.6 |
| Campaigned | 34.2 | 44.7 |
| Held office or belonged to political group | 11.8 | 4.8 |

There is no general agreement about what constitutes a satisfactory cumulative scale. Guttman has proposed a Coefficient of Reproducibility (CR), which is merely the proportion of all responses falling into "pure" scale patterns; he suggests that a minimum score of at least .90 be required. Judged by this standard, the PPS easily proves satisfactory for both races: The CR for whites is .98 and for Negroes is .95.

For a number of reasons, however, the CR is not always a very demanding test of unidimensionality.[1] Its value, for example, tends to be inflated by items with high modal popularity. The "expected value" of CR, even if the items comprising the scale are actually independent of one another, is often surprisingly high. It is possible to obtain a satisfactory CR even though one of the items in the scale is responsible for the bulk of the error. In view of these weaknesses of CR and the importance of the PPS to this study, the following additional properties of the measure are presented below:

|  | Negro | White |
|---|---|---|
| Coefficient of Reproducibility | .95 | .98 |
| Lowest possible CR | .75 | .81 |
| CR if items were independent | .92 | .96 |
| Percentage of respondents in nonscale patterns | 19% | 10% |
| Percentage of total error attributable to individual items | | |
|     Talking | 14% | 67% |
|     Voting | 63% | 21% |
|     Campaigning | 17% | 12% |
|     Belonging to political group, holding office | 6% | 0% |
| TOTAL | 100% (117) | 100% (67) |
| Percentages of each PPS Type that are errors | | |
|     Type I | 9% (67) | 7% (15) |
|     Type II | 3% (22) | 0% (65) |
|     Type III | 11% (105) | 12% (298) |
|     Type IV | 42% (160) | 8% (283) |
|     Type V | 41% (64) | 24% (33) |

It is apparent that the PPS possesses a number of technical weaknesses. Given the marginal distributions of the items, it is difficult to obtain low CR scores; the errors are not randomly distributed between the items but tend to cluster at the "voting" stage for Negroes and the "talking" stage for whites. A large proportion of the Negroes in types IV and V were assigned to these

[1] See B. F. Green, "Attitude Measurement," ch. 9 in Gardner Lindzey (ed.), *Handbook of Social Psychology* (Cambridge, Mass.: Addison-Wesley Publishing Co., 1954), vol. 1, pp. 353ff, and the works cited therein.

types despite errors. The actual CR scores are not much larger than they would be if the items were independent of each other.[2]

These imperfections were largely the result of the need for an identical measure of participation for the two races and the fact that Negro and white rates and patterns of participation are so different. A technically better measure could have been constructed for either race alone, but this, of course, would have rendered comparison across race lines impossible.

A second factor contributing to the technical limitations of the measure was a desire to use "natural" cutting-points in dichotomizing responses. If, for example, we had not used "ever talk about public problems" as the cutting-point between types I and II but had used, say, "ever talk politics to someone outside one's circle of friends or family," the technical properties of the measure would have been improved. But the scale's comprehensibility to laymen would have been largely destroyed in the process.

Since we are confident on intuitive and a priori grounds that the behaviors measured by PPS are all "political participation," these limitations of the measure as a demonstration of unidimensionality concern us less than they otherwise would. And since responses to one item are, in fact, highly predictive of responses to another—as indicated by the high CR scores—we believe that PPS, despite imperfections, is adequate for the purposes of this study. Indeed, as we argue in Chapter Three, some of the characteristics that weaken it as a scale are most revealing about the differences between white and Negro political behavior in the South.

### POLITICAL INFORMATION SCALE

Seven factual questions about government and politics were asked each Negro and white adult respondent (113–18 for Negro adults; 101–07 for whites). The Negro student sample was asked only four of these questions (91–94). The political information score consists of the number of correct answers given by each respondent.

### COMMUNITY RACE RELATIONS RATINGS

The respondents' ratings of race relations in their home community and in other communities are based on a "self-anchoring" scale explained in detail in Chapter Ten. Questions from which the scales were constructed are: Negro adults, 90–93f; white adults, 80–83f; Negro students, 68–71g. The ratings range from 10, the very best race relations the respondent can imagine, to 1, the very worst possible relations between the races. These judgments are made in terms of the respondent's own conception of the "best" and "worst" race relations.

[2] A technique for making this computation is given in M. L. Toby and M. Moore, "Object Scale Procedure," ch. 13 in M. W. Riley, J. W. Riley, Jr., J. Tobey (eds.), *Sociological Studies in Scale Analysis* (New Brunswick, N. J.: Rutgers University Press, 1954), pp. 317ff.

### INDEX OF MASS MEDIA EXPOSURE

Questions 16–19 for Negro adults, 15–18 for white adults, and 20–23 for Negro students ask whether the respondent was "more or less regularly" exposed to newspapers, magazines, radio, and television. The number of different media to which respondents reported exposure was used as an index of media exposure. Scores thus range from 0 (no regular exposure to any medium) to 4 (regular exposure to all four media).

### SENSE OF CIVIC COMPETENCE INDEX

Each respondent was presented with hypothetical problems and then asked if he would "do anything about it, or would you figure there wasn't much you could do?" (Negro adults, questions 20–24c; white adults, 19–21c; Negro students, 24–26c). The number of times each Negro adult respondent "definitely would take action" in three of these situations (questions 20, 21, 23) was counted as a rough index of subjective competence. Scores range from 0 (no action in any case) to 3 (action in all three cases). This index was not constructed for whites or for Negro students.

### ATTITUDE TOWARD CHANGE SCALE

A Guttman-type scale was constructed from agree-disagree responses to a set of statements on classical conservatism, or resistance to change, originally prepared by Herbert McClosky[3] (Negro adults, questions 107–11; white adults, 96–100; Negro students, 85–89). The Coefficients of Reproducibility for each sample are: Negro adults, .92; white adults, .93; Negro students, .93.

### PARTY IDENTIFICATION

The standard questions and coding procedures of the Survey Research Center of the University of Michigan were used to measure the direction and strength of partisan emotional attachments. The question numbers are: Negro adults, 76–78d; white adults, 65–68d; Negro students, 52–54d.

### PARTY IMAGE SCORE

Respondents were asked a series of questions concerning their likes and dislikes about the Democratic and Republican parties (Negro adults, 72–75; white adults, 61–64; Negro students, 48–51). The party image score was obtained by counting each favorable comment about the Democrats or unfavorable comment about the Republicans as a +1, and each unfavorable item about the Democrats or favorable item about the Republicans as a −1, and computing the net sum. These scores varied from +8 through 0 to −8, since up to four "likes" and "dislikes" for each party were coded. The larger the

[3] "Conservatism and Personality," *American Political Science Review*, vol. 52 (March, 1958), pp. 27-45.

positive score, the more favorable is the respondent's relative view of the Democratic party; the larger the negative score, the more favorable is the respondent's relative picture of the Republican party. A 0 score indicates no preference, so far as party images are concerned, for either party.

The total number of likes and dislikes mentioned by each respondent was taken as a measure of the cognitive "richness" of the respondent's picture of partisan realities.

## RACIAL STEREOTYPE INDEX

Four questions were asked each respondent about his views of the Negro and white races (Negro adults, 84–87; white adults, 74–77; Negro students, 62–65). A response indicating that the respondent felt that whites were smarter (behave better, are more dependable, try more) was counted as a $+1$; responses indicating that Negroes were smarter (behave better, are more dependable, try more) was counted as a $-1$; responses indicating no racial differences were counted as 0. The net sum of these scores, which varies from $+4$ (strongly pro-white) through 0 (races are the same) to $-4$ (strongly pro-Negro), was used as an index of racial stereotypes.

## OVERALL INDEX OF PSYCHOLOGICAL CHARACTERISTICS

In order to measure the collective influence of the psychological characteristics of Negroes on their political participation, eight psychological attributes (strength of partisanship, political interest, political information, sense of civic competence, sense of deprivation, sense of racial inferiority/superiority, attitude toward change, awareness of local intimidation) were combined into a single index using arbitrarily assigned weights. The measurement of all these variables except political interest and awareness of local racial incidents is described elsewhere in this appendix. These two factors were obtained from answers to questions 10 and 68 in the questionnaire for Negro adults.

The weighting of the responses was as follows:

|  | 2 | 1 | 0 |
|---|---|---|---|
| Strength of partisanship | Strong | Weak | Leaners, Independents, Apoliticals, DK, NA, RA |
| Political interest | Great deal | Somewhat | Not much, DK, NA, RA |
| Political information | 6–7 correct | 3–5 correct | 0–2 correct, DK, NA, RA |
| Sense of civic competence | 3 definite actions | 1–2 definite actions | 0 definite actions, DK, NA, RA |
| Sense of deprivation | Community ratings of 3–4, 7–8 | Community ratings of 5–6 | Community ratings of 1–2, 9–10, DK, NA, RA |

|                                   | 2                                                   | 1                        | 0                                |
|-----------------------------------|-----------------------------------------------------|--------------------------|----------------------------------|
| Sense of racial inferiority/superiority | Negroes better                                | No difference            | Whites better, DK, NA, RA        |
| Attitude toward change            | Types I–II                                          | Types III–IV             | Types V–VI, DK, RA, NA           |
| Awareness of local intimidation   | Heard scare stories about protest move-ment        | Heard no stories         | Heard other scare stories        |

Summing these weights for each respondent yields a composite score theoretically ranging from 0 (no psychological influences associated with participation) to 16 (all eight psychological factors strongly in support of participation).

### CONSERVATISM-LIBERALISM SCALE

This measure of domestic socioeconomic liberalism and conservatism was obtained by applying Guttman scaling procedures to agree-disagree responses to the following standard questions: Negro adults, 99–102; white adults, 90–93; Negro students, 77–80. The coefficients of reproducibility of these scales were: Negro adults, .97; white adults, .92; Negro students, .94.

### ACADEMIC QUALITY SCALE FOR SOUTHERN NEGRO COLLEGES

A Guttman scale of the academic quality of southern Negro colleges in our sample was constructed by Professor John Orbell using the following indicators and cutting points:

| | |
|---|---|
| Student/faculty ratio | 11.8 |
| Ph.D.'s on faculty | 22.5% |
| Books in library | 38,000 |
| Books per student | 25 |
| Budget dollars per student | $800 |

Information on Negro colleges was obtained from the American Council on Education[4] and other sources listed in John M. Orbell's *Social Protest and Social Structure: Southern Negro Participation in the Protest Movement*.[5] The Coefficient of Reproducibility for the scale is .89.

Two criteria often used (as in Lazarsfeld and Thielens' *The Academic Mind*[6]) in assessing academic quality of institutions—production of scholars and tuition fees—were excluded as inappropriate for this group of institutions.

[4] *American Universities and Colleges*, 8th ed. (Washington, D.C., 1960).
[5] (Unpublished Ph.D. dissertation, University of North Carolina, 1965).
[6] P. F. Lazarsfeld and W. Thielens, Jr., *The Academic Mind* (Glencoe, Ill.: The Free Press, 1958).

### NEGRO IDENTIFICATION WITH OTHER NEGROES

Negro adult respondents were asked about their identification with other Negroes (questions 26 and 27). Their responses were combined into index scores in the following fashion:

| INDEX SCORE | |
|---|---|
| 3 | feel pretty close; good deal of interest |
| 2 | feel pretty close; some interest |
| | feel pretty close; DK |
| | feel pretty close; NA |
| | can't decide; good deal of interest |
| | DK; good deal of interest |
| | NA; good deal of interest |
| 1 | feel pretty close; not much interested at all |
| | not closer than to others; good deal of interest |
| | not closer than to others; some interest |
| 0 | not closer than to others; not much interest at all |
| | can't decide; not much interest at all |
| | DK; not much interest at all |
| | not closer than to others; NA |
| | not closer than to others; DK |
| | RA; not much interest at all |

### WHITE IDENTIFICATION WITH THE SOUTH

White respondents, in questions 26 and 27, were asked how close they felt to other southerners. Their responses were combined into index scores following the same procedure outlined above.

*Index*

# Index

Abu-Laban, Baha, 180n
*Academic Mind, The*, 528
Age: and cumulative political experience, 73–74; and delayed registration by Negroes, 73; and effect of *Smith v. Allwright* on Negroes, 72; and effect of voting restrictions, 71; and late-starting activists, 72; and length of political experience, 72; and Negro generational effect, 71–72; of Negro leaders, 184; and Negro political participation, 101; and partisan regularity of voting, 70; and political involvement, 61; and political participation, 61; and racial differences in political participation, 71–73, 97; racial distribution by, 97–98; and white registration, 75n
Agger, Robert E., 179n
Aggregate data, use of, 32, 62, 112–14, 314
Aging effect, 33–34, 349. *See also* Age
Agrarianism, in South: measures of, 123; and Negro concentration, 123; and Negro registration, 123–24
Alabama: multifactionalism in, 160–61; Negro registration in, 148, 151; poll tax in, 153
Alexander, Holmes, 243
Alford, R. A., 475n
Almond, Gabriel, 142n, 276
Alsop, Joseph, 243
*American Dilemma, An*, 335–36
American political system, values of, 117

*Anatomy of Revolution*, 419
Apoliticals, defined, 374
Arkansas: absence of literacy test in, 153; bifactionalism in, 160–62; Negro registration in, 148–52; poll tax in, 153
Associated Press, 237, 241
*Atlanta Constitution*, 434
Attitudes: as immediate factors, 62; as individual attributes, 62; linkages with public policy-making, 477; and political participation, 312. *See also* Conflict of racial attitudes; Negro racial attitudes; Partisan attitudes; Party identification; Party image; Social change, attitude toward; White racial attitudes
Axelrod, Morris, 24n, 491n

Bachman, Jerald G., 28n
Barnes, James F., 117n
*Barr v. Columbia*, 413n
*Barrie v. Columbia*, 413n
Barth, Ernest A. T., 180n
"Basic" variables, linked with political participation, 89
Bell, W., 176n
*Bell v. Maryland*, 413n
Bennett, L., 10n
Berelson, B., 38n, 41n, 479n
Bettelheim, B., 12n, 126n
Bifactionalism, 159–60
Biracial political coalitions, effect of on political leadership, 479

## DATE DUE

| | | |
|---|---|---|
| JAN 3 1 | | |
| MAY 0 4 1995 | | |
| FE 26 '01 | | |
| | | |
| | | |
| | | |
| | | |
| | | |
| | | |
| | | |
| | | |
| | | |
| | | |
| | | |
| | | |
| | | |
| AYLORD | | PRINTED IN U.S.A. |